SOMETHING ABOUT THE AUTHOR®

Something about
the Author *was named
an "Outstanding
Reference Source,"*
*the highest honor given
by the American
Library Association
Reference and Adult
Services Division.*

ISSN 0276-816X

SOMETHING ABOUT THE AUTHOR®

*Facts and Pictures about Authors
and Illustrators of Books for Young People*

EDITED BY
ALAN HEDBLAD

VOLUME 98

GALE

DETROIT · LONDON

STAFF

Editor: Alan Hedblad
Associate Editors: Sheryl Ciccarelli, Melissa Hill, Thomas F. McMahon

Sketchwriters/Copyeditors: Joanna Brod, Marie Ellavich, Ronie Garcia-Johnson, Mary Gillis,
Motoko Fujishiro Huthwaite, Arlene M. Johnson, J. Sydney Jones, Gerard J. Senick, Pamela L. Shelton,
Crystal A. Towns, Arlene True, Stephen Thor Tschirhart, and Kathleen Witman

Managing Editor: Joyce Nakamura
Publisher: Hal May

Research Manager: Victoria B. Cariappa
Project Coordinator: Cheryl L. Warnock
Research Specialists: Michele P. LaMeau, Andrew Guy Malonis, Barbara McNeil
Research Associates: Jeffrey D. Daniels, Norma Sawaya
Research Assistants: Phyllis Blackman, Talitha A. Jean, Corrine A. Stocker

Permissions Manager: Susan M. Trosky
Permissions Specialist: Maria L. Franklin
Permissions Associates: Edna M. Hedblad, Michele Lonoconus

Production Director: Mary Beth Trimper
Production Assistant: Carolyn Fischer

Graphic Artist: Gary Leach
Image Database Supervisor: Randy Bassett
Imaging Specialists: Robert Duncan, Michael Logusz
Imaging Coordinator: Pamela A. Reed

Library of Congress Catalog Card Number 72-27107
ISBN 0-7876-1444-0 ISSN 0276-816X

Printed in the United States of America

10 9 8 7 6 5 4 3 2 1

Contents

Authors in Forthcoming Volumes viii
Introduction ix
Acknowledgments xi

Y-Z

Authors in Forthcoming Volumes

Below are some of the authors and illustrators that will be featured in upcoming volumes of *SATA*. These include new entries on the swiftly rising stars of the field, as well as completely revised and updated entries (indicated with *) on some of the most notable and best-loved creators of books for children.

Pierre Berton: Considered a Canadian national treasure, Berton is a writer, historian, and media personality whose body of work has greatly influenced the development of an authentic Canadian consciousness. His best-known children's book is *The Secret World of Og*.

Glenn Alan Cheney: In a style he calls creative nonfiction, Cheney writes award-winning young adult books examining political, social, and environmental issues. Among his best-known works are *They Never Knew: The Victims of Nuclear Testing* and *Teens with Physical Disabilities: Real Life Stories of Meeting the Challenges*.

*Chris Crutcher: Crutcher is regarded as a dynamic and insightful writer whose protagonists offer authentic reflections of the inner lives of young people. He has received the ALAN award for significant contributions to young adult literature.

Peter Golenbock: Golenbock is the best-selling author of sports books about major league baseball, stock car racing, professional football, and collegiate basketball. He has also received recognition for his children's title *Teammates,* which describes the trials of major league baseball's first black player, Jackie Robinson.

Mick Inkpen: British writer and illustrator Inkpen is best known for such award-winning titles as *Kipper, Threadbear,* and *Penguin Small*. His menagerie of picture book characters includes charming pigs, raucous mice, sleepy bears, and the puppy named Kipper.

*M. E. Kerr: Marijane Meaker, who writes for young adults almost exclusively as M. E. Kerr, addresses serious issues in an incisive and entertaining manner. Several of her novels, such as *Dinky Hocker Shoots Smack!* and *Gentlehands,* are among those acknowledged as landmarks of young adult literature.

Joy Nozomi Kogawa: Author and poet Kogawa is best known for the critically acclaimed novel *Obasan,* a fictionalization of her own experiences as a Japanese-Canadian during World War II. She has adapted *Obasan* for children under the title *Naomi's Road*.

*Ursula K. Le Guin: Le Guin is regarded as one of the most significant authors of science fiction and fantasy to have emerged in the twentieth century, and the first female writer to have made a major contribution to the genre. She has applied sophisticated themes and literary craftsmanship to many award-winning novels, picture books, and short stories.

Frank O'Keeffe: Irish-born Canadian author O'Keeffe produces books for children that celebrate the energy and resiliency of youth. His lively, insightful writing has led to several awards for books such as *Weekend at the Ritz* and *If It Rains Again Tomorrow, Can We Go Home?*

Kenneth Oppel: Since publishing his first book at age seventeen, Oppel has written many books for young people, ranging from picture books and first readers to young adult fiction. The Canadian Authors Association awarded him the 1995 Air Canada Award for promise demonstrated by a young Canadian writer.

*Julian F. Thompson: Thompson writes lengthy and sophisticated novels for young adults that portray intelligent and responsible teenagers who address contemporary concerns such as the nuclear threat, environmental problems, and international politics.

Teresa Toten: Croatian-born Canadian author Toten's first novel, *The Onlyhouse,* has been shortlisted for several important literary awards and has been included on the "best books" lists of both the Canadian Children's Book Centre and the Canadian Library Association.

Introduction

Something about the Author (*SATA*) is an ongoing reference series that examines the lives and works of authors and illustrators of books for children. *SATA* includes not only well-known writers and artists but also less prominent individuals whose works are just coming to be recognized. This series is often the only readily available information source on emerging authors and illustrators. You'll find *SATA* informative and entertaining, whether you are a student, a librarian, an English teacher, a parent, or simply an adult who enjoys children's literature.

What's Inside SATA

SATA provides detailed information about authors and illustrators who span the full time range of children's literature, from early figures like John Newbery and L. Frank Baum to contemporary figures like Judy Blume and Richard Peck. Authors in the series represent primarily English-speaking countries, particularly the United States, Canada, and the United Kingdom. Also included, however, are authors from around the world whose works are available in English translation. The writings represented in *SATA* include those created intentionally for children and young adults as well as those written for a general audience and known to interest younger readers. These writings cover the entire spectrum of children's literature, including picture books, humor, folk and fairy tales, animal stories, mystery and adventure, science fiction and fantasy, historical fiction, poetry and nonsense verse, drama, biography, and nonfiction.

Obituaries are also included in *SATA* and are intended not only as death notices but also as concise overviews of people's lives and work. Additionally, each edition features newly revised and updated entries for a selection of *SATA* listees who remain of interest to today's readers and who have been active enough to require extensive revisions of their earlier biographies.

Two Convenient Indexes

In response to suggestions from librarians, *SATA* indexes no longer appear in every volume but are included in alternate (odd-numbered) volumes of the series, beginning with Volume 57.

SATA continues to include two indexes that cumulate with each alternate volume: the Illustrations Index, arranged by the name of the illustrator, gives the number of the volume and page where the illustrator's work appears in the current volume as well as all preceding volumes in the series; the Author Index gives the number of the volume in which a person's Biographical Sketch or Obituary appears in the current volume as well as all preceding volumes in the series.

These indexes also include references to authors and illustrators who appear in Gale's *Yesterday's Authors of Books for Children, Children's Literature Review,* and *Something about the Author Autobiography Series.*

Easy-to-Use Entry Format

Whether you're already familiar with the *SATA* series or just getting acquainted, you will want to be aware of the kind of information that an entry provides. In every *SATA* entry the editors attempt to give as complete a picture of the person's life and work as possible. A typical entry in *SATA* includes the following clearly labeled information sections:

- *PERSONAL:* date and place of birth and death, parents' names and occupations, name of spouse, date of marriage, names of children, educational institutions attended, degrees received, religious and political affiliations, hobbies and other interests.

- *ADDRESSES:* complete home, office, electronic mail, and agent addresses, whenever available.

■ *CAREER:* name of employer, position, and dates for each career post; art exhibitions; military service; memberships and offices held in professional and civic organizations.

■ *AWARDS, HONORS:* literary and professional awards received.

■ *WRITINGS:* title-by-title chronological bibliography of books written and/or illustrated, listed by genre when known; lists of other notable publications, such as plays, screenplays, and periodical contributions.

■ *ADAPTATIONS:* a list of films, television programs, plays, CD-ROMs, recordings, and other media presentations that have been adapted from the author's work.

■ *WORK IN PROGRESS:* description of projects in progress.

■ *SIDELIGHTS:* a biographical portrait of the author or illustrator's development, either directly from the biographee—and often written specifically for the *SATA* entry—or gathered from diaries, letters, interviews, or other published sources.

■ *FOR MORE INFORMATION SEE:* references for further reading.

■ *EXTENSIVE ILLUSTRATIONS:* photographs, movie stills, book illustrations, and other interesting visual materials supplement the text.

How a SATA Entry Is Compiled

A *SATA* entry progresses through a series of steps. If the biographee is living, the *SATA* editors try to secure information directly from him or her through a questionnaire. From the information that the biographee supplies, the editors prepare an entry, filling in any essential missing details with research and/or telephone interviews. If possible, the author or illustrator is sent a copy of the entry to check for accuracy and completeness.

If the biographee is deceased or cannot be reached by questionnaire, the *SATA* editors examine a wide variety of published sources to gather information for an entry. Biographical and bibliographic sources are consulted, as are book reviews, feature articles, published interviews, and material sometimes obtained from the biographee's family, publishers, agent, or other associates.

Entries that have not been verified by the biographees or their representatives are marked with an asterisk (*).

Contact the Editor

We encourage our readers to examine the entire *SATA* series. Please write and tell us if we can make *SATA* even more helpful to you. Give your comments and suggestions to the editor:

BY MAIL: Editor, *Something about the Author,* Gale Research, 835 Penobscot Bldg., 645 Griswold St., Detroit, MI 48226-4094. NOTE: New address, effective September 15, 1998: Gale Research, 27500 Drake Rd., Farmington Hills, MI 48331-3535.

BY TELEPHONE: (800) 347-GALE

BY FAX: (313) 961-6599

Acknowledgments

Grateful acknowledgment is made to the following publishers, authors, and artists whose works appear in this volume.

ANDREWS, JAN. Wallace, Ian, illustrator. From an illustration in *Very Last First Time,* by Jan Andrews. McElderry Books, 1985. Illustrations copyright © 1985 by Ian Wallace. All rights reserved. Reproduced by permission of Groundwood Books/Douglas & McIntyre. In the U.S., its territories, dependencies, and the Philippine Islands by permission of Margaret K. McElderry Books, an imprint of Simon & Schuster Children's Publishing Division. / Cover of *Keri,* by Jan Andrews. Groundwood Books, 1996. Reproduced by permission of Groundwood Books/Douglas & McIntyre. / Andrews, Jan, photograph by Chislett Studio. Reproduced by permission of Jan Andrews.

BANFILL, A. SCOTT. Banfill, A. Scott, illustrator. From an illustration in *Nicholi,* by Cooper Edens. Simon & Schuster, 1997. Illustrations copyright © 1997 by A. Scott Banfill. All rights reserved. Reproduced by permission of Simon & Schuster Books for Young Readers, an imprint of Simon & Schuster Children's Publishing Division.

BAUER, CAROLINE FELLER. Westcott, Nadine Bernard, illustrator. From an illustration in *Thanksgiving: Stories and Poems,* edited by Caroline Feller Bauer. HarperCollins Publishers, 1994. Illustrations copyright © 1994 by Nadine Bernard Westcott, Inc. All rights reserved. Reproduced by permission of HarperCollins Publishers. / Bauer, Caroline Feller, photograph.

BIRDSEYE, TOM. Birdseye, Tom, photograph. Reproduced by permission of Tom Birdseye.

BIRNEY, BETTY G. O'Brien, John, illustrator. From an illustration in *Tyrannosaurus Tex,* by Betty G. Birney. Houghton Mifflin, 1994. Illustrations copyright © 1994 by John O'Brien. All rights reserved. Reproduced by permission of John O'Brien. In the U. S. and Canada by permission of Houghton Mifflin Company. / Birney, Betty G., photograph. Reproduced by permission of Betty G. Birney.

BLOOR, EDWARD. Johnson, Joel Peter, illustrator. From a jacket of *Tangerine,* by Edward Bloor. Harcourt Brace & Company, 1997. Jacket illustration copyright © 1997 by Joel Peter Johnson. Reproduced by permission. / Bloor, Edward, photograph by Pamela Bloor. Reproduced by permission of Edward Bloor.

BOLAND, JANICE. Boland, Janice, photograph by James Boland. Reproduced by permission of Janice Boland.

BORTON, LADY. Root, Kimberly Bulcken, illustrator. From an illustration in *Junkpile!,* by Lady Borton. Philomel Books, 1997. Illustrations copyright © 1997 by Kimberly Bulcken Root. All rights reserved. Reproduced by permission of Philomel Books, a division of Penguin Putnam Inc.

BREDESON, CARMEN. Bredeson, Carmen, photograph by Joseph Dybala, M. Photog., CPP. Reproduced by permission of Joseph Dybala Photography, Inc.

BROWN, KATHRYN. Brown, Kathryn, illustrator. From an illustration in *Tough Boris,* by Mem Fox. Harcourt Brace & Company, 1994. Illustrations copyright © 1994 by Kathryn Brown. All rights reserved. Reproduced by permission of Harcourt Brace & Company. / Brown, Kathryn, photograph. Reproduced by permission of Kathryn Brown.

BURLEIGH, ROBERT. Wimmer, Mike, illustrator. From an illustration in *Flight: The Journey of Charles Lindbergh,* by Robert Burleigh. Philomel Books, 1991. Illustrations copyright © 1991 by Mike Wimmer. All rights reserved. Reproduced by permission of Philomel Books, a division of Penguin Putnam Inc. / Burleigh, Robert, photograph. Reproduced by permission of Robert Burleigh.

CALHOUN, B. B. Cover of *His and Hers: New in Town,* by B. B. Calhoun. Avon Books, 1997. Copyright © 1997 by Christina Lowenstein. Reproduced by permission of Avon Books, Inc.

CAMPBELL, ROD. Campbell, Rod, illustrator. From an illustration in his *It's Mine.* Campbell Books, 1988. Original text and illustrations © Rod Campbell 1987. Reproduced by permission of Campbell Books, a division of Macmillan Children's Books. / Campbell, Rod, illustrator. From a jacket of his *The Pop-Up Farm.* Campbell Books, 1988. © Rod Campbell 1994 and 1998. Reproduced by permission of Campbell Books, a division of Macmillan Children's Books. / Campbell, Rod, photograph. Reproduced by permission of Rod Campbell.

CAVANAGH, HELEN. Goldstrom, Robert, illustrator. From a jacket of *The Last Piper,* by Helen Cavanagh. Simon & Schuster, 1996. Jacket illustration copyright © 1996 by Simon & Schuster. All rights reserved. Reproduced by permission of Simon & Schuster Books for Young Readers, an imprint of Simon & Schuster Children's Publishing Division. / Cavanagh, Helen, photograph by Glamour Shots. Reproduced by permission of Glamour Shots.

COLLICOTT, SHARLEEN. Collicott, Sharleen, illustrator. From an illustration in *The Chicken Sisters,* by Laura Numeroff. Laura Geringer Books, 1997. Illustrations copyright © 1997 by Sharleen Collicott. All rights reserved. Reproduced by permission of

SOMETHING ABOUT THE AUTHOR®

ADAIR, Gilbert

■ Personal

Born in Scotland.

■ Addresses

Agent—c/o HarperCollins, 10 East 53rd St., New York, NY 10022-5299.

■ Career

Writer.

■ Writings

FOR CHILDREN

Alice through the Needle's Eye (sequel to Lewis Carroll's *Alice in Wonderland* and *Through the Looking Glass*), illustrations by Jenny Thorne, Dutton, 1984.

(Adaptor) *Alice: And Her Friends from Wonderland,* illustrations by Thorne, Macmillan (London), 1986.

Peter Pan and the Only Children (sequel to J. M. Barrie's *Peter Pan*), illustrations by Thorne, Macmillan, 1987, Dutton, 1987.

(Editor with Marina Warner and translator) *Wonder Tales: Six French Stories of Enchantment,* illustrations by Sophie Herxheimer, Chatto and Windus (London), 1994, Farrar, Straus and Giroux (New York City), 1996.

NOVELS

The Holy Innocents: A Romance, Heinemann (London), 1988, Dutton, 1989.

Love and Death on Long Island, Heinemann, 1990.

The Death of the Author, Heinemann, 1992.

The Key of the Tower, Secker & Warburg, 1997.

OTHER

Hollywood's Vietnam: From "The Green Berets" to "Apocalypse Now," Proteus/Scribners (New York City), 1981.

(With Nick Roddick) *A Night at the Pictures: Ten Decades of British Film,* Columbus Books (London), 1985.

Myths and Memories: A Dazzling Dissection of British Life and Culture, Fontana Paperbacks (London), 1986.

(Translator) Francois Truffaut, *Letters,* edited by Gilles Jacob and Claude de Givray, foreword by Jean-Luc Godard, Faber and Faber (London), 1989, published in the United States as *Francois Truffaut: Correspondence, 1945-84,* Farrar, Straus and Giroux, 1990.

The Postmodernist Always Rings Twice: Reflections on Culture in the Nineties (essays), Fourth Estate (London), 1992.

Flickers: An Illustrated Celebration of One Hundred Years of Cinema, Faber and Faber, 1995.

(Translator) Georges Perec, *A Void* (novel), Harvill Press (London), 1995, HarperCollins, 1995.

Surfing the Zeitgeist, Faber and Faber, 1997.

Contributor to periodicals, including *Film Comment* and *Sight and Sound.*

■ Sidelights

A versatile writer who has published children's books, adult novels, criticism, and translations, Gilbert Adair is known for the intelligence and playfulness with which he invests his works, regardless of genre, and for the multiplicity of allusions that are likewise an inevitable aspect of his varied writings.

In Adair's first book for children, *Alice through the Needle's Eye,* a sequel to the noted "Alice" books by Lewis Carroll, Carroll's famous heroine meets a particularly helpful kangaroo and enters a world where it actually rains cats and dogs. John Fuller, writing in the *New York Times Book Review,* contended that *Alice through the Needle's Eye* sometimes lacks "the peculiar tension that exists between the original Alice and the characters she meets." Fuller conceded, however, that the book proves Adair "strong on lexical play and well able to keep the narrative proceeding at a brisk pace." In fact, "the pages bristle with word play and paradoxes that would have delighted Carroll," Fuller notes, "and the organization of the story is confident in its ability to entertain and, in a brilliantly delayed challenge, to surprise the reader." *Publishers Weekly* remarked that while there was "almost an excess of puns and rhymes and riddles" in Adair's version, they were "very clever inventions, bearing comparison with their inspiration." Although a *Kirkus Reviews* commentator lamented that "Adair's animal/letter characters lack the intense, sharp-edged charm of Carroll's scary/lovable creatures" and that "the land beyond the needle's eye doesn't have the compelling, dream-geography quality of Carroll at his best," the critic nevertheless concluded that for word-play and Alice enthusiasts, "this is a genial, hardworking imitation." A *Junior Bookshelf* critic commended: "Gilbert Adair is a brave man to attempt a sequel." In *Peter Pan and the Only Children,* Adair continues the adventures of J. M. Barrie's beloved character. In Adair's update on this childhood classic, a child hurls herself from a ship and discovers an undersea world in which Pan and his band once again do battle with the evil Captain Hook. Humphrey Carter proclaimed in the *Times Literary Supplement* that Adair "has caught the Barrie manner triumphantly." A reviewer for *Junior Bookshelf* wrote, "it is a clever feat of imagination and makes adults, to whom it is to be commended, think further about the original."

Adair is perhaps best known, however, for his various works of fiction for adults, which include his first novel, *The Holy Innocents: A Romance,* evoking Jean Cocteau's film *Les Infants Terrible; Love and Death on Long Island,* which has been perceived as a spoof of Thomas Mann's *Death in Venice,* and *The Death of the Author,* based on a controversy that ensued after the death of admired critic and educator Paul de Man, posthumously revealed to be the author of anti-Semitic works from the Nazi era. Adair has also gained recognition for several volumes of criticism. In the early 1980s he completed *Hollywood's Vietnam: From "The Green Berets" to "Apocalypse Now,"* in which he decries many Hollywood films. He also produced additional film criticism

in *Flickers: An Illustrated Celebration of One Hundred Years of Cinema,* which surveys the history of cinema by concentrating on a specific film for each year.

In 1994 Adair served as editor and translator with others of *Wonder Tales: Six French Stories of Enchantment* for children. He has also been praised for his translations from the French for adults.

■ Works Cited

Carpenter, Humphrey, in a review of *Peter Pan and the Only Children, Times Literary Supplement,* November 20, 1987, p. 1282.

Fuller, John, in a review of *Alice through the Needle's Eye, New York Times Book Review,* May 5, 1985, p. 42.

Review of *Alice through the Needle's Eye, Junior Bookshelf,* February, 1985, p. 33.

Review of *Alice through the Needle's Eye, Kirkus Reviews,* January 1, 1985, pp. 1-2.

Review of *Alice through the Needle's Eye, Publishers Weekly,* January 5, 1985, p. 86.

Review of *Peter Pan and the Only Children, Junior Bookshelf,* February, 1988, p. 14.

■ For More Information See

PERIODICALS

Books for Keeps, January, 1988, p. 5.
Library Journal, October 1, 1996, p. 78.
New Yorker, May 13, 1985, p. 147.*

*   *   *

ANDREWS, Jan 1942-

■ Personal

Born June 6, 1942, in Shoreham-by-Sea, Sussex, England; immigrated to Canada, 1963; became Canadian citizen, 1971; daughter of Sydney Frederick (an accountant) and Georgina (a dog breeder; maiden name, Welsman) Ellins; divorced; children: Miriam, Kieran. *Education:* University of Reading, B.A. (with honors), 1963; University of Saskatchewan, M.A. (English), 1969; attended Carson Grove Language Centre, 1975. *Hobbies and other interests:* Canoeing, kayaking, cross-country skiing, gardening, rock climbing.

■ Addresses

Home—R.R. #2, Lanark, Ontario K0G 1K0, Canada.

■ Career

CFQC-Radio, Saskatoon, Saskatchewan, copywriter, 1963; University of Saskatoon, Saskatchewan, instructor in English, summer, 1965; Murray Memorial Library, Saskatoon, library clerk, 1965; Office of the Secretary of State, Ottawa, Ontario, grants officer in citizenship branch, 1972, program officer with Native Citizens Program, 1973, literary projects officer, then

JAN ANDREWS

writing and publications officer and acting head of academic and cultural resources in Multicultural Directorate, 1976, 1978, 1984; freelance writer, editor, storyteller, and organizer of children's literature workshops, readings, exhibitions, and panel discussions, 1977—; Ottawa-Carleton Board of Education, presenter of workshops at public schools, 1979—, teacher of evening classes for adults, 1983; Counterpoint School (parent-run cooperative), Ottawa, coordinator, 1981, 1984-85; developer, oral history program "Out of Everywhere," Expo '86, 1985-86; Andrews-Cayley Enterprises, Ottawa, founder and partner, 1987—. Organizer of reading series, including "Come Hear a Writer," Glebe Community Centre, 1982-83, "The Chance to Give," 1986, and "Uncharted Territory," 1988; writer and coordinator for recording *A Band of Storytellers*, Ottawa, 1985; National Library of Canada, researcher for exhibitions "The Chance to Give," 1986-87, and "The Secret Self," 1988; programmer of summer performances at National Gallery of Canada and for Cultures Canada Festival, Ottawa, both 1988; MASC (arts education organization), Ottawa, co-founder, 1990—; Canada Council, member of jury, 1991-92; reader and performer at schools and storytelling festivals across Canada, 1990—. *Member:* Writers Union of Canada, Canadian Society of Children's Authors, Illustrators, and Performers, Storytellers of Canada / Conteurs du Canada (founding member; national coordinator, 1996, 1997).

■ Awards, Honors

Canada Council grants, 1983, 1987, 1991; Best Books for Young Adults, *School Library Journal,* Notable Books selection, American Library Association (ALA), Ruth Schwartz Award shortlist, Canada Council Children's Literature Prize, and Ontario Arts Council honor, all 1986, and Washington State Children's Choice Picture Book Award, 1989, all for *Very Last First Time,* which was exhibited at the Bologna International Children's Book Fair in 1985; Ontario Arts Council Writers-in-Schools grants, 1990, 1993, 1994, 1996; Regional Municipality of Ottawa-Carleton grant, 1991; Governor General's Literary Award and Ruth Schwartz Children's Literature Award, both for *The Auction;* Governor General's Literary Award shortlist, 1996, for *Keri.*

■ Writings

PICTURE BOOKS

Fresh Fish ... and Chips, illustrated by Linda Donnelly, Canadian Women's Educational Press (Toronto), 1973.

Ella, an Elephant / Ella, un elephant, illustrated by Pat Bonn, Tundra Books (Montreal), 1976.

Very Last First Time, illustrated by Ian Wallace, Groundwood Books, Douglas & McIntyre (Vancouver), 1985, Atheneum (New York City), 1986, published as *Eva's Ice Adventure,* Methuen (London), 1986.

Pumpkin Time, illustrated by Kim LaFave, Groundwood Books, Douglas & McIntyre (Toronto), 1990.

The Auction, illustrated by Karen Reczuch, Groundwood Books, Douglas & McIntyre, 1990.

YOUNG ADULT NOVELS

Keri, Groundwood Books, Douglas & McIntyre (Toronto), 1996.

OTHER

(Contributor) *The Canadian Family Tree,* Don Mills, 1979.

(Editor) *The Dancing Sun: Stories and Poems Celebrating Canadian Children,* illustrated by Renee Mansfield, Press Porcepic (Victoria, British Columbia), 1981.

Coming of Age (dramatic montage), produced at National Library of Canada, 1985.

Contributor to periodicals, including *Canadian Children's Annual, Cricket, Ahoy,* and language arts publications in Canada and the United States.

■ Work in Progress

Pa's Harvest, a children's picture book, set in New Brunswick during the Depression, forthcoming from Groundwood Books; *A Place for Truth* (working title), a young adult novel of growth and change about two girls on a canoe trip; *Who Will Say Yes, Yes?,* a collection of traditional stories with West African drummer and storyteller Yaya Diallo.

■ Sidelights

A British-born author and storyteller who makes her home in the Canadian countryside, Jan Andrews obtains much of her inspiration from the natural world around her. "Most of my writing seems to be very firmly rooted in some place or another," Andrews explained to *SATA.* "I often wonder whether, if I had not come to North America, I would ever have started writing at all. There is something about the way of the land—its vastness and strength, the space of it—that speaks to me very deeply." The way of the land is an element that runs throughout her picture books, which include *The Auction, Pumpkin Time,* and the highly praised *Very Last First Time,* as well as Andrews' young adult novel *Keri,* which was published in 1996.

Born in Shoreham-by-Sea, England, in 1942, Andrews earned her bachelor's degree in her native Great Britain before marrying and moving to Saskatchewan, Canada, in 1963. At first over-awed by the massive prairies that dominate the landscape of central Canada, Andrews was inspired by the stories she created for her children to begin writing and researching. Her first children's book, *Fresh Fish ... and Chips,* was published in 1973, followed by the bilingual *Ella, an Elephant / Ella, un elephant.* Beginning in the mid-1970s, Andrews began working independently as a writer and has since organized numerous workshops related to children's literature. A co-founder of Storytellers of Canada/Conteurs du Canada, she continues to perform before audiences throughout her adopted country. "I find that—as a storyteller—it is the old traditional folk and fairy tales that interest me the most," she explained. "They seem to carry the age-old wisdoms within them and yet speak very directly to us as we struggle with our problems today. Both storytelling and writing have brought travel to distant locations and that has meant new friends. Storytellers particularly like to gather. Perhaps that's part of the reason I organized twenty tellers and fifteen listeners to get together and tell Homer's *Odyssey* from beginning to end at my home one summer weekend. The telling took fourteen hours but nobody wanted to miss a word."

Andrews' most well-known work, the picture book *Very Last First Time,* was published in 1985 and later released in England under the title *Eva's Ice Adventure.* The story tells about Eva Padlyat, a young Inuit girl, and her first trip alone out under the ice covering Canada's Ungava Bay during the winter to collect the mussels accessible from the ocean floor during low tide. Lowering themselves through a hole cut through the thick ice into the bone-chilling darkness below during low tide has been a traditional way for Native Americans of the region to gather food, but it has also been dangerous; the mussel-gatherer, who must carry with him or her a candle at all times in order to see beneath the thick crust of ice, has to be sure to exit back through the hole to the ice's surface before the waters return. Lucy Young Clem, in her review for *School Library Journal,* called *Very First Last Time* "well developed, with just the right amount of suspense" and "an intriguing view of a little-

known way of life." Clem's praise was echoed by other reviewers, including Mary Ellen Binder of *Canadian Children's Literature.* "Children find it easy to identify with Eva's changing emotions as she moves from excited anticipation, through happiness and satisfaction as she completes her task, the terror of being alone in the darkness under the ice, and finally to the relief of finding herself back with her mother again," noted Binder in her review. *New York Times Book Review* contributor Selma G. Lanes lauded Andrews' work as "the very model of what a factual picture book can be." Lanes added: "How lean the prose, like that of a fable, and how artfully its well-chosen words hold the reader in thrall."

The Auction concerns a young boy's apprehensions at discovering that his grandfather is selling the family's farm; Gran has died and the farm is too much for one person to keep up. So, Todd spends the night before the auction with Gramps indulging in happy memories, goodbye tears, and a few of the remaining homemade pickles that Gran had put up the year before. By the end of the evening the pair has filled the auction site with scarecrows, a playful activity that transforms a sad occasion into a new memory that both will be able to recall with happiness. While *Quill & Quire* contributor Christtine Fondse noted that the "slow pace" of *The Auction* would discourage some young solo readers, she added that most "will enjoy sharing its nostalgic look at the past with a discerning adult."

Andrews' first longer work, the young-adult novel *Keri,* is a "spare, powerful story of a single weekend in the life of an adolescent Newfoundland girl," according to *Horn Book* critic Sarah Ellis. The daughter of a fisherman who has been forced to take a job away from his boats due to generations of overfishing, Keri fears the impending loss

An Inuit girl faces the challenge of her first solo expedition to the seabed under the ice to gather food for her tribe. (From *Very Last First Time,* written by Andrews and illustrated by Ian Wallace.)

Keri is desperate to save the whale. But why does it mean so much to her?

Keri
Jan Andrews

Newfoundlander Keri abandons her own concerns when she finds a beached whale and becomes immersed in altruistic attempts to save its life in Andrews' novel for young adults.

of her family's stability. Her worries are quickly compounded by the death of her beloved Gran. The girl's growing insecurity, anger, and resentment find a focus in her mother, and soon Keri has alienated herself from everyone in her family except her younger brother, Grae. Ultimately, a beached whale discovered during a morning walk draws thirteen-year-old Keri out of her self and prompts her to heroism in her efforts to save the animal from death. However, the novel's conclusion is somewhat un-conventional: the girl's efforts are ultimately unsuccessful and the whale dies. Despite such a tragic ending, however, the protagonist is redeemed by story's end. "*Keri* is not about saving a whale," noted Ellis. "It is about an encounter with grandeur, an encounter from which one cannot emerge unchanged." Julie Bergwerff agreed in *Books in Canada*, adding praise for the author's spare style and the novel's realistic outcome, an outcome reflected by nature. "There is a true sense of 'wordscaping' in all of Jan Andrews's books," explained Bergwerff, "words and language reflect and grow out of the landscape in her work.... *Keri*'s landscape is harsh, spare, and tough, and the novel's prose echoes this ruggedness."

Although making the transition from picture books to young adult novels, Andrews has no plans to write adult literature. "I write for young people because I can't seem to help it," she told *SATA*. Although admitting to a "passionate interest in adult life," stories about young people and nature continue to dominate her imagination. Despite the seeming solitude of a writer's life—especially a writer who lives in the countryside, as does Andrews—she has developed a network with other authors that helps to inspire everyone involved. "There are a number of other children's writers in my area. Four of us get together at least once a month to critique each other's work. Sometimes we even have sleepovers. We are strongly supportive of each other but also fiercely critical. We don't let anything get by us, if we can help it. I know the group has benefited my writing immensely and would strongly recommend the process for anyone, of any age, who is interested in improving their work."

"I cannot imagine not telling stories, not writing, not giving workshops to help others who want to do the same," Andrews admits. But she also makes an effort to balance her intellectual pursuits with those of a more athletic nature. "I ... know, however, that I need physical as well as mental activity. Apart from anything else, moving my body helps to move the writing along whenever it gets stuck. Perhaps that's why I've recently added rock climbing to my hobbies. I love the challenge of it and hope that I'll be able to make it part of one of my books some day. Inevitably, the events of my life and of my stories keep overlapping. That's also how I'm involved in a series of books about two girls who go on canoe trips, I suppose."

Having lived in and around the Ottawa area for several decades, Andrews set down new roots in 1995. "I moved to a house which is all by itself, down the end of a dirt road, on a lake," she told *SATA*. "In the summer I can see loons, ospreys, and the occasional otter from my office window. With the coming of the winter, the ice sings. Then, there is whiteness everywhere. I consider myself unbelievably lucky and do not intend to move from here for a very long time.

"Do I like being a storyteller and a writer? I love it, but not every day. All jobs have their frustrations and mine is no exception. Each book is a voyage of discovery; each has its times of struggle. Maybe that's why I like it. Maybe it's the hardest thing I know how to do."

■ Works Cited

Bergwerff, Julie, review of *Keri, Books in Canada,* October, 1997.

Binder, Mary Ellen, review of *Very Last First Time, Canadian Children's Literature,* No. 45, 1987, pp. 82-86.

Clem, Lucy Young, review of *Very Last First Time, School Library Journal,* May, 1986, p. 67.

Ellis, Sarah, review of *Keri, Horn Book,* September-October, 1996, pp. 662-63.

Fondse, Christtine, review of *The Auction, Quill & Quire,* December, 1990, p. 18.

Lanes, Selma G., review of *Very Last First Time, New York Times Book Review,* June 15, 1986, p. 38.

■ For More Information See

BOOKS

Sixth Book of Junior Authors & Illustrators, edited by Sally Holmes Holtze, H. W. Wilson (New York City), 1989.

PERIODICALS

Booklist, June 15, 1986, p. 1537.

Bulletin of the Center for Children's Books, February, 1991, p. 135.

Canadian Children's Literature, No. 64, 1991, p. 92; No. 88, Winter, 1997, pp. 74-76.

Canadian Materials, January, 1991, p. 25.

Children's Literature in Education, September, 1993, pp. 226-27.

Growing Point, July, 1986, p. 4657.

Junior Bookshelf, August, 1986, p. 137.

Kirkus Reviews, April 15, 1991, p. 542.

Quill & Quire, December, 1985, p. 24; November, 1990, p. 12; May, 1996, p. 33.

School Library Journal, May, 1991, p. 74.

*   *   *

ANDRIANI, Renee
See WILLIAMS-ANDRIANI, Renee

*   *   *

AUSTIN, Carrie
See SEULING, Barbara

B

BANFILL, A. Scott 1956-

■ Personal

Born September 10, 1956, in Grand Rapids, MI; son of Philip (a truck driver) and Lorna (a homemaker; maiden name, Bard) Banfill. *Education:* Kendall School of Design (now Kendall College), graduated, 1977.

■ Addresses

Home—19215 98th Ave. S., Apt. B, Renton, WA 98055.

■ Career

Teague Associates, Renton, WA, senior designer, 1978—.

■ Awards, Honors

Parents' Choice Award, 1991, for *Whisper from the Woods.*

■ Illustrator

Victoria Wirth, *Whisper from the Woods,* Green Tiger Press (New York City), 1991.
Marni McGee, *The Forest Child,* Green Tiger Press, 1994.
Cooper Edens, *Nicholi,* Simon & Schuster, 1996.

■ Sidelights

A. Scott Banfill told *SATA:* "I grew up in Michigan with five siblings: an older brother and sister, two younger brothers, and one younger sister. I was always encouraged by my parents to draw. Later, teachers in elementa-

Illustrator A. Scott Banfill captures the magical holiday spirit of Cooper Edens's *Nicholi.*

ry school recognized my interest in art and also encouraged me.

"After graduating from Kendall School of Design in 1977, I moved to Renton, Washington (near Seattle) for a job with Teague Associates, an industrial design firm. They mainly design the interiors of airplanes. My job is illustrating the interior (before it is made) for Boeing's clients.

"I got started in children's books when a friend from work brought me a newspaper advertisement from an author who was looking for an illustrator. My friend told me that, if I didn't answer the ad, she would do it for me. The author was Victoria Wirth. If we had asked anyone involved with publishers, *Whisper from the Woods* probably never would have been published. After meeting with Victoria and discussing her ideas and my ideas about the story, it was decided that I would do rough sketches and three illustrations. We would then put together a book mockup and send it out to publishers. After we received several rejections, I decided to continue doing illustrations and update the mockup as I finished each one. All this work was being done in my spare time. I was spending an average of one hundred hours on each piece. When I had one illustration to go, we finally found a publisher and five years had gone by. When people involved with children's books hear this, the usual response is something like 'you must be crazy!'

"The hardest thing about illustrating *Whisper from the Woods* was that the whole story occurs in little places in the woods. To make each page interesting and different from the next one, I zoomed in and out and had animals moving in and out.

"In comparison *Forest Child* was easy, because the main characters moved around quite a lot. I enjoyed that luxury. I think if an illustration is interesting to me, and I can't wait to start painting it, then it will appeal to other people, too. The best way I found to do this is to work out all the problems in pencil first.

"*Nicholi* is a completely different book because it takes place in the winter. I found it is not easy to paint snow when it's eighty-five degrees in the summertime. Normally I work on a painting from start to finish, but I worked differently on these illustrations. Because there was so much snow, I wanted to get all of it done at first, to keep it all looking the same."

■ For More Information See

PERIODICALS

School Library Journal, March, 1995, p. 184.*

BAUER, Caroline Feller 1935-

■ Personal

Born May 12, 1935, in Washington, D.C.; daughter of Abraham (a lawyer for the U. S. government and for the General Council of the United Nations) and Alice (an adviser of foreign students; maiden name, Klein) Feller; married Peter A. Bauer (president of White Stag sportswear company), December 21, 1968; children: Hilary. *Education:* Attended the University of Colorado; Sarah Lawrence College, B.A., 1957; Columbia University, M.L.S., 1958; University of Oregon, Ph.D., 1971. Attended the Cordon Bleu cooking school in Paris. *Politics:* Democrat. *Religion:* Jewish. *Hobbies and other interests:* Travel (Europe, the Far and Near East, India), skiing (member of the National Ski Patrol), jogging, tennis, ice skating, swimming, kayaking, horses, dogs, cooking (and eating), puppetry, magic, drawing, crafts.

■ Addresses

Home—10155 Collins Ave. #402, Miami Beach, FL 33154. *Electronic Mail*—cblovesbks@aol.com.

■ Career

Author, illustrator, editor, educator, and librarian. New York Public Library, New York City, children's librarian, 1958-59, 1961; Colorado Rocky Mountain School, Carbondale, CO, librarian, 1963-66; University of Oregon Graduate School of Librarianship, Eugene, OR, associate professor of library science, 1966-79. Lecturer and educational consultant. Producer of "Caroline's Corner" for KOAP-TV, 1973-74. Also worked as a radio announcer and commentator in Aspen. *Member:* American Library Association, Society of American Magi-

CAROLINE FELLER BAUER

cians, Puppeteers of America, Bedlington Terrier Club of America.

■ Awards, Honors

Ersted Award, 1968, for distinguished teaching; selection, *New York Times* Best Illustrated Books of the Year and American Institute of Graphic Arts Book Show, both 1981, and Christopher Award, picture book category, 1982, all for *My Mom Travels a Lot;* Dorothy McKenzie Award, Southern California Council on Literature for Children and Young People, 1986, for distinguished contribution to children's literature.

■ Writings

FOR CHILDREN

My Mom Travels a Lot (picture book), illustrated by Nancy Winslow Parker, Warne, Viking, 1981, (big book format) D.C. Heath, 1996.

Too Many Books! (picture book), illustrated by Diane Paterson, Warne, Viking, 1984.

Midnight Snowman (picture book), illustrated by Catherine Stock, Atheneum, 1987.

Putting on a Play, illustrated by Cyd Moore, Scott Foresman, 1993.

EDITOR; ANTHOLOGIES FOR CHILDREN

Rainy Day: Stories and Poems, illustrated by Michele Chessare, Lippincott, 1986.

Snowy Day: Stories and Poems, illustrated by Margot Tomes, Lippincott, 1986, illustrated by Lynn Gates Bredeson, H. W. Wilson, 1987.

Presenting Reader's Theater; Plays and Poems to Read Aloud, illustrated by Bredeson, H. W. Wilson, 1987.

Windy Day: Stories and Poems, illustrated by Dirk Zimmer, Harper, Lippincott, 1988.

Halloween: Stories and Poems, illustrated by Peter Sis, Lippincott, 1988, HarperCollins, 1989.

Valentine's Day: Stories and Poems, illustrated by Blanche Sims, HarperCollins, 1993.

Thanksgiving Day: Stories and Poems, illustrated by Nadine Bernard Westcott, HarperCollins, 1994.

OTHER

Handbook for Storytellers, illustrated by Kevin Royt, American Library Association, 1977, revised and published as *Caroline Feller Bauer's New Handbook for Storytellers: With Stories, Poems, Magic, and More,* illustrated by Bredeson, American Library Association, 1993.

This Way to Books, illustrated by Bredeson, H. W. Wilson, 1983.

Celebrations: Read-Aloud Holiday and Theme Book Programs, illustrated by Bredeson, H. W. Wilson, 1985.

Read for the Fun of It: Active Programming with Books for Children, illustrated by Bredeson, H. W. Wilson, 1992.

The Poetry Break; An Annotated Anthology with Ideas for Introducing Children to Poetry, illustrated by Edith Bingham, H. W. Wilson, 1995.

Leading Kids to Books through Magic, illustrated by Richard Laurent, American Library Association, 1996.

Leading Kids to Books Through Puppets, illustrated by Laurent, American Library Association, 1997.

VIDEOS AND AUDIOS

(Self-illustrated) *Children's Literature: A Teletext,* Oregon Educational Public Broadcasting Service, 1973.

(Self-illustrated) *Getting It Together with Books,* Oregon Educational Public Broadcasting Service, 1974.

(Self-illustrated) *Storytelling,* Oregon Educational Broadcasting Service, 1974; American Library Association, 1980.

Caroline's Corner, Oregon Educational Broadcasting Service, 1974.

Creative Storytelling Techniques: Mixing the Media With Dr. Caroline Feller Bauer, American Library Association, 1979.

Poetry, American Library Association, 1980.

My Mom Travels a Lot (cassette and sound filmstrip), Live Oak Media, 1982.

Storytelling with Caroline Feller Bauer, H. W. Wilson, 1985.

Stories to Tell (audio), Caroline's Corner, 1992.

Programming with Books; Ideas for Introducing Children to Books, Library Video Network, 1996.

Also author of other educational aids, teletexts, and videocassettes, including "Take a Poetry Break!" and a sound recording, "What's So Funny? Humor in Children's Literature." Contributor to periodicals including *Cricket* and *International Quarterly.*

Bauer's works are included in the de Grummond Collection at the University of Southern Mississippi.

■ Sidelights

Author/educator Caroline Feller Bauer is the creator of numerous books and videos designed to help teachers excite children about reading. She has also lectured to teachers, librarians, and parents in all fifty of the United States and in more than sixty countries. As a writer for children, Bauer has produced several picture books and has compiled well-received anthologies of poems and stories for children and young adults. Her picture books characteristically center on childhood experiences while her anthologies for young readers are arranged around the weather, holidays, and plays and poems suitable for reading aloud. In her works for adult professionals, Bauer provides suggestions for effective storytelling and compiles anthologies of poetry and read-aloud ideas for holidays. She also explains teaching enhancements such as using magic tricks and puppets in the classroom—techniques that she herself explored as a teacher—and has made audio and video recordings on storytelling and on introducing children to literature. Bauer's dedication to the education of young readers comes from her own childhood experience. She once told *Something about the Author* (SATA), "I guess I don't want the same thing that happened to me to happen to other children. I didn't read for fun until I was in the sixth grade. In fact,

I was passed on probation from the second to the third grade because of my poor (non-existent?) reading skills." Bauer revealed in her essay in *Something about the Author Autobiography Series* (*SAAS*), "I still wish that I had discovered reading sooner, for I will never have enough time to catch up on all the books I missed during those years in elementary school when I refused to read."

Born in Washington, D. C., Bauer grew up during World War II and its aftermath. Her father, a lawyer, worked to build the United Nations at the end of the war as its General Counsel. Given her father's career, Bauer lived in Washington, D.C.; in Brooklyn and Manhattan and on Long Island; and in Paris. She also spent many summers at camp in Maine, Massachusetts, and Vermont and lived for a summer in Switzerland and for another in France. Before graduating from high school, Bauer had attended more than a dozen schools. However, her home life provided a stimulating environment. She explained to *SATA*, "Lots of famous people came to our house for dinner and they had wonderful discussions about everything—art, music, politics. I always thought my Dad said the most intelligent things in the wittiest way. My Mom was very curious about people so she was a terrific hostess. She didn't fuss with fancy food or place settings. She just made sure everyone was comfortable so they could talk."

Bauer's parents, she recalled in *SATA*, "read all the time, big fat tomes like *The Rise and Fall of the Roman Empire* and they discussed what they read at the dinner table. They also discussed world politics and philosophical and ethical questions. My mother took me to the library every week and we had our own home library, too. I loved to hear books read aloud and I listened to stories on the radio in the form of children's adventure series ('Superman,' 'Terry and the Pirates,' 'Captain Midnight') and adult soap operas. I drew lots of pictures, played with paper dolls and woodcrafting sets while I listened." Bauer was also very active as a child and especially enjoyed sports. She told *SATA*, "I ice-skated, rode a bike, played softball, and swam whenever I had the chance. I loved exploring. My dog and I went by ourselves through the neighborhood, across the golf course, or through the woods pretending we were the characters we heard about on the radio." Finally, in the sixth grade, Bauer "discovered books and read everything" she could. "My favorites in those days are still in print; The 'Freddy the Pig' books by Walter Brooks, *Mary Poppins, Dr. Dolittle,* and any story about dogs or horses." As she elaborated in *SAAS*, "I began to read all the time, even after I was in bed. It was delicious to think that I was up after everyone was asleep, reading under the covers with my flashlight."

In high school, Bauer became especially interested in the theater and in fine art; she later provided the illustrations used in several of her videos. As a young adult, Bauer went to college at the University of Colorado and Sarah Lawrence, and earned a master's degree in library science from Columbia University. At Columbia, she was inspired to work with children's literature. She told

SAAS, "Remembering my own struggles, I began to think of ways to make reluctant readers more interested in what I now considered the most wonderful hobby of all time." After graduation, Bauer worked as a librarian at the New York Public Library and attended the Cordon Bleu cooking school in France. Returning to the United States, she worked in both public and school libraries. Her love of outdoor sports took Bauer to Colorado, where she accepted a job as a radio announcer and commentator. Offered a position as a professor at the University of Oregon's Graduate School of Librarianship, she taught children's literature and storytelling and used visual aids such as puppets, slides, and magic tricks in the classroom. "Naturally," she told *SAAS*, "I was thrilled when I won an award for my 'distinguished teaching.'" After marrying her husband, with whom she had a daughter, Bauer earned her Ph.D. in library science in 1971. She also began writing book reviews for the children's magazine *Cricket.*

Combining her interest in children's literature with her media experience, Bauer began teaching college courses on television and wrote a viewer's guide which later became her first published work for adults, *Handbook for Storytellers*. Since that time, she has produced several books and videos which, as she explained in *SAAS*, "are all about showing teachers, librarians, and parents how to bring children and books together." Bauer says that her projects for adults demonstrate her "passion for showing children and young adults that reading is fun." For instance, the anthology *Presenting*

Bauer's anthology of poems and stories highlight the holiday through the work of numerous authors for young readers.

Reader's Theater is a "collection of scripts, based on favorite stories, for children to read aloud." Bauer, who was named a Magic Castle magician by the famous Hollywood night club devoted to magic, published *Leading Kids to Books through Magic* in 1996.

Bauer's book *The Poetry Break: An Anthology with Ideas for Introducing Children to Poetry* guides teachers through an innovative way of working with poetry. Students take a "poetry break" when someone from the class, or a visitor, exclaims, "Poetry break!" and shares a poem. The book contains over two hundred pages of poems suggested for poetry breaks, along with helpful lists and bibliographies. According to Deborah Stevenson of *Bulletin of the Center for Children's Books, The Poetry Break* also includes "ideas for presentation, settings, and general poetry activities." Carolyn Phelan of *Booklist* describes the work as "upbeat and down-to-earth."

Bauer has also produced several theme programs for children in a series she calls "Celebrations." She explained in *SAAS,* "Some of the themes reflect traditional holidays, like Thanksgiving, Valentine's Day, and Halloween, but there are also my own special holidays, like National Pig Day, National Nothing Day, and a program celebrating baseball." Writing in the *Horn Book Magazine,* Margaret A. Bush called *Thanksgiving Day: Stories and Poems* an "amiable collection of familiar and new stories and poems reflecting the season, favorite foods, and the fellowship of family and friends."

Bauer's first work of fiction for children, *My Mom Travels a Lot,* was published in 1981. This book, as Denise M. Wilms explained in *Booklist,* "catalogs the good and bad points of mom's absence." A little girl relates how, when her mother is away, she gets to eat out more often and doesn't have to make her bed. Still, her mother cannot be at all her school events, and she wasn't home when the puppies were born. "Mom's missed, but she always comes back," reported a critic in *Bulletin of the Center for Children's Books,* noting that *My Mom* "may have the appeal of a familiar situation for some children; for others the concept ... may stretch their minds beyond the stereotypical parent roles." Wilms called the work an "engaging bit of bibliotherapy.... Nicely done."

Midnight Snowman, a story based on an experience of Bauer's daughter Hilary, begins with another children's book—Ezra Jack Keats's *The Snowy Day.* After a little girl hears this classic story at school, she wishes for snow. Although it rarely snows where the little girl lives, late one night her wish comes true. The child and her friends rush outside to play in the falling snow and they build a wonderful snowman; some adult neighbors also become involved in the project before the snow melts away. Betsy Hearne of *Bulletin of the Center for Children's Books* described *Midnight Snowman* as an "atmospheric seasonal read-aloud" while Cathy Woodward in *School Library Journal* concluded, "This is a beautiful book to share with younger students while older students will want to look at it themselves."

Bauer has created a series of popular anthologies which provides stories and poems about types of weather for children. The collections include poetry by such writers as Langston Hughes, John Ciardi, Myra Cohn Livingston, Ogden Nash, Eve Merriam, Jack Prelutsky, and Lilian Moore and stories from familiar and unfamiliar sources. The first volume in the series, *Rainy Day: Stories and Poems,* contains, as Carolyn Phelan of *Booklist* noted, "sayings, facts, and activities" in addition to stories and poems. Phelan observed that the collection would be "particularly handy for teachers and librarians." "An unusually pleasant anthology," commented a *Kirkus Reviews* critic, who concluded by claiming that the book is an "inviting volume for new readers or to read aloud to preschoolers." The next volume, *Snowy Day: Stories and Poems,* is, in the words of Ann A. Flowers of *Horn Book,* a "delightful confection of facts, fiction, poetry, and recipes" that is "just the thing for reading aloud to oneself in the cold midwinter.... [A] wintry treat." According to *School Library Journal* contributor Susan McCord, the volume, which contains poems, stories, recipes, craft projects, and facts about snow, "should save many librarians from slouching through a whole poetry collection for excellent lyrical material." *Windy Day: Stories and Poems,* as Ellen Fader of *Horn Book* noted, "explores the various moods of the wind." The anthology includes poems, short stories, and facts and sayings about the weather, along with weather-related activities. According to Fader, the book is a "diverse collection" that is "an inviting, enticing, unintimidating volume.... [A] worthy complement to the other volumes in the series." Carolyn Phelan of *Booklist* called *Windy Day* an "attractive anthology for independent reading."

Bauer has traveled all over the world to lecture and teach as well as explore. As she explained in *SAAS,* "I've ridden a camel in India, taken a jeep trip over the sand dunes in Dubai, and floated on a boat down the Nile in Egypt." When she is not traveling, she enjoys jogging and horseback riding, playing with her dog, working on her hobbies (magic and puppetry), and reading. "My husband, Peter, and my daughter, Hilary, and I always take a book with us wherever we go. We read at meal times, on planes, and in the bathtub," she confessed to *SATA.* "I may be in your town soon," she told readers in her *SAAS* entry. "You'll recognize me. I'm the woman carrying a book, wearing jogging shoes, and looking around for a dog to admire. Please say 'Hello!' We can talk about books together."

■ Works Cited

Bauer, Caroline Feller, autobiographical essay in *Something about the Author Autobiography Series,* Gale, Volume 24, 1997, pp. 17-24.

Bush, Margaret A., review of *Thanksgiving, Horn Book,* November-December, 1994, p. 709.

Fader, Ellen, review of *Windy Day, Horn Book,* January, 1989, p. 84.

Flowers, Ann A., review of *Snowy Day, Horn Book,* March-April, 1987, pp. 217-18.

Hearne, Betsy, review of *Midnight Snowman, Bulletin of the Center for Children's Books,* February, 1988, p. 110.

McCord, Susan, review of *Snowy Day, School Library Journal,* December, 1986, p. 69.

Review of *My Mom Travels a Lot, Bulletin of the Center for Children's Books,* December, 1981, p. 63.

Phelan, Carolyn, review of *Poetry Break, Booklist,* May 1, 1995, pp. 1581-82.

Phelan, Carolyn, review of *Rainy Day, Booklist,* July, 1986, p. 1616.

Phelan, Carolyn, review of *Windy Day, Booklist,* November 1, 1988, p. 488.

Review of *Rainy Day, Kirkus Reviews,* May 15, 1986, p. 792.

Stevenson, Deborah, review of *The Poetry Break, Bulletin of the Center for Children's Books,* May, 1995, p. 329.

Wilms, Denise M., review of *My Mom Travels a Lot, Booklist,* January 1, 1982, 595-96.

Woodward, Cathy, review of *Midnight Snowman, School Library Journal,* December, 1987, pp. 66-67.

■ For More Information See

PERIODICALS

Booklist, September 15, 1996, p. 253.
Growing Point, September, 1988, p. 5044.
Horn Book, September-October, 1985, pp. 585-87.
Instructor, November, 1996, p. 26.
Interracial Books for Children, no. 6, 1982, p. 42.
Kirkus Reviews, August 15, 1989, p. 1242.
New York Times Book Review, July 23, 1985, p. 27.
School Library Journal, June, 1993, pp. 94-95.
Wilson Library Bulletin, January, 1991, pp. 56-60.

* * *

BAUM, Allyn Z(elton) 1924-1997

OBITUARY NOTICE—See index for *SATA* sketch: Born October 22, 1924, in Chicago, IL; died of cancer, May 17, 1997, in New York, NY. Photographer, journalist, editor, and author. Baum was a highly regarded photojournalist who covered stories from around the globe, in places such as South Africa, Peru, Germany, England, and Antarctica. After serving in the U.S. Army Air Forces during World War II, Baum began work as the Berlin bureau chief for International News Photos, becoming general manager for Europe and Paris, France, a year later. After two years at United Press Photos as a general manager in Germany, he joined the staff of *American Daily* magazine in London for two more years. In 1957 he returned to the United States as an associate editor at *Coronet* and as a staff photographer for the *New York Times.* His work at the *Times* spanned a decade. He then was senior editor of *Medical Economics* magazine until his retirement in 1990. His photography is contained in permanent collections at the Eastman House, Museum of Modern Art, and the Metropolitan Museum of Art. He wrote two books:

Antarctica, the Worst Place in the World and *Glove Compartment Guide to Car Care.*

OBITUARIES AND OTHER SOURCES:

PERIODICALS

New York Times, May 20, 1997, p. D23.

* * *

BIRDSEYE, Tom 1951-

■ Personal

Born July 13, 1951, in Durham, NC; son of Irving Earl (a minister) and Mary Hughes (a librarian; maiden name, Carmichael) Birdseye; married Debbie Holsclaw (an educator), May 18, 1974; children: Kelsey, Amy. *Education:* Attended University of Kentucky, 1969-72; Western Kentucky University, B.A. (mass communications), 1974, B.A. (elementary education), 1977. *Hobbies and other interests:* Skiing, hiking, canoeing, camping, mountain climbing.

■ Addresses

Home and office—511 Northwest 12th St., Corvallis, OR 97330. *Agent*—Jean V. Naggar, 216 East 75th St., New York, NY 10021.

■ Career

Writer. Ocean Lake School, Lincoln City, OR, teacher, 1977-83; Washington Elementary School, Sandpoint,

TOM BIRDSEYE

ID, teacher, 1985-88. Has also taught English in Japan. *Member:* Authors Guild, Authors League of America, Society of Children's Book Writers and Illustrators.

■ Awards, Honors

Children's Choice Book Award, International Reading Association, 1989, for *Air Mail to the Moon,* and 1995, for *A Regular Flood of Mishap.* Winner of four state Children's Choice Awards.

■ Writings

I'm Going to Be Famous, Holiday House, 1986.
Air Mail to the Moon, illustrated by Stephen Gammell, Holiday House, 1988.
Song of Stars: An Asian Legend, illustrated by Ju-Hong Chen, Holiday House, 1990.
Tucker, Holiday House, 1990.
Waiting for Baby, illustrated by Loreen Leedy, Holiday House, 1991.
Just Call Me Stupid, Holiday House, 1993.
A Kids' Guide to Building Forts, illustrated by Bill Klein, Harbinger House (Tucson, AZ), 1993.
(Reteller) *Soap! Soap! Don't Forget the Soap! An Appalachian Folktale,* illustrated by Andrew Glass, Holiday House, 1993.
A Regular Flood of Mishap, illustrated by Megan Lloyd, Holiday House, 1994.
(With Debbie Holsclaw Birdseye) *She'll Be Comin' Round the Mountain,* illustrated by Andrew Glass, Holiday House, 1994.
Tarantula Shoes, Holiday House, 1995.
(With Debbie Holsclaw Birdseye) *What I Believe: Kids Talk about Faith,* photographs by Robert Crum, Holiday House, 1996.
(With Debbie Holsclaw Birdseye) *Under Our Skin: Kids Talk about Race,* photographs by Robert Crum, Holiday House, 1997.

■ Sidelights

Tom Birdseye readily admits that he never aspired to be a writer. As a young man growing up in North Carolina and Kentucky, he was more interested in sports, crawdads, mud balls, forts built in the woods, secret codes, bicycles without fenders, butter pecan ice cream, and snow. Birdseye, however, became published at the age of thirty-five after ten years of teaching, a year of living in Japan, and two unrelated degrees. The author once commented, "Life, it seems, is full of who'd-a-thought-its."

"At times it still amazes me that writing is my profession," Birdseye continued. "It was such a difficult process for me when I was a kid; I can really identify with the reluctant writer in school today." The author recalled how difficult it was for him to complete stories because of his poor grammatical skills. He acknowledges that if it were not for certain people offering him encouragement, he would not have prospered as a writer. Birdseye now carries a small notebook around just in case he comes across any new ideas or characters.

"True, I still labor through my stories," Birdseye admitted, "wrestling with the spelling beast and the punctuation monster, writing and rewriting, then rewriting some more, until I glean my best, but the process has become one of pleasure instead of pain. I love doing it, and I love sharing it with others. The boy who couldn't imagine himself a writer, now can't imagine himself anything else."

Birdseye's first published work for children, *I'm Going to Be Famous,* appeared in 1986. In this story, a fifth-grader, Arlo, focuses all of his energy on breaking the world record for eating bananas, which is seventeen bananas in two minutes. Arlo's feat begins as a personal endeavor but quickly becomes a major event at his school. He starts to wonder if breaking the record is worth the attention, especially since his parents disapprove. Arlo lies about the outcome, leaving him in an awkward position with his friends. Calling *I'm Going to Be Famous* a "furiously funny story," *Booklist* contributor Ilene Cooper states that the work has a "built-in appeal and a certain silliness that middle graders will adore."

Tucker addresses issues of divorce, sibling rivalry, and unemployment. The title character, eleven-year-old Tucker Renfro, lives with his divorced father, apart from his mother and nine-year-old sister Olivia. When Olivia comes to visit Tucker after seven years of absence, they do not get along. With time, however, the siblings grow more comfortable with each other. Olivia makes Tucker hopeful by telling him that their parents are getting back together. His hopes are crushed, however, after learning that his sister has been lying. The book also touches upon Tucker's passion to become an Indian hunter. He shoots a deer with his homemade bow and arrow despite being too young to receive a hunting license. After watching the deer suffer before dying, Tucker regrets killing the animal. The young boy's dilemmas are "treated sensitively and realistically," according to *School Library Journal* contributor Susan H. Williamson. Deborah Abbott, a reviewer for *Booklist,* contends that "readers will identify with the problems and the positive ending."

Waiting for Baby is another of Birdseye's well-known children's stories. In anticipation of becoming a big brother, a young boy envisions the fun he and his new sibling will have playing games, wrestling, and reading stories—but the activities he imagines are not appropriate for an infant. When his baby sister arrives, the older child is not disappointed because he likes to snuggle and hold her close to him. Ellen Mandel, a reviewer for *Booklist,* asserts that *Waiting for Baby* is "a beautifully executed, reassuring read for expectant families." "This idealized view of a new sibling is a good choice for sharing aloud," Virginia E. Jeschelnig notes in *School Library Journal.*

Just Call Me Stupid tells the struggle of a fifth-grader, Patrick, who reads below his grade level. Published in 1993, the book details the effects that parental verbal abuse and neglect has on a child. Every time Patrick tries to read, he begins to hyperventilate and the words blur together. His alcoholic father makes matters worse with his abusive comments. The only people who seem to care about Patrick are his teacher, Mrs. Romero, and his next door neighbor and classmate, Celina. Celina is bubbling with enthusiasm and motivates Patrick to explore his creativity. Thus, he recites an original story to Celina, which she records and secretly submits to a contest. When he wins, Patrick is furious with her. The boy later conquers his fear of books with his mother's unconditional love, Celina's confidence, and Mrs. Romero's encouragement. A contributor to *Kirkus Reviews* remarks that the book is "lively and well plotted, with funny ... scenes and a satisfying upbeat ending." Describing *Just Call Me Stupid* as a "dramatic, insightful novel," a *Publishers Weekly* reviewer proclaims the book "may also spark classroom discussion about self-esteem, disabilities, and talents."

In 1993, Birdseye turned his attention to folklore, in *Soap! Soap! Don't Forget the Soap! An Appalachian Folktale.* Plug Honeycut is a forgetful little boy who is sent to the store by his mother to purchase soap. Since the young man is easily distracted, he has to repeat, "Soap! Soap! Don't forget the soap!" Unfortunately, Plug ends up repeating whatever he hears from other people along the way. Each time he picks up a new phrase, he tells it to the next person he comes in contact with, unintentionally offending the stranger. When someone mentions soap again, Plug finally remembers his initial mission. A *Kirkus Reviews* contributor describes Birdseye's retelling of the book as "colorful and comical." *Booklist* reviewer Janice Del Negro adds that the "book will also work well in read-aloud programs ... or as a source for more traditional library storytelling."

■ Works Cited

Abbott, Deborah, review of *Tucker, Booklist,* July, 1990, p. 2086.

Birdseye, Tom, author comments in a Holiday House publicity flyer, c. 1997.

Cooper, Ilene, review of *I'm Going to Be Famous, Booklist,* December 1, 1986, p. 574-75.

Del Negro, Janice, review of *Soap! Soap! Don't Forget the Soap!, Booklist,* March 15, 1993, p. 314.

Jeschelnig, Virginia E., review of *Waiting for Baby, School Library Journal,* November, 1991, p. 90.

Review of *Just Call Me Stupid, Kirkus Reviews,* November 1, 1993, p. 1386.

Review of *Just Call Me Stupid, Publishers Weekly,* October 25, 1993, p. 62.

Mandel, Ellen, review of *Waiting for Baby, Booklist,* November 1, 1991, p. 530.

Review of *Soap! Soap! Don't Forget the Soap!, Kirkus Reviews,* May 1, 1993, p. 593.

Williamson, Susan H., review of *Tucker, School Library Journal,* June, 1990, p. 116.

■ For More Information See

PERIODICALS

Booklist, April 15, 1990, p. 1624-25; January 15, 1994, p. 930; July, 1994, p. 1952.
Bulletin of the Center for Children's Books, January, 1987, p. 82; June, 1993, p. 308.
Horn Book, May, 1988, p. 337; May, 1993, p. 338-39.
Kirkus Reviews, March 15, 1988, p. 450.
Publishers Weekly, March 18, 1988, p. 86; April 27, 1990, p. 60; August 1, 1994, p. 78.
School Library Journal, May, 1988, p. 76.

*   *   *

BIRNEY, Betty G. 1947-

■ Personal

Born April 26, 1947, in St. Louis, MO; daughter of Edgar J. (a businessman) and Ella (a homemaker; maiden name, Mohrmann) Griesbaum; first marriage dissolved; married Frank W. Birney (an actor), November 26, 1982; children: Walshe H. *Education:* Webster University, B.A. (cum laude), 1969; attended University of Missouri-Columbia, 1970-71. *Politics:* Independent. *Religion:* Presbyterian. *Hobbies and other interests:* "Reading (of course!), playing piano, computer stuff."

■ Addresses

Home—Sherman Oaks, CA. *Agent*—Todd Koerner, Writers & Artists, 924 Westwood Blvd., #900, Los Angeles, CA 90024. *Electronic mail*—bbirney @soca.com.

■ Career

Children's book author. Has worked as an advertising copywriter for various agencies in St. Louis, MO, and Chicago, IL; Disneyland, Anaheim, CA, advertising copywriter, 1977-79; Walt Disney Co., Burbank, CA, publicist, 1979-81; freelance television writer, 1982—. Trustee, the Humanitas Prize. *Member:* Society of Children's Book Writers and Illustrators, Authors Guild, PEN Center USA, Writers Guild of America-West.

■ Awards, Honors

ANDY Award, New York Ad Club; FLAIR Award, St. Louis Ad Club; Writers' Guild of America Award, Writers' Guild of America, 1991, Pappenheim Award, Jewish Family Services, both for "But He Loves Me"; Humanitas Prize, Human Family Educational and Cultural Institute, 1991, for "Wish upon a Fish," 1993, for "Big Boys Don't Cry," and 1996, for "Fast Forward"; Emmy Award nomination, Academy of Television Arts and Sciences, 1994, for "Big Boys Don't Cry"; Cybermania '94, Academy of Interactive Arts and Sciences, 1994, for "Berenstain Bears on Their Own"; Gold Apple, National Educational Media Network, 1996.

BETTY G. BIRNEY

■ Writings

Disney's Chip 'n Dale Rescue Rangers: The Rescue Rangers Save Little Red, illustrated by Don Williams, Western, 1991.
Oh Bother, Somebody's Not Listening, illustrated by Darrell Baker, Western, 1991.
Oh Bother, Somebody's Fibbing, illustrated by Sue DiCicco, Western, 1991.
(Adaptor) *Disney's The Little Mermaid,* illustrated by Kerry Martin and Fred Marvin, Western, 1992.
What's My Job?: A Riddle Flap Book, illustrated by Lisa Berrett, Simon & Schuster, 1992.
Who Am I?: A Riddle Flap Book, illustrated by Lisa Berrett, Simon & Schuster, 1992.
Oh Bother, Somebody's Grumpy, illustrated by Sue DiCicco, Western, 1992.
Walt Disney's Winnie the Pooh Half a Haycorn Pie, illustrated by Darrell Baker, Western, 1992.
Walt Disney's Winnie the Pooh and the Missing Pots, illustrated by Russell Hicks, Western, 1992.
Oh Bother, Somebody's Messy, illustrated by Nancy Stevenson, Western, 1992.
Disney's Beauty and the Beast: The Tale of Chip the Teacup, illustrated by Edward R. Gutierrez and Mones, Western, 1992.
Bambi's Snowy Day, illustrated by David Pacheco and Diana Wakeman, Western, 1992.
Walt Disney's Winnie the Pooh and the Little Lost Bird, illustrated by Russell Hicks, Western, 1993.
(Adaptor) *Disney's Beauty and the Beast,* illustrated by Mones, Western, 1993.

Oh Bother, Somebody Won't Share, illustrated by Nancy Stevenson, Western, 1993.
Raja's Story, St. Louis Zoo, 1993.
Walt Disney's Sleeping Beauty, illustrated by Mones, Western, 1993.
Walt Disney's Winnie the Pooh: The Merry Christmas Mystery, illustrated by Nancy Stevenson, Western, 1993.
Oh Bother, Somebody's Jealous, illustrated by Nancy Stevenson, Western, 1993.
Oh Bother, Somebody's Afraid of the Dark, illustrated by Darrell Baker, Western, 1993.
Walt Disney's I Am Winnie the Pooh, illustrated by Darrell Baker, Western, 1993.
(Adaptor) *Black Beauty,* Western, 1994.
Tyrannosaurus Tex, illustrated by John O'Brien, Houghton Mifflin, 1994.
(Adaptor) *Disney's Toy Story,* Western, 1995.
Meltdown at the Wax Museum, Western, 1995.
Pie's in the Oven, illustrated by Holly Meade, Houghton Mifflin, 1996.
Let's Play Hide and Seek, illustrated by Dara Goldman, Scholastic, 1997.

Co-author of *Disney Babies Bedtime Stories,* Mallard, 1990.

OTHER

Also author of scripts for live-action television series and special programs, including "Mary Christmas," to be aired, "My Indian Summer," a *CBS Schoolbreak Special* (Big Daddy Productions), "Fast Forward," an *ABC Afterschool Special* (also supervising producer; Wild Films), "Big Boys Don't Cry," a *CBS Schoolbreak Special* (Churchill Pictures), "But He Loves Me," a *CBS Schoolbreak Special* (Churchill Pictures), *The Puzzle Place* (PBS), *Talking with TJ* (Hallmark/UBU), *It Happened to Me* (Boy Scouts of America), *Zoobilee Zoo* (DIC/Syndication/PBS), *Too Smart for Strangers* (Disney Channel), *Welcome to Pooh Corner* (Disney Channel), *Dumbo's Circus* (Disney Channel), *Divorce Court,* and *Secret Lives* (Barry Enright Productions/Syndication).

Author of scripts for animated television programs, including *Book of Virtues* (Porchlight/PBS), *The Good Samaritan* (Sony Wonder), *Little Mouse on the Prairie* (Saban/Syn.), *Madeline* (DIC/ABC/Family Channel), *Where's Waldo* (Where's Waldo Productions/Goodtimes), *Camp Candy* (DIC/Saban/NBC/World Vision), *Doug* (Jumbo Pictures/Nickelodeon), *Prince Valiant* (Hearst/Family Channel), *Bobby's World* (Film Roman/Fox), *Maxie's World* (DIC/Syndication), *Once upon a Forest* (Hanna-Barbera), *The Chipmunks* (Bagdasarian/NBC), *Fraggle Rock* (Marvel/Henson/NBC), *The Moondreamers* (Marvel/Syndication), *The Snorks* (Hanna-Barbera/NBC).

Author of interactive software, including "The Crayon Factory" (Philips/Sega), "Berenstain Bears on Their Own" (Philips), "Wacky Tales" (Barry Interactive), "Storypainting: The Wizard of Oz" (Electronic Arts), "Richard Scarry's Busiest Disc Ever" (Philips), "Rich-

By the time the cattle came to their senses, they were safe and sound and rounded up again.

Pa thanked Tex and asked him to stay with the roundup.

"Sorry, partner," said Tex. "I gotta keep moving. But you got good help with these two youngsters."

He tipped that giant hat to Cookie and Pete.

And with a trembling of the tumbleweed and a shaking of the sagebrush, Tyrannosaurus Tex was gone.

In the tradition of American tall tales, Birney relates the legendary heroics of a dinosaur cowboy in *Tyrannosaurus Tex,* illustrated by John O'Brien.

ard Scarry's Busiest Neighborhood Ever" (Philips), "The Dark Fables of Aesop" I & II (Philips).

■ Sidelights

Betty G. Birney is the author of numerous works for children appearing in a variety of formats, including conventional picture books and lift-the-flap books as well as live-action and animated television programs and interactive software. Among her books for children is *Tyrannosaurus Tex,* a humorous story that plays upon the enduring popularity of dinosaurs among young audiences. .The story, which features a huge cowboy dinosaur, also relies upon common Texas mythology, in which everyone is a cowboy and everything is big. Thus Tyrannosaurus Tex shows up one night on the range, and after eating a pot of beans, pot and all, joins the other cowboys around the fire to tell tall tales. That night he saves the others by putting out a fire with his ten-thousand gallon hat. Birney's alliterative text delighted several reviewers, who recommended *Tyrannosaurus Tex*—"a tumbleweed-tumbling, rip-roaring good tale," according to Claudia Cooper in *School Library Journal*—for group readings.

Less a knee-slapping tall tale than a charming feel-good story, Birney's *Pie's in the Oven* was nonetheless equally warmly received by critics. When a boy and his grandfather arrive home with a basket full of freshly picked apples, the boy and his grandmother spend the day making apple pie. The smell of the pie as it bakes fills

not only the boy with delightful anticipation, but draws in aunts, uncles, friends, and even the mail carrier, each of whom is invited to join in the feast. "The narration offers the exuberant youngster's perspective on the events," noted Kathy Piehl in *School Library Journal.* The simplicity of the story, coupled with Birney's gently rhythmical prose, adds up to a "sweet celebration of family and friends," according to a critic in *Kirkus Reviews.*

Birney told *SATA:* "Some people find it strange that I've worked in so many mediums, from books to TV movies to animation to CD-ROM software. What links these different kinds of projects—and makes my career very interesting to me—is the fact that a story is a story and I am a storyteller. Some stories are better told in a small flap book. Others belong on the big screen. Once I get 'inside the story,' it doesn't matter whether I'm telling the story of a honey-loving bear or an abused teenager; the process of creating characters and plots is really the same and never, ever boring."

■ Works Cited

Cooper, Claudia, review of *Tyrannosaurus Tex, School Library Journal,* May, 1994, p. 84.

Piehl, Kathy, review of *Pie's in the Oven, School Library Journal,* September, 1996, p. 170.

Review of *Pie's in the Oven, Kirkus Reviews,* August 1, 1996, p. 1147.

■ For More Information See

PERIODICALS

Booklist, June 1, 1994, p. 1835; July, 1996, p. 1828.
Horn Book, May-June, 1994, p. 306.
Publishers Weekly, January 24, 1994, pp. 54-55; April 28, 1997, p. 77.

* * *

BLAIR, L. E.
See CALHOUN, B. B.

* * *

BLOOR, Edward (William) 1950-

■ Personal

Born October 12, 1950, in Trenton, NJ; son of Edward William Bloor and Mary Cowley Bloor; married Pamela Dixon (a teacher), August 4, 1984; children: Amanda Kristin, Spencer Dixon. *Education:* Fordham University, B.A., 1973.

■ Addresses

Home—12021 Windstone St., Winter Garden, FL 34787. *Electronic mail*—ebloor@harcourtbrace.com.

■ Career

Teacher in Florida public schools, 1983-86; senior editor, Harcourt Brace School Publishers, Orlando, FL, 1986—.

■ Awards, Honors

Books in the Middle, Outstanding Titles of 1997, *Voice of Youth Advocates, Horn Book* honor list, 1997, Pick of the List, American Booksellers Association, 1997, 100 Titles for Reading and Sharing, New York Public Library, 1997, Top Ten Best Books for Young Adults and Best Books for Young Adults citations, American Library Association, both 1998, and Edgar Allen Poe Award nominee for Best Young Adult Novel, 1998, all for *Tangerine.*

■ Writings

Tangerine, Harcourt Brace, 1997.

■ Work in Progress

Crusader, for Harcourt Brace.

■ Sidelights

Edward Bloor told *SATA:* "The current phase of my life started when I took a teaching job in a public school in south Florida. That's where I met my wife, Pam, who has made all of this possible and with whom I raise two children, Amanda and Spencer. My teaching job led to a

EDWARD BLOOR

job in educational publishing, where I was actually required to sit and read young adult novels all day long. So I decided to try it myself.

"I wrote most of *Tangerine* on my ride to work down the back roads of Florida, west of Orlando. To my dismay, I watched the daily destruction of the citrus groves along this route. This is how it happens: The citrus trees are uprooted and bulldozed into piles; the piles are set on fire; the charred remains of the trees are buried, and tons of white sand are dumped over their graves. After that, a completely different place is created, a place as fictional as any novel. A developer erects a wall, thinks of a theme, and gives the place a name. Then the place fills up with large houses and with people whose only common bond is that they qualified for the same amount of mortgage money.

"These daily sights, relentless and repulsive, made me think about this: Who are the people who used to make a go of it here? Who are the people now making their exit while we're making our entrance? And how do they feel about all this?

"These questions are part of what drives Paul Fisher, the story's protagonist, although the reader soon comes to realize that the demise of the citrus industry may be the least of Paul's worries. Paul lives in constant fear of his evil older brother, Erik. Paul also struggles mightily to lead a normal life and to see things as they really are despite the thick-framed glasses that cover his injured eyes. Playing goalie in soccer is at the core of Paul's life, and he gets to do it on two teams, one of which is a mixture of boys and girls. It is the clash of these two

Bloor's well-received first novel touches on environmental and social issues while exploring the trials of its seeing-impaired, soccer-playing protagonist, Paul Fisher. (Cover illustration by Joel Peter Johnson.)

teams, these two schools, and these two worlds that brings about the climactic scenes of the novel.

"I grew up in a city, Trenton, New Jersey, where children's soccer was taken very seriously. Different ethnic communities—Poles, Italians, Germans, Ukrainians—all had their kids' soccer clubs. Parents of the children on these teams raged and howled at the games as if their national pride was at stake. I was one of those little kids trying desperately to kick a soccer ball amidst the multilingual howling. I continued my soccer playing through high school, on a really good team, and into college, on a really bad team."

Set in the tangerine-growing region of Florida, Bloor's first novel touches on environmental and social issues while exploring the trials of the seeing-impaired, soccer-playing protagonist, Paul Fisher. *Bulletin of the Center for Children's Books* reviewer Deborah Stevenson stated that *Tangerine* "is a richly imagined read about an underdog coming into his own." Bloor deftly blends several plotlines into "a series of gripping climaxes and revelations," according to a *Kirkus Reviews* contributor. Well-rounded characterization and a humorous edge add to the appeal of the book. *Booklist* reviewer

Kathleen Squires asserted that "this dark, debut novel proves that Bloor is a writer to watch."

■ Works Cited

Squires, Kathleen, review of *Tangerine, Booklist,* May 15, 1997, p. 1573.
Stevenson, Deborah, review of *Tangerine, Bulletin of the Center for Children's Books,* March, 1997, p. 241.
Review of *Tangerine, Kirkus Reviews,* February 1, 1997, p. 219.

■ For More Information See

PERIODICALS

Horn Book, July-August, 1997, p. 449.
Publishers Weekly, March 24, 1997, p. 84; June 30, 1997, p. 27.
School Library Journal, April, 1997, p. 1334.

* * *

BOLAND, Janice

■ Personal

Born in Brooklyn, NY; daughter of Joseph Marino (a photoengraver) and Lena Marchetti Marino (a school teacher); married James Boland (in finance and real estate), 1960; children: Robert, John. *Education:* Fordham University, B.S. (education); attended Fordham University Graduate School of Education. *Politics:* Humanitarian. *Religion:* Roman Catholic. *Hobbies and other interests:* Education, herbalism, early music, the arts.

■ Addresses

Home—Box 352, Cross River, NY 10518. *Office*—Richard C. Owen Publishers, Inc., Box 585, Katonah, NY 10536.

■ Career

Writer and illustrator. Richard C. Owen Publishers, Katonah, NY, Director of Children's Books, 1990—; Mt. Pleasant Public Library, Pleasantville, NY, graphic artist. Former school teacher and adjunct professor of writing and children's book illustration. *Member:* Society of Children's Book Writers and Illustrators, National Teachers Association, National Federation of Teachers, Civil Service Employees Association, Reading Recovery Council of North America, American Association of University Women.

■ Awards, Honors

Pick of the List, American Booksellers Association, 1993, for *Annabel;* Children's Choice, International Reading Association—Children's Book Council, 1996-97, for *Annabel Again;* Washington Irving Award nomination, 1998, for *A Dog Named Sam.*

■ Writings

Annabel, illustrated by Megan Halsey, Dial, 1993.
Annabel Again, illustrated by Megan Halsey, Dial, 1994.
A Dog Named Sam, illustrated by G. Brian Karas, Dial, 1996.
The Fox, illustrated by Joe Boddy, R. C. Owen Publishers (Katonah, NY), 1996.
The Strongest Animal, illustrated by Gary Torrisi, R. C. Owen, 1996.
El Zorro, illustrated by Joe Boddy, R. C. Owen, 1996.
(And photographer) *The Pond,* R. C. Owen, 1997.
Zippers, illustrated by Judith Pfeiffer, R. C. Owen, 1997.
Breakfast with John, illustrated by Joe Veno, R. C. Owen, 1997.
Sunflowers, illustrated by Joe Veno, R. C. Owen, 1998.
Mrs. Murphy's Crows, R. C. Owen, in press.

A Dog Named Sam has been translated into Japanese and German; *The Strongest Animal* has been translated into Spanish.

■ Work in Progress

A book about carousels; further tales of Sam the dog's adventures; a picture book about a nonmusical child in a musical family; a book about elephants in New York City. Boland is also producing a series of fine art etchings.

■ Sidelights

Janice Boland told *SATA:* "Before I could read or write, I was drawing stories. My mother was a schoolteacher and a great advocate of literacy. My father was artistically and musically gifted. Our house was filled with books and drawing material and comic books. I remember understanding the stories in the comic books, before

JANICE BOLAND

I could read, by looking at the pictures. My family loved to tell each other stories about the past and about current happenings and daily home, work, and school experiences. Most of the stories ended in a humorous, dramatic, or memorable way. Every summer my mother, my sister, and I, and our various pets, including a bantam fighting rooster, headed to our country home. There, I explored the outdoors with my big red dog for protection. My mother encouraged my fascination with nature and my inclination to encounter it on my own. She fostered in me and my sister a sense of responsibility, independence, and curiosity.

"My first trade book, *Annabel,* is really a very brief autobiography. When I was writing it I wasn't aware of that. But after it was published I realized how much Mother Pig is like my mother. She expects Annabel to be successful in everything she does, and Annabel is. That's the way we were brought up.

"In college I majored in primary education. I took extra literature and art courses and studied with some very inspiring professors. I taught in the New York City public school system and in New York state and Connecticut public and private schools. I continued taking courses in children's literature, writing, communication, and the graphic and visual arts. I knew that I really wanted to create children's books from inception to the printed form.

"When my own children were infants their first gifts were books. They loved books. And I now had the perfect excuse to fill our home with children's literature, art, and poetry books.

"My second book, *Annabel Again,* was about an adventure I had as a child. My friend and I discovered an old barn on an abandoned road. It was filled with old spooky stuff and a brass-bound chest. While we were trying to unlock the chest, barn swallows looped and swooped over us. We never did get the chest open—but we knew it was filled with a treasure of gold and jewels.

"My third trade book, *A Dog Named Sam,* is the story of my children's adventures with their big yellow Labrador retriever. He was my children's companion and best friend for fifteen years, and did all the silly, endearing things Sam does in my stories.

"In 1990, I began a publishing career, working for Richard C. Owen Publishers, Inc., an educational publishing house. We developed a collection of children's author autobiographies and a collection of storybooks for children in kindergarten, first, and second grades. It started with a vision that Richard Owen had to create an ever-expanding core reading program of good literature books for beginning and fluent readers and aspiring young writers, books that the children could read on their own with success and enjoyment. With his support and encouragement we created a children's book department of which I am the director. My staff and I work with authors, illustrators, and photographers—ninety-five percent of whom are first timers—to develop their manuscripts and art into benchmark books for children at the critical beginning stages of literacy.

"My book *The Strongest Animal,* which is part of our Books for Young Learners collection, was inspired by a friend's visit to the Bronx Zoo while babysitting. *The Fox* is based on a fox who came each morning to see if the pet ducks and chickens my children were raising had forgotten to sleep in their house. *The Pond* is the story of the animals I see at a little pond two miles from my home. *Breakfast with John* is the story of my little hen, Rose, and her first egg. *Zippers* is the story of what happened to my suitcase in Boston. The book *Sunflowers* grew out of my pleasure in cultivating those fun flowers.

"I work on things simultaneously. I like to write two different books at the same time. I find that each stimulates ideas and enthusiasm for the other. I also love to do research for both my art and my stories. And of course I love to read. Lately, many of my choices for leisure reading have been all kinds of nonfiction such as autobiographies and travel memoirs. I love the books by Dervla Murphy and recently discovered the books of Elizabeth Von Arnim.

"As the director of children's books at R.C. Owen, I have opportunities to work with wonderful and gifted authors and artists, such as Verna Aardema, Eve Bunting, Paul Goble, Ruth Heller, James Howe, Jean Van Leeuwen, Jane Yolen, Jonathan London, and Frank Asch, to name just a few. Each one has an impact on my creativity and my commitment to children's literature.

"It is not easy to get published. It takes hard work, dedication, and enthusiasm. But what a great feeling it is when you see a child reading and enjoying a book you have created. It makes you feel that you have done something worthwhile.

"My advice to aspiring authors and artists is the same advice I gave my students when I taught courses in writing and illustrating children's books: 'Visit the children's room at your local library. Read all the books you can. Write every day. Hone your craft. And never give up.'"

■ For More Information See

PERIODICALS

Booklist, January 15, 1993, p. 918; April 1, 1996, p. 1375.
Kirkus Reviews, February 1, 1996, p. 223.
School Library Journal, March, 1993, pp. 170-71; August, 1995, p. 115; April, 1996, p. 99.

BORTON, Lady 1942-

■ Personal

Born September 8, 1942, in Washington, DC; daughter of John Carter (a public servant in the Department of Commerce) and Mary (a writer; maiden name, Newlin) Borton. *Education:* Attended University of Hawaii, 1962; Mount Holyoke College, A.B., 1964; further study at University of Pennsylvania, 1964-65, Temple University, 1967, Ohio University, 1972, 1975, and 1979, and Goddard College, 1979. *Religion:* Quaker. *Hobbies and other interests:* Reading, especially texts in Vietnamese.

■ Addresses

Home—1200 Stella Rd., Millfield, OH 45761. *Office*—Beacon School for Children with Mental Retardation and Developmental Disabilities, 801 West Union St., Athens, OH 45701. *Agent*—Meredith Bernstein, 2112 Broadway, No. 503A, New York, NY 10023.

■ Career

Westtown School, Westtown, PA, teacher of mathematics, 1964-67; Friends School, Philadelphia, PA, teacher of history, 1967-68; Overseas Refugee Program of American Friends Service Committee (AFSC), Philadelphia, assistant director, 1968-69; Quaker Service (physical rehabilitation center), Quang Ngai, Vietnam, assistant director, 1969-71; freelance writer and photographer, 1972—; Careline, Inc., Athens, OH, executive director, 1975-77; Pulau Bidong Refugee Camp, West Malaysia, health administrator, 1980. Beacon School for Children with Mental Retardation and Developmental Disabilities, Athens, bus driver, 1972—; home restoration worker, 1972—; B. Dalton Bookstore, Athens, clerk, 1985-88; Quaker Service—Vietnam, Hanoi, Vietnam, interim director, 1990-91, field director, 1993—. Independent radio producer, 1987—; columnist for *Akron Beacon Journal,* Akron, OH, 1989—; commentator for *Sunday Weekend Edition,* National Public Radio, 1990—; affiliated with Faculty Writers' Workshop at the Joiner Center for the Study of War and Social Consequences, University of Massachusetts, Boston, summers, 1993 and 1994. *Member:* PEN, Authors Guild, Society of Children's Book Writers and Illustrators, Association of Asian Scholars, National Association of Columnists.

■ Awards, Honors

Award for outstanding feature writing, Educational Press, 1975; fellowships for nonfiction writing, Ohio Arts Council, 1981, 1982, and 1988; Hannum-Warner travel fellowship, Mount Holyoke College, 1982; scholarship to Bread Loaf Writers' Conference; fellowship to Bread Loaf Writers' Conference, *Time,* Inc., 1984; named distinguished alumna by Mount Holyoke College, 1985; Sesquicentennial Award, Mount Holyoke College, 1987; fellowship to Wesleyan Writers' Conference, 1988; fellowship to Bennington Writers' Conference, 1990.

■ Writings

JUVENILE

Fat Chance!, Philomel Books, 1993.
Junk Pile, illustrated by Kimberly Bulcken, Philomel Books, 1995.

Also author of *Boat Boy,* Philomel Books.

OTHER

Sensing the Enemy: An American Woman among the Boat People of Vietnam (nonfiction), Doubleday, 1984.
Voyage of the Mekong Dragon, Wood Song Press, 1986.
Boat People and Vietnamese Refugees in the United States, Center for Social Studies Education, 1991.
After Sorrow: An American among the Vietnamese (nonfiction), Viking, 1995.

Contributor to *The Women's Almanac,* Armitage Press, 1976; *The Lessons of the Vietnam War,* edited by Don Luce, Center for Social Studies Education, 1986; *The Feminist Writers Guild Handbook,* edited by Celeste West, Dustbooks, 1986; *Women on War: Essential Voices for the Nuclear Age from a Brilliant International Assembly,* edited by Daniela Gioseffi, Simon and Schuster, 1988; *Visions of War, Dreams of Peace: Writings of Women in the Vietnam War,* edited by Lynda Van Devanter and Joan Fury, Warner Books, 1991; and *On Prejudice,* edited by Daniela Gioseffi, 1993. Contributor of articles to periodicals, including *Ms., Harvard Educational Review, Friends Journal, WIN, Focal Point, Harper's, Quaker Life,* and *Whole Earth Catalogue.*

■ Sidelights

"The book ... had dogged me for years," wrote Lady Borton (her real name, not a title) in the *Mount Holyoke Alumnae Quarterly.* "The book" is her own *Sensing the Enemy: An American Woman among the Boat People of*

Young Jamie Kay uses her imagination to transform her father's junkyard into a wondrous place. (From *Junk Pile!,* written by Lady Borton and illustrated by Kimberly Bulcken Root.)

Vietnam, the culmination of a decade-long odyssey that began in 1969, when Borton witnessed the ravages of the Vietnam War while working at an American Friends (Quaker) rehabilitation hospital in Quang Ngai. Throughout the 1970s, Borton tried to record her experiences with the Vietnamese people, first in journal form, then as a novel. She abandoned the effort in the face of what she called "my inability to recreate on paper the Vietnamese who had touched me."

Then in 1980 she accepted a position as a Red Cross health administrator at the Pulau Bidong Refugee Camp in West Malaysia. For six months she lived and worked with approximately thirteen thousand Vietnamese "boat people"—refugees who had fled Vietnam in ramshackle boats—on a barren volcanic island that, she says, was no bigger than her farm in southeastern Ohio. Her experience there finally broke the logjam: "Life on Bidong clawed at me with such intensity," she remembered in the *Mount Holyoke Alumnae Quarterly,* "that I could process it only by writing." The journal she kept at Bidong eventually became *Sensing the Enemy.*

Critics have noted that what distinguishes Borton's book from many other first-person accounts of Vietnam written by Westerners is, first, that the author looks at the tragedy of Vietnam from the perspective of the Vietnamese. "For years," Borton wrote in the *Mount Holyoke Alumnae Quarterly,* "I had been haunted by the perception that few Americans knew [the] Vietnamese except as victims, underlings, pimps and prostitutes." Second, Borton examines no political views or ideologies—she takes no interest in why the refugees she came to know had left Vietnam, nor does she explore the causes or the morality of the war there. Her goal simply is to record life in the camp, with its seemingly endless problems: disease, rats, monsoons, robberies, prostitution, erratic deliveries of United Nations rations, and the scores, if not hundreds, of unannounced refugees who arrived each day. In the *New York Times Book Review,* Henry Kamm found that "in artless words that stem from compassion, Miss Borton illuminates the refugee experience.... She illustrates the simple nobility of goals and the exceptional resources of spirit and determination that the refugees bring with them as their principal capital."

Borton continued her study of the Vietnamese people with *After Sorrow: An American among the Vietnamese.* "This book," the author once commented, "introduces the reader to the people who stayed in the country after the war. To my knowledge, I'm the only foreigner who has lived among the different sides in the war—I was in both South and North Vietnam during the war, and among boat people and former Vietcong (guerrilla members of the Vietnamese communist movement) southerners since. I continue to be haunted and, yes, driven to illuminate the pain that unites us all.

"For years I was the only foreigner whom the Vietnamese allowed to live in a village with a family. This was quite extraordinary, given that Vietnamese officials knew I'd written a book (*Sensing the Enemy*) that the

boat people find empathetic. But perhaps that speaks to the power of stories to heal. I worked on *After Sorrow* for more than ten years. It took more than three years to secure permission; I've been staying in the villages for a subsequent seven."

"My visits began during the period of collectivization, before the opening known here as *doi moi,* or 'renovation.' I was also among the first dozen Americans living in Hanoi. Although I did not set out to do this, *After Sorrow* also records from the inside, as they happened, the incredible changes that have transformed Vietnam. If I could have a wish for this book, it would be that readers feel the warmth and friendship towards Vietnamese that they, scarred from the war, have shown me."

From 1987 to 1993, Borton lived in three different communities in Vietnam. *After Sorrow* is her memoir of this period, a time spent listening to the peasant women recall the war. The stories reveal their active and varied roles in the war while still attending to the details of ordinary life. The stories also describe the devastation of the land and its people: the bombings, the terror, the soldiers still missing in action, and the long-term effects of the defoliant Agent Orange. Mary Ellen Sullivan, a critic in *Booklist,* remarked that the stories of these women are told with "deep compassion and respect ... bringing us fresh perspectives on the war." A contributor in *Kirkus Reviews* wrote that the coverage of the Vietnam War in *After Sorrow* is "rare for its honest, straightforward look at the ordinary people we fought."

■ Works Cited

Review of *After Sorrow: An American among the Vietnamese, Kirkus Reviews,* March 1, 1995, p. 281.

Kam, Henry, review of *Sensing the Enemy: An American Woman among the Boat People of Vietnam, New York Times Book Review,* April 29, 1984.

Mount Holyoke Alumnae Quarterly, summer, 1984.

Sullivan, Mary Ellen, review of *After Sorrow: An American among the Vietnamese, Booklist,* April 15, 1995, pp. 1469, 1476.

■ For More Information See

PERIODICALS

Booklist, October 15, 1993, p. 450; April 15, 1997, p. 1433.

Library Journal, March 15, 1995, p. 76.

Pacific Affairs, Spring, 1985, p. 186.

Publishers Weekly, February 24, 1984, p. 133; March 20, 1995, p. 50.

School Library Journal, December, 1993, p. 80.*

BREDESON, Carmen 1944-

■ Personal

Born November 3, 1944, in Norfolk, VA; daughter of Ralph (a professor and music critic) and Betty (Trader) Thibodeau; married Larry Dean Bredeson (an engineer), December 27, 1969; children: Dean, Lindsey. *Education:* Texas A & I University, B.S., 1967; Southern Illinois University, M.S., 1981. *Politics:* Republican. *Religion:* Christian.

■ Addresses

Home—Katy, Texas. *Electronic mail*—carmen @ tenet.edu.

■ Career

Writer. Taught high school English until 1972. Volunteered in neighborhood schools and libraries. *Member:* Society of Children's Book Writers and Illustrators, Texas Library Association, Texas Archaeological Society, Austin Writer's League, Maud Marks Friends of the Library (board member).

■ Writings

NONFICTION; FOR YOUNG PEOPLE

Jonas Salk: Discoverer of the Polio Vaccine, Enslow, 1993.
Henry Cisneros: Building a Better America, Enslow, 1995.
Ross Perot: Billionaire Politician, Enslow, 1995.
Ruth Bader Ginsburg: Supreme Court Justice, Enslow, 1995.
The Battle of the Alamo: The Fight for Texas Territory, Millbrook, 1996.
American Writers of the 20th Century, Enslow, 1996.
Presidential Medal of Freedom Winners, Enslow, 1996.
The Spindletop Gusher: The Story of the Texas Oil Boom, Millbrook, 1996.
Texas, Marshall Cavendish, 1997.
Gus Grissom: A Space Biography, Enslow, 1997.
Neil Armstrong: A Space Biography, Enslow, 1998.
The Moon, Franklin Watts, 1998.
Shannon Lucid, Millbrook, in press.

■ Work in Progress

Tide Pools for Franklin Watts; *I Know America: The Space Program* for Millbrook Press.

■ Sidelights

Carmen Bredeson has written a number of well-received nonfiction titles for middle graders and young adults. Her works on prominent twentieth-century Americans in such fields as science, politics, and the arts—men and women such as Dr. Jonas Salk, the discoverer of the polio vaccine; Supreme Court Justice Ruth Bader Ginsburg; astronaut Neil Armstrong; poet Maya Angelou; and Presidential Medal of Freedom winners Helen

CARMEN BREDESON

Keller, Cesar Chavez, and Colin Powell—are praised for providing a wealth of information, as do her books about historical places and events, several of which address subjects relevant to Bredeson's adopted home state of Texas. Commended for creating balanced, well-organized overviews that are considered good introductions to their topics and useful references for school reports, the author is also acknowledged for the in-depth discussions and vivid details of her books as well as for the clarity and liveliness of her writing style.

Bredeson developed a love of books as a child in Virginia. She told *Something about the Author* (*SATA*), "I grew up in a house filled with books. They lined the shelves, covered the tables, and piled up on the floor. Members of my family often traded books across the hallway at night and read favorite passages aloud for anyone who would listen." Later, as an English major at college in Texas, Bredeson discovered that she "always enjoyed writing research papers. Most of my classmates complained about the assignments, but I loved being in the library, digging through books for information. Making notes and arranging the facts into logical order appealed to me. These skills served me well in graduate school while I was studying to become a school librarian. I especially enjoyed the many reference assignments we were given. Although I never worked as a librarian, the things I learned didn't go to waste."

Bredeson's first career was as a high school English teacher. In 1972, she became a full-time mother. After she had married, Bredeson told *SATA,* she carried the love of books she had established as a child and young adult "to my new life. I began reading to my own children when they were still tiny babies, barely able to focus their eyes. When they got bigger, we made regular visits to the library and bookstore. There was always a pile of books sitting around in our house just waiting to be read. As a former English teacher, I knew that there was no substitute for good reading skills." While raising her two children, Bredeson volunteered at local schools and libraries. Since her own town did not have a public library, Bredeson and members of the community spent a lot of time and energy lobbying county officials to build one. Although it took ten years, their efforts were successful. Bredeson told *SATA,* "When our shiny new library opened, we had accumulated $100,000 to spend on extra books, equipment, and programs." In 1990, around the time the library was built and her children were entering college, Bredeson decided to write. She explained to *SATA,* "Since I love to do research, nonfiction was perfect for me. I wrote a short biography and spent the next two years sending it to publishers. I collected a big stack of rejection notices before finally getting the attention of an editor." Bredeson's first work, *Jonas Salk: Discoverer of the Polio Vaccine,* was published in 1993.

In *Jonas Salk,* Bredeson describes Salk's career from his days at medical school through his development of the polio vaccine and his research on a vaccine to combat the AIDS virus. In her *Appraisal* review, Janet K. Baltzell commented that the book "is especially notable for its in-depth discussion of the polio epidemic and the social and emotional importance of Dr. Salk's work in vaccine development." Baltzell concluded that the book "should be a valuable contribution" to biographies of leaders in the scientific field. Writing in *School Library Journal,* Joyce Adams Burner noted that the book is "a good overview" of Salk's life and work that would be "useful for reports" and "of interest to general science or biography readers."

In 1995, Bredeson published three biographies of well-known politicians: *Henry Cisneros: Building a Better America,* a study of the Mexican American who became a Texas mayor and Supreme Court official; *Ross Perot: Billionaire Politician,* the story of the businessman and Presidential candidate; and *Ruth Bader Ginsburg: Supreme Court Justice,* an outlining of the career of the second woman named to the United States Supreme Court. Writing in *Booklist* about *Ross Perot,* Mary Harris Veeder noted that Bredeson "presents a vivid detailing of her subject's early years." In her review of *Ruth Bader Ginsburg* in *Voice of Youth Advocates,* Mary Jo Peltier called the book an "informative biography" that is a "good source of current information on Ginsburg as well as a serviceable introduction to the Supreme Court." *School Library Journal* reviewer Katrina Yurenka concurred, noting that the "brief history of the U. S. Supreme Court will help readers understand just what [Ginsburg's] position entails."

In *American Writers of the 20th Century,* Bredeson introduces middle graders to ten major literary figures, including Willa Cather, John Steinbeck, Toni Morrison, and Ernest Hemingway. In her review in *Booklist,* Laura Tillotson commented that Bredeson "effectively capsules each [author] in a brief but thorough description." In *The Battle of the Alamo,* one of her first works focusing on a historical event, Bredeson offers readers a "brief, readable, and well-organized introduction to the historical background surrounding this momentous battle," in the words of Phyllis Graves of *School Library Journal.* Another of the author's books related to Texas, *The Spindletop Gusher,* tells the story of the discovery of oil at Spindletop Field in Beaumont, Texas in 1901 and provides information on petroleum and the oil industry. Writing in *Review of Texas Books,* Judith Linsley called *The Spindletop Gusher* "a must for any school and library," and added that it is "an excellent basic reference on the petroleum industry for adults as well." Bredeson has also focused her writing efforts on topics related to outer space and the people who have traveled there, such as Gus Grissom and Shannon Lucid.

"Writing nonfiction has been grand!" Bredeson told *SATA.* "I have learned so much in the process and enjoy the challenge of each new topic. Hopefully I can transfer some of my enthusiasm for reading and learning to the students who check out my books. Someone asked me one day how I happened to start writing. I answered that I had unknowingly been preparing for it my whole life."

■ Works Cited

Baltzell, Janet K., review of *Jonas Salk: Discoverer of the Polio Vaccine, Appraisal,* winter, 1994, p. 8.

Burner, Joyce Adams, review of *Jonas Salk: Discoverer of the Polio Vaccine, School Library Journal,* November, 1993, p. 113.

Graves, Phyllis, review of *The Battle of the Alamo: The Fight for Texas Territory, School Library Journal,* April, 1997, p. 144.

Linsley, Judith, review of *The Spindletop Gusher: The Story of the Texas Oil Boom, Review of Texas Books,* summer, 1996.

Peltier, Mary Jo, review of *Ruth Bader Ginsburg: Supreme Court Justice, Voice of Youth Advocates,* April, 1996, p. 47.

Tillotson, Laura, review of *American Writers of the 20th Century, Booklist,* June 1 & 15, 1996, p. 1706.

Veeder, Mary Harris, review of *Ross Perot: Billionaire Politician, Booklist,* April 15, 1995, p. 1494.

Yurenka, Katrina, review of *Ruth Bader Ginsburg: Supreme Court Justice, School Library Journal,* December, 1995, pp. 112-13.

■ For More Information See

PERIODICALS

School Library Journal, May, 1995, p. 112; July, 1995, p. 83; September, 1996, p. 230; June, 1997, p. 43.
Voice of Youth Advocates, February, 1994, p. 390.*

BROWN, Kathryn 1955-

■ Personal

Born March 20, 1955, in Twin Falls, ID; daughter of Devoe (a builder) and Colleen (a realtor; maiden name, Mooney) Brown; married Joseph O'Rourke (in media sales), July 22, 1988; children: Frances.

■ Addresses

Home and office—117 Hillside Rd., S. Deerfield, MA 01373. *Agent*—Ginger Knowlton, Curtis Brown Agency, 10 Astor Place, New York, NY 10003.

■ Career

Illustrator and author.

■ Awards, Honors

Pick of the List, American Bookseller Association, 1997, for *From Lullaby to Lullaby;* Notable Book citation, American Library Association, Outstanding Children's Book of the Year, *Parenting,* Joan Fassler Memorial Book Award from the Association for the Care of Children's Health, and Washington Children's Choice Picture Book Award, all for *Tough Boris.*

■ Writings

(Self-illustrated) *Muledred,* Harcourt Brace, 1990.

ILLUSTRATOR

Marilyn Singer, *The Lightey Club,* Four Winds, 1987.
Jane Yolen, *Eeny, Meeny, Miney Mole,* Harcourt Brace, 1992.
Mem Fox, *Tough Boris,* Harcourt Brace, 1994.

KATHRYN BROWN

Diane Marcial Fuchs, *A Bear for All Seasons,* Holt, 1995.
Cynthia Rylant, *The Old Woman Who Named Things,* Harcourt Brace, 1996.
Adele Geras, *From Lullaby to Lullaby,* Simon & Schuster, 1997.
Climb into My Lap (poems), edited by Lee Bennett Hopkins, Simon & Schuster, 1998.

■ Sidelights

Kathryn Brown is a children's book illustrator who has also written a work of her own, the self-illustrated *Muledred.* Her contribution to the picture books she illustrates lies in the details, which often add a whimsical, lively touch to a straightforward narrative. Working in watercolor, Brown imbues scenes with a warm, nostalgic aura, as in *Eeny, Meeny, Miney Mole,* or conveys the colorful ugliness of the pirate gang in *Tough Boris,* or takes on the magical world of dreams in *From Lullaby to Lullaby.*

Brown's picture book *Muledred,* which includes "colorful pastels [that] make the book inviting," according to *School Library Journal* contributor Nancy A. Gifford, centers on Muledred, who is always late to school because she finds something interesting to see or do along the way. When her grandfather gives Muledred his watch to help her keep track of the time, she loses it. The other children refuse to return the watch until the day she can get herself to school in time to ring the school bell. With a little ingenuity, Muledred is able to outsmart the other children and get to school on time. "Winsome mule children and wise mule adults populate this entertaining and original first effort," declared a critic in *Publishers Weekly.*

Brown next provided the illustrations for *Eeny, Meeny, Miney Mole,* written by Jane Yolen. In this well-received picture book, Eeny, the youngest mole, becomes curious about the world above the cozy burrow she shares with her older sisters, Meeny and Miney, who try to discourage her attempts to find out about the outside world. *Booklist* critic Hazel Rochman raved about the book: "The pictures have drama and homey detail, with rich characterization and a mythical sweep." Similarly, a reviewer for *Publishers Weekly* praised the "fanciful touches" added to the story by Brown's illustrations, which were described as "gracefully droll watercolors."

Brown is also the illustrator for Mem Fox's *Tough Boris,* a story that humanizes pirates by showing the depth of sorrow felt by Tough Boris when his pet parrot dies. Several critics noted that Brown's illustrations offer other stories to the observant reader's eyes, stories that are not mentioned in the book's narrative. "Brown has constructed a parallel world, expanding and enlarging upon the skeletal text to create a witty visual counterpart that is rife with potential subplots," noted Patricia T. O'Conner in the *New York Times Book Review.* The result, according to O'Conner, is "a picture book that luxuriates in pure possibility." Similarly, critic Rochman observed in *Booklist* that "for those who look

From *Tough Boris,* written by Mem Fox and illustrated by Brown.

carefully, the wordless story [told in the pictures] is a poignant counterpoint to the swashbuckling adventure scenes."

Brown was paired with author Cynthia Rylant for *The Old Woman Who Named Things,* a story that deals with "the sadness of loss and the necessity of continuing to love anyway," according to Susan Dove Lempke in *Booklist.* When an elderly woman realizes she has outlived most of her friends, she begins to give names only to those things that will outlive her, such as her car, which she names Betsy, and her house, which she calls Franklin. When a homeless puppy shows up at her gate, she feeds him but refuses to name him until the day he doesn't appear and she must go looking for him. Reviewers delighted in Brown's watercolor depiction of the feisty old woman and the lovable dog she eventually names Lucky. "Lucky the children who meet Lucky," quipped Mary Margaret Pitts in *School Library Journal.*

Brown's next project was to provide the illustrations for Adele Geras's fanciful story of a woman knitting a blanket for her daughter in *From Lullaby to Lullaby;* as an object appears in the blanket—like a doll, a moon, or a rainbow—the woman tells the story of its dreams. *From Lullaby to Lullaby* is told in a gently rhyming text and is illustrated by Brown's "elaborate" watercolors paintings, "filled with lots of wonderful details," according to Lauren Peterson in *Booklist.*

■ Works Cited

Review of *Eeny, Meeny, Miney Mole, Publishers Weekly,* February 3, 1992, p. 79.
Gifford, Nancy A., review of *Muledred, School Library Journal,* November, 1990, p. 86.

Lempke, Susan Dove, review of *The Old Woman Who Named Things, Booklist,* May 1, 1996, p. 1503.
Review of *Muledred, Publishers Weekly,* August 31, 1990, p. 65.
O'Conner, Patricia T., review of *Tough Boris, New York Times Book Review,* September 11, 1994, p. 22.
Peterson, Lauren, review of *From Lullaby to Lullaby, Booklist,* April 15, 1997, p. 1436.
Pitts, Mary Margaret, review of *The Old Woman Who Named Things, School Library Journal,* October, 1996, p. 105.
Rochman, Hazel, review of *Eeny, Meeny, Miney Mole, Booklist,* March 15, 1992, p. 1391.
Rochman, Hazel, review of *Tough Boris, Booklist,* March 1, 1994, p. 1269.

■ For More Information See

PERIODICALS

Horn Book, May-June, 1994, p. 313.
Publishers Weekly, March 17, 1997, p. 82.
School Library Journal, July, 1997, pp. 67-68.

*   *   *

BURLEIGH, Robert 1936-

■ Personal

Born January 4, 1936, in Chicago, IL; married; three children. *Education:* Attended DePauw University, 1953-57; University of Chicago, 1958-62.

■ Career

Author and artist. Worked for Society of Visual Education as a writer and artist.

■ Awards, Honors

Orbis Pictus Award, National Council of Teachers of English, 1992, for *Flight: The Journey of Charles Lindbergh.*

■ Writings

FOR CHILDREN

A Man Named Thoreau (picture book biography), illustrated by Lloyd Bloom, Atheneum, 1985.
Flight: The Journey of Charles Lindbergh (picture book biography), illustrated by Mike Wimmer, Philomel, 1991.
Home Run: The Story of Babe Ruth (picture book biography), illustrated by Mike Wimmer, Harcourt, 1996.
Who Said That? Famous Americans Speak (picture book biography), illustrated by David Catrow, Holt, 1997.
Black Whiteness: Admiral Byrd Alone in the Antarctic (picture book biography), illustrated by Walter Lyon Krudop, Atheneum, 1998.

OTHER

(With Mary Jane Gray) *Basic Writing Skills,* Society for
Visual Education, 1976.

The Triumph of Mittens: Poems (poetry), Boardwell-
Kloner, 1980.

Colonial America, illustrated by James Seward, Doubleday, 1992.

Hoops (picture book poetry), illustrated by Stephen T.
Johnson, Harcourt, 1997.

Also writer and producer of over one hundred filmstrips
and cassettes on educational subjects.

■ Work in Progress

I, Hercules for Harcourt.

■ Sidelights

A writer of informational books of biography and
history as well as a poet, Robert Burleigh is noted for
introducing difficult historical topics to young readers
in an accessible and effective manner. Characteristically
using a picture book format, the author presents facts
about his subjects—most often notable Americans such
as Henry David Thoreau, Charles Lindbergh, Babe
Ruth, and Admiral Richard Perry—in simple language

ROBERT BURLEIGH

and present-tense narration. Burleigh favors clipped,
staccato texts in both his prose and his poetry, a style
credited with expressing the ideas, drama, and importance of each of his topics in an evocative fashion.
Reviewers also note the successful marriage of the
author's texts with the illustrations of such artists as
Lloyd Bloom, Mike Wimmer, and Stephen T. Johnson.

Nineteenth-century writer and philosopher Henry David Thoreau is the subject of Burleigh's first biography,
A Man Named Thoreau. Considered a balanced overview of Thoreau's life and influence, the book addresses
its subject's time at Walden Pond, his love for nature,
his literary works, and his civil disobedience, among
other topics. Burleigh presents Thoreau and his ideas by
combining biographical facts with quotes from the
philosopher's popular work *Walden.* Writing in *School
Library Journal,* Ruth Semrau called *A Man Named
Thoreau* a book that "unfolds new pleasures on every
page" and deemed it an "exquisitely simple introduction to a difficult subject." David E. White observed in
Horn Book that the quotations "interspersed throughout
the text ... are beneficial in capturing the essence of
this noted figure." A reviewer for the *Bulletin of the
Center for Children's Books* declared that to "have
simplified concepts so much without distortion is a gift
to the younger reader or listener."

In his picture book *Flight: The Journey of Charles
Lindbergh,* Burleigh describes Lindbergh's famous non-
stop flight from New York to Paris in 1927. Basing his
text on Lindbergh's memoir *The Spirit of St. Louis,*
Burleigh focuses on the pilot's journey at the age of
twenty-five. Once again the author is credited with
successfully conveying a sophisticated concept, in this
case the difficulty of, in the words of *New York Times
Book Review* contributor Signe Wilkinson, "staying
awake, alert and in charge of a plane and one's life for
two days and a very long, lonely night before sleep" to
an audience "too young to appreciate what pulling an
all-nighter feels like." *Horn Book* reviewer Ann A.
Flowers remarked that the text conveys Lindbergh's
bravery, the drain on him personally, and the primitive
state of his plane in "completely convincing detail" and
noted that Burleigh's use of the present tense "keeps the
reader in suspense from the moment the plane takes off
until [its arrival in] Paris"; Flowers concluded that the
book is a "pioneer example of the 'right stuff,' splendid-
ly and excitingly presented." Burleigh's use of sentence
fragments and single-sentence paragraphs "conveys the
excitement of Lindbergh's historic flight," noted a critic
in *Kirkus Reviews,* who called *Flight* a book "that brings
new life to one of the stories of the century." Burleigh
received the Orbis Pictus Award in 1992 for this work.

Shifting to sports, Burleigh wrote a picture book biography of baseball's most widely known hero in *Home Run:
The Story of Babe Ruth,* as well as a picture book of
poetry, *Hoops,* that describes basketball in verses that
simulate the action of the players and the bouncing ball.
Filled with tactile imagery, *Hoops* outlines the way the
game feels to its players. "An ode to the game for older
children, veteran players, and NBA fans," declared a

He climbs into the boxlike cockpit that will be his only home
    for many, many hours.
He clicks on the engine. He listens as it catches, gurgles, and roars.
A few friends are here to say good-bye.
They are only a few feet away, and yet to Lindbergh how far off they seem.
They look up at him and wave. "Good luck! Keep safe!"

**Burleigh's award-winning account of Charles Lind-
bergh's 1927 transatlantic flight is based on the pilot's
memoir The Spirit of St. Louis.** (From *Flight*, illustrated by Mike Wimmer.)

Publishers Weekly reviewer, "this book will give language to teenagers' experience both on and off the
court." In his picture book *Black Whiteness: Admiral
Byrd Alone in the Antarctic*, Burleigh retells the explorer's incredible six-month stay alone in the Antarctic.
Based on Byrd's daily journal, *Black Whiteness* includes
detailed descriptions of Byrd's enduring hardships—
subzero temperatures, continuous darkness with limited
lighting equipment, and loneliness. "Burleigh's spare
prose eloquently captures the spartan surroundings in

which Byrd conducted daily meteorological studies,"
observed a critic in *Kirkus Reviews*, who concluded that
the explorer's story is "severe, often depressing, and
always riveting." Burleigh has also written several other
volumes of nonfiction and poetry, including an informational book about Colonial America and a collection of
the stories behind famous quotes and their speakers; in
addition, he served as the writer and producer of a
variety of educational filmstrips and cassettes and has
worked as a writer and artist for the Society of Visual
Education.

■ Works Cited

Review of *Black Whiteness: Admiral Byrd Alone in the
    Antarctic*, *Kirkus Reviews*, December 1, 1997, p.
    1773.
Review of *Flight: The Journey of Charles Lindbergh*,
    Kirkus Reviews, August 15, 1991, p. 1086.
Flowers, Ann A., review of *Flight: The Journey of
    Charles Lindbergh*, *Horn Book*, November, 1991, p.
    752.
Review of *Hoops*, *Publishers Weekly*, October, 6, 1997,
    p. 83.
Review of *A Man Named Thoreau*, *Bulletin of the
    Center for Children's Books*, December, 1985, p. 63.
Semrau, Ruth, review of *A Man Named Thoreau*, *School
    Library Journal*, January, 1986, p. 64.
White, David E., review of *A Man Named Thoreau*,
    Horn Book, March, 1986, pp. 215-16.
Wilkinson, Signe, review of *Flight: The Journey of
    Charles Lindbergh*, *New York Times Book Review*,
    January 26, 1992, p. 21.

■ For More Information See

PERIODICALS

Booklist, March. 15, 1986, p. 1079; March 1, 1997, p.
    1166.
Bulletin of the Center for Children's Books, November,
    1991, p. 58; February, 1998, p. 196.
Publishers Weekly, August 30, 1991, p. 81; December
    15, 1997, p. 58.
School Library Journal, October, 1991, p. 107; May,
    1997, p. 143.

C–D

CALHOUN, B. B. 1961-
(L. E. Blair)

■ Personal

Born June 26, 1961, in Brooklyn, NY; daughter of an architect/designer and an artist/teacher; married to an artist; children: one.

■ Addresses

Home—New York, NY. *Electronic mail*—bbcalhoun@earthlink.net. *Agent*—Fran Lebowitz, Writers House, 21 West 26th Street, New York, NY 10010.

■ Career

Writer. Taught pre-school, elementary, and junior high school for twelve years. *Member:* The Dinosaur Society, Society of Children's Book Writers and Illustrators.

■ Awards, Honors

Pick of the List, American Booksellers Association, 1995, for *The Competition.*

■ Writings

"GIRL TALK" SERIES; PUBLISHED BY WESTERN

The New You, 1990.
(Under pseudonym L. E. Blair) *The Ghost of Eagle Mountain,* 1990.
Odd Couple, 1990.
Baby Talk, 1991.
Beauty Queens, 1991.
(Under pseudonym L. E. Blair) *The Bookshop Mystery,* 1992.
(Under pseudonym L. E. Blair) *Allison, Shape Up!,* 1992.
(Under pseudonym L. E. Blair) *Allison to the Rescue!,* 1992.
(Under pseudonym L. E. Blair) *Allison's Babysitting Adventure,* 1992.

"PINK PARROTS" SERIES; PUBLISHED BY SPORTS ILLUSTRATED FOR KIDS

All That Jazz, illustrated by Jane Davila, 1990.
Fielder's Choice, 1991.

"DINOSAUR DETECTIVE" SERIES; PUBLISHED BY SCIENTIFIC AMERICAN

On the Right Track, illustrated by Daniel Mark Duffy, 1994.
Fair Play, illustrated by Duffy, 1994.
Bite Makes Right, illustrated by Duffy, 1994.
Out of Place, illustrated by Duffy, 1994.
Scrambled Eggs, illustrated by Duffy, 1995.
Night of the Carnotaurus, illustrated by Duffy, 1995.
The Competition, illustrated by Danny O'Leary, 1995.
The Raptor's Claw, illustrated by Leary, 1995.

"FORD SUPERMODELS OF THE WORLD" SERIES; PUBLISHED BY RANDOM HOUSE

The New Me, 1994.
Party Girl, 1994.
Having It All, 1994.
Making Waves, 1994.
Stepping Out, 1995.
High Style, 1995.
Model Sister, 1995.
Cover Girl, 1995.

"SILVER BLADES" SERIES; PUBLISHED BY BANTAM

Center Ice, 1995.
The Big Audition, 1995.
Nutcracker on Ice, 1995.
A New Move, 1996.
Wedding Secrets, 1996.
Rival Roommates, 1997.

"HIS & HERS" SERIES; PUBLISHED BY AVON

New in Town, Avon, 1997.
Summer Dreams, Avon, 1998.

Several of the author's books have been translated into other languages, including Turkish, Chinese, Japanese, and Spanish.

■ Sidelights

B. B. Calhoun has created and/or contributed to several series for young adults. Best known for her "Dinosaur Detective" series, Calhoun has also written series titles geared to adolescent girls interested in sports with her "Pink Parrot" series, and in the world of high fashion with her "Ford Supermodels of the World" series. She is often praised by critics for her smooth integration of realistic details from the diverse worlds that serve as background for her stories.

Fenton Rumplemayer, an eleven-year-old amateur sleuth and the son of two paleontologists, is the hero of Calhoun's "Dinosaur Detective" novels. While critics note that the books in the series show Fenton going through many experiences common to young people his age, including starting at a new school, dealing with a bully, and problems with friends, the plots are interwoven with story lines arising out of Fenton's interest in dinosaurs. "What makes this series special is the integration of computers, dinosaurs, [and] archaeology techniques with a mystery plot," Allison Smith observed in an *Appraisal* review. Indeed, averred Beverly A. Maffei also in *Appraisal,* "readers will pick up an abundance of facts about dinosaurs and about paleontology."

In the first book of the series, *On the Right Track,* Fenton and his father move to a dig site in Wyoming while Fenton's mother travels to a site in India. The story concerns Fenton's relationship with his mother, whom he misses, as well as his need to adapt to a new environment while meeting new friends and helping out his father at the dig site. A bully at school and a girl assigned as his partner for the local science fair are Fenton's biggest problems in the sequel *Fair Play,* in which a mystery involving a missing fossil at his father's dig site plays a part. Peter Roop noted in *Science Books and Films* that in both these books "the author tells an interesting story while weaving a great deal of information about dinosaurs into it."

In Calhoun's next "Dinosaur Detective" title, *Bite Makes Right,* the role of computers comes to the forefront—both in keeping Fenton in touch with his best friend Max back in New York City and in solving mysteries relating to the identification of dinosaur bones. Fenton's friendship with Max is put to the test in *Out of Place,* when Max comes to Wyoming for a visit. In *Scrambled Eggs,* the fifth volume in the series, Fenton and two new friends help scientists figure out why eggs found near a fossilized bird nest belong to a species too large to have built the nest. And when Fenton's father is hired as a consultant to a crew of filmmakers in *Night of the Carnotaurus,* Fenton becomes involved with one of the actors on the set. These installments in the "Dinosaur Detective" series proved to *Appraisal*'s Sarah Berman that "the author respects the fascination dinosaurs offer and tries to expand the knowledge of her readers as they also work toward the solution of the mystery she presents."

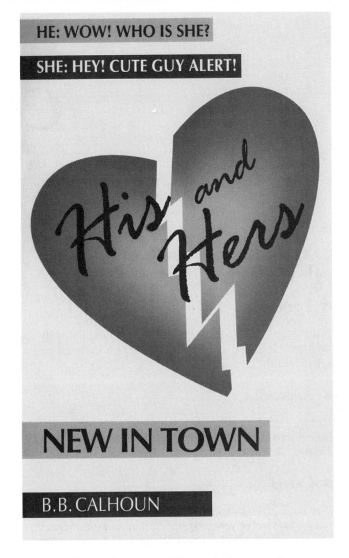

HE: WOW! WHO IS SHE?

SHE: HEY! CUTE GUY ALERT!

His and Hers

NEW IN TOWN

B.B. CALHOUN

B. B. Calhoun's young adult novel alternates between the perspectives of two central characters as a teenage boy and girl meet and become interested in one another.

"I was inspired to write the 'Dinosaur Detective' series," Calhoun explained to *SATA,* "by the students I used to teach, many of whom knew more about dinosaurs than any adult I have ever met. I've often heard it said that a paleontologist is just a kid who never grew out of liking dinosaurs. Maybe a children's author is just a kid who never grew out of liking to make up stories."

While the "Dinosaur Detective" and the "His and Hers" books are for both boys and girls to enjoy, Calhoun's other series, including "Girl Talk," "Silver Blades," "Pink Parrots," and the "Ford Supermodels of the World" sets, are directed exclusively to adolescent girls. In *All That Jazz* from the "Pink Parrots" series, Calhoun envisions the changing dynamics on a team of female baseball players when a fashion-conscious girl named Jazz joins the group. In turn, Jazz must reconcile the pull she feels toward her old gang of popular junior high school kids with her newfound enjoyment of playing on the baseball team. The story offers "appealing characters and interesting conflicts mixed with game action and the challenges of junior high social life," according to a *Booklist* reviewer.

The "Ford Supermodels of the World" series profiles the lives of various teenage girls pursuing modeling careers in New York City. For example, in the first title, *The New Me,* a farm girl from Nebraska is accepted by the Ford Modeling Agency and set up in a group apartment in New York City. The following title, *Party Girl,* focuses on a girl from Rio de Janeiro whose tendency to stay out all night causes problems with her new roommates and with the house mother. In *Stepping Out,* a girl arrives in New York from Russia, determined to shed her Russian past when she joins the other teenage models in their Ford-provided apartment. Calhoun's contributions to "Ford Supermodels of the World" provide "enough authentic details to enthrall its intended audience," noted a *Publishers Weekly* critic.

Calhoun explained to *SATA* how she first became interested in writing. "The first children's book I wrote was when I was six years old. My mother told me that I was going to have a younger brother or sister soon, and I sat down to write a collection of stories for the baby-to-be. I haven't stopped writing since!

"Growing up, I was always getting in trouble for reading under the covers with a flashlight when I was supposed to be asleep. My parents were divorced, and whenever my father and I visited together we read. He'd leaf through his newspaper, and I'd have my nose in whatever book I was in the middle of. To anyone else it must have seemed a funny way to spend time together, but it was our favorite activity. I still love to read—whether it's reading aloud to my own little girl or curling up in bed with a fat novel.

"These days, I probably read more of my own work than anything else—I seem to be forever re-reading, editing, and polishing. I find it helpful to make an outline before I begin writing—especially when I'm writing mysteries like my "Dinosaur Detective" books. I don't always stick to the outline once I begin writing, but it does help to have a plan.

"I used to be a teacher, and now I find that writing is a great way to stay in touch with kids. Not only do my books put me back in 'a kid's world,' but I have a chance to talk with many young readers by making author visits to schools. Next to writing, the thing I like best about what I do is hearing from readers who have enjoyed my books."

■ Works Cited

Review of *All That Jazz, Booklist,* December 15, 1990, p. 865.
Berman, Sarah, review of *Scrambled Eggs* and *Night of the Carnotaurus, Appraisal,* autumn, 1995, p. 65.
Maffei, Beverly A., review of *On the Right Track* and *Fair Play, Appraisal,* winter, 1995, p. 85.
Review of *The New Me, Publishers Weekly,* August 8, 1994, p. 440.

Review of *On the Right Track, Publishers Weekly,* April 11, 1994, pp. 65-66.
Roop, Peter, review of *On the Right Track, Science Books and Films,* November, 1994, p. 242.
Smith, Allison, review of *Bite Makes Right* and *Out of Place, Appraisal,* spring/summer, 1995, p. 63.

■ For More Information See

PERIODICALS

Booklist, May 15, 1994, p. 1679.
School Library Journal, February, 1991, p. 81; June, 1994, p. 126; March, 1995, p. 202; April, 1995, p. 130.
Voice of Youth Advocates, February, 1995, p. 336; August, 1995, p. 155.

* * *

CAMPBELL, Rod 1945-

■ Personal

Born May 4, 1945, in Scotland; son of Charles Edward (a carpenter) and Isabella (a homemaker; maiden name, Munro) Campbell. *Education:* University College of Rhodesia and Nyasaland (now University of Zimbabwe), B.Sc., 1966, M. Phil., 1968; attended University College of Cardiff, 1968-69; University of Nottingham, Ph.D., 1971; University College of Rhodesia and Nyasaland, postdoctoral study, 1971-72. *Hobbies and other interests:* "My work is my hobby. My interests extend to all aspects of art and design."

ROD CAMPBELL

■ Addresses

Home and office—c/o Macmillan Children's Books, 25 Eccleston Place, London SW1W 9NF.

■ Career

Author, illustrator, and paper engineer. Worked as a painter, 1972-81; freelance artist, 1981—. Has also worked part-time as a decorator and picture framer and in an art gallery.

■ Awards, Honors

American Institute of Graphic Arts Certificate of Excellence, 1983, and Book Show, 1984, for *Dear Zoo;* *Buster's Bedtime* was exhibited at Bologna International Children's Book Fair, 1985; Sheffield Children's Book Award, 1994, for *I Won't Bite.*

■ Writings

FOR CHILDREN; SELF-ILLUSTRATED (EXCEPT AS NOTED)

An ABC, Abelard-Schuman (London), 1980.
Dressing Up, Abelard-Schuman, 1980.
A Grand Parade Counting Book, Abelard-Schuman, 1980.
Great, Greater, Greatest, Abelard-Schuman, 1980.
Eddie Enginedriver, Abelard-Schuman, 1981.
Freddie Fireman, Abelard-Schuman, 1981.
Charlie Clown, Abelard-Schuman, 1981.
Nigel Knight, Abelard-Schuman, 1981.
Gertie Gardener, Abelard-Schuman, 1981.
Nancy Nurse, Abelard-Schuman, 1981.
Dear Zoo, Four Winds (New York), 1982, Abelard, 1982, Campbell (London), 1991, Macmillan (London), 1997.
Rod Campbell's Book of Board Games, Abelard-Schuman, 1982, Prentice-Hall, 1984.
Wheels!, Abelard-Schuman, 1982.
Look Inside! All Kinds of Places, Abelard-Schuman, 1983.
Look Inside! Land, Sea, Air, Abelard-Schuman, 1983.
Oh, Dear!, Scholastic, 1983.
My Farm, Blackie (London), 1983.
My Zoo, Blackie, 1983.
My Pets, Blackie, 1983.
My Garden, Blackie, 1983.
Rod Campbell's Noisy Book, Blackie, 1983.
Rod Campbell's Magic Circus, Abelard-Schuman, 1983.
Rod Campbell's Magic Fairground, Abelard-Schuman, 1983.
Henry's Busy Day, Viking Kestrel (New York), 1984.
Take the Wheel, Blackie, 1984.
Look Up at the Sky, Blackie, 1984.
How Many Hats?, Blackie, 1984.
What Color Is That?, Blackie, 1984.
Lots of Animals, Blackie, 1984.
Buster's Morning, Blackie, 1984.
Buster's Afternoon, Blackie, 1984.
From Gran, Blackie, 1984.
Toy Soldiers, Scholastic, 1984, Blackie, 1984.

Baby Animals, Scholastic, 1984.
Pet Shop, Scholastic, 1984.
Circus Monkeys, Scholastic, 1984.
Oh Dear!, Four Winds, 1984, Campbell, 1991.
Buster's Bedtime, Blackie, 1985.
Playwheels with Moving Parts!, Simon & Schuster, 1985.
Funwheels with Moving Parts!, Simon & Schuster, 1985, Blackie, 1985.
Big and Strong, Blackie, 1985.
Cars and Trucks, Blackie, 1985.
Road Builders, Blackie, 1985.
Speed!, Blackie, 1985.
Misty's Mischief, Viking, 1985.
My Bedtime, Blackie, 1985.
I'm a Mechanic, Barron (Hauppauge, NY), 1986, Simon & Schuster, 1988.
I'm a Nurse, Barron, 1986, Simon & Schuster, 1988.
My Bath, Blackie, 1986.
My Favorite Things, Blackie, 1986.
My Teatime, Blackie, 1986.
My Toys, Blackie, 1986.
My Day, Collins, 1986.
It's Mine, Blackie, 1987, Macmillan (New York), 1988, Barron, 1988.
Lift-the-Flap ABC, Blackie, 1987, Dutton, 1996.
Lift-the-Flap 123, Blackie, 1987.
Make a Word, Octopus, 1987.
Numbers, Campbell/Blackie, 1988.
Shapes, Campbell/Blackie, 1988.
Alphabet, Campbell/Blackie, 1988.
Buster Gets Dressed, Barron, 1988, Campbell Macmillan, 1996.
Buster Keeps Warm, Barron, 1988, Campbell Macmillan, 1996.
My Presents, Campbell, 1988, Simon & Schuster, 1989.
Colours, Campbell/Blackie, 1988.
Buster's Day, Macmillan, 1989.
The Pop-Up Pet Shop, Campbell, 1989, Simon & Schuster, 1990.
We Have a Pet, Campbell, 1990.
We Have a Rabbit, Campbell, 1990.
We Have a Dog, Campbell, 1990.
We Have a Cat, Campbell, 1990.
We Have a Guinea Pig, Campbell, 1990.
Noisy Farm, Campbell, 1990.
Look, Touch, and Feel with Buster, Campbell, 1991, Sandvik, 1992.
My Stand Up Baby Animals, Campbell, 1991.
My Stand Up Farm Animals, Campbell, 1991.
My Stand Up Wild Animals, Campbell, 1991.
Naughty Henry, Campbell, 1991.
Henry in the Park, Campbell, 1991.
A Simple Rhyming ABC, Campbell, 1991.
Rod Campbell's Lift-the-Flap Animal Book, Campbell, 1991, Macmillan, 1995.
A Simple Rhyming 1 2 3, Campbell, 1992.
I Won't Bite, Campbell, 1992.
Baby's First Counting Book, Sandvik, 1992.
My Pop-Up Garden Friends, Campbell, 1992, Simon & Schuster, 1993.
Let's Drive a-, Campbell, 1992.
Let's Go By-, Campbell, 1992.
Baby's First ABC Book, Sandvik, 1992.

Rod Campbell's Nursery School, Campbell, 1992.
A Simple Rhyming Colours, Campbell, 1993.
Misty, Campbell, 1993.
My Lift-the-Flap Nursery Book, Campbell, 1993.
Henry, Campbell, 1993.
Come into the Garden!, Harlow/Longman, 1994.
Garden Friends, Harlow/Longman, 1994.
I Can Spell! With Vowels A E I O U, Campbell, 1994.
I Can Spell! With Consonants B C D F G H, Campbell, 1994.
I Can Spell! With Consonants J K L M P, Campbell, 1994.
I Can Spell! With Consonants R S T V W Y Z, Campbell, 1994.
Henry's Ball, Campbell, 1994, Macmillan, 1996.
Hungry Animals!, Harlow/Longman, 1994.
Let's Go into the Jungle, Harlow/Longman, 1994.
Monkey's Banana, Harlow/Longman, 1994.
Playtime, Harlow/Longman, 1994.
Pop-Up Dinosaurs, Campbell, 1994.
The Pop-Up Farm, Campbell, 1994, Simon & Schuster, 1995.
Who's There?, Harlow/Longman, 1994.
Stroke Henry, Campbell, 1995.
The Pop-Up Jungle, Campbell, 1995.
Little Bird, Campbell, 1995.
My Farm (includes cassette), Collins, 1995.
My Zoo (includes cassette), Collins, 1995.
ABC Zoo, Campbell, 1996.
Creepy Things, Campbell, 1996.
Lift-the-Flap Farm 1 2 3, Campbell, 1996.
Fishy Things, Campbell, 1996.
Flying Things, Campbell, 1996.
Scary Things, Campbell, 1996.
Playschool, photographs by Tim Booth, Campbell, 1996.
This Baby! (includes mirror), Campbell, 1997.
Fluffy Chick: Touch and Feel, Campbell, 1997.
Noisy Ducks, Campbell, 1997.
Noisy Frogs, Campbell, 1997.

Several of Campbell's books have been published in multi-title editions and have been translated into Welsh.

■ Sidelights

A prolific author and illustrator of books for preschoolers and early readers, Campbell is the creator of more than a hundred works—characteristically concept, board, and toy books—that are noted for blending artistry and technology in an especially charming manner. Campbell introduces his young audience to such concepts as the alphabet, spelling, counting, and colors; to occupations such as nursing, firefighting, and gardening; and to interesting places such as a farm, the zoo, and the circus. In addition, he addresses subjects with particular interest to small children, such as animals and toys; relevant activities like playtime and bathtime; and transportation such as cars and boats. Campbell uses simple texts with a maximum of repetition in his books, which often reflect the author's tongue-in-cheek humor; he usually illustrates his works with double-page spreads composed of clear line drawings and decorated with bright colors. As a technician, Campbell uses various

techniques to provide the formats for his works; for example, he has created tactile books that children can touch and feel as well as toy books that include plastic wheels or other mechanisms. Campbell is perhaps best known as the creator of "flap books," titles that allow children to explore what is behind the flaps of the illustrations they are viewing—second pictures often containing surprises. Observers usually praise Campbell as an ingenious designer whose books contain both solid production and strong child appeal. *Books for Keeps* reviewer Judith Sharman says, "Rod Campbell's strength lies in his ability to pinpoint precisely what the young child wants to know and put it into a form which matches exactly the stage of interest, of development and of humor."

Born in Scotland, Campbell studied in Africa and England before abandoning a science career in the early 1970s and devoting himself to drawing and painting. He then pursued a career in the arts until the early 1980s, when he began producing books for preschoolers. He once told *SATA,* "I have come to the world of children's books quite late. I was brought up in Rhodesia and from an early age had an interest in and talent for drawing. There were no art schools, and the prevailing attitude regarded art as a hobby at best, so I went to university to train as a teacher. However, I stayed on after my degree and did research and eventually came to England on a scholarship to do a Ph.D. in organic chemistry. During this period I had continued to draw and paint, and I finally decided that this was what I really wanted to do, so I gave up a scientific career, to everyone's horror, and came to London, where I have been ever since. I supported myself with various part-time jobs while continuing to paint."

"Toward the end of 1978 I had produced some simple drawings of toys for my own amusement and sent them off to toy manufacturers, who commissioned a mobile and one or two other pieces of artwork. At about the same time, a friend took some work in to Blackie, the publisher, who was looking for an illustrator for some little books for very young children—a very happy coincidence. This was the beginning of a long association with them and my gradual absorption into the world of children's books. My area within this world is very much that of the under fives—indeed it is has found me, rather than the other way round! After the initial books I did, I regarded *Dear Zoo* as my real starting point as I wrote the words and did the pictures, in fact conceived the idea and layout. This has been true for all subsequent books."

Dear Zoo, which has become a British classic, begins with the young narrator writing to the zoo for a pet; the zoo responds by sending a variety of animals—an elephant, a giraffe, and a tiger, among others—that can be seen by lifting the flaps on their crates. All of these creatures are deemed unsuitable and returned to the zoo until the last, a puppy; the narrator responds, "He was perfect! I kept him." A reviewer for the *Bulletin of the Center for Children's Books* calls *Dear Zoo* one "of the nicest of toy books: simple, funny, and effective, this is

'It's mine!' says the crocodile.
'I swim in the river with it.'

《 إِنَّهُ لِي ! 》 قال التِّمْساح .
《 إِنِّي أَسْبَحُ بِهِ في النَّهر . 》

I can see a furry paw!
I wonder who that belongs to?

إِنِّي أَرَى كَفَّ حيوانٍ مَكْسُوًّا بالفَرَاء !
لِمَنْ يَأْتُرَى ذلك الكَفّ ؟

In *It's Mine,* author/illustrator Campbell introduces young readers to jungle animals by highlighting the unique characteristics of each.

just right for the ready-to-read audience." A *Junior Bookshelf* critic agrees, calling the title an "attractive, well-produced, ingenious book for first-time readers." Writing in the *Horn Book,* Ethel L. Heins compares *Dear Zoo* to the picture books of Bruno Munari and adds that despite the striking resemblance "one can acknowledge that the smaller volume has some inviting qualities of its own." *Dear Zoo* received a Certificate of Excellence from the American Institute of Graphic Arts in 1983.

Campbell continued in *SATA,* "I have done a number of flap books now, and feel that they are an important type of book for young children, especially those who can't yet read. The flaps appeal to children's curiosity and afford an element of physical participation. These sorts of books have been labelled 'novelty' books and have generally become rather complicated and specialized, in fact more for adults than children. This is certainly true of 'pop-ups.' I feel a novelty element will always be legitimate for certain books for the very young where one is bridging the toy/book gap, so long as the novelty element is simple and integral to the idea of the book." In addition to his flap books, Campbell has developed titles that feature play slots. In these works, which include such publications as *Toy Soldiers* and *Baby Animals,* figures can be manipulated into slots to enhance the illustrations. Campbell told *SATA,* "Apart from flap books I have done a book with plastic wheels which, on turning the board pages, becomes entirely different vehicles. On the last page of *Henry's Busy Day* where Henry the dog is asleep in his basket, one can stroke his furry coat because it is made of fake fur! *Magic Circus* and *Magic Fairground* were an attempt to use simple pop-up mechanisms in an appropriate way for the very young."

Throughout his career, most critics have responded favorably to Campbell's approach. For example, a reviewer in *Publishers Weekly* notes that the pictures in *Look Inside! All Kinds of Places,* a board book that provides views of such locations as a lighthouse, a garage, and a barn, "will appeal strongly to the tiniest children" and claims that its companion volume *Look Inside! Land, Sea, Air* is "just as much fun." *Books for Keeps* critic Judith Sharman comments on *Buster's Day,* a volume in Campbell's popular series about a lively tot, "What can one say about this book except, if you know

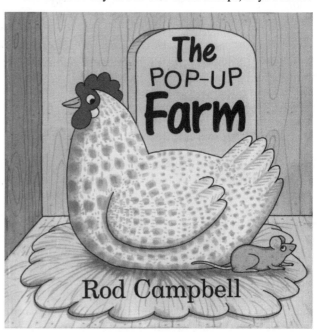

A mouse who travels across a farmyard introduces the child reader to typical farm animals in Campbell's picture book.

any babies or toddlers, go and buy it for them." Writing in the same publication, Moira Small says of *Noisy Farm,* a flap book about farm animals, "2- and 3-year-olds should get a lot from this book," while *Magpies* reviewer Cathryn Crowe notes that *I Won't Bite,* a touch-and-feel book featuring animals ranging from a mouse to a crocodile, is a work that young children "will delight in.... The touch spots are irresistible."

Campbell concluded in *SATA,* "The amount of writing I have done has been quite small, but it's very important to get it right. There are so many books for the very young that are too adult, in my view, presenting an adult's attitude and humor, often in a quirky way, too. I think any storyline should be quite simple, and, for the very young, repetitive elements are vital. Words which have a nice sound to them, or familiar words, will quickly be picked up by the child. To a small child, repetition is not boring. On completing the idea for *Dear Zoo,* I tried the dummy out on a friend's three-year-old. On reaching the last page, he said, "Again!," and this happened three times! I was fascinated that to the child repetition did not mean boredom but rather a re-experiencing of a pleasant experience. Also, knowing what is to come provides a wonderful sense of security which allows one to get excited, scared, etc., in complete safety.

"When people ask me what I do, I find it difficult to answer as I don't see myself as an illustrator or an author. I find playing around with an idea for a book a very exciting process—taking an idea and working out the means and format that suit it best, then developing the illustrations and story. I want to make books for under fives that are fun, warm, and reassuring. Well, that's a rationalization, I suppose! I actually make books that please me; they are done for me in the first instance, and the doing of them allows me free play with whatever childlike intuitions I may have, and personally I feel that the world of the young child should be warm, reassuring, and fun. Learning should be fun and completely unconscious at this age, and that's a great challenge—to convey simple ideas and concepts in an entertaining way, in a visual and written language that the child not only feels at home in, but positively delights in!

"My own childhood up to the age of six is an almost complete blank, so perhaps I have now been given the opportunity of discovering it, or at least participating in that very magical, innocent part of one's development. I go to schools and libraries from time to time, drawing for groups of children four to seven years old, which is very instructive. I think it important to keep in touch with children and, happily, I get on well with them. One does not get ideas directly from them, but it serves to remind one of what sort of things amuse them or they respond to. I find it a necessary part of my activity in children's books."

■ Works Cited

Crowe, Cathryn, review of *I Won't Bite, Magpies,* July, 1993, p. 27.

Review of *Dear Zoo, Bulletin of the Center for Children's Books,* November, 1983, p. 44.

Review of *Dear Zoo, Junior Bookshelf,* February, 1983, p. 10.

Heins, Ethel, L., review of *Dear Zoo, Horn Book,* August, 1983, p. 429.

Review of *Look Inside! All Kinds of Places, Publishers Weekly,* January 25, 1985, p. 93.

Sharman, Judith, review of *Buster's Day, Books for Keeps,* November, 1994, p. 10.

Sharman, Judith, review of *Buster Gets Dressed* and *Henry's Ball, Books for Keeps,* November, 1996, p. 7.

Small, Moira, review of *Noisy Farm, Books for Keeps,* May, 1994, p. 10.

■ For More Information See

PERIODICALS

Bulletin of the Center for Children's Books, March, 1985, p. 121.

Growing Point, November, 1982, p. 3972.

Junior Bookshelf, February, 1985, pp. 12-13; June, 1996, p. 101.

Observer (London), December 2, 1984, p. 25; December 8, 1985, p. 27; April 19, 1987, p. 23.

Times Educational Supplement, November 19, 1982, p. 36; January 13, 1984, p. 44.

—*Sketch by Gerard J. Senick*

*   *   *

CAVANAGH, Helen (Carol) 1939-

■ Personal

Born December 4, 1939, in Quincy, MA; daughter of Wapaa Albert (a construction worker) and Blanche Holmes (Magnant) Hanninen; married Lawrence Joseph Cavanagh (a corrections officer), June 18, 1960; children: Christopher (deceased), Lawrence Joseph, Jr., Patrick, Carin. *Education:* Attended Bay Path Junior College, 1957-58. *Hobbies and other interests:* Gardening, reading, and people.

■ Career

Worked as a clerk in Boston, MA, 1958-59; WEEI-Radio, Boston, secretary, 1959; *Sentinel,* East Brunswick, NJ, reporter, feature writer, and author of column, "Telling It Like It Is," 1970-78; Spotswood, NJ, town historian, 1976; free-lance writer, 1978—. Creative writing teacher at Old Bridge Community School. *Member:* Penmeisters.

HELEN CAVANAGH

■ Awards, Honors

Author Award, New Jersey Institute of Technology, 1979, for both *Second Best* and *Honey.*

■ Writings

Second Best, Scholastic, 1979.
Honey, Scholastic, 1979.
Superflirt, Scholastic, 1980.
Wildfire Diary, Scholastic, 1980.
The Easiest Way, Scholastic, 1980.
My Day by Day Diary with Special Poems for Me, Scholastic, 1980.
A Place for Me, Scholastic, 1981.
Just a Summer Girl, Scholastic, 1982.
Angel, Scholastic, 1984.
Kiss and Tell, Scholastic, 1984.
The Candy Papers, Simon & Schuster, 1985.
Panther Glade, Simon & Schuster, 1993.
The Last Piper, Simon & Schuster, 1996.
(Translator) *A Report of Murder,* by Yoryis Yatromano-lakis, Subterranean Company, 1997.

Contributor of poems and stories to magazines and newspapers, including *True Romance, Down East, Writer's Digest,* and *Co-Ed.*

■ Sidelights

Helen Cavanagh has been publishing novels for young adults since the 1970s. As she once explained to *SATA,* many of her titles address common struggles faced by teenagers. "In *Second Best,* I dealt with Shelly's struggles with jealousy and self-doubt, [in *Honey*] problems with [Honey's] mother and father, and [in] *Superflirt* Susan's confusion. Also, Abbie in *The Easiest Way* must struggle and suffer, and so does Colleen in *A Place for Me.* All these girls are me, and I feel their pain, but in my books

we always win and learn a little more about ourselves, and become better people."

Two titles which have appeared in the 1990s are *Panther Glade* and *The Last Piper.* In *Panther Glade* Cavanagh places an underachieving boy named Bill in the exotic locale of southern Florida, where he spends the summer with his great aunt Cait while his parents vacation in Europe. But Bill is afraid of the local flora and fauna in southern Florida and, initially at least, has little interest in archaeologist Cait's passion—the ancient burial sites of the Calusa, who once inhabited the Florida Everglades. Bill is befriended by a girl his age who works at his aunt's excavation site and together the two learn more about Calusa culture with the aid of an art class and Grant, an Indian friend. "Bill's growth ... is slow and steady, until he has a brief, climactic, and mystical survival adventure," noted Susan Oliver in *School Library Journal. Panther Glade* "is a good adventure story based on careful research which will circulate best by booktalking," maintained Carmen Oyenque in *Voice of Youth Advocates.*

Five-year-old Mikey Lauder is proven to be the reincarnation of a Scotsman wrongfully executed fifty years earlier in Cavanagh's thrilling novel. (Cover illustration by Robert Goldstrom.)

The spirit world, which appears in *Panther Glade* when Bill meets the spirit of King Calos while on a vision quest, comes to the forefront in *The Last Piper*. In this story, thirteen-year-old Christie and her five-year-old brother Mikey accompany their mother on a business trip to Scotland. Soon after their arrival, it becomes evident that Mikey is the reincarnation of a man wrongfully hanged for the murder of his fiancee fifty years before. Critics noted that Cavanagh takes the idea of reincarnation seriously in this novel, offering no other possible explanation for Mikey's knowledge of the facts of the case. This mystery, combined with "a vivid setting, interesting subplots, and complex characters ... add up to a gripping tale," concluded a critic for *Kirkus Reviews*.

Cavanagh once told *SATA:* "It's not just that I remember what it's like to be sixteen years old, or twelve; in my heart I still am! Just as I can look ahead and be eighty, sometimes I can go way back to when I was a year and a half. I can also be my true age when I *have* to be.

"Of course, what's true and what feels true gets all mixed together whenever I sit down to write. Who knows why? Maybe because I'm a mixture myself: part Finn, part French, part New England Yankee. Perhaps too because I'm left-handed (lefties often take liberties with logic). Very possibly it's because I gazed out the window too much when I should have been paying attention to the teacher.

"Daydreamer was a bad thing to be in those days, later, too, and sometimes I notice, even now. Not everyone approves of dreaming and not everyone believed I could be a writer. Except me—I did. Now I know my gazing and my dreaming were necessary and right. I dreamed of becoming a writer and *my dreams came true.*"

■ Works Cited

Review of *The Last Piper, Kirkus Reviews,* April 15, 1996, p. 599.
Oliver, Susan, review of *Panther Glade, School Library Journal,* June, 1993, p. 104.
Oyenque, Carmen, review of *Panther Glade, Voice of Youth Advocates,* October, 1993, pp. 214-15.

■ For More Information See

PERIODICALS

Booklist, July, 1996, p. 1826.
Bulletin of the Center for Children's Books, May, 1993, pp. 278-79; May, 1996, p. 295.
School Library Journal, May, 1996, p. 110.

*   *   *

COLE, Jennifer
See ZACH, Cheryl (Byrd)

COLLICOTT, Sharleen 1937-
(Sharleen Pederson)

■ Personal

Born April 10, 1937, in Los Angeles, CA; married Con Pederson (a special effects designer; divorced, 1985); children: Eric. *Education:* University of California at Los Angeles, B.A., 1969.

■ Addresses

Home and office—2960 Bel Air Dr., Las Vegas, NV 89109-1581. *Electronic mail*—rubincolli@aol.com.

■ Career

Writer, illustrator, ceramist, sculptor, and educator. Artist in residence, Duntog Foundation, 1983; teacher, Otis/Parson Design Institute, 1983; teacher, California State University, Long Beach, 1983-84. Panelist, National Endowment for the Arts, 1985; affiliated with India Ink Galleries, 1985-86, and Every Picture Tells a Story (art gallery), 1991-95. *Exhibitions:* Exhibitor at galleries in Los Angeles, CA, including India Ink Gallery, 1983; Los Angeles City College, 1984; Every Picture Tells a Story, 1991, 1994; Storyopolis, 1997.

■ Awards, Honors

Collicott has received several awards for her work from the Society of Illustrators, Los Angeles, the Art Directors Club of Los Angeles, and *Advertising Age* magazine.

SHARLEEN COLLICOTT

■ Writings

(Self-illustrated) *Seeing Stars,* Dial, 1996.

ILLUSTRATOR

(As Sharleen Pederson) Michael Hallward, *The Enormous Leap of Alphonse Frog,* Nash Publishing (Los Angeles, CA), 1972.

(As Sharleen Pederson) Suzanne Klein, *An Elephant in My Bed,* Follett (Chicago, IL), 1974.

Mouse, Frog, and Little Hen, DLM, 1990.

Sharon Lucky, *The Three Dinosaurs Dreadly,* DLM, 1991.

Karen Radler Greenfield, *The Teardrop Baby,* Harper-Collins, 1994.

Laura Numeroff, *The Chicken Sisters,* HarperCollins, 1997.

Also contributor of illustrations for *Elementary Math Series,* Addison-Wesley, *Frickles and Frackles,* DLM, and *Pattern Palace,* DLM. Contributor of illustrations to periodicals, including *Psychology Today, Westways, National Wildlife Federation, Human Behavior, Lady Bug,* and *Ranger Rick.*

■ Work in Progress

Writing and illustrating *Mildred and Sam* for Harper-Collins; a children's book for Houghton Mifflin, tentatively titled *Toestomper and the Caterpillars.*

■ Sidelights

Highly regarded both as a fine artist and a commercial artist, Sharleen Collicott has been illustrating picture books for children since the early 1970s; in 1996, she published *Seeing Stars,* the first of her works containing both original art and text. Her pictures—colorful, detailed paintings that range from intimate views to double-page spreads—characteristically feature fantastic animals and have been compared to such artists as Hieronymous Bosch for their imaginative quality and attention to detail.

In her early years as a professional artist, Collicott primarily illustrated advertising copy, magazine articles, educational material, and record covers. One of her most recognizable works was the first wide-screen version of the "Columbia Lady," the woman holding a torch at the beginning of movies produced by Columbia Pictures. Collicott has also taught art at the university level, served as an artist in residence in the Philippines, and formed affiliations with several Los Angeles art galleries. More recently, however, the illustrator has focused her efforts solely on illustrating and writing picture books.

In a promotional piece for one of her publishers, Collicott directed some comments about her early life to young readers: "You might not know about paper dolls, but when I was a child, we played with them all the time. I made my own paper dolls and designed their clothes. My love of animals comes, no doubt, from living on a farm with 3,000 rabbits and 12 chickens, and I used to go to the London Zoo every day and draw the animals. I love to paint fantasy pictures of things that no one has ever seen—like the dinosaurs in [Sharon Lucky's] *The Three Dinosaurs Dreadly.* You know, there's no reason not to picture a cardinal-red tyrannosaurus or a teal dimetrodon."

Although she earned a degree in sculpture from the University of California at Los Angeles (UCLA), Collicott's main interests were in ceramics and welding steel structures. She did not become seriously interested in illustrating until the early 1970s, while she was living in England. Because of rainy weather, she spent many days indoors at the London Zoo. In an interview with Marv Rubin in *Communication Arts,* the illustrator explained that being at the zoo "put me much closer to the animals than I had ever been. That inspired me to try sketching in my notebook, and to discover how much I enjoyed it." Collicott also told Rubin that seeing a centennial exhibit of Beatrix Potter's work convinced her "that drawing the things I imagined was indeed legitimate." After filling the pages of her notebook, she showed them to others, including director Stanley Kubrick, for whom she was sculpting alien creatures for the film *2001: A Space Odyssey.* Although her aliens were cut from the film, Kubrick encouraged her to add background to her animal sketches for exhibition or publication. She took his advice and has been illustrating ever since. "When I paint now," she told Rubin, "I'm revealing something from my imagination as realistically as possible."

Most of Collicott's early book illustrations were done for educational works. The first children's picture book that she worked on was Karen Greenfield's *The Teardrop Baby,* published in 1994. In this original fairy tale, a childless couple meet a magical woman who creates a child for them from their tears. When the boy is seven, the old woman comes back to claim him and makes him her servant; after tricking the woman with a fortune baked into a loaf of bread, the boy returns to his parents. "Collicott's illustrations, with many-eyed flowers and a deliciously scary depiction of the edge of the world, realize and enhance Greenfield's cryptic tale," declared a reviewer for *Publishers Weekly.* In a review in *School Library Journal,* Lisa Dennis called *The Teardrop Baby* an "unusual picture book" and noted that the illustrations "suit the fairy-tale flavor of the story." Dennis concluded that the Collicott's "decision to paint eyes on the flowers creates a distinctly creepy atmosphere."

In 1996, Collicott wrote illustrated her own picture book, *Seeing Stars.* The story describes how two small animals, Motley and Fuzzball, build a makeshift spaceship out of parts from a junkyard so they can reach the stars in outer space. Through Collicott's illustrations, the reader knows exactly where the ship lands—in the ocean. However, the pair thinks they are in space and that the starfish are actually stars. Writing in *School Library Journal,* Jane Marino noted that "younger readers may forgive the lapses in the story to enjoy the beautiful illustrations and may even sympathize with these two wayward passengers." A *Publishers Weekly*

Collicott's illustrations, with their lively detail, enhance Laura Numeroff's tale of three sister hens and their quirky personalities. (From *The Chicken Sisters.*)

reviewer wrote, "Aptly titled, this book is significantly more impressive for its eye-catching visuals than for its slightly cutesy story line." However, the critic noted that Collicott "adroitly pulls off the kid-pleasing contrivance" of letting young readers in on a secret of which her characters are unaware.

Published in 1997, *The Chicken Sisters,* by Laura Numeroff, became Collicott's next illustration project. The book features three hens, sisters whose hobbies—baking, knitting, and singing—annoy their neighbors because of the talent (or lack thereof) of their practitioners. When a wolf moves into the neighborhood and tries to ingratiate himself with the sisters, their demonstrations send him running home to his mother. The story "comes brilliantly alive in Collicott's pictures," declared *Booklist* contributor Ilene Cooper, who added that the artist's work "is chock-full and pretty darn adorable." *School Library Journal*'s Marino commented that the illustrations "reinforce the text, giving personality to the feathered siblings" and called *The Chicken Sisters* a

"winner that is sure to please at story time." A reviewer in *Publishers Weekly* predicted that toddlers will respond to the book's simple language as well as to "the bright colors in Collicott's intricately detailed art," which the critic concluded adds "spice to Numeroff's deadpan delivery."

Collicott began illustrating with colored pencils, then moved to watercolors. Currently, she prefers to paint with egg tempera, a blend of ground pigment powder and egg yolk, and has learned several of her recipes and techniques from books dating from the Middle Ages. In her interview with Marv Rubin in *Communication Arts,* Collicott claimed that every area of each of her pictures is "equally important. I don't like empty areas or unimportant areas." Furthermore, Collicott spends almost as much time preparing for an illustration as she does painting it. "I plan the pictures and their 'stories' carefully," she explained to Rubin. "I 'cast' all the characters before I begin. I do research on them and on their settings. I know all about them."

■ Works Cited

Review of *The Chicken Sisters, Publishers Weekly,* April 7, 1997, p. 90.

Collicott, Sharleen, interview in promotional piece, DLM Publishing.

Cooper, Ilene, review of *The Chicken Sisters, Booklist,* May 1, 1997, p. 1497.

Dennis, Lisa, review of *The Teardrop Baby, School Library Journal,* September, 1994, p. 184.

Marino, Jane, review of *Seeing Stars, School Library Journal,* April, 1996, p. 105.

Marino, Jane, review of *The Chicken Sisters, School Library Journal,* May, 1997, p. 109.

Rubin, Marv, "Sharleen Pederson," *Communication Arts,* January/February, 1983, pp. 66-70.

Review of *Seeing Stars, Publishers Weekly,* April 29, 1996, p. 70.

Review of *The Teardrop Baby, Publishers Weekly,* August 15, 1994, p. 95.

■ For More Information See

PERIODICALS

Artist Magazine, October, 1994.
Crayola Kids, June/July, 1998.
Today's Art, Volume 27, number 8.

* * *

CORDELL, Alexander
See GRABER, (George) Alexander

* * *

CORY, Rowena
See LINDQUIST, Rowena Cory

* * *

COUSTEAU, Jacques-Yves 1910-1997

OBITUARY NOTICE—See index for *SATA* sketch: Born June 11, 1910, in St. Andre-de-Cubzac, France; died after a long illness of respiratory infection and heart problems, June 25, 1997, in Paris, France. Underwater explorer, inventor, photographer, film and television producer, environmentalist, and writer. Cousteau fascinated the world with tales of explorations under the sea. He was a leader in marine research and is credited with turning oceanography into a popular science. Although he had no formal training in the field, Cousteau spent sixty years documenting underwater life, thrilling audiences with his films and adventure stories, technologically advancing the science of marine studies, and advocating the conservation of the Earth's resources. As a young man, Cousteau attended Ecole Navale, the French naval academy in Brest, beginning in 1930. In 1935 he began training as a flier with the French Navy, but a car accident prevented him from finishing. In 1936 he served in the artillery. It was at this time that Cousteau began conducting a series of diving experiments and developed a mask and fins used by French spear-fishermen. By 1942 World War II was well underway. Following the fall of France to the Germans, Cousteau joined the French Resistance where he put his camera skills to use by photographing enemy activities along the coast of France. For his efforts during the war, he received the Croix de Guerre and the Legion d'Honneur.

Also in 1942, Cousteau, along with Philippe Taillez and Frederic Dumas, began experimenting with underwater photography and produced their first documentary film *Par dix-huit metres de Fond* (*Through Eighteen Meters of Water*). The making of the film was later chronicled when *Par dix-huit metres de fond: Histoire d'un film* (*Through Eighteen Meters of Water: History of a Film*) was published in 1946. The year 1943 proved instrumental not only for Cousteau, but for oceanography and marine studies. Cousteau and engineer Emile Gagnan developed and patented the "aqualung"—the first self-contained underwater breathing apparatus (SCUBA)—by inserting a modified gas valve, hooked to an oxygen tank, into a diving mask. It revolutionized underwater diving. In the mid-1940s Cousteau and Taillez formed the Groupe d'Etudes et Recherches Sous-Marines for the French Navy to develop diving equipment.

During the 1950s, Cousteau and his crew converted a minesweeper into a research vessel called the Calypso. For the next forty-plus years, Cousteau and the Calypso sailed in search of the mysteries of the deep, funded by such groups as the National Oceanographic Society, Monaco's Oceanographic Institute, and the French government. (Calypso was sunk off the coast of Singapore in 1996 when it was struck by a barge while in dock.) In the early 1960s, Cousteau developed and documented the Conshelf II experiment in which five men lived beneath the sea in a man-made structure for one month. Cousteau's documentary film about Conshelf II, *World Without Sun,* won an Academy Award. Throughout his life, Cousteau produced numerous films and television shows, in addition to his written works. *The Silent World,* published in 1953, was transformed into a documentary film, which received honors at the Cannes Film Festival as well as an Academy Award. From 1968 to 1976 the American Broadcasting Corporation (ABC) aired *The Undersea World of Jacques Cousteau,* and later Cousteau produced shows for PBS and Turner Broadcasting System (TBS). His written works include *The Living Sea* (with James Dugan), *Jacques Cousteau's Amazon Journey* (with Mose Richards), *Jacques Cousteau—Whales* (with Yves Paccalet), and a twenty-volume encyclopedia titled *The Ocean World of Jacques Cousteau.* In the 1970s Cousteau founded the Cousteau Society in an effort to preserve marine life. His memoir, *Man, Octopus, and Orchids,* was published in 1997, it reflects his passion for protecting the Earth's water resources.

OBITUARIES AND OTHER SOURCES:

PERIODICALS

Chicago Tribune (electronic) June 26, 1997.
Detroit Free Press, June 26, 1997, pp. A12.
Los Angeles Times (electronic), June 26, 1997.
New York Times, June 26, 1997, pp. A1 and B7; July 1, 1997, p. D22.
Times (London; electronic), June 26, 1997; June 27, 1997; June 30, 1997.
USA Today (electronic), June 26, 1997.

* * *

CRABTREE, Judith 1928-

■ Personal

Born September 23, 1928, in Melbourne, Australia; daughter of Frank Richard (a professor of economics) and Nora (a high school teacher; maiden name, Bowls) Mauldon; married Peter Crabtree (a teacher), December 12, 1954; children: Rowena Crabtree Cowan, Jonathan. *Education:* University of Western Australia, B.A., 1954; Associated Teachers' Training Institution, Certificate of Education, 1967. *Hobbies and other interests:* Bush walking, meditation, handcrafts, reading children's books.

■ Addresses

Home—12 Bath Rd., Burwood, Victoria 3125, Australia.

■ Career

Author and illustrator. Teacher of high school English and history in Melbourne, Australia, 1965-79; Council of Adult Education, Melbourne, teacher of writing and illustrating children's books, 1979—. Participates in creative writing and illustration workshops and programs for children in the primary grades; lecturer on her working methods and approach to writing and illustration. *Exhibitions:* Seven of Crabtree's illustrations from *Song at the Gate* were included in a five-city Japanese exhibition of children's book illustrations, 1991. *Member:* Australian Society of Authors, Victorian Fellowship of Australian Writers.

■ Awards, Honors

Australia Council Literature Board Senior Fellowship, 1981; *The Sparrow's Story at the King's Command* was shortlisted for the Australian Children's Book Council Picture Book Award, 1984; Critici in Erba Prize Honorable Mention, Bologna Children's Book Festival, 1989, for *Song at the Gate.*

■ Writings

Emily Jean and the Grumphfs, illustrated by Susan O'Bryan, Wren (Melbourne), 1975.
Carolyn Two, illustrated by Cresside, Wren, 1975.

JUDITH CRABTREE

Skins and Shells and Peelings (young adult novel), Hyland House (Melbourne), 1979.

SELF-ILLUSTRATED

Nicking Off, Wren, 1975.
The High Rise Gang, Wren, 1975.
Legs, Penguin (Ringwood, Victoria), 1979, Oxford University Press (Melbourne), 1983.
The Sparrow's Story at the King's Command, Oxford University Press, 1983.
Stolen Magic, Oxford University Press, 1983.
Song at the Gate, Oxford University Press, 1987.
Night of the Wild Geese, Oxford University Press, 1990.
Skew-whiff, Hodder & Stoughton (Sydney, Australia), 1995.
A Strange and Powerful Magic: A Sea Tale of Love and Jealousy, Hodder Headline (Rydalmere, New South Wales), 1996.

ILLUSTRATOR

Judith Bathie, *The Princess and the Painter,* Wren, 1975.
Jan Harper, *A Family of Potters,* Wren, 1975.
Jan Harper, *Marina,* Women's Movement Children's Literature Cooperative (Box Hill, Victoria), 1977.
Joe Heard, *Tides of Time,* Council of Adult Education (Melbourne), 1980.
Heather Fidge, *Yes I Can,* Oxford University Press, 1984.

OTHER

Author of short stories for educational publications and scripts for the Australian Broadcasting Corporation.

■ Adaptations

A video of *The Sparrow's Story at the King's Command* was produced by Reva Lee Studios in 1985.

■ Sidelights

An author and illustrator of picture books and fiction for primary graders and older children, Judith Crabtree is perhaps best known as the creator of picture books that draw on elements from folk and fairy tales and are praised for their depth, beauty, and appeal. Considered among the few contemporary Australian writers for children to work chiefly with fantasy rooted in European sources, she is credited with writing and illustrating books that reflect a timeless quality. Crabtree is also celebrated for her illustrations, luminescent watercolors and vibrant acrylics surrounded by intricate borders that are influenced by the works of such artists as Arthur Rackham, Kay Nielsen, and Edmund Dulac, and that demonstrate her design sense and attention to detail. In addition, she is praised for the authenticity of her pictures, which are often set in periods such as medieval times and the Victorian Age. Noted for the levels of meanings that her stories provide, Crabtree, who studies philosophy, psychology, and metaphysics as well as art and literature, often underscores her works with allegorical themes such as the power of love and the recognition of the individual; she also includes archetypal characters such as talking animals and holy fools in her books. Writing in *Magpies*, Edel Wignell says that Crabtree has "a rare talent, writing and illustrating with

equal skill. . . . She invites readers to enter her stories and shape them to the truth they choose, according to their age, experience, and imagination."

Legs is considered one of Crabtree's most distinctive picture books. The book depicts characters in an unfinished painting, who move around and interact when the painter departs. These figures are in a painting of people who are on their way to the market in order to exhibit animals in a contest. While the painter is away, one character, Lotta, walks out of the painting and discovers the artist's sketchpad, which includes a doodle of a figure comprised solely of a pair of legs. Lotta takes "Legs" back into the painting, and though the other characters are unable to complete Legs's figure, "Legs proves that, whatever its top half might have been, it is gentle, kind, brave and strong," observed reviewer Marcus Crouch in *Junior Bookshelf*. Because of these qualities, Legs wins the prize for the most beautiful animal at the market. Calling *Legs* "a tough, idiosyncratic picture book," Crouch concluded that "there is a lot in this book, and children who think that a single reading will reveal all have missed much." Writing in *Growing Point*, Margery Fisher found *Legs* "an examination in values" and noted that Crabtree's illustrations "are full of movement and expression and underline the point of an unusual parable."

Like Lotta, Eliza in *Night of the Wild Geese* climbs out of her bedroom window and joins in the flight of her beloved geese despite the remonstrances of her strict Victorian father, who wants to kill the geese, and the

From *The Sparrow's Story at the King's Command,* written and illustrated by Crabtree.

aunts who have cared for her since the death of her mother. When Eliza returns, she is a goose herself, a transformation whose effects extend to each member of her family. "Judith Crabtree matches a delicately humorous story with a sequence of powerful drawings, some suitably magical, others richly funny. . . . Beautifully designed, thoughtful, direct—an excellent picture book for a wide range of ages," remarked Marcus Crouch in *Junior Bookshelf.* Writing in *School Librarian,* Audrey Laski noted that Crabtree's picture of the three aunts singing in church "is a gem." Commenting on *Night of the Wild Geese* to *Magpies* interviewer Edel Wignell, Crabtree said, "Eliza lives in a repressive household and longs for the freedom to be herself, a freedom represented by the wild geese. But the geese are shot at and are driven away and so are no longer free to come and go. In giving them back their freedom, Eliza frees herself and brings freedom to her household."

In her picture book *A Strange and Powerful Magic,* Crabtree tells the story of a young girl wrongfully imprisoned by the well-meaning but wrongheaded adults who care for her. In a work that is considered to have echoes of the Hans Christian Andersen story "The Little Mermaid," the author, who was inspired to write this book by a series of dreams, introduces Selina, a mermaid who falls in love with the Lord of the Wind, the sworn enemy of her father, King Neptune. When her jealous sisters imprison her in the sea, Selina's love and courage help her to break free. A critic in *Reading Time* remarked, "This is a rather beautiful picture book. . . . [The] loveliness of the story is melded with the loveliness of the illustrations. . . . This is a wonderful picture book to share with a child, or for individual reading."

In her *Magpies* interview, Crabtree was asked how themes emerge in her writing: "The message that comes simply 'happens.' An image with a particular feeling tone comes first. Its thought content hasn't emerged but is implicit in it. For me, story, and therefore meaning, arise out of the image-feeling. For example, *Night of the Wild Geese* started with the image of a little girl in her nightdress flying through the night, her arms around the neck of a wild goose. The feeling tone was mixed— longing, joy, excitement, a sense of freedom. *A Strange and Powerful Magic* had its genesis in a very strong image of a blue-toned sea maid swimming languidly, all grace and beauty, deep beneath the sea. The feeling was of profound sadness, listlessness, a sense of loss. The story emerged through questions I posed to the character in the image: Q. *Why are you so sad?* A. *Because I can't rise into the world of air.* Q. *What prevents you?* and so on, until the story line was clear."

"Since I began writing and illustrating fantasy stories," Crabtree once told *SATA,* "I have frequently been asked if I would ever consider writing for adults. My answer has always been the same. When all the universal human concerns can be woven into tales that are simple, yet endlessly varied, resonant and rich in dramatic imagery, what more could a writer-illustrator wish for?

"The best fairy tales are always allegorical. Like poetry, they are models of conciseness and address issues of the greatest importance in a form that gives clarity and vision. They are as timeless and as placeless as 'Once there was . . .' can be, and they appeal to old and young and everybody in between.

"But for me the greatest beauty of these stories is in those omissions that give them their universality, those gaps through which the reader is drawn into inner spaces that give room to intuition and creative dreaming. When a story is complete in all its details, it leaves the reader still confined within the familiar and the commonplace self. In contrast, the gaps in an allegory are byways into the reader's creative self and beyond it.

"[In some of my books] I have left some incidents not fully explained and have used in my illustrations recurring images not mentioned in the text and not essential to the story line. I believe that both of these devices can give stories greater resonance, if not deeper meaning.

"When children write to ask for explanation of my stories, I hand on the ones given to me by children I have worked with. Many of their accounts are surprisingly close to my own, and even when they aren't, they are still useful because they make the story richer and more satisfying to those who give them. Some of these accounts express violence and anger, but these are feelings that the kindly fairy tale can comfortably encompass."

■ Works Cited

Crouch, Marcus, review of *Legs, Junior Bookshelf,* February, 1980, p. 17.

Crouch, Marcus, review of *Night of the Wild Geese, Junior Bookshelf,* April, 1992, p. 53.

Fisher, Margery, review of *Legs, Growing Point,* November, 1979, p. 3607.

Laski, Audrey, review of *Night of the Wild Geese, School Librarian,* May, 1992, p. 55.

Review of *A Strange and Powerful Magic, Reading Time,* May, 1997, p. 21.

Wignell, Edel, "Judith Crabtree: Folly and Wisdom," *Magpies,* May, 1997, pp. 16-18.

■ For More Information See

BOOKS

Alderman, Belle, and Stephanie Owen Reeder, *A History of Australian Children's Book Illustration,* Oxford University Press, 1982.

Crabtree, Judith, "A True Tale," in *The Lu Rees Archives: Notes, Books, and Authors,* Children's Book Council of Australia, ACT Branch, Canberra, 1992.

Dunkle, Margaret, editor, *The Story Makers: A Collection of Interviews with Australian and New Zealand Authors and Illustrators for Young People,* Oxford University Press, 1987.

Holden, Robert, *Koalas, Kangaroos and Kookaburras: 200 Australian Children's Books and Illustrations, 1857-1988,* James Hardie Industries, 1988.
McVitty, Walter, *Authors and Illustrators of Australian Children's Books,* Hodder & Stoughton, 1989.
Muir, Marcie, *A History of Australian Children's Book Illustration,* Oxford University Press, 1982.

PERIODICALS

British Book News, January, 1980, p. 15.
Emergency Librarian, September, 1984, p. 20.
School Librarian, September, 1980, p. 251.
Times Educational Supplement, May, 1992, p. 55.

* * *

CRAVATH, Lynne W. 1951-

■ Personal

Surname is accented on second syllable; born March 6, 1951, in Miles City, MT; daughter of Walter B. and Mary Lou Woodcock; married Jay Cravath (a teacher), September 7, 1975; children: Chloe, Jeff. *Education:* University of Montana, B.A. (with high honors). *Politics:* Democrat. *Religion:* Episcopalian.

■ Addresses

Home—10438 South 45th Pl., Phoenix, AZ 85044. *Agent*—Paige Gillies, Publisher's Graphics, 251 Greenwood Ave., Bethel, CT 06801.

LYNNE W. CRAVATH

■ Career

Children's book illustrator. Chico Chism Chicago Blues Band, bass player. *Member:* Society of Children's Book Writers and Illustrators.

■ Illustrator

Debbie Driscoll, *Three Two One Day,* Simon & Schuster, 1994.
Tony Geiss, *My Little Teddy Bear: A Jewelry Book,* Random House, 1994.
Natalie Standiford, *Brave Maddie Egg,* Random House, 1995.
Margaret Yatsevitch Phinney, *Will You Play with Us?,* Mondo (Greenvale, NY), 1995.
Ellen Weiss and Mel Friedman, *The Plug at the Bottom of the Lake; And Other Wacky Camp Stories,* HarperCollins, 1996.
Ellen Weiss and Mel Friedman, *The Flying Substitute,* HarperCollins, 1996.
Allan Trusell-Cullen, *No Singing Today,* Mondo, 1996.
Linda Tracey Brandon, *The Little Flower Girl,* Random House, 1997.
Alice Lyne, *A, My Name Is . . . ,* Whispering Coyote Press (Dallas, TX), 1997.
A Poem a Day (poetry anthology), Scholastic, 1997.
JoAnn Vandine, *Play Ball,* Mondo, 1997.
Sharon Dennis Wyeth, *Tomboy Trouble,* Random House, 1997.
Patricia Reilly Giff, *Kidnap at the Catfish Cafe* (first book from the "Minnie and Max" series), Viking, 1998.
Stuart J. Murphy, *The Penny Pot,* HarperCollins, 1998.
Sheila Kelly Welch, *Little Prince Know-It-All,* Golden Books, 1998.
Over the River and Through the Woods, HarperCollins, in press.
The Prince's Pets, Golden Books, in press.
Carol Trojanowski and Margaret Holtschlag, *Buttons,* Random House, in press.

"FLOWER GIRLS" SERIES

Kathleen Leverich, *Daisy,* HarperCollins, 1997.
Kathleen Leverich, *Heather,* HarperTrophy, 1997.
Kathleen Leverich, *Rose,* HarperCollins, 1997.
Kathleen Leverich, *Violet,* HarperTrophy, 1997.

Illustrator of *The Random House 1997 Calendar for Kids.* Contributor to magazines, including *Ladybug, Spider, Clubhouse Jr., Brio,* and *Highlights for Children.*

■ Work in Progress

Illustrating an Advent calendar, Publications International, in press; *Tiny and Bigman,* by Phillis Gershator, for Marshall Cavendish (Freeport, NY), 1999; *One, Two, Three Little Pilgrims,* by B.G. Hennessy, for Viking, 1999; *The Adventures of Minnie and Max,* a four-book mystery series, by Patricia Reilly Giff, for Viking, 1999.

From *Daisy,* written by Kathleen Leverich and illustrated by Cravath.

Sidelights

Lynne W. Cravath told *SATA:* "I like to paint with gouache, since it gives you bright, rich color, it's versatile, and it's a very forgiving medium. If you make a mistake, you can lift it out or paint over it. You can make it very opaque, or you can add water or acrylic medium to make it transparent.

"I have a friend who says that all my characters are just myriad little self-portraits of myself. In a sense that's probably true. We can only paint what we know, and we paint the world the way we want to see it. As an illustrator, exposure to all types of people and events in the world around you is very important, along with a good sense of humor. Watching people—their characteristics, clothing, etc.—I carry around a sketchbook at all times and try not to be too obvious about scribbling down a stranger's best and worst features. Animals seem more oblivious to it.

"All our experiences feed our art. I play the bass in a blues band, and then in the morning I'm a mom with two kids. I love to travel and talk to people wherever I go. Other artists are strong influences on my work. Charlotte Voake was a strong influence on me when I started illustrating, and so was Ludwig Bemelmans, the creator of *Madeline.*"

For More Information See

PERIODICALS

Publishers Weekly, February 17, 1997, p. 218.
School Library Journal, May, 1997, p. 106.

*   *   *

CROOK, Connie Brummel
See CROOK, Constance

*   *   *

CROOK, Constance
(Connie Brummel Crook)

Personal

Born in Ameliasburg Township, Ontario, Canada; daughter of Elick (a farmer) and I. V. Pearl (a homemaker; maiden name, Carr) Thorton Brummel; married F. Reginald Brown (a minister), July 7, 1956 (died April 9, 1961); married Albert W. Crook (a farmer), July 12, 1969; children: (first marriage) Elisabeth Ann Beranger, Deborah Lois Floyd. *Education:* Queens University, Kingston, B.A.; University of Toronto, education diploma; further study at Wheaton College, Wheaton, IL. *Hobbies and other interests:* Reading, writing, walking, swimming, baby-sitting five grandchildren.

Addresses

Home and office—Peterborough, Ontario, Canada.

Career

Writer. Taught English and Latin for thirty years in secondary schools in Ontario, Canada.

Awards, Honors

Nellie L. was shortlisted for the Geoffrey Bilson Award for Historical Fiction for Young People, Canadian Children's Book Centre, 1995; several of Crook's works have been placed on booklists in Canadian schools.

Writings

HISTORICAL FICTION, EXCEPT AS NOTED

Flight, Stoddart (Toronto), 1991.
Laura's Choice: The Story of Laura Secord, Windflower Communications (Winnipeg), 1993.
Nellie L., Stoddart, 1994.
Meyers' Creek (sequel to *Flight*), Stoddart, 1995.
Maple Moon (picture book), illustrated by Scott Cameron, Stoddart, 1997.
Nellie's Quest (sequel to *Nellie L.*), Stoddart, 1998.

Contributor to the periodical *Canadian Children's Literature. Flight* was published by CNIB as a Braille edition in 1973.

CONSTANCE CROOK

■ Adaptations

Teacher's guides to *Laura's Choice,* published by Windflower Communications, and *Nellie L.,* released by Irwin Publishing, were written by Cynthia Rankin; guides to *Flight* and *Meyers' Creek* were also released by Irwin Publishing. *Flight* was made into a sound recording by the library services branch of Vancouver, British Columbia, in 1993.

■ Work in Progress

A picture book and a young adult suspense novel.

■ Sidelights

Canadian author Constance Crook, known to her readers as Connie Brummel Crook, is credited for writing well-researched historical novels for young adults that celebrate Canadian history. Calling her historical fiction "dramatized biography," Crook is perhaps best known as the creator of works featuring two notable nineteenth-century Canadian women, Laura Secord and Nellie McClung. She is also highly regarded for writing two novels about an American family loyal to the British Crown who relocate to Canada during the Revolutionary War. The author's detailed and often unique research methods include library research, corresponding with the descendants of her characters, visiting cemeteries, and in one case, actually retracing the journey made by one of her heroines. In addition to her young adult novels, Crook has written a picture book for children.

Crook has lived in the Peterborough area of Ontario, Canada, for most of her life. After attending elementary schools near Belleville, she moved with her parents to a farm north of Norwood, where she walked three miles to high school. Crook showed an aptitude for writing as a student; at the end of high school, she won scholarships to Queen's University and the College of Education at the University of Toronto. Crook began her career as an educator after receiving her teaching certificate from Toronto. Two years after her marriage to minister F. Reginald Brown, Crook left teaching to start a family. When her husband died of leukemia, Crook resumed teaching to help raise her two young daughters.

Eight years after the death of her first husband, she married Albert W. Crook. The author taught English in Ontario secondary schools in Owen Sound, Sault Ste. Marie, Norwood, and Peterborough for thirty years; in Peterborough, she taught at Peterborough Collegiate and Vocational School for twenty-six years and also started that city's first reading lab. Between raising her family and teaching, Crook was unable to find the time to seriously pursue her writing interests. Upon retiring, however, Crook finally started, as she told *SATA,* "taking the creative English lessons to heart that she gave others" and began to write.

Crook's first historical novel, *Flight,* was published in 1991. In this book, the author describes the coming of age of twelve-year-old George Waltermyer during the American Revolution. Because his United Empire Loyalist father Hans is a top courier for the British, George is forced to take care of his family and their farm in Albany, New York. Angry at his father for leaving the family, George is also proud of his work for the British. When the rest of his family heads to New York City to meet Hans, George is forced to stay behind; his adventures in trying to reunite with his family, who eventually move from Albany to Canada, form the majority of the book.

Crook is a descendant of John W. Meyers, the founder of the city of Belleville, Ontario, who is a member of the family in *Flight;* the author was familiar with her subject since, as she wrote in *Canadian Children's Literature,* "I had grown up hearing about his family's adventures." As a member of the United Empire Loyalists' Association of Canada, Crook depicts the persecution by the Rebels of those who pledged allegiance to the Crown. Darleen Golke, a reviewer in *CM: A Reviewing Journal of Canadian Materials for Young People,* declared that *Flight* "will appeal to young adult readers interested in Canada's history.... Crook ... applauds the determination and courage of [the Loyalists]." In 1995, Crook published *Meyers' Creek,* a sequel to *Flight* that focuses on nineteen-year-old Mary Meyers, who longs to be recognized as an adult by her family.

Crook's second book, *Laura's Choice: The Story of Laura Secord,* is set during the War of 1812. The author dramatizes the life of Canadian heroine Laura Secord and describes her twenty-mile, life-threatening journey by foot from her home in Queenston, Ontario, to a

British outpost on the Niagara Peninsula. While on this trip, Secord endures quicksand, snakes, mosquitoes, and other natural elements in order to warn the British of an impending American attack. Crook admitted that researching this novel was much more complicated than her first. In addition to visiting many of the locations, libraries, and museums that mark Secord's life, Crook actually walked and drove the entire stretch of Secord's journey. Writing in *Canadian Children's Literature,* Crook said that by retracing Secord's steps, "I got a sense of the lay of the land, the height of the terrain, and the kinds of trees she would have encountered. I needed that to make my description of her walk believable." In a promotional piece released by Windflower Communications, Canadian author and broadcaster Roy Bonisteel stated that, as with *Flight,* Crook brought Canadian history "to life in an exciting and dramatic fashion. *Laura's Choice* is a marvelous read and a real page-turner...." Bonisteel concluded that the novel is "a must for every Canadian family and certainly should be in every school library."

Crook's second book on Canadian suffragette, reformer, legislator and author Nellie McClung picks up where her first left off—with McClung, a young schoolteacher, beginning her adult life.

After publishing Secord's story, Crook wrote about another courageous Canadian woman, suffragist Nellie McClung, in *Nellie L.* Called "Canada's most famous woman activist" by Helen Norrie in the Winnipeg *Free Press,* McClung was elected to the Alberta legislature and was the first woman to sit on the CBC Board of Governors; she also helped to obtain the vote for women in Manitoba, the first Canadian province to grant this privilege, and was a best-selling author. Although Crook talks about McClung's life as a mother, author, activist, and civil servant, she focuses more on her childhood in the early twentieth century, a time when the young tomboy was known as Nellie L. Mooney.

Much of Crook's novel is based on Nellie McClung's autobiographies. Through her research and a little serendipity, Crook was able to locate family members of the Mooney family. Speaking to the descendants of her subjects "made me even more aware that researching a dramatized historical biography is much more than paperwork," Crook wrote in *Canadian Children's Literature,* adding, "[You] have a more immediate sense of the family and you realize what a great responsibility you have to present the person's life in an accurate way." Norrie called *Nellie L.* "interesting reading for any age" and referred to its subject as "a heroine with whom many girls will identify, and whom even boys may admire." The reviewer concluded that the work is a "lively, enjoyable book" that imparts "a good deal of little-known information...." With the help of McClung's family, Crook wrote *Nellie's Quest,* a sequel to *Nellie L.* that was published in 1998.

Maple Moon is Crook's fictionalized account of the discovery of maple syrup. Rides the Wind (also called Limping Leg) is a young native boy who has a limp that keeps him from doing all the things other boys can do. During a solitary walk in the woods, he discovers sap running from a maple tree and collects some in a bucket. This "sweet water" helps feed his hungry people, giving him new status in his community and a new name, Wise Little Raven. Anne Louise Mahoney, a critic for *Quill & Quire,* noted that Crook's "sensitive telling and ear for language make the story echo in the reader's heart long afterward. She captures the boy's loneliness, his curiosity, and his need to find a place in this community."

As an author, Crook believes that presenting Canadian history in a novel helps to foster Canadian unity. She explained to *SATA,* "All of my novels and my picture book are true stories of our Canadian heritage. This is one of my purposes—to give credit to great Canadians of the past and to bring them to life for students. The Americans pay tribute to their founding heroines and heroes. We should also, for we have many worthy Canadians to remember."

In her essay in *Canadian Children's Literature,* Crook remarked, "Though I always try to write an exciting story, it is just as important to write something that is accurate enough that the subject of the book would also enjoy reading. If John W. Meyers, Laura Secord, and

Nellie McClung were alive today, I hope they would find their lives honoured and accurately reflected in the books I have written about them."

■ Works Cited

Bonisteel, Roy, commentary in promotional piece for *Laura's Choice,* Windflower Communications.

Crook, Connie Brummel, "Treading the Line Between Fact and Fiction," *Canadian Children's Literature,* Number 83, 1996, pp. 84-86.

Golke, Darleen, review of *Flight, CM: A Reviewing Journal of Canadian Materials for Young People,* May, 1992, p. 166.

Mahoney, Anne Louise, review of *Maple Moon, Quill & Quire,* January, 1998, p. 38.

Norrie, Helen, "Nellie Brought to Life," *Free Press* (Winnipeg), January 22, 1995, p. D5.

■ For More Information See

PERIODICALS

Canadian Children's Literature, fall, 1995, pp. 76-78; summer, 1997, p. 75.

Examiner (Peterborough, Ontario), May 29, 1993, p. D4.

School Library Journal, April, 1998, p. 98.*

*   *   *

CURLEE, Lynn 1947-

■ Personal

Born October 9, 1947, in North Carolina. *Education:* Attended College of William and Mary, 1965-67; University of North Carolina, B.A., 1969; University of North Carolina, M.A., 1971.

■ Addresses

Home and office—P.O. Box 699, Jamesport, NY 11947.

■ Career

Exhibiting gallery artist, 1973—; freelance writer, 1991—.

■ Writings

FOR CHILDREN

(Illustrator) Dennis Haseley, *Horses with Wings,* HarperCollins, 1993.

(And illustrator) *Ships of the Air,* Houghton Mifflin, 1996.

(And illustrator) *Into the Ice: The Story of Arctic Explorations,* Houghton Mifflin, 1997.

■ Work in Progress

Writing and illustrating a nonfiction picture book for Scholastic, expected 1999.

Lynn Curlee's self-illustrated *Ships of the Air* documents the invention and subsequent refinement of the steerable balloon.

■ Sidelights

An exhibiting gallery artist for over twenty years, Lynn Curlee started displaying his artwork to a larger audience when he illustrated his first children's book, *Horses with Wings,* in 1993. *Booklist* contributor Kay Weisman hailed Curlee's work in *Horses with Wings*—an account of a balloon escape from Paris during the Franco-Prussian War—as "stunning." *Ships of the Air,* which Curlee wrote and illustrated, continues with the flight motif. It is a brief history of balloon and dirigible crafts. A *Kirkus Reviews* critic found that the book "delights as well as ... informs."

■ Works Cited

Review of *Ships of the Air, Kirkus Reviews,* June 1, 1996, p. 821.

Weisman, Kay, review of *Horses with Wings, Booklist,* November 15, 1993, p. 630-31.

■ For More Information See

PERIODICALS

Booklist, September 1, 1996.

Bulletin of the Center for Children's Books, October, 1996, pp. 53-55.

Horn Book, November-December, 1996, p. 757.

Publishers Weekly, September 13, 1993, pp. 132-37.

School Library Journal, December, 1993, pp. 88-89.

DRAPER, Sharon M(ills)

■ Personal

Born in Cleveland, OH; daughter of Victor (a hotel manager) and Catherine (a gardener) Mills; married Larry E. Draper (an educator); children: Wendy, Damon, Crystal, Cory. *Education:* Pepperdine University, B.A.; Miami University (Oxford, OH), M.A.

■ Addresses

Office—2650 Highland Ave., Cincinnati, OH 45219.

■ Career

Junior- and senior-high school teacher, 1972—. Public speaker, poet, and author. *Member:* International Reading Association, American Federation of Teachers, National Board for Professional Teaching Standards (Board of Directors, 1995—), National Council of Teachers of English, Ohio Council of Teachers of English Language Arts, Conference on English Leadership, Delta Kappa Gamma, Phi Delta Kappa, Women's City Club.

■ Awards, Honors

First prize, *Ebony* Magazine Literary Contest, 1991, for short story, "One Small Torch"; Coretta Scott King Genesis Award for an outstanding new book, American Library Association (ALA), 1995, for *Tears of a Tiger;* Best Book for Young Adults, ALA, Best Books, Children's Book Council and Bank Street College, Books for the Teen Age, New York Public Library, and Notable Trade Book in the Field of Social Studies, National Council for the Social Studies, 1995, for *Tears of a Tiger,* and 1998, for *Forged by Fire;* Coretta Scott King Award, ALA, 1998, for *Forged by Fire.*

Outstanding High School English Language Arts Educator, Ohio Council of Teachers of English Language Arts, 1995; Midwest regional winner of the NCNW Excellence in Teaching Award, 1996; Governor's Educational Leadership Award from the Governor of Ohio, 1996; National Teacher of the Year, 1997.

■ Writings

FOR CHILDREN

Ziggy and the Black Dinosaurs, Just Us Books (East Orange, NJ), 1994.
Ziggy and the Black Dinosaurs: Lost in the Tunnel of Time, Just Us Books, 1996.
Ziggy and the Black Dinosaurs: Shadows of Caesar's Creek, Just Us Books, 1997.

FOR YOUNG ADULTS

Tears of a Tiger, Simon and Schuster, 1994.
Forged by Fire, Simon and Schuster, 1997.

Also author of *Let the Circle Be Unbroken* (children's poetry), and *Buttered Bones* (poetry for adults). Contrib-

SHARON M. DRAPER

utor of poems and short stories to literary magazines, and of an award-winning essay, "The Touch of a Teacher," to *What Governors Need to Know About Education,* Center for Policy Research of the National Governor's Association.

■ Sidelights

Sharon Draper told *SATA:* "On April 18, 1997, I was honored as the 1997 National Teacher of the Year by President Clinton at the White House. It is a wonderful honor, but also an awesome responsibility—to be the spokesperson and advocate for education in America. I was ready for this challenge, however, because I had been preparing for this work my entire life.

"I have been a public school teacher for twenty-five years. I know what kids like, what they will read, and what they won't. Although I have nothing against Charles Dickens, many teenagers would rather gag than read him. Dickens wrote for his contemporaries—young people of a hundred and fifty years ago. American students might need to know about the world of London in the 1860s, but they would much rather read about their own world first. Not only will they read about recognizable experiences with pleasure, but they will also be encouraged to write as well. So I started writing books for young people.

"*Tears of a Tiger* is written for high school students—on their level, in their style, about their world. The main characters are African American males, but it's written for all teenagers. The characters are just ordinary kids trying to get through high school. The book does not deal with drugs or gangs or sex. It does, however, deal with parents, girlfriends, and homework. It also discusses the problems of drinking and driving, racism and teen suicide. I sent it to twenty-five publishing companies and got twenty-four rejection notices. The very last letter was a letter of acceptance from Simon and Schuster.

"While I was waiting for that one to finish the publication process, I wrote another book for younger students. It is called *Ziggy and the Black Dinosaurs*. It is written for boys ages six to twelve. *Ziggy* is funny and a mystery, dealing with club houses and buried treasure, and even includes hidden history lessons for young readers. The response has been so wonderful that it has been made into a series. In the second book, *Lost in the Tunnel of Time*, Ziggy and his friends find an old, abandoned tunnel of the Underground Railroad and get lost in it. The third book in this series is called *Shadows of Caesar's Creek*, and deals with the forgotten connections between African Americans and Native Americans, again through humor, excitement, and solid literary development. Students can read this series and learn as well as enjoy the tale. Teachers can use these to teach.

"Although it was not planned that way, both *Tears of a Tiger* and *Ziggy and the Black Dinosaurs* hit the bookstores on the very same day! The response was tremendous and overwhelming. Parents have asked, 'Where have you been?' Young readers are clamoring for the sequels. I don't think I have ever had a young person read *Tears of a Tiger* and not like it. Actually, many of the teenagers who read it tell me they have never read a whole book before in their lives, but they read that one in one night.

"*Tears of a Tiger* has received wonderful reviews, several national awards, and was awarded the Coretta Scott King Genesis Award, as well as being selected as an ALA Best Book for Young Adults for 1995. The sequel, *Forged by Fire*, is a powerful piece for young people on child abuse and survival. I was surprised and pleased when it received the Coretta Scott King Award in 1998.

"I feel very blessed that I have had so much success in such a short time. I hope that my books can continue to make a difference in the lives of young people."

Draper's debut novel, *Tears of a Tiger*, delves into the gritty issues of teen suicide, alcoholism, and racism, exploring what happens in the wake of a car accident in which the intoxicated driver's best friend is killed. Andy, a high school basketball star, tries to cope with his feelings of guilt and loss. When teachers, counselors, coaches, and even his girlfriend are unable to help him, Andy commits suicide. The story is told through homework assignments, newspaper articles, police reports, and conversations. According to Kathy Fritts in *School Library Journal*, "the character's voices are strong, vivid and ring true." Roger Sutton, in *Bulletin of the Center for Children's Books*, maintains the book will "provoke lots of thought and debate among young adults." *Voice of Youth Advocates* contributor Dorothy M. Broderick asserts that *Tears of a Tiger* "is as compelling a novel as any published in the last two decades."

■ Works Cited

Broderick, Dorothy M., review of *Tears of a Tiger, Voice of Youth Advocates*, February, 1995, p. 338.
Fritts, Kathy, review of *Tears of a Tiger, School Library Journal*, February, 1995, p. 112.
Sutton, Roger, review of *Tears of a Tiger, Bulletin of the Center for Children's Books*, January, 1995, p. 164.

■ For More Information See

PERIODICALS

Booklist, November 1, 1994, p. 492; February 15, 1997, p. 1016.
Publishers Weekly, October 31, 1994, p. 64; March 25, 1996, p. 85; December 16, 1996, p. 61.
School Library Journal, March, 1995, p. 202; March, 1997, p. 184.

F–G

FLOWERS, Sarah 1952-

■ Personal

Born December 8, 1952, in Emporia, KS; daughter of Donald E. (a retired school administrator) and Gloria June (a retired preschool teacher and storyteller; maiden name, Wright) Inbody; married Philip L. Flowers (a computer programmer), September 14, 1975; children: Stephen, Mark, Thomas. *Education:* Kansas State University, B.A. (history), 1974; University of California at Berkeley, M.A. (history), 1976; San Jose State University, M.L.S., 1992. *Religion:* Catholic.

■ Addresses

Home—2455 Fountain Oaks Dr., Morgan Hill, CA 95037. *Office*—Morgan Hill Public Library, 17575 Peak Ave., Morgan Hill, CA 95037. *Electronic mail*—sflowers@scinet.co.santa-clara.ca.us.

■ Career

Santa Clara County Library, Morgan Hill, CA, librarian, 1991-93, adult program librarian, 1995—; Los Gatos Public Library, Los Gatos, CA, young adult librarian, 1993-95. *Member:* American Library Association, Young Adult Library Services Association (chair of Youth Participation Committee), Phi Beta Kappa.

■ Writings

NONFICTION FOR CHILDREN

The Reformation, Lucent Books (San Diego, CA), 1995.
Sports in America, Lucent Books, 1996.
Age of Exploration, Lucent Books, in press.
Space Exploration, Enslow Publishers, in press.

■ For More Information See

PERIODICALS

Booklist, September 1, 1996, p. 71.

School Library Journal, November, 1992, pp. 37-38; March, 1996, pp. 224-25.

* * *

FORD, Carolyn (Mott) 1938-

■ Personal

Born November 26, 1938, in Staten Island, NY; daughter of Ellison Jesse (a marine engineer) and Loretto (a homemaker; maiden name, Donovan) Mott; married Jon Ford, Sr., December 14, 1956 (died November 1, 1993); children: Elizabeth Ford Wilson, Victoria Ford Thomas, Jon, Timothy, Mary (deceased), Patrick. *Hobbies and other interests:* Reading, attending the theater, dancing, writing poetry, "spending time with my children and grandchildren."

■ Addresses

Home—548 Ocean Blvd., No. 20, Long Branch, NJ 07740.

■ Career

Writer. Monmouth Medical Center, Long Branch, NJ, former guest services representative; also worked as library assistant, tax clerk, and stringer for a local radio station. *Member:* Society of Children's Book Writers and Illustrators.

■ Writings

Nothing in the Mailbox, illustrated by Sally Schaedler, Richard C. Owen (Katonah, NY), 1996.

Work represented in anthologies, including *From Eulogy to Joy.* Contributor of articles and reviews to periodicals, including *Highlights for Children, Ladybug, Sports Illustrated for Kids,* and *Children's Literature.* Other essays found in various newsletters and newspapers.

CAROLYN FORD

■ Work in Progress

Fifty/Fifty: Fifty Wonderful Reasons to Enjoy Your Fifties; biographical research on Katherine Lee Bates.

■ Sidelights

Carolyn Ford told *SATA:* "Writing for children is a joy and a privilege. The love of reading I have enjoyed since early childhood is a blessing to be shared. I have been particularly happy to have my first published book be an early reader and to have stories accepted by magazines such as *Highlights for Children* and *Ladybug.*

"In addition to writing for children and reviewing books for *Children's Literature,* I also enjoy writing essays, which have been published in various newsletters and newspapers, and I have just had a short story and a poem accepted for a forthcoming anthology.

"I have been working on a manuscript titled *Fifty/Fifty: Fifty Wonderful Reasons to Enjoy Your Fifties.* The first of those reasons? You can plan what to do with the second half of your life. My plan? To try and take myself seriously as a writer. As my children were growing up, our family relocated often, due to my husband's career with the Department of the Army, so I always held part-time or temporary jobs. We lived in various areas of New Jersey, in El Paso, Temple, and Belton, Texas, in Huntsville, Alabama, Colorado Springs, Colorado, and

in Stuttgart, Germany. I have been a library assistant, a tax clerk, a stringer for a radio station, and so on, but the focus was always on my family. I have just left my position as a guest services representative at Monmouth Medical Center and intend to focus on writing.

"My other interests are reading, attending the theater, enjoying the company of my children and grandchildren, dancing, and occasionally writing poetry. I am fortunate to live a block from the beach, so I walk three or four miles on the boardwalk almost every day. I visit New York City often to attend plays or go to museums, and I find the dynamics of the city invigorating. During the school year, I volunteer to work with very young children one morning a week, and I am a volunteer driver on occasion through the county Board of Social Services. I am a member of the Society of Children's Book Writers and Illustrators and get together for informal meetings with other members in the Jersey shore area.

"I think that our attitudes about careers, aging, and making changes are undergoing a beneficial transformation. I feel that we should be aware of our options and cherish the opportunities and joys in every stage of our lives. Writing, as well as reading, makes my life more interesting, productive, and fulfilling."

*   *   *

FREY, Darcy

■ Personal

Education: Graduated from Oberlin College.

■ Addresses

Home—Boston, MA. *Office*—c/o Houghton Mifflin, 222 Berkeley St., Boston, MA 02116.

■ Career

Journalist. Worked for business and law magazines following graduation; staff editor at *Harper's* for a year.

■ Awards, Honors

National Magazine Award, for an article on college basketball recruiting.

■ Writings

The Last Shot: City Streets, Basketball Dreams (nonfiction), Houghton Mifflin (Boston, MA), 1994.

Also contributor of articles to periodicals, including *Harper's* and *Rolling Stone.*

■ Sidelights

Journalist Darcy Frey turned his award-winning article on college basketball recruiting into the critically acclaimed volume *The Last Shot: City Streets, Basketball Dreams*. In the book, Frey examines the lives of four high school basketball stars in order to expose the darker truths behind the myth of escaping from the slums via professional basketball. As Brent Staples explained in the *New York Times Book Review:* "Fewer than one percent of the half-million young men who play high school ball will win scholarships.... Fewer than one in a hundred of those who play in college will go on to careers in professional basketball. Of this final, golden few, most ... will last no longer than four years—has-beens at the age of twenty-six."

The Last Shot profiles four basketball superstars from New York's Lincoln High School. Once surrounded by the glittery opulence of Coney Island, the school now stands amid bleak housing projects inhabited by poor African Americans. Frey details how the students, casualties of a lackluster educational system, pin all their hope on landing first a college scholarship, which will hopefully lead to a lucrative National Basketball Association (NBA) contract. Two of the students Frey portrays miss their goal because they lack the academic scores for admission to four-year colleges. One succeeds

Darcy Frey chronicles the process of college athletic recruitment through his stories of four inner-city high school basketball stars, their dreams, goals, and future prospects.

at Seton Hall University, while another has bloomed so early in his basketball skills that Frey's narrative ends while he is still in high school, hounded by college recruiters who are encouraged by his ambitious father.

In the course of the book, Frey follows the most successful boy to a Nike-sponsored basketball camp, a place James North in *Chicago Tribune Books* described as "swarming with college coaches." North called *The Last Shot* "outstanding," while Staples asserted that the book was "compellingly written, with elegance, economy and just the right amount of outrage." John Skow in *Time* praised the volume as "thoughtful" and "sharply observed," while Evan Thomas in *Newsweek* hailed it as "an achingly good book." Calling the book "a heartbreaking, gritty piece of work," a *Kirkus Reviews* critic ascribed the emotional force of *The Last Shot* to "the psychological drama and physical beauty of the game, and the joy it brings those who play it and see it played at its best."

■ Works Cited

North, James, review of *The Last Shot, Chicago Tribune Books,* November 27, 1994, p. 5.

Review of *The Last Shot, Kirkus Reviews,* September 1, 1994, p. 1185.

Staples, Brent, review of *The Last Shot, New York Times Book Review,* November 13, 1994, pp. 3, 66-67.

Thomas, Evan, review of *The Last Shot, Newsweek,* November 21, 1994, p. 101.

Skow, John, review of *The Last Shot, Time,* November 28, 1994, p. 91.

■ For More Information See

PERIODICALS

Booklist, December 1, 1994, pp. 650-51.
Publishers Weekly, September 12, 1994, p. 74.*

*   *   *

GORBACHEV, Valeri 1944-

■ Personal

Born June 10, 1944, in the U.S.S.R. (now Ukraine); immigrated to the United States, 1991; son of Gregory and Polina (Koishman) Gorbachev; married; wife's name, Victoria, October, 1970; children: Konstantin (son), Shoshana Aleksandra (daughter). *Education:* Attended Academy of Art, Kiev, U.S.S.R. (now Ukraine).

■ Addresses

Home—1440 East 14th St., Apt. F-5, Brooklyn, NY 11230.

■ Career

Artist; author and illustrator of children's books.

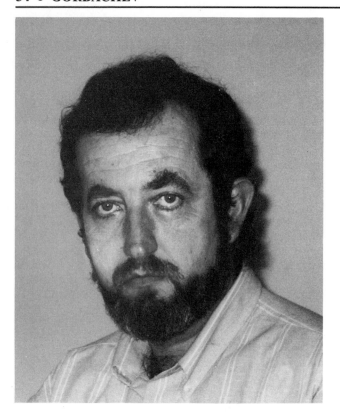

VALERI GORBACHEV

■ **Writings**

SELF-ILLUSTRATED CHILDREN'S BOOKS

The Three Little Pigs: Full-color Sturdy Book, Dover, 1995.
Arnie the Brave, Grosset & Dunlap, 1997.
(With Warren Longmire) *The Flying Ship,* Star Bright, 1997.
Fool of the World and the Flying Ship, Star Bright, 1998.
Nicky and the Big, Bad Wolves, North-South, 1998.

ILLUSTRATOR

Joy N. Hulme, *What If? Just Wondering Poems,* Boyds Mills (Honesdale, PA), 1993.
Laurie A. Jacobs, *So Much in Common,* Boyds Mills, 1994.
Pamela J. Farris, *Young Mouse and Elephant: An East African Folktale,* Houghton Mifflin, 1996.
Miriam Kosman, *Red, Blue, and Yellow Yarn: A Tale of Forgiveness,* Hachai Publications (Brooklyn, NY), 1996.
Patricia Blanchard and Joanne Suhr, *There Was a Mouse,* Richard C. Owens (Katonah, NY), 1997.

Author and illustrator of several dozen books published in Russian. Contributor to magazines.

■ **Sidelights**

Valeri Gorbachev told *SATA:* "I arrived in the United States in 1991 with my wife, my two children, my suitcases, and dozens of characters I had created. Since then I have illustrated five books by American writers. In my native Ukraine, I illustrated forty children's books, half of which I also wrote. They have been translated into Finnish, German, and Spanish, and I have participated in many exhibitions of children's books in the former Soviet Union and abroad. I have also had solo exhibitions in Moscow and St. Petersburg. For many years government officials denied me the right to leave the country. The demise of communism at last cleared the way for me and my family to move to the United States.

"When I illustrate a book, the drawings and the text become one, and it is not really possible for me to separate the drawings from the text. I love to draw for children and to create books when I am both author and illustrator. I think that my work in children's magazines helped me to connect with the reading audience. Now I am enjoying my work with American magazines. I also love American children's books because they have strong visual appeal, and the connection between author and illustrator is close. Often the author and artist are the same person. That is how I understand children's literature. I hope that American children will love my books as much as Russian children do. My characters will take on nuances of American culture, but the basic qualities of the characters show the similarities among people all over the world."

Similarities and differences among people is the theme of Laurie A. Jacobs's book *So Much In Common,* a 1994 work that Gorbachev illustrated. Philomena Midge, a hippo, and Horace Abercrombie, a goat, are two friends who share different interests. The pair, however, easily acknowledge what they enjoy about each other—Philomena enjoys Horace's sense of humor while Horace savors Philomena's cooking. Other friends tell the hippo and goat that they have nothing in common, but the duo only grow closer. Unfortunately, a minor disagreement causes the friends to isolate themselves from each other, causing much unhappiness. The two are reunited when they both tie for first place in a floral arrangement contest. The story ends by promoting acceptance and diversity between the characters. Gorbachev adds to the theme with "cheerful pen-and-ink and watercolor drawings of the animal village," says *School Library Journal* reviewer Janet M. Bair. A *Publishers Weekly* contributor notes that the illustrator's drawings "bring the characters playfully to life."

Young Mouse and Elephant: An East African Folktale by Pamela J. Farris is another well-known children's book that includes Gorbachev's drawings. The humorous folktale focuses on Young Mouse, who claims to be the strongest animal on the African plains. Mouses's grandfather bruises his ego when he disagrees and states that Elephant is the strongest. Young Mouse goes out looking to challenge Elephant, proclaiming that he will "break Elephant apart and stomp her to bits." On his journey, Mouse encounters several other larger animals who are fearful of him after thinking that he has control over an approaching storm. When the mouse reaches the elephant, he ends up being blown across the savanna by her water-filled trunk. Instead of feeling defeated, Mouse thinks that Elephant has been washed away by a storm when he doesn't see her after gathering himself. Thus, Mouse considers Elephant lucky that she doesn't have to battle with him. According to *School Library Journal* reviewer Jennifer Fleming, Gorbachev perfectly pairs his drawings to the folktale by making them "full of mischief and fun" and a "delightful match for this clever retelling." *Booklist* contributor Annie Ayres adds that the "sprightly ink-and-watercolor illustrations should amuse the small and swaggering."

Gorbachev both wrote and illustrated *Nicky and the Big, Bad Wolves,* a picture book about a small bunny named Nicky who awakens one night terrified by a nightmare he has had. As Nicky relates his dream to his mother and four siblings, Gorbachev "wrings every last ounce of humor from the action" with his "particularly droll" pen-and-ink and watercolor illustrations, according to a reviewer for *Publishers Weekly.* The same commentator concluded that *Nicky and the Big, Bad Wolves* has a "fresh, friendly sensibility" that will "keep little ones coming back for more."

■ **Works Cited**

Ayres, Annie, review of *Young Mouse and Elephant: An East African Folktale, Booklist,* May 1, 1996, p. 1509.

Bair, Janet M., review of *So Much In Common, School Library Journal,* December, 1994, p. 76.

Farris, Pamela J., *Young Mouse and Elephant: An East African Folktale,* Houghton Mifflin, 1996.

Fleming, Jennifer, review of *Young Mouse and Elephant: An East African Folktale, School Library Journal,* April, 1996, p. 124.

Review of *Nicky and the Big, Bad Wolves, Publishers Weekly,* April 13, 1998, p. 74.

Review of *So Much In Common, Publishers Weekly,* June 13, 1994, p. 63.

■ **For More Information See**

PERIODICALS

Publishers Weekly, June 21, 1993, p. 104.
School Library Journal, August, 1993, p. 158.

GRABER, (George) Alexander 1914-1997 (Alexander Cordell)

OBITUARY NOTICE—See index for *SATA* sketch: Born September 9, 1914, in Colombo, Ceylon (now Sri Lanka), to British parents; body found in a stream, July 9, 1997, near Llangollen, Denbighshire, Wales. Soldier, surveyor, author. Graber was a popular novelist who penned historical yarns under the pseudonym Alexander Cordell. The son of a British soldier, he also pursued military service first as a British Army sapper from 1932 to 1936, then with the Royal Engineers during World War II, becoming a major. From 1936 to 1939 and after 1945, Graber worked as a civil surveyor in Wales and eventually settled there. He was a member of the Welsh Nationalist Party and advocated self-government in his adopted country. He began his writing career in earnest in 1950 and at one time served as vice president of the Cardiff Writers' Circle. Credited with writing nearly thirty books, Graber is best remembered for his novel *Rape of the Fair Country,* which focused on the struggles of workers to obtain various labor rights. The book was part of the "Welsh Trilogy," which also included *Robe of Honour* and *Song of the Earth.* Among his other books are *A Thought of Honour, If You Believe the Soldiers, Land of My Fathers, To Slay the Dreamer, Tales from Tiger Bay, Tunnel Tigers, Requiem for a Patriot, Land of Heart's Desire,* and *Send Her Victorious.* He also wrote a number of books for children, including *The White Cockade, Witches Sabbath,* and *The Healing Blade.* At the time of his death, his novel about Owain Glyndwr, a medieval Welsh prince, was incomplete.

OBITUARIES AND OTHER SOURCES:

PERIODICALS

Chicago Tribune, August 11, 1997, section 4, p. 8.
New York Times, August 10, 1997, section 1, p. 37.
Times (London), July 12, 1997.

* * *

GRAHAM, Ennis
See MOLESWORTH, Mary Louisa

* * *

Greybeard the Pirate
See MACINTOSH, Brownie

H

JESSIE HAAS

HAAS, (Katherine) Jessie 1959-

■ Personal

Born July 27, 1959, in Westminster, Vermont; daughter of Robert Joseph (a truck driver and freight manager) and Patricia Anne (a farmer and housewife; maiden name, Trevorrow) Haas; married Michael Joseph Daley (a writer and educator), April 25, 1981. *Education:*

Wellesley College, B.A. (English), 1981. *Politics:* Progressive Democrat. *Hobbies and other interests:* Horseback riding, animals, cooking, knitting, drawing, reading, Scottish dancing, politics.

■ Addresses

Home—RFD #3, Box 627, Putney, VT 05346.

■ Career

Writer, 1981—. Worker at a vegetable stand, early 1980s; yarn mill laborer, mid-1980s to 1991. Trustee, Westminster West Library, 1984-87; Westminster Cares (Meals-on-Wheels delivery). *Member:* Society of Children's Book Writers and Illustrators, Authors Guild, Vermont Consumer's Campaign for Health.

■ Awards, Honors

Dorothy Canfield Fisher Award Master List, Volunteer State Book Award Master List, and Northwest Territories (Australia) Children's Choice Award Master List, all 1983, all for *Keeping Barney;* Dorothy Canfield Fisher Award Master List, 1993-94, for *Skipping School;* Pick of the Lists, *American Bookseller,* 1993, and Sequoyah Children's Book Award Master List, 1995-96, both for *Beware the Mare;* Dorothy Canfield Fisher Award Master List, 1995-96, Bluebonnet Award Master List, Mark Twain Award Master List, and South Carolina Children's Book Award Master List, all 1996-97, all for *Uncle Daney's Way;* Pick of the Lists, *American Bookseller,* 1995, for *No Foal Yet;* Dorothy Canfield Fisher Award Master List, 1996-97, and West Virginia Children's Book Award Master List, 1997-98, both for *A Blue for Beware;* Pick of the Lists, *American Bookseller,* for *Busybody Brandy;* Dorothy Canfield Fisher Award Master List, 1997-98, and Children's Book of the Year, Child Study Association, both for *Be Well, Beware;* Pick of the Lists, *American Bookseller,* Children's Book of the Year, Child Study Association, both 1996, and Volunteer State Book Award Master List, 1998-99, all for *Clean House;* Notable Children's Book in the Field of Social Studies, NCSS/CBC, and Children's Book of the

56

Year, Child Study Association, both 1997, both for *Sugaring*. Several of Haas's books have been chosen as Junior Literary Guild titles.

■ Writings

FOR CHILDREN

Keeping Barney, Greenwillow, 1982, Apple Paperbacks, 1983, Beechtree Books, 1998.

Working Trot, Greenwillow, 1983.

The Sixth Sense and Other Stories, Greenwillow, 1988.

Skipping School, Greenwillow, 1992.

Beware the Mare, illustrated by Martha Haas, Greenwillow, 1993, Beech Tree Books, 1996.

Chipmunk!, illustrated by Jos. A. Smith, Greenwillow, 1993.

A Horse Like Barney, Greenwillow, 1993.

Mowing, illustrated by Jos. A. Smith, Greenwillow, 1994.

Uncle Daney's Way, Greenwillow, 1994, Beech Tree Books, 1997.

Busybody Brandy, illustrated by Yossi Abolafia, Greenwillow, 1994.

Safe Horse, Safe Rider, Storey Communications, 1994.

A Blue for Beware, illustrated by Jos. A. Smith, Greenwillow, 1995, Beech Tree Books, 1997.

No Foal Yet, illustrated by Jos. A. Smith, Greenwillow, 1995.

Be Well, Beware, illustrated by Jos. A. Smith, Greenwillow, 1996, Beech Tree Books, 1997.

Clean House, illustrated by Yossi Abolafia, Greenwillow, 1996.

Sugaring, illustrated by Jos. A. Smith, Greenwillow, 1996.

Westminster West, Greenwillow, 1997.

Fire! My Parents' Story, Greenwillow, 1998.

Beware and Stogie, self-illustrated, Greenwillow, 1998.

Haas's works have been translated into Swedish, Finnish, and German.

■ Work in Progress

The Weathervane Colt, the story of a girl who is orphaned in a horse and buggy accident and the colt she must train, expected 1999; *Runaway Radish,* a chapter book about a pony whose riders keep outgrowing him.

■ Sidelights

Jessie Haas is the author of some twenty novels and picture books for children, most of which deal with one of Haas's reigning passions—horses. In award-winning titles such as *Keeping Barney, Beware the Mare, Uncle Daney's Way, A Blue for Beware,* and *Sugaring,* Haas illuminates the life of farming and of working with farm animals, a topic that comes naturally for Haas who was herself raised on a Vermont farm which she still calls home.

"My childhood was full of haying, gardening, horseback riding, and animals," Haas told *SATA.* "I trained my own horse. I was given a goat for my sixteenth birthday.

My mother was the town poundkeeper, so we had an endless stream of stray cats and dogs coming through. Lots of them stayed." But if animals were a vital part of Haas's growing up, so was reading, an activity that was not limited to the confines of an easy chair. Haas read everywhere, as she explained to *SATA:* "Even in the bathtub. I read all the horse stories ever written, as first choice, and then anything else printed on a page." This magpie curiosity stood her in good stead when she went to college, at Wellesley, studying English literature and writing. Influenced by the British novelist Jane Austen and by the loads of horse stories she had earlier consumed, Haas wrote her first novel while still a college student. One of her teachers recommended she try to publish the book, supplying the name of a former student who had become editor-in-chief at Greenwillow publishers. The novel, *Keeping Barney,* was initially rejected, but with helpful suggestions for a re-write, suggestions which Haas followed. Upon its second submission, the novel was accepted by Greenwillow, a month before Haas graduated from college. That same month, Haas married and settled on property near her parents' farm, building a simple cabin. "We had one room at first," Haas told *SATA,* "with no insulation, no phone, no plumbing, and no electricity—but a very small mortgage. The little house gave us—still gives us—the freedom to pursue our interests without having to get 'real jobs.' I've worked at a vegetable stand, a village store, and a yarn mill, all part-time, while concentrating mainly on my writing."

After Tess and her mother labor to prepare the house for a visit from their relatives, they decide they like it more comfortably messy.

Meanwhile, *Keeping Barney* was published to favorable reviews, earning several awards to boot. Barney is a cranky and stubborn horse who causes his young owner no end of trouble. Sarah Miles is thirteen and has long waited for the day she would have her own horse, imagining a lovely partnership between human and animal. But Barney is a far cry from the sleek stallion of her imagination, and his feistiness is intimidating. Finally, Sarah learns that the "secret of success is frequently self-control," according to Mary M. Burns, writing in *Horn Book,* and the realization that Barney "would never really be hers was not only the moment of demarcation between childhood and adolescence but is also the climax of the story." *Booklist* critic Denise M. Wilms noted that "there is much truth in the portrayal of Sarah's struggles with a real rather than a dream horse, and her girlish joy in horses and riding will surely be communicated to readers." A contributor in *Kirkus Reviews* dubbed this first novel a "nicely managed girl-gets-horse story—with individuated characters and some unexpected twists.... [S]atisfying *and* sustaining."

Haas's second title, *Working Trot,* again features horses, but this time her protagonist is a young male. James graduates from high school with plans far different from his parents, who want him to attend college and pursue a business career. Instead James wants to train as a dressage rider, working with a somewhat dilapidated Lippizan stallion at his uncle's riding establishment in Vermont. Demands of a professional riding career prove harder than James first imagined, however, and he struggles to balance his study with his social life, attempting to fit in with a young equestrian who wants to ride on the Olympic team. Pat Harrington, writing in *School Library Journal,* observed that "Haas conveys an impressive knowledge of her subject," and that she "has written a novel that is realistic and satisfying."

Haas turned to the short story format for her next work, *The Sixth Sense and Other Stories,* a collection of nine "wonderful stories" according to *Horn Book* reviewer Elizabeth Watson, dealing with the relationship between humans and animals. Haas employs two main characters, James and Kris, who tie many of the stories together, and examines themes of loyalty, death, responsibility, love, and understanding in tales which deal with cats, dogs, and horses. Watson concluded that this was a "superb collection with deeply felt emotion for animal lovers." Betsy Hearne noted in *Bulletin of the Center for Children's Books* that Haas's tales "make a real contribution to the short story genre, being both resonant and readable."

Ultimately, Haas has been able to reduce her other part-time work and concentrate solely on her writing. "Car trips, horseback rides, and long walks are times when I ask myself questions about my characters, and when I listen to the answers," Haas explained to *SATA.* "Bad habits are excess reading and excess public radio, which occupy brain space I should keep free." For Haas, the writing process is similar to riding—one that demands balance and profound concentration. "Each novel is

Lily, with her horse Beware, unwillingly competes against her best friend in a horse show. (Cover illustration by Gregg Thorkelson.)

different, and requires a different process. Some come inch by inch, arriving in polished sentences which remain the same from first draft to printed book. Others come scattershot; you catch the fragments and press them into shape like a meat loaf."

With *Skipping School,* Haas left horses behind for the time being. Fifteen-year-old Phillip feels isolated and confused as he learns to cope with his father's terminal illness. Still reeling from the move from a farm to the suburbs, Phillip finds solace at a nearby abandoned farmhouse, where he spends afternoons chopping wood and caring for a pair of kittens. His skipping school ultimately pays off, for Phillip slowly comes to terms with his father's impending death. A *Publishers Weekly* reviewer commended Haas on her "eye for telling details" that "give this heartwarming novel its subtle power," and concluded that "this is a book to savor." *Horn Book* critic Watson observed that Haas created "a provocative, satisfying novel that contrasts the value of life against the constant presence of death. . . . A wonderful book to read and discuss—probably the only time skipping school resulted in an A+."

Haas returned to her initial equine creation with *A Horse Like Barney,* a sequel to *Keeping Barney* in which Sarah continues the search for a horse of her own.

Again, the search is more difficult than Sarah imagined: Should she pick the lively Roy or the older and needier Thunder? Watson, writing in *Horn Book,* felt that the story had "depth and texture, provided by insights into the emotions Sarah feels," while Hazel Rochman, writing in *Booklist,* noted that Haas's short chapters made the book ideal "for young readers ready to go beyond illustrated fiction. A wholesome, introspective novel, just right for horse enthusiasts."

Other notable Haas titles in novel-length fiction are *Uncle Daney's Way, Westminster West,* and *Fire!* In the first of these, young Cole learns important lessons about life and managing a work horse when his disabled uncle moves into the family's barn. Watson noted in *Horn Book* that the "middle-grade reader will identify with Cole's growing enthusiasm fueled by increasing accomplishment in this refreshing treatment of a loving family's successful attempt to cope with a challenge. . . ." Deborah Stevenson observed in *Bulletin of the Center for Children's Books* that the novel was "a good old story told with affection and subtlety." Haas has also written historical fiction, as in *Westminster West,* in which two sisters in 1884 must deal with their

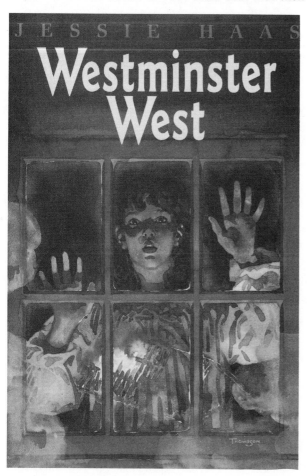

Set in 1884, Haas's historical novel treats the relationship between two sisters struggling with their role as women and with the unsettling activities of an arsonist threatening their rural New England community. (Cover illustration by Ellen Thompson.)

roles as women both in the family and society when an arsonist threatens their Vermont village, and *Fire!,* the story of how Haas's mother's house burned when she was eight. "*Westminster West* is based on real events which took place within three miles of my home, over a hundred years ago," Haas explained to *SATA.* "I fictionalized the story, trying to understand and make convincing one version of why people might have behaved as they did. A story about arson and about taking to one's bed with the vapors, it was poised between melodrama and no drama at all, and required a complex understructure." In the event, Haas's technical efforts with the book proved successful. *Horn Book* reviewer Mary M. Burns concluded that "the book grapples effectively with the conflicting issues of personal freedom and family responsibilities," and Elizabeth Bush noted in *Bulletin of the Center for Children's Books* that "Haas builds a rich and sensitive portrait of a late nineteenth-century Vermont farm family. . . ." *Fire!* is a book that Haas tried to write for years, "in various complex ways," she told *SATA.* "It only worked when I found the way to tell it in the eight-year-old voice, as simply as possible."

In addition to her novels for juveniles and young readers, Haas has also created a number of award-winning picture books and beginning chapter readers. *Beware the Mare* was the first of her illustrated books for younger readers, as well as the first in a series to feature the mare named Beware. In this initial title, Gramps gets a good bargain on a seemingly perfect mare for young Lily, though the horse's name does make him suspect something might be wrong. Haas uses this mystery "to provide enough tension to hold this charming vignette together," according to a critic in *Kirkus Reviews.* "Horse lovers who like their fiction short and easy are frequently disappointed," noted Stevenson in *Bulletin of the Center for Children's Books,* "but here's a well-written offering that conveys a flavorful lot in a small space." Lily and her horse Beware continue their adventures in further titles in the "Beware" series. A horse show ribbon is won in *A Blue for Beware,* a book to be "greeted with unbridled enthusiasm," according to Stevenson in *Bulletin of the Center for Children's Books,* and a case of colic has to be treated in *Be Well Beware,* a book in which the "plot takes off from the first page and maintains intensity right until the end," according to Christina Linz in *School Library Journal.* A fourth work in the series is the self-illustrated *Beware and Stogie.* "My newest adventure is illustration—chapter headers for *Beware and Stogie,*" Haas told *SATA.* "It's exciting to be learning something completely new, and to go beyond what I thought were limits."

Another early reader is *Clean House,* in which Tess and her mother have to tidy the house for the arrival of Tess's cousin, Kate. The more they clean, however, the messier things get, but finally the house is spotless yet also very boring and antiseptic. But once the relatives arrive, they help to mess things up nicely again. Roger Sutton noted in *Bulletin of the Center for Children's Books* that the book admits "the little-acknowledged truth about house work: why bother? . . . . Cognizant of both parent and child demands, this easy chapter book would make a fine intergenerational read-together."

Haas's books aimed at preschool and first grade readers include the companion volumes *Mowing, No Foal Yet,* and *Sugaring,* featuring the winning duo of Gramp and Nora. Nora helps her Gramp in the first title with horse-drawn mowing, avoiding a fawn and a killdeer nest in the process. A *Kirkus Reviews* critic noted that "the warm interaction between Nora and Gramp grows naturally from their companionable dialogue, while art and text work beautifully together to bring out the story's quiet drama." In *No Foal Yet,* Nora and Gramp are back on the farm waiting for Bonnie to give birth to her foal, and in *Sugaring,* Nora helps Gramp make maple syrup and sugar, a "satisfying story," according to Caroline Ward in *School Library Journal,* and one that "will be a welcome addition during any season."

Literary awards and a growing readership have not greatly changed Haas's lifestyle. "I still live the same kind of life I did growing up," she reported to *SATA.* "I ride a horse I trained myself. A cat sleeps on my desk as I work. I walk to my parents' farm every day, and can pick out the exact spot in the pasture where my horse Josey gave me *Beware the Mare.* It's an immense privilege to live this way—to make up stories and people, to spend all day drawing pictures of cows, to find a way to tell a family story so it will reach a wider audience, move perfect strangers, and be preserved. Another great benefit is being master, more or less, of my time, which allows me to be politically active." Much of Haas's political activity is directed at campaigning for a national health care system which will cover all citizens.

Haas also meets her reading public regularly. "When I speak in schools I show slides of my house, to try and challenge kids' ideas of what's possible and necessary. I show my animals, because that's where many of my ideas come from. It's fascinating to hear their questions, to find out where I'm reaching them and where I miss. Each of us has only one life to live, but a writer gets to try on others, and then send ideas out into the lives of people she will never meet, to affect them in unknown and private ways."

■ Works Cited

Review of *Beware the Mare, Kirkus Reviews,* May 15, 1993, p. 661.

Burns, Mary M., review of *Keeping Barney, Horn Book,* August, 1982, pp. 403-4.

Burns, Mary M., review of *Westminster West, Horn Book,* May-June, 1997, p. 321.

Bush, Elizabeth, review of *Westminster West, Bulletin of the Center for Children's Books,* April, 1997, p. 284.

Harrington, Pat, review of *Walking Trot, School Library Journal,* January, 1984, p. 86.

Hearne, Betsy, review of *The Sixth Sense and Other Stories, Bulletin of the Center for Children's Books,* January, 1989, p. 122.

Review of *Keeping Barney, Kirkus Reviews,* April 1, 1982, pp. 417-18.

Linz, Christina, review of *Be Well Beware, School Library Journal,* April, 1996, p. 132.

Review of *Mowing, Kirkus Reviews,* May 14, 1994, p. 698.

Rochman, Hazel, review of *A Horse Like Barney, Booklist,* September 15, 1993, p. 152.

Review of *Skipping School, Publishers Weekly,* November 9, 1992, p. 87.

Stevenson, Deborah, review of *Beware the Mare, Bulletin of the Center for Children's Books,* July-August, 1993, p. 345.

Stevenson, Deborah, review of *Uncle Daney's Way, Bulletin of the Center for Children's Books,* April, 1994, p. 259.

Stevenson, Deborah, review of *A Blue for Beware, Bulletin of the Center for Children's Books,* March, 1995, pp. 236-37.

Sutton, Roger, review of *Clean House, Bulletin of the Center for Children's Books,* March, 1996, p. 227.

Ward, Caroline, review of *Sugaring, School Library Journal,* October, 1996, pp. 94-96.

Watson, Elizabeth, review of *The Sixth Sense and Other Stories, Horn Book,* March-April, 1989, pp. 216-17.

Watson, Elizabeth, review of *Skipping School, Horn Book,* January-February, 1993, pp. 90-91.

Watson, Elizabeth, review of *A Horse Like Barney, Horn Book,* November-December, 1993, p. 744.

Watson, Elizabeth, review of *Uncle Daney's Way, Horn Book,* July-August, 1994, p. 452.

Wilms, Denise M., review of *Keeping Barney, Booklist,* June 1, 1982, p. 1312.

■ For More Information See

PERIODICALS

Booklist, November 15, 1988, pp. 566-67; November 15, 1992, p. 590; June 1, 1994, p. 1638; May 1, 1996, p. 1506; November 15, 1996, p. 594.

Bulletin of the Center for Children's Books, April, 1984, p. 147; February, 1993, p. 177; March, 1998, p. 243.

Horn Book, May-June, 1993, p. 333; May-June, 1994, p. 315; May-June, 1995, p. 349; May-June, 1996, pp. 332-33.

Kirkus Reviews, July 15, 1993, p. 934; October 15, 1993, p. 1330; February 15, 1996, p. 295; February 1, 1997, p. 223.

Publishers Weekly, July 8, 1988, p. 58.

School Library Journal, April, 1993, p. 118; July, 1993, p. 33; October, 1993, p. 124; February, 1994, p. 84; April, 1994, p. 128; May, 1995, p. 106; June, 1995, p. 81.*

—Sketch by J. Sydney Jones

SUSAN HAMPSHIRE

HAMPSHIRE, Susan 1942-

■ Personal

Born May 12, 1942, in London, England; daughter of George Kenneth and June (Pavey) Hampshire; married Pierre Granier-Deferre (divorced, 1974); married Sir Eddie Kulukundis (a shipbroker and impresario), April, 1981; children: (first marriage) Christopher, Victoria (deceased). *Education:* Attended Hampshire School.

■ Addresses

Office—c/o Chatto and Linnett, 123A Kings Road, London SW3 4PL, England.

■ Career

Writer and actress. Has appeared on BBC-TV, with the Royal Shakespeare Company, and in the West End Theatre. Gardening correspondent for *Mail on Sunday*, 1986-88. *Member:* Population Concern (executive committee), Dyslexia Institute (patron, founding member of bursary fund, and president).

■ Awards, Honors

Emmy Award, 1970, for "The Forsyte Saga," 1971, for "The First Churchills," and 1973, for "Vanity Fair"; Honorary Doctor of Literature, City University (Lon-

don), 1984; Honorary Doctor of Literature, St. Andrews University (Scotland), 1986; Honorary Doctor of Education, Kingston University (London), 1994; Honorary Doctor of Arts, Pine Manor College (Boston), 1994; Order of the British Empire Award, 1995.

■ Writings

FOR CHILDREN

Rosie's Ballet Slippers (picture book), illustrated by Maria Teresa Meloni, HarperCollins, 1996, published as *Rosie's First Ballet Lesson*, Heinemann, 1996.

"LUCY JANE" SERIES

Lucy Jane at the Ballet, illustrated by Vanessa Julian-Ottie, Collins, 1987.
Lucy Jane on Television, illustrated by Vanessa Julian-Ottie, Methuen, 1989.
Lucy Jane and the Dancing Competition, illustrated by Honey De Lacey, Methuen, 1990.
Lucy Jane and the Russian Ballet, illustrated by Honey De Lacey, Methuen, 1993.

OTHER; NONFICTION

Susan's Story: An Autobiographical Account of My Struggle with Dyslexia, Sidgwick & Jackson, 1981, St. Martin's, 1982.
The Maternal Instinct: A Book for Every Woman Who Wants a Child, Sidgwick & Jackson, 1984.
Trouble Free Gardening, Elm Tree Books, 1989.
Every Letter Counts, Bantam, 1990.
Susan Hampshire's My Secret Garden, illustrated by Hugh Palmer, Collins & Brown, 1993.

■ Sidelights

Susan Hampshire is an award-winning British actress who has written books for adults and for children. Among her works for adults is an autobiography entitled *Susan's Story: An Autobiographical Account of My Struggle with Dyslexia,* in which the author focuses on her lifelong struggle with dyslexia, a condition that prevents her from recognizing written symbols in a conventional fashion. Hampshire's account of her glamorous life in the world of British theatre, television, and film "will induce readers to smile and laugh as often as they feel compassion for the author," observed a reviewer for *Publishers Weekly.* Hampshire has also written several children's books that draw upon her experiences, as the author once told *SATA,* from her "early childhood as a dancer and in film." Hampshire's critics consider her a charming writer for children whose stories are filled with realistic details and an emphasis on the hard work as well as the joy of being a performer.

Hampshire introduced popular young protagonist Lucy Jane in *Lucy Jane at the Ballet,* which begins when the title character goes to stay with her aunt while her mother has a baby. Lucy Jane's aunt is wardrobe mistress at the Royal Opera House and allows her niece to wander the theater at will, an opportunity that finds Lucy Jane accidentally wandering onto the stage during

Hampshire presents the basics of ballet in her picture book about a little girl's preliminary dance lesson. (From *Rosie's Ballet Slippers,* illustrated by Maria Teresa Meloni.)

a performance, stumbling into the royal box, and eventually winning an audition for *The Nutcracker.* "Miss Hampshire writes with unassuming enthusiasm, and gets all the technical details right," observed *Junior Bookshelf* reviewer Marcus Crouch. Similarly, *Growing Point* reviewer Margery Fisher appreciated the way Hampshire blended "technical detail" with "a happy tale."

In the second book of the "Lucy Jane" series, *Lucy Jane on Television,* Hampshire's young protagonist is spending the summer with her grandmother in Scotland and lands a role in a television film being made in a nearby town. "[Hampshire's] inside knowledge of making a film for television adds valuable extra authority to this story," noted another *Junior Bookshelf* critic. In *Lucy Jane and the Russian Ballet,* Hampshire's young dancer auditions for, and ultimately wins, a chance to study ballet in Russia. "The children's rivalries, friendships, hopes and setbacks are realistically portrayed," remarked a critic for *Junior Bookshelf.*

Rosie's Ballet Slippers, aimed at the picture book audience, draws upon the energy and enthusiasm of a young girl's first ballet lesson. Critics remarked favorably, as they had with the "Lucy Jane" books, upon Hampshire's inclusion of realistic touches that demonstrate the author's firsthand knowledge of the settings she employs. "Young readers will take away a healthy dollop of nuts-and-bolts ballet terminology and intensi-

fied enthusiasm for dance," asserted a reviewer for *Publishers Weekly.*

Hampshire once explained to *SATA:* "My books are usually written about a consuming passion—be it dyslexia, gardening, or having a child—and on the whole they have a philanthropic theme: to help people who are perhaps experiencing the same difficulties. I think it is also fair to say that as much as the love of writing, it is the desire to prove that I am not illiterate (as I am dyslexic) that has been the driving force behind the books—in the same way a disabled athlete not only loves sport but also wants to be considered in the same light as the able bodied."

■ Works Cited

Crouch, Marcus, review of *Lucy Jane at the Ballet, Junior Bookshelf,* February, 1986, p. 23.
Fisher, Margery, review of *Lucy Jane at the Ballet, Growing Point,* March, 1986, p. 4593.
Review of *Lucy Jane and the Russian Ballet, Junior Bookshelf,* August, 1994, pp. 134-35.
Review of *Lucy Jane on Television, Junior Bookshelf,* February, 1990, pp. 26-27.
Review of *Rosie's Ballet Slippers, Publishers Weekly,* April 15, 1996, p. 68.
Review of *Susan's Story: An Autobiographical Account of My Struggle with Dyslexia, Publishers Weekly,* August 20, 1982, p. 60.

■ For More Information See

PERIODICALS

Booklist, September 1, 1982, pp. 12-13; April 1, 1996, p. 1371.
Books for Keeps, May, 1995, p. 10.
School Library Journal, March, 1996, p. 175.

*   *   *

HARD, Charlotte (Ann) 1969-

■ Personal

Born June 2, 1969, in Watford, England; daughter of Peter Charles (a teacher) and Mary Ann (a craft artist) Hard; partner of Richard Holdsworth (an engineer). *Education:* Manchester Polytechnic, degree in design for communications media.

■ Addresses

Home and office—54 Chapel Lane, Headingley, Leeds LS6 3BW, England.

■ Career

Children's book illustrator, 1990—. Volunteer at local primary school. *Member:* Society of Authors.

CHARLOTTE HARD

■ Writings

One Green Island (self-illustrated), Candlewick Press (Cambridge, MA), 1995, published as *One Green Island: An Animal Counting Gamebook,* Walker (London), 1996.

ILLUSTRATOR

Heather Maisner, *Find Mouse in the Garden,* Walker, 1993, published as *Find Mouse in the Yard,* Candlewick Press, 1994.
Heather Maisner, *Find Mouse in the House,* Walker, 1993, reprinted, Candlewick Press, 1994.
Heather Maisner, *Save Brave Ted,* Candlewick Press, 1996, reprinted, Walker, 1996.
(With Sienna Artworks) *Body Facts,* Collins Children's Books (London), 1996.
(With Gary Slater) *Major Disasters,* Collins Children's Books, 1996.
(With Tony Smith) *Unsolved Mysteries,* Collins Children's Books, 1996.
(With Tony Smith and Kevin Madison) Carol Watson, *Datefinder,* Collins Children's Books, 1996.
Sarah Allen, *Cats,* Barron's (Hauppauge, NY), 1996.
Sandy Ransford, *Dogs,* Barron's, 1996.
Sandy Ransford, *Horses and Ponies,* Barron's, 1996.
Marjorie Newman, *The Wonderful Journey of Cameron the Cat,* Walker, 1997, reprinted, Candlewick Press, 1998.

Kathy Henderson, *Cars, Cars, Cars,* Frances Lincoln, 1998.
Andrea Shavick, *The Truth about Babies,* Oxford University Press, 1998.

Contributor to periodicals, including *BBC Learning Is Fun, BBC Playdays, Ideal Home,* and *Horse and Pony.*

■ Work in Progress

Books in the "Educational Fax Finders" series, for HarperCollins; *Poly Molly Woof Woof,* for Walker Books.

■ Sidelights

Charlotte Hard told *SATA:* "I gravitated toward illustration in a totally natural way. I came from a very artistic background. At home, painting and drawing were all around, so it seemed the only course to take. I do believe, however, that a great deal of luck is involved in getting a career in the arts off the ground.

"My working habits, when illustrating, involve large cups of coffee and trashy television. My working day is punctuated by dog walking and pottering around (usually when trying to avoid starting something!) my house, in which I have my office."

■ For More Information See

PERIODICALS
Publishers Weekly, May 2, 1994, p. 306.

*   *   *

HINDS, P(atricia) Mignon

■ Personal

Born in New York, NY. *Education:* Hampton University, B.S.; City University of New York, M.S.

■ Addresses

Home—333 East 55th St., New York, NY 10022.

■ Career

Writer. Mignon Communications, owner; Essence Books, director.

■ Awards, Honors

Three CEBA Awards; Leaf of Life Award.

■ Writings

Kittens Need Someone to Love, illustrated by Alan Phillips, Golden Press, 1981.
Puppies Need Someone to Love, illustrated by June Goldsborough, Golden Press, 1981.
Baby Pig, illustrated by Jim Kritz, Golden Books, 1988.

Baby Calf, Golden Books, 1990.
A Day in the Life of Morgan Freeman, McGraw/Macmillan, 1994.
(Editor) Audrey Edwards, *Essence: Twenty-Five Years Celebrating Black Women,* introduction by Susan L. Taylor, foreword by Maya Angelou, Abrams (New York City), 1995.
What I Want to Be, illustrated by Cornelius Van Wright, Western Publishing (Racine, WI), 1995, published as *Essence: What I Want to Be,* Golden Books, 1997.
My Best Friend, illustrated by Van Wright, Golden Books, 1996, published as *Essence: My Best Friend,* Golden Books, 1997.
Best Friends, Golden Books, 1997.
The King's Daughters, Golden Books, 1997.

■ For More Information See

PERIODICALS

American Visions, October-November, 1995, p. 37.
Booklist, November 1, 1995, p. 441.*

*   *   *

HORNIMAN, Joanne 1951-

■ Personal

Born November 2, 1951, in Murwillumbah, New South Wales, Australia; daughter of J. W. R. (an overseer of works) and J. A. (a chef; maiden name, Tunsted) Horniman; married Tony Chinnery (a potter), 1978; children: Ry, Kay (both sons). *Education:* Macquarie University, B.A. (English), 1973; Armidale College of Advanced Education, graduate diploma (infants/primary education), 1988.

■ Addresses

Home—602 Cawongla Rd., Via Lismore, New South Wales 2480, Australia. *Agent*—Margaret Connolly and Associates, P.O. Box 945, Wahroonga, New South Wales 2076, Australia.

■ Career

New South Wales Department of Education's *School Magazine,* Sydney, New South Wales, Australia, assistant editor, 1973-77; writer. Part-time lecturer in children's literature at Southern Cross University; adult literacy teacher at New South Wales department of technical and further education. *Member:* Australian Society of Authors.

■ Awards, Honors

Sand Monkeys, Jasmine, Bad Behaviour, and *Billygoat Goes Wild* were all named CBCA Notable Books; *The Serpentine Belt* was shortlisted for New South Wales Premier's Award, 1994, and Australian Multicultural Children's Literature Award, 1995; Category A Fellowship, Literature Board of the Australia Council, 1995.

JOANNE HORNIMAN

■ Writings

The End of the World Girl, Collins Dove (Melbourne, Australia), 1988.
The Ghost Lasagne, illustrated by Margie Chellew, Omnibus, 1992.
Sand Monkeys, Omnibus, 1992.
The Serpentine Belt, Omnibus, 1994.
Furry-Back and the Lizard-Thing, illustrated by Samone Turnbull, Omnibus, 1995.
Jasmine, illustrated by Margaret Power, Omnibus, 1995.
(With Jacqueline Kent) *Bad Behaviour* (stories), Omnibus, 1996.
Billygoat Goes Wild, illustrated by Robert Roennfeldt, Omnibus, 1996.
Loving Athena, Omnibus, 1997.

■ Work in Progress

Sophie in the Sky (working title), a book for younger readers about a child's adventures with three talking animals, for Omnibus.

■ Sidelights

Joanne Horniman is an Australian author of novels and short stories for children and young adults centering on the realistic portrayal of unusual relationships. Many of her books are linked by setting; they often take place in the rainforest countryside. In addition, three of her works, *Sand Monkeys, The Serpentine Belt,* and *Loving Athena,* all involve the search for a lost parent, as well as the establishment of strong bonds between characters who are not blood relations.

The Ghost Lasagne, published in 1992, concerns a mysterious invisible lasagne that replenishes itself after each bite. Antonella and Dip discover the ghost lasagne in a deserted restaurant and enjoy it daily, until the owner of the place catches them there. The ending emphasizes the importance of friendship and community. *Magpies* commentator Nola Cavallaro called the work "appealing and accessible for newly independent readers."

The Serpentine Belt also deals with friendship. In this case, long-time friends Emily and Kat, who are both sixteen, find themselves growing apart as each learns more about her own unique background. While Kat becomes interested in her Koori heritage, Emily discovers that her own past may in fact be different from what she's been told. In the end, both girls learn to take a broader view of friendship. Horniman employs an unusual structural device in the novel, which is told as a series of interconnecting stories. *The Serpentine Belt* has "strongly-drawn characters and lots of ideas for the reader to chew on," according to *Magpies* contributor Moira Robinson. She added that the book is "leisurely, reflective and highly enjoyable."

Jasmine, a 1995 work, is a realistic tale of one girl's difficulties growing up. In particular, Jazz has trouble making friends, especially with the new boy at school. Then she discovers an enchanting, fairy-like new shop and its equally fascinating owner, Rosie. Jazz wonders if Rosie might be able to help her solve her problem. Writing in *Magpies,* Alan Horsfield commented that the children's and adults' "fears, anxieties, confusion and their pleasures all contribute to the portrayal of characters with which the reader can empathise."

Horniman told *SATA* that another of her recent books, *Billygoat Goes Wild,* "was written for my son Kay about his pet hen (what we call in Australia a 'chook'). It was only afterwards that I considered I might offer it for publication. At the heart of it is the idea of what goes on outside at night when we are normally asleep, through the eyes of a domestic hen. It is really a much more difficult and dangerous other world."

The author continued, "All my books are about the interaction of people and animals with the natural world, not in the usual adventurous sense but in a more spiritual way. We are all connected with forces that we are only aware of some of the time, which is probably why people like to get out and experience nature when they have a chance to get away from their workaday lives. Living away from big cities has been enormously sustaining for me and has led to the kind of books I write."

■ Works Cited

Cavallaro, Nola, review of *The Ghost Lasagne, Magpies,* November, 1992, p. 30.
Horsfield, Alan, review of *Jasmine, Magpies,* September, 1995, pp. 31-32.
Robinson, Moira, review of *The Serpentine Belt, Magpies,* March, 1995, p. 32.

■ For More Information See

BOOKS

Niewenhuizen, Agnes, *More Good Books for Teenagers,* Reed (Australia), 1996.

PERIODICALS

Magpies, July, 1996.
Viewpoint, Winter, 1997.

*   *   *

HUBBARD, Woodleigh Marx

■ Personal

Born in Sharon, CT; daughter of Earl (an artist) and Barbara (a writer and speaker; maiden name, Marx) Hubbard. *Education:* Evergreen State College, B.A.

■ Addresses

Home and office—6240 NE Tolo Road, Bainbridge Island, WA 98110. *Electronic mail*—wmh@aol.com.

WOODLEIGH MARX HUBBARD

■ Career

Writer and illustrator.

■ Awards, Honors

American Institute of Graphic Arts Award for Excellence, and Parent's Choice selection, Parent's Choice Foundation, both 1990, and Notable Children's Book citation, American Library Association, all for *C Is for Curious: An ABC of Feelings;* Parent's Choice illustration honor book designation, Parent's Choice Foundation, 1993, for *The Moles and the Mireuk: A Korean Folktale;* Society of Children's Book Writers and Illustrator's Award, and Bookbuilder's West Award, both 1993, both for *Hip Cat,* which was also featured on the PBS television program *Reading Rainbow,* 1997; "Pick of the Lists" selection, American Booksellers Association, 1996, for *The Precious Gift: A Navajo Creation Myth.*

■ Writings

SELF-ILLUSTRATED

C Is for Curious: An ABC of Feelings, Chronicle Books, 1990.
Two Is for Dancing: A 1, 2, 3 of Actions, Chronicle Books, 1991.
The Friendship Book, Chronicle Books, 1993.
C Is for Curious: An Emotional Address Book, Chronicle Books, 1993.
Visual Feast Recipe Journal, Chronicle Books, 1995.
Woodleigh Marx Hubbard's Twelve Days of Christmas, Chronicle Books, 1996.

ILLUSTRATOR

Holly H. Kwon (reteller), *The Moles and the Mireuk: A Korean Folktale,* Houghton Mifflin, 1993.
Jonathan London, *Hip Cat,* Chronicle Books, 1993.
Margaret Wise Brown, *Four Fur Feet,* Hyperion, 1994.
Ellen Jackson, *The Precious Gift: A Navajo Creation Myth,* Simon & Schuster, 1996.
Layne Longfellow, *Imaginary Menagerie,* Chronicle Books, 1997.

Hubbard's works have been translated into other languages, including French, Japanese, and Korean.

■ Work in Progress

I Used to Be an Alphabet by Niki Leopold, for Putnam; *The Birthday Book,* for Putnam.

■ Sidelights

An award-winning author and illustrator of picture books for children, Woodleigh Marx Hubbard is praised as an especially talented artist as well as an inventive creator of concept books. Celebrated for her originality and imagination, she graces both her own books and the works of other authors with bold, colorful, and vibrant paintings in gouache that reflect the artist's impressionistic style. Hubbard is the creator of several well-received concept books—such as an alphabet book, a counting book, and a book about friendship—as well as a modish version of the traditional Christmas carol "The Twelve Days of Christmas." She has also provided the illustrations for such works as retellings of a Navajo creation myth and a Korean folktale, an original picture book about a feline jazzman, and a new edition of a classic story by Margaret Wise Brown. As an illustrator, Hubbard favors whimsical animals and stylized shapes and patterns to complement or enhance her texts; her paintings have received comparisons to such artists as Pablo Picasso, Henri Matisse, and Joan Miro. Writing in *School Library Journal,* Marie Orlando called Hubbard's work "A unique blend of brilliant color, abstract art, and imaginative graphic design with a duality of concept."

Born in Sharon, Connecticut, Hubbard grew up in an artistic home; her father was an artist and her mother a writer. Hubbard explained to *SATA,* "I was a *terrible* student, in part because I was a visual child; thinking in words and concepts was both awkward and challenging. I was made to feel stupid because my linear thinking process was not as developed as other students. When I illustrate a book or give a school presentation, my sole aim is to make children feel joyful and confident about learning."

Hubbard's first self-illustrated work, *C Is for Curious: An ABC of Feelings,* was published in 1990. In this picture book, the author offers an emotion for every letter of the alphabet, from angry through zealous. With each word, Hubbard includes an illustration of an animal depicting that emotion. For "angry", for example, Hubbard created a red-faced beast while "happy" features serene-looking cows jumping over the moon. "Artistically," declared Karen James in *School Library Journal, C Is for Curious* "is an exceptional work—colorful, original, unique." While some reviewers felt that terms like "xenophobic" are more appropriate for older readers, *Booklist* contributor Carolyn Phelan noted that "parents and teachers seeking books to stimulate discussions of feelings may find the book a refreshing alternative to ... volumes more typical of the genre." The critic also commented that its graphics distinguish *C Is for Curious* from "the hundreds of other ABCs and picture books on feelings." Writing in *Bulletin of the Center for Children's Books,* Roger Sutton claimed that unlike "too many other picture books mining the postmodern vein, this one never seems self-consciously arty or smirking in its weirdness."

Hubbard's next two works, *Two Is for Dancing: A 1, 2, 3 of Actions* and *The Friendship Book,* are considered similar in style and form to *C Is for Curious.* In *Two Is for Dancing,* actions such as dreaming, singing, and reading are paired with numbers from one through twelve. Each action is characterized by Hubbard's distinctive animal illustrations. "As before, emotional content is creatively conveyed by the art," noted a critic in *Kirkus Reviews,* who concluded that the "joyous enthusiasm in each picture is pleasantly contagious." *School Library Journal* reviewer Marie Orlando claimed

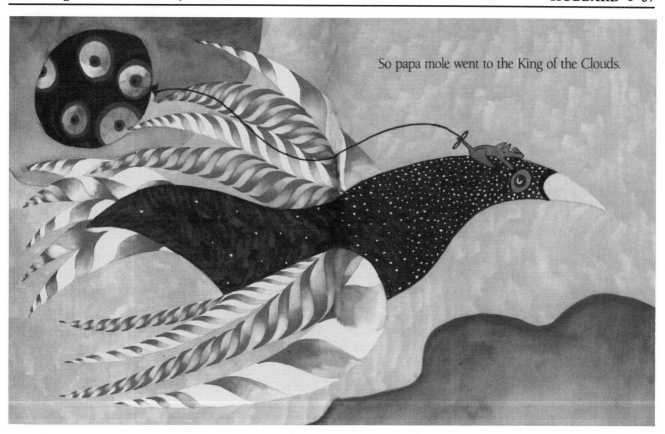

So papa mole went to the King of the Clouds.

Hubbard's unaffected illustrations grace Holly H. Kwon's retelling of the Korean folktale about a mole who embarks on an extensive journey to find the perfect husband for his daughter.

that Hubbard is "even more successful [than in her previous book], providing a treat for children to discover again and again." In *The Friendship Book*, Hubbard examines twelve adages about friendship, such as "Friends don't always agree" and "a friend keeps your secrets." "Again," noted a critic in *Kirkus Reviews*, "the artist's contrasted colors and decorative animal figures ... deftly express the subtleties of emotion." The critic concluded that children and adults "will be amused by the humor and the strength of the visual expression." In 1996, Hubbard published her illustrated version of Clement Moore's "The Twelve Days of Christmas," a work in which the artist enhances the song lyrics with, in the words of a reviewer in *Publishers Weekly*, "waggish gouache paintings and a playful cursive typeface" as well as twelve punch-out ornaments. Critics noted the invention and dazzling quality of Hubbard's paintings; a reviewer in *School Library Journal* commented, "There's no denying this rendition's color and energy."

Expanding her artistic talents, Hubbard began illustrating books for other authors in the early 1990s. She made her initial contributions to Holly H. Kwon's *The Moles and the Mireuk: A Korean Folktale*, a retelling of a Korean folktale about a mole father whose search for the perfect mate for his daughter takes him to the Mireuk, a tall, powerful statue. The Mireuk is only susceptible to the burrowing of moles, a fact that leads father mole to his future son-in-law, "the most perfect mole in the whole universe." Writing in *Horn Book*, Ellen Fader noted that the tale's "inherent humor is reinforced by

the bold yet naive illustrations, which are easily large enough for group sharing...." Michael Shapiro of the *New York Times Book Review* claimed that both the text and the "impressionistic earth-tone illustrations ... are well-suited to preschool listeners." Hubbard also provided the pictures for *Hip Cat* by Jonathan London, a picture book that received favorable reviews, won several awards for its illustration, and was featured on the popular PBS show *Reading Rainbow*. In this tale, Oobie-do John—a cool, saxophone-playing cat—travels to San Francisco to make his musical mark. At first, Oobie-do is rejected by the big clubs, which are owned by dogs; however, he keeps practicing and playing until he becomes a sensation on the jazz scene. "Here is a one-of-a-kind book with a great message.... Hubbard's vivid illustrations ... offer just the right accompaniment to the jazzy text," applauded Virginia E. Jeschelnig of *School Library Journal*, who concluded by suggesting, "Just pop in a cassette by Dizzy or Miles, and read, man, read." A reviewer in *Publishers Weekly* predicted, "Only squares won't dig ... this beboppable, unstoppable tale" and noted that Hubbard creates "vibrant spreads that ideally complement the narrative...."

While Hubbard's work is often compared to the colorful, abstract styles of Impressionist and Expressionist painters like Matisse and Picasso, she told *SATA* that "Saul Steinberg and James Thurber rule the planet as far as illustration goes. Steinberg makes the most mundane thing imaginable (a rug or a bug) and wildly fascinating.

Thurber's illustrations, in conjunction with his hilariously witty writing, have kept me in good spirits for years. I picked two artists that work for the most part in pen and ink, also my roots. Pen and ink is wickedly difficult and, when mastered, wow! As far as my contemporaries, many of them are fine artists and I am frequently humbled by the skill level of my peers. Also, I find illustrators as a group generous, deliciously eccentric, and very funny."

As for her own work, the author and illustrator told *SATA* that she hopes "to make learning fun, interesting, and easy." She further added that her purpose behind writing or illustrating a specific book "is always the same: to make the art as original and beautiful as possible while allowing learning to be a joy. Knowledge is power, knowledge is freedom; there's nothing that motivates me more than playing whatever small part I can in bringing this into the lives of children." When asked what advice she might give aspiring illustrators, Hubbard told *SATA*, "It's a privilege to be published. What I mean is, getting the chance to touch the lives and minds of young children. Make sure you fill your books with things that will inspire and uplift the soul."

■ Works Cited

Fader, Ellen, review of *The Moles and the Mireuk: A Korean Folktale, Horn Book,* July, 1993, p. 470.

Review of *The Friendship Book, Kirkus Reviews,* December 1, 1992, p. 1504.

Review of *Hip Cat, Publishers Weekly,* August 14, 1993, p. 102.

Hubbard, Woodleigh Marx, *The Friendship Book,* Chronicle Books, 1993.

James, Karen, review of *C Is for Curious: An ABC of Feelings, School Library Journal,* January, 1991, p. 76.

Jeschelnig, Virginia E., review of *Hip Cat, School Library Journal,* January, 1994, p. 93.

Kwon, Holly H., *The Moles and the Mireuk: A Korean Folktale,* Houghton Mifflin, 1993.

Orlando, Marie, review of *Two Is for Dancing: A 1, 2, 3 of Actions, School Library Journal,* January, 1992, p. 92.

Phelan, Carolyn, review of *C Is for Curious: An ABC of Feelings, Booklist,* March 1, 1991, pp. 1391, 1394.

Shapiro, Michael, review of *The Moles and the Mireuk: A Korean Folktale, New York Times Book Review,* October 31, 1993, p. 26.

Sutton, Roger, review of *C Is for Curious: An ABC of Feelings, Bulletin of the Center for Children's Books,* January, 1991, p. 121.

Review of *Woodleigh Marx Hubbard's Twelve Days of Christmas, Publishers Weekly,* September 30, 1996, p. 88.

Review of *Woodleigh Marx Hubbard's Twelve Days of Christmas, School Library Journal,* October, 1996, p. 41.

Review of *Two Is for Dancing: A 1, 2, 3 of Actions, Kirkus Reviews,* November 1, 1991, p. 1404.

■ For More Information See

PERIODICALS

Horn Book, March-April, 1994, p. 225.
Kirkus Reviews, November 1, 1997, p. 1646.
Publishers Weekly, April 1, 1996, p. 76.
School Library Journal, July, 1993, p. 81; January, 1995, pp. 81-82; May, 1996, p. 105.

*   *   *

HUNTER, Sara Hoagland 1954-

■ Personal

Born March 28, 1954, in Dover, MA; daughter of John H. (a media consultant) and Sara R. (a Christian Science practitioner) Hoagland; married Andy Hunter (an executive recruiter), June 10, 1978; children: John, Abigail. *Education:* Dartmouth College, B.A., 1976; Harvard University, Ed.M., 1986. *Religion:* Christian Scientist. *Hobbies and other interests:* Skiing, rollerblading, spending time with family, reading, singing, playing piano.

■ Addresses

Office—8C Pleasant St., South Natick, MA 01760. *Agent*—Palmer & Dodge, LLP, 1 Beacon St., Boston, MA 02108. *Electronic mail*—sarahunter@aol.com.

SARA HOAGLAND HUNTER

■ Career

Christian Science Monitor, writer and radio producer, 1976-80; Massachusetts Public School system, teacher of English, drama, and public speaking, 1982-94; Sara Hunter Productions, Inc. (producer of children's videos, books, and music), South Natick, MA, founder and president, 1994—.

■ Awards, Honors

Spur Award finalist, Western Writers of America; Gold Award, Charleston Film Festival, and Bronze Award, Houston Film Festival, both for *Born Journey,* a video documentary; Notable Books for Children citation, *Smithsonian,* 1996, for *The Unbreakable Code.*

■ Writings

Miss Piggy's Night Out, illustrated by Tom Leigh, Viking/Puffin, 1995.

Rondo's Stuff, illustrated by Nate Evans, ("Allegra's Window" series), Aladdin, 1996.
The Good, the Bad, and the Tweety, Landoll, 1996.
Beauty and the Feast, Landoll, 1996.
The Unbreakable Code, illustrated by Julia Miner, Northland (Flagstaff, AZ), 1996.
Chocolate Yak-A-Lot, Landoll, 1997.

Lyricist for *Born to Sing,* Volumes 1 and 2, Kid Rhino Records/Warner Bros., 1996. Created videos "A Symphony of Voices" and "Born Journey."

■ Sidelights

"When I was in second grade," wrote Sara Hoagland Hunter, the author of the award-winning *Unbreakable Code,* "my grandmother brought me to the home of Louisa May Alcott in Concord, Massachusetts. She knew I loved reading and writing and thought it would be good for me to visit the home of a famous author. What I remember most, besides the fact that my

Hunter's story concerns the little-known historical fact of the use of Navajo language as a basis for communication codes during World War II. (From *The Unbreakable Code,* illustrated by Julia Miner.)

grandmother had made me feel so important, was seeing Louisa May Alcott's writing desk in the window. Writing children's books while looking out over Walden Pond seemed to me the most wonderful existence one could hope for. From then on, no matter where we lived, I always had a desk facing a window. Even today, my office looks out over the Charles River where I can look and think and write (in that order!)"

Hunter has written a number of light, humorous tales based on familiar characters. In her first book, *Miss Piggy's Night Out,* published in 1995, Miss Piggy is too wrapped up in her own dreams of stardom to pay attention to her loyal friend Kermit. Kermit takes her to a restaurant where she can meet the rich and famous, but despite Kermit's attempts to warn her, Miss Piggy makes a fool of herself in front of a big-time movie director. Writing in *Bulletin of the Center for Children's Books,* Heather McCammond-Watts noted that Hunter "puts a secure and comfortable face on the everyday worries of smaller children" who will be able to relate to Miss Piggy's plight. "Readers will find the story predictable but humorous," Mary Ann Bursk commented in *School Library Journal.*

The following year Hunter author published *The Unbreakable Code,* which she calls "my favorite of the books I have written so far. Like any project we love the most," she told *SATA,* "it also took the most out of me to write and to research.

"The book began as a conversation with a close friend who was a Nez Perce Indian," the author explained. "This college friend was so creative and full of ideas, she was always telling me stories I couldn't wait to write down. When she told me about a code invented by the Navajos and used during World War II, I told her she should write it as a children's book, but she wanted me to do it. So I did."

The Unbreakable Code tells of a little-known historical fact by embedding it in a work of fiction set in the present. When a young Navajo boy's family is moving away from the Reservation for the first time, he expresses his anxiety about living in the outside world to his grandfather. His grandfather tells him the story of the time he, too, once had to leave the reservation. He had served in the Marine Corps during World War II, and, along with other Navajo Marines, was given the special assignment of creating a code that the Japanese would not be able to penetrate.

The Navajo language was selected as a basis for this code because it was an oral language. It had never been written down and was known by very few outside the tribe. The Japanese were not able to unscramble American radio messages transmitted using the Navajo code, and countless American lives were saved. The older man tells his grandson that the boy carries with him this heritage, this unbreakable code, and that it will protect him as he goes out into the world. A *Publishers Weekly* reviewer stated, "Hunter's lengthy but absorbing story ... casts a well-deserved spotlight on these skilled

soldiers and on a wartime role that is almost guaranteed to interest readers."

Hunter commented, "I learned so much from the inventors of the code whom I interviewed on the Navajo Reservation in Arizona and New Mexico. Their kindness, modesty, and generosity knew no bounds. They wanted a book to share with their grandchildren, and that became my motivation. My desire to accurately convey their sacrifices and achievements and to capture some of their phrases, images, and rhythms of speech formed the basis of the text.

"To have the illustrator be a close friend involved in the process from the first day of research is a phenomenon. Julia Miner and I set off together to our first meeting of the Navajo Code Talkers Association. On the way we gasped at the scenery of the Canyon de Chelly and worked in a third grade classroom on the Reservation. While I interviewed, Julia drew and interjected questions. Artistic collaboration, when it works, is the most satisfying experience there can be."

■ Works Cited

Bursk, Mary Ann, review of *Miss Piggy's Night Out, School Library Journal,* March, 1996, p. 176.

McCammond-Watts, Heather, review of *Miss Piggy's Night Out, Bulletin of the Center for Children's Books,* October, 1995, p. 58.

Review of *The Unbreakable Code, Publishers Weekly,* April 8, 1996, pp. 68-69.

■ For More Information See

PERIODICALS

School Library Journal, August, 1996, p. 123.
Smithsonian, November, 1996.

*   *   *

HYNES, Pat

■ Personal

Religion: Roman Catholic.

■ Addresses

Office—Castle Jordan, Tullamore, Offaly, Ireland.

■ Career

Secondary school teacher.

■ Writings

FOR CHILDREN

Land of Deep Shadow, Wolfhound Press (Dublin, Ireland), 1993.
Dawn Flight, Wolfhound Press, 1994.
Chase the Wind, Wolfhound Press, 1996, Irish American Book Company, 1997.

Pat Hynes's books featuring hares as protagonists are adventure tales tackling such fundamental issues as loyalty, racism, and environmental concerns. (Cover illustration by Patrick Billington.)

■ Sidelights

Pat Hynes told *SATA:* "[My first] three books are animal stories featuring hares as the main characters. They can be enjoyed by both adults and children alike. The books can be enjoyed simply as adventure stories, but they are also allegorical so that a teacher reading them with a class group can bring out the underlying meanings. These include such issues as friendship, loyalty, sacrifice, bullying, racism, blood sports, pollution, and ethnic cleansing.

"The chapters are purposely short and often end on a knife edge. This helps maintain interest. Most importantly, the stories are a quest for justice. Sometimes, in order to arouse a sense of justice, injustice is described.

"Visiting schools in Ireland where the books have been read has been very enlightening. Teachers have informed me that there were times when pupils didn't want to stop reading! If the books help children to read, transport them to another world, which, at the same time, they recognize as part of their own, then I hope that something good can come of them. For all of us, young readers and adults alike, a good story stays with us for a long time."

■ For More Information See

PERIODICALS

Junior Bookshelf, April, 1994, p. 68.
School Library Journal, July, 1994, p. 119.

J

JANECZKO, Paul B. 1945-

■ Personal

Born July 27, 1945, in Passaic, NJ; son of Frank John and Verna (Smolak) Janeczko. *Education:* St. Francis College, Biddeford, ME, A.B., 1967; John Carroll University, M.A., 1970. *Hobbies and other interests:* Swimming, cooking vegetarian meals, biking, working with wood.

PAUL B. JANECZKO

■ Addresses

Home—Rural Route 1, Box 260, Marshall Pond Rd., Hebron, ME 04238.

■ Career

Poet and anthologist. High school English teacher in Parma, OH, 1968-72, and Topsfield, MA, 1972-77; Gray-New Gloucester High School, Gray, ME, teacher of language arts, 1977-1990; visiting writer, 1990—. *Member:* National Council of Teachers of English, Educators for Social Responsibility, New England Association of Teachers of English, Maine Teachers of Language Arts, Maine Freeze Committee.

■ Awards, Honors

English-Speaking Union Books-across-the-Sea Ambassador of Honor Book award, 1984, for *Poetspeak: In Their Work, about Their Work; Don't Forget to Fly: A Cycle of Modern Poems, Poetspeak, Strings: A Gathering of Family Poems,* and *Pocket Poems: Selected for a Journey* were selected by the American Library Association as Best Books of the Year.

■ Writings

Loads of Codes and Secret Ciphers (nonfiction), Simon & Schuster, 1981.
Bridges to Cross (fiction), Macmillan, 1986.
Brickyard Summer (poetry), illustrated by Ken Rush, Orchard Books, 1989.
Stardust otel (poetry), illustrated by Dorothy Leech, Orchard Books, 1993.
That Sweet Diamond (poetry), illustrated by Carole Katchen, Simon & Schuster-Atheneum, 1998.

POETRY ANTHOLOGIST

The Crystal Image, Dell, 1977.
Postcard Poems, Bradbury, 1979.
Don't Forget to Fly: A Cycle of Modern Poems, Bradbury, 1981.

Poetspeak: In Their Work, about Their Work, Bradbury, 1983.

Strings: A Gathering of Family Poems, Bradbury, 1984.

Pocket Poems: Selected for a Journey, Bradbury, 1985.

Going over to Your Place: Poems for Each Other, Bradbury, 1987.

This Delicious Day: 65 Poems, Orchard Books, 1987.

The Music of What Happens: Poems That Tell Stories, Orchard Books, 1988.

The Place My Words Are Looking For: What Poets Say about and through Their Work, Bradbury, 1990.

Preposterous: Poems of Youth, Orchard Books, 1991.

Looking for Your Name: A Collection of Contemporary Poems, Orchard Books, 1993.

Poetry from A to Z: A Guide for Young Writers, illustrated by Cathy Bobak, Simon & Schuster, 1994.

Wherever Home Begins: One Hundred Contemporary Poems, Orchard Books, 1996.

(With Naomi Shihab Nye) *I Feel a Little Jumpy around You: A Book of Her Poems and His Poems Collected in Pairs,* Simon & Schuster, 1996.

Home on the Range: Cowboy Poetry, illustrated by Bernie Fuchs, Dial, 1997.

OTHER

Author of "Back Pages," a review column in *Leaflet,* 1973-76. Contributor of numerous articles, stories, poems (sometimes under pseudonym P. Wolny), and reviews to newspapers, professional and popular magazines, including *Armchair Detective, New Hampshire Profiles, Modern Haiku, Dragonfly, Friend, Child Life,* and *Highlights for Children.* Also contributor of articles to books, including *Censorship: A Guide for Teachers, Librarians, and Others Concerned with Intellectual Freedom,* edited by Lou Willett Stanek, Dell, 1976; *Young Adult Literature in the Seventies,* edited by Jana Varlejs, Scarecrow, 1978; and *Children's Literature Review,* Volume 3, Gale, 1978. Guest editor of *Leaflet,* spring, 1977.

■ Work in Progress

Very Best (Almost) Friends: A Collection of Friendship Poetry, for Candlewick Press.

■ Sidelights

"Paul Janeczko is the best collector of poems working on behalf of young adults today," according to Beth and Ben Nehms in their *English Journal* review of *Strings: A Gathering of Family Poems.* Poems from internationally known poets appear alongside those of young upstarts in the more than a dozen anthologies Janeczko has assembled. The books are distinctive because each provides multiple ways of understanding the experiences of young people through poetry while at the same time maintaining a distinct focus. Janeczko, who taught language arts for twenty-two years before becoming a full-time writer, is popular with young adults because he treats them with respect; the poems he selects are complex and challenging, and they never condescend to the reader. In his own collection of poetry, *Brickyard*

Summer, Janeczko uses short, narrative poems to depict two teenage boys enjoying a summer away from school.

When Janeczko was growing up, it seemed highly unlikely that he would one day be a writer. He ranked in the middle of his class in school, but says in an interview with *Author and Artists for Young Adults (AAYA)* that he was more interested in baseball and riding bikes with his three brothers than he was in school. His mother, however, had other ideas about how he should spend his time, and in the fifth grade she made him read for twenty minutes each day. "I didn't want to read for twenty minutes," Janeczko remembers, "I had done my school work, that was reading, that was enough. I wanted to be out with my brothers, playing ball, getting into trouble." His mother prevailed, and at first Janeczko says that he started getting headaches from keeping one eye on his book and the other on the clock. Eventually, he says, "I started reading for longer and longer times, not because she was making me, but because I was finally starting to get into it. The Hardy Boys were exciting, dangerous, mysterious and funny. I didn't find out until much later that they were racist and sexist."

Janeczko attended the same schools as his older brothers, and remembers that when he was going to the Catholic High School his brother was "a thug and an outlaw and I was just this short little ninth-grader who called attention to himself by wearing a loud sweater vest." When his older brother graduated from high school his mother saw the chance to get her young son into a better school, so she transferred him to a school run by Christian brothers noted for their discipline and corporal punishment. The brothers failed to instill in him a great love for school, and his dislike is reflected in his novel, *Bridges to Cross,* which recalls some of the difficulties of attending such a strict Catholic school.

Upon graduation from high school, Janeczko was accepted at St. Francis College, a small Catholic college in Maine. There, he explains, "I really began to change my attitude towards study, towards knowledge, towards intellectual pursuits. I saw that many of the people were just far better students than I was and realized at that point that I had wasted a lot of time. I needed to work harder just to tread water, and as I worked harder school became more interesting and satisfying." Eventually he decided to major in English. "Writing some bad poetry for the school's literary magazine," he recalls, "was almost a graduation requirement for an English major, so I did it." His English degree also taught him how to recognize and understand good poetry, though his discrimination developed slowly. Janeczko admitted in an *English Journal* essay that in high school he thought sentimental poet Rod McKuen was great: "I was touched by the Guru of Gush ... and I hadn't been exposed to much poetry except the Greats, which to me and many of my friends meant poems difficult to read and impossible to understand. It was no surprise that I graduated from high school thinking there was an Official Approved List of Subjects You Can Write Poems About." When he graduated from St. Francis,

Janeczko continues, he realized that the Official Approved List of Subjects You Can Write Poems About "was as wide as the universe. And the universe doesn't always rhyme."

Janeczko entered teaching after graduate school, he says, because "I wanted to be the teacher I never had." His enthusiasm and joy in teaching soon led him into the two activities that have dominated his professional life: writing and collecting good poems. "The late 1960s was a hell of a time to be a teacher," he remembers in his *AAYA* interview. "Paperback books were the god of the classroom, so we were reading *The Outsiders, The Pigman* and other young adult books and I read them and taught them and said 'I could do this.' As it turned out I couldn't, but I was motivated to try. The other thing that got me interested in writing was that I started writing for teaching magazines like *English Journal* and I started experiencing the narcotic of seeing my name in print in a serious way. I've never looked back since then."

Janeczko began collecting poetry as a practical response to his needs as a teacher. He recalls being encouraged to "do his own thing" in the classroom, and one of the things he wished to do was to introduce his students to poetry. He combed the huge poetry anthology that was available to him for good poems, but insists that the book "just wasn't cutting it. This was the 'Age of Aquarius' and some really challenging people were writing. Poetry was going through a period of change and I wanted the kids to experience some of that new poetry. I've always felt that any kid will read if you give him or her the right stuff, and that applies to poetry as well. I felt like if kids found contemporary poetry to their liking then somewhere down the line they may, in fact, discover and enjoy some of the classics." Janeczko was soon bringing in some of the better poems he remembered from graduate school and copying poems out of the small magazines that publish contemporary poetry. The students responded enthusiastically, hints Janeczko, partly because they liked what they were reading, and partly because they were rebels and enjoyed exploring the cutting edge of poetry.

Although Janeczko was building up quite a collection of poetry that he used in his teaching, he had no intention of doing anything with his collection—until he bumped into an editor at a teacher's convention in Las Vegas, Nevada. Soon they had agreed to publish *The Crystal Image,* Janeczko's first poetry anthology. "I had no idea then that anthologies were going to be what I would wind up doing or that poetry was going to be such an important part of my life," he tells *AAYA.* Some ten anthologies later, Janeczko has become more systematic in his compilation of poems for his anthologies. His anthologies tend to center on an idea or a theme: *Postcard Poems,* his second book, contains poems short enough to fit on a postcard sent to a friend; *Strings: A Gathering of Family Poems* collects poems about family; and *Pocket Poems: Selected for a Journey* is organized around the idea of being at home and then going out into the world and returning. Despite their thematic

coherence, each of the volumes contains a wide variety of poems. In fact, Janeczko claims that the organization of any of his anthologies is more apparent to him than to anyone who might read the books. "When I put a book together it's very similar to writing a novel in the structural sense," he says. "I hope the whole book tells a story, even though nobody is going to sit down and read one of my anthologies from cover to cover like they do a novel. But if they were to do that they would begin to find a sense of continuity in the book."

One of the ways Janeczko gathers poems for his anthologies is by reading widely. "I read some poetry every day," he remarks in his *AAYA* interview, "and when I find a good poem I simply mark it off in the book, make a photocopy of it, and put it in a file that says 'New Poems.' Every so often I'll read through those and I'll say 'This is about flowers' and I'll put it in a flower folder. I don't really start thinking about a book until I say 'Boy, this flower folder or this love folder is really getting fat.'" Not all of Janeczko's groupings of poems become books, however. He remembers that at one point he had a number of wonderful poems about old age and aging, so he suggested to his editor that they do a book about this topic. The editor did not think it was a good subject for a whole book for young readers, but suggested that a book of poems about families might

In his collection of original poems, *Brickyard Summer,* Janeczko uses short, narrative verse to describe two teenage boys enjoying a summer away from school. (Illustrated by Ken Rush.)

work. That idea was published as *Strings*. But rarely does Janeczko look for poems to fit a specific theme. "I look for poems that strike me," he says, "ones that I hope I'll be able to share with somebody someday."

Janeczko has ironed out many of the wrinkles of his selection process over the years. He learned after his second book that he did not want to write introductions to his anthologies. "What could I say in an introduction?" he asks. "I wrote one for *Postcard Poems* and it was just 'lah dee dah, lah dee dah,' here's how this idea came about, and so on. For the three pages that took I would rather have had, in retrospect, three more poems." This same principle has led him to generally exclude his own poetry as well. At first he excluded his own poetry because, when he compared his work to the other possible entries, he felt that it just was not as good. As time has gone on, however, he has made it his goal to include new poets, and that has excluded his work. "If my book has a hundred poems in it, it might have sixty poets," he remarks. "So if it comes down between putting my poems in the book or somebody else who is a new poet, I almost always go with the other person. If I write something good, I'll put it in one of my own books."

Janeczko has developed other methods of gathering poems, in part because he has come to know many of the poets he includes in his books. "What I've done for the last five or six books," he maintains, "is print out on my computer 100 postcards and send them to poets that I've used before and tell them what I'm looking for." He almost always asks for humorous poems and poems about baseball, the former because he figures that kids always need a laugh, and the latter because he is a diehard baseball fan. (Though he grew up a fan of the New York Giants and Mets, his allegiance has switched to the Boston Red Sox since he moved to New England.) He also asks his network of poets and friends to tell him about other poets he should read. Janeczko credits this network with helping him introduce new poets and new voices in his anthologies.

Janeczko's *Preposterous: Poems of Youth,* published in 1991, is primarily a book about boys, boys who are not quite men but feel the pull of manhood nonetheless. The opening poem, "Zip on 'Good Advice'" by Gary Hyland, sets the tone for the entire book by calling into question the authority of parents and their good advice. From that point on Janeczko groups his poems around such themes as anger, budding sexuality, the loss of a friend, and the delight to be found in mischief. In "Economics," a poem by Robert Wrigley, a young boy boils with rage at the man who owns everything he sees—and has a pretty daughter who seems unattainable. The boy strikes out where he can, but remains trapped in the impotence of his youth. Jim Wayne Miller's "Cheerleader" is no less striking a poem, though it deals with a very different pain of adolescence. In language reminiscent of a Catholic service, Miller condenses the sexual longing of adolescence in the image of a high school cheerleader who lives to share herself with others. She is "a halftime Eucharist"

distributed to the adoring basketball fans who fill the high school gym to watch her perform. As her spin ends "The sweating crowd speaks tongues and prophecies." The poems speak to a young man's vague yearnings to have more—more knowledge, more freedom, more control—and they convey the feelings of youthful frustration.

Many of the poems Janeczko includes in these anthologies explore challenging and potentially controversial subject matter, and his decision to include such poems indicates his refusal to make easy distinctions between adult and young adult poetry. Janeczko insists that one of his goals is to challenge young readers, to get them to stretch their minds. At the same time, he feels that there are important differences between poetry for adults and poetry for young adults. "Young adults don't have the life experiences to understand a poem written by a man who is going through a divorce," he contends in his *AAYA* interview, "but they do understand the end of relationships, so I pick poems that deal with levels of experience that a teenager can understand." Another factor that differentiates the two types of poetry is the sophistication of the language, or syntax. "I would think twice," he admits, "about giving kids the poetry of Wallace Stevens [a twentieth-century poet who constructs elaborately metaphorical poems that treat language almost as a musical medium rather than a medium to convey ideas]." The poems that Janeczko selects *mean* something, though they may also be musical or metaphorical. Janeczko says that his anthologies have been successful because "they deal with themes that kids can understand, or they are told from an experience point of view, or they get readers to reach a little bit. There is something there for everyone."

In *Pocket Poems* Janeczko arranges the poems to suggest the passage of time and the passage from the security of childhood to the responsibilities of growing up. The book contains about 120 poems broken up into three sections. The first fifty poems "are about being someplace," the anthologist tells *AAYA,* and reflect the concerns of childhood and young adulthood; this first section ends with poems about going away. The middle section contains twelve seasonal poems, roughly representing the twelve months of the year, that suggest the passing of time. The final fifty poems are about being out in the world, about taking responsibility and growing up, but the section ends with poems about going back to someplace. If read continuously, the poems suggest a cyclical movement of time but, says Janeczko, "if you pick and choose your favorite poet or interesting titles you don't catch the structure. Missing the structure is not a big deal, it's just an extra thing that I do with the books." In *Don't Forget to Fly: A Cycle of Modern Poems,* however, a reviewer from *English Journal* found the book's organization to be one of its greatest strengths, commenting that "the poems are arranged like a symphony with similar subject matter grouped together."

"I put a lot of thought and effort into how the poems are arranged," claims Janeczko, "and people may not see the overall structure from beginning to end but I hope they see how poems are clustered, two or three or four together." In fact, Janeczko arranges the poems in such a way that it would be hard to read just one: the poems physically touch each other on the page. It is rare to find a poem alone on a page; instead one poem will end halfway down the page and the next will start directly below it. The reader is lured into reading that next poem and it leads to the next and so on. *Preposterous* contains a number of good examples of this type of organization. Miller's "Cheerleader" is preceded by Rodney Torreson's "Howie Kell Suspends All Lust to Contemplate the Universe," and followed by Bob Henry Baber's "Fat Girl with Baton." Torreson's poem pits Howie Kell's glib belief in creationism against the animal magnetism of Valerie Marslott, and Howie admits that his beliefs "would be shaken by [her] milky kiss." This poem is light and playful, but it also sets the stage for Miller's almost erotic consideration of a cheerleader by showing how shaken a young boy can be when he discovers physical attraction. Baber's fat girl serves as a counterpoint to these poems, for she is evidence that while some girls move in a nearly magic realm of male attention, others are destined to have their "Majorette Dreams ... meet the ground/untouched," and for no better reason than their weight. The combination of the three poems allows a reader to consider the idea of male attraction in three very different ways, and suggests the effects that this attention has on both boys and girls. Similar groupings can be found throughout Janeczko's anthologies and they exist because, he says in his *AAYA* interview, "when people are reading the poems I want them to be thinking of things like 'Why is this poem here?,' or 'In this poem she took this point of view and I like this one better because....' Although the poems speak for themselves, the alignment has something to say too."

Although each of Janeczko's anthologies has a different story to tell, the books are all similar in that they all encourage the reader to think, to play with words, and possibly to write poetry themselves. One anthology that conveys this message well is *Poetspeak: In Their Work, about Their Work,* which *English Journal* reviewer Dick Abrahamson called "a real find for teachers of poetry." In preparing this book, Janeczko asked all of his contributors to write a little note, no more than five hundred words, about one of the poems, about their writing process, or about anything else they wanted. The short essays encourage the young reader to dream, to imagine, to be a poet, for they remind the reader that poets are just people shaping their thoughts into words. Janeczko feels that this is an important message for kids to understand. He notes that the message was best expressed by Al Young's poem "Don't Forget to Fly," the last poem in the collection of the same name. "I think for some kids 'Don't Forget to Fly' is a very important message, because they need to fly personally, creatively. As school budgets get cut and classes become more regimented it's going to be harder and harder for kids to fly. I do hope they get that message from my books, because I try to put in different ways of looking

Fourteen-year-old Leary composes poems about the girl of his dreams, his best friend, and his life at his parents' time-worn hotel. (From *Stardust otel,* written by Janeczko and illustrated by Dorothy Leech.)

at life and I'm hoping that there are going to be poems that connect with these kids."

While the poems that Janeczko includes in his anthologies and the poems he writes are often uplifting, he feels that he can also use poetry to show young people that "life is not all glamour and glitz. There is that dark side." In "The Bridge," a poem from *Brickyard Summer,* Janeczko describes a group of boys' stoic reaction when one of their friends falls through the old railway trestle that their parents had warned them about: "The only words we said about it/were Raymond's/'We were lucky'/after we watched Marty/slide into the ambulance/wrapped in a rubber sheet." In the book of poetry that he is currently working on, Janeczko has a number of poems about a girl who is abused by her father. However, he recognizes that there are dangers in exploring the darker side of life. While developing his next anthology, entitled *Looking for Your Name: Poems of Conflict,* he worried that the book's focus on conflict was too negative: "I'm aware that there are a lot of unhappy kids and I really don't want to add to that by giving a book that's just a real downer. My wife has been the head of a child abuse agency for the last five years, and after listening to her and just being more aware of what happens to families, I'm amazed that kids turn out as alright as they do."

Janeczko tells *AAYA*, "I don't want to be the 'Captain Bring Down' on poetry, so I try to strike a balance between the dark and the light poems, I try to write goofier ones or more 'hanging out with the guys' kind of poems. Part of what I want to do in a book is give kids some hope and some escape. If their life is a drag maybe reading one of the poems like "The Kiss" (in *Brickyard Summer*) will just give them a little spark and that's good." Many of the poems in *Brickyard Summer* explore the relationship between the narrator and his best friend, Raymond. The two boys share a deep bond, though the word "love" is never used to describe their relationship. When the glass-eyed town prophet in "Glass-Eyed Harry Coote" tells the narrator "Your gift is friendship," Raymond mutters "Should be against the law/to take money/for telling something/as plain as bark on a tree." In the course of the book the two boys share shoplifting, running from the town bullies, and secrets. Raymond is forgotten only at the end, when the narrator experiences his first kiss beside a moonlit pond. Though there is great excitement in the poem, there is also a melancholy sense that the friendship between the boys must change as a result of the kiss.

Janeczko quit teaching in 1990 in order to concentrate on his own writing and to spend more time visiting schools. Leaving teaching was a big step, for he had been teaching for twenty-two years. But, he declares, "It feels great! I always said that when I left teaching I wanted to leave at a time when I felt I could still do it well. I didn't want to be one of those burned out cases that just collects his pay check and counts the years to retirement. Now I can do what I want to do." His first year away from teaching was actually planned as a leave of absence, and during that year he became a father for the first time and spent a great deal of time with his new daughter, Emma. He discovered during that year how much he enjoyed writing, visiting schools, and talking to students, so he decided to make his retirement from teaching permanent. "I still get to work with kids, which is why I went into teaching in the first place," he comments, "but now I don't have to deal with the politics at the faculty meetings or correcting papers. I visit a school, I do my thing, and I leave." He misses the camaraderie of working with his friends, but says that he has made an effort to get together with those friends to watch a Boston Celtics game or a Boston Red Sox game.

Though Janeczko does not care much for the flying that being a visiting writer requires, he enjoys the time that he spends visiting schools and talking with his young readers and their teachers and librarians. In 1991 he spent about forty-five days actually visiting schools, and he describes what he does at the school in his *AAYA* interview: "Often I meet with a large group, like seventy kids, and I talk about the writing process, how it works for me. I show them how I get an idea and how I sometimes come up with a good poem or a funny poem. I read from *Brickyard Summer* or from whatever book I

am currently working on, and then I answer questions. The other thing I'll do is hold a writing workshop with two or three classes for a period, but I've done more of the informal chatting and reading than I have the writing workshops."

One of the things that Janeczko talks to students about is the process by which he creates poems. Anyone reading Janeczko's *Brickyard Summer* would imagine that it is a collection of reminiscences about his childhood. The short poems describing the life of two boys passing the summer between eighth and ninth grade contain such clear images, such telling details, that they seem to grow out of the poet's memory. But Janeczko says that there is very little in *Brickyard Summer* that actually happened to him. "There was nothing spectacular about my childhood, but when I write I can make it funny, I can make it interesting, and I can make it exciting. I don't write the truth but I try to write what's true." Part of the difficulty in getting young people to write poems is getting them to let go of the facts of their experience when those facts do not suit the poem. "You take one little bit of your life," he advises, "and then you do something different with it, that's okay, this isn't history, this is a poem and you go with that."

Most of Janeczko's poems spring from his imagination, and begin as only an abstract idea. "Roscoe," a poem from *Brickyard Summer,* is a good example. In this poem two boys accidentally chase a neighbor's cat in front of a truck, and then hide their responsibility from the neighbor. Janeczko describes the poem's origins in his *AAYA* interview: "One of the things you grow up with when you're a Catholic is guilt. I wanted to write a poem about guilt and 'Roscoe' was my vehicle for doing that, because guilt was the experience, but I never did anything with a cat." Janeczko describes another such idea he is developing for a work in progress: "I wanted to write a poem about a dare, a group of kids saying 'I dare you to do this.' So the dare was that the narrator, much like the narrator in *Brickyard Summer,* would go to the graveyard and kiss the tombstone of this girl who died twenty years ago at the age of sixteen, very mysteriously, nobody knows how she died or who paid for the stone angel that's above her tombstone. The dare was the idea for the poem and I tried to put clothes on it and see if it could walk around." Janeczko encourages young writers to stretch their imagination in similar ways, reminding them that they are not chained to the facts.

Another way Janeczko gets poems to work is by developing believable characters. "Sometimes I start with an idea, but a lot of times my poems are about characters. When I develop interesting characters, chances are they are going to do interesting things and so a lot of times I just come up with an interesting character and see what he or she does." One of the most convincing characters in *Brickyard Summer* is the narrator's friend Raymond. Janeczko never had such a friend when he was young; he hung around with his brothers. But whenever the author visits schools students ask him if he really knew Raymond. He did not, but enjoys the flattery.

Janeczko has promised himself a number of times that he would retire from anthologizing, not because he does not like it but because he would like to spend more time on his own writing. Though he has already published a novel, *Bridges to Cross,* and a nonfiction book on secret writing, *Loads of Codes and Secret Ciphers,* his eventual goal is to write in even more areas. "If the poetry or the writing muse came in and sat in my chair—which, by the way, is an old seat from Comiskey Park in Chicago—and said 'I will grant you success in one field of writing. Which will it be?,' I would take mysteries, with poetry a close second." His favorite mystery writers are Robert Parker and Ed McBain: he likes the wise, smart-aleck, American private eyes. He would also like to write something about baseball, though he cannot decide whether it will be for kids or for adults, fiction or nonfiction. "Until I have the security of knowing that my writing will be my income," he tells *AAYA,* "I'll just continue doing different kinds of writing."

"The great thing about writing," Janeczko tells young people, "is that you can try different things. W. Somerset Maugham [a noted English novelist] said there are three rules about writing a novel, and unfortunately nobody remembers what they are. I think that is also part of what I like about writing. I'm a disciplined person and I have my routine where I write, but as my wife has told me a number of times, I have this thing about authority, and I suspect that that applies to rules too. Rules? You can break the rules, and I think that is the biggest attraction about writing."

■ Works Cited

Abrahamson, Dick, Betty Carter, and Barbara Samuels, review of *Don't Forget to Fly* in "The Music of Young Adult Literature," *English Journal,* September, 1982, pp. 87-88.

Abrahamson, D., review of *Poetspeak: In Their Work, about Their Work, English Journal,* January, 1984, p. 89.

Baber, Henry, "Fat Girl with Baton," *Preposterous: Poems for Youth,* compiled by Paul B. Janeczko, Orchard Books, 1991, pp. 27-28.

Janeczko, Paul B., *Don't Forget to Fly: A Cycle of Modern Poems,* Bradbury, 1981.

Janeczko, Paul B., essay in "Facets: Successful Authors Talk about Connections between Teaching and Writing," *English Journal,* November, 1984, p. 24.

Janeczko, Paul B., *Brickyard Summer* (poetry), illustrations by Ken Rush, Orchard Books, 1989.

Janeczko, Paul B., *Preposterous: Poems of Youth,* Orchard Books, 1991.

Janeczko, Paul B., interview with Tom Pendergast for *Authors and Artists for Young Adults,* Gale Research, conducted February 18, 1992.

Miller, Jim Wayne, "Cheerleader," *Preposterous: Poems for Youth,* compiled by Paul B. Janeczko, Orchard Books, 1991, p. 27.

Nehms, Beth and Ben Nehms, "Ties That Bind: Families in YA Books," *English Journal,* November, 1984, p. 98.

Torreson, Rodney, "Howie Kell Suspends All Lust to Contemplate the Universe," *Preposterous: Poems for Youth,* compiled by Paul B. Janeczko, Orchard Books, 1991, pp. 26-27.

■ For More Information See

BOOKS

Children's Books and Their Creators, edited by Anita Silvey, Houghton Mifflin, 1995.

Sixth Book of Junior Authors and Illustrators, Wilson, 1989.

Something about the Author Autobiography Series, Vol. 18, Gale Research, 1994, pp. 151-64.

Twentieth-Century Young Adult Writers, St. James Press, 1994.

PERIODICALS

ALAN Review, spring, 1997, pp. 12-16.

Horn Book, March-April, 1990, p. 215; May-June, 1990, p. 343.

New York Times Book Review, April 27, 1980, p. 61; October 7, 1990, p. 30.

Publishers Weekly, March 16, 1998, p. 64.

School Library Journal, May, 1990, p. 118; March, 1991, p. 223.

—Sketch by Tom Pendergast

*   *   *

JENKINS, Jean
(Jean Loewer)

■ Personal

Born in Buffalo, NY; father, a writer; mother, a physician; married H. Peter Loewer (a writer and illustrator). *Education:* University of Buffalo (now State University of New York at Buffalo), B.F.A.; Hunter College of the City University of New York, degree in art education; studied book illustration at School of Visual Arts, New York City.

■ Addresses

Home and office—Asheville, NC.

■ Career

Freelance book illustrator, c. 1972—. Works at Graphos Studio; Asheville-Buncombe Library System, part-time employee at children's library; art teacher in public schools; teacher of adult education classes in art. *Member:* Society of Children's Book Writers and Illustrators, South-Eastern Bookseller's Association, Phi Beta Kappa.

■ Writings

(With husband Peter H. Loewer) *The Moonflower* (self-illustrated), Peachtree Publishers (Atlanta, GA), 1998.

ILLUSTRATOR

Andre Norton and Dorothy Madlee, *Star Ka'at World,* Walker, 1978.

Norton and Madlee, *Star Ka'ats and the Plant People,* Walker, 1979.

Norton and Madlee, *Star Ka'ats and the Winged Warriors,* Walker, 1981.

David A. Adler, *Jeffrey's Ghost and the Leftover Baseball Team,* Holt, 1984.

Athena V. Lord, *Today's Special: Z.A.P. and Zoe,* Macmillan, 1984.

Adler, *Jeffrey's Ghost and the Fifth Grade Dragon,* Holt, 1985.

Patrick Skene Catling, *John Midas in the Dreamtime,* Morrow, 1986.

Adler, *Jeffrey's Ghost and the Ziffel Fair Mystery,* Holt, 1987.

Lord, *The Luck of Z.A.P. and Zoe,* Macmillan, 1987.

Loewer, *The Inside-Out Stomach: An Introduction to Animals without Backbones,* Atheneum, 1990.

Loewer, *Pond Water Zoo: An Introduction to Microscopic Life,* Atheneum, 1996.

Campbell, Stu, *Let It Rot: The Gardener's Guide to Composting,* Storey Communications (Pownell, VT), 1998.

Some work appears under the name Jean Loewer. Illustrator for trade and textbook publishers, newspapers, and magazines, including *Greenprints: The Weeder's Digest.*

JEAN JENKINS

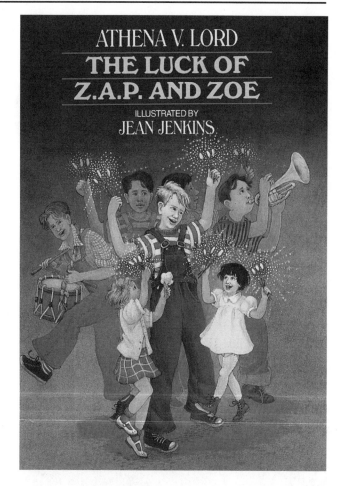

Jenkins's spirited illustrations capture the character of Athena V. Lord's tale of uninhibited twelve-year-old Zach Poulos, whose determination to conquer his fear of moving brings happy results.

■ Sidelights

Jean Jenkins told *SATA:* "I have worked for the past twenty-five years as a freelance illustrator, creating art for newspapers, magazines, textbooks, and trade books. For twelve years I worked with the Theatre Access Project of the Theatre Development Fund, in New York City. The project produced signed performances of Broadway shows for the deaf community, and I created line art of character sign logos for the performances. The art was also used as promotional material. We worked by phone, fax, photos, and FedEx, and all went smoothly, even with tight deadlines and little turn-around time.

"I am a regular contributor to a small magazine, started by one of the former editors of the *Mother Earth News.* This magazine, *Greenprints,* is about the whys, rather than the hows of gardening, and I have created both inside and cover art."

■ For More Information See

PERIODICALS

School Library Journal, March, 1987, p. 152; January, 1988, p. 75; January, 1991, p. 102.

K

KAMEN, Gloria 1923-

■ Personal

Born April 9, 1923, in New York City; daughter of Herman and Tillie Kamen; married Elliot Charney (a research scientist), June 22, 1947; children: Tina, Ruth, Juliet. *Education:* Attended Pratt Institute, 1939-42, and Art Students' League of New York, 1942-45.

GLORIA KAMEN

■ Addresses

Home—R.R. 1, Box 29, Hartland, VT 05048.

■ Career

Illustrator and author. Fairchild Publications, New York City, member of promotion department staff, 1947-49; freelance designer and illustrator, New York City, 1949—; freelance author and illustrator, 1957—. Volunteer reading tutor in local schools; speaker to children's groups. *Exhibitions:* Fourth International Exhibit of Best Illustrated Books, Catalonia, Spain. *Member:* Artists' Equity Association, Children's Book Guild (Washington, DC; president, 1975-76), Authors Guild.

■ Awards, Honors

Awards from Educational Press Association of America, 1969, 1974, for a series of magazine covers for the *National Education Association Journal,* and 1974, for magazine covers for *Red Cross Magazine;* Ohio State University Awards, Institute for Education by Television and Radio, 1975, 1977, 1978, for television programs *The Sea Egg: Children's Poetry Program, The Upstairs Room,* and John Robbin's series, *Cover-to-Cover;* Best Illustrated Books, New York Public Library, 1990, for *The Ringdoves.*

■ Writings

NONFICTION FOR CHILDREN; SELF-ILLUSTRATED

Fiorello: His Honor, the Little Flower, Atheneum (New York City), 1981.
Charlie Chaplin, Atheneum, 1982.
Kipling, Storyteller of East and West, Atheneum, 1985.
Edward Lear, King of Nonsense: A Biography, Atheneum, 1990.
Hidden Music: The Life of Fanny Mendelssohn, Atheneum, 1996.

FICTION FOR CHILDREN; SELF-ILLUSTRATED

(Reteller) *The Ringdoves: From the Fables of Bidpai,* Atheneum, 1988.

"Paddle," Said the Swan, Atheneum, 1989.

The Second-Hand Cat, Atheneum, 1992.

ILLUSTRATOR

Hughie Call, *The Little Kingdom,* Houghton (Boston), 1964.

Elizabeth Goudge, *A Book of Comfort,* Coward, 1964.

Betty Crocker Cookbook for Boys and Girls, Western Publishing, 1966.

Ann Guy, *One Dozen Brownies,* Abingdon (Nashville), 1965.

Ethelyn M. Parkinson, *The Operation That Happened to Rupert Piper,* Abingdon, 1966.

Joan Lexau, *Three Wishes for Abner,* Ginn (Boston), 1967.

Phyllis Naylor, *To Shake a Shadow,* Abingdon, 1967.

Barbara Klimowicz, *The Strawberry Thumb,* Abingdon, 1968.

Lila Sheppard, *Wiki Wants to Read,* Whitman, 1968.

Ruth Hooker, *Gertrude Kloppenberg (Private),* Abingdon, 1970.

Barbara Klimowicz, *When Shoes Eat Socks,* Abingdon, 1971.

Valerie Pitt, *Let's Find Out about the Family,* F. Watts (New York City), 1971.

Ethelyn M. Parkinson, *Rupert Piper and Megan, the Valuable Girl,* Abingdon, 1972.

Barbara K. Todd, *Juan Patricio,* Putnam (New York City), 1972.

Ruth Hooker, *Gertrude Kloppenberg II,* Abingdon, 1974.

Jean Leifheit, *Drugs Your Friends, and Drugs Your Enemies,* Standard Publications, 1974.

Edna S. Levine, *Lisa and Her Soundless World,* Human Sciences Press (New York City), 1974.

Ethelyn M. Parkinson, *Rupert Piper and the Dear, Dear Birds,* Abingdon, 1976.

Barbara Brooks Wallace, *Hawkins,* Abingdon, 1977.

Miriam Anne Bourne, *White House Children,* Random House, 1979.

Alfred Meyer, editor, *A Zoo for All Seasons: The Smithsonian Animal World,* Smithsonian Exposition Books, 1979.

Barbara Brooks Wallace, *The Contest Kid Strikes Again,* Abingdon, 1980.

Wallace, *Hawkins and the Soccer Solution,* Abingdon, 1981.

Miriam Anne Bourne, *The Children of Mount Vernon: A Guide to George Washington's Home,* Doubleday (New York City), 1980.

K. C. Tessendorf, *Look Out! Here Comes the Stanley Steamer,* Atheneum (New York City), 1984.

Peggy Thomson, *Siggy's Spaghetti Works,* Tambourine Books (New York City), 1993.

Peggy Thomson, *Take Me Out to the Bat and Ball Factory,* Whitman, 1998.

ILLUSTRATOR; OTHER

Judith Martin, *Miss Manners' Guide to Excruciatingly Correct Behavior,* Atheneum, 1982.

Martin, *Miss Manners' Guide to Rearing Perfect Children,* Atheneum, 1984.

Martin, *Miss Manners' Guide for the Turn-of-the-Millennium,* Pharos Books (New York City), 1989.

Martin, *Miss Manners on Painfully Proper Weddings,* Crown Publishers, 1995.

Creator of art work for educational television program *Cover-to-Cover,* WETA (Washington, DC). Contributor of illustrations to periodicals, including *Woman's Day* and publications for children.

■ Sidelights

Gloria Kamen began her career in children's publishing as an illustrator, but has since expanded her efforts into writing both nonfiction and fiction for young readers. While her art work has been featured in books by authors such as Elizabeth Goudge and Phyllis Naylor, Kamen's more recently revealed talent as a writer has produced several well-received works of nonfiction for children, including *Kipling: Storyteller of East and West* and *Hidden Music: The Life of Fanny Mendelssohn,* the latter published in 1996. Her contributions to children's fiction include a retelling of the Indian fable of "The Ringdoves" as well as *Second-Hand Cat,* a humorous

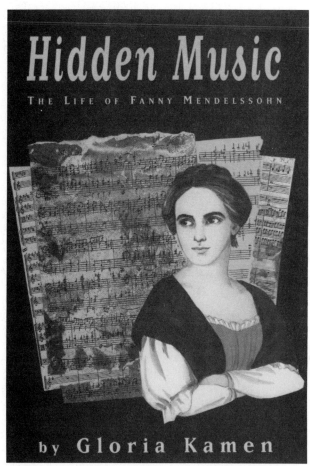

Kamen relates the life story of Felix Mendelssohn's sister Fanny, a talented musician and composer whose career was thwarted by the restrictions placed on women during her lifetime.

Peggy Thomson's *Siggy's Spaghetti Works*, illustrated by Kamen, demonstrates the process of making spaghetti in a factory while offering some historical facts about pasta.

picture book that reflects its author/illustrator's strong sense of a child's perspective.

Born in 1923 in New York City, Kamen was exposed to the arts from an early age. After completing high school she attended the prestigious Pratt Institute, transferring to New York's Art Students' League in 1945. After several years of course work at the League, Kamen ended her studies and obtained a job at Fairchild Publications, moving on from there to become a freelance designer and illustrator. Raising a family occupied much of her time during the 1950s; by the early 1960s Kamen had resumed her focus on design and illustration.

The 1960s and 1970s proved to be productive decades for Kamen: the illustrator lent her artistic talents to more than twenty book-length projects. In 1981, she published her first self-written work, *Fiorello: His Honor, the Little Flower*. The biography of Fiorello La Guardia, a former U.S. Congressman and one of the most beloved mayors in New York City's history, *Fiorello* delves into the popular politician's childhood and the beginning of his rise up the political ladder in the early years of the twentieth century. Praising Kamen's pen-and-ink drawings, Anna Biagioni Hart noted in a review for *School Library Journal* that Kamen's book is a "fine introduction" to Fiorello La Guardia and a "much better than average junior biography."

Kamen's first successful work of nonfiction encouraged the author/illustrator to produce others. Her *Charlie Chaplin* offered an illustrated history of the most famous film actor of the silent-movie era, from his impoverished childhood in England to his success as a film star and director in the United States. Noting that many of the problems that dogged Chaplin throughout his later life were primarily "adult fare," *School Library Journal* critic Helen Gregory maintained that Kamen handles such events "with taste and discretion. There is dialogue and description of feelings ... [that] ring true." Other British-born notables covered by Kamen in book form include Rudyard Kipling, the author of *The Jungle Book, Captains Courageous, Just-So Stories* and many other classics, and limerick-writer Edward Lear, whose biography Kamen subtitled *King of Nonsense*. "It is gratifying to read a biography that is fluent, lively, based on careful research, and ... balanced in treatment," stated *Bulletin of the Center for Children's Books* reviewer Zena Sutherland. "Lear seems very much present in this volume," added Kathleen Whalin in her review of the book for *School Library Journal*. Whalin also commented on Kamen's ability to supplement Lear's pen-and-ink cartoons with her own artwork in illustrating the story of the nineteenth-century writer's life.

Hidden Music: The Life of Fanny Mendelssohn paints the portrait of a lesser-known nineteenth-century creative talent. The sister of world-renowned composer

Felix, Fanny Mendelssohn was born to a wealthy German-Jewish family that reverted to Christianity when Fanny was a young girl due to the anti-Semitism that was gaining sway in that country. Basing her story on family letters, Kamen shows how Fanny's talent as both a composer and a pianist was underappreciated by those around her due to her gender and overshadowed by the fame of her brother; as a *Kirkus Reviews* contributor noted, despite the obvious feminist slant to Kamen's text, "it is not hard to ache for the suppression of a clearly radiant talent." Roger Sutton added in *Bulletin of the Center for Children's Books* that Kamen fortunately "does not lean on [her feminist theme] too heavily and avoids turning her early-nineteenth-century subject into a twentieth-century heroine."

In addition to nonfiction, Kamen has written and illustrated several popular works of fiction for the younger set. In *The Ringdoves*, she introduces Indian fables collectively known as the "Bidpai" and "Hitopadesha" by retelling a story of friendship and cooperation among different species of animals. *The Ringdoves* begins as a flock of doves, trapped by the net of a hunter, flap their wings in unison and rise into the sky, net and all. Their efforts to escape are assisted by a tiny mouse, who gnaws through the rope holding the net to the ground. A crow witnesses the mouse's unselfish act and starts up a friendship that several other animals soon join in. Ultimately, the hunter's efforts to capture any of the circle of friends are thwarted by the other animals, and he retreats from the forest to allow nature's creatures to live in peace. Praising Kamen's Persian-influenced illustrations, a *Kirkus Reviews* critic remarked that *The Ringdoves* is "a rare instance of a lively tale that convincingly demonstrates the value of peaceful cooperation."

Original fiction by Kamen includes the picture books *"Paddle," Said the Swan* and *Second-Hand Cat*, both illustrated by the author with humorous paintings. In *"Paddle,"* small animals are urged by their parents to take their first steps towards independence, although by nightfall—and the book's end—all are urged to sleep. Based on the traditional children's song "Over in the Meadow," Kamen's story features rhymes that, according to Mary M. Burns of *Horn Book*, "demonstrat[e] that traditional forms can comfortably enrich ... contemporary perspectives." Burns also praised Kamen's imagery as "elegantly composed" and "thoughtfully detailed." In *Second-Hand Cat*, Kamen describes the growing relationship between a boy and a cat that the boy inherits from a neighbor who is moving away; the longer the two are together, the more the cat's idiosyncrasies are revealed. In addition to commending Kamen's story, *School Library Journal* contributor Debra S. Gold praised the book's illustrations, writing that the "whimsical watercolor drawings ... capture the lighthearted tone of this story."

"I enjoy children—all kinds," Kamen once told *SATA*. Her own three children inspired her with much of the insight that has characterized her illustrations and writing, and she encouraged each of them in their own

creative endeavors: "one with theatre lighting, one with modern dance, the other ... [with] painting," Kamen recalled. "They [were] dragged to museums since they were little." When not working on illustrations or texts for a new book, Kamen sometimes takes on more large-scale projects, drawing on large sheets of paper. The results of these "large-scale" as opposed to page-sized efforts have been exhibited at art galleries in one-woman shows.

■ Works Cited

Burns, Mary M., review of *"Paddle," Said the Swan, Horn Book,* May-June, 1989, p. 359.

Gold, Debra S., review of *Second-Hand Cat, School Library Journal,* June, 1992, p. 96.

Gregory, Helen, review of *Chaplin, School Library Journal,* March, 1983, pp. 178-79.

Hart, Anna Biagioni, review of *Fiorello: His Honor, the Little Flower, School Library Journal,* February, 1982, p. 77.

Review of *Hidden Music: The Life of Fanny Mendelssohn, Kirkus Reviews,* February 15, 1996, p. 296.

Review of *The Ringdoves, Kirkus Reviews,* February 1, 1988, p. 202.

Sutherland, Zena, review of *Edward Lear, King of Nonsense, Bulletin of the Center for Children's Books,* November, 1990, pp. 63-64.

Sutton, Roger, review of *Hidden Music: The Life of Fanny Mendelssohn, Bulletin of the Center for Children's Books,* May, 1996, p. 304.

Whalin, Kathleen, review of *Edward Lear, King of Nonsense, School Library Journal,* November, 1990, p. 128.

■ For More Information See

PERIODICALS

Booklist, January 1, 1986, p. 685; March 15, 1989, p. 1032; February 1, 1992, p. 1040; October 1, 1993, p. 349.

Bulletin of the Center for Children's Books, January, 1982, p. 87; March, 1986, p. 130.

Horn Book, September-October, 1996, pp. 615-16.

School Library Journal, November, 1988, p. 104; January, 1994, p. 111.

Voice of Youth Advocates, June, 1996, p. 118.

* * *

KATZ, William Loren 1927-

■ Personal

Born June 2, 1927, in Brooklyn, NY; son of Bernard (a researcher) and Madeline (Simon) Katz; married Dr. Laurie Lehman, September 10, 1994; children: (first marriage) Naomi, Michael. *Education:* Syracuse University, B.A., 1950; New York University, M.A., 1952. *Religion:* Jewish.

■ Career

Educator and author. New York City Public Schools, teacher of American history, 1955-60; Greenburgh District Eight School System, Hartsdale, NY, high school teacher, 1960-68; New School for Social Research, New York, instructor in U.S. history, 1977—. Scholar-in-residence, Teachers College, Columbia University, 1971-73; lecturer on African American history at teacher institutes; has taught courses at New York University, University of California, Los Angeles, and at the Tombs Prison. Producer of classroom audiovisual materials on minorities. Consultant to President John F. Kennedy's committee on juvenile delinquency and youth development and to organizations, including the Smithsonian Institution, U.S. Air Force Schools in Europe, British House of Commons, *Life* magazine, and CBS-TV. Has testified before the U.S. Senate on African American history and has appeared on numerous television and radio programs in the United States and Europe. *Military service*—U.S. Navy, 1945-46. *Member:* United Federation of Teachers.

■ Awards, Honors

Gold Medal Award for nonfiction, National Conference of Christians and Jews, and Brotherhood Award, both 1968, both for *Eyewitness: The Negro in American History;* Oppie Award, 1971, for *The Black West;* Children's Book Showcase, 1976, for *Making Our Way: America at the Turn of the Century in the Words of the Poor and Powerless;* Carter G. Woodson Outstanding Merit designation, 1991, for *Breaking the Chains: African-American Slave Resistance.*

■ Writings

NONFICTION

Eyewitness: The Negro in American History, Pittman, 1967, revised edition published as *Eyewitness: A Living Documentary of the African American Contribution to American History,* Touchstone/Simon & Schuster, 1995.
Five Slave Narratives, Arno/New York Times, 1968.
Teachers' Guide to American Negro History, Anti-Defamation League, 1968, rev. ed., Quadrangle (Chicago), 1971.
(With Warren J. Halliburton) *American Majorities and Minorities: A Syllabus of United States History for Secondary Schools,* Arno, 1970.
The Black West: A Documentary and Pictorial History, Doubleday, 1971, revised edition, 1973.
(With Halliburton) *A History of Black Americans,* Harcourt, 1973.
An Album of the Civil War, F. Watts, 1974.
An Album of Reconstruction, F. Watts, 1974.
(With Bernard Gaughran) *The Constitutional Amendments,* F. Watts, 1974.
Black People Who Made the Old West, Crowell, 1977, new edition, Africa World Press, 1992.
The Great Depression, F. Watts, 1978.
An Album of Nazism, F. Watts, 1979.

The Invisible Empire: The Ku Klux Klan Impact on History, Open Hand (Washington, DC), 1986.
Black Indians: A Hidden Heritage, Atheneum, 1986.
The Lincoln Brigade: A Picture History, Atheneum, 1989.
Breaking the Chains: African-American Slave Resistance, Atheneum, 1990.
(With Paula A. Franklin) *Proudly Red and Black: Stories of Africans and Native Americans,* Atheneum, 1993.
Black Women of the Old West, Atheneum, 1995.
Black Legacy: A History of New York's African Americans, Simon & Schuster/Atheneum, 1997.

NONFICTION; "MINORITIES IN AMERICAN HISTORY" SERIES

Early America: 1492-1812, F. Watts, 1973.
Slavery to Civil War: 1812-1865, F. Watts, 1973.
Reconstruction and National Growth: 1865-1900, F. Watts, 1974.
From the Progressive Era to the Great Depression: 1900-1929, F. Watts, 1974.
Years of Strife: 1929-1956, F. Watts, 1975.
Modern America: 1957 to the Present, F. Watts, 1975.

NONFICTION; "HISTORY OF MULTICULTURAL AMERICA" SERIES

Exploration to the War of 1812, 1492-1814, Steck-Vaughn, 1993.
The Westward Movement and Abolitionism, 1815-1850, Steck-Vaughn, 1993.

The result of several decades of research, William Loren Katz's "History of Multicultural America" series begins with a study of Native American peoples and ends with a discussion of current immigration and ethnic diversity in America.

The Civil War to the Last Frontier, 1859-1880s, Steck-
    Vaughn, 1993.
The Great Migrations, 1880s-1912, Steck-Vaughn, 1993.
The New Freedom to the New Deal, Steck-Vaughn, 1993.
World War II to the New Frontier, 1940-1963, Steck-
    Vaughn, 1993.
The Great Society to the Reagan Era, 1964-1990, Steck-
    Vaughn, 1993.
Minorities Today, Steck-Vaughn, 1993.

EDITOR

The American Negro: His History and Literature, 146
    volumes, Arno, 1968-71.
Picture Histories of American Minorities, six volumes, F.
    Watts, 1972-73.
(With Jacqueline Hunt Katz) *Making Our Way: Ameri-
    ca at the Turn of the Century in the Words of the
    Poor and Powerless,* Dial, 1975.
Pamphlets in American History (series), Microfilm
    Corp. of America/New York Times, 1978-82.
(And author of introduction) *Flight from the Devil: Six
    Slave Narratives,* Africa World Press (Trenton, NJ),
    1996.

Also editor of *Teaching Approaches to Black History in
the Classroom,* 1973. Editor of the series "The Anti-
Slavery Crusade in America," sixty-nine volumes, Arno,
and "Vital Sources of American History for High School
Students," 179 volumes, 1980.

OTHER

Contributor to periodicals, including *Freedomways,
Journal of Black Studies, Journal of Negro Education,
Journal of Negro History, Reader's Digest, Saturday
Review, Southern Education Report,* and *Teachers Col-
lege Record.*

■ Sidelights

Educator and author William Loren Katz has been
interested in the lives and unique history of the "grass-
roots" citizens of the United States since his teen years.
Well known for his expertise within the field of African-
American history, Katz is the author of numerous
books—including his highly acclaimed debut work
Eyewitness: The Negro in American History—detailing
centuries of contributions by blacks, Native Americans,
and other ethnic minorities to social and political
progress in the United States. He has also served as
editor of several collections of original documents and
photographs that illuminate, enrich, and preserve America's historical legacy for students. With Jacqueline
Hunt Katz, he has also edited *Making Our Way:
America at the Turn of the Century in the Words of the
Poor and Powerless,* an illustrated selection of first-
person narratives detailing the hardships endured by
immigrants during the early years of the twentieth
century.

Born in 1927 and raised amid the ethnic diversity of
New York City, Katz watched as World War II unfolded
during his high school years. After graduating, he served
in the U.S. Navy for the last year of the war and then

earned degrees from Syracuse and New York Universities before beginning his career as an educator. "I then
began teaching high school social studies, only to find
that school texts and courses ignored the role Black
Americans played in history, or caricatured their contributions," the author once explained to *SATA.* "Through
my own research I introduced eyewitness accounts to
my students, documenting the neglected part [African
Americans] had always taken in American growth."
These eyewitness accounts served as the basis of Katz's
Eyewitness: The Negro in American History, an award-
winning textbook that has recently been revised and
updated.

Eyewitness, which collects actual reports from the
Colonial Era through the civil rights movement of the
twentieth century, was the first of many books Katz
would write about the history of African Americans.
Containing numerous photographs, the book was hailed
by critics for bringing to light a formerly obscured view
of U.S. history—a view that Katz would dedicate much
of his later career to further illuminating. His *Black
Legacy: A History of New York's African Americans*
further explores the history of African Americans by

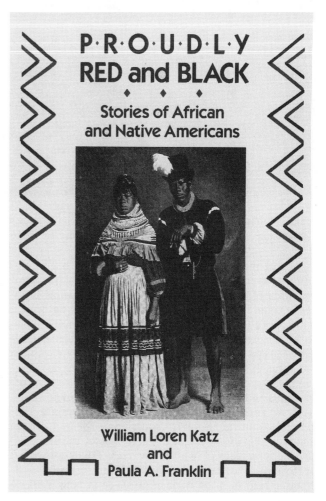

**Katz's work, cowritten with Paula A. Franklin, is a
compilation of short biographies of famous Americans
who are of mixed Native American and African ances-
try.**

Katz highlights the efforts of African American women who took advantage of the opportunities offered by westward expansion and contributed to American culture in these pioneering communities.

presenting the story of blacks in New York, beginning with the seventeenth-century group of Dutch slaves who first attempted to settle in the area then known as New Amsterdam. These earliest black residents laid the groundwork for what would eventually grow to be New York City, and Katz goes on to outline the continuing contributions of African Americans in the area since that time; his book covers such topics as the Harlem Renaissance of the 1920s, the civil rights movement of the 1950s and 1960s, and the election of David Dinkins as New York City's first black mayor. Despite the volume's subtitle, *Booklist* contributor Ilene Cooper remarked that *Black Legacy* "encompasses the story of all American blacks," while *New York Times* contributor Rosemary L. Bray called the work "an accessible and engaging record of the African presence in New York."

In 1971 Katz published *The Black West: A Documentary and Pictorial History,* a profile of the role of African Americans in the growth of the "Old West." Praised by a *Publishers Weekly* critic for containing "some dramat-

ic ... chapters that expand the common knowledge," *The Black West* presents detailed biographies of a variety of African Americans who helped settle the western reaches of the United States. From soldiers and lawmen to gamblers, explorers, and even villains, *The Black West* provides readers with a fresh perspective on a much-romanticized era in American history.

The Old West serves as Katz's focus in several other books, including *Black Indians: A Hidden History.* This volume, like *The Black West,* seeks to expand its readers' traditional notions of America's past. Calling the book "inherently dramatic, moving, and absorbing," a reviewer for the *Bulletin of the Center for Children's Books* praised Katz's work while noting the author's tendency to use subjective rather that impartial words to describe the relationship between blacks and Native Americans in establishing communities apart from white settlers. While commenting on the difficulty of reconstructing such a history when much of what transpired was never written down, Helen E. Williams praised *Black Indians* in a review for *School Library Journal,* noting that "this highly readable and sad chronology of a hidden heritage is needed and welcomed." Katz again expands young readers' understanding of the century-old contributions of former slaves in his 1995 work *Black Women of the Old West.* Called an "eye-opener" by *Booklist* contributor Chris Sherman, *Black Women* uses numerous photographs and prints from the time period to convey the efforts of African American women to participate fully in the educational, economic, and social opportunities offered as United States boundaries expanded.

Although the contributions of African Americans to the westward expansion of the United States have been sparsely documented in mainstream history texts, their role in other political and cultural movements has been somewhat better referenced. Since the early 1970s, through television programs like the award-winning miniseries *Roots,* along with the book by Alex Haley that inspired it, and films such as *Glory* and other documentaries, the role of blacks before and during the Civil War has been afforded increased attention. Katz attempts to address this interest from a black, rather than white abolitionist perspective in 1990's *Breaking the Chains: African-American Slave Resistance.* Containing actual accounts of fugitive slaves and their black contemporaries—including Frederick Douglass, Harriet Tubman, and Dred Scott—*Breaking the Chains* documents the many forms that black people's resistance to their own slavery and oppression took in the early to mid-nineteenth century. Calling the book "powerful and authentic," a *Publishers Weekly* critic noted that Katz's well-illustrated work "will be welcomed by those seeking to reclaim the truth behind their heritage."

Katz has continued his dedication to expanding the understanding of students of U.S. history by highlighting the contributions of diverse races, cultures, and genders through his "Minorities in American History" series, as well as through a more recent eight-volume series entitled "History of Multicultural America." In the first two volumes of the "Minorities in American History" series—covering the years 1492 to 1865—Katz "asserts the role economics play in shaping prejudice," according to a *Booklist* reviewer. The "Minorities in American History" books were cited as a "matter-of-fact look at the darker side of American history" by a *Booklist* contributor critiquing the volumes that cover the years from Reconstruction to the Great Depression. Although faulting Katz's "History of Multicultural America" for lacking a list of references with which to locate much of its source material, *Booklist* contributor Janice Del Negro noted that the author "provides a tremendous amount of material" illuminating the many contributions of both minorities and women to life in the United States. *Voice of Youth Advocates* contributor Laura L. Lent maintained that "Katz's unique approach to American history will pique the reader's interest and begin to fill a gap in research that has been neglected for too long."

In *Black Legacy,* Katz traces the role of African Americans in the founding of New York City and their influence on the city's outstanding artistic and political movements of the twentieth-century.

Throughout Katz's published works, the historian makes use of source materials written or narrated by those who actually lived through the events and times he discusses. In several works, Katz also relies upon historic photographs and prints to tell the story. *An Album of the Civil War,* published in 1974, as well as its companion volumes—*An Album of Reconstruction, An Album of the Great Depression,* and *An Album of Nazism*—provide reluctant readers with insight into some of the most significant events shaping America's past. Drawing on the author's own private collection of images, *An Album of the Civil War* divides the period from the signing of the Emancipation Proclamation through the end of the war and its aftermath into more than forty simply written chapters, thus isolating and highlighting facts that might have become lost in longer chapters. Similar in design, *An Album of the Great Depression* provides crucial background to the economic downturn of the 1930s; a reviewer in *Bulletin of the Center for Children's Books* called the work "a comprehensive study ... made dramatic by the many photographs."

In addition to teaching and writing, Katz has testified before the U.S. Senate on the matter of African-American history, has appeared on the *Today Show* and a host of other television and radio programs in the United

States and in England, and has lectured on black history in schools from Florida to California, as well as overseas. Since beginning his career Katz has taken the responsibility of being a historian seriously and has directly confronted such accepted beliefs as the dictum that "history is that which is set down by the victors." As Katz once stated, "I agree with the idea that the historian who condoned a crime was perpetuating it throughout history—his guilt was greater than that of the original perpetrator of the crime, not only because the effect of his sin was more enduring, but also because his motive was less pressing." In contrast, Katz has worked to "offer a history that enables us to look at the past intelligently and shape our future with the knowledge of the past in mind. My concentration on minorities has been pursued because I believe that society is only as strong as its weakest members, and that the responsibility of our nation is to spread justice to all within its borders. The first line of defense of all of us is protection for the least of us."

■ Works Cited

Review of *An Album of the Great Depression, Bulletin of the Center for Children's Books,* March, 1979, p. 120.

Review of *Black Indians: A Hidden History, Bulletin of the Center for Children's Books,* April, 1986, p. 150.

Review of *The Black West, Publishers Weekly,* August 2, 1971, p. 57.

Bray, Rosemary L., review of *Black Legacy: A History of New York's African Americans, New York Times Book Review,* July 20, 1997.

Review of *Breaking the Chains: African-American Slave Resistance, Publishers Weekly,* September 28, 1990, p. 104.

Cooper, Ilene, review of *Black Legacy: A History of New York's African Americans, Booklist,* February 15, 1997, p. 1012.

Del Negro, Janice, review of *Exploration to the War of 1812, 1492-1814,* and *The Westward Movement and Abolitionism, 1815-1850, Booklist,* June 1 and 15, 1993, p. 1803.

Lent, Laura L., review of *Exploration to the War of 1812, 1492-1814, Voice of Youth Advocates,* October, 1993, p. 244.

Review of "Minorities in American History" series: *Early America, 1492-1812,* and *Slavery to the Civil War, 1812-1865, Booklist,* May 1, 1974, p. 1004.

Review of "Minorities in American History" series: *From the Progressive Era to the Great Depression, 1900-1929,* and *Reconstruction and National Growth, 1865-1900, Booklist,* November 15, 1974, p. 344.

Sherman, Chris, review of *Black Women of the Old West, Booklist,* December 15, 1995, pp. 696-97.

Williams, Helen E., review of *Black Indians: A Hidden Heritage, School Library Journal,* August, 1996, p. 101.

■ For More Information See

PERIODICALS

Booklist, June 1, 1974, p. 1105; January 15, 1976, p. 686; December 15, 1977, p. 684; December 1, 1978, p. 617; June 15, 1986, pp. 1529-30; December 1, 1993, p. 687.

Bulletin of the Center for Children's Books, September, 1989, p. 8; January, 1996, p. 163.

Horn Book, March, 1991, p. 214.

Kirkus Reviews, February 15, 1974, pp. 193-94; February 1, 1975, p. 130; November 1, 1975, p. 1243; September 15, 1977, p. 997; June 1, 1989, p. 838.

Publishers Weekly, November 20, 1967, p. 55; August 29, 1977, pp. 366-67; June 9, 1989, p. 71.

School Library Journal, March, 1975, p. 106; September, 1975, p. 121; January, 1976, p. 54; January, 1994, p. 137.

Voice of Youth Advocates, April, 1996, p. 55.

*   *   *

KIM, Helen 1959-

■ Personal

Born in Korea in 1959; immigrated to New Jersey, 1971. *Education:* Boston University, B.A., New York University, M.A.

■ Addresses

Home—Seattle, WA.

■ Career

Writer and educator. Instructor of literature and creative writing in Seattle, WA.

■ Awards, Honors

Grant from the New Jersey State Council on the Arts, 1991; Delogu Scholarship for outstanding woman fiction writer, Stonecoast Writers Conference, and Jacobson Scholarship for writers of unusual promise, Wesleyan Writer's Conference, both 1993; Best Books selection, *Publishers Weekly,* 1996, National Book Award finalist for young adult fiction, National Book Foundation, 1996, and finalist, Children's Books of Distinction Award for young adult fiction, *Hungry Mind Review,* 1997, all for *The Long Season of Rain.*

■ Writings

The Long Season of Rain, Holt, 1996.

Contributor to *Goldfinch* and *Global City Review.*

■ Work in Progress

A sequel to *The Long Season of Rain.*

■ Sidelights

Helen Kim is a young adult author and poet of Korean descent whose first novel, *The Long Season of Rain,* met with great success. Dubbed a "master of understatement" by Elizabeth Devereaux and Diane Roback in *Publishers Weekly,* Kim received tremendous praise for her sensitive, detailed narrative. Set in Seoul, Korea, in 1969, *The Long Season of Rain* describes the life of a Korean family from the perspective of eleven-year-old Junehee, the second oldest of four daughters. Conflict arises when Junehee's mother wants to adopt an orphaned boy, Pyungsoo, who has been living with the family. While Junehee agrees that her mother should adopt her new friend, her often absent and domineering father and her strict paternal grandmother forbid it. It is during this family struggle, which takes place during the *changma,* or rainy season, that Junehee realizes the difficult demands placed on her mother, who has been close to despair. At the conclusion of the novel, Junehee and her mother confront Father about his frequent absences; the man admits that he has been unfaithful. Junhee's mother leaves the family for a time; when she returns, it appears that she will be granted more rights and that Father will be more involved with his wife and children. However, Junhee has experienced a loss of innocence through both the breakdown of her family and her exposure to the demands placed upon women in a patriarchal society.

Born in Korea, Kim enjoyed writing from an early age. When she was in the third grade, Kim won first prize in a writing contest for her story about an event in the life of Junhee, who would later become the protagonist of *The Long Season of Rain.* It was not until Kim moved to the United States at age twelve that she found it difficult to express herself. "I wrote in 'Konglish,' first using English words with Korean syntax then doing the reverse," the author explained to Lynda Brill Comerford in an interview in *Publishers Weekly.*

At Boston University, Kim majored in premed before becoming an English major; she earned a Bachelor's degree in English from BU followed by a Master's degree in British and American literature from New York University. It was during one of her writing workshops that Kim started *The Long Season of Rain.* Begun as an assignment to write the first sentence of a short story, the novel, which is described by its author as half autobiography and half fiction, "triggered moments of my past that seemed both close and far away. I had fallen out of touch with my childhood in Korea and it surprised me how fresh it all seemed as I wrote."

After completing the first fifty pages, Kim applied for—and received—a grant from the New Jersey Council on the Arts, an honor that led to the acceptance of *The Long Season of Rain* by publishers Henry Holt and Company. Initially, another publisher offered to buy the book as adult fiction, but the author chose to publish her book as a young adult novel. She explained to Comerford, "I was eager to launch my career as an adult author, but I knew I might never have another chance to publish a YA book." The publication of *The Long Season of Rain,* which was nominated for a National Book Award, has also led to some personal triumphs for Kim: her sisters, who appear as fictionalized versions of themselves in the book, have, she says, "gotten to know me better" through her writing, and she now feels more confident in her literary abilities. "I feel more visible, more heard," Kim told Comerford, adding, "I can really consider myself a writer now."

Reviewers have generally found *The Long Season of Rain* to be an especially effective first novel and Kim to be an insightful observer of human nature. Martha V. Parravano of the *Horn Book* called the book a "devastatingly clear-eyed view of societal restrictions and their effects on the young narrator's family.... Despite the wealth of cultural information conveyed, this is a universal novel...." *Booklist* contributor Hazel Rochman wrote that, although Kim includes a bit too much local color and culture, this "unforgettable novel ... will appeal as much to adults as to older teens." The critic concluded that, as in Laura Esquivel's adult novel *Like Water for Chocolate,* the "domestic details tell a heartfelt story of women in family and community." Writing in *School Library Journal,* Carolyn Noah called *The Long Season* a "compelling novel" and noted that Kim's vivid imagery "captures each thoughtfully ren-

HELEN KIM

dered character . . . . Despite the age of the protagonist, the book's thematic sophistication make it an outstanding choice for thoughtful YAs."

■ Works Cited

Comerford, Lynda Brill, "Flying Starts," *Publishers Weekly,* December 16, 1996, p. 36.

Devereaux, Elizabeth, and Diane Roback, review of *The Long Season of Rain, Publishers Weekly,* November 4, 1996, p. 77.

Noah, Carolyn, review of *The Long Season of Rain, School Library Journal,* December, 1996, p. 139.

Parravano, Martha V., review of *The Long Season of Rain, Horn Book,* January-February, 1997, pp. 59-60.

Rochman, Hazel, review of *The Long Season of Rain, Booklist,* November 1, 1996, p. 490.

■ For More Information See

PERIODICALS

Kirkus Reviews, October 15, 1996, p. 1534.
New York Times Book Review, March 16, 1997, p. 26.
Voice of Youth Advocates, February, 1997, p. 328.

* * *

KIPPAX, Frank
See NEEDLE, Jan

* * *

KITAMURA, Satoshi 1956-

■ Personal

Born June 11, 1956, in Tokyo, Japan; moved to England, 1983; son of Testuo (a retail consultant) and Fusae (Sadanaga) Kitamura; married Yoko Sugisaki (an interior designer), December 15, 1987. *Education:* Attended schools in Japan.

■ Career

Freelance illustrator, 1975—.

■ Awards, Honors

Mother Goose Award, Books for Children Book Club, 1983, for *Angry Arthur; What's Inside* was selected one of *New York Times* Notable Books, 1985; Children's Science Book Award (Great Britain) and Children's Science Book Award, New York Academy of Sciences, both 1987, both for *When Sheep Cannot Sleep.*

■ Writings

SELF-ILLUSTRATED

What's Inside: The Alphabet Book, Farrar, Straus (New York City), 1985.

Paper Jungle: A Cut-out Book, A. & C. Black (London), 1985.

When Sheep Cannot Sleep: The Counting Book, A. & C. Black, 1986, Farrar, Straus, 1986.

Lily Takes a Walk, Blackie (London), 1987, Dutton (New York City), 1987.

Captain Toby, Blackie, 1987, Dutton, 1988.

UFO Diary, Andersen (London), 1989, Farrar, Straus, 1990.

From Acorn to Zoo, Andersen, 1991, as *From Acorn to Zoo and Everything In Between in Alphabetical Order,* Farrar, Straus, 1992.

Sheep in Wolves' Clothing, Andersen, 1995, Farrar, Straus, 1996.

Squirrel Is Hungry, Andersen, 1996, Farrar, Straus, 1996.

Cat Is Sleepy, Andersen, 1996, Farrar, Straus, 1996.

Dog Is Thirsty, Andersen, 1996, Farrar, Straus, 1996.

Duck Is Dirty, Andersen, 1996, Farrar, Straus, 1996.

Bathtime Boots, Andersen, 1997.

A Friend for Boots, Andersen, 1997.

Goldfish Hide-and-Seek, Andersen, 1997, Farrar, Straus, 1997.

ILLUSTRATOR

Hiawyn Oram, *Angry Arthur,* Andersen, 1982, Harcourt (New York City), 1982.

Hiawyn Oram, *Ned and the Joybaloo,* Anderson, 1983, Farrar, Straus, 1988.

Roger McGough, *Sky in the Pie* (poems), Viking, 1983.

Hiawyn Oram, *In the Attic,* Andersen, 1984, Holt, 1985.

The Flying Trunk (anthology), Andersen, 1986.

Alison Sage and Helen Wire, compilers, *The Happy Christmas Book,* A. & C. Black, 1986.

Pat Thomson, *My Friend Mr. Morris,* Gollancz, 1987, Delacorte, 1987.

The Happy Christmas Book (anthology), Hippo (London), 1987.

Andy Soutter, *Scrapyard,* A. & C. Black, 1988.

A Children's Chorus (anthology), Dutton, 1989.

Hiawyn Oram, *A Boy Wants a Dinosaur,* Andersen, 1990, Farrar, Straus, 1991.

Hiawyn Oram, *Speaking for Ourselves* (poems), Methuen (London), 1990.

Carl Davis and Hiawyn Oram, *A Creepy Crawly Song Book,* Farrar, Straus, 1993.

Mick Fitzmaurice, *Morris Macmillipede: The Toast of Brussels Sprout,* Andersen (London), 1994.

Stephen Webster, *Inside My House,* Riverswift, 1994.

Richard Edwards, *Fly with the Birds: An Oxford Word and Rhyme Book,* Oxford University Press, 1995, as *Fly with the Birds: A Word and Rhyme Book,* Orchard (New York City), 1996.

Brenda Walpole, *Hello, Is There Anyone There?,* Riverswift, 1995.

Brenda Walpole, *Living and Working Together,* Riverswift, 1995.

Stephen Webster, *Me and My Body,* Riverswift, 1995.

John Agard, *We Animals Would Like a Word with You,* Bodley Head, 1996.

■ Sidelights

Praised for his ability to interweave Japanese and Western visual traditions in the engaging illustrations he has contributed to the works of numerous writers, Satoshi Kitamura has also become well known as an author of children's books. With strong technical abilities and a gift for visual humor, Kitamura adds a whimsical, often unconventional touch to many traditional children's book formats, including alphabet and counting books. He is widely recognized for his use of simplified angular shapes and a rich palette of earth and sky tones. As David Wiesner noted in the *New York Times Book Review,* Kitamura's books "are suffused with both warmth and wit .... The simplicity of Mr. Kitamura's art is deceptive. A superb draftsman and colorist, he uses pen and brush to create remarkably lush and textured illustrations." Among the author/illustrator's most well-received titles are the award-winning counting book *When Sheep Cannot Sleep, Sheep in Wolves' Clothing,* and *UFO Diary,* a 1989 work that *School Librarian* contributor Sue Smedley praised as "a sophisticated book acknowledging that children deserve quality texts and illustrations."

Kitamura was born and raised in Tokyo, Japan. In 1983, he moved to England, making his permanent home in London. By the time he became a resident of Great Britain, Kitamura's first children's book illustration project, Hiawyn Oram's *Angry Arthur,* had already been published in both England and the United States. An award-winning book, *Angry Arthur* caused publishers to take notice of the young Japanese illustrator and his work; numerous projects were soon awarded him in quick succession.

In 1985, Kitamura published *What's Inside: The Alphabet Book,* the first of his many solo children's book projects. Full of visual clues to help lead children through alphabetically ordered pairs of lower-cased letters, *What's Inside* was dubbed "gloriously exuberant" by a *Junior Bookshelf* critic and praised by *School Library Journal* contributor Patricia Homer as a book "which will delight readers who are up to a verbal and visual challenge." Denise M. Wilms echoed such praise in *Booklist,* maintaining that the "imaginative quality" of Kitamura's full-color line and wash illustrations "make for a fresh, engaging display of letters that will stand up to more than one close look."

In yet another alphabet book, Kitamura builds young readers' vocabulary, one letter at a time. *From Acorn to Zoo* features pages chock-full of illustrated objects that begin with the same letter, allowing children's vocabularies to be "expanded almost painlessly and [their] capacity for observation sharpened," in the opinion of a *Junior Bookshelf* reviewer. Each illustration features energetic pen-and-ink renderings of an unusual assortment of animals and objects, richly colored and positioned on the page in ways that readers will find humorous. For example, on one page a hefty hippo tests the strength of a hammock by sitting in it and playing his harmonica while a harp and coat hanger can be found nearby. In a similar vein, Kitamura tackles introductory mathematics by illustrating the quandary of an insomniac named Woolly in *When Sheep Cannot Sleep,* a 1-2-3 book. Rather than lay about in the dark, Woolly goes on a search for objects grouped first in pairs, then in threes, fours, and so on up to twenty-two, before tiring himself out and falling asleep in an abandoned country cottage. But Kitamura does not make things any too easy for his reader; on each page the object Woolly finds must also be discovered by the reader and its quantity totaled up. Calling *When Sheep Cannot Sleep* "a joy to look at," *Horn Book* contributor Anita Silvey added that Kitamura's "slightly primitive drawing style is delightful, making counting the objects or just looking at the book a great deal of fun." Ilene

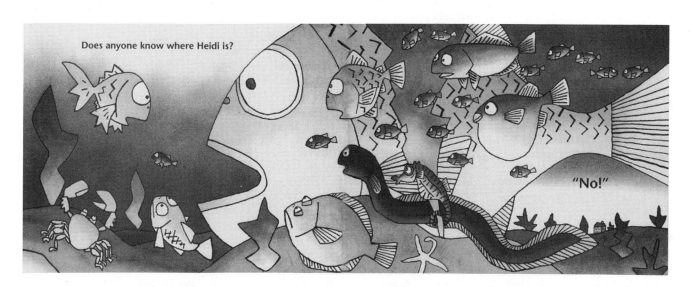

From *Goldfish Hide-and-Seek,* written and illustrated by Satoshi Kitamura.

Cooper of *Booklist* noted that Kitamura's "squared-off sheep has an endearingly goofy look that kids and adults will love."

Goofy looking sheep serve as the focus of Kitamura's *Sheep in Wolves' Clothing.* Hubert, Georgina, and Gogol are sheep who hoof it on down to the seashore for one last dip in the ocean before the chill of winter sets in. Near the beach, they meet a group of wolves enjoying the fall afternoon by taking time off from work at their knitwear factory to take in a round of golf. The wolves generously offer to watch the sheep's warm wool coats while the seabound swimmers take their plunge; not surprisingly, neither wolves nor wool are anywhere to be found when the soaked sheep return. Fortunately, the sheep call in the services of Elliott Baa, a fully-fleeced ace detective, who follows the woolly trail to its conclusion. "Younger children will delight in the climactic brouhaha and will also find [*Sheep in Wolves' Clothing*] a satisfying mystery story," according to *Horn Book* reviewer Margaret Bush.

Other books by Kitamura that showcase his vivid imagination and ability to capture a child's attention include *UFO Diary,* the observations of an outer-space visitor who accidentally lands on Earth and is befriended by a young boy. Although never depicted in Kitamura's colorful drawings, the alien provides readers with an opportunity to "see our planet's natural abundance and beauty with fresh eyes," according to John Peters, a *School Library Journal* contributor. In *Captain Toby,* a young boy becomes convinced that the storm raging outside his bedroom window has blown his house out to sea. And in *Lily Takes a Walk,* a young girl's pet dog has a vivid imagination, scaring up shadows of everything from vampires to monsters as his owner takes him for his evening walk around the block.

"I am interested in different angles of looking at things," Kitamura once told *SATA.* "I find great potential in picture books where visual and verbal fuse to experience and [I also] experiment with these angles. Also, there is an advantage of universality of expression in this medium due to the clarity required for young readers."

■ Works Cited

Bush, Margaret, review of *Sheep in Wolves' Clothing,* *Horn Book,* July, 1996, p. 450.

Cooper, Ilene, review of *When Sheep Cannot Sleep,* *Booklist,* October 1, 1986, p. 273.

Review of *From Acorn to Zoo, Junior Bookshelf,* June, 1992, p. 104.

Homer, Patricia, review of *What's Inside: The Alphabet Book, School Library Journal,* September, 1985, p. 120.

Peters, John, review of *UFO Diary, School Library Journal,* January, 1990, p. 84.

Silvey, Anita, review of *When Sheep Cannot Sleep, Horn Book,* November, 1986, pp. 736-37.

Smedley, Sue, review of *UFO Diary, School Librarian,* November, 1989, p. 145.

Review of *What's Inside: The Alphabet Book, Junior Bookshelf,* October, 1985, p. 212.

Wiesner, David, "A Job for Elliott Baa, Private Eye," *New York Times Book Review,* May 19, 1996, p. 27.

Wilms, Denise M., review of *What's Inside: The Alphabet Book, Booklist,* September 1, 1985, p. 64.

■ For More Information See

PERIODICALS

Booklist, July, 1992, p. 1943; May 1, 1996, p. 1512.

Growing Point, January, 1987, p. 4745; February, 1990, p. 5269.

Horn Book, March, 1990, pp. 190-91; May, 1992, p. 330.

Junior Bookshelf, February, 1987, p. 21; August, 1989, p. 162.

Kirkus Reviews, November 1, 1987, p. 1575; August 15, 1989, p. 1247; June 15, 1996, p. 906; January 1, 1998, p. 58.

New York Times Book Review, June 16, 1985, p. 30; March 6, 1988, p. 29.

Publishers Weekly, September 30, 1988, p. 65; June 24, 1996, p. 62.

School Librarian, February, 1988, p. 16.

School Library Journal, December, 1986, p. 90; November, 1987, pp. 93-94; March, 1989, p. 164; July, 1992, p. 60.

* * *

KUSHNER, Ellen (Ruth) 1955-

■ Personal

Born October 6, 1955, in Washington, DC; daughter of Irving (a medical doctor) and Enid (a social worker and lawyer; maiden name, Lupeson) Kushner. *Education:* Attended Bryn Mawr College, 1973-75; Columbia University, A.B., 1977. *Religion:* Jewish. *Hobbies and other interests:* World travel, eating at various restaurants, singing, socializing.

■ Addresses

Agent—Julie Fallowfield, McIntosh and Otis, 310 Madison Ave., New York, NY 10017.

■ Career

Writer. Ace Books, New York City, editorial assistant, 1977-79; Pocket Books, New York City, associate editor, 1979-80; freelance copywriter, reviewer, and artist's representative, 1980-87; Public Radio International/WGBH Radio, Boston, MA, producer/announcer, beginning 1987, *Sound and Spirit* (public radio show), host/producer, 1996—.

■ Awards, Honors

World Fantasy Award, 1991, Mythopoeic award, 1991, and "Book for the Teen Age" Citation, New York

Public Library, all for *Thomas the Rhymer;* 1997 NFCB Silver Reel award, for *Sound and Spirit* radio show.

■ Writings

FANTASY NOVELS

Swordspoint: A Melodrama of Manners, Arbor House (New York City), 1987.
Thomas the Rhymer: A Romance, Morrow, 1990.
St. Nicholas and the Valley Beyond: A Christmas Legend, illustrated by Richard W. Burhans, Viking Studio, 1994.

FOR CHILDREN; "CHOOSE-YOUR-OWN-ADVENTURE" SERIES

Outlaws of Sherwood Forest, illustrated by Judith Mitchell, Bantam, 1985.
The Enchanted Kingdom, illustrated by Judith Mitchell, Bantam, 1986.
Statue of Liberty Adventure, illustrated by Ted Enik, Bantam, 1986.
The Mystery of the Secret Room, illustrated by Judith Mitchell, Bantam, 1986.
Knights of the Round Table, illustrated by Judith Mitchell, Bantam, 1988.

PLAYS

Author of radio plays, including (co-author) *Which Way's Witch: A June Foray Halloween Spell,* 1991; (also producer, director, and narrator) *Festival of Liberation: The Passover Story in World Music,* 1992; (also producer, director, and narrator) *A Door Is Opened: A Jewish High Holiday Meditation,* 1992; and (also producer, director, and narrator) *Beyond 1492: 500 Years of Jewish Song and Legend,* 1992.

OTHER

(Editor) *Basilisk,* Ace, 1980.
(Editor with Donald G. Keller and Della Sherman) *The Horns of Elfland,* Dutton, 1997.

■ Sidelights

"When I was a kid," Ellen Kushner recalled in an article for *Locus,* "the things that meant the most to me were really good books, especially fantasy, and I thought the people who wrote those books were the happy of the earth, the blessed singing in the heavenly choir. And I wanted to be like *that.* I was a geeky kid, or perceived as one.... I put on plays with the other kids, I did all the artistic stuff, but writing is what I got a lot of strokes for, from my family and my teachers."

Kushner entered publishing as an editorial assistant at Ace Books. "I was the baby there," she wrote in *Locus.* "Three weeks after Jim [Baen] started, I was assisting him. Because I knew fantasy really well, and I had read a lot of stuff that had been in hardcover but never in paper, I moved up. Also, because I was such a complete incompetent as an assistant. So they hired Susan Allison. My whole generation is in charge now...."
Kushner eventually went to work for David Hartwell at Pocket Timescape. She remarked: "I don't like doing

ELLEN KUSHNER

things unless I can be successful at them, so thank God I was quite successful quite fast, and was able therefore to bow out at a high enough level that I knew what the ride was gonna be like, and I didn't want to stay on it. I moved up to associate editor at Pocket/Simon and Schuster, and I think they were about to either promote me or give me a raise. I thought, 'This is not what I want to do with my life.' I don't regret leaving."

In 1987, Kushner moved to Boston and began a career in public radio at WGBH-FM. With her unusual blend of classical and contemporary music, she created the diverse music mix of *NightAir.* On Sunday afternoons she hosted *Caravan,* a program of folk, roots, and worldbeat music. Taking her upbeat style in a new direction, Kushner hosted *The International Music Series* from 1989 to 1991. Her innovative program consisted of classical music which was heard by over 130 stations on American Public Radio. In 1992, she produced, hosted, wrote, and directed three award-winning Jewish holiday specials. She has also been heard on National Public Radio as a contributor to *A Note to You* and *Performance Today.* Kushner is perhaps best known as the host and producer of the award-winning public radio program *Sound and Spirit.* Launched in April, 1996, *Sound and Spirit* is currently on over ninety stations around the United States and on Europe's RadioOne.

Kushner's *Swordspoint: A Melodrama of Manners,* published in 1987, depicts a fantasy world of antiheroes, class differences, and non-traditional romance. Richard St. Vier is a master swordsman who lives amongst thieves and beggars in a district called Riverside. The aristocrats on the Hill look to settle their differences by soliciting brave swordsmen to fight for them. Richard finds himself in a sequence of unpredictable events when he is hired to kill Michael Goduin, a young nobleman. The swordsman accidentally kills someone else instead. When his lover, Alec, is kidnapped, Richard kills again, which leads to his arrest for two deaths. Kushner combines dissimilar subjects, "persuasively drawing readers into this distinctive fantasy world," contends *Booklist* contributor Peter L. Robertson. A reviewer for *Publishers Weekly* calls the book "intelligent, humorous and dramatic with a fine, malicious feeling for the operation of gossip in a close society."

Based on a traditional Scottish ballad, and rich with British folklore, *Thomas the Rhymer: A Romance* highlights Kushner's skill as a fantasy writer. An accomplished harper and rhymer, Thomas intrigues a curious neighbor, Elspeth, with his interesting stories. Just when Elspeth and the rhymer become friends, Thomas is seduced and held captive by the Queen of Elfland in her domain for seven years. When the Queen finally releases Thomas, she gives him the gift of prophecy, allowing him to speak only the truth. Once Thomas returns to the real world, his new way of life causes problems. According to a reviewer for *Publishers Weekly,* the novel is a "happy blend of discreet scholarship and literary style." *Booklist* contributor Roland Green adds that it is an "excellent" book "recommended for medium-size or large fantasy collections."

■ Works Cited

Green, Roland, review of *Thomas the Rhymer: A Romance, Booklist,* March 15, 1990, p. 1420.

Kushner, Ellen, "Ellen Kushner: True Fantasy," *Locus,* April, 1992, pp. 5, 65-66.

Robertson, Peter L., review of *Swordspoint: A Melodrama of Manners, Booklist,* November 15, 1987, pp. 541-42.

Review of *Swordspoint: A Melodrama of Manners, Publishers Weekly,* October 2, 1987, p. 86.

Review of *Thomas the Rhymer: A Romance, Publishers Weekly,* February 16, 1990, p. 71.

■ For More Information See

PERIODICALS

Quill and Quire, September, 1994, p. 68.

School Library Journal, September, 1986, p. 151; April, 1987, p. 116.

Voice of Youth Advocates, June, 1989, p. 110.

L

LEITCH, Patricia 1933-

■ Personal

Born July 13, 1933, in Paisley, Renfrewshire, Scotland; daughter of James Ritchie (an engineer) and Anna (Mitchell) Leitch. *Education:* Craigie College of Education, primary teacher's diploma, 1967.

■ Career

Glasgow Corporation and Renfrewshire County Library, Library assistant, 1954-59; Kilmacolm Riding School, instructor, 1960-61; shop assistant in various book shops, 1962-63; Troon Primary School, Ayrshire, Scotland, 1968-70; typist for various employers, 1971-73; writer, 1974—.

■ Writings

A Pony of Our Own, Blackie & Son, 1960.
To Save a Pony, Hutchinson, 1960.
Rosette for Royal, Blackie & Son, 1963.
Janet Young Rider, Constable, 1963, published in the United States as *Last Summer to Ride,* Funk, 1965.
The Black Loch, Collins, 1963, Funk, 1968.
Highland Pony Trek, Collins, 1964.
Riding Course Summer, Collins, 1965.
Cross Country Pony, Blackie & Son, 1965.
Treasure to the East, Gollancz, 1966.
Jacky Jumps to the Top, Collins, 1973.
First Pony, Collins, 1973.
Afraid to Ride, Collins, 1973.
Rebel Pony, Collins, 1973.
Pony Surprise, Collins, 1974.
Dream of Fair Horses, Collins, 1975, published in the United States as *The Fields of Praise,* Lippincott, 1978.
Gallop to the Hills [and] *Horse in a Million,* Armada, 1976.
For Love of a Horse [and] *A Devil to Ride,* Collins, 1976.
Summer Riders, Collins, 1977.
Windows: Poems, New Leaves, 1978.
Night of the Red Horse, Lions, 1978.

The Magic Pony, Fontana, 1982.
Ride Like the Wind, Armada, 1983.
Chestnut Gold, Armada, 1984.
Jump for the Moon, Fontana, 1985.
Horse of Fire, Armada, 1986.
Running Wild, Armada, 1988.
Night of the Red Horse [and] *Gallop to the Hills,* Armada, 1988.
Three Great Jinny Stories, Armada, 1989.
Gallop to the Hills, Lions, 1992.
For Love of a Horse, Lions, 1992.
The Special Pony, Lions, 1992.
A Pony to Jump, Lions, 1992.
For Love of a Horse, A Devil to Ride, [and] *The Summer Riders,* Armada, 1992.
Night of the Red Horse, Gallop to the Hills, [and] *Horse in a Million,* Lions, 1993.
For Love of a Horse [and] *A Devil to Ride,* Lions, 1993.
The Summer Riders [and] *Night of the Red Horse,* Lions, 1994.
Horse of Fire [and] *Running Wild,* Collins, 1995.
The Pony Ride [and] *Ride Like the Wind,* Lions, 1995.
Pony Puzzle, Lions, 1995.
The Stolen Pony, Lions, 1995.
Chestnut Gold [and] *Jump for the Moon,* Lions, 1995.
The Special Pony, A Pony to Jump, [and] *Cross-Country Gallop,* Collins, 1996.
Mystery Horse, HarperCollins, 1997.

"HORSESHOES" SERIES

Cross-Country Gallop, Lions, 1993, HarperCollins, 1996.
Pony Club Rider, Lions, 1993, HarperTrophy, 1996.
The Perfect Horse, HarperTrophy, 1996.
Jumping Lessons, HarperTrophy, 1996.
Show Jumper Wanted, HarperCollins, 1997.

■ Sidelights

Patricia Leitch once told *SATA:* "I have always had a vivid imagination being typical of the Jungian category of introverted intuitive.... I have neither a visual nor an aural imagination. It is something else. Most of my books are 'pony books,' some are fantasies but really

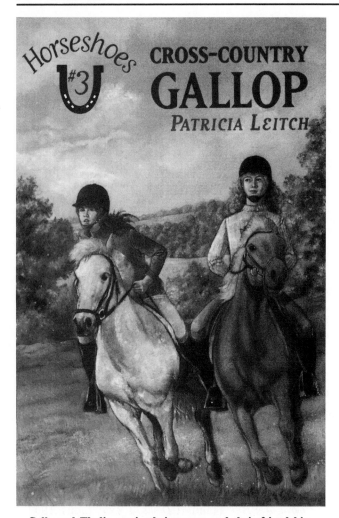

Sally and Thalia strain their nerves and their friendship when they decide to compete together in a horse show in this installment of Patricia Leitch's "Horseshoes" series. (Cover illustration by Stephen Marchesi.)

they all say the same thing—'Sin is behovely, but all shall be well, and all manner of thing shall be well.'"

In *The Fields of Praise,* Gillian dreams of owning a pony and riding in the Horse of the Year competition, but her father is a critically acclaimed novelist whose works earn plenty of respect but little money. Finally, he compromises his high artistic principles, writes a best-selling crime novel, buys his boyhood home, and moves the family to the country. Then Gillian's dreams begin to materialize when their neighbor, Mr. Ramsey, chooses her to train and ride his fine pony, Perdita, for competition. According to *Booklist*'s Denise M. Wilms, Leitch gives "food for thought" in depicting "the price paid by the [family] for their father's artistic principles." Whitney Rogge, in *School Library Journal,* noted that Leitch develops her theme with "understanding and delicacy," and Ann A. Flowers of *Horn Book* praised the novel as a "well-written, first-class horse story."

Leitch has written a number of "pony book" series, one of which features a young girl and her horse as central characters. Set in Scotland, the tales revolve around twelve-year-old Jinny and Shantib, the Arab mare she

rescues from a circus. Regarding one such work, *The Night of the Red Horse,* Margery Fisher of *Growing Point* noted that, unlike the narrowly defined characters of many other horse stories, Jinny is "more lively" because she "is allowed a range of feeling and opinion outside stable and tack-room life." Jinny's relationship with her horse, her family, and the mystical goddess Epona form the core of the novel. *Growing Point*'s Fisher also noted the importance of character in Leitch's tales. About *Chestnut Gold,* another of the books featuring Jinny as central protagonist, Fisher stated that "events are arranged round and justified by certain ideas which depend as much on character as they do on action." Leitch's emphasis on character becomes evident when Jinny's concern for her horse and the open Scottish countryside she calls home is tested by a film director whose values are contrary to her own.

Another series of horse stories by Leitch centers on two young friends, Sally and Thalia. In *Cross-Country Gallop* and *Pony Club Rider,* the pair engage in some "rollicking adventures," according to Jill Warren in *School Librarian.* Warren also commented that Leitch "skillfully captured the pony-mad world of the young riders" in both novels. *School Library Journal* contributor Betty Teague recommended *Pony Club Rider* for

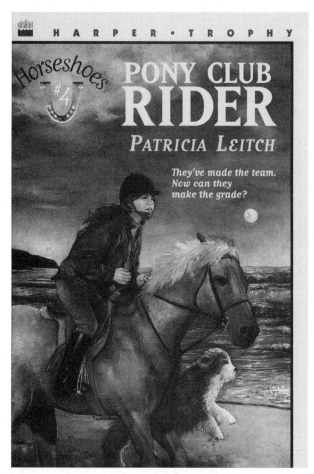

Sally and Thalia, old friends and horse riding enthusiasts, try to hone their skills for the benefit of the Pony Club team. (Cover illustration by Stephen Marchesi.)

"horse enthusiasts." The story revolves around a horse show in which Sally and Thalia, as part of the Tarent Pony Club team, practice to compete in the Junior One-Day Event. Teague noted that readers will enjoy the suspense of who will be chosen to compete and the detailed descriptions of events, and maintained that episodes about a bearded collie and a hound running parallel to the main plot make the story attractive to even more young animal lovers.

■ Works Cited

Fisher, Margery, review of *Chestnut Gold, Growing Point,* May, 1984, p. 4253.
Fisher, Margery, review of *The Night of the Red Horse, Growing Point,* November, 1978, pp. 3408-09.
Flowers, Ann A., review of *The Fields of Praise, Horn Book,* August, 1978, p. 403.
Rogge, Whitney, review of *The Fields of Praise, School Library Journal,* September, 1978, p. 160.
Teague, Betty, review of *Pony Club Rider, School Library Journal,* December, 1996, p. 123.
Warren, Jill, review of *Cross-Country Gallop* and *Pony Club Rider, School Librarian,* November, 1993, p. 155.
Wilms, Denise M., review of *The Fields of Praise, Booklist,* May 1, 1978, p. 1435.

■ For More Information See

PERIODICALS

School Library Journal, May, 1997, p. 136.*

*   *   *

LEVINE, Gail Carson 1947-

■ Personal

Born September 17, 1947, in New York, NY; daughter of David (an owner of a commercial art studio) and Sylvia (a teacher; maiden name, Jacobson) Carson; married David Levine (a software developer), September 2, 1967. *Education:* City College of the City University of New York, B.A., 1969.

■ Addresses

Home and office—Brewster, NY. *Agent*—Ginger Knowlton, Curtis Brown Ltd., 10 Astor Pl., New York, NY 10003. *Electronic mail*—gclevine@cloudq.net.

■ Career

Children's book author. New York State Department of Labor, New York City, employment interviewer, 1970-82; New York State Department of Commerce, New York City, administrative assistant, 1982-86; New York State Department of Social Services, New York City, welfare administrator, 1986-96; New York State Department of Labor, New York City, welfare administrator, 1986—.

GAIL CARSON LEVINE

■ Awards, Honors

Best Books for Young Adults and Quick Picks for Young Adults citations, American Library Association, and Newbery Honor Book, American Library Association, all 1998, all for *Ella Enchanted.*

■ Writings

Ella Enchanted, HarperCollins, 1997.

Author of the script for the children's musical *Space-napped,* produced in Brooklyn, NY.

■ Work in Progress

The Wish (tentative title), a contemporary novel for children, dealing with the subject of popularity; *Dave at Night* (tentative title), a historical novel for children, about an orphanage and the Harlem Renaissance, completion expected in 1998; a four-book series of fractured fairy tales for children ages seven to ten.

■ Sidelights

Gail Carson Levine told *SATA:* "I grew up in New York City. My father was interested in writing, and my mother wrote full-length plays in rhyme for her students to perform. Both of them had an absolute reverence for creativity and creative people, a reverence that they passed along to my sister and me. My sister, Rani, is a wonderful painter of Jamaican subjects and a professor of fine arts.

"I didn't plan to be a writer, even though I started writing early. In elementary school I was a charter member of the Scribble Scrabble Club, and in high school my poems were published in an anthology of student poetry, but my ambition was to act or to be a painter like my older sister. My interest in the theater led to my first writing experience as an adult. My husband David wrote the music and lyrics, and I wrote the book for a children's musical, *Spacenapped,* and that was produced by a neighborhood theater in Brooklyn.

"It was painting that brought me to writing in earnest for children. I took a class in writing and illustrating children's books and found that I was much more interested in the writing than in the illustrating. Before *Ella Enchanted,* I wrote several picture books and a novel loosely based on my father's childhood in an orphanage in Harlem in the 1920s (all unpublished so far). I'm revising that first novel, bringing in elements of the Harlem Renaissance, an exciting time in our history.

"*Ella Enchanted* began in another class. I had to write something and couldn't think of a plot, so I decided to write a Cinderella story because it already had a plot! Then, when I thought about Cinderella's character, I realized she was too much of a goody-two-shoes for me, and I would hate her before I finished ten pages. That's when I came up with the curse: she's only good because she has to be, and she is in constant rebellion.

"The meaning of what one writes is rarely transparent. Many people are cursed with obedience and with attending too much to other people's expectations. We are cursed with constraints on our freedom to act as we wish, even uncertainty about what we wish. I know I am!

"As a child I loved fairy tales because the story, the what-comes-next, is paramount. As an adult I am fascinated by their logic and illogic. Ella's magic book gave me the chance to answer a question that always plagued me about *The Shoemaker and the Elves:* why the elves abandon the shoemaker. I came up with one answer, but many are possible—and I think the real solution goes to the heart of gratitude and recognition, an example of the depth in fairy tales.

"Most of my job life has had to do with welfare, first helping people find work and finally as an administrator. The earlier experience was more direct and satisfying, and I enjoy thinking that a bunch of people somewhere are doing better today than they might have done if not for me. The issues in welfare are so complex and are reduced to such heated one-liners that it's no wonder we never get anywhere in solving the problem. Most of the recipients I've known have been extraordinarily decent and good-natured under terrible circumstances. I haven't yet found a way to write about the subject, but I hope to someday.

"My husband David and I, and our Airedale Jake, live in Brewster, New York, in a two-hundred-year-old farmhouse. While I worked in New York City, I did most of my writing on Metro North, and I am most grateful to my fellow passengers for their vast indifference to the scribbler at their elbows.

"My advice to aspiring writers is: suspend judgment of your work and keep writing. Take advantage of the wonderful community of writers for children—who are always ready with helpful criticism and support in the struggle to succeed. And be patient—writing and glaciers advance at about the same pace!"

■ For More Information See

PERIODICALS

ALAN Review, fall, 1997.
Booklist, April 15, 1997, p. 1423.
Horn Book, May-June, 1997, p. 325.
Kirkus Reviews, February 1, 1997, p. 225.
Publishers Weekly, March 31, 1997, p. 75; June 30, 1997, p. 28.
School Library Journal, April, 1997, p. 138.

* * *

LINDQUIST, Rowena Cory 1958-
(Rowena Cory)

■ Personal

Born February 5, 1958, in Brisbane, Australia; children: six.

■ Addresses

Home—65 School Rd., Wynnum West, Queensland 4178, Australia. *Electronic mail*—rowena@powerup. com.au.

■ Career

Writer. *Member:* Australian Society of Authors.

■ Writings

UNDER NAME ROWENA CORY

Sport-Billy at the Ancient Olympics (stories), illustrated by Christopher Johnston, Budget Books (Melbourne, Australia), 1984.
Sport-Billy at Vanda's Space Games (stories), illustrated by Stephen Campbell, Budget Books, 1984.
Sport-Billy Climbs Mt. Everest (stories), illustrated by Christopher Johnston, Budget Books, 1984.
Sport-Billy Meets Leonardo da Vinci (stories), illustrated by Stephen Campbell, Budget Books, 1984.
(And illustrator with Christopher Johnston) *Splishes and Sploshes* (poems), edited by Debbie Powell and Andrea Butler, Mimosa Publications (Hawthorn, Australia), 1989.
(With Tony Barber; and illustrator with Christopher Johnston) *The Lost Forests,* Matchbooks (South Melbourne, Australia), 1989.

ROWENA CORY LINDQUIST

AS ROWENA CORY LINDQUIST

Capped!, illustrated by David Stanley, Scholastic Australia (Sydney), 1996.
Big or Little, Scholastic Australia, 1997.
How Did It Happen?, Scholastic Australia, 1997.
Mum Went to Get Pizza, Scholastic Australia, 1997.
The Intruder, illustrated by Christopher Johnston, Lothian Books (Port Melbourne, Australia), 1997.
Faceless Fear, Macmillan, 1997.
The Insiders, Macmillan, 1997.
A Stone on the Gate Post, Macmillan, 1997.

■ Sidelights

Rowena Cory Lindquist told *SATA:* "As a mother of six children, I work at the 'coal face.' My kids keep me in touch with the concerns of modern youngsters. Our house is never quiet. I sometimes feel like I'm living in a manic episode of *The Brady Bunch.* I keep waiting for the laugh track!

"I've sold more than a dozen books, ranging from early readers to young adult works. I like producing books for children because you can write about characters who feel things intensely. They might be intensely happy, or just plain naughty, but they are never boring!"*

LISLE, Holly 1960-

■ Personal

Born in October, 1960, in Salem, OH. *Education:* Richmond Community College, associate degree in nursing, 1982.

■ Addresses

Agent—Russell Galen, Scovil, Chichak, Galen Literary Agency, 381 Park Avenue South, Suite 1020, New York, NY 10016. *Electronic mail*—Holly.Lisle@sff.net.

■ Career

Writer. Worked as an advertising representative for a newspaper, sang in restaurants, taught guitar, did commercial artwork, and worked as a registered nurse for ten years, primarily in emergency and critical care units; became full-time writer, 1993—. *Member:* Science Fiction Writers of America.

■ Awards, Honors

Compton Crook Award for Best First Novel, 1993; finalist for John W. Campbell Award for Best New Writer, 1993 and 1994.

■ Writings

"ARHEL" NOVELS

Fire in the Mist, Baen (Riverdale, NY), 1992.
Bones of the Past, Baen, 1993.
Mind of the Magic, Baen, 1995.

"GLENRAVEN" NOVELS

(With Marion Zimmer Bradley) *Glenraven,* Baen, 1996.
(With Marion Zimmer Bradley) *In the Rift,* Baen, 1998.

"DEVIL'S POINT" NOVELS

Sympathy for the Devil, Baen, 1996.
(With Walter Spence) *The Devil and Dan Cooley,* Baen, 1996.
(With Ted Nolan) *Hell on High,* Baen, 1997.

"BARD'S TALE" NOVELS

(With Aaron Allston) *Thunder of the Captains,* Baen, 1996.
(With Aaron Allston) *Wrath of the Princes,* Baen, 1997.
Curse of the Black Heron, Baen, in press.

OTHER NOVELS

Minerva Wakes, Baen, 1993.
(With Mercedes Lackey) *When the Bough Breaks,* Baen, 1993.
(With S. M. Stirling) *The Rose Sea,* Baen, 1994.
(With Chris Guin) *Mall, Mayhem and Magic,* Baen, 1995.
Hunting the Corrigan's Blood, Baen, 1997.
Diplomacy of Wolves, Warner, 1998.

Contributor of short stories to anthologies, including *Women at War,* edited by Lois McMaster Bujold, Tor, 1992; *The Enchanter Reborn,* edited by L. Sprague de Camp and Christopher Stasheff, Baen, 1992; and *Chicks in Chainmail,* edited by Esther Friesner, Baen, 1995.

■ Work in Progress

Vengeance of Dragons and *Courage of Falcons.*

■ Sidelights

Holly Lisle is an author of fantasy novels that often center on female protagonists who possess or come under the influence of magical powers. In her first novel, *Fire in the Mist,* Lisle presents the story of Faia, a young shepherdess who exhibits a natural talent for magic. Faia joins a group of more advanced practitioners in order to develop her abilities but ultimately rebels against the strict social arrangement of the society, in which men and women reside separately and are celibate. Carolyn Cushman, reviewing *Fire in the Mist* in *Locus,* called the novel "exceptionally well-crafted and

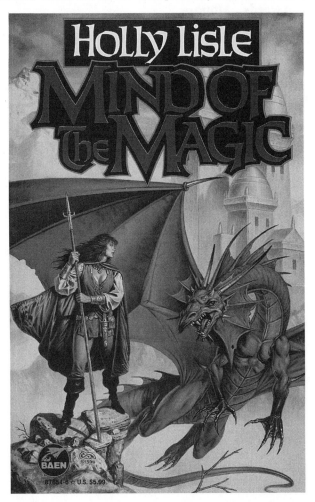

Powerful but ill-fated mage Faia Rissedotte must control the chaos that erupts when all the inhabitants of her town acquire magic powers in Holly Lisle's science fiction thriller. (Cover illustration by Clyde Caldwell.)

readable," concluding that the work is "a real page-turner that should be highly popular with genre fans."

In *Minerva Wakes,* protagonist Minerva Kiakra inadvertently gains possession of a wedding ring with magical powers, setting off a series of fantasy adventures that include an encounter with a dragon, the abduction of Minerva's children, and a trip to an alternate universe. Susan E. Chmurynsky, reviewing Lisle's second novel in *Kliatt,* called *Minerva Wakes* "a good natured and breezy tale that moves along at a rapid clip."

In *Mind of the Magic,* Lisle returns to the saga of Faia, the protagonist of *Fire in the Mist,* who has grown into adulthood and is now the mother of a five-year-old child. The novel centers on circumstances that evolve when all the inhabitants of the town of Arhel suddenly develop magical abilities, then just as suddenly lose their gifts, leaving the town in a nightmarish state of ruin. Through Faia the community is reborn and establishes harmonious contacts with the Klaue, nonhuman beings who cohabit the region. Commenting on *Mind of the Magic,* Sister Avila Lamb in *Kliatt* wrote that "there are instances of very fine writing.... [R]eaders will be charmed by the delightful characters."

Coauthored with Chris Guin, Lisle's young adult fantasy novel *Mall, Mayhem and Magic* was published in 1995. In the story, magic wreaks havoc in a local mall when a bookstore clerk attempts to cast a love spell on the girl he admires. Karen S. Ellis, reviewing *Mall, Mayhem and Magic* in *Kliatt,* noted that coauthors Lisle and Guin "have created an interesting combination of fantasy, horror and humor." Ellis called the pace of the novel "quick and exciting."

In *Sympathy for the Devil,* a young woman's wish that all those in Hell receive a second chance at redemption brings the condemned back to earth. "Character development is well done," remarked Lesley S. J. Farmer, reviewing *Sympathy for the Devil* in *Kliatt,* "and the tone is actually light-hearted."

Glenraven, cowritten with noted fantasy writer Marion Zimmer Bradley, follows the adventures of two women who visit Glenraven, a fictitious country that harbors secrets of "Europe's mystical forgotten past." Recommending *Glenraven* in a review in *Library Journal,* a critic noted that "Bradley and Lisle expertly juxtapose contemporary women and a medieval, magical culture."

■ Works Cited

Chmurynsky, Susan E., review of *Minerva Wakes,* *Kliatt,* March, 1994, p. 18.

Cushman, Carolyn, review of *Fire in the Mist, Locus,* July, 1992, p. 33.

Ellis, Karen S., review of *Mall, Mayhem and Magic,* *Kliatt,* November, 1995, p. 17.

Farmer, Lesley S. J., review of *Sympathy for the Devil, Kliatt,* May, 1996, p. 18.

Review of *Glenraven, Library Journal,* August, 1996, p. 120.
Lamb, Sister Avila, review of *Mind of the Magic, Kliatt,* September, 1995, p. 23.*

* * *

LOEWER, Jean
See JENKINS, Jean

* * *

LOEWER, Peter 1934-

■ Personal

Born February 13, 1934, in Buffalo, NY; son of Henry Christian (a designing engineer) and Ruth Isabelle (a fashion designer; maiden name, Duerstein) Loewer; married Jean Jenkins (an artist), February 13, 1959. *Education:* University of Buffalo, Albright Art School, B.F.A., 1958.

■ Addresses

Home—Asheville, NC. *Office*—P.O. Box 5039, Biltmore Sta., Asheville, NC 28813.

■ Career

Graphos Studio, Asheville, NC, art director, 1968—; *Upper Delaware* magazine, art director, 1979-80; *Warwick Photo Adviser,* production manager, 1983-86. Host of *Back to the Garden,* for Asheville's public broadcasting station, WCQS. Illustrator, with work held in permanent collection at Carnegie-Mellon University. J. C. Raulston Arboretum, member of advisory board; Botanical Gardens at Asheville, member of board; member of Asheville Tree Commission. *Member:* American Society of Journalists and Authors, American Rock Garden Society, Royal Horticultural Society, Asheville Chamber Music Society.

■ Awards, Honors

Philadelphia Book Clinic Award, 1987, for *Gardens by Design; The Annual Garden* was cited as one of the fifty great garden books by the National Agricultural Library, 1988; Mack Beckmann fellow, Brooklyn Museum Art School; eight awards from Garden Writers Association of America.

■ Writings

FOR YOUNG PEOPLE

Letters to Sarah, Fort Delaware Museum (Narrowsburg, New York), 1989.
The Inside-Out Stomach: An Introduction to Animals without Backbones, illustrated by Jean Jenkins, Atheneum, 1990.

PETER LOEWER

Pond Water Zoo: An Introduction to Microscopic Life, illustrated by Jean Jenkins, Simon & Schuster, 1996.

NONFICTION

(Editor) *Taylor's Guide to Annuals,* Houghton Mifflin, 1986.
(Editor) *Garden Ornaments,* Brooklyn Botanic Garden, 1987.
(Editor) *Ornamental Grasses,* Brooklyn Botanic Garden, 1988.
A World of Plants: The Missouri Botanical Garden, Abrams, 1989.
(With Anne Halpin) *Secrets of the Great Gardeners: The Brooklyn Botanic Garden,* Summit, 1991.
Organic Gardener's Annuals, reprinted, Van Patten, 1993.
The Winter Garden: Planning and Planting for the Southeast, illustrated by Larry Mellichamp, Stackpole, 1997.
The Moonflower, illustrated by Jean Jenkins, Peachtree Books, 1997.

NONFICTION; SELF-ILLUSTRATED

The Indoor Water Gardener's How-to Handbook, Walker, 1973.

Bringing the Outdoors In, Walker, 1974, second edition, Contemporary Books, 1988.

Seeds and Cuttings, Walker, 1975.

Growing and Decorating with Grasses, Walker, 1977.

Growing Plants in Water, Penguin, 1980.

Evergreens: A Guide for Landscape, Lawn, and Garden, Walker, 1981.

The Month-by-Month Garden Almanac, Perigee/Putnam, 1983.

Gardens by Design, Rodale, 1986.

The Annual Garden, Rodale, 1988.

American Gardens, Simon & Schuster, 1988.

A Year of Flowers, Rodale, 1989.

The Indoor Window Garden, Contemporary Books, 1990.

The Wild Gardener: On Flowers and Foliage for the Natural Border, Stackpole, 1991.

Tough Plants for Tough Places, Rodale, 1991.

The Evening Garden, Stackpole, 1993.

The New Small Garden: Plans and Plants that Make Every Inch Count, Stackpole, 1994.

Seeds: The Definitive Guide to Growing, History, and Lore, Macmillan, 1995.

Thoreau's Garden: Native Plants for the American Landscape, Stackpole, 1996.

Bartram's Garden, Stackpole, 1998.

ILLUSTRATOR

Alan E. Simmons, *Growing Unusual Fruit,* Walker, 1972.

Craig Tufts, *The National Wildlife Federation Guide to Gardening for Wildlife: How to Create a Beautiful Backyard Habitat for Birds, Butterflies, and Other Wildlife,* Rodale, 1995.

Bebe Miles, *Wildflower Perennials for Your Garden: A Detailed Guide to Years of Bloom from America's Native Heritage,* Stackpole, 1996.

Author of "Back to the Garden," a column in *Sullivan County Democrat,* 1977—. Contributor of articles and illustrations to periodicals, including *Woman's Day, Green Scene, American Horticulturist, Garden Design,* and *Hudson Valley.* Editor, *Sullivan County Democrat,* 1979-81, *Quill and Trowel,* 1988-91, and *American Conifer Society Bulletin,* 1991; contributing editor, *Carolina Gardener.*

■ Sidelights

Peter Loewer is a prolific and award-winning author and illustrator of books for gardeners. He has also written books on natural science topics for children, including *The Inside-Out Stomach,* on invertebrates, and *Pond Water Zoo,* which examines microscopic life in pond water. In *The Inside-Out Stomach,* Loewer explains the difference between vertebrates and invertebrates for an audience of third-to-fifth graders, and then discusses each of the eleven phyla in the class of invertebrates

Loewer explains how to collect samples of pond water and examine them for microscopic life forms in this nonfiction study for young people. (Cover illustration by Jean Jenkins.)

with regard to structure, function, life cycle, and behavior. "The book is thorough for its intended audience and scope," remarked Jacqueline Elsner in *School Library Journal.* For a slightly older audience, Loewer wrote *Pond Water Zoo,* in which he places emphasis on how to collect and study samples of pond water, examining them for microscopic life forms. Susan DeRonne, who reviewed *Pond Water Zoo* in *Booklist,* concluded that this "very detailed book will serve the young researcher well."

■ Works Cited

DeRonne, Susan, review of *Pond Water Zoo: An Introduction to Microscopic Life, Booklist,* September 15, 1996, p. 235.

Elsner, Jacqueline, review of *The Inside-Out Stomach: An Introduction to Animals without Backbones, School Library Journal,* January, 1991, p. 102.

■ For More Information See

PERIODICALS

School Library Journal, February, 1997, p. 120.

Science Books and Films, January, 1991, p. 20.

M

MACINTOSH, Brownie 1950-
(Greybeard the Pirate, John Young)

■ Personal

Born February 15, 1950, in Haverhill, MA; son of Gardner Brown (a salesman) and Marcia Harkin (a homemaker; maiden name, Brown) Macintosh; married Karen Porter Kirk (a teacher, photographer, and gardener); children: Gardner III. *Education:* Attended Emerson College.

BROWNIE MACINTOSH

■ Addresses

Home—New Hampshire. *Electronic mail*—GBM2NH @aol.com.

■ Career

Songwriter, performing artist, actor, and writer. Guest on television and radio programs, including *Folk Song America* and *Woody's Children;* performed on stage with recording artists, including Theodore Bikel, Eric Weissberg, Doc Watson, Pure Prairie League, Jerry Jeff Walker, Steve Goodman, and Tom Paxton. *Member:* Broadcast Music, Inc.

■ Writings

The Streamlined Double Decker Bus (with audio cassette), illustrated by Wayne Geehan, Covered Bridge Press, 1995.
(With Julie Thompson) *A Pirate's Life for Me!: A Day Aboard a Pirate Ship* (with audio cassette), illustrated by Patrick O'Brien, Charlesbridge Publishing (Watertown, MA), 1996.

Author (and co-producer) of the radio series *American Folk Theatre.* Wrote, produced, arranged, and performed commercial radio and television jingles, and public service announcements. Also wrote two educational radio programs for children. Some writings appear under the pseudonyms Greybeard the Pirate and John Young.

■ Work in Progress

Books on multiculturalism and fantasy, some with audio cassettes; a book of quotations by creative New Englanders, past and present.

■ Sidelights

Brownie Macintosh told *SATA:* "I studied briefly at Emerson College in Boston, but I learned songwriting, general writing, and musical performance by doing it. I have been writing poetry and songs since childhood, and I became a performing artist at age fifteen.

"My main focus is writing songs and working as a performing artist. I have written for the Kingston Trio, the Irish Rovers, and many other international touring acts, as well as for Atlantic Music Corporation and the public television series *Nova*. I have written, produced, and arranged more than three hundred commercial jingles for radio and television, and I have appeared in television and radio commercials as an actor.

"I am currently working on combination book/tape song collections for children, but I have dabbled in ghost stories as well. I am always working on a new song and new stories.

"I am an active collector of folk music in all forms (recordings and print), and I enjoy meeting people who share the interest and love to sing. I am a classically trained 'whiskey' baritone with a vocal range of two-and-a-half octaves. I also play guitar, banjo, mandolin, concertina, and tenor guitar, and am self-taught on all."

*   *   *

MARTIN, Jacqueline Briggs 1945-

■ Personal

Born April 15, 1945, in Lewiston, ME; daughter of Hugh C., Jr. (a dairy farmer) and Alice (a homemaker and cook; maiden name, Prince) Briggs; married Richard Martin (a college professor), June 17, 1967; children: Sarah E., Justin A. *Education:* Wellesley College, B.A., 1966; University of Minnesota Institute of Child Development, M.A., 1971. *Hobbies and other interests:* Camping, hiking, growing roses and hot peppers.

■ Addresses

Office—312 Second Ave. N., Mt. Vernon, IA 52314.

■ Career

Author. *Member:* Society of Children's Book Writers and Illustrators, Authors Guild.

■ Awards, Honors

Notable Children's Trade Book in the Field of Social Studies commendation, National Council for the Social Studies/Children's Book Council, 1995, for *Washing the Willow Tree Loon*, and 1997, for *The Green Truck Garden Giveaway: A Neighborhood Story and Almanac;* Notable Book commendation, American Library Association, and Lupine Award, Maine Librarians, both 1996, and Children's Book of Distinction, *Hungry Mind Review,* all for *Grandmother Bryant's Pocket.*

JACQUELINE BRIGGS MARTIN

■ Writings

Bizzy Bones and Uncle Ezra, illustrated by Stella Ormai, Lothrop (New York City), 1984.

Bizzy Bones and Moosemouse, illustrated by Stella Ormai, Lothrop, 1986.

Bizzy Bones and the Lost Quilt, illustrated by Stella Ormai, Lothrop, 1988.

Good Times on Grandfather Mountain, illustrated by Susan Gaber, Orchard (New York City), 1992.

The Finest Horse in Town, illustrated by Susan Gaber, HarperCollins (New York City), 1992.

Washing the Willow Tree Loon, illustrated by Nancy Carpenter, Simon & Schuster (New York City), 1995.

The Second Street Gardens and the Green Truck Almanac, illustrated by Alec Gillman, Four Winds Press (New York City), 1995, as *The Green Truck Garden Giveaway: A Neighborhood Story and Almanac,* Simon & Schuster, 1997.

Grandmother Bryant's Pocket, illustrated by Petra Mathers, Houghton (Boston), 1996.

Higgins Bend Song and Dance, illustrated by Brad Sneed, Houghton, 1997.

Button, Bucket, Sky, illustrated by Vicki Jo Redenbaugh, Carolrhoda, 1998.

Snowflake Bentley, illustrated by Mary Azarian, Houghton, 1998.

■ Work in Progress

A work titled *Black Mountain Crow.*

■ Sidelights

Jacqueline Briggs Martin's books for young readers reflect both their author's love of the past and her respect for the environment. While her tales may wander as far afield as the rocky coastline of Maine is to a bustling city street, or recount events that have taken place as long ago as the late eighteenth century or as recently as yesterday, they are unified by their author's enthusiasm for the people and places that make up her fictional worlds, and for sharing those worlds with young readers. "I hope readers will find friends in my stories," she explained to *SATA,* "people they want to visit again and again, people who become part of their memories, and their own stories."

"Since I was a child I have loved the sounds of words," Martin confided. "And I have loved stories. Though writing books is not always easy, I cannot imagine doing anything else. Every day I get to work with words that tell a story." Born in Lewiston, Maine, in 1945, she was raised in the countryside, where her appreciation for nature and her interest in the history of both her family and her town grew. "As a child I spent much time wandering in the fields and forests of our farm in Maine, wondering about the generations who lived there before we did," the author recalled. Several of Martin's books, such as 1996's *Grandmother Bryant's Pocket,* reflect this childhood questioning. Drawn by Martin back to the year 1787, the reader of *Grandmother Bryant's Pocket* meets eight-year-old Sarah Bryant, who is haunted by bad dreams after her dog is killed in a horrible fire. Convinced that a change of scene will help their daughter recover from her pet's death, Sarah's parents send the girl to stay with her grandmother. Grandmother Bryant is a woman full of wonderful stories and knowledgeable in the ways of natural medicines and healing—she carries herbs and bandages in her pocket, a drawstring pouch worn tied around the waist by women of the period. Describing Martin's text as "eloquent ... [with] the force of a prose poem," a *Publishers Weekly* critic hailed *Grandmother Bryant's Pocket* as "a pleasingly timeless historical tale." Comparing the book to the "Little House" stories of Laura Ingalls Wilder, Deborah Stevenson praised the work in *Bulletin of the Center for Children's Books,* noting that while Martin's "telling use of detail effectively creates a world very far away from now, [her] respectful and understanding treatment of Sarah's fear ... and of her enduring grief ... adds a timeless touch."

Good Times on Grandfather Mountain was inspired by an article Martin read concerning a man who created musical instruments out of wood—his whittling included everything from fence posts to abandoned cabins. "I have always been fascinated by people who make beautiful objects out of what others might call junk," recalled Martin, "and wanted to make up a story of such a person." In *Good Times,* Old Washburn turns bad

Martin offers young readers a compendium of gardening tips along with her story of a rundown neighborhood transformed when the residents are given small gardens to cultivate. (Cover illustration by Alec Gillman.)

situations around with his pocket knife. When his milk cow runs away, or his vegetable garden becomes infested with insects, he gathers up whatever wood remains, applies his pocket knife, and creates something musical. Ultimately, his home is destroyed during a bad storm, but, undaunted, Old Washburn whittles himself up a fiddle from the floorboards that remain and starts playing a jig. His jaunty melody not only calls the mischievous cow back home, but draws out his neighbors as well, and the old man's affairs are soon set to rights with some neighborly help. Martin's "wry, nicely cadenced narration gives her tale a hearty folk-tale flavor," noted a *Kirkus Reviews* critic who deemed *Good Times on Grandfather Mountain* "Entertaining, original, and beautifully produced."

Higgins Bend Song and Dance is another book in the folk tale, tall-tale genre. It is the story of a single-minded fisher named Simon Henry who vows to catch a crafty catfish named Oscar. "I'll sleep in my boots until I bring him in," Simon Henry vows. Oscar proves too wily for the man who could catch anything that "swam, crawled or floated," until Simon Henry comes up with one last overpowering bait.

"I wrote this book because I love rivers," Martin told *SATA.* "I like the notion of a contest between an old grouch and a smart catfish. And I love the banter between two old friends who don't always agree." A contributor in *Kirkus Reviews* called the work "A meaty tale of the quest for an uncatchable fish named Oscar ... told in folksy, irresistible language," while Jody McCoy, writing in *School Library Journal,* stated that the book is "pure pleasure for any who are or know dedicated (obsessed) fishermen," adding "this whopper of a fish tale also makes a good read-aloud."

Another book that takes readers into the past, *The Finest Horse in Town,* also has its roots in the author's own family history. The story involves two sisters— Martin's great-aunts Stella and Cora—who owned a dry-goods and clothing store in a small Maine town. And they owned a beautiful, grey, carriage horse named Prince, the "finest horse in town," according to an old watchmaker who remembered the horse. The watchmaker's memories are few, though, and the author speculates on adventures the sisters might have had with the horse. Each of these three episodes ends with the refrain "We don't really know what happened. We only know the sisters had the finest horse in town. The watchmaker told us. And he was there." A *Publishers Weekly* reviewer praised the book's "nostalgic sing-song language and descriptions of village life." Deborah Abbott complimented the story in her *Booklist* review, writing that *The Finest Horse in Town* "transports readers back in history to reflect upon the joys and cares of people and a horse named Prince."

Among Martin's stories dealing with more contemporary themes is the award-winning *Washing the Willow Tree Loon.* Published in 1995, the book recounts the efforts of people living along the coast of Turtle Bay to rescue a loon who has become soaked in oil leaked by a barge that hit a bridge while traversing the bay. Found hiding under a willow tree, the bird is cared for by a caring group of citizens who are varied in age and occupation. "The well-drawn text has a gentle rhythm and infuses an appealing story with interesting information," according to *Horn Book* reviewer Margaret Bush, who praised Martin's inclusion of endnotes describing bird rehabilitation. *Washing the Willow Tree Loon* ends with a plea to readers to help in whatever way each of them can; "Who knows who has seen the willow tree loon since then," Martin asks. "Maybe me, maybe you. The world is full of birds. And we have work to do."

Often, Martin is inspired with an idea for a new book by something she has read. "When I read about Dan Barker building and giving away gardens in Portland, Oregon, I knew I wanted to write a children's book about giving away gardens," she told *SATA.* "And I wanted readers to be able to make gardens for themselves, or gardens to give away." *The Green Truck Garden Giveaway: A Neighborhood Story and Almanac,* first published in 1995, would be the result of Martin's interest in Barker's work. The story opens on a Saturday morning, as a strange, green truck full of soil and seeds rolls down an unkempt city street. The truck's two passengers persuade even the most reluctant residents to attempt a seed garden; they also pass out pamphlets full of gardening tips and inspiration. Soon, the entire neighborhood has been transformed into a paradise, as the residents become inspired to clean up yards and vacant lots and rescue untamed tangles of raspberry plants from rubbish and weeds. Martin is an avid gardener and has included a wealth of gardening lore in addition to the central story. "I wanted this book to have enough information to be the gift of a garden in itself," Martin told *SATA.*

In addition to stories that mirror her family's history or deal with contemporary issues of importance to her, Martin has also written a series of stories in a lighter vein. In *Bizzy Bones and Uncle Ezra,* which was her first published book for children, two mice set up housekeeping in an abandoned work boot. When the younger mouse, Bizzy Bones, worries that the shoe will blow away in the brisk, whistling March winds, the elder mouse, Uncle Ezra, finds a way to calm him by constructing a colorful carousel that captures the early spring gusts and sets them spinning. Other books featuring the young Bizzy Bones include *Bizzy Bones and Moosemouse* and *Bizzy Bones and the Old Quilt.*

"My stories often start with something that has happened to me, or to people that I love," Martin told *SATA* in discussing her development as a children's book author. "Sometimes they start with a question. For example, *Washing the Willow Tree Loon* began when I read an article about bird washing and asked myself, 'Who would want to wash birds?' *Higgins Bend Song and Dance* began with the question 'Who wins when a crafty old fisherman vows to catch a catfish that is just as crafty?'

"Some books begin with things I love to do, such as collecting acorns to plant oak trees (*Button, Bucket, Sky*), or watching crows (*Black Mountain Crows,* in progress). One of my books began with a snowflake and a memory of a brief article about a man who said he 'loved snow more that anything else in the world.' I read Wilson Bentley's articles about snow, looked at some of the thousands of photographs he took of individual snow crystals, read about his life, visited the farmhouse where he had lived, and eventually wrote *Snowflake Bentley.*

"When I am writing I become obsessed with the world of my work and have been known to walk into shelves, or other people, because I am thinking so hard about my characters. I live with them and am always a little sad to finish a story."

■ Works Cited

Abbott, Deborah, review of *The Finest Horse in Town, Booklist,* June 15, 1992, pp. 1849-50.

Bush, Margaret, review of *Washing the Willow Tree Loon, Horn Book,* September/October, 1995, p. 591.

Review of *The Finest Horse in Town, Publishers Weekly,* June 22, 1992, p. 61.

Review of *Good Times on Grandfather Mountain, Kirkus Reviews,* February 1, 1992, pp. 186-87.

Review of *Grandmother Bryant's Pocket, Publishers Weekly,* February 5, 1996, p. 89.

Review of *Higgins Bend Song and Dance, Kirkus
   Reviews,* July 1, 1997, p. 1032.
Martin, Jacqueline Briggs, *The Finest Horse in Town,*
   HarperCollins, 1992.
Martin, Jacqueline Briggs, *Washing the Willow Tree
   Loon,* Simon & Schuster, 1995.
Martin, Jacqueline Briggs, *Higgins Bend Song and
   Dance,* Houghton, 1997.
McCoy, Jody, review of *Higgins Bend Song and Dance,
   School Library Journal,* September 19, 1997, pp.
   187-88.
Stevenson, Deborah, review of *Grandmother Bryant's
   Pocket, Bulletin of the Center for Children's Books,*
   July/August, 1996, pp. 363-64.

■ For More Information See

PERIODICALS

Booklist, September 1, 1984, p. 68; September 15, 1986,
   p. 133; March 15, 1988, p. 1266; December 15,
   1995, p. 709; May 1, 1997, pp. 1501-2.
Bulletin of the Center for Children's Books, March, 1992,
   p. 186; July, 1992, p. 300.
Five Owls, September/October, 1997, p. 8.
Horn Book, May/June, 1992, pp. 332-33.
Kirkus Reviews, October 15, 1995, p. 1496.
New Advocate, fall, 1996, p. 340.
New York Times Book Review, April 27, 1997, p. 29.
Publishers Weekly, April 7, 1997, p. 92.
School Library Journal, November, 1984, p. 112; Octo-
   ber, 1986, p. 164; June/July, 1988, p. 93; August,
   1992, p. 144; October, 1995, p. 108; June, 1996, p.
   105; June, 1997, p. 98.

*   *   *

MARTINEZ, Ed(ward) 1954-

■ Personal

Born January 2, 1954, in Buenos Aires, Argentina; son
of Gabriel (in advertising) and Nelly Martinez; married
Deborah L. Chabrian (an artist); children: Oliver. *Education:* Attended Parsons School of Design. *Religion:*
Roman Catholic. *Hobbies and other interests:* "Restoring an eighteenth-century farmhouse."

■ Addresses

Home and office—28 Spooner Hill Rd., South Kent, CT
06785.

■ Career

Illustrator.

■ Illustrator

Gary Soto, *Too Many Tamales,* Putnam, 1993.
Mary Calhoun, *Tonio's Cat,* Morrow, 1996.
Dennis Fradin, *Maria de Sautuola: The Discoverer of the
   Bulls in the Cave* (nonfiction), Silver Press (Parsip-

ED MARTINEZ

pany, NJ), 1996, published as *Maria de Sautuola:
The Bulls in the Cave,* 1997.
Sarah Glasscock, *My Prairie Summer,* Steck-Vaughn
   (Austin, TX), 1998.
Lori M. Carlson, *Reyes: Three Kings' Day,* Lodestar,
   1998.

■ Sidelights

Ed Martinez told *SATA:* "I enjoy painting pure and
simple. Although I studied illustration and wanted to
become an illustrator, I am finding it more exciting to
paint outdoors, [especially] the landscapes in the rural
area where I live. This way of painting has found its way
back into my illustration work with the rich textures and
painterly brushwork I use in my outdoor paintings.
Although I have been an illustrator for fifteen years, I
only recently started doing children's books. My first
book *Too Many Tamales* is selling like hotcakes.

"My hobby is restoring an eighteenth-century farmhouse with my wife and son Oliver, who is pretty good
with a hammer for someone so young."

■ For More Information See

PERIODICALS

Booklist, September 15, 1996, p. 245.
School Library Journal, September, 1996, p. 171.

*   *   *

MERRIMAN, Rachel 1971-

■ Personal

Born August 8, 1971, in Liverpool, England; daughter of William and Hilda (Leather) Merriman. *Education:* John Moores University, Foundation Diploma in Art and Design (with distinction), 1990; Manchester Metropolitan University, B.A. (with first class honors), 1993.

■ Addresses

Home and office—Flat 3, 45 Queen Elizabeth's Walk, London N16 5UG, England.

■ Career

Freelance illustrator, including textile design, editorial work, animation sequences, greeting cards, and gift wrap; presents workshops at primary and secondary schools. *Exhibitions:* Has exhibited works at shows and galleries, including Greenfish Gallery, Liverpool, England.

■ Awards, Honors

Autumn Prize, *Picture Book Quarterly,* 1996, for *The Tale of Tobias.*

■ Illustrator

Jan Mark, *The Tale of Tobias,* Candlewick (Cambridge, MA), 1995.
Betsy Bang, *The Old Woman and the Red Pumpkin,* Walker (London, England), 1998.

■ Sidelights

Rachel Merriman told *SATA:* "I don't think I ever chose to be an illustrator. I feel as though illustration chose me. I read fiction and drew continually as a child, making my own miniature books, casting myself and my best school friend as central characters. I suppose I've never really grown up.

"Beatrix Potter and E. H. Shepard were favorites when I was a very young child, and I still return to them now as something to aspire to in terms of draftsmanship. Modern picture books have a much stronger 'design' bias, which is also something I enjoy enormously. I am helped by the great fortune of working with wonderful designers at Walker Books and rewarded by the inclusion of *The Tale of Tobias* in British Books '96, an exhibition of British book design and production held at the British Printing Industries Federation in London.

"As a beginning illustrator, I don't have a definite working routine. Work comes in, and I do it. Until now the work has been as varied as compact disc covers, stained glass windows, textiles, and, of course, picture books. Reference comes from anywhere and everywhere. I've recently moved to London, so I'm still finding my environment really exciting. I especially love film and theater, and I have been lucky enough to dabble in theater during the past year in a design capacity."

I saw a great fish and barked and ran in circles. Azarias said to Tobias: "Catch the fish and we will have supper." So Tobias caught the fish and Azarias said to Tobias: "Cut up the fish and keep the guts. We will roast the rest and eat it for supper." I thought: That is strange. I am the one who gets the guts. But I said nothing. I am only a dog.

Rachel Merriman illustrated *The Tale of Tobias,* a biblical tale retold by Jan Mark from the viewpoint of Tobias's dog.

■ For More Information See

PERIODICALS

Horn Book, January-February, 1997, p. 77.
Picture Book Quarterly, autumn, 1996.
School Librarian, May, 1996.
School Library Journal, October, 1996, p. 115.

* * *

MITCHARD, Jacquelyn 1952-

■ Personal

Born in 1952; married Dan Allegretti (a journalist; died, 1993); children: five.

■ Addresses

Home—Madison, WI. *Agent*—Jane Gelfman, Gelfman, Schneider Literary Agents Inc., 250 West 57th St., New York, NY 10107.

■ Career

Newspaper reporter; newspaper columnist, *Milwaukee Journal Sentinel,* beginning in 1985; author of nonfiction and fiction.

■ Writings

Mother Less Child: The Love Story of a Family, Norton, 1985.
Jane Addams: Pioneer in Social Reform and Activist for World Peace, Gareth Stevens (Milwaukee, WI), 1991.
(With Barbara Behm) *Jane Addams: Peace Activist,* Gareth Stevens, 1992.
The Deep End of the Ocean, Viking, 1996.
The Rest of Us: Dispatches from the Mother Ship, Viking, 1997.
The Most Wanted, Viking, 1998.

Also author (with Amy Paulsen) of the screenplays *The Serpent's Egg* and *Typhoid Mary.* Author of essays, including "Mother to Mother," anthologized in *The Adoption Reader,* Seal Press (Seattle, WA), 1995.

■ Adaptations

A movie option, for *The Deep End of the Ocean,* was sold to Peter Guber's Mandalay Entertainment, in conjunction with Michelle Pfeiffer's production company, in 1996.

■ Sidelights

Heralded as a first-rate storyteller, Jacquelyn Mitchard of Madison, Wisconsin, sold her 1996 book *The Deep End of the Ocean* after writing a mere one hundred pages. The book concerns a Midwestern family, the Cappadoras, that collapses in on itself after three-year-

JACQUELYN MITCHARD

old Ben Cappadora is kidnapped from a hotel lobby in Chicago.

Before Mitchard's success as a novelist, she worked as a newspaper columnist for the *Milwaukee Journal Sentinel.* Her strong desire to have children, a nearly fatal tubal pregnancy, and her efforts to cope with her inability to conceive and overcome the emotional and psychological aspects of infertility compelled Mitchard to write an account of her ordeal in *Mother Less Child.* In *Publishers Weekly,* Genevieve Stuttaford advised, "The casual reader may feel she covers the material too thoroughly, but those faced with a similar reality will empathize with the couple's plight. Mitchard writes frankly and well of a painful subject that haunts all too many." That frankness even extends to discussion of the near failure of Mitchard's marriage due to the strain resulting from her desire to conceive a child.

Mitchard's skill and thoroughness as a writer is evidenced in her 1991 nonfiction book, *Jane Addams: Pioneer in Social Reform and Activist for World Peace,* which was written for children. In 1993, when her husband, journalist Dan Allegretti, died of cancer, Mitchard was determined to keep freelancing. She used her competence as a reporter and columnist to write "*everything* for *anybody* to pay the bills. I wrote warning labels: 'Don't point the paint-sprayer at your face while operating.' I put up with a lot of horrible rejection, but I wouldn't give in," as she related to Jeff Giles in *Newsweek.*

That persistence paid off. Mitchell was rewarded with a big advance for *The Deep End of the Ocean;* she secured a distribution deal with the Book of the Month Club; and she sold the book's movie rights to *Batman* producer Peter Guber's film production company. With five children to support, financial success is no small matter for Mitchard.

Critics have noted the heart-squeezing anxiety of *The Deep End of the Ocean,* specifically remarking on the intriguing characters. Donna Seaman wrote in *Booklist,* "She describes [Ben's mother] Beth's unraveling with clinical finesse, then proceeds to chronicle every aspect of the high-profile search for the missing child, the media feeding frenzy over this ideal prime-time tragedy, and the psychological toll such a cruel and mysterious disappearance exacts."

Nine years pass in the suspenseful plot, giving adequate time to explore the various family member's feelings, especially those of teenage Vincent Cappadora, who was seven when his brother disappeared. It was Vincent who was instructed to watch Ben in the crowded hotel lobby while his mother checked in. During these years, Beth's anxiety and grief has led her to neglect Vincent, her daughter Kerry, and her husband Pat. Reviewer Sybil S. Steinberg, in *Publishers Weekly,* declared that Mitchard's plot is permeated with "disturbingly candid" revelations regarding familial relationships. Gail Collins, in the *New York Times Book Review,* described the book as "not so much a thriller as a gut wrencher." Mitchard delves into all the relationships, Giles insisted in *Newsweek,* "Don't bother predicting the end: there's a plot twist that'll spin you around no matter which way you're looking."

■ Works Cited

Collins, Gail, review of *The Deep End of the Ocean, New York Times Book Review,* August 18, 1996, p. 22.
Giles, Jeff, review of *The Deep End of the Ocean, Newsweek,* June 3, 1996, pp. 72-74.
Seaman, Donna, review of *The Deep End of the Ocean, Booklist,* April 1, 1996, p. 1324.
Steinberg, Sybil S., review of *The Deep End of the Ocean, Publishers Weekly,* April 1, 1996, p. 54.
Stuttaford, Genevieve, review of *Mother Less Child: The Love Story of a Family, Publishers Weekly,* February 1, 1985, p. 353.

■ For More Information See

PERIODICALS

Booklist, March 15, 1985, p. 1019.
Choice, October, 1991, p. 245.
Kirkus Reviews, January 15, 1985, p. 81; March 15, 1996, p. 400; April 1, 1998, p. 429.
Library Journal, March 15, 1985, p. 67; April 15, 1996, p. 123.
Publishers Weekly, February 1, 1985, p. 353.

MOERBEEK, Kees 1955-

■ Personal

Name is pronounced *Kays Mow-beek;* born April 10, 1955, in Halsteren, the Netherlands; married Carla Dijs (a children's book author and illustrator), 1983; children: Lizawela, Anna Felice. *Education:* Studied graphic design in art school in Arnhem, 1978-81.

■ Addresses

Home—Usquert, the Netherlands.

■ Writings

FOR CHILDREN; SELF-ILLUSTRATED

Brave Billy, Price Stern Sloan, 1987.
Cindy's Circus, Price Stern Sloan, 1987.
Patrick's Problem, Price Stern Sloan, 1987.
Have You Seen a Pog?, Price Stern Sloan, 1988.
Who's Peeking at Me?, Western, 1988.
Beware of the Pog!, Child's Play, 1989.
New at the Zoo: A Mix-and-Match Pop-Up Book, Child's Play, 1989.
Fancy That!, Child's Play, 1991.
Let's Go!, Child's Play, 1991.
Penguins Slide, Child's Play, 1991.
Four Courageous Climbers, World International, 1992.
Hi Mom, I'm Home!: Another Pop-Up Adventure, Price Stern Sloan, 1992.
Oh No, Santa!, World International, 1992.
Night before Christmas, Price Stern Sloan, 1992.
The Museum of Unnatural History: A Pop-Up Book, Orchard, 1993.
New at the Zoo 2: A Mix-and-Match Pop-Up Book, Random House, 1993.
Boo Whoo?: A Spooky Mix-and-Match Pop-Up Book, Golden, 1993.
All Mixed Up: An Enchanted Mix-and-Match Pop-Up Book, Western, 1994.
Can't Sleep, Golden, 1994.
Am I a Frog?, McClanahan, 1996.
Am I a Tiger?, McClanahan, 1996.
Crabs Grab!, McClanahan, 1996.
Owls Fly!, McClanahan, 1996.
Undersea, Price Stern Sloan, 1997.
Jungle King, Price Stern Sloan, 1997.

WITH CARLA DIJS

Bee Says Buzz, Child's Play, 1986.
Hiding Places, Child's Play, 1986.
Let's Play, Child's Play, 1986.
Peek-a-boo, H. Holt, 1986.
Hot Pursuit: A Forward-and-Backward Pop-Up Book, Price Stern Sloan, 1987.
Six Brave Explorers: A Pop-Up Book, Collins, 1988.
When the Wild Pirates Go Sailing: A Pop-Up Book, World International, 1992.

ILLUSTRATOR

Peter Seymour, adapter, *Little Red Riding Hood: A Pop-Up Book with Action Characters*, Price Stern Sloan, 1990.

■ Sidelights

Kees Moerbeek has created numerous well-received pop-up books for children, many with his wife Carla Dijs, whom he met while they were in the same art school. These books, which are considered suitable for preschoolers and primary graders, combine pop-ups and other elements of sophisticated paper engineering with minimal stories, resulting in books that critics have praised as humorous and inventive.

Six Brave Explorers, co-authored by Dijs, is a triangular-shaped book out of which leap ferocious animals who conquer the brave explorers of the title in a "brilliant example of Pop-Up engineering," according to a reviewer for *Junior Bookshelf. Hot Pursuit*, another co-authored effort, reads both backwards and forwards, as a chase is depicted across the pages and then up the edge of the last page and back across the book backwards and upside-down. The back of the head of each character becomes another character in the reverse position, thus the book (and the chase it depicts) are "circular and neverending," as Joanne Robertson pointed out in *Canadian Materials.* "With its bright colours and large pop-ups, *Hot Pursuit* is guaranteed to delight young children," Robertson maintained.

With *New at the Zoo* and *The Museum of Unnatural History*, two solo efforts, Moerbeek continued to stretch the ingenuity of his paper engineering. In *New at the Zoo*, animals open and shut their mouths as the pages are turned, revealing their names inside each mouth, with little bits of information about each one at the bottom of the page. Then the book may be manipulated so that the top and bottom of each illustration is mixed with another, creating a new, nonsensical creature with a hybrid name, such as a hipger—a combination hippo and tiger. *Bulletin of the Center for Children's Books* critic Betsy Hearne noted that, though a large number of paper-engineering books have been created in recent years for children, "this scores high for invention, information, and amusement." Similarly, a reviewer for *Junior Bookshelf* noted that, although the creatures in Moerbeek's *Museum of Unnatural History* have never been found in real life or in a museum, they are "all rather good fun, and very vividly coloured fun at that." The book follows the path of a visitor through the museum, while animals and creatures of the imagination pop out at the reader as he or she pulls tabs, spins wheels, and lifts flaps.

■ Works Cited

Hearne, Betsy, review of *New at the Zoo, Bulletin of the Center for Children's Books*, November, 1989, p. 66.
Review of *The Museum of Unnatural History, Junior Bookshelf*, April, 1994, p. 58.

Robertson, Joanne, review of *Hot Pursuit, Canadian Materials,* September, 1988, p. 182.
Review of *Six Brave Explorers, Junior Bookshelf,* June, 1988, p. 139.

■ For More Information See

PERIODICALS

Books for Your Children, spring, 1994, p. 16.

* * *

MOLESWORTH, Mary Louisa 1839-1921 (Ennis Graham)

■ Personal

Born May 29, 1839, in Rotterdam, Holland; moved to Manchester, England; died 1921; daughter of Charles Augustus (a senior partner in a shipping business) and Agnes Janet Wilson Stewart; married Major Richard Molesworth (an officer in the Royal Dragoons), 1861 (separated 1879); children: Violet, Richard Walter, Cicely, Juliet, Olive, Richard Bevil, Lionel Charles.

■ Career

Author and essayist.

■ Writings

(As Ennis Graham) *Lover and Husband* (three volumes), Skeet (London), 1870.
(As Graham) *She Was Young and He Was Old* (three volumes) Tinsley (London), 1872.
(As Graham) *Not Without Thorns* (three volumes) Tinsley, 1873, (one volume), Osgood (Boston), 1873.
(As Graham) *Cicely: A Story of Three Years* (three volumes) Tinsley, 1874.
(As Graham) *Tell Me a Story*, illustrated by Walter Crane, Macmillan (London), 1875, Macmillan (New York City), 1893.
(As Graham) *"Carrots": Just a Little Boy*, Macmillan (London), 1876, (as Mary Louisa Molesworth) 1879, Burt (New York City), 1890?.
(As Graham) *The Cuckoo Clock*, illustrated by Walter Crane, Macmillan, 1877, (as Mary Louisa Molesworth) Caldwell (New York City), 1877?, Macmillan (London), 1882, illustrated by Charles E. Brock, Mayflower, 1980, published as *The Cuckoo Clock and the Tapestry Room*, illustrated by Walter Crane, with a preface by Angela Bull, Garland, 1976.
Grandmother Dear: A Book for Boys and Girls, Burt, n.d., Macmillan, 1878.
Hathercourt Rectory (three volumes) Hurst & Blackett (London), 1878, republished as *Hathercourt*, Holt (New York), 1878.
The Tapestry Room: A Child's Romance, illustrated by Walter Crane, Macmillan, 1879, Burt, 1879, published as *The Cuckoo Clock and the Tapestry Room*, with a preface by Angela Bull, Garland, 1976.

MARY LOUISA MOLESWORTH

A Christmas Child: A Sketch of a Boy-Life, Macmillan, 1880.

Miss Bouverie (three volumes) Hurst & Blackett (London), 1880.

The Adventures of Herr Baby, Macmillan, 1881, Macmillan (New York City), 1886.

Hermy: The Story of a Little Girl, Routledge (London), 1881.

Hoodie, Routledge, 1882.

Summer Stories for Boys and Girls, Macmillan, 1882.

Rosy, Macmillan, 1882, Macmillan (New York City), 1896.

Two Little Waifs, Macmillan, 1883, Macmillan (New York City), 1890.

Christmas-Tree Land, Macmillan, 1884, republished in *Christmas-Tree Land and A Christmas Posy,* Macmillan, 1893.

Lettice, Society for Promoting Christian Knowledge (London), 1884, Young (New York City), 1884.

The Little Old Portrait, Society for Promoting Christian Knowledge, 1884, republished as *Edmee: A Tale of the French Revolution,* Macmillan (London), 1916.

Us: An Old-Fashioned Story, Macmillan, 1885, Harper (New York City), 1885.

Silverthorns, Hatchards (London), 1886, Dutton, 1900?

A Charge Fulfilled, Society for Promoting Christian Knowledge, 1886.

The Abbey by the Sea, Society for Promoting Christian Knowledge, 1886.

Four Winds Farm, Macmillan, 1887, published with *The Children of the Castle* as *Four Winds Farm and the Children of the Castle,* with a preface by Roger Lancelyn Green, Garland, 1977.

Little Miss Peggy: Only a Nursery Story, Macmillan, 1887, Burt, 1891?

Marrying and Giving in Marriage, Hurst, n.d., Longmans (London), 1887.

A Christmas Posy, Macmillan, 1888, republished in *Christmas-Tree Land and A Christmas Posy,* Macmillan, 1893.

The Third Miss St. Quentin, Whittaker (New York City), 1888, Hatchards (London), 1889.

Five Minutes' Stories, Society for Promoting Christian Knowledge, 1888.

Great Uncle Hoot-Toot, Society for Promoting Christian Knowledge, 1889.

A House to Let, Society for Promoting Christian Knowledge, 1889.

French Life in Letters, Macmillan, 1889.

The Rectory Children, Macmillan, 1889.

That Girl in Black, and Bronzie, Chatto & Windus (London), 1889, Lovell (New York City), 1889.

Nesta: On Fragments of a Little Life, Chambers (London), 1889.

Neighbours, Hatchards, 1889, Whittaker (New York City), 1890.

The Old Pincushion, or Aunt Clotilda's Guests, Farran (London), 1889, Dutton, 1890.

Little Mother Bunch, Cassell (London), 1890.

The Story of a Spring Morning, and Other Tales, Longmans, Green, 1890.

The Children of the Castle, Macmillan, 1890, published with *Four Winds Farm* as *Four Winds Farm and the Children of the Castle,* with a preface by Roger Lancelyn Green, Garland, 1977.

The Green Casket, and Other Stories, Chambers, 1890.

Family Troubles, Society for Promoting Christian Knowledge, 1890, Young, 1890.

Twelve Tiny Tales, Society for Promoting Christian Knowledge, 1890?

The Lucky Ducks, and Other Stories, Society for Promoting Christian Knowledge, 1891.

The Bewitched Lamp, Chambers, 1891.

The Red Grange, Methuen (London), 1891, Whittaker, 1891.

Sweet Content, Farran, 1891, Dutton, 1891?

Nurse Heatherdale's Story, Macmillan, 1891, republished in *Nurse Heatherdale's Story and Little Miss Peggy,* Macmillan, 1893.

The Girls and I: A Veracious History, Macmillan, 1892.

Leona, Cassell, 1892.

An Enchanted Garden: Fairy Stories, Unwin, 1892, Cassell, 1892.

Stories of the Saints for Children, Longmans, 1892.

Farthings: The Story of a Stray and a Waif, Gardner, Darton (London), 1892, Young (New York City), 1892.

Imogen, or Only Eighteen, Chambers, 1892, Whittaker (New York), 1892.

Robin Redbreast: A Story for Girls, Chambers, 1892, Burt, 1892.

The Man with the Pan Pipes, and Other Stories, Society for Promoting Christian Knowledge, 1892.

The Thirteen Little Black Pigs, and Other Stories, Society for Promoting Christian Knowledge, 1893, illustrated by J. Watson Davis, Burt, 1901.

The Next-Door House, Chambers, 1893, Cassell, 1893.

Studies and Stories, Innes (London), 1893.

Mary: A Nursery Story for Very Little Children, Macmillan, 1893.

My New Home, Macmillan, 1894, Macmillan (New York City), 1898, illustrated by L. Leslie Brooke, with an introduction by Gillian Avery, Gollancz, 1968.

Blanche: A Story for Girls, Chambers, 1894.

Olivia: A Story for Girls, Chambers, 1894, Lippincott, 1895.

White Turrets, Chambers, 1895, Whittaker, 1895.

The Carved Lions, Macmillan, 1895.

Opposite Neighbours, and Other Stories, Society for Promoting Christian Knowledge, 1895.

Friendly Joey, and Other Stories, Society for Promoting Christian Knowledge, 1896.

The Oriel Window, Macmillan, 1896.

Phillipa, Chambers, 1896, Lippincott, 1896.

Uncanny Tales, Hutchinson (London), 1896, Longmans, Green (New York), 1896, Arno Press, 1976.

Meg Langhome, or The Day After Tomorrow, Chambers, Lippincott, 1897.

Miss Mouse and Her Boys, Macmillan, 1897.

Stories for Children in Illustration of the Lord's Prayer, Gardner, Darton, 1897.

The Laurel Walk, Ibister, 1898, Biddle (Philadelphia, PA), 1898.

Greyling Towers: A Story for the Young, Chambers, 1898.

The Magic Nuts, Macmillan, 1898, Altemus (Philadelphia, PA), 1899?

This and That: A Tale of Two Tinies, Macmillan, 1899.

The Grim House, Nisbet (London), 1899.

The Children's Hour, Nelson (London), 1899.

The House That Grew, Macmillan, 1900.

The Three Witches, Chambers, 1900.

My Pretty and Her Little Brother Too, and Other Stories, 1901, Dutton, 1901.

The Wood-Pigeons and Mary, Macmillan, 1901.

The Blue Baby, and Other Stories, Unwin (London), 1901.

Peterkin, Macmillan, 1902.

The Mystery of the Pinewood and Hollow Tree House, Nister, 1903.

The Ruby Ring, Macmillan, 1904.

The Wrong Envelope, and Other Stories, Macmillan, 1906.

Jasper: A Story for Children, Macmillan, 1906.

The Bolted Door, and Other Stories, Chambers, 1906.

The Little Guest: A Story for Children, Macmillan, 1907.

Fairies—Of Sorts, Macmillan, 1908.

The February Boys: A Story for Children, 1909, Dutton, 1909?

The Story of a Year, Macmillan, 1910.

Fairies Afield, Macmillan, 1911.

OTHER

Contributor to *The Art of Authorship: Literary Reminiscences, Methods of Work, and Advice to Young Beginners*, edited by George Bainton, Clarke, 1890, and *Women's Mission: Papers on the Philanthropic Work of Women*, edited by Baroness Burdett-Coutts, Scribners (New York), 1893. Also contributor of essays and short stories to various nineteenth-century British periodicals, including *Longman's, Contemporary Review*, and *Chamber's Journal*. Author of letters, held in the British Library.

■ Sidelights

Mary Louisa Molesworth, or Mrs. Molesworth, as she was known by readers of the nineteenth century, was one of the most popular and influential children's writers of her time. Her books were read by children around the world, and her fans included the Princess of Wales, who read Molesworth's books to her children. The future Victor Emmanuel II of Naples wrote Molesworth to say that her books helped him to survive the period of mourning after the death of his grandfather. In addition to religious or moral tales, Molesworth wrote stories about the everyday lives of middle-class children as well as purely imaginative fantasies, and is praised as an exemplary author of both types of fiction. She is considered among such groundbreaking creators of children's literature as Hans Christian Andersen, Lewis Carroll, and E. Nesbit, authors who wrote their books for the pure enjoyment of children rather than for their instruction. Although Molesworth attempted to teach Christian values to children through her works, most of them are only subtly didactic; she is usually regarded as a writer who understood children and childhood and did not condescend to her audience, which ranged from preschool through young adult. As a writer, she pioneered the concept of addressing the child reader directly and often included sophisticated language in order to increase the vocabulary of her audience. Molesworth also peppered the dialogue of some of her child characters with baby talk, a fashion of the time that current critics note as damaging to the effectiveness of her books. This fact, along with the opinion that her books declined in quality and became more overtly instructive as she became more prolific, is generally considered the reason that her books fell out of favor in the later twentieth century. However, even though much of her work has been forgotten, some of her books—especially her fantasies *The Cuckoo Clock, The Tapestry Room: A Child's Romance*, and *The Carved Lions* and the realistic story *"Carrots": Just a Little Boy*—are still regarded as classics.

Molesworth was born Mary Louisa Stewart in Rotterdam, Holland, to a Scottish businessman and his wife. When she was about two years old, her family, which included two other sisters and three brothers, moved to Manchester, England; Molesworth grew up in that city and its suburbs. She was raised as a Calvinist in a strict religious environment; this experience led her to decide to teach children about a religion that was not based on fear. Molesworth was taught by her mother at home and attended school in Switzerland. She was also instructed by the Reverend William Gaskell, the husband of Elizabeth Cleghorn Gaskell, a popular English novelist who influenced writers such as George Eliot; Gaskell is credited with helping Molesworth to develop her literary style. As a girl, Molesworth visited her grandmother Mary Wilson, who was an accomplished storyteller, in Scotland each year; after Wilson's death in 1849, Molesworth took it upon herself to continue the story-telling tradition with her brothers and sisters. A voracious reader, Molesworth began to devise her own stories when she was still a child and began publishing some of them in magazines as a teenager.

At twenty-one, Mary Louisa Stewart married Major Richard Molesworth of the Royal Dragoons. The couple had seven children, but their marriage was not a happy one. Richard Molesworth had been wounded in a battle in Crimea, and the shrapnel that remained in his head supposedly caused him to act violently. In addition, the couple's first daughter and son died. After the death of her daughter, Molesworth, under the pseudonym Ennis Graham, the name of a deceased childhood friend, published a three-volume adult novel concerning marriage and the unhappiness that it sometimes causes. Molesworth wrote three similar novels before she and her husband received a legal separation in 1879. After the separation, she lived in France and Germany, where she translated French and German books and wrote

Molesworth's classic book relates the tale of Griselda, a lonely young girl who is befriended and tutored by a magical cuckoo from the clock in her aunt's home. (From *The Cuckoo Clock,* illustrated by Ernest H. Shepard.)

essays before returning to England to settle permanently in 1883.

Although Molesworth had difficulties with her husband, she had a better relationship with her surviving children. She told them stories and read to them frequently. Molesworth began to write down some of her original tales and tried to gain an objective opinion about them from her children by slipping them between the covers of other books that she was reading aloud. Still, Molesworth did not think of publishing her children's stories until a friend, the artist Sir Noel Paton, suggested that she send some to the publisher Macmillan, who purchased Molesworth's stories and published them in a book, *Tell Me a Story.* This collection, which contains six stories, includes "Good-night, Winny," which according to Linda Anne Julian in the *Dictionary of Literary Biography (DLB)* "bears a striking resemblance to the circumstances surrounding the death of Molesworth's daughter Violet." Another story from this collection, "The Reel Fairies," describes a girl who imagines that spools of thread become fairies and take her away to fairyland; however, at the end of the story she becomes cross with the fairies and wants to return home. Molesworth based this character on herself as a child.

Molesworth's second published book for children, *"Carrots": Just a Little Boy,* was very popular during the late nineteenth century. "Rather than presenting magical adventures or fantasy," asserted Julian of the *DLB,* "it invites the reader to share the day-to-day happenings in a middle-class family" and thus "signaled a new kind of realism in children's literature." In *Carrots,* red-headed Fabian, the new addition to a family of six children, learns about the world through the influence of his affectionate older sister Floss, a nurse, and an aunt. Fabian, who grows from infancy to school-age through the course of the book, is also told stories—both fairy tales and Biblical references—that are interspersed throughout the narrative. Molesworth's next book, *The Cuckoo Clock,* was also very popular. The story focuses on Griselda, a little girl whose mother has died and who has been sent to live with her two elderly aunts. Griselda is lonely, but she is soon befriended by a magical cuckoo from the clock in her aunts' home; the cuckoo acts as teacher. Writing in *Horn Book,* Paula Fox noted that the "cuckoo encourages [Griselda's] curiosity and her interest in things outside of herself." The cuckoo, who is somewhat curmudgeonly, takes Griselda to Butterfly-Land, the Land of the Mandarins, and the Other Side of the Moon before disappearing when Griselda becomes friends with a little boy from a neighboring estate. In his *Tellers of Tales,* Roger Lancelyn Green called *The Cuckoo Clock* Molesworth's most famous book, one that "set her definitely in the forefront of writers for children, and showed her deep understanding of the imaginative life of children." Paula Fox remembered the story from her childhood and, upon reading it fifty years later, reported, "I found the book's voice as compelling as ever, a warm, confiding voice touched with melancholy here and there, yet often carefree, even jaunty, and very, very patient, willing to spend time on

Basing her novel on her own childhood experiences, Molesworth portrays Geraldine, whose imagination offers her escape from the unhappiness of life at her boarding school. (From *The Carved Lions,* illustrated by Lewis Hart.)

every element in its beguiling and intricate story." Analyzing this voice in *Children's Literature,* Sanjay Sircar explained that it "invites the active participation of the narrattee, and therefore indirectly of all its listeners or readers." Writing in 1988, Nigel Spencer of *Books for Keeps* found *The Cuckoo Clock* a "pleasant, old-fashioned story [that] encapsulates the flavour of the Victorian children's story" and is "full of advice."

Molesworth began to use her own name (for a second publication of *The Cuckoo Clock*) in 1877. She continued to write popular books for children, such as the fantasies *The Tapestry Room* and *Christmas-Tree Land,* and the realistic stories *Christmas Child: A Sketch of a Boy-Life,* the story of a boy who dies young and the only one of Molesworth's books to include the death of a child, *The Adventures of Herr Baby,* and *Two Little Waifs.* One of Molesworth's most highly regarded works is *The Carved Lions.* The author based this book on her own childhood; in it, young Geraldine goes from a happy home in Manchester to the horrors of boarding school. After she runs away, she finds shelter in a shop where she meets the Carved Lions, who come to life in

her dreams and help her come to cope with her problems. Roger Lancelyn Green stated that *The Carved Lions* is "[probably] the best book that [Molesworth] ever wrote, and certainly the best of the real-life stories"; he concludes that of all her works "it is the most memorable and the most convincing: the best example of the shared experience that is the secret of most of the greatest books."

Molesworth continued to write books for both children and adults into the twentieth century. In addition to the books she published with Macmillan and other publishers, Molesworth, an Anglican, wrote Bible stories and morality tales, many of which were published by the Society for Promoting Christian Knowledge. As a novelist and short story writer for adults, Molesworth commented on the middle-class of the late Victorian and early Edwardian period; she also published two collections of supernatural stories and several essays about children's literature and writing for children. Although Molesworth was respected as an adult writer, the popularity of her books for this audience was far surpassed by that of her stories for children. By the end of the nineteenth century, she had stopped writing for adults entirely.

Molesworth had specific ideas about books for children. She thought, as *DLB* essayist Linda Anne Julian explained, that children's books should contain words that would force children to understand meaning through context and would strengthen vocabularies. She also believed that children, as characters, should be rendered in a realistic fashion, even if they were depicted in fantastic environments. Finally, according to Julian, Molesworth believed that children should read books that do not make them sad, but that also do not "deceive children about the sober concerns of the world." Careless writing for children, Molesworth noted in her essay "Juliana Horatia Ewing" in the *Contemporary Review,* is an extremely serious matter because "the evil such may do can *never* be undone." In her essay "On the Art of Writing Fiction for Children," Molesworth wrote, "The great thing is to make the acquaintance of your characters and get to know them as well and as intimately as you possibly can.... I always feel as if *somewhere* the children I have *learnt* to love are living, growing into men and women like my own real sons and daughters."

Molesworth published her last book for children in 1911; in 1921, she died of heart failure. During her lifetime and well into the twentieth century, she received many critical accolades. The first major critic to acknowledge her was Algernon Charles Swinburne, the noted English poet and man of letters. Writing in the *Nineteenth Century Review* in 1884, Swinburne said that among women writers since the death of George Eliot, "there is none left whose touch is so exquisite and masterly, whose love is so thoroughly according to knowledge, whose bright and sweet invention is so fruitful, so truthful or so delightful as Mrs. Molesworth's. Any chapter of *The Cuckoo Clock* or *The Adventures of Herr Baby* is worth a shoal of the very best novels dealing with the characters and fortunes of mere adults." During the course of the twentieth century, Molesworth's books for children fell out of favor. Julian speculated that this is "perhaps because the didactic tone is not palatable a century later and because her kind of fairy tales has been supplanted by stories whose characters are products of toy manufacturers and animation." Julian concluded that it "is unlikely that any of her work, except for five or six of her best children's stories, will regain an audience." However, other contemporary reviewers view Molesworth as a solid presence in current literature for children. In his *How to Find Out about Children's Literature*, Alec Ellis called her "the last great writer of fantasy in the nineteenth century." Roger Lancelyn Green concluded that Molesworth "wrote books for children which children loved dearly then and can enjoy now.... [Adults], who although they may see her faults, can still return again and again to a great many of her books and be sure of that kind of delight which has earned her the description of 'the Jane Austen of the nursery.'"

■ Works Cited

Ellis, Alec, *How to Find Out about Children's Literature*, Pergamon, 1973, p. 121.

Fox, Paula, "A Second Look: *The Cuckoo Clock*," *Horn Book*, September, 1987, pp. 592-93.

Green, Roger Lancelyn, "Mrs. Molesworth," *Tellers of Tales: British Authors of Children's Books from 1800-1964*, Watts, 1965, pp. 104-15.

Julian, Linda Anne, "Louisa Molesworth," *Dictionary of Literary Biography, Vol. 135: British Short-Fiction Writers, 1880-1914—The Realist Tradition*, Gale, 1994, pp. 226-33.

Molesworth, Mary Louisa, "Juliana Horatia Ewing," *Contemporary Review*, May, 1886, pp. 675-86.

Sircar, Sanjay, "The Victorian Auntly Narrative Voice and Mrs. Molesworth's *Cuckoo Clock*," *Children's Literature*, 17, 1989, pp. 1-24.

Spencer, Nigel, review of *The Cuckoo Clock, Books for Keeps*, September, 1988, p. 10.

Swinburne, Algernon Charles, *Nineteenth Century Review*, 1884.

■ For More Information See

BOOKS

Carpenter, Humphrey and Mari Pritchard, *Oxford Companion to Children's Literature*, Oxford University Press, 1984, p. 355.

Green, Roger Lancelyn, *Mrs. Molesworth*, Bodley Head, 1961.

Laski, Marghanita, *Mrs. Ewing, Mrs. Molesworth, and Mrs. Hodgson Burnett*, Folcroft Library Editions, 1976.*

MORRIS, (Margaret) Jean 1924- (Kenneth O'Hara)

■ Personal

Born January 15, 1924, in Sevenoaks, Kent, England; children: one daughter. *Education:* University of London, B.A. (with honors).

■ Addresses

Home—Flat 1, 56 Pevensey Road, Eastbourne, East Sussex BN21 3HT, England.

■ Career

Writer. *Member:* PEN.

■ Awards, Honors

Arts Council of Great Britain bursary award, 1955, for drama; *The Donkey's Crusade* was a runner-up for the Whitbread writer's award, 1983.

■ Writings

FOR CHILDREN

The Path of the Dragons, Hutchinson (London), 1980.
Twist of Eight (short stories), Chatto & Windus (London), 1981.
The Donkey's Crusade, Bodley Head (London), 1983.
The Song under the Water, Bodley Head, 1985.
The Troy Game, Bodley Head, 1987.
The Paper Canoe, Bodley Head, 1988.
A New Magic, Bodley Head, 1990.
A New Calling, Bodley Head, 1992.

NOVELS

Man and Two Gods, Cassell (London), 1953, Viking (New York), 1954.
Half of a Story, Cassell, 1957.
The Adversary, Cassell, 1959.
The Blackamoor's Urn, Cassell, 1962.
A Dream of Fair Children, Cassell, 1966.

NOVELS; AS KENNETH O'HARA

A View to a Death, Cassell, 1958.
Sleeping Dogs Lying, Cassell, 1960, Macmillan (New York), 1962.
Underhandover, Cassell, 1961, Macmillan, 1963.
Double Cross Purposes, Cassell, 1962.
Unknown Man, Seen in Profile, Gollancz (London), 1967.
The Birdcage, Gollancz, 1968, Random House (New York), 1969.
The Company of St. George, Gollancz, 1972.
The Delta Knife, Gollancz, 1976.
The Ghost of Thomas Penry, Gollancz, 1977.
The Searchers of the Dead, Gollancz, 1979.
Nightmares' Nest, Gollancz, 1982, Doubleday (Garden City, NY), 1983.
Death of a Moffy, Doubleday, 1987.

PLAYS

The Spongees, published in *Eight Plays 1,* edited by Malcolm Stuart Fellows, Cassell, 1965.

Anne of Cleves, televised 1970, published in *The Six Wives of Henry VIII,* edited by J. C. Trewin, Elek (London), 1972.

Author of the stage play *Island of Gulls,* 1956; author of numerous radio plays for the British Broadcasting Corporation (BBC), including *Safety of the City,* 1961, *The Heretic,* 1962, *The Mislaid Cause,* 1964, and *Travelling in Winter,* 1971.

OTHER

(Translator, with Radost Pridham) *The Peach Thief and Other Bulgarian Stories,* Cassell, 1968.

The Monarchs of England, Charterhouse (New York), 1975.

■ Adaptations

The television play *Anne of Cleves* was adapted for the stage by Herbert E. Martin, Dramatic Publishing (Chicago), 1973.

■ Sidelights

Jean Morris is a British author of historical fantasy novels for young readers, including such popular titles as *The Path of the Dragons, The Song under the Water,* and the award-winning *Donkey's Crusade.* The last-mentioned title, set in the thirteenth century, involves a young novice monk and a wise and cynical donkey that speaks in human language, both forming part of a band of characters on a mission to help rescue Jerusalem from the non-Christian "infidels." Often dealing in quest tales, Morris also ladles up large doses of magic in her young adult books. Under the name Kenneth O'Hara, Morris has also written adult suspense novels noted for their blend of mystery and the supernatural. In addition to these young adult and adult fiction titles, Morris has also written an illustrated history of the kings and queens of England entitled *The Monarchs of England,* as well as plays and radio scripts, including the television play, *Anne of Cleves.* In all her work, she creates a rich blend of melodic language and depth of characterization and detail. As Geoffrey Trease noted in his review of *The Donkey's Crusade* in the *Times Educational Supplement,* Morris's style is akin to "listening to some strange melody played on a wind instrument with effortless command."

Morris already had many adult novels under her belt when she wrote her first for young readers, *The Path of the Dragons.* She hit the ground running, for, according to Naomi Lewis writing in *Twentieth-Century Children's Writers,* that first is "by far the most complex and demanding of her novels." Dealing with Greek myth and the legend of Atlantis, *The Path of the Dragons* tells the story of that advanced ancient civilization, including the fall of Atlantis and its replacement by the newer Greek Olympian powers. In Morris's rendering, the Atlantids, or inhabitants of Atlantis, are a gifted lot,

replete with not only mind-reading capabilities, but also many modern inventions such as computers, radio transmission, and air travel. Their mission is to bring enlightenment to the lesser-gifted, emerging civilizations of the world. The dragons of the title are an intelligent, music-loving life form, leaving paths in the sky where they have passed—guides to even the super-smart Atlantids. But the Atlantid society is ultimately doomed by the invasion of the much baser Olympians, announced by the arrival of the brutish Herakles, covered in a stinking lion skin and with club in hand. A reviewer in *British Book News, Children's Supplement* considered the novel "a really outstanding work," while a *Junior Bookshelf* contributor noted the complexity of the tale and concluded that if the reader "can share the vivid imagination of the author he will enjoy this excursion into a possible world which ends with the destruction of Atlantis."

With her second book for young adults, Morris collected eight familiar legendary, folk, and fairy tales, and stood them on their head. "Easily the most accessible of Morris's books," according to Lewis, *Twist of Eight* includes such reworkings as "The Waking Beauty," in which Sleeping Beauty takes on a new meaning. In this rendition, the beautiful princess has grown bored with her soft life and exchanges places with a young maid, running off with a stable boy instead. An evil witch then puts the fabled curse on the maid instead of the princess, which in turn sets the stage for the magic waking kiss from the handsome prince. Rumpelstiltskin and Cinderella also get a new lease on life in this "witty" collection of tales that is "likely to create new interest in old stories," according to Frances Ball in *School Librarian.* Margery Fisher, writing in *Growing Point,* felt that the stories would be appreciated by "anyone who enjoys quick wit and stylish prose." Ruth K. MacDonald, however, pointed out in *School Library Journal* that some of the stories were "not usually included in America's fairy-tale hit parade," and therefore the ironic twist Morris supplies might cause more "puzzlement" than illumination.

One of Morris's most popular titles and a runner-up for the British Whitbread writer's award, *The Donkey's Crusade* is "historical fiction in the best sense," according to Gerry Young, writing in *School Library Journal.* Thomas, fifteen and a novice monk apprenticed to a French abbey, receives a commission to search for Prester John, the fabled Christian prince and king of Asia. Thomas is born of a family of Travellers, professional guides, and his mission in finding Prester John is to win his help in combating the enemies of thirteenth-century Christendom—the Saracens. Accompanied by a street-wise Arab boy, Aubrey, an old knight, and a sentient donkey, Ears, Thomas leaves his home of Acre to travel the ancient Silk Route in search of Prester John. As the pilgrims travel farther east, adventures accrue and Thomas is taught many lessons by his loyal and sage donkey, who at times communicates to him in human language. Slowly the band discovers, however, that they have been chasing a fantasy, that Prester John is only a legend, and they agree to end their quest.

Returning to Acre, Thomas finds the city sacked and the remainder of his family killed. As a reviewer for *The Junior Bookshelf* pointed out, Thomas learns through his adventures "that religion and politics have little to do with the real things in life." The reviewer concluded that *The Donkey's Crusade* "is a gripping narrative, recreating the worlds of the East ... and its central characters are very well drawn." A reviewer for *Bulletin of the Center for Children's Books* applauded the book's "humor and sometimes barbed wit." And Fisher, in a *Growing Point* review, concluded that a "note of irony underlies the adventure, an implied comment on civilisation as the various characters understand it, which gives the book a substance beyond the immediate action."

Another of Morris's novels for young readers, *Song under the Water*, explores themes of foreignness and the difference between poverty and wealth. It is at heart an exotic coming-of-age adventure set in medieval Europe. The son of the local miller, Jem has grown up on the water and loves it. The sound of water and images of it suffuse the pages of the novel, as Jem makes friends with a strange boy, Thorn, and a flood threatens the village. The locals do not like either Thorn or the old Lady Esclairemond at the chateau, both of whom are considered outsiders; but it is at the chateau where the villagers take refuge from the rising waters. *Growing Point*'s Fisher felt that a "message for peace lies behind a tale of shifting colours and ideas which sweeps the reader into its atmosphere by the power of imagination." A *Kirkus Reviews* critic noted that the book "strikes its own satisfying tone" and serves as a good choice "for those who already have an appetite for fantasy." S. E. Chippendale, writing in the *School Librarian*, observed that the novel offers a deeper dimension for older readers, particularly the ending, in which "Jem realises that the world extends beyond his narrow community." A *Junior Bookshelf* contributor also commented on the levels of meaning in the book, finding it to be an "eventful story with drama and suspense" most memorable for "the evocative descriptions of the river and the countryside."

A quest is the focus of another Morris title, *The Troy Game*, in which the younger son of a king, Bannock, is sent on a journey by the magician, Mennon. Again, as with *The Donkey's Crusade*, the young traveler is accompanied by a loyal animal, his dog, Goldeneye, and here too the main character is shaped and educated by the adventures experienced on his journey. Mennon wants Bannock to go to the hall of his order, giving him a golden brooch to help him in his search, for on the brooch is engraved the tracks of a maze that will guide him there. Bannock is eventually joined by his cousin, the girl Eilian, and her cat, both of whom become "indispensable on the long and teasing journey with its terrors, joys, and marvels," according to Lewis in *Twentieth-Century Children's Writers*. Set loosely in the time between the fall of Roman power in England and the imposition of Saxon rule, the story harkens back to ancient English tradition, when the landscape was dotted with so-called Troy mazes, which were part

magical incantation, part spiritual ritual. The journey and search are somewhat aided by the fact that Bannock possesses psychic powers for guidance. A reviewer for *Junior Bookshelf* praised the work as "deeply fascinating" and also commented that "the power of Jean Morris' narrative carries the reader irresistibly to the last satisfying page." Fisher similarly applauded the book in her *Growing Point* review, writing that "Jean Morris's tales are always unexpected and always finely wrought—this one is no exception."

Morris turned her hand to more contemporary events with three later novels, *The Paper Canoe* and the companion volumes, *A New Magic* and *A New Calling*. Magic and fantasy are at the center of each, though in *The Paper Canoe,* the supernatural is replaced by a daydream. Young Carly has a summer job in a garden center with two older boys, Jonathan and Raff. Where Jonathan is bossy and good-looking, Raff is a kindly country boy. All three of them are anxiously awaiting their school exam scores, and for Carly this is especially nerve-wracking, for she fears she has failed in geography, the specialty of her recently-deceased father. Carly begins a powerful daydream, a journey down an African river, and subtly, the dual tales of the here-and-now and the African voyage interweave in what a *Junior Bookshelf* reviewer called a "very clever book." Morris "is one of the most subtle and thoughtful of writers," the same reviewer commented, concluding that "teenage girls who persist beyond the first few pages will find something of themselves in this portrait of one who lives in two worlds."

Very different in style are the books *A New Magic* and *A New Calling*. Both deal with the attempts of the evil witch Miss Maldrew to first recover the lost estates of her ancestors and then to enslave the citizens of Great Britain by the use of modern technology. Her nefarious schemes are battled by a quartet of children: Aspasia, Gareth, Sophie, and Leo. Employing the motif of a computer game and its virtual reality in *A New Magic,* Morris has her four protagonists foil the plot of Miss Maldrew, who is serving as their summertime governess, and her villainous co-conspirator, Dr. Cynack. Margery Fisher, reviewing the first of these volumes in *Growing Point,* commented that "optical detail and some brisk dialogue" help to make this "fresh and robust adventure" appealing to young readers. In *A New Calling,* Miss Maldrew is up to her old tricks again, but now on a larger scale—she hopes for no less than total domination of the world, beginning with England—and employs magic, shape-altering video equipment as part of her nasty arsenal. A *Junior Bookshelf* critic observed of this last title that it "has pace and great suspense and the action is a model of controlled energy."

Jessica Yates, in a review of *A New Calling* in *School Librarian,* summed up Morris's achievement as a writer for young people. The critic called Morris a "quality author ... with, sadly, a minority appeal." Expressing optimism that Morris would broaden her audience with the use of more contemporary themes, Yates concluded,

"I look forward to Jean Morris's further discoveries at the interface of science and magic."

■ Works Cited

Ball, Frances, review of *Twist of Eight, School Librarian,* September, 1981, pp. 238-39.

Chippendale, S. E., review of *The Song under the Water, School Librarian,* December, 1985, p. 356.

Review of *The Donkey's Crusade, Junior Bookshelf,* April, 1984, p. 87.

Review of *The Donkey's Crusade, Bulletin of the Center for Children's Books,* February, 1986, p. 115.

Fisher, Margery, review of *Twist of Eight, Growing Point,* July, 1981, p. 3925.

Fisher, Margery, review of *The Donkey's Crusade, Growing Point,* January, 1984, p. 4180.

Fisher, Margery, review of *The Song under the Water, Growing Point,* March, 1985, pp. 4582-83.

Fisher, Margery, review of *The Troy Game, Growing Point,* May, 1987, pp. 4804-05.

Fisher, Margery, review of *A New Magic, Growing Point,* March, 1991, p. 5493.

Lewis, Naomi, "Jean Morris," *Twentieth-Century Children's Writers,* St. James Press, 1995, pp. 683-84.

MacDonald, Ruth K., review of *Twist of Eight, School Library Journal,* August, 1982, p. 103.

Review of *A New Calling, Junior Bookshelf,* April, 1993, pp. 72-73.

Review of *The Paper Canoe, Junior Bookshelf,* February, 1989, pp. 38-39.

Review of *The Path of the Dragon, British Book News, Children's Supplement,* August, 1980, p. 8.

Review of *The Path of the Dragon, Junior Bookshelf,* August, 1980, p. 196.

Review of *The Song under the Water, Junior Bookshelf,* August, 1985, p. 188.

Review of *The Song under the Water, Kirkus Reviews,* November 15, 1987, p. 1631.

Trease, Geoffrey, review of *The Donkey's Crusade, Times Educational Supplement,* January 13, 1984.

Review of *The Troy Game, Junior Bookshelf,* June, 1987, pp. 136-37.

Yates, Jessica, review of *A New Calling, School Librarian,* May, 1993, p. 73.

Young, Gerry, review of *The Donkey's Crusade, School Library Journal,* March, 1986, p. 178.

■ For More Information See

PERIODICALS

British Book News, autumn, 1981, p. 17; September, 1987, p. 41.

Observer, November 30, 1980, p. 36; November 29, 1981, p. 27; December 11, 1983, p. 35; April 19, 1987, p. 23; August 6, 1989, p. 40; December 31, 1989, p. 36; August 5, 1990, p. 6.

Times Educational Supplement, January 5, 1981, p. 39; November 15, 1985, p. 46; January 5, 1987, p. 64; March 10, 1989, p. B14; January 11, 1991, p. 31; February 19, 1993, p. R6.

Times Literary Supplement, November 29, 1985, p. 1357; April 3, 1987, p. 355.*

—Sketch by J. Sydney Jones

N

NEEDLE, Jan 1943-
(Frank Kippax)

■ Personal

Born February 8, 1943, in Holybourne, England; son of
Bernard Lionel (an engineer) and Dorothy Mary (Brice)
Needle; children: Hugh, Sadie, David, Matti, Wilf.
Education: Victoria University of Manchester, drama
degree (with honors), 1971. *Hobbies and other interests:*
Drama, European travel (especially France), sailing.

■ Addresses

Home—Rye Top, Knowl Top Ln., Uppermill, Oldham,
Lancashire, England. *Agent*—David Higham Asso-
ciates, 5-8 Lower John St., Golden Square, London
W1R 4HA, England.

JAN NEEDLE

■ Career

Portsmouth Evening News, Portsmouth, England, reporter, 1960-64; *Daily Herald and Sun,* Manchester,
England, reporter and sub-editor, 1964-68; freelance
writer, 1971—.

■ Awards, Honors

Guardian Award for Children's Fiction commended
book, 1979, for *My Mate Shofiq;* Carnegie Medal
commended book, 1980, for *A Sense of Shame and
Other Stories;* children's books of the year list, National
Book League, 1982, for *Piggy in the Middle;* best books
list, Federation of Children's Book Groups, 1987, for
Wagstaffe the Wind-up Boy.

■ Writings

FICTION FOR YOUNG ADULTS

Albeson and the Germans, Deutsch, 1977.
My Mate Shofiq, Deutsch, 1978.
A Fine Boy for Killing, Deutsch, 1979, restored edition,
    HarperCollins, 1996.
A Sense of Shame and Other Stories, Deutsch, 1980.
Piggy in the Middle, Deutsch, 1982.
The Wicked Trade, Burnett Books, 1983.
Going Out, Deutsch, 1983.
A Pitiful Place and Other Stories, Deutsch, 1984.
Tucker's Luck, Deutsch, 1984.
Tucker in Control, Deutsch, 1985.
The Thief (also see below), Hamish Hamilton, 1989.
The Bully, Hamish Hamilton, 1993.

PLAYS FOR YOUNG ADULTS

(With Vivien Gardner and Stephen Cockett) *A Game of
    Soldiers,* Collins, 1985.
(With Vivien Gardner and Stephen Cockett) *The Rebels
    of Gas Street,* Collins, 1986.
(With Vivien Gardner and Stephen Cockett) *The Thief,*
    Collins, 1990.

FOR CHILDREN

Rottenteeth (picture book), illustrated by Roy Bentley, Deutsch, 1979.

The Bee Rustlers, illustrated by Paul Wright, Collins, 1980.

The Size Spies, illustrated by Roy Bentley, Deutsch, 1980.

Losers Weepers, illustrated by Jane Bottomley, Methuen, 1981.

Another Fine Mess, illustrated by Roy Bentley, Armada, 1982.

Behind the Bike Sheds (also see below), Methuen, 1985.

A Game of Soldiers, Deutsch, 1985.

Great Days at Grange Hill, Deutsch, 1985.

Skeleton at School, illustrated by Robert Bartelt, Heinemann, 1987.

Uncle in the Attic, illustrated by Robert Bartelt, Heinemann, 1987.

Wagstaffe the Wind-up Boy, illustrated by Roy Bentley, Deutsch, 1987.

In the Doghouse, illustrated by Robert Bartelt, Heinemann, 1988.

The Sleeping Party, illustrated by Robert Bartelt, Heinemann, 1988.

Mad Scramble, illustrated by Kate Aldous, Heinemann, 1990.

As Seen on TV, illustrated by Kate Aldous, Heinemann, 1990.

The War of the Worms, illustrated by Kay Widdowson, Hamish Hamilton, 1992.

Wagstaffe and the Life of Crime, illustrated by Roy Bentley, Collins Lions, 1992.

Bogeyman, illustrated by Liz Tofts, Deutsch, 1992.

FICTION FOR ADULTS

Wild Wood, illustrated by William Rushton, Deutsch, 1981.

(Under pseudonym Frank Kippax) *The Scar* (dramatized as television series *Underbelly*), HarperCollins, 1990.

(Under pseudonym Frank Kippax) *The Butcher's Bill,* HarperCollins, 1991.

(Under pseudonym Frank Kippax) *Other People's Blood,* HarperCollins, 1992.

(Under pseudonym Frank Kippax) *Fear of Night and Darkness,* HarperCollins, 1993.

OTHER

(With Peter Thomson) *Brecht* (criticism), University of Chicago Press, 1981.

Also author of television series *A Game of Soldiers,* 1984, *Behind the Bike Sheds,* 1985-86, *Truckers* (for adults), 1987-88, and *Soft Soap,* 1988. Author of radio plays broadcast in England and New Zealand between 1971 and 1980.

■ Sidelights

Jan Needle is a British author of books for children, young adults, and adults whose style and content area are as varied as his audiences. His works include such hard-hitting, realistic titles for young adults as *My Mate Shofiq* and *Piggy in the Middle,* both of which deal with racism and employ street argot as well as scenes of violence. Needle has also written zany comedies for younger readers such as *Wagstaffe the Wind-up Boy* and a subtler, ironic book for adults, *Wild Wood,* which turns the famous *Wind in the Willows* on its head. Under the name Frank Kippax, Needle has penned a quartet of thrillers for adults, and in addition he has written both adult and children's scripts for television and radio. If he is prolific and diverse, his twenty-plus books for children and young adults nonetheless are all "unified by a sense of humour which is always linked to a skeptical distrust of authority," according to Ann Wright in the *School Librarian.* Wright went on to point out that though Needle's "contemporary idiom and realistic subject-matter have been criticised as reflections of an over-grim reality ... they are balanced by a persuasive blend of social criticism and ironic humor."

Needle was in need of both these traits to survive his childhood. Born in Holybourne, England, he grew up in Portsmouth, a rough-and-ready port town on the south coast. His early years were punctuated with the blasts from German Nazi bombers which destroyed a third of the city during World War II; growing up, he and his friends used the bombed-out houses and factories as their playgrounds. The son of working class parents, Needle was somewhat amazed when the family moved to Wales to take up farming when he was four. Needle's father, a restless man who was always looking for his calling in life, had earned good money during the war years working in Spitfire airplane factories; with savings in hand he led his family to North Wales where the severest winter in a century ate up their capital. By spring, the family was back in Portsmouth living in a derelict factory, huddling around a single gas stove for heat and wondering how they would make ends meet. Needle's father had a succession of jobs thereafter, from editor of a Labour party newspaper to lathe operator to company director. Recalling the time spent in the old factory, Needle, writing in *Something about the Author Autobiography Series* (*SAAS*), noted that "being young, I loved it; I thought it was my private castle." This, however, was not the case with his parents or his older sister, Valerie, who made her distaste for the place only too vocal.

At school Needle excelled at "imagination things," as he stated in *SAAS.* His English and storytelling skills were well-honed, and he did not reserve such skills to story hour at school, but was forever making up tales about everything in his life. Something of a loner, short and a bit pudgy, he learned early on how to fend off attacks by bullies: "I'd run away," he wrote in *SAAS.* "Fighting's ridiculous." Needle won a scholarship to secondary school, the exclusive Portsmouth Grammar School attended by sons of naval officers. There, according to Needle in *SAAS,* "Class ... did indeed rear its ugly head, and extraordinarily quickly." His classmates, and those of that social level, "don't speak English, they quack it," according to Needle.

An outcast because of his accent—which he quickly worked on—and because he was a son of a working class family, his one saving grace at school was his skill with boats. He eventually found his place in the school as a fellow handy with the tiller and who knew his way around a sailboat. "Sadly, though," Needle recalled in *SAAS,* "not much of my school life was very pleasurable, least of all the work." When it became apparent that he would not graduate with high enough grades to win a place at a university, Needle left school. With the help of his father, who had a friend on the local paper, Needle, at age seventeen, became a cub reporter.

"Journalism, I have to say, suited me," Needle wrote. It was easy for him to write straight news stories, as he had always had a facility with language. At age eight, in fact, he had published his first work: the opening chapter of a planned novel which appeared in the paper his father was editing at the time. For three years after beginning work as a journalist, he lived at home, writing for the Portsmouth newspaper. Then, at twenty, he was offered a much more lucrative position in Manchester. Until 1968, he wrote and edited news copy, earning a good living. He married and also discovered another passion—writing fiction.

Eventually this avocation of writing came front and center in his life. By age twenty-five he had determined to become a playwright. He quit journalism and went to university, with the aid of his teacher wife, and eventually earned an honors degree in drama. "By the time I left the university," Needle said in *SAAS,* "I was a playwright, for stage and radio. However, I was ridiculously poor. I didn't have the proverbial red cent."

For a time, Needle worked solely on plays, creating vehicles for local dramatic companies. Then one day he had an idea that eventually changed his direction as a writer. A fan of the Kenneth Grahame story *Wind in the Willows,* he asked himself what it would be like to rewrite that story from the perspective of the supposed villains of the piece—the forest creatures who take over Toad Hall when the plump Mr. Toad is carted off to jail. In Needle's tongue-in-cheek version, Toad and his friend are not simply pleasure-loving and droll protagonists, they are decadent aristocrats, while the weasels and stoats in Needle's version become lower class victims who act out of desperation. Though the resulting book, *Wild Wood,* was kept from publication for many years because of copyright problems, it did plant the idea of novel-writing in Needle's head. More importantly, and quite by accident, it made his agent think he was a children's writer.

Asked to create another, and this time totally original, book for young readers, Needle obliged. In four weeks he wrote his first published novel for young readers, *Albeson and the Germans,* a book that used many of his own experiences growing up in post-war Portsmouth. Albeson runs away from school when it is announced that two German children are being enrolled. Having gleaned negative feelings about people of that nationality from both his grandfather's war stories and from comics, Albeson and his buddy, Smithie, decide to "hop the wag" as they put it and play truant from school. They indulge in shoplifting and vandalism, and finally Albeson runs away to sea—on a German boat—where the crew manages to disabuse him of his prejudices by their kindly behavior. Needle, in *SAAS,* described the story as the sort of novel "I would have liked to have read when I'd been ten to fourteen." This book was not about rich children and their adventures, but about a child much like Needle himself had been. Albeson is something of a proletarian anti-hero, controlled by self-satisfied adults yet never giving in to them. Reviewing the novel in the *Times Educational Supplement,* Roy Blatchford noted that Needle's insight into the view of a child "is remarkably forceful, and the pacing of the plot finely judged." Margaret Meek concluded her review of *Albeson and the Germans* in the *School Librarian* by commenting that Needle's brand of realism "will make us less comfortable, for a start, but young readers will see the point."

Young readers did indeed see the point, but many reviewers, teachers, and librarians found this new realism too extreme and agitating, and thus refused to review or use many of Needle's books. "From my point of view," Needle commented in *SAAS,* "these reactions were fascinating.... What the objectors seemed to be wanting was what I thought was a lie—that adults could, and would, 'look after' children, and that everything would therefore be 'made all right.'" When Needle set about writing his second novel for young readers, he first did some reading himself, surveying the contemporary world of children's literature to see if things had changed since his childhood, when he was unable to find the sort of books he wanted to read. "My overall impression was that the driving force behind them was pretty well unchanged. English children's literature, it seemed to me, existed to promote the values of an older middle class that was smug, prescriptive, and irrelevant to the mass of children 'out there'; children like I had been, but twenty years further on."

So Needle kept writing the kind of books that interested him. His second novel, *My Mate Shofiq,* deals with racism and integration. When Shofiq, a Pakistani boy, runs afoul of a local gang, young Bernard is reluctantly drawn into the fight on the Pakistani's side. The book features hard language and violent scenes as well—such as when an eye is put out in the final encounter—and through these Needle draws an unflinching portrait of a working class life lacking in comfort and hope. Gillian Cross, reviewing the novel in the *Times Literary Supplement,* noted that the "complicated story is excellently told and moves at a fast, exciting pace" and concluded that while not always "convincing," the book avoids simplistic solutions. Meek, writing in the *School Librarian,* felt that Needle's second young adult novel was "a strongly committed, outspoken book," while Terry Jones, in *Children's Literature in Education,* wondered if Needle didn't "paint so bleak a picture of that life that the reader is disinclined to go beyond the first few chapters." For Leila Berg, in the *Times Educational Supplement,* however, there were no doubts. "No one who has read [the book] ... will ever be the same again; which gives our society a chance of improvement," the critic concluded.

Needle changed direction with his third book, writing the comedy *The Size Spies* for juveniles, an act that Needle looks at now, as he explained in *SAAS,* as "the big mistake in my career as a writer for young people." This comment, however, is partly tongue-in-cheek, for Needle prides himself on the fact that he is all over the map with his books, not content to simply reproduce past successes. "One of the reasons, indeed, that I write comedies as well as darker books is because I find many children's stories do not engage children enough for them to really *care* about what's going on," Needle wrote in *SAAS. The Size Spies* deals with the adventures of young George and Cynthia and their eccentric friend, the Prof, as they get the best of a nest of spies who are after a weapon which will insure world peace. A reviewer for the *Book Window* thought the story was "an extremely funny and imaginative tale which will appeal to both boys and girls."

Following this, Needle returned to a more somber mood with *A Fine Boy for Killing,* a historical tale of conditions in the British Navy during the time of eighteenth-century British Admiral Horatio Nelson. Young Jesse Broad is impressed into the navy, literally kidnapped into such duty. But it is Broad who ultimately helps to challenge corrupt authority, only to get the noose for his troubles. This richly detailed novel was cut for the young adult market; a 1996 edition restored these cuts for an intended adult audience. While Needle seemingly dismisses the novel in *SAAS* as "deeply serious and too harrowing for all but teenagers and adults," Fred Inglis, in *Stories and Society: Children's Literature in Its Social Context,* called *A Fine Boy for Killing* "Needle's master-piece," and Peter Hollindale dubbed it a "minor classic" in *Twentieth-Century Young Adult Writers.* Inglis noted that behind "this good craftsman's prose is a driving anger and hatred at class cruelty and arrogance which he forces any halfway decent reader to share."

Needle continued to stay one step ahead of the reviewers in his eclectic mix of styles and themes with such adventure stories as *The Bee Rustlers* and *Losers Weepers,* with a picture book for the very young, *Rottenteeth,* and with a collection of short stories, *A Sense of Shame and Other Stories,* which Neil Philip in the *Times Educational Supplement* commented had "a depth of feeling and understanding" as their "two outstanding qualities." In 1982, Needle tackled another serious theme with *Piggy in the Middle,* the story of a young policewoman who encounters racism in her fellow officers and is forced to choose between her career and her beliefs. When an elderly Pakistani is brutally murdered, his son, a former classmate of the policewoman, Sandra, is held for questioning then released for lack of evidence. This is obviously a race crime, yet no one is charged for the murder, and soon Sandra is caught between her boyfriend David and those on the police force who are racist. Ultimately Sandra resigns and she and David plan to work together to battle racism and

corruption. "A thought-provoking, deeply disturbing book," is how A. Thatcher characterized *Piggy in the Middle* in the *Junior Bookshelf.* Writing in *Growing Point,* Margery Fisher admired the author's "strong, direct prose, his gift for establishing individual voices in dialogue and his uncompromising view of urban tensions."

During the mid-1980s, much of Needle's creative energy was focussed on writing for television, and some of these projects resulted in tie-in novels, as well, such as *Behind the Bike Sheds, Great Days at Grange Hill,* and *A Game of Soldiers,* about the Falkland War. It was during this time also that Needle wrote what he called in *SAAS* his "favourite book of all," *Wagstaffe the Wind-up Boy.* Written for one of his children who was a reluctant reader, the novel is a compilation of nonsense, a "crazy book," as Needle described it in *SAAS.* Wagstaffe is such an awful child that his own mother and father run away from home to be rid of him. Wagstaffe goes playing on the freeway and gets flattened by a truck and then is revived with clockwork innards. When he discovers that his parents have been kidnapped by an American circus, Wagstaffe sets off across the Atlantic to free them. Needle came in for another round of criticism for *Wagstaffe the Wind-up Boy,* from both librarians and reviewers. Jenny Woolf commented in *Punch* that "Needle miscalculated badly" with the comedy, and Chris Stephenson dubbed the story a "gruesome little book" in the *School Librarian.* Yet Stephenson had to admit that despite the "lavatory jokes" and the fact that the book was "relentlessly tasteless," there was also the "odd snicker" from his students. "The eleven-year-olds are finding it 'wickedly funny'—and that just about sums it up," Stephenson concluded. And such was, indeed, Needle's purpose in the first place. "Children's taste is not the same as adults'," Needle wrote in *SAAS.* "If I have a mission as a children's writer, that could be it: Listen to the children." Needle followed the original Wagstaffe title up with a second, *Wagstaffe and the Life of Crime.*

Returning to more serious themes, in 1989 Needle published the young adult work *The Thief,* which deals with a boy who is falsely accused of stealing. In 1993 he released *The Bully,* a book with a similar premise. Both books explore what Needle calls "the underbelly of childhood experience." Reviewing *The Bully* in the *Times Educational Supplement,* David Buckley called it "a good case study and a cracking piece of storytelling." Such writing efforts, however, were put on hold after Needle was involved in a serious traffic accident in 1992. The experience, he explained in *SAAS,* "caused a gap in my writing career.... I still find it hard to plan ahead what I *ought* to be writing next, however, and my ideas still range from comedy to tragedy.... Children's books, comic and serious, keep bubbling."

■ Works Cited

Berg, Leila, review of *My Mate Shofiq, Times Educational Supplement,* March 26, 1982, pp. 28-29.

Blatchford, Ray, review of *Albeson and the Germans, Times Educational Supplement,* January 13, 1978, p. 22.

Buckley, David, review of *The Bully, Times Educational Supplement,* February 25, 1994, p. 14.

Cross, Gillian, review of *My Mate Shofiq, Times Literary Supplement,* September 29, 1978, p. 1082.

Fisher, Margery, review of *Piggy in the Middle, Growing Point,* March, 1982, p. 4029.

Hollindale, Peter, "Needle, Jan," *Twentieth-Century Young Adult Writers,* St. James Press, 1994, pp. 484-85.

Inglis, Fred, "Social Class and Educational Adventures: Jan Needle and the Biography of a Value," *Stories and Society: Children's Literature in Its Social Context,* Macmillan, 1992, pp. 84-96.

Jones, Terry, review of *My Mate Shofiq, Children's Literature in Education,* summer, 1982, pp. 59-60.

Meek, Margaret, review of *Albeson and the Germans, School Librarian,* March, 1978, p. 60.

Meek, Margaret, review of *My Mate Shofiq, School Librarian,* December, 1978, p. 361.

Needle, Jan, *Albeson and the Germans,* Deutsch, 1977.

Needle, Jan, essay in *Something about the Author Autobiography Series,* Volume 23, Gale, 1996, pp. 179-95.

Philip, Neil, review of *A Sense of Shame and Other Stories, Times Educational Supplement,* November 7, 1980, p. 24.

Review of *The Size Spies, Book Window,* winter, 1980, p. 29.

Stephenson, Chris, review of *Wagstaffe the Wind-up Boy, School Librarian,* May, 1988, pp. 57-58.

Thatcher, A., review of *Piggy in the Middle, Junior Bookshelf,* February, 1983, p. 51.

Woolf, Jenny, review of *Wagstaffe the Wind-up Boy, Punch,* October 21, 1987, p. 42.

Wright, Ann, "Something for Everyone? A Study of Jan Needle," *School Librarian,* December, 1985, pp. 301-5.

■ For More Information See

BOOKS

Children's Literature Review, Volume 43, Gale, 1997, pp. 123-43.

—*Sketch by J. Sydney Jones*

*   *   *

NICHOLS, Grace 1950-

■ Personal

Born January 18, 1950, in Georgetown, Guyana; moved to England, 1977; companion of John Agard (a poet); children: Lesley Miranda, Kalera. *Education:* University of Guyana, diploma in communications.

■ Addresses

Agent—Anthea Morton-Saner, Curtis Brown, 162-68 Regent Street, London W1R STB, England.

■ Career

Poet, author of fiction, and editor. Teacher, 1969-70; Georgetown *Chronicle,* Guyana, reporter, 1972-73; Government Information Services, information assistant, 1973-76; freelance journalist, Guyana, until 1977.

■ Awards, Honors

Commonwealth Poetry Prize, 1983, for *I Is a Long-Memoried Woman;* British Arts Council bursary, 1988.

■ Writings

STORIES AND POETRY FOR CHILDREN

Trust You, Wriggly!, Hodder and Stoughton (London), 1980.

Baby Fish and Other Stories from Village to Rainforest, Islington Community Press (London), 1983.

Leslyn in London, Hodder and Stoughton, 1984.

The Discovery, Macmillan (London), 1986.

Come on into My Tropical Garden (poetry), illustrated by Caroline Binch, A. and C. Black (London), 1988, Lippincott, 1990.

(With John Agard) *No Hickory No Dickory No Dock: A Collection of Caribbean Nursery Rhymes,* Viking (London), 1990, published in the United States as *No Hickory No Dickory No Dock: A Collection of*

GRACE NICHOLS

Nursery Rhymes, illustrated by Cynthia Jabar, Candlewick Press (Cambridge, MA), 1995.

(Editor) *Can I Buy a Slice of Sky?: Poems from Black, Asian and American Indian Cultures,* illustrated by Liz Thomas, Blackie (London), 1991.

(Editor with John Agard) *A Caribbean Dozen: Poems from Caribbean Poets,* illustrated by Cathie Felstead, Walker Books (London), 1994, published in the United States by Candlewick Press, 1994.

Give Yourself a Hug (poems), illustrated by Kim Harley, A. and C. Black, 1994.

Asana and the Animals, illustrated by Sarah Adams, Walker, 1997.

OTHER

I Is a Long-Memoried Woman, Caribbean Cultural International, 1983.

The Fat Black Woman's Poems, Virago Press (London), 1984.

(Editor) *Black Poetry,* illustrated by Michael Lewis, Blackie, 1988, published as *Poetry Jump-Up,* Penguin (Harmondsworth, England), 1989.

Lazy Thoughts of a Lazy Woman, and Other Poems, Virago Press, 1989, Random House (New York), 1990.

Whole of a Morning Sky (novel), Virago Press, 1989.

Sunris, Virago, 1996.

Work represented in several anthologies, including *A Dangerous Knowing: Four Black Women Poets,* Sheba Feminist Publishers (London), 1984.

■ Adaptations

Nichols contributed to the audio recording *Contemporary Literature on Tape,* National Sound Archive Publications, 1987; *I Is a Long-Memoried Woman* was adapted as a video by Women Make Movies, Leda Serene/Yod Video Productions, 1990.

■ Sidelights

As critic Brenda F. Berrian explained in *Dictionary of Literary Biography (DLB),* Grace Nichols is considered "among the most important of Guyana's prolific women writers.... Nichols has established herself as a black woman writer based in Britain who is busy carving out her own space and language." In addition to poems and a novel for adults, Nichols has crafted stories and poetry for children that draw upon or reflect her own identity as a Guyanese woman; she is also an anthologist who has worked on several books with her companion, the noted English poet John Agard. "Whether Nichols writes children's books, novels, or poetry," noted Berrian, "certain themes reoccur: the experience of migration, the validation of a Caribbean history told from a Caribbean perspective, the importance of the collective voice and identity, and the survival tactics and spirituality of black woman." As a poet, Nichols draws upon the history, myths, proverbs, riddles, and, especially, the language of Guyana; she writes her poems in both Creole dialect and standard English. Nichols is acknowledged as a political and social writer whose works often reflect women's issues and the author's feminist perspective. Her work for adults has been lauded; considered a groundbreaking writer who celebrates both black women and universal emotions, she won the 1983 Commonwealth Prize for Poetry for her collection, *I Is a Long-Memoried Woman.* Nichols's work for children, too, has prompted singular praise from critics. As Judith Nicholls of *Books for Your Children* observed, Nichols "has a wonderful gift for making words sing for younger children."

Nichols was born in Georgetown, Guyana in 1950, the fifth of seven children. During her early childhood she lived in Highdam, a small village, and attended the elementary school where her father worked as headmaster and her mother gave piano lessons. She was eight years old when the family relocated to Georgetown. Nichols left high school at sixteen with the hope of working as a teacher, and ended up completing a degree in communications at the University of Guyana. She began her professional career as a journalist at the Georgetown *Chronicle* and later became a freelance writer for the Government Information Services of Guyana. While working as a journalist, Nichols covered current events and travel and wrote features; her tenure in this profession also led to her becoming a poet and writer of fiction. Nichols told Maggie Butcher in *Wasafiri,* "We used to bring out what we'd call a house organ, a small magazine with pieces from members of staff, a story, a poem, anything; and we put it together in this magazine. I had a few poems published in that, and I also had a short story published in Guyana. That was my first."

In 1977, Nichols moved from Guyana to Sussex, England, with her eldest daughter Lesley and John Agard; the couple later had a daughter of their own, Kalera. While the move took her far from home, it also caused Nichols to think and dream about Guyana. She read her poetry publicly, and began to write children's books set in the Caribbean. According to Berrian in her *DLB* essay, Nichols wrote for children because of her "love for children and belief that Caribbean children need to read books about themselves and their countries." Nichols's first book for children, *Trust You, Wriggly!,* features the adventures of a young Guyanese girl, Evangeline (Wriggly), in her village of Lowdam. *Baby Fish and Other Stories from Village to Rainforest* is a collection of five stories Nichols culled from Guyanese and Amerindian folklore; her nine-year-old daughter Lesley illustrated the book. *Leslyn in London* presents another young Guyanese protagonist, a girl coping with her move from her homeland to London. "This book is appropriate for all students to read to gain more understanding and sensitivity to foreign students in their classrooms," explained Berrian. In *The Discovery,* a work Nichols wrote for use in British primary schools, the author tells of an Amerindian girl, Tanya, whose discovery of cave paintings saves her village from being flooded by the Guyanese government to make electricity from a neighboring river.

THINGS I LIKE IN THE SEA
THAT GO BY SWIMMINGLY

Jellyfish
Starfish
Flying fish
Seals

Dolphins
Octopuses
Otters
Eels

Crabs
Turtles
Weevers
Manatees

Sea lions
Walruses
Shrimps
Whales

But best of all
I like Mermaids

Asana, who is very fond of animals, describes several of them in this collection of poems by Nichols. (From *Asana and the Animals,* illustrated by Sarah Adams.)

Come on into My Tropical Garden contains thirty poems replete with the imagery and sounds of the Caribbean; in this work, Nichols takes the point of view of a child to portray a typical South American childhood. Critics praised the book for being both specific and relevant to children from many backgrounds. Jill Bennett of *Books for Keeps* called *Garden* a "superb collection" and concluded that the poet's "words ... paint colours in the imagination." While Nichols presents some "universal experiences," as John Peters of *School Library Journal* pointed out, "the frequent use of rhythmic non-standard English establishes a lyrical sense of place.... An inviting mix of the exotic and the familiar."

Give Yourself a Hug, published after *Come on into My Tropical Garden*, "deserves a wave of applause in its own right!" as *School Librarian* contributor Chris Routh exclaimed. This collection features poems that, in Routh's words, "offer a variety of rhythm and rhyme" and seem to be set in England as well as in the Caribbean. Critics especially appreciate the poem in which a Caribbean grandmother comes to visit her family in England; she finds the place cold, but states that she is at home "wherever there's God's earth." *Give Yourself a Hug,* in the words of *Books for Keeps* reviewer Pam Harwood, is a "bright, zingy collection.... A fabulously rich resource."

Nichols teamed up with John Agard on *No Hickory, No Dickory, No Dock,* a collection of thirty-nine poems that parodies Mother Goose rhymes in a Caribbean setting; although six of these are traditional Caribbean verses, the remainder have been written by the couple. Hazel Rochman of *Booklist* called the book "a lively collection that takes Mother Goose to the Caribbean in all her dancing energy and nonsense" and concluded that it will "appeal to those who've had enough of Little Miss

Muffet." Barbara Osborne Williams, however, found that the collection was disappointing "in view of the extraordinary execution" of the other contributions of Nichols and Agard. *A Caribbean Dozen: Poems from Caribbean Poets* is a collection of fifty-four poems written by thirteen Caribbean poets; first-person memoirs begin each poet's section. The "poems are deeply rooted in the details of West Indian culture," explained Julie Corsaro of *Booklist,* who called the book a "winner on several counts." Most of the entries, wrote a *Publishers Weekly* critic, "address the universal concerns of children in language saturated with the sounds and colors" of the Caribbean. "An excellent venue for multicultural appreciation," concluded Barbara Osborne Williams of *School Library Journal.* In addition to presenting the lyricism of the Caribbean to young readers, Nichols has collected and presented the poetic products of other cultures. Her collection *Can I Buy a Slice of Sky?: Poems from Black, Asian and American Indian Cultures* features diverse poems from people around the world, represents different languages and dialects, and includes oral poetry, nursery rhymes, and even the verses of children. "The overall mood is one of celebration," observed *Books for Keeps* commentator George Hunt, who called the book "an uncommonly varied anthology.... An essential collection."

In her essay "The Battle with Language," Nichols has explained her philosophy of writing: "I would say that I write because writing is my way of participating in the world and in the struggle for keeping language and the human spirit alive (including my own)." She adds that her work is "a way of sharing a vision that is hopefully life-giving."

■ Works Cited

Bennett, Jill, review of *Come on into my Tropical Garden, Books for Keeps,* May, 1993, p. 10.

Berrian, Brenda F., "Grace Nichols," *Dictionary of Literary Biography, Volume 157: Twentieth-Century Caribbean and Black African Writers,* Gale, 1995, pp. 235-40.

Review of *A Caribbean Dozen, Publishers Weekly,* November 28, 1994, p. 62.

Corsaro, Julie, review of *A Caribbean Dozen, Booklist,* December 1, 1994, p. 665.

Harwood, Pam, review of *Give Yourself a Hug, Books for Keeps,* July, 1996, p. 12.

Hunt, George, review of *Can I Buy a Slice of Sky, Books for Keeps,* January 1994, p. 9.

Nicholls, Judith, review of *Come on into my Tropical Garden, Books for Your Children,* summer, 1993, p. 21.

Nichols, Grace, "The Battle with Language," *Caribbean Women Writers: Essays from the First International Conference,* edited by Selwyn Cudjoe, Calaloux, 1990, pp. 283-89.

Nichols, Grace, "Grace Nichols in Conversation with Maggie Butcher," *Wasafiri,* spring, 1988, pp. 17-19.

Peters, John, review of *Come on into my Tropical Garden, School Library Journal,* April, 1990, p. 136.

Rochman, Hazel, review of *No Hickory, No Dickory, No Dock, Booklist,* May 1, 1995, p. 1576.

Routh, Chris, review of *Give Yourself a Hug, School Librarian,* May, 1995, p. 75.

Williams, Barbara Osborne, review of *A Caribbean Dozen, School Library Journal,* December, 1994, p. 94.

Williams, Barbara Osborne, review of *No Hickory, No Dickory, No Dock, School Library Journal,* August, 1995, pp. 131-32.

■ For More Information See

BOOKS

Blain, Virginia and others, *The Feminist Companion to Literature in English: Women Writers from the Middle Ages to the Present,* Yale University Press, 1990.

Buck, Claire, editor, *The Bloomsbury Guide to Women's Literature,* Prentice Hall, 1992.

Mgcobo, Lauretta, editor, *Let It Be Told: Black Women Writers in Britain,* Virago, 1987, pp. 95-104.

Penguin Modern Poets, Vol. 8, Penguin, 1996.

Williams, Patrick, "Difficult Subjects: Black British Women's Poetry," in *Literary Theory and Poetry: Extending the Canon,* edited by David Murray, B. T. Batsford, 1989, pp. 108-26.

Woodcock, Bruche, "'Long Memoried Women': Caribbean Women Poets," in *Black Women's Writing,* edited by Gina Whisker, St. Martin's Press, 1993, pp. 55-77.

PERIODICALS

Choice, Spring, 1991, p. 47.

Publishers Weekly, June 5, 1995, p. 64.

School Librarian, August, 1997, p. 132.

Third World Quarterly, April, 1988, pp. 995-98.

O

O'HARA, Kenneth
See MORRIS, (Margaret) Jean

* * *

OSBORNE, Mary Pope 1949-

■ Personal

Born May 20, 1949, in Ft. Sill, OK; daughter of William P. (a U.S. Army colonel) and Barnette (maiden name, Dickens) Pope; married Will Osborne (an actor and writer), May 16, 1976. *Education:* University of North Carolina at Chapel Hill, B.A., 1971.

■ Addresses

Agent—Gail Hochman, Brandt and Brandt, 1501 Broadway, #2310, New York, NY 10036.

■ Career

Writer, 1980—. Also worked variously as a window dresser, medical assistant, travel consultant, waitress, bartender, and editor for a children's magazine. *Member:* PEN International, Authors Guild (elected council member; chairman of Children's Book Committee; president, 1993-97), Authors Guild Foundation (vice-president, 1996—).

■ Awards, Honors

Woodward Park School Annual Award (Brooklyn, NY), and Children's Choice from the International Reading Association and the Children's Book Council, both 1983, and chosen Most Popular Children's Novel of the Northern Territory of Australia, 1986, all for *Run, Run, as Fast as You Can;* Children's Books of the Year list, Child Study Association of America, 1986, for *Last One Home;* Pick of the List, *American Bookseller,* 1986, for *Mo to the Rescue;* "outstanding and worthy of note" citation, Virginia Library Association, 1990, for *The Many Lives of Benjamin Franklin;* Pick of the List, *American Bookseller,* and Best Books of the Year,

MARY POPE OSBORNE

Parents' Magazine, both 1991, both for *Moonhorse;* one of Bank Street's Best Books of the Year, 1992, for *Spider Kane and the Mystery under the May-Apple;* one of Bank Street's Best Books of the Year, 1992, for *Dinosaurs before Dark;* Best Books of the Year List, *School Library Journal,* Blue Ribbon Book, *Bulletin of the Center for Children's Books,* Notable Children's Trade Book in the Field of Social Studies, National Council for the Social Studies/Children's Book Council, all 1991, and Utah Children's Book Award, 1993, all for *American Tall Tales;* Edgar Award finalist, Best Juvenile Mystery, 1993, for *Spider Kane and the Mystery at Jumbo Nightcrawler's;* Notable Children's Trade Book in Social Studies, National Council for the Social Studies/Children's Book Council, 1993, for *Mermaid Tales from around the World;* Orbis Pictus Honor Award, National Council of Teachers of English, 1996, for *One World, Many Religions: The Ways We Worship.*

■ **Writings**

FOR YOUNG PEOPLE

Run, Run, as Fast as You Can, Dial, 1982.
Love Always, Blue, Dial, 1983.
Best Wishes, Joe Brady, Dial, 1984.
Mo to the Rescue, illustrated by Dyanne Disalvo-Ryan, Dial, 1985.
Last One Home, Dial, 1986.
(Reteller) *Beauty and the Beast,* illustrated by Winslow Pinney Pels, Scholastic, 1987.
The Story of Christopher Columbus: Admiral of the Ocean Sea, illustrated by Stephen Marchesi, Dell, 1987, Gareth Stevens, 1997.
Pandora's Box, illustrated by Lisa Amoroso, Scholastic, 1987.
(With Will Osborne) *Jason and the Argonauts,* illustrated by Steve Sullivan, Scholastic, 1988.
(With Will Osborne) *Deadly Power of Medusa,* illustrated by Steve Sullivan, Scholastic, 1988.
(Reteller) *Favorite Greek Myths,* illustrated by Troy Howell, Scholastic, 1989.
Mo and His Friends, illustrated by Dyanne Disalvo-Ryan, Dial, 1989, Puffin, 1997.
A Visit to Sleep's House, illustrated by Melissa Bay Mathis, Knopf, 1989.
The Many Lives of Benjamin Franklin, Dial, 1990.
(Editor) *The Calico Book of Bedtime Rhymes from around the World,* illustrated by T. Lewis, Contemporary Books, 1990.
(Compiler) *Bears, Bears, Bears: A Treasury of Stories, Songs, and Poems about Bears,* illustrated by Karen L. Schmidt, Silver Press, 1990, Simon and Schuster, 1992.
Moonhorse, illustrated by S. M. Saelig, Knopf, 1991.
George Washington: Leader of a New Nation, Dial, 1991.
(Reteller) *American Tall Tales,* illustrated by Michael McCurdy, Knopf, 1991.
Spider Kane and the Mystery under the May-Apple, illustrated by Victoria Chess, Knopf, 1992.
Dinosaurs before Dark, illustrated by Sal Murdocca, Random House, 1992.
Spider Kane and the Mystery at Jumbo Nightcrawler's, illustrated by V. Chess, Knopf, 1993.
The Knight at Dawn, illustrated by Sal Murdocca, Random House, 1993.
Mummies in the Morning, illustrated by Sal Murdocca, Random House, 1993.
(Reteller) *Mermaid Tales from around the World,* illustrated by Troy Howell, Scholastic, 1993.
Molly and the Prince, illustrated by Elizabeth Sayles, Knopf, 1994.
Pirates Past Noon, illustrated by Sal Murdocca, Random House, 1994.
Night of the Ninjas, illustrated by Sal Murdocca, Random House, 1995.

Afternoon on the Amazon, illustrated by Sal Murdocca, Random House, 1995.
Sunset of the Sabertooth, illustrated by Sal Murdocca, Random House, 1996.
One World, Many Religions: The Ways We Worship, Knopf, 1996.
Midnight on the Moon, illustrated by Sal Murdocca, Random House, 1996.
Haunted Waters, Candlewick Press, 1996.
(Reteller) *Favorite Norse Myths,* Scholastic, 1996.
Rocking Horse Christmas, illustrated by Ned Bittinger, Scholastic, 1997.
Dolfins at Daybreak, illustrated by Sal Murdocca, Random House, 1997.
Ghost Town at Sundown, illustrated by Sal Murdocca, Random House, 1997.
(Reteller) *Favorite Medieval Tales,* illustrated by Troy Howell, Scholastic, 1998.
Lions at Lunchtime, illustrated by Sal Murdocca, Random House, 1998.
Standing in the Light: The Captive Diary of Catherine Carey Logan, Delaware Valley, Pennsylvania, 1763, Scholastic, 1998.
Polar Bears Past Bedtime, Random House, 1998.
Vacation under the Volcano, Random House, 1998.
Day of the Dragonking, Random House, 1998.
Viking Ships at Sunrise, Random House, 1998.
Hour of the Olympics, Random House, 1998.
The Life of Jesus in Masterpieces of Art, Viking/Penguin, 1998.

■ **Work in Progress**

The Family Animal, a dramatic play about the late 1960s; *Manifest Destiny,* a stage musical about expansion into the American West, in collaboration with three other authors; *Adaline Falling Star,* a novel of a girl on the Mississippi River in 1843.

■ **Sidelights**

Mary Pope Osborne is the author of over forty works for children and young adults, including award-winning picture books, biographies for middle-grade readers, fantasies, retellings of tall tales and mythologies, and novels. Osborne's highly-acclaimed and popular books such as the best-selling "Magic Tree House" series, the middle grade reader *One World, Many Religions: The Ways We Worship,* and her collection of retellings, *American Tall Tales,* are reflective of the author's eclectic interests. She explores the wonders of the world in her books and novels, drawing heavily on mythology, history, and her personal experiences for material.

Osborne's personal material will not soon run out. The daughter of a military father, she lived in Oklahoma, Austria, Florida, and various army posts in Virginia and North Carolina before the age of fifteen. Far from finding this wandering life a burden, she revelled in the constant change, building close family ties not only with her parents, but also with her twin brother, older sister, and younger brother. Traumatic for Osborne was staying in one place, which the family did upon her father's

Toda trembled when he saw her.

THE SERPENT AND THE SEA QUEEN

The Sea Queen of Japan lavishly rewards a brave man who has rescued her from a serpent in one tale from Osborne's collection of mermaid stories. (From *Mermaid Tales from around the World*, illustrated by Troy Howell.)

retirement, settling in a small town in North Carolina. Osborne was consumed by boredom until one day she discovered a community theater—a place that changed her life. Thereafter, she spent all available free time at the theater, both acting and working backstage. Attending the University of North Carolina at Chapel Hill, she first studied drama, and then in her junior year became interested in comparative religions and mythology, majoring finally in religion.

Graduating in 1971, Osborne spent the next several years traveling: living for a time in a cave on Crete, and then caravaning with friends through sixteen Asian countries to Katmandu where she contracted a life-threatening case of blood poisoning. Back in the U.S., Osborne moved first to Monterey, California, working as a window dresser and medical assistant. By the mid-1970s she was back on the east coast, working as a travel consultant in Washington, D.C. One night at the theater in Washington, viewing a musical version of the life of Jesse James, she fell in love with the actor playing Jesse, Will Osborne. A year later they were married and on tour.

Osborne's first novel was about an eleven-year-old girl living in the South, who was not unlike Osborne herself. Employing many of the incidents that happened to her during her childhood, Osborne finished the book and Dial Press bought it. In 1982 this first novel, *Run, Run, as Fast as You Can,* was published. Substituting Virginia for North Carolina, Osborne explored many of her own emotional states when her father retired from the army and settled down. Her protagonist, Hallie Pines, worries about her popularity and deals with a family tragedy when her younger brother is diagnosed with cancer. Karen M. Klockner, writing in *Horn Book,* noted that in her first book, Osborne "shows a family in crisis, unable to communicate with or help one another; and she writes naturally about the interaction among children and of children with adults." A critic in *Publishers Weekly* felt that the novel was "a sensitive, moving and remarkably honest delineation of conflicting values that affect children during puberty," while a *Growing Point* reviewer concluded that *Run, Run, as Fast as You Can* "has a candour and directness which are refreshing." Osborne's first novel also earned her several awards and honors both in the United States and abroad.

With her next titles, Osborne continued to explore the genre of young adult fiction. *Love Always, Blue* and *Best Wishes, Joe Brady* both feature teenage female protagonists: in the former, Blue Murray is fourteen and has to learn to cope with her parents' recent separation; in the latter, eighteen-year-old Sunny suffers the pangs of first love when she falls for an older actor. Reviewing *Love Always, Blue* in *School Library Journal,* Denise L. Moll felt the book was "much better than many in the plethora of dealing-with-divorce titles," while *Booklist*'s Ilene Cooper found it to be an "engrossing story of family relationships that will give young people a perception about adult depression and how it manifests itself." Gayle Keresey, reviewing *Best Wishes, Joe Brady*

in *Voice of Youth Advocates,* noted that the book would be "highly appealing because it deals with first love and soap opera stars" but that Osborne's novel displayed more "substance, character development, and regional flavor . . . than is found in the typical series romances." In *Last One Home,* Osborne rounded out a quartet of young adult and juvenile novels from her early writing period. In the novel, twelve-year-old Bailey struggles to overcome her loneliness after her parents' divorce, her father's subsequent planned remarriage, and her brother's preparations to leave for the service. Phyllis Graves, writing in *School Library Journal,* observed that Osborne's "finely crafted characterization enhances this affecting story about the difficulties of coping," while a reviewer in *Bulletin of the Center for Children's Books* noted that the "writing style has vitality and pace; the dialogue is excellent."

With *Mo to the Rescue,* Osborne branched out into easy-to-read picture books. Mo is an amiable beaver-cum-sheriff who keeps the peace around his pond. He welcomes a newcomer, Chicken Lucille, decked out in bermuda shorts and tennis shoes, and manages to settle a family argument in the Bluejay family, among other tales. "Mo is an engaging newcomer to a long line of animal easy-to-read protagonists," observed Denise M. Wilms in *Booklist,* and a critic in *Publishers Weekly* found Osborne's stories "droll" and "tender." Osborne visited Mo again in *Mo and His Friends,* a "fine addition to the easy-to-read shelves," according to Gale W. Sherman in *School Library Journal.*

Further easy-to-read picture books by Osborne include the retelling of *Beauty and the Beast;* a fantasy inspired by Ovid's *Metamorphoses, A Visit to Sleep's House;* the award-winning *Moonhorse;* and *Molly and the Prince.* Osborne's *Beauty and the Beast* foreshadows much of her later work in the retelling of myth and folk tales, twin passions that go back to her college days. Her *Beauty and the Beast* adapts the French fairy tale in a story told "elementally but smoothly," according to Betsy Hearne in *Bulletin of the Center for Children's Books.* Osborne later teamed up with her husband, Will Osborne, to adapt Greek myths in *Jason and the Argonauts* and *The Deadly Power of Medusa.* Bedtime gets a different take with Osborne's *A Visit to Sleep's House,* following the progress of a little girl who ventures along a mountain path to the house where sleep lives. Patricia Pearl noted in *School Library Journal* that the "combination of soothing, melodious words and peaceful evening pictures makes an unusual and pleasant bedtime story." A *Publishers Weekly* critic observed that "This imaginative concept provides a comfortingly different look at bedtime." *Moonhorse* details a moonlit ride on a winged horse, a book filled with "gracefully phrased text," according to a contributor in *Kirkus Reviews.* More fantasy is served up in *Molly and the Prince,* the story of a little girl who finds a stray dog by a river and follows it deep into the forest where magic in the form of a satyr awaits her. "Dog lovers and lovers of magic will respond to this brief but intense idyll," concluded *Kirkus Reviews.* A reviewer for *Publishers Weekly* felt that Osborne's "original tale touches the

In this tale from the "Magic Tree House" series, Jack and Annie are transported back to the Wild West, where they experience both excitement and danger. (From *Ghost Town at Sundown,* illustrated by Sal Murdocca.)

deep ground where children find secrets hidden from adult knowledge," and that "Elegant prose and deceptively simple dialogue couch the rare accomplishment of a genuinely childlike voice." Osborne's best-selling picture book, *Rocking Horse Christmas,* also explores mythical journeys in the imagination. A *Publishers Weekly* critic wrote, "Osborne's prose is masterfully subtle."

Osborne returned to juvenile fiction with *Haunted Waters,* adapted from the German fairy tale, *Undine,* about the water sprite who marries a human. Osborne endowed her tale with a gothic twist, as Lord Huldbrand travels through the frightening woods, stumbling onto the cottage of a fisherman where he meets the foundling Undine. Trapped by a sudden storm, the knight marries Undine, the child of nature, who ultimately leaves her human form to return to her watery home. Carrie Eldridge, writing in *Voice of Youth Advocates,* found the novel to be "well written" and felt that it "will appeal to

those interested in fairly tales and fantasy." A critic in *Kirkus Reviews* noted that the "lushly atmospheric narrative will draw readers who enjoy dark, otherworldly fantasies," while a *Publishers Weekly* reviewer dubbed the book a "sweepingly romantic novel." The reviewer went on to note that Osborne "chooses details elegantly and economically, using just a few descriptive phrases to evoke a sumptuously imagined chivalric age. Lustrous as a pearl."

Humor and fantasy inform the books Osborne has written for middle and beginning readers. In *Spider Kane and the Mystery under the May-Apple,* she presents a "bug-saga," according to Roger Sutton in *Bulletin of the Center for Children's Books,* that will keep its audience "amused and slightly breathless at the fast action and twisting plot." Leon, a young butterfly, falls in love with gossamer Mimi, who promptly disappears. Enter the brilliant detective Spider Kane to help put matters to right. In an extensive review in the *New York Times Book Review,* Scotia W. MacRae noted that Osborne's work was "more a book about coming of age than it is a mystery," and observed that there "is lots of plot lightly spun out in this beguiling fantasy." The insect detective made a curtain call in *Spider Kane and the Mystery at Jumbo Nightcrawler's.*

Osborne has also developed a best-selling series of beginning chapter books in the "Magic Tree House" series, time-travel fantasies about Jack and his younger sister Annie who find a tree house filled with books. Wishes turn to reality when pages of the books form real-life adventures for the children. Encounters with dinosaurs, ninjas, mummies, knights, pirates, and saber-tooth tigers are but a sampling of the adventures in store for the siblings. Reviewing the first title in the series, *Dinosaurs before Dark,* Louise L. Sherman in *School Library Journal* called the work an "enjoyable time-travel fantasy" and "a successful beginning chapter book." A contributor in *Kirkus Reviews* stated that it was "a fast-paced tale offering both mystery and dinosaurs—powerful enticements for newly independent readers." Osborne has helped develop a Magic Tree House Club for young readers, a Web site, and a classroom program. She speaks extensively around the country about the series and is planning to write a total of twenty-four "Magic Tree House" books.

Osborne has also carved out a place for herself in two further areas of children's literature: biography and retellings of myths and folk tales. In the former category she has told the life stories of such well-known men as Christopher Columbus, Ben Franklin, and George Washington. Phyllis Wilson, writing in *Booklist,* called Osborne's *The Story of Christopher Columbus: Admiral of the Ocean Sea* "an objective, sober text," and Mary Mueller noted in *School Library Journal* that "Osborne presents Columbus as a hero, but also as a man who had both strengths and weaknesses in his nature," concluding that "Overall, this title would be a good addition to libraries needing biographies which are written from a modern standpoint and are without many of the prejudices and distortions common in older books for children." A critic in the *New York Times Book Review* observed that Franklin himself "might well be pleased" by Osborne's "briskly written" *Many Lives of Benjamin Franklin,* and *Booklist*'s Deborah Abbott dubbed Osborne's *George Washington: Leader of a New Nation* "a pithy biography."

Retellings of Greek, Norse, and medieval myths, as well as American tall tales and mermaid tales, also find their way into Osborne's varied writings. Reviewing Osborne's *Favorite Greek Myths* in *Bulletin of the Center for Children's Books,* Betsy Hearne noted that the author's "mix of narrative and dialogue makes for an informal tone that will disarm readers unfamiliar with the tales." *Horn Book*'s Mary Burns observed of Osborne's *Favorite Norse Myths* that it "would be difficult to find a more useful or appealing source for these timeless tales." For her award-winning *American Tall Tales,* Osborne chose nine stories about such figures as Pecos Bill, Paul Bunyan, and Johnny Appleseed, in a "superlative offering," according to Luann Toth in *School Library Journal.* Osborne was also able to indulge her interest in comparative religions with *One World, Many Religions: The Ways We Worship,* an "exceptionally handsome volume" which "offers middle readers a thoughtful overview of major world religions," according to Elizabeth Bush in *Bulletin of the Center for Children's Books.* Ilene Cooper, writing in *Booklist,* thought that the work would be an "excellent choice for religion shelves." A reviewer in *Newsweek* magazine said that "Osborne's clear, precise style serves her subject very well. This book has an unforced dignity that's rare in children's literature."

Osborne has also been a leading advocate of author's rights. She was only the second children's book author to be elected president of the Authors Guild (the leading organization in the United States for professional book authors) in the Guild's eighty-five year history. She is also one of the founding directors of the Authors Registry and vice-president of the Authors Guild Foundation.

Osborne divides her time between her New York City apartment and a cabin in the Pennsylvania woods, and if her work is varied, it is also reflective of the life of the author. As she once told *SATA,* "I feel that the years I spent traveling in Asia, the different jobs I've held, the theater career of my husband, our life in New York among a small community of writers, actors, musicians, and artists, my southern military background, my family, my editor, my work with runaway teenagers, and my interests in philosophy and mythology have all informed and shaped my work."

■ Works Cited

Abbott, Deborah, review of *George Washington: Leader of a New Nation, Booklist,* August, 1991, p. 2143.

Burns, Mary, review of *Favorite Norse Myths, Horn Book,* July-August, 1996, pp. 471-72.

Bush, Elizabeth, review of *One World, Many Religions: The Ways We Worship, Bulletin of the Center for Children's Books,* January, 1997, p. 183.

Cooper, Ilene, review of *Love Always, Blue,* and *Best Wishes, Joe Brady, Booklist,* January 15, 1984, p. 750.

Cooper, Ilene, review of *One World, Many Religions: The Ways We Worship, Booklist,* October 1, 1996, p. 336.

Review of *Dinosaurs before Dark, Kirkus Reviews,* August 1, 1992, p. 993.

Eldridge, Carrie, review of *Haunted Waters, Voice of Youth Advocates,* February, 1995, p. 350.

Graves, Phyllis, review of *Last One Home, School Library Journal,* May, 1986, p. 108.

Review of *Haunted Waters, Kirkus Reviews,* August 15, 1994, p. 1137.

Review of *Haunted Waters, Publishers Weekly,* August 15, 1994, p. 96.

Hearne, Betsy, review of *Beauty and the Beast, Bulletin of the Center for Children's Books,* July, 1987, p. 216.

Hearne, Betsy, review of *Favorite Greek Myths, Bulletin of the Center for Children's Books,* June, 1989, pp. 261-62.

Keresey, Gayle, review of *Best Wishes, Joe Brady, Voice of Youth Advocates,* June, 1985, p. 134.

Klockner, Karen M., review of *Run, Run, as Fast as You Can, Horn Book,* June, 1982, pp. 291-92.

Review of *Last One Home, Bulletin of the Center for Children's Books,* June, 1986, p. 192.

MacRae, Scotia W., review of *Spider Kane and the Mystery under the May-Apple, New York Times Book Review,* June 7, 1992, p. 22.

Review of *The Many Lives of Benjamin Franklin, New York Times Book Review,* March 17, 1991, p. 27.

Moll, Denise L., review of *Love Always, Blue, School Library Journal,* January, 1984, p. 88.

Review of *Molly and the Prince, Kirkus Reviews,* July 15, 1994, p. 992.

Review of *Molly and the Prince, Publishers Weekly,* August 15, 1994, p. 94.

Review of *Moonhorse, Kirkus Reviews,* May 15, 1991, p. 678.

Review of *Mo to the Rescue, Publishers Weekly,* November 29, 1985, p. 49.

Mueller, Mary, review of *The Story of Christopher Columbus: Admiral of the Ocean Sea, School Library Journal,* March, 1988, p. 208.

Review of *One World, Many Religions: The Ways We Worship, Newsweek,* December 2, 1996.

Pearl, Patricia, review of *A Visit to Sleep's House, School Library Journal,* January, 1990, pp. 87-88.

Review of *Rocking Horse Christmas, Publishers Weekly,* October 6, 1997.

Review of *Run, Run, as Fast as You Can, Growing Point,* January, 1984, p. 4187.

Review of *Run, Run, as Fast as You Can, Publishers Weekly,* September 17, 1982, pp. 114-15.

Sherman, Gale W., review of *Mo and His Friends, School Library Journal,* July, 1989, p. 74.

Sherman, Louise L., review of *Dinosaurs before Dark, School Library Journal,* September, 1992, p. 209.

Sutton, Roger, review of *Spider Kane and the Mystery under the May-Apple, Bulletin of the Center for Children's Books,* May, 1992, pp. 244-45.

Toth, Luann, review of *American Tall Tales, School Library Journal,* December, 1991, pp. 125-26.

Review of *A Visit to Sleep's House, Publishers Weekly,* October 27, 1989, p. 63.

Wilms, Denise M., review of *Mo to the Rescue, Booklist,* October 15, 1989, pp. 342-43.

Wilson, Phyllis, review of *The Story of Christopher Columbus: Admiral of the Ocean Sea, Booklist,* March 1, 1988, p. 1189.

■ For More Information See

PERIODICALS

Booklist, November 1, 1984, p. 361; August, 1986, p. 1692; June 1, 1989, p. 1728; August, 1989, p. 1981; March 15, 1992, p. 1352; May 1, 1992, p. 1602; October 15, 1993, pp. 436-37.

Bulletin of the Center for Children's Books, January, 1984, p. 94; January, 1992, p. 135; February, 1994, p. 197.

Junior Bookshelf, December, 1985, p. 262; February, 1992, p. 12.

Kirkus Reviews, May 1, 1989, p. 695; October 15, 1991, p. 1347; April 15, 1992, p. 541; January 1, 1996, p. 72; August 1, 1996, p. 1156.

New York Times Book Review, December 1, 1985, p. 39; April 1, 1990, p. 26; December 22, 1991, p. 15.

Publishers Weekly, June 21, 1991, p. 66.

School Library Journal, January, 1985, p. 87; December, 1987, p. 82; August, 1991, p. 153; November, 1993, p. 118; September, 1994, pp. 190-91; December, 1994, p. 111; April, 1996, p. 148; November, 1996, pp. 116-17.

Wilson Library Bulletin, June, 1994, p. 130.

—*Sketch by J. Sydney Jones*

*   *   *

OTTEN, Charlotte F. 1926-

■ Personal

Born March 1, 1926, in Chicago, IL; daughter of Edward E. (a communications sales representative) and Anna (DeBeer) Fennema; married Robert T. Otten (a professor of classical languages and literature), December 21, 1948; children: Gillis R., Justin E. *Education:* Calvin College, B.A., 1949; University of Michigan, M.A., 1969; Michigan State University, Ph.D., 1971.

■ Addresses

Home—2271 Whisper Cove Dr., S.E., Grand Rapids, MI 49508-3780. *Office*—Department of English, Calvin College, Grand Rapids, MI 49546.

■ Career

Grand Valley State University, Allendale, MI, assistant professor, 1972-74, associate professor of English, 1974-77; Calvin College, Grand Rapids, MI, professor of English, 1977-1991. Consultant to National Endowment for the Humanities. *Member:* Modern Language Association of America, Milton Society, Children's Literature Association, Shakespeare Association of America, Society for Textual Scholarship.

■ Awards, Honors

American Council of Learned Societies Grant-in-Aid, Summer 1973; Grand Valley State College Research Grant, 1976-77; Calvin Foundation Grant, 1978; University of Chicago Occasional Fellowship, 1980 and 1982; Calvin College Faculty Research Grant, 1985-86; Newberry Library Fellowship, 1985-86; Calvin College Summer Research Grant, 1987.

■ Writings

FOR CHILDREN

January Rides the Wind: A Book of Months (poetry), illustrated by Todd L. W. Doney, Lothrop, Lee & Shepard, 1997.

OTHER

Environ'd With Eternity: God, Poems, and Plants in Sixteenth and Seventeenth Century England, Coronado Press (Lawrence, KS), 1985.

(Editor) *A Lycanthropy Reader: Werewolves in Western Culture,* Syracuse University Press (Syracuse, NY), 1986.

(Editor with Gary D. Schmidt) *The Voice of the Narrator in Children's Literature,* Greenwood Press (Westport, CT), 1989.

CHARLOTTE F. OTTEN

(Editor) _English Women's Voices, 1540-1700,_ University of Florida Press, 1991.

(Editor) _The Virago Book of Birth Poetry,_ Virago (London, England), 1993.

(Editor) _The Book of Birth Poetry,_ Bantam, 1995.

Contributor of articles to journals such as _English Language Notes, The Explicator, Milton Studies, Notes and Queries, Shakespeare Quarterly,_ and _Signal._ Otten's poems have appeared in many journals, including _Manhattan Poetry Review, Commonweal, Southern Humanities Review, Anglican Theological Review, Skylark,_ and _South Coast Poetry Journal._

■ Sidelights

Charlotte F. Otten once commented, "_A Lycanthropy Reader_ sprang from my work in Renaissance literature. Not a wayward study of the irrational, it addresses the problems, struggles, conflicts, anxieties, triumphs, and joys of human life through the study of this particular phenomenon—metamorphosis.

"I started writing poetry when I took a group of students to Wales. When my Welsh colleague (and poet) asked me why I wasn't writing poetry along with my students, I was nonplussed. I thought that coteaching them excused me from doing the assignments. The question festered in my mind. I wrote my first poem in Wales about the ruins left by Eric Gill in Wales, the next poem about my students at the grave of Henry Vaughan. After that came poems about other people and places: Le Corbusier at Harvard; the Keweenaw Peninsula and Sleeping Bear Dune in Michigan; Abraham Lincoln in Hodgenville, Kentucky; Chicago. Then came poems on war—World War I, World War II, Vietnam—and poems on family and fishing."

Otten's first book for children is a poetic calendar entitled _January Rides the Wind: A Book of Months,_ in which she has crafted a small gem of a poem for each month of the year. Bypassing holiday themes, Otten concentrates on painting vivid word pictures of the changing seasons. "Each phrase resonates, capturing a tiny moment that crystallizes an experience or sight for the reader," commented _Booklist_ contributor Susan Dove Lempke. According to _Bulletin of the Center for Children's Books_ reviewer Deborah Stevenson, "Otten's deft use of soundplay—internal rhymes, alliteration, repetition, assonance—combines with fresh and vivid imagery to make the poems musical and atmospheric evocations." Each poem is accompanied by a two-page spread of an oil painting depicting a natural setting or children involved in a seasonal activity such as sledding

In her collection of original verse, Charlotte Otten celebrates the seasons in poems about each month. (From _January Rides the Wind,_ illustrated by Todd L. W. Doney.)

or collecting fireflies. _School Library Journal_ contributor Kathleen Whalin noted that "words and paintings together form a glowing, sensual salute to the seasons."

■ Works Cited

Lempke, Susan Dove, review of _January Rides the Wind, Booklist,_ October 15, 1997, p. 403.

Stevenson, Deborah, review of _January Rides the Wind, Bulletin of the Center for Children's Books,_ January, 1998, p. 171.

Whalin, Kathleen, review of _January Rides the Wind, School Library Journal,_ October, 1997, p. 121.

■ For More Information See

PERIODICALS

Kirkus Reviews, September 15, 1997, p. 1461.

Library Journal, March 1, 1995, p. 75.

New York Times Book Review, April 5, 1987, p.33.

School Library Journal, June, 1990, p. 64.

P

PATON, Priscilla 1952-

■ Personal

Born October 12, 1952, in Brattleboro, VT; daughter of Philip (a dairy farmer) and Marian (a dairy farmer; maiden name, Rumgay) Paton; married David Anderson (a college dean), August 5, 1979; children: James, Elizabeth. *Education:* Bowdoin College, B.A., 1974; Boston College, Ph.D., 1979. *Politics:* Democrat. *Religion:* Lutheran. *Hobbies and other interests:* Ecology, photography.

■ Addresses

Home—Decorah, IA. *Electronic mail*—PPaton@salamander.com.

■ Career

University of Texas at Austin, lecturer in English, 1982-83; Texas A&M University, College Station, assistant professor of English, 1986-93; Florida Atlantic University, Boca Raton, assistant professor of English, 1994-97; Luther College, Decorah, IA, assistant professor of English, 1997—. *Member:* Society of Children's Book Writers and Illustrators, Phi Beta Kappa.

■ Writings

Howard and the Sitter Surprise, illustrated by Paul Meisel, Houghton, 1996.

■ Work in Progress

Crane Famous for Weeping, "an original fable"; research for a scholarly book on American landscape and art in the twentieth century; research for a middle-grade novel on the fashion wars of the 1890s.

■ Sidelights

Priscilla Paton told *SATA:* "I grew up on a Maine dairy farm where I had time to read, dream, and roam outside. Because I loved books, I went on to become an English professor, who occasionally dreamed of writing her own stories. When my son was born, I began to write him stories, even though he couldn't understand a word yet! This continued with the birth of my daughter, and I began to take the stories more seriously. Then three things happened that made my first book, *Howard and the Sitter Surprise,* possible. First, my daughter began to bang her head on the floor when a babysitter would

PRISCILLA PATON

136

Howard revolts each time he is left with a sitter until his mother hires Sarah, a bear, to take charge. (From *Howard and the Sitter Surprise,* written by Paton and illustrated by Paul Meisel.)

come. Then I had two feet in casts (no fun at all), and I got a new computer. Now I had plenty of opportunity to sit still and write a book. I'm not wearing casts anymore, but I continue to love books and love writing them. I've learned that it takes much work to write something that seems simple and light. I work on balancing careful revision with a spark that makes the story unpredictable and alive.

"I read and admire many children's authors, including Jane Yolen, Cynthia Rylant, Lloyd Alexander, Avi, Jennifer Armstrong, Katherine Paterson, Allen Say, Susan Meddaugh, and Kevin Henkes (especially his sense of humor). I owe a large debt to Kathi Appelt, who encouraged me and showed me where to start with writing and marketing.

"In writing a book like *Howard,* I address young children's fears and frustration through humor and a touch of absurdity. I like to mix human and animal characters in these stories. I'm also beginning to write more serious pieces, one about a girl who survives a flood and another about a nineteenth-century girl who wonders why women around her are obsessed with fashion. In these pieces, I'm exploring young girls' feelings of strength and vulnerability and their thoughts about the natural world around them, which can be

beautiful, terrifying, and fragile. I find it a challenge to place myself in the child's world, but I also find freedom in imagining that world."

Paton's *Howard and the Sitter Surprise,* published in 1996, effectively displays her ability to understand children and their dilemmas. Howard is not fond of babysitters and he expresses his disapproval by throwing temper tantrums. His outbursts, which are witnessed by his brother and sister, cause most of the babysitters not to come back. Howard, however, meets his match with the new hire, Sarah. Sarah is different than other sitters; she is a bear. Now when Howard yells, she yells louder and gives him and his siblings a great big bear hug. Sarah tells Howard about a cub who thought his mother left him with a sitter because she did not love him. This story helps to draw Howard closer to Sarah in the end. A *Publishers Weekly* reviewer called *Howard* an "entertaining and comforting" story. *School Library Journal* contributor Heide Piehler added that the book is "an acceptable addition for libraries in need of babysitter trauma stories."

■ Works Cited

Review of *Howard and the Sitter Surprise, Publishers Weekly,* November 4, 1996, p. 75.
Piehler, Heide, review of *Howard and the Sitter Surprise, School Library Journal,* October, 1996, p. 103.

■ For More Information See

PERIODICALS

Horn Book Guide, spring, 1997, p. 42.

*   *   *

PEDERSON, Sharleen
See COLLICOTT, Sharleen

*   *   *

PLOWDEN, Martha Ward 1948-

■ Personal

Born February 24, 1948, in Atlanta, GA; daughter of Isiah Paul, Sr. (a minister) and Annie Mae (a nurse's aide; maiden name, Haley) Ward; married Nathaniel Plowden (a United Parcel Service supervisor), December 31, 1972; children: Natalie Ward. *Education:* Clark College, B.S., 1969; Atlanta University, M.S.L.S., 1975, Specialist Degree, 1977; further graduate study at Georgia State University and Walden University, 1980, 1995. *Politics:* Democrat. *Religion:* Baptist.

■ Addresses

Home—3104 Topaz Lane S.W., Atlanta, GA 30331.
Electronic mail—nplowden@compuserv.com.

MARTHA WARD PLOWDEN

■ **Career**

Southern Bell Telephone Co., Atlanta, GA, operator; Taliaferro County Elementary and High School, Crawfordville, GA, librarian; Grady Memorial Hospital, Atlanta, food service supervisor; Clark College, Atlanta, librarian; Atlanta Public Schools, Atlanta, media specialist; Metro Atlanta Skills Center, Atlanta, mathematics instructor. Clark Atlanta University, adjunct professor; Young Men's Christian Association, member of board of directors, 1975-79; volunteer for American Red Cross, Oakhill Homes, United Negro College Fund, and Martin Luther King's Center for Nonviolent Social Change. *Member:* National Association of Educators, National Association of Black School Educators, American Library Association, National Association for the Advancement of Colored People (member of Atlanta board of directors; chairperson of ACT-SO Program), National Council of Negro Women, Georgia Association of Educators, Georgia Library Media Association, Georgia Nutrition Association, Atlanta Association of Educators, Atlanta Urban League Guild (past president), Greater Atlanta Panhellenic Council (vice-president), Phi Delta Kappa, Delta Sigma Theta, Kappa Delta Epsilon, Eta Phi Beta, Atlanta Epicureans, Continental Colony Community Association.

■ **Awards, Honors**

Academic Incentive Award Area II in Media; fellowship for study of Library Science, Atlanta University; Million Dollar Club Medallion, NAACP, 1982 and 1984.

■ **Writings**

Famous Firsts of Black Women, illustrated by Ronald Jones, Pelican Publishing (Gretna, LA), 1993.
Olympic Black Women, illustrated by Ronald Jones, Pelican Publishing, 1996.

Regional editor, *Library Scene.*

■ **Work in Progress**

Updating *Famous Firsts of Black Women;* another book on the Olympics.

■ **For More Information See**

PERIODICALS

Horn Book Guide, fall, 1996, p. 362.
School Library Journal, March, 1994, p. 244.
Skipping Stones, winter, 1995, p. 31; February-March, 1996, p. 31.

*   *   *

POULIN, Stephane 1961-

■ **Personal**

Name is pronounced "poo-lan"; born December 12, 1961, in Montreal, Canada; children: Gabriel, Camille. *Education:* Attended College Ahunstic, studied graphic arts.

■ **Addresses**

Home—4597 des Erables, Montreal, Canada H2H 2E1.

■ **Career**

Illustrator, 1984—.

■ **Awards, Honors**

First prize for children's illustration, Communication-Jeunesse, 1984; Canada Council Children's Literature Prize, French language, illustration, 1986, for *Album de Famille* and *As-tu vu Josephine?;* Elizabeth Mrazik-Cleaver Canadian Picture Book Award, 1988, for *Peux-tu attraper Josephine?* and its English translation, *Can You Catch Josephine?;* Boston Globe Award of Excellence, 1988; Vicky Metcalf Award for a body of work, 1989; Governor General's Literary Award in Children's Literature for best illustrations in a French book, 1989, for *Benjamin et la saga des oreillers;* Mr. Christie Book Award, French-language illustrations, 1991, and IBBY Honour List, 1994, for *Un Voyage pour deux: contes et mensonges de mon enfance* and its English translation,

Travels for Two: Stories and Lies from My Childhood;
Mr. Christie's Book Award, French-language illustration, 1996, for *Poil de serpent, dent d'araignee;* IBBY
Hans Christian Andersen Award for a body of work,
1996.

■ Writings

SELF-ILLUSTRATED

Ah! belle cite!/A Beautiful City ABC, Tundra Books,
1985.
Album de famille, Editions Michel Quintin, 1986,
English edition, *Family Album,* Editions Quintin,
1991.
As-tu vu Josephine?, Tundra Books, 1986, English edition, *Have You Seen Josephine?,* Tundra Books,
1986.
Peux-tu attraper Josephine?, Tundra Books, 1987, English edition, *Can You Catch Josephine?,* Tundra
Books, 1987.
Les Jeux zoolympiques, Editions Quintin, 1988.
Pourrais-tu arreter Josephine?, Tundra Books, 1988,
English edition, *Could You Stop Josephine?,* Tundra
Books, 1988.
Benjamin et la saga des oreillers, Annick Press, 1989,
English edition, *Benjamin and the Pillow Saga,*
Annick Press, 1989.
*Les Amours de ma mere: contes et mensonges de mon
enfance,* Annick Press, 1990, English edition as *My*

Mother's Loves: Stories and Lies from My Childhood, Annick Press, 1990.
*Un Voyage pour deux: contes et mensonges de mon
enfance,* Annick Press, 1991, English edition as
Travels for Two: Stories and Lies from My Childhood, Annick Press, 1991.

ILLUSTRATOR

Raymond Plante, *Le Record de Philibert Dupont,* Boreal, 1984.
Mimi Legault, *Le Robot concierge,* Heritage, 1984.
Louise Beaudin, *Les Animaux de la basse-cour,* Editions
du Nomade, 1985.
Marie Page, *Vincent, Sylvie et les autres,* Heritage, 1985.
Plante, *Minibus: nouvelles,* Quebec/Amerique, 1985.
Beaudin, *Les Animaux en hiver,* Editions Quintin, 1987,
English edition, *Animals in Winter,* Editions Quintin, 1991.
Helene Lamarche, *Le Leonard des enfants, petits et
grands,* Musee des beaux-arts de Montreal, 1987,
English edition, *Leonardo for Children Young and
Old,* Montreal Museum of Fine Arts, 1987.
Henriette Major, *Les lutin de Noel,* Heritage, 1987,
English edition, *The Christmas Elves,* McClelland
and Stewart, 1988.
Kathy Stinson, *Teddy Rabbit,* Annick Press, 1988,
French-language edition, *Nounours-Lapin,* Annick
Press, 1988.
Dennis Cote, *Les Prisonniers du zoo,* Les editions la
courte echelle, 1988.
Dennis Cote, *Le Voyage dans le temps,* Les editions la
courte echelle, 1989.
Michel Quintin, *Les Animaux en danger,* Editions
Quintin, 1989, English edition translated by Alan
Brown, *Endangered Animals,* Editions Quintin,
1992.
Dennis Cote, *Les Geants de Blizzard,* Les editions la
courte echelle, 1990.
Dennis Cote, *La Nuit du Vampire,* Les editions la courte
echelle, 1990.
Dennis Cote, *Les Yeux d'emeraude,* Les editions la
courte echelle, 1991.
Michel Quintin, *Les Dinosaures,* Editions Quintin,
1992, English edition, *Dinosaurs,* Editions Quintin,
1992.
Cecile Gagnon, Roger Poupart, and Robert Soulieres,
Liberte . . . surveillee: roman a six mains, Editions
Paulines, 1993.
Dennis Cote, *Le Parc aux sortileges,* Les editions la
courte echelle, 1994.
Dennis Cote, *La Trahison du vampire,* Les editions la
courte echelle, 1995.
Dennis Cote, *L'Ile du savant fou,* Les editions la courte
echelle, 1996.
Danielle Marcotte, *Poil de serpent, dent d'araignee,* Les
400 coups, 1996.
Jack Zipes, editor, *The Outspoken Princess and the
Gentle Knight: A Treasury of Modern Fairy Tales,*
Bantam, 1996.
Mary Jo Collier and Peter Collier, *The King's Giraffe,*
Simon and Schuster, 1996.
Gilles Tibo, *Choupette et son petit papa,* Heritage, 1997.

STEPHANE POULIN

Also illustrator of a puppeteer how-to book, *Pellicule et les animaux en danger,* by Michel Quintin, 1989. *Have You Seen Josephine?* was anthologized in *Duncan Really Likes Me: Stories about Cats and Dogs,* Houghton Mifflin, 1992.

■ Adaptations

The "Josephine" books were adapted for filmstrip as *The Misadventures of Josephine,* Society for Visual Education, Inc., 1990.

■ Sidelights

Stephane Poulin is an award-winning Canadian writer and illustrator of children's books noted for his offbeat humor and sophisticated design. He delights in featuring his hometown, Montreal, in his books which serve as an introduction to the province of Quebec for young readers. His self-illustrated books have texts in both French and English, and as an illustrator he has also

worked on a score of French-language picture books and novels for young readers. Known for his blend of fantasy, reality, and humor, Poulin uses themes such as family, togetherness, and love, and works in primary colors to create striking images. His most popular books make up the "Josephine" series, which chronicles the adventures of a mischievous cat as it attempts to stay one step ahead of its young owner.

Poulin was born in Montreal in 1961, one of nine children. He grew up in a French-speaking household, and with the departure of his father when Poulin was twelve, his mother was left to fend for the large and rambunctious collection of children. While completing his studies in graphic arts at College Ahunstic, he won an award for children's illustration that set him on the career path he continues to follow.

His first picture book, a bilingual alphabet book, was published in 1985 and warmly received by critics and young readers alike. *A Beautiful City ABC* employed

Daniel's frisky cat leads him through a farm in the Quebec countryside in Poulin's self-illustrated picture book *Could You Stop Josephine?*

In the winter, after playing outside, we had to look for cups and spoons in the snow. Then my mother would make us some delicious hot chocolate.

My Mother's Loves is Poulin's self-illustrated tale of a large blended family joyously overfilling their tiny one-room house.

Montreal as the backdrop for this first introduction to the alphabet. To gather images of the city where he grew up, Poulin pedaled a bicycle around the old quarters of the city, taking photos from which he created oil paintings. Employing only four colors, Poulin managed to create paintings "alive with colour, feeling, action and realism," according to Barbara Egerer Walker in *Canadian Materials*. Bernie Goedhart, writing in *Quill and Quire*, noted that Poulin's book was a "delight . . . . The paintings are evocative and full of humour." Poulin's humor could be seen in pictures such as that for the letter N, which shows *nombril* or navel. "This is a book to be shared by children and adults," *Canadian Material*'s Walker noted, and is the "perfect book for reading aloud."

The first of Poulin's "Josephine" books, *Have You Seen Josephine?*, is set in Montreal's east end and has the cream-colored cat eluding its owner, Daniel, through that picturesque part of the city. Again, working from photographs and in oil with primary colors, Poulin blended his images with a simple and sometimes lyrical text. Finally Daniel tracks Josephine down to the neighbors, Mr. and Mrs. Gagnon, who have a party for the cats of the neighborhood every weekend. Part of the fun of this initial book and with the subsequent "Josephine" titles is the fact that Poulin partially hides the cat in his richly detailed paintings, and the reader must search for her along with Daniel. A critic in *Kirkus Reviews* felt that Poulin employed a "strange perspective and solemn atmosphere to lend an air of sophistication to a simple, reassuring story," and concluded that

this was a picture book for readers "who enjoy using their eyes to extend the bounds of the plot."

Poulin has noted that he enjoys juxtaposing naturalistic scenes with stylized characters—people who have short, squat bodies or long necks and protruding eyes. Sometimes he even includes illustrations of himself as a child in his books. *Quill and Quire*'s Susan Perren dubbed *Have You Seen Josephine?* "a loving look at an east-end Montreal neighborhood," and went on to comment that it was "an intriguing book and a harbinger, one hopes, of more good things to come." That it was, for Poulin followed up this first "Josephine" book with two more titles, *Can You Catch Josephine?* and *Could You Stop Josephine?*, the last of which is set in the Quebec countryside where Poulin himself spent ten years of his youth. Perren, writing in *Books for Young People*, noted of *Can You Catch Josephine?* that "Poulin shows how masterful he is at setting a droll story in a droll landscape," and concluded that the "weird little world of Poulin's illustrations . . . coupled with his minimal, poetic prose style, makes his books distinctive and rewarding for readers of all ages." Of that same title, a reviewer in *Maclean's* noted that Poulin's artwork "has an unconventional beauty and—and considerable wit." Of *Could You Stop Josephine?*, Peter Carver, writing in *Books for Young People*, remarked that Poulin's "rich colours, the child's-eye and bird's-eye perspectives of the oil paintings" make the book a "fittingly upbeat finish to the Josephine series."

With his award-winning *Benjamin and the Pillow Saga*, Poulin visited a fabulist theme with the story of shy Benjamin who works in a pillow factory. Benjamin loves to hum as he works, and his pillows are not ordinary ones: They guarantee the user a wonderful night's sleep. The fame of the pillows spreads far and wide, and one day when a group from Italy is touring the factory, Benjamin is heard humming and is invited to hum at an Italian opera house. While he and his family are away, the pillows lose their magic power. But when it is discovered that Benjamin's humming is the magic ingredient in the pillows, purchasers begin bringing the pillows to Benjamin's concerts to have them filled with his voice. Allan Sheldon, writing in *Canadian Children's Literature*, noted that Poulin's story "in words and pictures is evocative of old Europe," and Patricia Fry wrote in *Canadian Materials* that "Poulin has once again created what is sure to become a favourite picture-book for children."

Poulin explores his own past in two titles, *My Mother's Loves* and *Travels for Two*, both of which have the evocative sub-title, *Stories and Lies from My Childhood*. Recalling the days of his single mother bringing up nine children, Poulin has fashioned stylized recollections, a "blend of nostalgia and whimsy," according to Anne Denoon in *Books in Canada*. The first in the series tells of the family living in a tiny one-room house. The mother meets and falls in love with another man, and soon marries him, increasing the size of the family with the man's own numerous children. "Here's a picture book that begins with a happy family and ends with a happy, albeit changed, family," noted Ellen Pauls in *Canadian Materials*. Fred Boer, writing in *Quill and Quire*, commented that Poulin's artwork in *My Mother's Loves* "is up to his usual high standards," noting in particular the illustrator's use of "detail, action, and humour." With *Travels for Two*, Poulin continued the adventures of this family as they parachute from an airplane, are marooned on a desert island, and are set upon by pirates. "The humour of the story is infectious, and is carried through in the illustrations," noted Rebecca Raven in *Canadian Materials*. Reviewing the book in *Canadian Children's Literature*, Sheila O'Hearn commented on the "surreal disquiet" of Poulin's artwork.

Poulin's illustrations for the texts of other authors have proven equally as successful as his self-illustrated titles, winning illustration awards and a wider international audience for this French-Canadian with the wry sense of humor.

■ Works Cited

Boer, Fred, review of *My Mother's Loves: Stories and Lies from My Childhood*, *Quill and Quire*, February, 1991, p. 22.

Review of *Can You Catch Josephine?*, *Maclean's*, December 7, 1987, pp. 54, 56.

Carver, Peter, "Quebec Illustrators' Welcome Invasion," *Books for Young People*, December, 1988, p. 8.

Denoon, Anne, review of *My Mother's Loves: Stories and Lies from My Childhood*, *Books in Canada*, April, 1991, p. 37.

Fry, Patricia, review of *Benjamin and the Pillow Saga*, *Canadian Materials*, January, 1990, pp. 14-15.

Goedhart, Bernie, "Picture-Books: Some Succeed, Others Better Read Than Seen," *Quill and Quire*, December, 1985, p. 24.

Review of *Have You Seen Josephine?*, *Kirkus Reviews*, October 15, 1986, p. 1580.

O'Hearn, Sheila, "Picture Books Packed with Humour and Action," *Canadian Children's Literature*, Number 70, pp. 84-86.

Pauls, Ellen, review of *My Mother's Loves: Stories and Lies from My Childhood*, *Canadian Materials*, January, 1991, p. 30.

Perren, Susan, "Picture-Book Plums for Christmas Gift-Giving," *Quill and Quire*, December, 1986, p. 16.

Perren, Susan, "Annabel and Goldie Go to the Sea, Josephine Goes to School," *Books for Young People*, October, 1987, pp. 18-19.

Raven, Rebecca, review of *Travels for Two: Stories and Lies from My Childhood*, *Canadian Materials*, March, 1992, p. 84.

Sheldon, Allan, "Secret Marriages: Unified Text and Visuals," *Canadian Children's Literature*, Number 61, 1990, pp. 96-99.

Walker, Barbara Egerer, review of *Ah! belle cite/A Beautiful City ABC*, *Canadian Materials*, May, 1986, p. 137.

■ For More Information See

BOOKS

Children's Books and Their Creators, Houghton Mifflin, 1995, pp. 535-36.

Children's Literature Review, Volume 28, Gale, 1992, pp. 192-99.

PERIODICALS

Bulletin of the Center for Children's Books, March, 1986, p. 135.

Canadian Children's Literature, Number 46, 1987, p. 108; Numbers 57-58, 1990, pp. 106-07; Number 69, 1993, pp. 65-67.

Canadian Materials, March, 1992, pp. 76-7.

Emergency Librarian, March, 1988, p. 23; November, 1988, p. 47; March, 1989, pp. 21, 51; March, 1990, p. 60; May, 1990, p. 59.

Horn Book, September-October, 1991, pp. 632-33.

School Library Journal, April, 1986, p. 78; August, 1987, p. 74; May, 1988, p. 87.

Times Educational Supplement, June 3, 1988, p. 46.

—*Sketch by J. Sydney Jones*

PRICE, Beverley Joan 1931-
(Beverley Randell)

■ Personal

Born in 1931, in Wellington, New Zealand; daughter of William Harding and Gwendolyn Louise (Ryall) Randell; married Hugh Price (a book publisher), October 17, 1959; children: Susan. *Education:* Victoria University of Wellington, B.A., 1952; Wellington Teachers College, Diploma of Teaching, 1953.

■ Addresses

Home and office—24 Glasgow St., Kelburn, Wellington, New Zealand 6005.

■ Career

Freelance writer and editor. Teacher at primary schools in Wellington, Raumati, and Marlborough, New Zealand, 1953-59, and London, England, 1957-58; Price Milburn and Co. Ltd., Wellington, editor, 1962-84; Thomas Nelson Australia, Melbourne, PM Library editor, 1993—. *Member:* International PEN, New Zealand Women Writers Society, Australian Society of Authors.

■ Writings

JUVENILES; UNDER NAME BEVERLEY RANDELL

Tiny Tales, sixteen volumes, Wheaton, 1965.
PM Commonwealth Readers, sixteen volumes, A. H. and A. W. Reed, 1965.
John, the Mouse Who Learned to Read, illustrated by Noela Young, Collins, 1966, reprinted, Penguin (London), 1986.
Methuen Number Story Caption Books, sixteen volumes, Methuen, 1967.
Methuen Caption Books, Volumes I-IV: *Blue Set,* Volumes V-VIII: *Green Set,* Volumes IX-XII: *Orange Set,* Volumes XIII-XVI: *Purple Set,* Volumes XVII-XX: *Red Set,* Volumes XXI-XXIV: *Yellow Set,* Methuen, 1967, 2nd edition, 1974, series published as *PM Starters Two* (with Jenny Giles and Annette Smith), twenty volumes, Price Milburn, 1995.
Bowmar Primary Reading Series: Supplementary to All Basic Reading Series, sixty volumes, Bowmar, 1969.
Instant Readers, sixteen volumes, Price Milburn (Wellington, New Zealand), 1969-70.
Listening Skillbuilders, twenty-four volumes, Price Milburn, 1971, published as *PM Alphabet Starters,* twenty-six volumes, Price Milburn, 1995.
Mark and Meg Books, five volumes, Methuen, 1971.
Guide to the Ready to Read Series, and Supporting Books, Price Milburn, 1972.
PM Story Books, one hundred two volumes, Price Milburn, 1972-76, also published as *New PM Story Books,* sixty-four volumes, Nelson Price Milburn, 1994.
First Phonics, twenty-four volumes, Methuen, 1973.

BEVERLEY JOAN PRICE

PM Creative Workbooks, nine volumes, Price Milburn, 1973.
(With Robin Robilliard) *Country Readers,* eighteen volumes, Price Milburn, 1974, published as *Country Books,* four volumes, Methuen, 1974.
(With Clive Harper) *Animal Books,* sixteen volumes, Thomas Nelson, 1978.
Readalongs, eighteen volumes, Price Milburn and Methuen, 1979-81.
Phonic Blends, twenty-four volumes, Methuen, 1979, also published as *PM Alphabet Blends,* thirty-four volumes, Price Milburn, 1995.
Singing Games, Price Milburn, 1981.
Joining-In Books, sixteen volumes, Nelson, 1984.
Rhyme and Rhythm Books, four volumes, Heinemann, 1985.
Look and Listen, twenty-four volumes, Heinemann, 1985.

EDITOR; UNDER NAME BEVERLEY RANDELL

Red Car Books, Price Milburn, 1967, revised edition, 1974.
Instant Readers, thirty-six volumes, Price Milburn, 1969-70, published as *PM Starters One* (with Jenny Giles and Annette Smith), twenty volumes, Price Milburn, 1995.
PM Town Readers, Price Milburn, 1971.
Dinghy Stories, Methuen, 1973.
PM Everyday Stories, Price Milburn, 1973-80.
PM Science Concept Books, Price Milburn, 1974.
PM People at Work, Price Milburn, 1974.
PM Seagulls, Price Milburn, 1980.
PM Early Days, Price Milburn, 1982.

OTHER

(Under name Beverley Randell) *A Crowded Thorndon Cottage,* Gondwanaland Press, 1992.

Also author of *Readalongs,* eighteen volumes; *Pets* (with Clive Harper), five volumes, 1996, *Animals in the Wild,* six volumes, 1997, *Farm Animals,* six volumes, 1997, *Time and Seasons,* six volumes, 1997; *PM Storybooks,* nine volumes, 1997, five volumes, 1998.

Contributor to books, including *Reading Is Everybody's Business,* International Reading Association (Wellington), 1972. Price's books have been translated into several languages, including Italian, Greek, Chinese, Japanese, Welsh, and Australian Aboriginal languages.

■ Sidelights

Beverley Joan Price, better known as Beverley Randell, once wrote: "In 1972 I traveled to England to lecture on reading at teachers' centers, and I have several times lectured in Australia. My interest is in understanding how children learn to read, and writing (and editing) the sorts of books that can help them. The school books I dislike most are those that are narrow and restricting— mere reading exercises (often 'based on linguistic principles'). But I like those that strike a spark—that are sensible and worth reading as well as easy."

■ For More Information See

PERIODICALS

School Librarian, January, 1979, p. 132.
Times Educational Supplement, March 11, 1983, p. 47; July 4, 1997, p. 8.
Times Literary Supplement, December 4, 1969, p. 1392.

R

RADLAUER, Ruth (Shaw) 1926-

■ Personal

Born August 18, 1926, in Wyoming; married Edward Radlauer (a writer), June 28, 1947; children: David Preston Radlauer, Robin Joy Radlauer-Cramer, Daniel Kurt Radlauer. *Education:* University of California, Los Angeles, B.A., 1950. *Hobbies and other interests:* Basket making.

■ Addresses

Home—620 West Rd., La Habra Heights, CA 90631-8054. *E-mail*—radlauer2@earthlink.net.

■ Career

Writer, 1958—; Childrens Press, editor, 1972-78; photographer, 1970—. *Member:* Society of Children's Book Writers and Illustrators, Authors Guild of America.

■ Awards, Honors

Award for Service on Behalf of Children and Reading, Southern California Council on Literature for Children and Young People, 1982.

■ Writings

Fathers at Work, Melmont, 1958, published as *About Men at Work*, 1967.
Women at Work, Melmont, 1959.
Of Course, You're a Horse, Abelard, 1959.
Mothers Are That Way, Abelard, 1960.
About Four Seasons and Five Senses, Melmont, 1960.
(Self-illustrated) *Good Times Drawing Lines*, Melmont, 1961.
Good Times with Words, Melmont, 1963.
Stein, the Great Retriever, Bobbs-Merrill, 1964.
(With Marjorie Pursel) *Where in the World Do You Live?*, Franklin, 1965.
From Place to Place, Franklin, 1965.
Food from Farm to Family, Franklin, 1965.

RUTH RADLAUER

Clothes from Head to Toe, Franklin, 1965.
Get Ready for School, Elk Grove Press, 1967.
What Can You Do With a Box?, Childrens Press, 1973.
Yellowstone National Park, Childrens Press, 1975.
Everglades National Park, Childrens Press, 1975.
Yosemite National Park, Childrens Press, 1976.
Great Smoky Mountains National Park, Childrens Press, 1976.
Mesa Verde National Park, Childrens Press, 1976.
Grand Canyon National Park, Childrens Press, 1977.

Rocky Mountain National Park, Childrens Press, 1977, revised edition, 1984.
Glacier National Park, Childrens Press, 1977.
Olympic National Park, Childrens Press, 1978.
Mammoth Cave National Park, Childrens Press, 1978.
Volcanoes, Childrens Press, 1981.
(With Henry M. Anderson) *Reefs*, Childrens Press, 1983.
(With Charles H. Stembridge) *Comets*, Childrens Press, 1984.
(With Charles H. Stembridge) *Planets*, Childrens Press, 1984.
(With Lisa Sue Gitkin) *The Power of Ice*, Childrens Press, 1985.
(With Carolynn Young) *Voyagers I & II: Robots in Space*, Childrens Press, 1987.
Molly, Prentice-Hall, 1987.
Molly Goes Hiking, Prentice-Hall, 1987.
Molly at the Library, Simon & Schuster, 1988.
Breakfast by Molly, Simon & Schuster, 1988.
Honor the Flag, Forest House, 1992.

WITH HUSBAND, ED RADLAUER

About Missiles and Men, Melmont, 1959.
About Atomic Power for People, Melmont, 1960.
Atoms Afloat: The Nuclear Ship Savannah, Abelard, 1963.
What Is a Community?, Elk Grove Press, 1967.
Get Ready for School, Elk Grove Press, 1967.
Whose Tools Are These?, Elk Grove Press, 1968.
Water for Your Community, Elk Grove Press, 1968.
Father Is Big, Bowmar, 1968.
Colors, Bowmar, 1968.
Evening, Bowmar, 1968.
Quarter Midget Challenge, Childrens Press, 1969.
We Go on Wheels, Elk Grove Press, 1970.
Some Basics About Women's Gymnastics, Childrens Press, 1978.
Chopper Cycle Mania, Childrens Press, 1980.
Baseball Mania, Childrens Press, 1980.
Dolls, Childrens Press, 1980.
Miniatures, Childrens Press, 1980.
Hot Rod Mania, Childrens Press, 1980.
Pet Mania, Childrens Press, 1980.
Horse Mania, Childrens Press, 1981.
Bird Mania, Childrens Press, 1981.
Clown Mania, Childrens Press, 1981.
Contest Mania, Childrens Press, 1981.
Reptile Mania, Childrens Press, 1981.
Volcano Mania, Childrens Press, 1981.
Some Basics about Karate, Childrens Press, 1981.
Cowboy Mania, Childrens Press, 1981.
Motorcycle Winners, Childrens Press, 1982.
Parade Mania, Childrens Press, 1982.
Dog Mania, Childrens Press, 1982.
Minibike Winners, Childrens Press, 1982.
Truck Mania, Childrens Press, 1982.
Some Basics about Women's Basketball, Childrens Press, 1982.
Karting Winners, Childrens Press, 1982.
Low Rider Mania, Childrens Press, 1982.
Guide Dog Winners, Childrens Press, 1983.
Soap Box Winners, Childrens Press, 1983.

BMX Winners, Childrens Press, 1984.
Radio Tech Talk, Childrens Press, 1984.
(With others) *Satellite Tech Talk*, Childrens Press, 1984.
(With Jean and Bob Mather) *Computer Tech Talk*, Childrens Press, 1984.
Nuclear Tech Talk, Childrens Press, 1985.
(With others) *Robot Tech Talk*, Childrens Press, 1985.
Truck Tech Talk, Childrens Press, 1986.
Auto Tech Talk, Childrens Press, 1987.
Earthquakes, Childrens Press, 1987.

AND COPHOTOGRAPHER WITH HUSBAND, ED RADLAUER

Acadia National Park, Childrens Press, 1978.
Zion National Park, Childrens Press, 1978.
Haleakala National Park, Childrens Press, 1979.
Hawaii Volcanoes National Park, Childrens Press, 1979.
Grand Teton National Park, Childrens Press, 1980.
Bryce Canyon National Park, Childrens Press, 1980.
Carlsbad Caverns National Park, Childrens Press, 1981.
(With additional photos by Rick McIntyre) *Denali National Park and Preserve*, Childrens Press, 1981.
(With additional photos by Henry M. Anderson) *Virgin Islands National Park*, Childrens Press, 1981.
Shenandoah National Park, Childrens Press, 1982.

COAUTHOR AND COPHOTOGRAPHER WITH HUSBAND, ED RADLAUER

Horses Pix Dix: A Picture Dictionary, Bowmar, 1970.
Buggy-Go-Round, F. Watts, 1971.
On the Drag Strip, F. Watts, 1971.
Scramble Cycle, F. Watts, 1971.
Chopper Cycle, F. Watts, 1972.
Horsing Around, F. Watts, 1972.
On the Sand, F. Watts, 1972.
Bonneville Cars, F. Watts, 1973.
On the Water, F. Watts, 1973.
Horse Show Challenge, Childrens Press, 1973.
Mototcycle Mutt, F. Watts, 1973.
Salt Cycle, F. Watts, 1973.
Foolish Filly, F. Watts, 1974.
Racing on the Wind, F. Watts, 1974.
Horses, Bowmar, 1975.
Gymnastics School, F. Watts, 1976.

PHOTOGRAPHER

Ed Radlauer, *Dirt Riders* Childrens Press, 1983.
Ed Radlauer, *Model Fighter Planes*, Childrens Press 1983.
Ed Radlauer, *Model Rockets*, Childrens Press, 1983.
Ed Radlauer, *Model Trucks*, Childrens Press, 1983.
Ed Radlauer, *Warships*, Childrens Press, 1984.
Ed Radlauer, *Wheels, Wheels, and More Wheels*, Forest House, 1992.
Ed Radlauer, *Bears, Bears, and More Bears*, Forest House, 1992.
Ed Radlauer, *Cats, Cats, and More Cats*, Forest House, 1992.

PLAYS

(With Dan Radlauer and Barbara Slade) *Reach for the Magic: A Tale Mostly Ghostly* (musical), Lorenz, 1987.

(With Dan Radlauer and Barbara Slade) *Spring Fling* (musical), Lorenz, 1989.

■ Work in Progress

A novel, *The Diary Club,* for children ages eight to twelve; *Mammoth Cave,* an addition to the series about national parks; several picture books in the marketing stage.

■ Sidelights

Since 1958, when she published her first work, Ruth Radlauer has written or collaborated on more than 200 books, as well as games, skill development materials, tapes, and filmstrips. She has covered a wide range of nonfiction topics, including educational materials for the language arts and sciences. For her series on America's National Parks she served as author and sometimes cophotographer along with her husband, Ed, and others. In the late 1980s, Radlauer created a successful fiction series featuring Molly, a sprightly youngster. She has also written two musicals with her son, Dan, and Barbara Slade, to be performed by children.

Yellowstone National Park and *Yosemite National Park* are two of Radlauer's books from a series about the National Parks of the United States. Her text covers the main physical features of the parks and the various activities available to visitors. According to *Booklist* critic Judith Goldberger, the photographs are "beautiful" and the "considerable" information found in the works is useful for travel as well as school work. Reviewing the books in *School Library Journal,* Ralph J. Folcarelli called the text "lucid" and praised the "truly awe-inspiring photographs."

Reviewing *Everglades National Park, School Library Journal* contributor Gale K. Shonkwiler noted that the book is "attractive and useful." Barbara Elleman, a critic for *Booklist,* described the work as a "valuable resource." Radlauer's husband, Ed, joined her to coillustrate *Hawaii Volcanoes National Park.* Clarence L. Vinge, in *Science Books and Films,* noted that the book is full of "interesting information," and *School Library Journal* reviewer Mary V. Ratzer complimented the "immediate and visually attractive" format. Of the twenty books on national parks Ruth published, eleven were illustrated with her and Ed's photographs. Recalling the work involved with those books, Ruth commented, "Poor me, I had to go to all those wonderlands set aside for our enjoyment."

In a departure from her nonfiction titles, Radlauer produced a series of books about the fictional character Molly. The "Molly" series features a charming, enthusiastic, energetic little girl as the central character. In *Molly,* the youngster carefully tidies up her appearance for preschool, only to have it fall apart during an active day at school. Her father shares her enthusiasm, even though she arrives home looking a mess. Patricia Pearl, a critic for *School Library Journal,* wrote that Molly is

Radlauer's book instructs young readers on the appropriate treatment of the American flag. (Cover illustration by J. J. Smith-Moore.)

"appealing" and the story displays an understanding for a child's need for "new experiences within safe and acceptable limits." A reviewer in *Publishers Weekly* described the story as "pleasant" and Molly as a "charmer." In *Molly at the Library,* Molly talks too loud in her excitement over all the many books. Then she chooses to take home ten books covering a wide range of topics. A contributor for *Kirkus Reviews* described Molly as a "liberated pre-schooler with unusual spunk and appeal."

■ Works Cited

Review of *Breakfast by Molly* and *Molly at the Library, Kirkus Reviews,* February, 1, 1988, p. 206.

Elleman, Barbara, review of *Everglades National Park, Booklist,* June 1, 1976, p. 1409.

Folcarelli, Ralph J., review of *Yellowstone National Park* and *Yosemite National Park, School Library Journal,* February, 1976, p. 48.

Goldberger, Judith, review of *Yellowstone National Park* and *Yosemite National Park, Booklist,* January 15, 1976, p. 687.

Review of *Molly, Publishers Weekly,* May 29, 1987, p. 76.

Pearl, Patricia, review of *Molly* and *Molly Goes Hiking, School Library Journal,* August, 1987, p. 74.

Ratzer, Mary V., review of *Hawaii Volcanoes National Park, School Library Journal,* February, 1980, p. 60.

Shonkwiler, Gale K., review of *Everglades National Park, School Library Journal,* October, 1976, p. 110.

Vinge, Clarence L., review of *Hawaii Volcanoes National Park, Science Books and Films,* March, 1980, p. 226.

■ For More Information See

PERIODICALS

Booklist, October 15, 1992, p. 427.

* * *

RAHAMAN, Vashanti 1953-

■ Personal

Born July 15, 1953, in Trinidad, West Indies; daughter of Hari P. (a dental surgeon) and Marjory (a homemaker; maiden name, Gayadeen) Ramcharan; married Mohamed N. Rahaman (a professor of ceramic engineering), June 13, 1981; children: Lennard I., Ronald O. *Education:* Mt. Allison University (New Brunswick, Canada), Bsc., 1974; *Religion:* Presbyterian.

■ Addresses

Home—Rolla, MO.

■ Career

Trinidad and Tobago Teaching Service, secondary school teacher, 1977-83; writer and homemaker. Substitute teacher and public school volunteer. Elder and education chair at Rolla First Presbyterian Church, 1995-98. *Member:* Society of Children's Book Writers and Illustrators.

■ Awards, Honors

Notable children's trade book in the field of social studies, Children's Book Council/National Council for the Social Studies, 1996, for *O Christmas Tree;* Author of the Month citation, *Highlights Magazine,* 1997; Honor Book, Society of School Librarians International, 1997, for *Read for Me, Mama.*

■ Writings

O Christmas Tree, illustrated by Frane Lessac, Boyds Mills Press, 1996.

Read for Me, Mama, illustrated by Lori McElrath-Eslick, Boyds Mills Press, 1997.

A Little Salmon for Witness, illustrated by Sandra Speidel, Lodestar Books, 1997.

Contributor of stories and articles to *Highlights for Children, Cricket, Spider, Ladybug, Once Upon a Time* and *Children's Writer.*

VASHANTI RAHAMAN

■ Sidelights

Vashanti Rahaman is the author of picture books with strong messages and rich cultural settings, often based in the author's native West Indies. In *O Christmas Tree,* Rahaman's first book, Anslem, a young West Indian boy, feels that Christmas on his island is fake because there's no ice or snow and the only evergreen trees are those imported from elsewhere. Anslem decides to rescue one of these trees, discarded because they have arrived brown and lifeless, and ends up making a mess as he attempts to decorate it. Having given up hope of having a real Christmas, Anslem slowly becomes aware of the island's holiday traditions, such as ginger beer, smoked ham, and poinsettias, and he develops a new appreciation for the unique West Indian Christmas he's always taken for granted.

Told in West Indian dialect and rich with cultural references in both the text and the illustrations, *O Christmas Tree* was lauded as an unusual Christmas story with a message "delivered with just the right tone," according to a *School Library Journal* contributor. Susan Dove Lempke noted in *Booklist* that the text has a "delightful, rollicking quality." She added, "In a sea of conventional Christmas titles from the religious to the commercial, this warm and touching book stands out." "The moral is pretty predictable," Deborah Stevenson remarked in *Bulletin of the Center for Children's*

Books, "but the turns the story takes to get there are lively and vivid."

Read for Me, Mama, published in 1997, concerns a young African American boy and his mother. Joseph loves to read and to be read to, but although his mother is considered an excellent storyteller, she claims she is too tired from working all day to read to him. Eventually his mother admits that she is illiterate. She then enrolls in adult classes and begins to read with Joseph. Several reviewers found this story to be a moving celebration of both literacy and the love between mother and son. As Pat Mathews stated in *Bulletin of the Center for Children's Books, Read for Me, Mama* is "a compelling and realistic tribute to the power of literacy." A *Kirkus Reviews* critic called it a "poignant story that is at its best in simple moments."

A Little Salmon for Witness, also published in 1997, is set in Trinidad. Rajiv's grandmother laments their inability to afford the traditional salmon for Good Friday, and Rajiv is especially sorry because his grandmother's birthday falls on the same day. The young boy sets about trying to earn the tin of salmon. He is discouraged when none of the neighbors can help him, until he has an idea that pays off. Writing in *School Library Journal,* Martha Topol noted that in *A Little Salmon for Witness,* "The customs, the clipped language, and ethnic foods all work to lend a cultural atmosphere." A *Publishers Weekly* critic felt that the dialect and exotic dishes "add a dash of local color." A contributor in *Kirkus Reviews* praised the values central to the story, such as hard work, living simply, and respecting one's elders.

Rahaman told *SATA:* "I began writing to find out whether I could write, as a sort of exercise for my brain. Following my husband's career to the U.S.A. had, because of visa restrictions, put a stop to my own and taught us that a stay-at-home mom was the kind we preferred.

"Writing seemed like a good occupation for a stay-at-home mom. I didn't expect to enjoy it as much as I did, but written words were like the playdough I cooked for my sons—malleable and responsive in a wonderfully satisfying way. With writing, I could show my boys the people and ideas and stories and perspectives that would have surrounded them in the Caribbean if we had not come to America. With writing, I can share the world of my experiences with others.

"When publishers began publishing my work and readers began reading it, that was icing on a cake that already seemed too sinfully rich to eat."

■ Works Cited

Lempke, Susan Dove, review of *O Christmas Tree, Booklist,* September 1, 1996, p. 137.
Review of *A Little Salmon for Witness, Kirkus Reviews,* January 1, 1997, p. 62.
Review of *A Little Salmon for Witness, Publishers Weekly,* January 13, 1997, p. 75.
Mathews, Pat, review of *Read for Me, Mama, Bulletin of the Center for Children's Books,* March, 1997, pp. 255-56.
Review of *O Christmas Tree, School Library Journal,* October, 1996, p. 39.
Review of *Read for Me, Mama, Kirkus Reviews,* January 1, 1997, p. 63.
Stevenson, Deborah, review of *O Christmas Tree, Bulletin of the Center for Children's Books,* November, 1996, p. 111.
Topol, Martha, review of *A Little Salmon for Witness, School Library Journal,* February, 1997, p. 84.

■ For More Information See

PERIODICALS

Booklist, February 15, 1997, p. 1028.
Publishers Weekly, September 30, 1996, p. 90.

*   *   *

RANDELL, Beverley
See PRICE, Beverley Joan

*   *   *

RAWN, Melanie (Robin) 1954-

■ Personal

Born June 12, 1954, in Santa Monica, CA; daughter of Robert Dawson and Alma Lucile (Fisk) Rawn. *Education:* Scripps College, B.A. (history), 1975; attended graduate school at University of Denver, 1975-76; California State University at Fullerton, teacher credentials, 1980.

■ Addresses

Home—Los Angeles, CA. *Agent*—Russell Galen, Scovil Chichak Galen, Inc., 381 Park Avenue S., New York, NY 10016.

■ Career

Writer. *Member:* Science Fiction and Fantasy Writers of America.

■ Writings

FANTASY NOVELS

(With Jennifer Roberson and Kate Elliot) *The Golden Key,* DAW (New York City), 1996.
Knights of the Morningstar ("Quantum Leap" series), Boulevard, 1996.
The Diviner (prequel to *The Golden Key*), DAW, 1997.

"DRAGON PRINCE" TRILOGY

Dragon Prince, DAW, 1988.
The Star Scroll, DAW, 1989.

MELANIE RAWN

Sunrunner's Fire, DAW, 1990.

"DRAGON STAR" TRILOGY

Stronghold, DAW, 1990.
The Dragon Token, with map by Marty Siegrist, DAW, 1992.
Skybowl, DAW, 1993.

"EXILES" SERIES

The Ruins of Ambrai, DAW, 1994.
The Mageborn Traitor, DAW, 1997.

■ Sidelights

Popular fantasy novelist Melanie Rawn published her first novel, *Dragon Prince,* in 1988, beginning a succession of fiction trilogies and also a long-lasting association with a single publisher, New York City's DAW Books. The prince of the "Dragon Prince" trilogy is Rohan. In the series' opening novel, Rohan's father, Zehava, has recently died, leaving their desert kingdom open to threats from High Prince Roelstra, whose seventeen daughters give him considerable leverage in concluding alliances with nearby domains. Dragons are included in the adventures too, as is love in the person of an orphaned acolyte, Sioned. Commenting on the length and extravagance of this romantic saga, a *Publishers Weekly* critic felt it would appeal to readers of specific tastes, adding, "Rawn moves her large cast swiftly and colorfully through their expected motions."

The second volume in the trilogy, *The Star Scroll,* finds Prince Rohan settled into peaceful rulership of his realm fourteen years after the conflicts of the first novel have been resolved. This peace is mistaken for weakness by some, who wish for a change of leadership. A new conflict arises through a star scroll which discloses the magic techniques of an ancient people who were able to control starlight. Two reviewers, Karen S. Ellis in *Kliatt*

and John Christensen in *Voice of Youth Advocates,* cautioned that a reading of *Dragon Prince* was necessary to an understanding of the complicated feuds and character relationships in *The Star Scroll;* but both reviewers enjoyed the book on its own terms as well. Ellis called it "involved fantasy fare" in which the characters "are all woven together by intrigue and magic." Christensen labelled it a "struggle of good against evil.... The main characters," he continued, "are well developed and it is a very compelling fantasy."

The "Dragon Prince" trilogy ended in 1990 with *Sunrunner's Fire,* and Rawn's sequel-trilogy, "Dragon Star," began that same year with *Stronghold.* A change of generations takes place, with Prince Rohan dying, his son Pol taking charge of the kingdom, and the kingdom's stronghold being destroyed. In the trilogy's second volume, 1992's *The Dragon Token,* Pol must deal with an attack from an army of unidentified invaders; to do so, he returns to his desert roots and consults the wise dragons who live there (and who communicate by means of color). Sally Estes, in *Booklist,* found the dragon-human relationship in *The Dragon Token* to be one of its most interesting aspects, both in itself and in

Set in the mythical planet of Lenfell, Rawn's fantasy is the tale of three sisters whose varied strengths promise a viable future for a world nearly destroyed by devastating wars. (Cover illustration by Michael Whelan.)

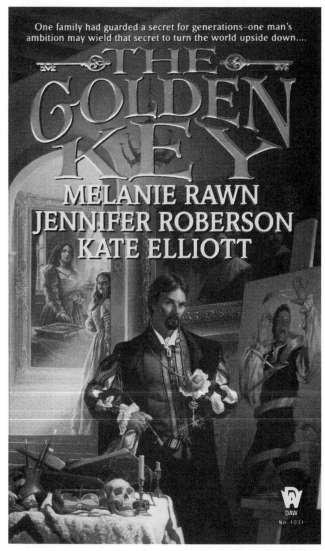

One family had guarded a secret for generations—one man's ambition may wield that secret to turn the world upside down....

THE GOLDEN KEY

MELANIE RAWN
JENNIFER ROBERSON
KATE ELLIOTT

Rawn and two other fantasy writers penned this novel of a family of artists who can influence reality by means of their painting. (Cover illustration by Michael Whelan.)

comparison to dragon-human relationships in other works of fantasy. Writing that "Rawn demonstrates a fine sense of world building and characterization," Estes called the novel "challenging fantasy well worth the effort." Estes noted the challenge involved in keeping track of a huge cast of characters and interrelationships, many of them from Rawn's four previous novels. Reviewer Margaret Miles, in *Voice of Youth Advocates,* offered the same caveat to readers. However, Miles, like Estes, gave the novel a clear thumbs-up, opining that Rawn's "fully imagined historical and cultural backgrounds, and her absorbing systems of Sunrunners' and sorcerers' magic all give this series a tremendous and well-deserved appeal." Similar views were voiced by a critic for *Publishers Weekly,* who called *The Dragon Token* "unusually sophisticated" for its genre. The reception for the trilogy's finale, *Skybowl,* was less enthusiastic, as critics in both *Publishers Weekly* and *Kirkus Reviews* complained of the novel's massive length and intricate cast of characters. Sally Estes, in *Booklist,* once again commented favorably, however,

saying that the novel was a fully satisfying wrap-up to the series—briskly paced, involving, and boasting a gripping denouement.

Rawn's next fantasy series, "Exiles," takes the reader to a different land, Lenfell, which was colonized in the distant past by a population of mages who gained control of—and polluted through warfare—the natural environment. *The Ruins of Ambrai,* which opens the series, brings the reader up-to-date on this matriarchal society's past and introduces three orphaned sisters: Glennin, Sarra, and Cailet. Raised apart from one another, each sister has different strengths and attitudes and each separately, and together, has the potential to affect the planet's future. *Voice of Youth Advocates* reviewer Rosemary Moran praised Rawn's "great attention to detail," and called *The Ruins of Ambrai* "engrossing." She especially appreciated Rawn's delineation of the structure of a matriarchy, as did *Kliatt* reviewer Judith H. Silverman, who, despite complaining of the novel's length and complexity, said, "Fantasy readers hungry for a good matriarchy will not be disappointed."

Rawn's career took a turn in 1996, when she collaborated with two other fantasy writers, Jennifer Roberson and Kate Elliott, to create a three-generation novel that aimed to preserve both novelistic unity and authorial individuality. Set in the fantasy duchy of Tira Virte, *The Golden Key* examines the relationship among art, love, and magic, for this is a world in which paintings constitute the recorded history of the society, and some of the paintings—those made by the magical Grijalva family—can actually affect history. The Grijalva artists, called Limners, are sterile, and insert their vital essence into the paintings, at the cost of the painters' early, painful deaths. *Booklist* reviewer Roland Green found the novel not only "original in concept and superior in execution," but clearly the best work any of its three authors had produced to that point. "[T]he romance justifies every one of its nearly 800 pages," Green declared.

■ Works Cited

Christensen, John, review of *The Star Scroll, Voice of Youth Advocates,* December, 1989, p. 291.

Review of *Dragon Prince, Publishers Weekly,* October 28, 1988, p. 74.

Review of *Dragon Token, Publishers Weekly,* December 6, 1991, pp. 60-61.

Ellis, Karen S., review of *The Star Scroll, Kliatt,* September, 1989, p. 20.

Estes, Sally, review of *The Dragon Token, Booklist,* March 15, 1992, p. 1344.

Estes, Sally, review of *Sky Bowl, Booklist,* February 15, 1993, p. 1041.

Green, Roland, review of *The Golden Key, Booklist,* September 1, 1996, p. 69.

Miles, Margaret, review of *The Dragon Token, Voice of Youth Advocates,* August, 1992, p. 179.

Moran, Rosemary, review of *The Ruins of Ambrai, Voice of Youth Advocates,* February, 1995, p. 351.

Silverman, Judith H., review of *The Ruins of Ambrai,*
    Kliatt, March, 1996, p. 20.
Review of *Sky Bowl, Kirkus Reviews,* December 15,
    1992, p. 1542.
Review of *Sky Bowl, Publishers Weekly,* November 30,
    1992, pp. 38-39.

■ For More Information See

PERIODICALS

Kirkus Reviews, January 1, 1992, p. 24.
Library Journal, October 15, 1994, p. 90.
Publishers Weekly, August 19, 1996, p. 57.
Voice of Youth Advocates, April, 1989, p. 45; February,
    1997, p. 340.*

* * *

RICHLER, Mordecai 1931-

■ Personal

Born January 27, 1931, in Montreal, Quebec, Canada;
son of Moses Isaac and Lily (Rosenberg) Richler;
married Catherine Boudreau (divorced); married Florence Wood, July 27, 1960; children: (second marriage)
Daniel, Noah, Emma, Martha, Jacob. *Education:* Attended Sir George Williams University, 1949-51. *Religion:* Jewish.

■ Addresses

Home and office—1321 Sherbrooke St. W., Apt. 80C,
Montreal, Quebec, Canada H3G 1J4. *Agent*—(literary
and film) Janklow and Nesbit Associates, 598 Madison
Ave., New York, NY 10022.

■ Career

Author and scriptwriter. Left Canada in 1951 to become
freelance writer in Paris, France, 1952-53, and London,
England, 1954-72; returned to Canada, 1972. Writer in
residence, Sir George Williams University, 1968-69;
visiting professor, Carleton University, 1972-74.

■ Awards, Honors

President's Medal for nonfiction, University of Western
Ontario, 1959; art fellowships, Canadian council: junior
art fellowships, 1959 and 1960, senior arts fellowship,
1967; creative writing fellowship, Guggenheim Foundation, 1961; humor prize, *Paris Review,* 1967, for section
from *Cocksure;* Governor General's Award for fiction,
1969, for *Cocksure;* Governor General's Award for
literature and London *Jewish Chronicle* Literature
Award, both 1972, both for *St. Urbain's Horseman: A
Novel;* Berlin Film Festival Golden Bear, Academy
Award nomination, and Screenwriters Guild of America
Award, all 1974, all for screenplay, *The Apprenticeship
of Duddy Kravitz;* first Ruth Schwartz Children's Book
Award, *New York Times* Outstanding Book, 1975,
Canadian Bookseller's Award for best children's book,
and Book of the Year for Children Award, Canadian

MORDECAI RICHLER

Library Association, all 1976, all for *Jacob Two-Two
Meets the Hooded Fang;* London *Jewish Chronicle*/H. H.
Wingate Award for fiction, 1981, for *Joshua Then and
Now;* Commonwealth Writers Award, 1990, for *Solo-
mon Gursky Was Here;* Giller Fiction Prize, Canada,
1997.

■ Writings

JUVENILE FICTION

Jacob Two-Two Meets the Hooded Fang, illustrated by
    Fritz Wegner, Knopf, 1975, McClelland & Stewart
    (Toronto), 1975.
Jacob Two-Two and the Dinosaur, illustrated by Nor-
    man Eyolfson, Knopf, 1987, McClelland & Stewart,
    1987.
Jacob Two-Two's First Spy Case, illustrated by Michael
    Chesworth, McClelland & Stewart, 1995, Farrar,
    Straus & Giroux, 1997.

ADULT NOVELS

The Acrobats (also see below), Putnam, 1954, Deutsch
    (London), 1954, published as *Wicked We Love,*
    Popular Library (New York), 1955.
Son of a Smaller Hero, Collins (Toronto), 1955, Paper-
    back Library, 1965.
A Choice of Enemies, Collins, 1957.
The Apprenticeship of Duddy Kravitz (also see below),
    Little, Brown, 1959.
The Incomparable Atuk, McClelland & Stewart, 1963,
    published as *Stick Your Neck Out,* Simon & Schus-
    ter, 1963.

Cocksure: A Novel, Simon & Schuster, 1968, McClelland & Stewart, 1968.

St. Urbain's Horseman: A Novel, Knopf, 1971, McClelland & Stewart, 1971.

Joshua Then and Now: A Novel (also see below), Knopf, 1980, McClelland & Stewart, 1980.

Solomon Gursky Was Here, Viking (Markham, Ontario), 1989, Knopf, 1990.

Barney's Version, Knopf Canada, 1997, Knopf, 1998.

SCREENPLAYS

(With Nicholas Phipps) *No Love for Johnnie,* Embassy, 1962.

(With Geoffrey Cotterell and Ivan Foxwell) *Tiara Tahiti,* Rank, 1962.

(With Nicholas Phipps) *The Wild and the Willing,* Rank, 1962, released as *Young and Willing,* Universal, 1965.

Life at the Top, Royal International, 1965.

The Apprenticeship of Duddy Kravitz (adapted from Richler's novel; also see below), Paramount, 1974.

(With David Giler and Jerry Belson) *Fun with Dick and Jane,* Bart/Palevsky, 1977.

Joshua Then and Now (adapted from Richler's novel), Twentieth Century-Fox, 1985.

TELEVISION SCRIPTS

The Acrobats (based on Richler's novel; also see below), Canadian Broadcasting Corp. (CBC-TV), 1957.

Friend of the People, CBC-TV, 1957.

Paid in Full, ATV (England), 1958.

The Trouble with Benny (based on Richler's short story), ABC (England), 1959.

The Apprenticeship of Duddy Kravitz (based on Richler's novel), CBC-TV, 1960.

The Fall of Mendel Krick, British Broadcasting Corp. (BBC-TV), 1963.

RADIO SCRIPTS

The Acrobats (based on Richler's novel), CBC-Radio, 1957.

Benny, the War in Europe, and Myerson's Daughter Bella, CBC-Radio, 1958.

The Spare Room, CBC-Radio, 1961.

Q for Quest (excerpts from Richler's fiction), CBC-Radio, 1963.

It's Harder to Be Anybody, CBC-Radio, 1965.

Such Was St. Urbain Street, CBC-Radio, 1966.

The Wordsmith (based on Richler's short story), CBC-Radio, 1979.

OTHER

Hunting Tigers under Glass: Essays and Reports (essays), McClelland & Stewart, 1969.

The Street: Stories, McClelland & Stewart, 1969, New Republic (Washington, D.C.), 1975, as *The Street: A Memoir,* Weidenfeld and Nicholson (London), 1972.

(Editor) *Canadian Writing Today* (anthology), Peter Smith, 1970.

Shoveling Trouble (essays), McClelland & Stewart, 1972.

Notes on an Endangered Species and Others (essays), Knopf, 1974.

(With Andre Fortier and Rollo May) *Creativity and the University,* York University Press (Toronto), 1975.

The Suit (animated filmstrip), National Film Board of Canada, 1976.

Images of Spain (nonfiction), photographs by Peter Christopher, Norton, 1977, McClelland & Stewart, 1977.

The Great Comic Book Heroes and Other Essays (essays), McClelland & Stewart, 1978.

(Editor) *The Best of Modern Humor,* Knopf, 1983.

Home Sweet Home: My Canadian Album (essays), Knopf, 1984, published in paperback as *Home Sweet Home,* Penguin, 1985.

(Author of book) *Duddy* (play; based on Richler's novel *The Apprenticeship of Duddy Kravitz*), first produced in Edmonton, Alberta, at the Citadel Theatre, April, 1984.

Broadsides: Reviews and Opinions, Viking (Markham, Ontario), 1990.

(Editor) *Writers on World War II: An Anthology,* Knopf, 1991.

Oh Canada! Oh Quebec! Requiem for a Divided Country (humor), Knopf, 1992.

The Language of Signs (humor), David McKay, 1992.

This Year in Jerusalem (nonfiction), Knopf, 1994.

(Editor and author of afterword) Mavis Gallant, *The Moslem Wife and Other Stories,* McClelland & Stewart, 1994.

(Introduction) Mark Twain, *The Innocents Abroad,* edited by Shelley F. Fishkin, Oxford University Press, 1996.

Book columnist for *Gentleman's Quarterly* (*GQ*). Contributor to Canadian, English, and American periodicals, including *New Statesman, Spectator, Observer, Punch, Holiday, New York Review of Books, Commentary, Encounter,* and *London Magazine.* Member of editorial board, Book-of-the-Month Club, 1972-89. Richler's books have been translated into Finnish, French, Dutch, German, Hebrew, Italian, and Spanish and have been published in Braille. His papers are housed in a permanent collection at the University of Calgary Library in Alberta, Canada.

■ Adaptations

The Street was made into an animated filmstrip by the National Film Board of Canada, 1970; *Son of a Smaller Hero* and *St. Urbain's Horseman* (sound recordings) were released by Crane Library, Vancouver, 1972; Paramount, in conjunction with Astral Films (Canada), released the film *The Apprenticeship of Duddy Kravitz,* starring Richard Dreyfuss, 1974; *Jacob Two-Two Meets the Hooded Fang* was adapted by Cinema Shares International (Canada) as a film starring Alex Karras, as a recording made by Caedmon and narrated by Christopher Plummer, and as a sound recording made by the Crane Library, Vancouver, all in 1977; *Jacob Two-Two* was adapted as a play, with book and lyrics by Peg McKelvey, Pat Patterson, and Dodi Robb and music by Patterson and Joy Alexander, Playwrights Canada, 1981; Twentieth Century-Fox produced the film *Joshua Then and Now,* starring James Woods and Alan Arkin,

1985; *Bambinger* (short story) was made into a film by Atlantis Films/Beacon Films, the National Film Board of Canada, 1985; *Mortimer Griffin and Shalisky* (short story) was made into a film by Atlantis Films/Beacon Films, the National Film Board of Canada, 1986; *Jacob Two-Two Meets the Hooded Fang* was made into a primary/junior whole language literature unit by Bookmates in 1987; *Jacob Two-Two and the Dinosaur* was recorded for Caedmon by Christopher Plummer, 1988. Sound recordings of most of Richler's works have been released by BMG Kidz, CNIB, the Crane Library, the Ontario Library Service, and other Canadian companies and organizations.

■ Work in Progress

Two books on literary feuds.

■ Sidelights

Mordecai Richler is a novelist, essayist, scriptwriter, journalist, and editor who is considered one of Canada's most important and controversial writers as well as a celebrated international figure. As a novelist and essay-

Eight-year-old Jacob hides his pet diplodocus from the adults who fear the dinosaur and hope to destroy it. (From *Jacob Two-Two and the Dinosaur,* written by Richler and illustrated by Norman Eyolfson.)

ist for adults, he has written literature—much of it autobiographical or semi-autobiographical—that reflects his characteristic dark humor and penetrating view of society in general and Canadians, especially Canadian Jews. As a writer for children, Richler is the creator of three stories about Jacob Two-Two, a small boy based on his youngest son who has a series of fantastic adventures; Richler is also well known among young people as the author of *The Apprenticeship of Duddy Kravitz,* a novel originally published for adults that describes the progression of an aggressively materialistic Montreal teenager from a conniving fifteen-year-old to a ruthless entrepreneur. Often considered Richler's best book, *Duddy Kravitz* has long been a favorite of Canadian adolescents and has been studied as a textbook in Canadian schools. *Duddy Kravitz* and the books about Jacob Two-Two are generally embraced with enthusiasm by the young, who appreciate Richler's sensitivity to their plight, the colloquial liveliness of his style, and the humor and fast pace of his narratives.

As a novelist, Richler is praised as a gifted social critic who fills his works, which often blend reality and fantasy, with lively narratives, caustic humor, and rich, pointed characterizations. Skewing popular tastes and pretensions in acidic prose, Richler usually depicts contemporary society as a barbaric world inhabited by insecure, alienated individuals; his typical protagonists are morally disillusioned men who find self-knowledge and inner stability difficult to attain. Although Richler is sometimes faulted for excessive vulgarity and for his views of both Canadian nationalism and Jewish culture, most observers regard him as a brilliant writer whose works are both funny and incisive. In his essay on Richler in *Dictionary of Literary Biography,* R. H. Ramsey claims that he "has something fresh to say about humanity and says it in a well-crafted form, which even with its comic exuberance, stands firmly in the tradition of moral and intellectual fiction. Richler writes novels out of a compulsion to produce a work that approaches a definitive statement, fully realized artistically—an aim that, in his own opinion, always fails.... [In] spite of his own harsh criteria, the body of writing he has already produced has earned him the stature he enjoys."

Born in Montreal to Moses Isaac and Lily Rosenberg Richler, Richler grew up on St. Urbain Street, an area that at the time was populated almost exclusively by working-class Jewish immigrants who fled Russia after the Russo-Japanese war. As Leah Rosenberg, Richler's mother wrote a memoir of her early years in Montreal, *The Errand Runner: Reflections of a Rabbi's Daughter.* In his own book *Home Sweet Home: My Canadian Album,* published in 1984, Richler remembers, "In my day, St. Urbain Street was the lowest rung on a ladder we were all hot to climb.... [On] St. Urbain, our fathers worked as cutters or pressers or scrap dealers and drifted into cold-water flats, sitting down to supper in their freckled Penman's long underwear, clipping their nails at the table. Mothers organized bazaars, proceeds for the Jewish National Fund, and jockeyed for position on the ladies' auxiliary of the Talmud Torah or the

Folkschule, both parochial schools. Visiting aunts charged into the parlor, armed with raffle books, ten cents a ticket." The landscape of Richler's youth has become the setting for several of his most famous novels, including *The Apprenticeship of Duddy Kravitz.*

As a child, Richler recalls in an essay in *Canadian Literature,* "I never read children's books myself, but cut my intellectual teeth on Superman, Captain Marvel, and The Batman, moving from Ellery Queen and Perry Mason, and finally, at the age of twelve or thereabouts, to the first novel that I ever read, *All Quiet on the Western Front.*" As an Orthodox Jew, Richler received a traditional upbringing: "I attended parochial school (studying English, modern Hebrew, and French)," he continues in *Home Sweet Home,* "and after classes, three afternoons a week, I knuckled down to the Talmud with Mr. Yalofsky's class in the back room of the Young Israel Synagogue. Our parents were counting on us—a scruffy lot, but, for all that, the first Canadian-born generation—to elbow our way into McGill [University]." In 1946, Richler's parents were divorced, "an all-but-unheard-of scandal in its time," the author writes in *Esquire.*

After graduating from United Talmud Torah and Baron Byng High School, Richler attended Sir George Williams University in Montreal for two years as an English major and worked part-time for the *Montreal Herald.* "I did very badly in high school," Richler remembers in an interview in *Tamarack Review,* "but I was expected to go to Sir George William. I was very quickly disappointed.... I found that all the people I knew and liked had graduated. So I quit." At the age of nineteen, Richler cashed in an insurance policy his mother had taken out on him and used the money to go to Europe; "I decided the best thing," he tells *Tamarack Review,* "was to cut myself off and find out if I could write." While living in Paris, he wrote a novel, lived a bohemian lifestyle, and became friends with other expatriate authors such as Allen Ginsberg, Terry Southern, and Mavis Gallant, whose collection *The Moslem Wife and Other Stories* Richler would later edit. A year later, he ran out of money and returned to Canada, where he took on a series of jobs, including work in the newsroom of the Canadian Broadcasting Company. The novel Richler had written in Paris, *The Acrobats,* was published in 1954; influenced by such authors as Hemingway, Camus, Sartre, and Celine, it describes the life and death of a young existentialist artist who has moved from Montreal to Spain during that country's civil war. In the same year, Richler moved to London and began his literary career in earnest; he was also married and divorced within a few years.

Published when Richler was only twenty-eight, *The Apprenticeship of Duddy Kravitz* established the author as a major figure and humorist. The book chronicles Duddel (Duddy) Kravitz's rise from a bright, motherless schoolboy to a prominent landowner who has alienated his family and friends. Duddy lives on St. Urbain Street in Montreal's Jewish ghetto—the area in which Richler grew up—in a world dominated by dishonest business-

In this third book about Jacob Two-Two, Richler describes how the young boy and his neighbor, master spy X. Barnaby Dinglebat, claim victory over the mean-spirited headmaster at Jacob's school. (From *Jacob Two-Two's First Spy Case,* illustrated by Michael Chesworth.)

men and petty criminals. Raised by a father who teaches him to idolize small-time racketeer Jerry "Boy Wonder" Dingleman and rebuffed by his family in favor of his scholarly older brother, Duddy searches for a hint that someone does—or could—love him. Misinterpreting his grandfather's advice that "a man without land is nobody," Duddy sets out to acquire property by any means possible. At the end of the novel, Duddy is a nineteen-year-old landowner with valuable property in the Laurentians, a popular Canadian resort area, but he has been snubbed by his girlfriend and best friend as well as by the one person he has genuinely tried to impress—his grandfather. Duddy is, however, embraced by his father, who sees in him the promise of another Boy Wonder. Duddy Kravitz reappears in minor roles in Richler's adult novels *St. Urbain's Horseman* and *Joshua Then and Now;* in these works, he is depicted as an unscrupulous, unloved millionaire.

Compared to classic coming-of-age stories such as James Joyce's *Portrait of the Artist as a Young Man,* D. H. Lawrence's *Sons and Lovers,* and the "Studs Lonigan" books by James T. Farrell, *The Apprenticeship of Duddy Kravitz* established Richler as a gifted comic novelist, satirist, and moralist as well as a superior creator of character. Observers note that Richler's ambivalence toward Duddy, whom he portrays as both a grasping, self-centered opportunist and an underprivileged, confused teenager, forces readers to constantly reassess the character. Considered both harsh and tender, *Duddy Kravitz* is also noted for Richler's searingly accurate picture of life on St. Urbain Street and its surrounding society. Duddy is considered among Richler's finest creations; Warren Tallman of *Canadian Literature* deems him "a naive yet shrewd latter-day Huck Finn" while *Journal of Canadian Fiction* critic John Ferns calls him "in many ways a North American everyman." Writing in *New Leader*, Pearl Kazin notes that *Duddy Kravitz* is "extremely skillful and has a rambunctious vitality not often encountered in novels about any world these days.... Richler can understand both the wonder and cruelty of family feeling without underestimating either. It is an enormously impressive achievement." In his essay on *Duddy Kravitz* in the collection *Mordecai Richler*, A. R. Bevan says, "Written by a Canadian and about Canadians in Canada's largest city, this novel with its satiric-tragic-comic attitude to man in the modern world is much more than a 'mere' Canadian work. Richler's novel, it seems to me, can stand on its own by any standard."

Although *Duddy Kravitz* received a generally favorable critical reception, it was not an instant popular success. However, the novel's reputation continued to grow, especially among young people. In 1973, Richler tells interviewer Graeme Gibson in *Eleven Canadian Novelists*, "I don't think I really found my own style until *Duddy Kravitz* and then it all became easier in a way because it was all my own. I felt confident, then, for better or for worse this was the way I wanted to write. Until then I was all hit and miss and groping around." In 1974, Richler wrote the screenplay for the film version of *Duddy Kravitz*. The movie, which starred Richard Dreyfuss, was nominated for an Academy Award for best screenplay. Response to the film regenerated interest in Richler's original book, which by this time was being used as a textbook in high school classrooms in Canada. In 1978, Richler wrote a draft for a musical comedy playscript based on his novel. In 1984, the musical *Duddy*—with songs by Jerry Leiber and Mike Stoller, who had written hits for Elvis Presley, the Coasters, and other popular performers—opened at the Citadel Theatre in Edmonton, Alberta; unfortunately, the play did not move on to Toronto and New York as expected. In "Why I Write," an essay published in 1974, Richler comments on *Duddy Kravitz:* "Of all the novels I've written, it is *The Apprenticeship of Duddy Kravitz* and *Cocksure* which come closest to my intentions and, therefore, give me the most pleasure."

In the years following the publication of *Duddy Kravitz*, Richler continued to build his reputation as a novelist and essayist while producing screenplays and scripts for television and radio. In 1960, Richler married Florence Wood, a Canadian model with whom he had five children. When his youngest child, Jacob, asked Richler if he could read any of his father's books, the author promised that he would write something just for his children; in response, he created *Jacob Two-Two Meets the Hooded Fang,* published in 1975.

Prompted by a bedtime story told to Jacob Richler, *Jacob Two-Two Meets the Hooded Fang* is a satiric view of adulthood through a child's eyes. The youngest of five children, six-year-old Jacob has acquired his nickname from having to repeat everything twice before anyone will listen to him. Living in a world planned by—and for—grownups and teased by his siblings, whose names are those of Richler's other children, Jacob dreams that he is spirited away to the horrible Slimers' Isle and put on trial by a group of adults simply for being a child. He is imprisoned in a dungeon presided over by the dreaded Hooded Fang, an ogrelike ex-wrestler. Undaunted, Jacob uncovers the weaknesses of his jailer and saves the other children with whom he has been incarcerated.

Reviewers greeted *Jacob Two-Two* with enthusiasm, recognizing the author's sympathy toward children as well as his characteristic indictment of society. Writing in *Saturday Night,* John Ayre says, "As black satirist, fearless lambaster of Jewish and WASP, dirty comic writer, Mordecai Richler has consistently displayed a resolute sneer. But in his first children's book, Richler stands revealed.... Richler knows and loves children. Astonishingly, he accepts them for what they are ... *Jacob Two-Two* [is] a subversive but happy accomplishment." John Parr of *Canadian Children's Literature* claims that it is "evidently to Richler's credit that he has remained true to his artistic vision, turning in a genuinely creative performance, rather than hackishly reproducing some standard item for the young set.... [One] would like to think that Mordecai Richler has created a Canadian children's literature classic. For this is a compellingly presented tale, replete with comic detail and story-line inventiveness." Writing in the same publication, Perry Nodelman asserts, "*Jacob Two-Two* is a subversive book—a comical attack on grownup supremacy that undermines the control grownups have over children.... It is a large part of Richler's genius as a novelist for children that he recognizes, and allows his youthful protagonist to enjoy, the pleasures of paranoia.... [For] Jacob ... a vengeful imagination turns out to be a boon and not a failing." Although some critics are dissatisfied that Richler fashioned Jacob's adventure as a dream, most observers see *Jacob Two-Two* as a successful contribution to children's literature as well as a book consistent with Richler's other works.

In an essay he wrote for *Canadian Literature* on writing *Jacob Two-Two*, Richler comments, "I decided if I ever got round to writing a book for my kids, its intention would be to amuse. Pure fun, not instruction, is what I had in mind. But I resisted sitting down to *Jacob Two-Two* for more than a year, because I ... have a prejudice against children's books, too many of which are written by third-rate writers for children already old enough to at least enjoy some adult books.... I wrote it, first of all, for my own pleasure (and in fulfillment of a rash promise). Of course, I hoped, as I always do, that it would appeal to a large audience, but that is never a consideration in the actual writing." Richler concludes, "The success of *Jacob Two-Two* surprised, even embarrassed me.... Ironically, I suppose, *Jacob Two-Two,* in hard cover, has already outsold even my most successful adult novel, *St. Urbain's Horseman.* Maybe I missed my true vocation."

A bestseller in Canada, *Jacob Two-Two Meets the Hooded Fang* was translated into several languages, was made into a musical play, and was adapted into a film starring Alex Karras. In 1987, Richler completed the first of his sequels to the novel, *Jacob Two-Two and the Dinosaur.* In this book, Jacob—now eight years old—is given a small reptile as a gift. To his surprise, it grows into a huge dinosaur, a diplodocus. Pursued by, in the words of Peter Carver of *Books for Young People,* "a collection of refugees from Richler's adult satirical mind," who wish to try and use the dinosaur for their own selfish ends, Jacob and Dippy flee to the Rocky Mountains of British Columbia. Organizations such as the government and the army work to try and destroy Jacob's pet, who speaks joke-filled English. After spending a month together on the run, Jacob and Dippy part company after a misunderstanding; Jacob is captured and Dippy is presumed to have been exterminated. However, the story ends happily: Dippy makes it to British Columbia, finds a mate, and reconciles with Jacob by leaving him a confirming message in a mountain valley that is shown on television. Some reviewers found *Dinosaur* to be a lesser achievement than *Hooded Fang.* For example, Carver predicts, "The story will entertain kids, but it may not have the shelf life of the original," while Michael Darling of *Canadian Children's Literature* calls it "a mean-spirited book, which promotes an Us vs. Them philosophy, and suggests that Canadian scientists, politicians, and military men are corrupt, self-serving, and vicious.... One hopes and expects that children will not care for this book." However, not all reviewers found the social and political satire of *Dinosaur* to be unappealing. "Indeed," writes Brian D. Johnson in *Maclean's,* "the ogre-and-dungeon fantasy of *The Hooded Fang* seems positively lugubrious next to the Swiftian satire of *Dinosaur,* a fable cunningly designed to delight children and parents alike."

Jacob Two-Two's First Spy Case, published in 1995, is Richler's third book about his young protagonist. In this story, Jacob turns the tables on Perfectly Loathsome Leo Louse, the nasty cook at his private school, with the help of his next-door neighbor, master spy X. Barnaby Dinglebat, and his four siblings. Using swindles and subterfuge, Jacob triumphs over Leo as well as his headmaster, Mr. Greedyguts, and his geography teacher, Miss Sour Pickle; in an appendix, Richler explains the mind reading trick that Jacob and Mr. Dinglebat pull on Perfectly Loathsome Leo Louse. *New York Times Book Review* critic Jim Gladstone deems *Jacob Two-Two's First Spy Case* to be "good silly fun" and says that young readers "will be baffled by the sophisticated scam, and

delighted to find an appendix that teaches them how to replicate it." Writing in *Books in Canada,* Howard Engel describes *Spy Case* as a "wonderfully funny and cunning tale," and adds that it "is not every serious novelist who can successfully turn out material for children.... It is the trick of the clever writer of children's stories to engage both parent-reader and child-listener in his lines.... Each will pull different but equally savoury morsels from this satisfying story."

In his essay "Why I Write," Richler quotes George Orwell's essay of the same name in citing four main reasons for creating literature: "sheer egotism," "aesthetic enthusiasm," "historical impulse," and "political purpose." Regarding Orwell's second point, Richler says, "The agonies involved in creating a novel, the unsatisfying draft, the scenes you never get right, are redeemed by those rare and memorable days when, seemingly without reason, everything falls right. Bonus days. Blessed days when, drawing on resources unexpected, you pluck ideas and prose out of your skull that you never dreamt capable of. Such, such are the real joys." He concludes, "Like any serious writer, I want to write one novel that will last, something that will keep me remembered after death, so I'm compelled to keep trying."

■ Works Cited

Ayre, John, "Mordecai Richler's Subversive Accomplishment," *Saturday Night,* July-August, 1975, pp. 65-66.

Bevan, A. R., "'The Apprenticeship of Duddy Kravitz,'" *Mordecai Richler,* edited by G. David Sheps, Ryerson Press, 1971, pp. 84-91.

Carver, Peter, review of *Jacob Two-Two and the Dinosaur, Books for Young People,* April, 1987, p. 9.

Darling, Michael, "An Unappealing Sequel," *Canadian Children's Literature,* Number 49, 1988, pp. 43-45.

Engel, Howard, "Two-Two's Apprenticeship," *Books in Canada,* December, 1995, p. 34.

Ferns, John, "Sympathy and Judgement in Mordecai Richler's 'The Apprenticeship of Duddy Kravitz,'" *Journal of Canadian Fiction,* winter, 1974, pp. 77-82.

Gibson, Graeme, *Eleven Canadian Novelists,* Anansi, 1973.

Gladstone, Jim, "Magical Mysteries," *New York Times Book Review,* May 18, 1997, p. 29.

Johnson, Brian D., "Jacob Two-Two in Love," *Maclean's,* June 1, 1987, p. 52.

Kazin, Pearl, "Chicken Soup and the Jewish Novel," *New Leader,* March 21, 1960, pp. 18-19.

Nodelman, Perry, "Jacob Two-Two and the Satisfactions of Paranoia," *Canadian Children's Literature,* Numbers 15 & 16, 1980, pp. 31-37.

Parr, John, "Richler Rejuvenated," *Canadian Children's Literature,* autumn, 1975, pp. 96-102.

Ramsey, R. H., "Mordecai Richler," *Dictionary of Literary Biography,* Volume 53: *Canadian Writers since 1960,* Gale, 1986, pp. 328-37.

Richler, Mordecai, "A Conversation with Mordecai Richler," *Tamarack Review,* winter, 1957.

Richler, Mordecai, "My Father's Life," *Esquire,* August, 1962.

Richler, Mordecai, "Why I Write," *Notes on an Endangered Species and Others,* Knopf, 1974, pp. 36-48.

Richler, Mordecai, "Writing *Jacob Two-Two,*" *Canadian Literature,* autumn, 1978, pp. 6-8.

Richler, Mordecai, *Home Sweet Home: My Canadian Album,* Knopf, 1984.

Tallman, Warren, "Wolf in the Snow, Part Two: The House Repossessed," *Canadian Literature,* autumn, 1960, pp. 41-48.

■ For More Information See

BOOKS

Children's Literature Review, Gale, Volume 17, 1989, pp. 63-81.

Contemporary Literary Criticism, Gale, Volume 18, 1981, Volume 46, 1988, Volume 70, 1992.

Helbig, Alethea K., and Agnes Regan, *Dictionary of Children's Fiction from Australia, Canada, India, New Zealand, and Selected African Countries,* Greenwood, 1992.

Landsberg, Michele, *Reading for the Love of It: Best Books for Young Readers,* Prentice-Hall, 1987, p. 82.

New, W. H., *Articulating West: Essays on Purpose and Form in Modern Canadian Literature,* New Press, 1972, pp. 108-27.

Ramraj, Victor J., *Mordecai Richler,* Twayne, 1983.

Woodcock, George, *Mordecai Richler,* McClelland & Stewart, 1970.

PERIODICALS

Children's Book News, Spring, 1996, p. 20.

Esquire, August, 1982.

Maclean's, May 7, 1984.

Modern Canadian Fiction, winter, 1974, pp. 77-82.

New York Times Book Review, October 18, 1987, p. 38.

Quill and Quire, November, 1995, p. 45.

Times Literary Supplement, April 2, 1976, p. 376.

—*Sketch by Gerard J. Senick*

*   *   *

ROEDER, Virginia Marsh 1926-

■ Personal

Born October 19, 1926, in Knoxville, TN; daughter of Frank Henry (a sales representative) and Margaret (a government employee; maiden name, Barton) Marsh; married Richard C. Roeder (a designer), June, 1951; children: Ramsay Weatherford, Lee, Parke Wellman, Margaret Ferranti. *Education:* Pratt Institute, Certificate in Illustration, 1946; University of Houston, B.F.A., 1976. *Politics:* Democrat. *Hobbies and other interests:* Travel.

■ Addresses

Home—8111 Bromley, Houston, TX 77055.

■ Career

Sterling Advertising Agency, New York City, illustrator, 1948-51; Joskes, Battlesteins, McCain Typographer, Inc., Houston, TX, freelance illustrator, 1952-60; St. John's School, Houston, art teacher, 1963-93, consultant, 1993—. *Member:* Society of Children's Book Writers and Illustrators, Museum of Fine Arts, Houston, Phi Kappa Phi.

■ Awards, Honors

Emeritus status, St. John's School.

■ Illustrator

Mary Wade, *I'm Going to Texas/Yo Voy a Tejas,* translated by Quadalupe C. Quintanilla, Colophon House (Houston, TX), 1994.

Jo Harper, *Deaf Smith, Texas Hero,* Eakin Publications (Austin, TX), 1994.

Mary Wade, *I'm Going to California/Yo Voy a California,* translated by Juan M. Aguayo, Colophon House, 1997.

O. D. Lachtman, *Call Me Consuelo,* Arte Publico, 1997.

Jo Harper, *Bigfoot Wallace,* Eakin Publications, 1998.

Mary Wade, *Jane Long's Journey,* Colophon House, 1998.

Also illustrator of book cover for *A Yank among Us* by Wanda Dionne.

VIRGINIA MARSH ROEDER

■ Sidelights

Virginia Marsh Roeder told *SATA:* "I can't remember a time when I didn't draw, and I can't remember a time when drawing didn't turn into an illustration or story. Even the paper dolls I drew had elaborate backdrops to add to the make-believe. I still find that I react to storytelling visually.

"It followed that my major at Pratt Institute in New York would be illustration. The last project that I remember was a series of illustrations for a children's book about a leprechaun.

"Much later, I used my own four children as models and inspiration for spots that were used in the *Houston Post* in the Entertainment Section. I did a great deal of freelance illustration, advertising children's clothing for several department stores in Houston. My work was shown in a gallery for many years although, with four children, I was not very prolific. Through the years, I have accepted commissions for portraits of children. They hang in homes in Houston, Austin, and Dallas, Texas, and in New York, California, New Mexico, Tennessee, and Paris, France.

"As my children grew to school age, I accepted a position teaching art at St. John's School in Houston. Even though I enjoyed sparking an interest in art in my students, I always enjoyed the non-teaching elements, like doing program covers, invitations, and announcements for the school, more than the actual teaching. As an outgrowth of my teaching art in the upper school, I began a program of taking a group of students to Europe each summer to study art and architecture. This opened a wider area for drawing. I now have several sketchbooks full of France, Italy, and the Greek islands. I also came back with a number of stories waiting to be written.

"Finally, after retiring from more than twenty-five years of teaching art, I have come full circle and find myself totally captivated by children's illustration again. I spend part of my time completing children's portraits, which keeps me interested in detail, and the rest of my time working on two picture books I have written and illustrated.

"I am busier now than I would like to be with outside commitments to speak at a number of conferences about illustrating for children's books, but this also involves book signings, which give me the opportunity to see where the books are going and who is buying them. Everything seems to have a picture and, now with grandchildren, I find that I have a whole new batch of models."

■ For More Information See

PERIODICALS

School Library Journal, July, 1997, p. 77.

ROGERS, Paul 1950-

■ Personal

Born June 16, 1950, in London, England; son of Franklin (a company director) and Alice (Nuttman) Rogers; married Emma Jane Rothwell-Evans (a writer), October 15, 1977; children: Toby, Thea, Joshua. *Education:* University of Sussex, B.A. (with honors), 1973; attended University of Freiburg. *Hobbies and other interests:* Playing folk and classical guitar, ancient Hebrew.

■ Career

Northease Manor School, Lewes, Sussex, England, teacher, 1974-78; Tideway School, Newhaven, Sussex, teacher, 1978-81; Sydenham Community School, Bridgwater, Somerset, England, language teacher and head of language department, 1981—.

■ Writings

FOR CHILDREN

Forget-Me-Not, illustrated by Celia Berridge, Viking, 1984.
Sheepchase, illustrated by Celia Berridge, Viking, 1986.
From Me to You, illustrated by Jane Johnson, Orchard, 1987.

PAUL ROGERS

Rand and Shine, illustrated by Chris Burke, Orchard, 1987.

Tumbledown, illustrated by Robin Bell Corfield, Walker, 1987.

Lily's Picnic, illustrated by John Prater, Bodley Head, 1988.

Somebody's Awake, illustrated by Robin Bell Corfield, Bodley Head, 1988.

Somebody's Sleepy, illustrated by Robin Bell Corfield, Bodley Head, 1988.

Me and Alice Go to the Gallery, illustrated by John Prater, Bodley Head, 1989.

What Will the Weather Be Like Today?, illustrated by Kazuko, Orchard, 1989.

Me and Alice Go to the Museum, illustrated by John Prater, Bodley Head, 1989.

Don't Blame Me!, illustrated by Robin Bell Corfield, Bodley Head, 1990.

The Shapes Game, illustrated by Sian Tucker, Orchard, 1989.

Surprise, Surprise!, illustrated by Sian Tucker, Orchard, 1990.

Funimals, illustrated by Charles Fuge, Bodley Head, 1991.

A Letter to Granny, illustrated by John Prater, Bodley Head, 1994.

(With John Prater) *Nearly but Not Quite,* Bodley Head, 1997.

FOR CHILDREN; WITH WIFE, EMMA ROGERS

The Get Better Book, illustrated by Jo Burroughes, Orchard Books, 1988.

Boneshaker, illustrated by Maureen Bradley, Viking, 1989.

What's Wrong, Tom?, illustrated by Colin Robinson, Viking, 1989.

Amazing Babies, illustrated by Dee Shulman, Dent, 1990.

Boneshaker Rides Again, illustrated by Maureen Bradley, Viking, 1990.

Do You Dare?, illustrated by Sonia Holleyman, Orchard Books, 1991.

Bat Boy, illustrated by Toni Goffe, Dent, 1991.

Zoe's Tower, illustrated by Robin Bell Corfield, Walker, 1991.

Billy Buzoni & Friends, illustrated by Dee Shulman, Dent, 1991.

Our House, illustrated by Priscilla Lamont, Walker, 1991.

Billy the Kid, illustrated by Toni Goffe, Dent, 1993.

Little Boat, illustrated by Siobhan Dodds, Dent, 1993.

Little Train, illustrated by Siobhan Dodds, Dent, 1993.

Ten Terrible Pirates, illustrated by Norman Johnson, David Bennett, 1994.

Quacky Duck, illustrated by Barbara Mullarney Wright, Orion, 1995.

Cat's Kittens, Viking, 1996.

Giant Pie, illustrated by Nick Schon, Viking, 1997.

OTHER

Alles Klar: German Grammar through Cartoons, Harrap, 1982.

Understanding Grammar, Harrap, 1982.

La Grammaire en clair: French Grammar through Cartoons, Harrap, 1983.

(With Bryan Goodman-Stephens and Lol Briggs) *Zickzack* (German textbook), three volumes, Arnold-Wheaton, 1987-89, revised as *Zickzack neu,* Nelson, 1995.

(With Goodman-Stephens) *Route nationale* (French textbook), Nelson, 1993.

■ Sidelights

Children's book author and educator Paul Rogers got his start as a writer by creating foreign-language grammar texts. Fortunately, he made the transition to children's fiction by putting formality aside and getting down to fun. Picture books and beginning readers by Rogers include *Sheepchase, Tumbledown,* and *Don't Blame Me!,* as well as a host of popular books written in partnership with his wife, Emma Rogers.

Born in London, England, in 1950, Rogers's childhood attention was drawn more to what was going on on-stage than to what lay between the covers of books. "As a child I was not very interested in books," the author once admitted to *SATA.* "I preferred to be drawing pictures or climbing up a tree.... Theatre, in fact, excited me much more than books, and I was lucky to be taken quite often to musicals in the west end of London by my father. He was happy to encourage my interest in the theatre by taking me backstage during the interval, but was very disappointed when my choice of musical instrument turned out to be nothing more tuneful than the drums."

Rogers's interest in music and theatre stayed with him throughout secondary school and even into his student days at the University of Sussex. "I produced plays, made films, and played in bands. In their own way, I think these contributed to my interest in the visual side of storytelling and to my fascination with the rhythm of words." It was during Rogers's time as a student that he also discovered the joy of books, and "began to feel that writing was what I would really like to do."

After college graduation, Rogers went to live and teach in Spain. He also wrote, as he later admitted, "lots of very bad poetry, inspired by the poet I admired most, the German, Rilke." Returning to England in 1974, he taught French, German, and Spanish part time at a school in Sussex. It was there that he met Emma Rothwell-Evans, whom he later married. "I shall never forget the first time I benefited from her literary criticism," Rogers recalled of the woman who also eventually collaborated with him on many books for children. "Her reaction, when I read her a poem I had been working on, was to say: 'You mean you've spent all afternoon doing *that?!*' I went off to cut the spinach for supper with uncustomary cruelty. Since that time her criticisms have never failed to help."

The birth of the author's first child, Toby, inspired him to begin writing children's book. "Reading to Toby made [my wife and I] aware of the shortage of well-

"Aha!" said the heron.
"She's back!" said the cat.

"Well," said the farmer,
"just look at that!"

From *Quacky Duck,* **written by Paul and Emma Rogers and illustrated by Barbara Mullarney Wright.**

written, well-constructed books for young children," Rogers explained to *SATA*. As luck would have it, he soon met award-winning illustrator Celia Berridge. "I asked her if she would be interested in doing some drawings for a text I had written called *Forget-Me-Not*. A sales representative at a book fair cautioned me about the number of unsolicited manuscripts submitted, but gave me the address of Penguin Books. We decided to try anyway. The book came out in 1984."

Forget-Me-Not is a "hide-and-seek" book, where young readers follow an absentminded lion named Sidney as he attempts to visit a cousin and return home without mislaying everything in his possession. Having been awarded many positive reviews for its humor and warmth, *Forget-Me-Not* encouraged Rogers to continue writing for young people. The book was followed shortly by Rogers's *Sheepchase,* a curiously titled rhyming tale about a young sheep on the lam. Frisky Flossie escapes the watchful eye of her shepherd and heads off to town to visit the fair, but is eventually tracked down and chased back to the flock by her owner, all in brightly colored illustrations by Berridge.

Rhyming text is also used by Rogers in *From Me to You,* as an elderly woman tells her granddaughter the history of her family from the grandmother's own birth eighty years earlier to the birth of her granddaughter's mother. Running through the story is the passing down of a family heirloom—a piece of lace—which the granddaughter learns will be passed on to her to wear on her wedding dress. A *Junior Bookshelf* critic praised the story as "an authentic piece of social history presented in a way which must bring delight to many little girls." In a more humorous vein, an entire village must clean up its act when the Prince schedules a visit in *Tumbledown.* Unfortunately, even after a few nails, oil on the hinges, and a fresh coat of paint, the town's true character comes through: "A comic vision of the com-

fortable, cheerful, lackadaisical life," according to Ann A. Flowers in her *Horn Book* review.

In addition to original stories, Rogers has also written books designed to teach beginning concepts to young listeners. In *What Will the Weather Be Like Today?*, designed for very young children, a number of different climates and types of weather are illustrated through the use of animals and their diverse habitats—from the "frog in the bog" to a lizard basking in the dry heat of a desert sun. *Horn Book* reviewer Margaret A. Bush described the book as "a cheerful invitation" to take notice of the weather and noted that it would be useful "for introducing weather concepts in nursery school." And in *The Shapes Game,* published in 1990, Rogers includes a wide variety of named shapes—from oval and square to crescent and spiral—that all come together on the final page to form a Christmas tree with all the trimmings. *School Library Journal* reviewer Dorcas Hand praised the work both for its "original approach" and Rogers's "clever verses," which she noted are "easily read aloud."

In 1988 Rogers and his wife, Emma, published their first collaborative effort, *The Get Better Book.* The couple's successful writing partnership has continued through numerous titles, including *Amazing Babies*—five stories recounting the exploits of such precocious tots as the first baby in space, the greediest baby on earth, and a child so noisy that his voice could be used to rescue travellers in a dense fog. While noting that other children's books have described infants who are "mildly naughty," a *Junior Bookshelf* critic maintained that the Rogers' humorous protagonists "are truly terrible." In *Zoe's Tower,* a gentler tale is told, as a young girl travels to her favorite spot in the whole world—an old stone tower from the top of which she can see all the way home, "and a little bit further." Praising the picture book in *School Librarian,* reviewer

David Lewis called *Zoe's Tower* "a book of some considerable charm and subtlety." And in *Cat's Kittens,* the Rogers illustrate the growth of independence among a litter of kittens with what a *Junior Bookshelf* contributor called "a blend of excitement and security."

A prolific writer, Rogers once commented: "I like to work on several things at once and greatly enjoy working with a variety of illustrators. But I am still looking forward to the day when I have more time for reading."

■ Works Cited

Review of *Amazing Babies, Junior Bookshelf,* April, 1991, p. 62.

Bush, Margaret A., review of *What Will the Weather Be Like Today?, Horn Book,* March-April, 1990, pp. 222-23.

Review of *Cat's Kittens, Junior Bookshelf,* October, 1996, pp. 187-88.

Flowers, Ann A., review of *Tumbledown, Horn Book,* July, 1988, pp. 484-85.

Review of *From Me to You, Junior Bookshelf,* April, 1988, p. 86.

Hand, Dorcas, review of *The Shapes Game, School Library Journal,* November, 1990, p. 98.

Lewis, David, review of *Zoe's Tower, School Librarian,* February, 1992, p. 17.

■ For More Information See

PERIODICALS

Booklist, October 15, 1986, p. 356; February 15, 1988, p. 1002; February 15, 1997, p. 1029.

Books for Keeps, November, 1996, p. 8.

Bulletin of the Center for Children's Books, May, 1988, p. 187; February, 1989, p. 156; May, 1990, p. 225.

Growing Point, July, 1984, pp. 4294-95; September, 1986, p. 4691; January, 1991, p. 5467; January, 1992, p. 5631.

Junior Bookshelf, October, 1984, p. 204; August, 1986, p. 139; December, 1987, p. 271; February, 1988, p. 36; October, 1988, p. 235; August, 1989, p. 165; October, 1989, p. 231; February, 1990, p. 18; April, 1992, p. 58.

Kirkus Reviews, March 15, 1988, p. 458; June 15, 1988, p. 903.

Publishers Weekly, July 8, 1988, p. 55; February 24, 1989, p. 229.

School Librarian, December, 1986, pp. 333-34; August, 1990, p. 104; November, 1990, p. 144; August, 1991, p. 102.

School Library Journal, September, 1984, p. 108; March, 1987, p. 149; April, 1988, p. 90; December, 1988, p. 92; December, 1989, p. 88; December, 1991, p. 100.

ROHAN, Michael Scott 1951-
(Mike Scott Rohan; Michael Scot, a joint pseudonym)

■ Personal

Born January 22, 1951, in Edinburgh, Scotland; son of Renaud-Philippe (a doctor and dental surgeon) and Vera (Forrest) Rohan; married Deborah (an instructor in archival conservation). *Education:* Oxford University, M.A., 1973. *Politics:* "Highly suspect." *Religion:* "Sympathetic agnostic, with fire insurance." *Hobbies and other interests:* Music, home entertainment technology, anthropology, paleontology, archery, and travel.

■ Addresses

Home—Cambridge, England. *Agent*—c/o Maggie Noach Literary Agency, 21 Redan Street, London W14 0AB, England. *E-mail*—mike.scott.rohan@asgard. zetnet.co.uk.

■ Career

Writer. Entered publishing as a reference book editor and became senior editor of two general encyclopedias, as well as other publications; also runs Asgard, an editorial company specializing in international reference titles, with two other senior editors. Worked for a short time as a technical author.

■ Awards, Honors

All Time Great Fantasy Short Story, Gamesmaster International, 1991, for *Findings;* William F. Crawford Award for Best First Fantasy Novel, International Association for the Fantastic Arts, 1991, for the "Winter of the World" trilogy.

■ Writings

FANTASY NOVELS

(With Allan Scott) *Fantastic People,* Pierrot (London), 1980, NAL/Dutton, 1981.

(With Scott, under joint pseudonym Michael Scot) *The Ice King,* New English Library (London), 1986, published as *Burial Rites,* Berkley, 1987.

(With Scott) *A Spell of Empire: The Horns of Tartarus,* Orbit (London), 1992.

The Lord of Middle Air, Gollancz (London), 1994.

FANTASY NOVELS; "WINTER OF THE WORLD" SERIES

The Anvil of Ice, Morrow, 1986.

The Forge in the Forest, Morrow, 1987.

The Hammer of the Sun, Morrow, 1988.

FANTASY NOVELS; "SPIRAL" SERIES

Chase the Morning, Morrow, 1990.

The Gates of Noon, Morrow, 1992.

Cloud Castles, Morrow, 1993.

Maxie's Demon, Little, Brown, 1997.

SCIENCE-FICTION NOVELS

(Under name Mike Scott Rohan) *Run to the Stars,* Arrow (London), 1983, Ace, 1986.

NONFICTION

(With Scott) *The Hammer and the Cross,* Alder (Oxford), 1980.
First Byte: Choosing and Using a Home Computer, E. P. Publishing, 1983.
(With Scott and Phil Gardner) *The BBC Micro Add-On Guide,* Collins (London), 1985.
(Editor) *The Classical Video Guide,* Gollancz, 1994.

OTHER

Work represented in anthologies, including *Aries 1* and *Andromeda 2.* Author of various computer titles. Translator of various German and French works, including a number of arts and crafts books. Contributor of articles, columns, and reviews to magazines and newspapers, including *Opera Now, Times, Classic CD, Gramophone,* and *Music.*

■ Work in Progress

A prequel to the "Winter of the World" series; a sequel to *Maxie's Demon,* tentatively titled *The Cabinet of Dr. Maxie.*

■ Sidelights

Michael Scott Rohan has published both science-fiction and fantasy novels. Notable among his fantasy writings is the "Winter of the World" trilogy comprised of *The Anvil of Ice, The Forge in the Forest,* and *The Hammer of the Sun.* This series, published in the late 1980s, concerns the classic conflict between good and evil during an Ice Age replete with wizards, knights, and strange creatures. Among the many memorable characters in these volumes are Alv (later known as Elof), a foundling trained by the sinister necromancer Mylio, who eventually becomes Alv's foe, and Kermorvan, a great warrior who joins Alv in his battle against Mylio. There are also—in addition to Mylio—a host of villains, including hordes of demonic Ekwesh who seek to overcome all who conduct their lives in opposition to the evil Ekwesh ways.

The Anvil of Ice, a "compelling" novel, according to Gail Stubblefield of *School Library Journal,* blends "strong characterization ... with the story" and added interest in the way of "friendship and a little romance." A *Kirkus Reviews* critic praised it for its "bold imaginings [and] some original touches," while a reviewer for *Publishers Weekly* described Rohan's style as "taut, lyrically haunting" with an "element of suspense" that brought this fantasy to a satisfying end, at the same time leaving the reader eager for more. A *Publishers Weekly* reviewer described the adventures of Elof, Kermorvan, and band in the second volume, *The Forge in the Forest,* as a "string of Homeric terrors and wonders."

Rohan is also the author of the "Spiral" trilogy comprised of *Chase the Morning, Gates of Noon,* and *Cloud*

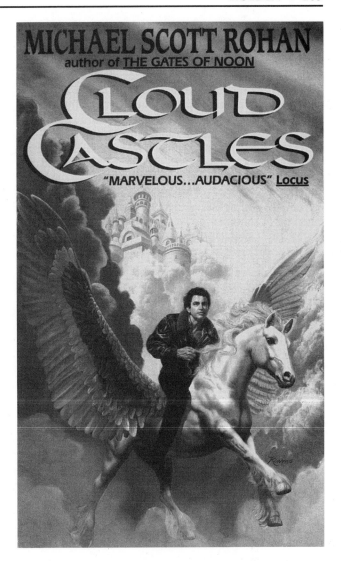

The third book of a trilogy, Michael Scott Rohan's fantasy novel depicts Stephen Fisher who, after discovering a supernatural world in which mythology is real, journeys to a legendary city in the clouds which is the source of great power. (Cover illustration by Rowena A. Morrill.)

Castles. In this series, which appeared in the early 1990s, Rohan writes of Stephen Fisher, an inventor and prominent businessperson who discovers the Spiral, a supernatural world in which mythology is real. Fisher embarks on various adventures in each of the "Spiral" tales. In *Chase the Morning,* "a marvelously written, richly imaginative novel, with characters readers will want to meet again," according to Sister Avila Lamb in *Kliatt,* Fisher encounters all manner of battles and challenges as he pursues the kidnappers of his faithful secretary Clare. Faren Miller, writing in *Locus,* hails Rohan's trilogy as "a breath of fresh sea air, infused with the energies of the classic adventure novels and ... the exotica of Asian cultures." In *The Gates of Noon,* which a *Publishers Weekly* reviewer called "a welcome change from standard sword-and-sorcery quests," Fisher and a band of pirates undertake a perilous journey that leads them into conflict with supernatural forces attempting to undermine Fisher's shipping business. In *Cloud Castles,* Fisher travels across a futuristic Europe as he attempts to return the magical lance associated with the Holy Grail, also the origin of worldwide benevolence. Fisher's journey, as one might expect, is hardly an uneventful one, for neo-fascists threaten to cause political and social instability throughout the land, and the spear itself is sought by evil powers. *Voice of Youth Advocates* contributor Kathleen D. Hutchins called *Cloud Castles* a "swashbuckling, fast-paced adventure [that] will sweep the reader to a satisfying conclusion," and a *Publishers Weekly* reviewer concluded that the author has created a "vivid fantasy, drawing on some of the most powerful of ancient myths as well as the most enduring of modern ones."

Among Rohan's other writings are *First Byte: Choosing and Using a Home Computer* and, with co-authors Allan Scott and Phil Gardner, *The BBC Micro Add-On Guide.* In addition, Rohan has translated and edited Agnes Marie-Therese Masias's *Painting on China,* as well as many other French and German titles, and edited *The Classical Video Guide,* published in 1994. Rohan comments: "I try to write, above all, the kinds of books I want to read myself. I love knowledge and scholarship. I love hard science, wild myth and legend, and the possibilities of the imagination. Above all, I love weaving all of these together. Music feeds my imagination, music of all kinds, the more timeless the better, whether it is Wagner, Basin Street or ancient folk melodies. My literary heroes range from Shakespeare and Chaucer to Goethe, the great Edinburgh men Robert Louis Stevenson and Sir Arthur Conan Doyle, the late Fritz Leiber, Avram Davidson, Mikhail Bulgakov, and, of course, J. R. R. Tolkien.

"What I write may be escapist; but I believe escape is a necessary function which every author of fiction must to some extent fulfill, and which can often allow us to confront our condition with greater clarity. Ask yourself, as Tolkien said to C. S. Lewis, 'Who is most interested in preventing escape?—Jailers.'"

■ Works Cited

Review of *The Anvil of Ice, Kirkus Reviews,* September 1, 1986, p. 1330.

Review of *The Anvil of Ice, Publishers Weekly,* August 22, 1986, p. 83.

Review of *Cloud Castles, Publishers Weekly,* August 8, 1994, p. 392.

Review of *Forge in the Forest, Publishers Weekly,* October 9, 1987, p. 81.

Review of *The Gates of Noon, Publishers Weekly,* June 7, 1993, p. 57.

Hutchins, Kathleen D., review of *Cloud Castles, Voice of Youth Advocates,* April, 1995, pp. 38-39.

Lamb, Sister Avila, review of *Chase the Morning, Kliatt,* November, 1992, p. 18.

Miller, Faren, review of *The Gates of Noon, Locus,* October, 1992, p. 56.

Stubblefield, Gail, review of *The Anvil of Ice, School Library Journal,* February, 1987, p. 99.

■ For More Information See

BOOKS

Encyclopedia of Science Fiction, edited by John Clute and Peter Nicholls, St. Martin's Press (New York City), 1993, p. 1024.

PERIODICALS

Kirkus Reviews, May 1, 1993, p. 562; June 1, 1994, p. 742.

Locus, January, 1994, p. 48.

Wilson Library Bulletin, November, 1994, pp. 102-03.*

*   *   *

ROHAN, Mike Scott
See ROHAN, Michael Scott

S

SAUL, John 1942-

■ Personal

Born February 25, 1942, in Pasadena, CA; son of John and Elizabeth (Lee) Saul. *Education:* Attended Antioch College, Ohio, 1959-60; Cerritos College, Norwalk, CA, 1960-61; Montana State University, Missoula, MT, 1961-62; and San Francisco State College, 1963-65. *Politics:* Democrat. *Hobbies and other interests:* Playing bridge, cooking.

JOHN SAUL

■ Addresses

Office—P.O. Box 17035, Seattle, WA 98107. *Agent*—Jane Rotrosen Agency, 318 E. 51st St., New York, NY 10022. *Electronic mail*—authorjs@aol.com.

■ Career

Writer. Spent several years traveling around the United States, writing and supporting himself by odd jobs; worked for a drug and alcohol program in Seattle, WA; director of Tellurian Communities, Inc., 1976-78; director, Seattle Theater Arts, Seattle, 1978—; trustee and vice-president, The Chester Woodruff Foundation (a philanthropic organization), New York. *Member:* Authors Guild, Authors League of America, Maui Writers Conference (advisory board member).

■ Awards, Honors

Lifetime Achievement Award, Pacific Northwest Writers Conference.

■ Writings

NOVELS

Suffer the Children, Dell, 1977.
Punish the Sinners, Dell, 1978.
Cry for the Strangers, Dell, 1979.
Comes the Blind Fury, Dell, 1980.
When the Wind Blows, Dell, 1981.
The God Project, Bantam, 1982.
Nathaniel, Bantam, 1984.
Brainchild, Bantam, 1985.
Hellfire, Bantam, 1986.
The Unwanted, Bantam, 1987.
The Unloved, Bantam, 1988.
Creature, Bantam, 1989.
Sleepwalk, Bantam, 1990.
Second Child, Bantam, 1990.
Darkness, Bantam, 1991.
Shadows, Bantam, 1992.

Guardian, Ballantine, 1993.
The Homing, Ballantine, 1994.
Black Lightning, Ballantine, 1995.
The Blackstone Chronicles, Ballantine, 1997.
The Presence, Ballantine, 1997.

■ Adaptations

Cry for the Strangers was produced by Gerber Productions and MGM as a CBS movie; *The Blackstone Chronicles* is projected as a six-hour miniseries for ABC, to be aired in 1998.

■ Sidelights

John Saul is the author of over two dozen horror novels and suspense thrillers, many of which employ children as the victims or agents of malevolent, unnatural forces. From his first title, *Suffer the Children,* Saul has been a bestselling author, churning out at least a book per year. That his novels have not been highly praised by critics does not faze Saul, who has had over 50 million copies of his works published in 19 different languages and in 24 different countries. And that critics also take him to task for the violence in his books no longer bothers Saul, either. "Originally, I thought [my novels] were a bit strong for children," Saul said in a *Publishers Weekly* interview with Robert Dahlin, "but since then, I've talked to school librarians who are happy with them. Young people like my books, and as it turns out, in this way I've introduced many of them to the act of reading. Librarians aren't concerned that any of my violence is going to affect children. They would rather have them reading, and these kids have told me they don't read the books for the violence. They read them for the plot."

As a youngster, Saul himself experienced none of the horrors of some of his fictional protagonists. Born in Pasadena, California, in 1942, he grew up in Whittier, enjoying what he termed a normal childhood. In an interview with Andrea Chambers in *People* magazine, Saul noted that he had been an audience-pleaser even as a youth. "If you had to write 300 words on a subject," Saul told Chambers, "300 words was exactly what you got. I sat there and counted them." By college, he was hard at work on technique, writing a "technically correct" twenty-line poem daily. Saul studied anthropology, theater, and liberal arts at five different colleges, but finally left San Francisco State in 1965 without a degree.

Deciding that the best thing for a college dropout to do was become a writer, he spent the next fifteen years working variously as a technical writer and office helper, all the while attempting to write a novel that someone would want to publish. He had little success, producing among other rejected novels a comic murder mystery and a book about the citizen band (CB) radio craze of the 1970s. Finally a New York agent suggested he try a horror novel, a genre then becoming quite popular. Never having read such a novel, Saul studied some published works, put together an outline for his own creation, and his world subsequently changed forever.

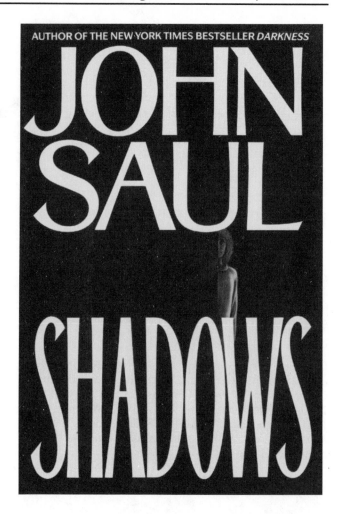

Several gifted children are used for evil psychological experiments in Saul's suspense novel. (Cover illustration by Tom Hallman.)

Both his agent and Dell publishers thought the outline held promise to become a bestseller. It took Saul a month to write the book, which was promoted with television advertising, and within another month his *Suffer the Children* was on all the bestseller lists in the U.S. and reached the number one spot in Canada, as well. "I'd never really tried writing horror before," Saul told Dahlin in *Publishers Weekly,* "but when I began, I found it fascinating. There were times I was writing certain scenes that I had to stop because I even scared myself, but I'm convinced that it helps to be a total coward when it comes to writing a book like this. If you can't scare yourself, how can you scare anyone else?"

Suffer the Children is set in a small New England town and tells the tale of the young daughter of a severely dysfunctional family who becomes a suspect in the disappearances of some of the town's children. In this first novel, Saul introduced two ingredients that would become hallmarks of most of his fiction: the use of children and teenagers either as victims or evil-doers, and the final ambiguity as to whether events in the book are caused by unnatural forces or warped psychology and/or science. Saul's first novel also initiated a critical squabble over his use of violence that has accompanied publication of many of his later titles. A reviewer for *Publishers Weekly,* for example, knocked this first novel for its "graphically violent scenes against children which are markedly tasteless." Though few of Saul's later novels include the level of brutality found in *Suffer the Children,* many of them have been criticized for formulaic plot devices and thinly drawn characters.

Saul is, however, a novelist of situation and story-line rather than one of character. "After [*Suffer the Children*]," Saul explained in his *Publishers Weekly* interview, "my books got progressively less violent because I really saw no reason for gore for gore's sake. It seems to me that what makes a book good is the tension in wondering what's going to happen next." What happened next in Saul's writing career was *Punish the Sinners,* a story involving strange sexual rituals in an order of priests. With *Cry for the Strangers,* Saul revisited the theme of a small, closed community with his fictional Clark's Harbor, a town in the Pacific Northwest which has no time for outsiders. When artist Glen Palmer and his wife settle there because of the curative effects of the ocean on their hyperactive child, they choose to ignore hostile signs. Death and mayhem follow and are linked to long-distant events. "Terror and suspense are trademarks of Saul," noted a reviewer for *Publishers Weekly,* "and there is plenty of both in this latest chilling tale." The novel, like most of Saul's, reached the bestseller ranks and was produced for television. Yet another small, closed community, as well as visitation of forces from the past, come to play in *Comes the Blind Fury.* In this tale, the ghost of a blind 12-year-old girl who was taunted and eventually killed by her classmates a century ago returns to wreak vengeance on the descendants of her tormentors. "Five children meet horrific deaths," tallied a reviewer for *Publishers Weekly.* Priscilla Johnson, writing in *School Library Journal,* commented: "This depressing story is written in a spare style which highlights its lurid details and chilling suspense."

In his *Publishers Weekly* interview, Saul went on to explain the use of children in much of his fiction: "Children are very imaginative. They share a lot of fear based on the unknown, or what might happen in the dark.... Also children are very appealing, both as villains and as victims. It's hard to stay mad at a kid, no matter what he does." Children again figure in Saul's sixth novel, but otherwise it is something of a departure for the novelist. Instead of ghosts from the past, Saul looks at terror in the future with *The God Project,* a techno-thriller about a secret government project involving genetic engineering. The first of his novels to be published in hardback, *The God Project* was, at the time, Saul's attempt at spreading his literary wings. "It seems as if I'm starting all over again," Saul told Dahlin in *Publishers Weekly.* "I feel just like a first novelist wondering how my book will do, but I'm looking forward to reading the professional criticism—constructive criticism, I hope—that will be written about it." *Voice of Youth Advocates* found the book a "creepy read" that could provoke school discussions on "research ethics, the military, and eugenics." Mary Mills in

School Library Journal felt that while the "characters are predictable and one-dimensional," the "twisty plot is clever, fast-paced and suspenseful...."

Sales of *The God Project* were not as strong as with earlier titles, and with *Nathaniel* Saul returned to his ghostly formulas. *Booklist*'s Stephanie Zvirin noted of *Nathaniel* that "although supernatural and mysterious doings take precedence here over logic and characterization, Saul's novel is spooky stuff, bound to lure readers along and keep them guessing until the end." With *Brainchild,* Saul managed to combine themes of distant revenge with a futuristic fable to create something of a medical thriller. Revenge in this setting is had by a Mexican-American surgeon whose ancestors were killed in the 1850 annexation of California. Performing brain surgery on young Alex Lonsdale, the surgeon turns the Anglo into a marked man. *Hellfire* continued Saul's trademark use of a revenge-seeking ghost from the past, as did *The Unloved,* both novels with gothic atmosphere and plenty of gore.

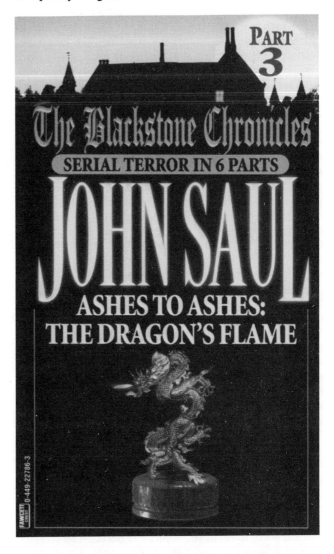

Best-selling author Saul has penned a six-part series about the small New England Town of Blackstone, whose inhabitants are threatened by the mystifying power in various strange objects.

Saul's twelfth novel, *Creature,* deals with contemporary problems of steroid abuse among young athletes. Something of a mad scientist, Dr. Marty Ames is posing as a physical trainer at a local high school in an endeavor to create the perfect physical specimen with drug therapy. But instead of studs, Ames gets violent freaks, and puny, 16-year-old Mark Tanner is witness to it all. Ray Olson in *Booklist* compared the book to *The Island of Dr. Moreau* by H. G. Wells, and concluded that Saul had produced "a riveting thriller that implicitly raps the win-at-all costs philosophy of both competitive sports and big business." Anne Paget, writing in *School Library Journal,* felt that "*Creature* will be widely read by athletes and sports fans." Another sleepy town and experiments on teenagers are featured in Saul's next thriller, *Sleepwalk,* which also contains Native American folklore. Reviewing that title, *Publishers Weekly* concluded that "Saul's suspenseful tale leaves the reader with no doubt on the question of who wins and loses in the struggle of good against evil."

Once again a vengeful ghost from another century pulls the strings in Saul's *Second Child.* In this tale, 15-year-old Melissa is responsible for the fire that killed her mother and stepfather, and when she goes to live with her biological father, she is ready for more evil business. *Darkness* continues in the same vein, employing a cast of teenagers who suffer from nightmares about the same old man. This time the little town is in Florida, but the gothic atmosphere is still in place. *Booklist*'s Olson called the book a "genuine descendant of the eighteenth-century style of gothic fiction in which something only seemingly supernatural's afoot." Another group of young children is at risk in *Shadows,* set at an elite private school which seems to be suffering from a rash of suicides. Soon the protagonist, ten-year-old Josh, begins to wonder if the suicides are real or not and why it is always the brainiest kids who die. *Kirkus Reviews* dubbed the book "one of [Saul's] best—or least offensive—tales of psychological suspense."

With his next novel, *Guardian,* Saul changed publishers to Ballantine, but maintained the twin pillars of his craft: juvenile protagonists as either "vehicle or victim of unnatural forces," as *Publishers Weekly* once noted in a review of *Creature,* and "terrors that seem to be supernatural but turn out to be the fault of evil science," as *Booklist*'s Olson noted in a review of *Guardian.* Evil scientists get another rap from Saul in *The Homing,* "a contrived but fast-paced thriller," according to *Kirkus Reviews,* which "does for insects what Hitchcock's *The Birds* did for our feathered friends." The same reviewer concluded that the story was a "skillful manipulation of primal fears about the natural world and the corruption of innocence." *Publishers Weekly* found that "fast pacing and skillful narrative misdirection" made Saul's next book, *Black Lightning,* one of his best—"and one of his few not to focus on children in peril." The story of a serial killer whose bent spirit enters that of a journalist's husband upon execution in the electric chair, *Black Lightning* "promises to raise [teens] to the edge of their seats," according to Barbara Hawkins, writing in *School Library Journal.*

Saul has continued to produce more than a novel per year with his new publishers, including the six-part *Blackstone Chronicles* and *The Presence,* set in Hawaii. *The Blackstone Chronicles* are scheduled for a six-part television mini-series that should only consolidate Saul's reputation for craftsman-like suspense and thrills.

■ Works Cited

Review of *Black Lightning, Publishers Weekly,* May 29, 1995, p. 66.

Review of *Comes the Blind Fury, Publishers Weekly,* April 11, 1980, p. 73.

Review of *Creature, Publishers Weekly,* March 10, 1989, p. 74.

Review of *Cry for the Strangers, Publishers Weekly,* April 23, 1979, p. 79.

Review of *The God Project, Voice of Youth Advocates,* August, 1982, p. 36.

Hawkins, Barbara, review of *Black Lightning, School Library Journal,* December, 1995, p. 144.

Review of *The Homing, Kirkus Reviews,* June 1, 1994, p. 732.

Johnson, Priscilla, review of *Comes the Blind Fury, School Library Journal,* September, 1980, p. 93.

Mills, Mary, review of *The God Project, School Library Journal,* October, 1982, p. 170.

Olson, Ray, review of *Creature, Booklist,* February 15, 1989, p. 961.

Olson, Ray, review of *Darkness, Booklist,* May 1, 1991, p. 1675.

Olson, Ray, review of *Guardian, Booklist,* June 1, 1993, p. 1735.

Paget, Anne, review of *Creature, School Library Journal,* July, 1989, p. 99.

Saul, John, interview with Robert Dahlin, *Publishers Weekly,* August 13, 1982.

Saul, John, interview with Andrea Chambers, *People,* June 26, 1989.

Review of *Shadow, Kirkus Reviews,* April 15, 1992, p. 495.

Review of *Sleepwalk, Publishers Weekly,* December 14, 1990, p. 62.

Review of *Suffer the Children, Publishers Weekly,* April 25, 1977, p. 73.

Zvirin, Stephanie, review of *Nathaniel, Booklist,* May 1, 1984, p. 1380.

■ For More Information See

BOOKS

Bail, Paul, *John Saul: A Critical Companion,* Greenwood Press, 1996.

Contemporary Literary Criticism, Volume 46, Gale, 1988.

PERIODICALS

Booklist, September 1, 1990, p. 394; May 1, 1992, p. 1563; June 1, 1994, p. 1726; June 1, 1995, p. 1684.

Kirkus Reviews, June 1, 1993, p. 684; June 1, 1995, p. 736.

Publishers Weekly, May 25, 1984, p. 56; June 28, 1985,
　　p. 71; March 10, 1989, p. 74; April 12, 1991, p. 45;
　　June 21, 1992, p. 84.
School Library Journal, April, 1998, p. 159.
Voice of Youth Advocates, December, 1983, p. 267;
　　February, 1985, p. 332; February, 1991, p. 367.

—Sketch by J. Sydney Jones

*　　*　　*

SCARBOROUGH, Elizabeth Ann 1947-

■ Personal

Born March 23, 1947, in Kansas City, MO; daughter of
Donald Dean (a telephone installer) and Betty Lou (a
registered nurse) Scarborough; married Richard G.
Kacsur, June 15, 1975 (divorced January 1, 1982).
Education: Bethany Hospital School of Nursing (Kansas
City, MO), R.N., 1968; University of Alaska, Fairbanks,
B.A., 1968. *Politics:* "Pragmatic humanist." *Religion:*
"Disorganized Christian universalist."

■ Addresses

Home and office—Port Townsend, WA. *Agent*—Merri-
lee Heifetz, 21 West 26th St., New York, NY 10010.

■ Career

Author and journalist. Formerly associated with Gallup
Indian Medical Center and with Bethany Hospital,
Kansas City, MO; former medical/surgical nurse at St.
David's Hospital, Austin, TX. Freelance writer, 1979—.
Military service: U.S. Army, Nurse Corps; served in
Vietnam; became captain. *Member:* Science Fiction
Writers of America, Society for Creative Anachronism.

■ Awards, Honors

Nebula Award, Science Fiction Writers of America,
1989, for *The Healer's War.*

■ Writings

FANTASY NOVELS

The Harem of Aman Akbar; or, The Djinn Decanted,
　　Bantam, 1984.
The Drastic Dragon of Draco, Texas, Bantam, 1986.
The Goldcamp Vampire; or, The Sanguinary Sourdough,
　　Bantam, 1987.
The Healer's War, Doubleday, 1989.
Nothing Sacred, Doubleday, 1991.
Last Refuge, Bantam, 1992.
The Godmother, Ace Books, 1994.
The Godmother's Apprentice, Ace Books, 1995.
Carol for Another Christmas, Ace Books, 1996.

"ARGONIA" SERIES

Song of Sorcery, Bantam, 1982.
The Unicorn Creed, Bantam, 1983.
Bronwyn's Bane, Bantam, 1983.

ELIZABETH ANN SCARBOROUGH

The Christening Quest, Bantam, 1985.
Songs from the Seashell Archives (contains *Song of
　　Sorcery, The Unicorn Creed, Bronwyn's Bane,* and
　　The Christening Quest), two volumes, Bantam,
　　1987-88.

"SONGKILLER" SERIES

Phantom Banjo, Bantam, 1991.
Picking the Ballad's Bones, Bantam, 1991.
Strum Again?, Bantam, 1992.

"POWER" SERIES; WITH ANNE McCAFFREY

Powers that Be, Del Rey Books (New York City), 1993.
Power Lines, Del Rey Books, 1994.
Power Play, Del Rey Books, 1995.

OTHER

An Interview with a Vietnam Nurse, Bantam, 1989.

Contributor to magazines and newspapers, including
Alaskafest and *Alaska Today.*

■ Sidelights

Recognized as a popular and influential author of comic
fantasy, Elizabeth Ann Scarborough has written works
that characteristically blend humor and fantasy to
describe earthy protagonists, chiefly female, and charming animals who embark on exciting quests; Scarborough has also collaborated with fantasist Anne McCaffrey on a series of science fiction novels. Published for
adults but appreciated by young people, her books are
acknowledged for their originality, intelligence, and
unconventionality as well as for their wit, fast pace, and

light-hearted approach. In the fantasy genre, Scarborough is perhaps best known as the creator of the "Argonia" and "Songkiller" series; in the former, the author describes the adventures of a cheerful young witch, Maggie Brown, and her mother Bronwyn in the secondary world Argonia, while the latter describes how a group of courageous figures restore folk music to the world after it has been eliminated by demons. Scarborough is also well regarded for writing *The Healer's War,* a semi-autobiographical novel set during the Vietnam War that combines fantasy and mysticism with stark reality. Winner of the Nebula Award in 1989, the story focuses on an army nurse who is given special healing powers by a magic amulet. Writing in the *St. James Guide to Fantasy Writers,* Cosette Kies comments, "Scarborough's output to date gives proof of her importance in the contemporary fantasy-genre scene. It is probable that she has influenced some newer writers, who also create humorous fantasy with down-to-earth heroines and delightful animal companions. Scarborough's own development as a writer appears to be leading her into a spare and lean phase with more emphasis on stories of the future rather than on the alternative worlds of high fantasy."

Born in Kansas City, Missouri, Scarborough was educated as a nurse and served in the U.S. Army Nurse Corps both in the United States and in Vietnam before becoming a full-time writer in 1979; she also received a degree in history from the University of Alaska at Fairbanks in 1987. "I started out," she said in the *St. James Guide to Fantasy Writers,* "writing humorous fantasy—at first traditional and then historical western and Arabian Nights, which interested me after I studied Middle Eastern dance." Scarborough's first books are contributions to the "Argonia" series, fantasies that include archetypal characters from folk and fairy tales such as witches, dragons, magicians, and unicorns and center on quests by what Cosette Kies calls "very human protagonists," adding: "There is playfulness and cheerfulness throughout the stories, with puns and comic situations to create humor as fast-paced as the action."

Scarborough's first departure from "Argonia" was *The Harem of Aman Akbar,* a comic novel set in the Middle East about how a young bride reverses a spell placed on her unfaithful husband by a genie. *Los Angeles Times Book Review* critic Kristiana Gregory claims that Scarborough's story "is fun, a wild fantasy ... pulsing with color and noise like a marketplace at noon," while *Booklist* reviewer Roland Green says, "This excellent piece of humorous fantasy is witty, fast-paced, intelligent, and features excellent characterization." With *The Christening Quest,* Scarborough returns to Argonia; in this novel, according to Margaret Miles in *Voice of Youth Advocates,* the author "uses her accustomed blend of fairy tale, gypsies, and Arabian Nights to produce another chuckle-filled light fantasy adventure." The novel describes the rescue of Princess Romany, the first-born daughter of Princess Bronwyn, who has been kidnapped by money-hungry magicians; the baby is rescued by Bronwyn's brother and cousin in an adventure, according to Roland Green of *Booklist,* "as filled

with action and humor as any of the preceding books." Writing in *Fantasy Review,* Douglas Barbour says that *The Christening Quest* is "light entertainment and ... enjoyable because it does try in its small way to undercut some of the sexist conventions of the genre, unlike most of what passes for writing ... these days." *Songs from the Seashell Archives* is a two-volume omnibus containing the four volumes of the "Argonia" quartet.

Scarborough's next two novels, *The Drastic Dragon of Draco, Texas* and *The Goldcamp Vampire,* are fantasies with historical settings that feature author/journalist Pelagia Harper as their protagonist; in *The Drastic Dragon,* Pelagia is captured by Indians and meets a fire-breathing dragon in her attempt to write about the romance of the Wild West, while in *The Goldcamp Vampire* Pelagia encounters the son of Count Dracula, who is masquerading as the potential buyer of an Alaskan saloon during the Gold Rush. Writing in *Library Journal,* Jackie Cassada calls *The Drastic Dragon* a "superbly told tale that may even attract some Western fans," while *Voice of Youth Advocates* reviewer Pat Pearl calls *The Goldcamp Vampire* a "cheerfully macabre, amusingly told story with a frostily vivid Klondike-of-the-Gold Rush background." Cosette Kies says of *The Goldcamp Vampire* that "Scarborough's originality is evident in the fact that she sets her vampire story in a land where night goes on for months, wonderful for recruiting vampires but not so great for unwilling recruits," and notes of the two novels that the settings "of the frontier, both in Texas plains and the Yukon goldfields, provide the journalist heroine ... with colorful milieus in which to pursue mystery, magic and the supernatural."

The publication of *The Healer's War* marked a departure in Scarborough's literary style: the author moved from her characteristic humorous fantasy to creating a strongly realistic antiwar novel about a young woman's coming of age that contains fewer fantastic elements than her other books. In the words of *Booklist* reviewer Mary Banas, Scarborough "expertly blends suspense, dark humor, and realism into a powerful, soul-stirring mix that, for the first time, shows the Vietnam War from a woman's perspective." Cosette Kies concurs, acknowledging that the novel, the author's first to be published in hard cover, is "in amazing contrast" to Scarborough's earlier fantasies. *The Healer's War* focuses on twenty-one-year-old Kathleen (Kitty) McCully, a character that the author based largely on herself. A nurse from Kansas who is stationed in a Vietnam hospital, Kitty is given an amulet by an old Vietnamese mystic just before he dies. The amulet allows Kitty to sense the aura of each person she meets and to learn their true motives; in addition, she receives the power to heal. Kitty experiences the horrors of war but also goes on a spiritual journey, coming to realize the special qualities of Vietnam and its people. While trying to save the life of a young amputee, Kitty is captured by the Viet Cong but uses her skills as a healer to survive. After being rescued by American troops and sent back to America, Kitty tries to adjust to Stateside life and to find purpose in her new existence. Writing in *Voice of Youth Advocates,* Syrul Lurie says that Scarborough's "depiction of a time and place in American history [is one] which every young adult should internalize and never forget," while *Kirkus Reviews* notes that the author "writes powerfully and convincingly of the war itself." Sybil Steinberg of *Publishers Weekly* states, "Although the moralizing invites comparison with TV's *M*A*S*H* and *Twilight Zone,* Scarborough's light, fluid storytelling and the authentic, pungent background keep this novel interesting." In her author's note in the paperback edition of *The Healer's War,* Scarborough says, "I chose to write the book as fiction because, as somebody is frequently misquoted as saying, fiction is supposed to make sense out of real life. And if there was ever an episode in my life that needed sense made out of it, it was Vietnam. In a nonfiction account, I could talk only about myself, what I saw and felt. I wasn't very clear about that when I started writing." In 1988, Scarborough published a second book about her Vietnam experience, *An Interview with a Vietnam Nurse.*

With her "Songkiller" saga, Scarborough created a comic fantasy series that is considered a thinly veiled and incisive depiction of the censorship of contempo-

Fairy godmother Felicity Fortune helps an overwrought social worker with her caseload of destitute clients. (Cover illustration by Tara McGovern.)

rary music. She bases the series on the premise that a cabal of devils, who realize that music—especially folk music—is one of the few things that truly edifies the human race, attempts to wipe out the art form off the face of the earth. In the first volume, *Phantom Banjo,* the devils kill folk musicians and destroy the folk music archives at the Library of Congress, among other unsavory activities; as each artist dies and each medium preserving the music is ruined, human beings find that they have lost their familiarity with popular songs. In addition, little music is allowed on the airwaves; the radio, for example, broadcasts mostly news. Before his death, legendary folk artist Sam Hawthorne wills his banjo to Mark Mosby, a singer and fan. Before he dies in a car accident, Mosby goes to see Willie MacKai, a Texas resident and retired singer, and gives the banjo—named Lazarus—to him. This act begins a journey that takes Willie and Lazarus, a remarkable instrument that plays music with or without human hands, on a quest to save the music. "Good fun," writes *Voice of Youth Advocates* contributor Penny Blubaugh, "and very close to the bone." Writing in *Booklist,* Roland Green concludes that *Phantom Banjo* has "just about every virtue one can reasonably expect in a contemporary fantasy tale."

In the second volume of the series, *Picking the Ballad's Bones,* Willie and other keepers of the flame go to England, meet the ghost of Sir Walter Scott, and agree, as part of a deal, to spend seven years living out the stories told by the old ballads so that they might be retrieved for humanity; the deal is arranged by the former Faerie Queen, who is also known as Lady Luck, and, in recent years, has gone by the name of Torchy. "The second part [of the saga]," writes Tom Whitmore in *Locus,* "is a good continuation of the first . . . . It's light, amusing, and quick; once again, the very real background to this story . . . sits in the background and is not obviously real. It doesn't take demons to keep the music out of our ears, unfortunately." *Booklist* reviewer Roland Green concurs, saying that this volume of the "superior black comedy fantasy trilogy . . . . is contemporary fantasy of a very high order." In the conclusion to the series, *Strum Again?,* the questers return to the United States and—with Torchy's assistance—reintroduce folk songs into the national consciousness while fighting opposition from public and private institutions which, it turns out, are controlled from Hell. Green calls the book an "absorbing, tension-filled story that demands a good deal of erudition of its readers but repays their efforts."

In addition to her other works, Scarborough has made several well-received contributions to the science fiction genre. *Nothing Sacred* is a novel based on a vivid dream had by the author while completing *The Healer's War.* In the words of Gerald Jonas in the *New York Times Book Review,* Scarborough "heralds a new subgenre that might be called New World Order Science Fiction." Set in the year 2069 and written in the form of a prison journal, the book describes a post-holocaust world where the Pentagon has become part of the North American Continental Allied Forces (NACAF), a group that supplies professional soldiers to international war-makers. NACAF allies are involved in a conflict with Russia, China, and India. After a forty-two-year-old warrant officer, Vivika Jeng Vanachek, is shot down during an aerial mapping mission in the mountains of Tibet, she is captured by local guerrillas, who imprison, torture, and brainwash her. As the novel progresses, it becomes clear that Viv is in Shambala, an enchanted paradise reminiscent of Shangri-La that is the last safe spot in a decimated world. While she helps organize an old library, Viv eventually becomes reconciled to her new situation. Jonas writes that Viv "is an engaging sort once she gets her wits about her . . . . [Her] irrepressible flippancy nicely undercuts the creeping pietism that seems to be an occupational hazard of Tibetan sagas." Scarborough notes in the *St. James Guide to Fantasy Writers* that she introduces *Nothing Sacred* at author readings with the comment, "There's good news and bad news. The bad news is, I end the world. The good news is, there's a sequel." *Last Refuge* is that sequel: set twenty years after the conclusion of *Nothing Sacred,* the novel features the granddaughter of Viv Vanachek, Chime Cincinnati, who is Shambala's emissary to the outside world. Accompanied by her father Mike, Viv's son, Chime goes on a quest to discover what is causing Shambala's babies to be born without souls. After Chime and Mike find another enchanted valley, ruled by the evil Master Meru, the pair outwit Meru and guide the living and the dead, whose souls will be used to infuse the children of Shambala, to safety. A critic in *Kirkus Reviews* notes, "Any exoticism the Buddhist background might have added is lost in Scarborough's paradoxically rationalistic explanation of the supernatural . . . . The novelties that made the first book interesting cannot rescue this one." *Booklist*'s Roland Green disagrees, noting that "a vivid and powerful yarn awaits the many fans who have made Scarborough so popular."

Powers that Be, Scarborough's first collaboration with Anne McCaffrey, is set in a future with a definite militaristic bent. When Major Yanaba Maddock, a female soldier, is sent to the frontier planet Petaybee as a spy, she discovers a rebel plot to destroy the corporation that controls the planet. After becoming sympathetic to the settlers, who are environmentally conscious and humane, as opposed to the coldly bureaucratic corporation, Yanaba decides to become a rebel. The sequels, *Power Lines* and *Power Play,* describe the conflict between the settlers and the corporation.

Scarborough is also the author of the "Godmother" books, stories that center on a fairy godmother named Felicity Fortune who assists those in need. Felicity belongs to the Godmothers' Union and is hampered by strict union regulations as well as budget cutbacks. In *The Godmother,* which is set in Seattle, she manages to help an overwrought social worker with her caseload of destitute clients. Writing in *Voice of Youth Advocates,* Denise M. Thornhill calls *The Godmother* "not just a fantasy novel—it is also a problem novel." *The Godmother's Apprentice* finds Felicity in Ireland with her new apprentice, fifteen-year-old Sno Quantrill. Drawing on folklore, fairy tales, and mythology, Scarborough tells

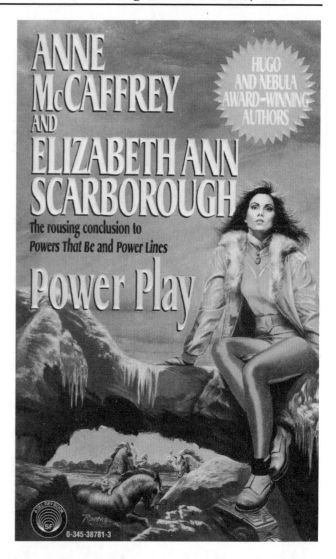

In Scarborough's novel, cowritten with Anne McCaffrey, Yanaba Maddock is taken hostage in an attempt to destroy her treasured planet, Petaybee.

a complex tale involving an Irish terrorist, house spirits, and a talking toad; *Voice of Youth Advocates* contributor Donna L. Scanlon notes that the author draws "the various threads . . . together into a well-woven, compelling plot with a satisfactory ending."

Scarborough comments, "After fifteen years of nursing, an important job for which I was not temperamentally suited, I'm finally doing what I always wanted to do. I am getting paid for my ridiculous ideas and off-the-wall jokes, the same sort that always got me into trouble in other lines of work. (I was lucky they didn't court martial me before I got out of the Army Nurse Corps!)" Commenting in the *St. James Guide to Fantasy Writers,* she adds, "Lately, I've been trying to blend some serious content with humor in *The Godmother* and to some extent in the books I've been writing in Ireland with Anne McCaffrey set in our new world. My experience living in Fairbanks, Alaska, for 15 years, and in the military, helped me to make my contributions to Petaybee, the world Anne and I created together. My many friendships with concerned and caring social workers and other non-cynical types inspired [my "God-mother" books]."

■ Works Cited

Banas, Mary, review of *The Healer's War, Booklist,* November 1, 1988, p. 450.

Barbour, Douglas, "Too Nice a Quest," *Fantasy Review,* October, 1985, p. 20.

Blubaugh, Penny, review of *Phantom Banjo, Voice of Youth Advocates,* December, 1991, p. 326.

Cassada, Jackie, review of *The Drastic Dragon of Draco, Texas, Library Journal,* May 15, 1986, p. 81.

Green, Roland, review of *The Christening Quest, Booklist,* October 1, 1985, pp. 195-96.

Green, Roland, review of *The Harem of Aman Akbar, Booklist,* December 15, 1984, p. 561.

Green, Roland, review of *Last Refuge, Booklist,* June 15, 1992, p. 1787.

Green, Roland, review of *Phantom Banjo, Booklist,* June 15, 1991, p. 1937.

Green, Roland, review of *Picking the Ballad's Bones, Booklist,* December 1, 1991, p. 684.

Green, Roland, review of *Strum Again?, Booklist,* April 15, 1992, p. 1509.

Gregory, Kristiana, review of *The Harem of Aman Akbar, Los Angeles Times Book Review,* December 9, 1984, p. 14.

Review of *The Healer's War, Kirkus Reviews,* September 15, 1988, p. 1366.

Jonas, Gerald, review of *Nothing Sacred, New York Times Book Review,* April 21, 1994, p. 24.

Kies, Cosette, essay in *St. James Guide to Fantasy Writers,* St. James Press, 1996, pp. 514-16.

Review of *Last Refuge, Kirkus Reviews,* June 15, 1992, p. 754.

Lurie, Syrul, review of *The Healer's War, Voice of Youth Advocates,* June, 1989, p. 118.

Miles, Margaret, review of *The Christening Quest, Voice of Youth Advocates,* February, 1986, p. 397.

Pearl, Pat, review of *The Goldcamp Vampire, Voice of Youth Advocates,* June, 1988, p. 97.

Scanlon, Donna L., review of *The Godmother's Apprentice, Voice of Youth Advocates,* June, 1996, p. 110.

Scarborough, Elizabeth Ann, *The Healer's War,* Double-day, 1989.

Scarborough, Elizabeth Ann, commentary in *St. James Guide to Fantasy Writers,* St. James Press, 1996, pp. 514-16.

Steinberg, Sybil, review of *The Healer's War, Publishers Weekly,* September 16, 1988, p. 63.

Thornhill, Denise M., review of *The Godmother, Voice of Youth Advocates,* December, 1994, p. 290.

Whitmore, Tom, review of *Picking the Ballad's Bones, Locus,* October, 1991, p. 56.

■ For More Information See

PERIODICALS

Analog, February, 1995, p. 159; May, 1996, p. 144.

Booklist, September 1, 1994, p. 28; December 15, 1995, p. 689.

Kirkus Reviews, July 1, 1994, p. 892; October 15, 1995, p. 1462.

Kliatt, March, 1996, p. 20.

Library Journal, November 15, 1995, p. 103.

Locus, August, 1994, p. 62.

Magazine of Fantasy and Science Fiction, March, 1996, p. 56.

Publishers Weekly, August 29, 1994, p. 64; November 27, 1995, p. 56.

—Sketch by Gerard J. Senick

*   *   *

SCHROEDER, Alan 1961-

■ Personal

Born January 18, 1961, in Alameda, CA; son of Walter R. (a draftsman) and Hilda (Henningsen) Schroeder. *Education:* Received degree (with honors) from University of California, Santa Cruz, 1982.

■ Addresses

Home—1225 College Ave., Alameda, CA 94501.

■ Career

Writer.

■ Awards, Honors

Parent's Choice Award Winner, *Booklist* Children's Editors' Choice, Notable Book of the Year, American Library Association, Teachers' Choice, International Reading Association, IRA-CBC Favorite Picture Book, 1994, all for *Ragtime Tumpie;* Best Book for the Teen Age, New York Public Library, for *Josephine Baker;* Bank Street Book of the Year, for *The Stone Lion;* Marion Vannett Ridgway Honor Book, for *Lily and the Wooden Bowl;* Notable Book of the Year, American Library Association, Bank Street Book of the Year, Keystone to Reading Book Award nominee, Notable Children's Book, Association for Library Services to Children, all for *Carolina Shout!;* Notable Book of the Year, American Library Association, Silver Medal for Children's Literature, Commonwealth Club of California, Best Children's Books Round-Up, *Time* magazine, Golden Kite Honor Book for Picture-Illustration, 1996, Coretta Scott King Award for Illustration, 1996, Christopher Award, 1996, IRA/CBC Teachers' Choice, 1997, Nebraska Golden Sower Award (Grades 4-6) nominee, 1998-99, all for *Minty: A Story of Young Harriet Tubman;* Smithsonian's Notable Books for Children, 1996, NAPPA Honors Award, 1996, Paterson Prize for Books for Young People (Grades 4-6), 1997, IRA Teachers' Choice, 1997, all for *Satchmo's Blues.*

■ Writings

PICTURE BOOKS

Ragtime Tumpie, Joy Street Books, 1989.

ALAN SCHROEDER

Lily and the Wooden Bowl, Doubleday, 1994.
The Stone Lion, Scribner's, 1994.
Carolina Shout!, Dial, 1995.
Satchmo's Blues, Doubleday, 1996.
Minty: A Story of Young Harriet Tubman, Dial, 1996.
Smoky Mountain Rose: An Appalachian Cinderella,
    Dial, 1997.
The Tale of Willie Monroe, Clarion Books, 1998.

BIOGRAPHY; FOR YOUNG PEOPLE

Josephine Baker, Chelsea House, 1991.
Booker T. Washington, Chelsea House, 1992.
Jack London, Chelsea House, 1992.
James Dean, Chelsea House, 1994.
Charlie Chaplin: The Beauty of Silence, Watts, 1997.

■ Work in Progress

A picture book about the childhood of abolitionist
Frederick Douglass; a picture book about blues singer
Bessie Smith.

■ Sidelights

Alan Schroeder's *Ragtime Tumpie* gives a fictionalized
rendering of African American entertainer Josephine
Baker's childhood. With strong memories of her father,
who played drums in a ragtime band, Josephine grows
up in St. Louis, Missouri, in a poor, struggling family.
Nicknamed Tumpie, Josephine rises from the crowd

one night to win a dance contest. The story trumpets the
rising dreams of an artist who becomes a dancer
extraordinaire, living and working in Paris during the
Jazz Age. Liz Rosenberg, a critic for the *New York
Times Book Review,* wrote that *Ragtime Tumpie* "inspire[s] children to dream and hold on to stubborn
hope." Rosenberg described Tumpie winning the dance
contest as that "moment of reward in which an artist's
determination is born." A critic in *Kirkus Reviews*
stated that the picture book "powerfully evokes" St.
Louis in 1915, and a *Publishers Weekly* contributor
described the work as "irresistible" with a "saucy
exuberance, spicy as a gingersnap." The critic also noted
that while "the plot is simple the book's emotional
reverberations are complex."

In *Carolina Shout!* Schroeder's young narrator, Delia,
guides the reader along the streets of Charleston, South
Carolina, describing the clamor and charming cadence
of the city. The voices of street vendors and the noisy
sounds of everyday life harmonize into a city song. The
sounds of a carpenter's hammer, a bullfrog's croaking,
the cries of the vegetable man, milk bottles clinking, and
a metal gate closing combine as the streets of Charleston
become a place full of music. A reviewer for *Publishers
Weekly* found the language in this "stunning" picture
book "image-rich." According to Ruth Semrau of *School
Library Journal,* the "best songs arise from the throats
of the city's workers as they start the day." Leone
McDermott, a critic for *Booklist,* wrote that the book is
an "irresistible tribute to a vanished urban lyricism."

Schroeder told *SATA:* "Kids are always asking me, 'Of
all the books you've written, which one is your favorite?'
That's a hard question to answer, but in the end, I guess
I'd have to say *Minty.* Writing a book about her
childhood was one of the happiest experiences of my
career. I've always admired Harriet Tubman. She was
an incredibly brave woman!"

Though little is known about Tubman's early life, in
Minty: A Story of Young Harriet Tubman, Schroeder
builds a fictional account of her childhood using information garnered from many sources, including *Harriet
Tubman: The Moses of Her People,* written in 1869.
Minty (a nickname derived from Tubman's "cradle"
name, Araminta) is opinionated and independent, behavior that is punished in a slave on a Southern
plantation. She is removed from the main house and
sent into the fields where the work is harder. Recognizing his daughter's growing intolerance for the inhumane
treatment of the slaves, Minty's father teaches her
survival skills that she will later use to help bring the
slaves to freedom in the North. Maria Salvadore, a
reviewer for *Horn Book,* stated that the author's "quick
action and dialogue" create a tight story. Schroeder
"successfully combines fact and fiction to present a
plausible account" of Tubman's early childhood, wrote
Vivienne Grant, a critic for *School Librarian.* She
further noted that this "moving and poignant" story
could be a valuable learning tool.

■ Works Cited

Review of *Carolina Shout!, Publishers Weekly,* August 28, 1995, p. 113.

Grant, Vivienne, review of *Minty: A Story of Young Harriet Tubman, School Librarian,* February, 1997, p. 34.

McDermott, Leone, review of *Carolina Shout!, Booklist,* October 1, 1995, p. 309.

Review of *Ragtime Tumpie, Kirkus Reviews,* September 15, 1989, p. 1409.

Review of *Ragtime Tumpie, Publishers Weekly,* September 8, 1989, p. 67.

Rosenberg, Liz, review of *Ragtime Tumpie, New York Times Book Review,* February 25, 1990, p. 33.

Salvadore, Maria, review of *Minty: A Story of Young Harriet Tubman, Horn Book,* September, 1996, pp. 589-90.

Semrau, Ruth, review of *Carolina Shout!, School Library Journal,* October, 1995, pp. 118-19.

■ For More Information See

PERIODICALS

Booklist, September 15, 1996, p. 251; May 15, 1997, p. 1578.

Bulletin of the Center for Children's Books, June, 1991, p. 249; February, 1994, p. 201.

Five Owls, September/October, 1994, pp. 14-15.

Kirkus Reviews, March 1, 1994, pp. 309-10; October 15, 1994, pp. 1415-16.

New York Times Book Review, December 8, 1996, p. 78.

Publishers Weekly, October 31, 1994, p. 62; October 14, 1996, p. 84; May 12, 1997, p. 76.

School Library Journal, December, 1994, p. 102; September, 1996, p. 191; June, 1997, pp. 111-12, 144.

Teaching and Learning Literature, January-February, 1998, p. 89.

*   *   *

SCHUR, Maxine Rose 1948-

■ Personal

Born October 21, 1948, in San Francisco, CA; married Stephen Schur; children: Aaron, Ethan. *Education:* University of California at Berkeley, B.A. (dramatic arts); Stanford University, M.L.A. *Hobbies and other interests:* Reading, traveling, visiting art museums.

■ Addresses

Agent—Curtis Brown Ltd., Ten Astor Place, New York, NY 10003.

■ Career

New Zealand National Film Unit, Wellington, New Zealand, film editor, 1972-75; actress in television program *Close to Home,* New Zealand Broadcasting Corp.; freelance writer, 1977—; Addison-Wesley Publishing Co., staff writer, 1978-82; Wordwright, co-

MAXINE ROSE SCHUR

founder and educational software designer, 1981-84. Currently marketing communications consultant, copywriter, travel essayist, and children's book author. *Member:* Society of Children's Book Writers and Illustrators, PEN, Authors Guild, Bay Area Travel Writers, International Association of Business Communicators.

■ Awards, Honors

Work-in-Progress grant, Society of Children's Book Writers, 1981, for *The Circlemaker;* nominee, National Jewish Book Award, 1987, for *Hannah Szenes: A Song of Light;* Louis B. Dessauer grant, 1994; Parents Choice Award, 1994, for *Day of Delight: A Jewish Sabbath in Ethiopia;* Sydney Taylor Award, Association of Jewish Libraries, 1997, and Sugarman Family Award, Washington, D.C. Jewish Community, 1997, both for *When I Left My Village;* Finalist, National Jewish Book Award, 1997, for *Sacred Shadows.*

■ Writings

Weka Won't Learn, illustrated by Victor Ambrus, Viking/Sevenseas (New Zealand), 1977.
The Witch at the Wellington Library, illustrated by Ambrus, Viking/Sevenseas, 1978.
Shnook the Peddler, illustrated by Dale Redpath, Dillon, 1985.
Hannah Szenes: A Song of Light, illustrated by Donna Ruff, Jewish Publication Society (Philadelphia), 1986.
Gullible Gregory, Little, Brown (New York City), 1986.

Samantha's Surprise: A Christmas Story, illustrated by Nancy Niles and R. Grace, Pleasant Co., 1986.

The Reading Woman, Pomegranate Art Books, 1991.

The Circlemaker, Dial (New York City), 1994.

Day of Delight: A Jewish Sabbath in Ethiopia, illustrated by Brian Pinkney, Dial, 1994.

When I Left My Village, illustrated by Pinkney, Dial, 1995.

The Marvelous Maze (picture book), illustrated by Robin DeWitt and Patricia DeWitt-Grush, Stemmer House (Owings Mills, MD), 1995.

Enchanted Islands, Pomegranate Art Books, 1996.

Sacred Shadows, Dial, 1997.

Contributor of articles and reviews to periodicals, including *Australia/New Zealand Bookworld, Carribean Travel and Life, Christian Science Monitor, Escape Magazine, Los Angeles Times, San Francisco,* and *San Francisco Examiner.*

■ Adaptations

Samantha's Surprise: A Christmas Story was adapted as an audiocassette, Pleasant Co., 1986.

■ Work in Progress

The Peddler's Gift, for Dial Books.

■ Sidelights

An author of both picture books and historical novels, Maxine Rose Schur has set her writing against such diverse backgrounds as mid-nineteenth-century Russia, the rural highlands of Ethiopia, and prewar Poland. Many of her books feature Jewish characters whose lives, set against these diverse backgrounds, illuminate the Jewish past, gaining the understanding and compassion of contemporary readers. Among Schur's award-winning work for young readers are *The Circlemaker* and *Day of Delight,* both published in 1994, and *Day of Delight*'s sequel, *When I Left My Village.*

Schur was born in San Francisco, California. As a child, she had what she later termed the "good fortune" to contract rheumatic fever, which required a considerable period of rest during the recovery stage. This allowed the young Schur to spend a lengthy period of time learning to read and to enjoy books—unlike today, there was no television to distract her. Her favorite books were those that transported her to far-off places or back in time: *Black Beauty, Heidi, Little Women, Little Lord Fauntleroy,* and *Anne of Green Gables,* among others. These books strongly influenced Schur's career as a writer in the decades to come: she still enjoys writing books that focus on historical periods.

However, despite her love of books at an early age, Schur did not plan to be a writer. Graduating from high school in the mid-1960s, she majored in drama and received a degree in theatre arts from the University of California, Berkeley. Soon after graduation, she married and set out with her husband for a year-and-a-half-long

trip around the world, traveling by buses, trains, cars, donkeys, trucks, and tramp steamers during their adventures in over forty countries. In 1972, the Schurs began a five-year stop-over in Wellington, New Zealand, where Schur became a documentary and feature film editor, children's book critic, and actress. However, her thoughts were "haunted by exotic scenes, unforgettable people, and incredible anecdotes, 'traveller's tales,'" as she recalled to *SATA.* Schur began to write, first about the adventures she and her husband had in southern Turkey. These first autobiographical writings were made into story books illustrated by the Caldecott Award-winning illustrator Victor Ambrus. "These first small beginnings got me hooked on writing as a means of remembering and communicating," Schur revealed. "I've been hooked ever since. Much of my writing is still drawing inspiration from that journey [around the world] . . . , but much also takes its inspiration from the journeys I made in distance . . . and time in my own mind."

Returning with her husband to the United States in 1977, Schur was unsure what direction her life should take. Now a mother with a small child at home, she quickly realized that writing was a more practical occupation than acting, so she began taking on freelance writing assignments. A year later, Schur was hired as an in-house writer for Addison-Wesley Publishing Co. "I didn't know such dream jobs existed," she recalled of the position. "Each day I'd come to work and brainstorm with a wonderful group of crazy, creative types and then go into my office to write original poems, stories, riddles, and articles. It was not only bliss, but a great training that really honed my writing skills."

In 1981, Schur and a partner founded Wordwright, a company that conceived of and created educational software for young people. "This became an exciting time," the author recalls; "we worked with several of the pioneering companies in computer games and we learned a tremendous amount about not only computer design but marketing children's products." Schur later began work as a marketing communications manager for the high-tech industry. For several years she balanced her growing responsibilities with her writing projects, still managing to find time to work on several children's book projects, including *Shnook the Peddler* and *Hannah Szenes.* Finally, after three of her books—*The Circlemaker, Day of Delight,* and *When I Left My Village*—were sold to Dial in quick succession, Schur was able to return to her writing full time.

Characteristic of Schur's work is *Hannah Szenes: A Song of Light,* a biography of the World War II resistance fighter and poet who was executed for treason in 1944 at the age of twenty-three. The book, which was nominated for the National Jewish Book Award, is based upon the diaries of Szenes, whose idealism prompted her to parachute into war-torn Hungary to aid resistance fighters during the Nazi takeover of Europe. As Betsy Hearne noted in *Bulletin of the Center for Children's Books,* Szenes' biography provides "an appealing model for youngsters who have absorbed *The*

Diary of Anne Frank" and want to find out more about young peoples' lives during World War II. Schur would return to the World War II period in her 1997 book *Sacred Shadows,* which describes the life of a German Jew living in Poland during the rise of Adolf Hitler.

In *The Circlemaker,* readers are introduced to twelve-year-old Mendel, a Russian Jew living in the Ukraine who disguises his Jewish heritage and flees from the Russian soldiers who have come to his town to conscript children for service in the czar's army. The year is 1852, and Mendel, along with fellow runaway Dovid, must make it to the Hungarian border without being caught; in addition to serving as a story of a boy's taking on of the moral responsibilities of adulthood, *The Circlemaker* was described by *Booklist* critic Hazel Rochman as "an exciting story of terror and disguise, of leaving home and outwitting the enemy." A *Publishers Weekly* commentator called the book "atmospheric and suspenseful ... maintaining an edge-of-the-seat tension until the very last words."

Two books that reveal a less familiar Jewish world are Schur's award-winning *Day of Delight: A Jewish Sabbath in Ethiopia* and *When I Left My Village.* Both books focus on black African Jews who inherited the Jewish traditions many centuries ago while living in the remote Gondar province of Ethiopia. Their culture was so isolated from the rest of the world that many Beta Israel (Ethiopian Jews) did not even realize that other Jews existed in the world. Unfortunately, the famine that plagued their country in the 1980s forced many of the Beta Israel to leave for the Sudan and Israel, and many of the old ways were lost. In *Day of Delight,* Schur records these traditions, including the weekly preparations for what the Beta Israel called the "Day of Delight," the Sabbath. Described from the point of view of a twelve-year-old boy named Menelik, "the story portrayed here is of a vanishing way of life" according to *Horn Book* contributor Hanna Zeiger. Menelik's family's exodus to Israel in the face of famine and civil war is brought to life in *When I Left My Village,* a 1996 book that Maria Salvador described in *Horn Book* as "provocative and emotional." *When I Left My Village* was awarded the 1997 Sydney Taylor Award by the Association of Jewish Libraries for the most outstanding contribution to Jewish children's literature.

Schur divides her time between her travel writing, children's books, and consulting work. She enjoys talking to her readers—especially her young readers—at bookstores, libraries, conferences and schools. She travels the world as a travel writer, and also still likes to "noodle around" with game ideas and designs for gift products—she's developed calendars, bookmarks, and journals. "I have a busy, diverse, satisfying life right now," Schur says, adding "with just enough time to read."

■ Works Cited

Review of *The Circlemaker, Publishers Weekly,* December 6, 1993, p. 73.

Hearne, Betsy, review of *Hannah Szenes: A Song of Light, Bulletin of the Center for Children's Books,* October, 1986, p. 36.
Rochman, Hazel, review of *The Circlemaker, Booklist,* January 15, 1994, p. 919.
Salvador, Maria, review of *When I Left My Village, Horn Book,* May-June 1996, pp. 333-34.
Zeiger, Hanna, review of *Day of Delight, Horn Book,* November-December 1994, p. 747.

■ For More Information See

PERIODICALS

Booklist, November 1, 1985, p. 414; October 1, 1994, p. 334.
Bulletin of the Center for Children's Books, February, 1994, p. 201; November, 1994, p. 103; February, 1996, p. 202.
Kirkus Reviews, January 1, 1994, p. 74; October 15, 1994, p. 1416; October 15, 1997, p. 1588.
Publishers Weekly, January 8, 1996, p. 79.
School Library Journal, February, 1986, p. 78; March, 1996, p. 198.

*   *   *

SCHWENINGER, Ann 1951-

■ Personal

Born August 1, 1951, in Boulder, CO; daughter of Ivan F. (a teacher) and Alice M. (a teacher; maiden name, Hill) Schweninger. *Education:* Attended the University of Colorado, 1969; California Institute of the Arts, B.F.A., 1975.

■ Career

Author and illustrator.

■ Writings

FOR CHILDREN; SELF-ILLUSTRATED, EXCEPT AS NOTED

The Hunt for Rabbit's Galosh, illustrated by Kay Chorao, Doubleday, 1976.
A Dance for Three, Dial, 1979.
(Compiler and editor) *The Man in the Moon as He Sails the Sky, and Other Moon Verse,* Dodd, 1979.
On My Way to Grandpa's, Dial, 1981.
(Adaptor) *Silent Night,* Golden Press, 1983.
Halloween Surprises, Viking, 1984.
Christmas Secrets, Viking, 1984.
Birthday Wishes, Viking, 1986.
Off to School!, Viking, 1987.
(Compiler) *My Christmas Tree and Other Poems of the Season,* Golden Book, 1987.
Valentine Friends, Viking, 1988.
(Compiler) *Favorite Mother Goose and Animal Tales,* co-illustrated by Christopher Santoro, Western, 1989.
Wintertime, Viking, 1990.
Autumn Days, Viking, 1991.

Summertime, Viking, 1992.
Springtime, Viking, 1993.

ILLUSTRATOR

Jean Marzollo, *Amy Goes Fishing,* Dial, 1980.
Janice May Udry, *Thump and Plunk,* Harper, 1981.
Jim Erskine, *Bedtime Story,* Crown, 1982.
Jean Van Leeuwen, *Amanda Pig and Her Big Brother Oliver,* Dial, 1982.
Mary Caldwell, *Morning, Rabbit, Morning,* Harper, 1982.
Dewitt Conyers, compiler, *Animal Poems for Children,* Western, 1982.
Alan Benjamin, *Ribtickle Town,* Crown, 1983.
Jean Van Leeuwen, *Tales of Amanda Pig,* Dial, 1983.
Ben Cruise, reteller, *The Musicians of Bremen,* Golden Press, 1983.
Nancy Jewell, *ABC Cat,* Harper, 1983.
Maida Silverman, *Peter's Welcome,* Golden Book, 1985.
Jean Van Leeuwen, *More Tales of Amanda Pig,* Dial, 1985.
Mabel Watts, *Henrietta and the Hat,* Golden Book, 1985.
Doris Orgel, reteller, *Godfather Cat and Mousie,* Macmillan, 1986.
Clara A. Nestor, editor, *Mother Goose and Other Nursery Rhymes,* Golden Book, 1986.
Jean Van Leeuwen, *Oliver, Amanda, and Grandmother Pig,* Dial, 1987.
Melanie Donovan, selector, *The Mother Goose Word Book,* Golden Book, 1987.
Linda Hayward, *The Runaway Christmas Toy,* Random House, 1988.
Mary Packard, adaptor, *Two-Minute Fairy Tales,* Golden Book, 1988.
Joanna Cole and Stephanie Calmenson, compilers, *The Read-Aloud Treasury,* Doubleday, 1988.
Jean Van Leeuwen, *Oliver and Amanda's First Christmas,* Dial, 1989.
Jean Marzollo, *The Teddy Bear Book,* Dial, 1989.
Linda Hayward, *Alphabet School,* Random House, 1989.
Jean Van Leeuwen, *Oliver Pig at School,* Dial, 1990.
Jean Van Leeuwen, *Amanda Pig on Her Own,* Dial, 1991.
Jean Van Leeuwen, *Oliver and Amanda's Halloween,* Dial, 1992.
Sarah Josepha Buell Hale, *Mary Had a Little Lamb,* Western, 1992.
Beatrix Potter, *The Tale of Peter Rabbit,* Western, 1992.
Frances Zweifel, *The Make-Something Club: Fun with Crafts, Food, and Gifts,* Viking, 1994.
Jean Van Leeuwen, *Oliver and Amanda Pig and the Big Snow,* Dial, 1995.
Jean Van Leeuwen, *Amanda Pig, Schoolgirl,* Dial, 1997.
Frances Zweifel, *The Make-Something Club Is Back! More Fun with Crafts, Food, and Gifts,* Viking, 1997.

■ Sidelights

Author and illustrator Ann Schweninger is noted for her gentle, well-detailed watercolor-and-ink illustrations.

With picture books such as *A Dance for Three* and *The Man in the Moon as He Sails the Sky, and Other Moon Verse* to her credit, her watercolor renderings have also graced the works of other writers, including those of Jean Van Leeuwen, Frances Zweifel, and Beatrix Potter, whose classic, *The Tale of Peter Rabbit,* was reillustrated by Schweninger in 1992.

Born in 1951 in Boulder, Colorado, Schweninger was the daughter of two teachers who provided her with an upbringing that included an early love of books in all shapes and sizes. After graduating from high school in 1968, she attended the University of Colorado for a year before taking a break from her education. Classes in art and illustration would follow at California's Institute of the Arts, where Schweninger received her bachelor of fine arts degree in 1975.

Schweninger's first written work for children was *The Hunt for Rabbit's Galosh.* Her only work that was not self-illustrated, *The Hunt for Rabbit's Galosh* was followed by numerous other stories, including *A Dance for Three, The Man in the Moon as He Sails the Sky, and Other Moon Verse,* and *On My Way to Grandpa's.* Augmented with watercolor pictures that *Horn Book* critic Karen Klockner called "delicately painted ... in soft muted colors," *The Man in the Moon* contains twenty-one poems collected from both traditional and modern sources that describe nighttime. Verse from Mother Goose and limericist Edward Lear to such poets as Vachel Lindsay and Kathryn Maxwell Smith are all represented, making the volume "a sometimes mellow, sometimes sprightly collection especially appropriate for sleepy-time reading," according to Barbara Elleman in her *Booklist* critique. Darkness makes way to a colorful rainbow in *On My Way to Grandpa's,* as a young girl ventures out into a late spring shower to walk down her country road to Grandpa's house. With subdued color washes depicting squirrels, ants, and rabbits each awaiting the downpour's end, Schweninger's gentle story was praised by a *Publishers Weekly* reviewer as "a low-keyed, soothing adventure [that] is a winning candidate for bedtime reading."

Awaiting special days of the year provides much of childhood's excitement, and Schweninger captures this spirit of anticipation in a series of books that focus on holidays and other important events in a child's life. In *Christmas Secrets,* a family of rabbits makes preparations for Christmas—writing letters to Santa Claus, baking Christmas-only cookies, and decorating their small, rabbit-sized tree—while still taking time out to make snow-bunnies and enjoy the season. Divided into three vignettes, *Christmas Secrets* was praised by a *Publishers Weekly* reviewer as "all but irresistible." Schweninger's *Halloween Surprises* continues the rabbit family's tale, as tricks and treats among family and friends become the order of the day—and night. In *Birthday Wishes,* the celebration surrounding newly five-years-old Buttercup are detailed. "Soft, glowing pastel watercolors outlined in ink successfully convey the festive mood of this warm, whimsical family and capture the frenzied excitement of the day," noted Jean

Gaffney in her review of *Birthday Wishes* for *School Library Journal.* And, in addition to a pleasant story, *Valentine Wishes* contains directions young readers can follow to cut out a perfect heart shape. "Charmingly depicting joy in creativity and sharing, [*Valentine Wishes*] will inspire children's own industrious efforts," maintained *Booklist* reviewer Ellen Mandel.

The changing seasons are given a fresh lustre through Schweninger's creative renderings. In the "Let's Look at the Seasons" series of books that begins with *Wintertime,* her popular animal characters engage in a host of activities characteristic of each season of the year. *Wintertime* shows how frost forms, explains the importance of feeding birds when the snow falls, and describes how animals hibernate and otherwise survive the cold, snow, and ice that blanket the earth during the winter months. While noting that Schweninger's illustrations will be enjoyed by young children, *Appraisal* reviewer Patsy Ann Giese expressed concern that such youngsters would become confused with the illustrations' mix of human-like, jacket-and-trouser-wearing bears with more realistically portrayed animals. However, the mixture of fact and fiction in *Springtime* was met with more positive response, *Appraisal* contributor Nancy L. Bluntzer calling it "a book that will spark a young child's interest in nature and thus lead to more questions and an early interest in science."

The Jean Marzollo-penned picture book *Amy Goes Fishing* was Schweninger's first project as a contributing illustrator. Since this initial effort, Schweninger has provided pictures for the works of such authors as Mary Caldwell, Frances Zweifel, and Joanna Cole. In Caldwell's *Morning, Rabbit, Morning,* Schweninger presents a young rabbit's efforts to greet the coming of day in detailed, gently colored watercolors, and Frances Zweifel's *The Make-Something Club Is Back!* includes illustrated step-by-step instructions that *Booklist* reviewer Julie Corsaro characterized as "sweetly appealing." Schweninger's most winning collaboration, though, has been with author Jean Van Leeuwen, whose books featuring Amanda and Oliver Pig have become increasingly popular with young readers. These easy-to-read books, which include *Amanda Pig and Her Big Brother Oliver, Oliver and Amanda's First Christmas,* and *Oliver Pig at School,* showcase a close-knit family engaging in everyday pursuits, all brought to life through Schweninger's stylized, whimsical drawings. As *Booklist* critic Ilene Cooper noted, Schweninger's round-faced, jovial pigs "will make friends as well as fans" among their many young readers.

■ Works Cited

Bluntzer, Nancy L., review of *Springtime, Appraisal,* spring-summer, 1993, pp. 55-56.

Review of *Christmas Secrets, Publishers Weekly,* August 17, 1984, p. 60.

Cooper, Ilene, review of *Oliver and Amanda's Halloween, Booklist,* October 1, 1992, p. 339.

Corsaro, Julie, review of *The Make-Something Club Is Back, Booklist,* February 1, 1997, p. 944.

Elleman, Barbara, review of *The Man in the Moon as He Sails the Sky, and Other Moon Verse, Booklist,* November 15, 1979, p. 507.

Gaffney, Jean, review of *Birthday Wishes, School Library Journal,* May, 1986, p. 84.

Giese, Patsy Ann, review of *Wintertime, Appraisal,* autumn, 1991, pp. 53-54.

Klockner, Karen, review of *The Man in the Moon as He Sails the Sky, and Other Moon Verse, Horn Book,* December, 1979, pp. 673-74.

Mandel, Ellen, review of *Valentine Friends, Booklist,* February 1, 1988, pp. 936-37.

Review of *On My Way to Grandpa's, Publishers Weekly,* May 29, 1981, p. 43.

■ For More Information See

PERIODICALS

Booklist, November 1, 1976, p. 412; October 15, 1984, p. 312; August, 1991, p. 2151; January 1-15, 1996, p. 852.

Bulletin of the Center for Children's Books, September, 1984, pp. 14-15; July, 1986, p. 217.

Canadian Materials, July, 1988, p. 147.

Growing Point, November, 1984, p. 4345.

Horn Book, December, 1982, pp. 637-38; November, 1989, p. 754; September-October, 1990, p. 599; September, 1995, p. 628; May-June, 1997, p. 329.

Publishers Weekly, February 5, 1979, p. 95; August 20, 1979, p. 81; September 26, 1986, p. 88; February 10, 1989, p. 68; September 29, 1989, p. 71.

School Library Journal, April, 1979, p. 48; September, 1981, p. 115; October, 1984, p. 175; February, 1985, p. 68; August, 1987, p. 75; February, 1988, p. 64; January, 1991, p. 80; July, 1992, p. 64; April, 1993, p. 114; December, 1995, p. 92.*

*   *   *

SCOT, Michael
See ROHAN, Michael Scott

*   *   *

SEIDLER, Tor 1952-

■ Personal

Born June 26, 1952, in Littleton, NH; son of John M. (an investor) and Jean (an actress; maiden name, Burch) Falls. *Education:* Stanford University, B.A., 1972.

■ Addresses

Home—121 West 78th St., New York, NY 10024.

■ Career

Harcourt, Brace, Jovanovich, New York City, freelance contributor to language arts program, 1976-78; freelance writer, 1978—.

■ Awards, Honors

Fiction award, Washington State Writer's Day, 1980, for *The Dulcimer Boy; Terpin* was named one of *New York Times*'s Outstanding Children's Books, 1982; Best Books selection, *Publishers Weekly,* Children's Books of the Year, Library of Congress, 1986, and Silver Giffel (Dutch translation), all for *A Rat's Tale;* Notable Book selection, American Library Association, and Parent's Choice Storybook Award, both 1993, both for *The Wainscott Weasel;* Best Books, *Publishers Weekly* and *School Library Journal,* and finalist, National Book Award, 1997, all for *Mean Margaret.*

■ Writings

The Dulcimer Boy, illustrated by David Hockney, Viking, 1979.
Terpin, Farrar, Straus, 1982.
A Rat's Tale, illustrated by Fred Marcellino, Farrar, Straus, 1985.
The Tar Pit, Farrar, Straus, 1987.
(Reteller) Hans Christian Andersen, *The Steadfast Tin Soldier,* illustrated by Fred Marcellino, HarperCollins, 1992.
The Wainscott Weasel, illustrated by Marcellino, HarperCollins, 1993.

TOR SEIDLER

Mean Margaret, illustrated by Jon Agee, HarperCollins, 1997.

OTHER

Take a Good Look (adult novel), Farrar, Straus, 1990.

Contributor of articles and reviews to art magazines.

■ Sidelights

Tor Seidler mixes elements of fairy tale and realism in his highly imaginative novels for young readers. Fate and chance, and the personal risks that people sometimes take when their way of life is threatened, all figure prominently in his books, which include *The Dulcimer Boy, A Rat's Tale,* and the whimsical *The Wainscott Weasel.*

Seidler lived in Burlington, Vermont, before moving with his mother and stepfather to Seattle, Washington. Because his parents were divorced when he was very young and he would visit his father, he recalled growing up in two different families, with two different sets of rules. Seidler's mother was an actress; his stepfather was very interested in the stage and established theatre groups in both Vermont and Seattle, so Tor's childhood memories include watching rehearsals of such productions as Shakespeare's *Richard III,* rich with language, duplicity, and mystery.

Although an early introduction to Thorton Wilder's *The Bridge of San Luis Rey* convinced Seidler that he wanted to be an author, he never actively pursued writing during his school years. Instead, he studied math and science at Stanford University while competing in sports. After graduating from Stanford in 1972, Seidler moved to New York City and accepted a position with a publishing company that would finally inspire him to begin writing with an eye to publication. "I started trying to write children's books after working on elementary school readers for a language arts program at Harcourt, Brace," he once explained to *SATA.* "I always liked children's literature. My stepfather used to tell terrific bedtime stories to my older brother and me. He made up 'episodes' which featured animal characters whose foibles were, in fact, ours."

Seidler's first book, *The Dulcimer Boy,* is a fantasy set in New England. The story follows the adventures of William, whose life has an unusual beginning: he is placed, with his twin brother Jules, in a basket outside the door of some distant relatives—Mr. and Mrs. Carbuncle—before his widowed father goes off to sea. The only other object the father leaves in the basket is a dulcimer, which William eventually learns to play quite well, using its tones to entertain Jules, who cannot speak. Unfortunately for the boys, the Carbuncles are very selfish people. Mistreating the twins for many years, they finally attempt to take the dulcimer and sell it; William is forced to run away to save his precious instrument, and goes in search of his father and of answers to who he really is and how he may rescue his brother from the clutches of the Carbuncles. A *Junior*

Bayley Brown Jr., a weasel living in the wooded areas of eastern Long Island, befriends a fish and saves her life in Seidler's *The Wainscott Weasel*, illustrated by Fred Marcellino.

Bookshelf reviewer hailed *The Dulcimer Boy* as "exquisitely formed, with a fine irony of style, trenchant and economic yet also poetic," noting that Seidler's work incorporates more than a little social satire. Zena Sutherland of the *Bulletin of the Center for Children's Books* agreed, noting that in his debut novel the author makes the "Alger-like adventures of the dulcimer boy almost believable and certainly touching."

Seidler's next work of fiction, *Terpin,* tells the story of a U.S. Supreme Court justice who returns to the town where he was raised, after a thirty-year absence, to attend a celebration in his honor. The trip back home brings to mind an event from the distant past that had formed the crux of Terpin's personal philosophy: he recalls an incident from his youth where he told a lie that he believed led to a tragic suicide. A dream occurring shortly after the incident reinforced the young Terpin's decision: always to live and speak the truth. This way of life, of course, made the young man unpopular with both family and friends, in whose opinion his penchant for truthfulness became annoying. *Terpin* was not viewed by critics as a simple story, but rather, in the words of *Bulletin of the Center for Children's Books* reviewer Sutherland, a multi-layered tale containing "a wry commentary" on failing to reach one's potential and the superficiality of interpersonal relationships, as well as a "rejection" of several commonplace ethical and moral standards in place in modern society. "The trouble with *Terpin,*" opined a *Junior Bookshelf* critic, "is that at the end one wishes there were much more of it."

In *A Rat's Tale,* Seidler tells the story of Montague Mad-Rat the Younger, a sleek, frisky fellow whose habits are not those of his friends. Instead of the usual rat pursuits through the sewers in his Central Park home, Montague enjoys helping his mother make feathered hats, watching his father build mud castles, and painting. Realizing that he scuttles to a different drummer, Montague ventures outside the park and meets up with the Wharf Rats, who are trying to scout up enough lost loose change to pay off the wharf owner before he hires an exterminator to rid the area of their kind. Here Montague's talents can ultimately be of some use, as his paintings—detailed miniature drawings done on sea shells—prove popular with buyers and bring in the much-needed cash. Noting the satire that runs through *A Rat's Tale, Horn Book* critic Ann A. Flowers maintained that the story is "clever in its use of language" and called it "a study of the problems and rewards of nonconformity." Lyle Blake Smythers agreed in his *School Library Journal* assessment, noting that "although seemingly light entertainment, the novel tackles such topics as death, strength of character, and self-acceptance, and handles them well."

Anthropomorphized weasels and woodchucks and other wildlife serve as the protagonists of Seidler's *Wainscott Weasel* and *Mean Margaret.* In the former, which takes place in the wooded areas of eastern Long Island, we find Bagley Brown Jr., whose amorous interests are seemingly misplaced when he falls for a green-striped fish named Bridget instead of the smooth-coated weasel Wendy Blackish, who is also an excellent dancer. Although Bridget rejects Bagley's advances, she finally agrees to friendship, although her destiny will be to go out to sea with the rest of her kind. Comparing the author's warm-hearted approach to that of E. B. White in the classic *Charlotte's Web, New York Times Book Review* contributor Karen Brailsford maintained that Seidler "is prodding young readers [toward] tolerance and cooperation with the environment—and with themselves." Praising the author's imaginatively plotted story, Stephen Fraser added in *Five Owls* that Seidler's "language is elegant without sounding high-minded, creating a sophisticated yet wholly engaging read." *Horn Book* commentator Martha V. Parravano also praised Seidler's prose in a review of his well-received *Mean Margaret,* a comical tale of woodchuck newlyweds whose lives are completely disrupted by the arrival of a human toddler named Margaret who has been abandoned near their burrow. Margaret quickly turns the woodchucks' quiet home into an uninhabitable mess in what Parravano described as a "very funny commentary on the demands and rewards of parenthood." Parravano added: "Best of all is the language, which enhances the simple story with a sophisticated, precise vocabulary that rivals Beatrix Potter's famous *soporific.*"

Despite the praise that his fiction has received, Seidler remains modest about his accomplishments as a writer. "I've been writing pretty much regularly for [several] years," he once told *SATA,* "and every once in the while I think I'm beginning to get the hang of it, but most of the time I really wonder."

■ Works Cited

Brailsford, Karen, review of *The Wainscott Weasel, New York Times Book Review,* November 14, 1993, p. 52.

Review of *The Dulcimer Boy, Junior Bookshelf,* October, 1981, p. 217.

Flowers, Ann A., review of *A Rat's Tale, Horn Book,* March, 1987, pp. 212-13.

Fraser, Stephen, review of *The Wainscott Weasel, Five Owls,* February, 1994, pp. 62-63.

Parravano, Martha V., review of *Mean Margaret, Horn Book,* January-February, 1998, pp. 80-81.

Smythers, Lyle Blake, review of *A Rat's Tale, School Library Journal,* January, 1987, p. 79.

Sutherland, Zena, review of *The Dulcimer Boy, Bulletin of the Center for Children's Books,* February, 1980, p. 118.

Sutherland, Zena, review of *Terpin, Bulletin of the Center for Children's Books,* December, 1982, p. 77.

Review of *Terpin, Junior Bookshelf,* June, 1984, p. 144.

■ For More Information See

BOOKS

Sixth Book of Junior Authors and Illustrators, edited by Sally Holmes Holtze, H. W. Wilson (New York City), 1989.

PERIODICALS

Booklist, August, 1987, p. 1752.
Bulletin of the Center for Children's Books, February, 1987, p. 118; July, 1987, p. 217; November, 1993, p. 99; February, 1998, p. 218.
Growing Point, March, 1988, p. 4948.
Horn Book, March-April, 1993, pp. 192-93; November, 1993, p. 772.
Junior Bookshelf, April, 1988, p. 109; October, 1988, p. 254.
Kirkus Reviews, August 15, 1982, p. 941; June 1, 1987, p. 862; September 1, 1993, p. 1151.
New York Times Book Review, October 18, 1987, p. 38.
Publishers Weekly, June 25, 1979, p. 113; September 20, 1993, p. 74.
School Library Journal, November, 1979, pp. 81-82; March, 1983, p. 197.

* * *

SEULING, Barbara 1937-
(Carrie Austin; Bob Winn, a joint pseudonym)

■ Personal

Surname pronounced "Soo-ling"; born July 22, 1937, in Brooklyn, NY; daughter of Kaspar Joseph (a postman) and Helen Veronica (Gadie) Seuling (a homemaker). *Education:* Attended Hunter College (now Hunter College of the City University of New York), 1955-57, Columbia University, 1957-59, and School of Visual Arts and the New School for Social Research; also studied art and illustration privately. *Hobbies and other interests:* Movies, travel, reading, music.

■ Addresses

Home—New York, NY, and Landgrove, VT. *Agent*—Miriam Altshuler Literary Agency, RR #1, Box 5, 5 Old Post Road, Red Hook, NY 12571.

■ Career

Freelance writer and illustrator, 1968—. Has worked for an investment firm, for Columbia University, and at the General Electric Co. exhibit at the 1964 New York World's Fair. Dell Publishing Co., New York City, children's book editor, 1965-71; J. B. Lippincott Co., New York City, children's book editor, 1971-73. Director, The Manuscript Workshop, 1982—. Lecturer, teacher, and consultant on children's books and writing for children. Served as a consultant to the New York Foundling Hospital. *Member:* Society of Children's Book Writers and Illustrators (board of directors).

■ Awards, Honors

Award from American Institute of Graphic Arts, 1979, for *The Teeny Tiny Woman: An Old English Ghost Story;* Christopher Award, 1979, for *The New York Kid's Book;* first place, Harold Marshall Solstad Prize, Camer-

on University Children's Short Story Competition, 1982.

■ Writings

SELF-ILLUSTRATED NONFICTION

Freaky Facts, Xerox Education Publications (Middletown, CT.), 1972.
More Freaky Facts, Xerox Education Publications, 1973.
The Last Legal Spitball and Other Little-Known Facts about Sports, Doubleday, 1975.
Abracadabra!: Creating Your Own Magic Show from Beginning to End, Messner (New York), 1975.
You Can't Eat Peanuts in Church and Other Little-Known Laws, Doubleday, 1975.
The Loudest Screen Kiss and Other Little-Known Facts about the Movies, Doubleday, 1976.
The Last Cow on the White House Lawn and Other Little-Known Facts about the Presidency, Doubleday, 1978.
You Can't Count a Billion Dollars and Other Little-Known Facts about Money, Doubleday, 1979.
You Can't Show Kids in Underwear and Other Little-Known Facts about Television, Doubleday, 1982.
Elephants Can't Jump and Other Freaky Facts about Animals, Dutton/Lodestar, 1985.
You Can't Sneeze with Your Eyes Open and Other Freaky Facts about the Human Body, Dutton/Lodestar, 1986.
The Man in the Moon Is Upside Down in Argentina and Other Freaky Facts about Geography, Ivy Books/Ballantine (New York), 1991.
Too Cold to Hatch a Dinosaur and Other Freaky Facts about Weather, Ivy Books/Ballantine, 1993.

NONFICTION

(Editor and contributor) *The New York Kid's Book,* Doubleday, 1979.
Stay Safe, Play Safe: A Book about Safety Rules, illustrated by Kathy Allert, Western Publishing (New York), 1985.
(With Winnette Glasgow) *Fun Facts about People around the World,* illustrated by Leslie Connor, Xerox Education Publications, 1986.
It Is Illegal to Quack Like a Duck and Other Little-Known Laws, illustrated by Gwenn Seuling, Field/Weekly Reader, 1987, published as *Is It Illegal to Quack Like a Duck and Other Freaky Laws,* Dutton/Lodestar, 1988.
Natural Disasters, Kidsbooks, 1994.
Bugs That Goes Blam! And Other Creepy Crawly Trivia, Willowisp, 1995.
To Be a Writer: A Guide for Young People Who Want to Write and Publish, Twenty-First Century Books, 1997.
Winter Lullaby, illustrated by Greg Newbold, Harcourt, 1998.

SELF-ILLUSTRATED FICTION

The Teeny Tiny Woman: An Old English Ghost Tale (retelling), Viking, 1976.

The Great Big Elephant and the Very Small Elephant, Crown, 1977.

The Triplets, Houghton Mifflin/Clarion, 1980.

Just Me, Harcourt, 1982.

FICTION

What Kind of Family Is This? A Book about Stepfamilies, illustrated by Ellen Dolce, Western Publishing, 1985.

I'm Not So Different: A Book about Handicaps, illustrated by Pat Schories, Western Publishing, 1986.

Who's the Boss Here?: A Book about Parental Authority, illustrated by Eugenie, Western Publishing, 1986.

Boo the Ghost Has a Party, Xerox Educational Publications, 1986.

Boo the Ghost and the Robbers, Xerox Educational Publications, 1987.

Boo the Ghost and the Magic Hat, Xerox Education Publications, 1988.

(Under pseudonym Carrie Austin) *Julie's Boy Problem* ("Party Line" series), Berkeley (New York City), 1990.

(Under pseudonym Carrie Austin) *Allie's Wild Surprise* ("Party Line" series), Berkeley, 1990.

PUZZLE AND ACTIVITY BOOKS

Monster Mix, Xerox Education Publications, 1975.

Monster Madness, Xerox Education Publications, 1976.

(With Winnette Glasgow) *Fun with Crafts,* Xerox Education Publications, 1976.

Dinosaur Puzzles, Xerox Education Publications, 1976.

Did You Know?, Xerox Education Publications, 1977.

Monster Puzzles, Xerox Education Publications, 1978.

(With Winnette Glasgow; under joint pseudonym Bob Winn), *Christmas Puzzles,* Scholastic, 1980.

Valentine Puzzles, Xerox Education Publications, 1980.

Space Monster Puzzles, Xerox Education Publications, 1980.

Goblins and Ghosts, Xerox Education Publications, 1980.

Scary Hairy Fun Book, Xerox Education Publications, 1981.

My Secrets, Xerox Education Publications, 1984.

ILLUSTRATOR

Wilma Thompson, *That Barbara!,* Delacorte, 1969.

Nan Hayden Agle, *Tarr of Belway Smith,* Seabury Press (New York), 1969.

Stella Pevsner, *Break a Leg!,* Crown, 1969.

Antonia Barber, *The Affair of the Rockerbye Baby,* Delacorte, 1970.

Stella Pevsner, *Footsteps on the Stairs,* Crown, 1970.

Moses L. Howard, *The Ostrich Chase,* Holt, 1974.

Melinda Green, *Bembelman's Bakery,* Parents' Magazine Press (New York), 1978.

NONFICTION FOR ADULTS

How to Write a Children's Book and Get It Published, Scribner, 1984, revised and expanded edition, 1991.

Contributor to books and periodicals for and about children, including *Cricket, Ladybug,* and *Once Upon a Time....*

■ Work in Progress

A biography; a middle-grade novel.

■ Sidelights

The author and illustrator of fiction, nonfiction, and picture books for young readers and the illustrator of works by such writers as Stella Pevsner and Antonia Barber, Barbara Seuling is perhaps best known as the creator of the "Freaky Facts" books. These informational books, organized thematically, provide middle graders with little-known facts, myths, and legends on such subjects as sports, law, money, television, geography, the weather, the human body, and the presidency. Reflecting the author's fascination with her subjects, the "Freaky Fact" books are generally considered both edifying and entertaining.

Seuling is also the author of individual volumes of middle grade nonfiction on such topics as natural disasters, safety, and creating a magic show. In addition, she has written books on the art of writing and being published and has edited a popular guide to New York City for children. As the creator of picture books for preschoolers and early readers, Seuling is the author and illustrator of a well-received retelling of an English folktale; works that address such topics as friendship and individuality; and three stories about Boo, a ghost. For older children, she has written bibliotherapy titles on being handicapped, adjusting to a new stepfamily, and establishing personal independence with parents as well as two stories for middle graders published under the pseudonym of Carrie Austin. Seuling is also the creator of activity books on some of children's favorite subjects, such as monsters, ghosts, dinosaurs, crafts, and holidays.

"My early years," Seuling wrote in her essay in *Something about the Author Autobiography Series* (*SAAS*), "were the part of my childhood that left the deepest impression, and it is where I feel most connected." Born and raised in the Bensonhurst section of Brooklyn, New York, Seuling was the middle child and only girl in her family, which also includes two brothers. Her parents, Kaspar and Helen Seuling, were influential figures in Barbara's decision to create books for children. "My mother," Seuling said in *SAAS,* "passed on to me her love of reading, of fairy tales and mythology and stories in general.... While my mother filled my head with a love of books, it was my father who fostered the magic and wonder in our childhood, especially around the holidays." Her father, Seuling recalled in *SAAS,* "had a unique, witty [writing] style. I like to think I inherited some of my feeling for writing from him."

Growing up in the richly varied area of Bensonhurst, Seuling absorbed neighborhood life as well as the stories passed on by members of her family. "I didn't know then, of course," she recalled in *SAAS,* "that I was collecting details—the colors, the sounds, the language, the sights, the emotions, of my world—and that I would later use them as a writer and artist." She was also

Barbara Seuling retells the Old English ghost story *The Teeny Tiny Woman* in her self-illustrated picture book.

greatly influenced by the popular culture of the time: radio shows like "Gangbusters," "The Green Hornet," and "Inner Sanctum"; the comics; and movies, which, Seuling wrote in *SAAS*, "left a great impression on me, and it's no wonder that one of my freaky fact books—*The Loudest Screen Kiss and Other Little-Known Movie Facts*—is about them."

While Seuling was developing her love of story, she was also establishing her talent as an artist. "I showed talent for drawing as soon as I could hold a pencil," she recalled in *SAAS*. "For a long time, my talent for drawing became an important part of my identity. My family was close, but never showed affection openly. The praise and encouragement I received through my drawing, however, seemed to make up for that, giving me a sense of importance. All through my school years, my skill in drawing served as a kind of reminder to an otherwise not-very-confident youngster that I was really good at something." In addition to her interest in art, Seuling was developing a love of nature, fostered by the summers she spent outside of New York City. "These summers," she wrote, "instilled in me a deep love of the country and of space and time to explore and discover the natural world. They balanced my view so that I did not grow up thinking city life was the only life."

In grade school, Seuling was, she recalled, a "good student, if rather passive." In junior high she experienced some difficulties, both social and academic—"I just wasn't ready for all the changes in my life, physical and social, happening all at once." However, she made some friends and learned to cope with her problem subjects, science and algebra. In addition, she was voted wittiest in her class, claiming, she once told *SATA,* "I've been clowning around ever since." In the summer between junior high and high school, Seuling went to

Indiana to live with one of her cousins, an experience that she feels helped her to gain self-confidence. "My trip to Indiana—seeing a slice of another way of life," she recalled, "set off something inside of me.... I didn't know what I wanted, but it seemed to be outside school, even outside Brooklyn. I began to question what I would do with my life, what I might accomplish. I wanted to see so much of the world, do so much, be *useful*." By the time Seuling reached high school, there "was certainly none of the trauma that junior high had for me," she wrote in *SAAS*.

At fourteen, Seuling saw the movie *With a Song in My Heart,* the story of singer Jane Froman, who learned to walk again after surviving a plane crash that occurred while she was traveling as part of the USO. Froman's "strength and courage," wrote Seuling, "became my model for all that a person could be." Becoming a member of the Jane Froman fan club, Seuling met Froman in person and became friends with her. "It was through Jane," Seuling wrote, "that I began writing." Becoming the assistant editor of the Froman fan club journal, she wrote and illustrated stories and edited features. "I developed my love for editing at this point," she recalled in *SAAS,* "and while I still didn't think of myself as a writer, I was becoming one. I was, at that time, more confident in my abilities as an artist." The editor of the fan club journal, Winnette Glasgow, has remained Seuling's lifelong friend and has collaborated with her on several works.

Seuling attended night school at Hunter College in the Bronx while working at an insurance company during the day; at nineteen, she changed jobs and schools, taking a position at Columbia University, which offered free college credits as a benefit. She took a room with a single mother in exchange for part-time child care help. Struggling with the balance of work and school, Seuling decided to take a full-time position as the office manager of an investment company. In charge of hiring temporary help, she hired Winnette Glasgow and Nancy Garden, a budding writer who later became a successful children's author. Seuling and Garden collaborated on a tale for young readers—"a long story about a bookworm," Seuling remembers—with Garden doing the text and Seuling the pictures. When the investment company went bankrupt, Seuling found a position at Dell Publishing Company as a secretary in the adult trade department; when Dell created a new department for children's books, Seuling transferred into it. Working with editor Lee Hoffman, she began to learn about the craft of editing and about the principles of successful writing for children. Seuling then became an assistant children's book editor and also began writing her own works. Her first book, *Freaky Facts,* was written for the Weekly Reader Book Club and published in paperback. *Freaky Facts* compiles hundreds of humorous and outrageous facts on a wide range of subjects, from, Seuling wrote in *SAAS,* "language and hair to animal behavior and diseases." This compilation, she continued, "came from my own love of the strange and fascinating. As a child I had devoured Ripley's *Believe It or Not* in the Sunday funnies and later on in paperback books.... I knew strange and funny facts would entertain kids, and I could illustrate them humorously as well. This little book began a long trail of fact books for me that has not stopped yet."

While creating her own books, Seuling continued to work at Dell with Lee Hoffman's successor, George Nicholson. "My association with children's books and publishing," she wrote in *SAAS,* "only whetted my appetite for illustrating. George liked some samples of my drawings that I showed him, and he gave me a middle grade novel to illustrate. My illustrations were mentioned in a couple of reviews, and my career as an illustrator was started." Seuling showed Nicholson, who had moved from Dell to Viking, her first ideas for a version of the English folktale "The Teeny Tiny Woman." When she had completed the book, Nicholson accepted it for publication. *The Teeny Tiny Woman: An Old English Ghost Tale* is a picture book version of the ghost story in which a small woman in a miniature house finds a small bone on top of a tiny grave. When she gets home, the woman puts the bone in some soup and hears a voice saying, "Give me my bone." She doesn't give up the bone; instead, she tells the voice to take it. Seuling illustrates the tale in soft pencil with rosy overlays and incorporates hand-lettering into her drawings. A critic in *Publishers Weekly* noted that this "just-for-fun ghost story ... is embellished with exuberant pictures," while a *School Library Journal* reviewer called *The Teeny Tiny Woman* "a fine new retelling.... [The] gentle pencil drawings soften the scare so even the most timid beginning readers will enjoy this." Writing in the *Horn Book,* Virginia Haviland concluded that the drawings "have a neatness that allows its detail its precise place in pictures appropriate to lines filled with 'teeny tiny.'"

Seuling based her next picture book, *The Great Big Elephant and the Very Small Elephant,* on her friendship with Winnette Glasgow. Seuling describes this book, which is comprised of three gentle stories illustrated in inks and watercolors that stress the affection of her title characters for each other, as "a picture storybook about two friends who are opposite personalities and who see things differently but who ultimately get along by contributing what they each do best." A contributor in *Publishers Weekly* said that Seuling "tells and shows with equal skill in three stories of friendship.... Seuling has given beginners a funny, enduring, and altogether lovely book." *The Great Big Elephant* has received comparisons to Arnold Lobel's "Frog and Toad" books and James Marshall's "George and Martha" series. For example, a reviewer in *Bulletin of the Center for Children's Books* said, "This hasn't the tenderness of the Lobel stories or the humor of the Marshall books, but it's adequate, both in writing style and as a testament to the give-and-take of friendship."

Two of Seuling's picture books published in the early 1980s have personal identity as their theme. In *The Triplets,* sisters Pattie, Mattie, and Hattie, who have been dressed and treated alike since birth, sequester themselves in their room and refuse to emerge until they

are recognized as individuals. A contributor in *Kirkus Reviews* noted that the book contained "An obvious problem-solution contrivance, but there is some zip in the specific examples and in the author's simple two-color cartoons," while *Horn Book* reviewer Kate M. Flanagan noted the "guileless text" and that the illustrations of the "three round-faced triplets, though identical in appearance, exhibit subtle but distinct differences in facial expressions and mannerisms." In the easy reader *Just Me,* Seuling depicts a little girl who, over a three-day period, imagines herself as a horse (with hooves made by blocks on her feet), a dragon (with a jump rope for a tale), and a robot (with a box for a body); finally, she decides to just be herself when her supportive mother says, "I like you best of all." *Booklist* reviewer Judith Goldberger said, "With this unimposing set of first-person stories, Seuling shines a true yet carefully framed mirror on the younger reader," while a reviewer in *School Library Journal* noted that the "blend of real life and imagination in both text and pictures will strike a chord within any child who's ever ... been sent to his room for refusing to go against dragon nature and 'be nice.'" In the piece she wrote for *SAAS,* Seuling said, "Of all I have written, the work I love best is in picture books. Picture books offer the greatest challenges and bring the most satisfaction.... Every word must count, so I have to choose my words carefully, and to hone and polish for the best effect. This has made me a better writer in all forms, not just in picture books."

While contributing books to other genres, Seuling continues to write and illustrate her nonfiction collections of arcane information. One of the earliest "Freaky Facts" titles, *You Can't Eat Peanuts in Church and Other Little-Known Laws,* is a collection of obscure and offbeat laws gathered from around the United States

It Is Illegal to Quack Like a Duck **is Seuling's second book on the subject of outrageous and obscure laws.** (Illustrated by Gwenn Seuling.)

and illustrated in cartoonlike line drawings that underscore the incongruous nature of the laws; writing in *School Library Journal*, Linda Kochinski called *You Can't Eat Peanuts in Church* "[just] the ticket for upper elementary and junior high trivia buffs." Seuling's research for *The Last Cow on the White House Lawn and Other Little-Known Facts about the Presidency,* a collection of facts, firsts, and unique accomplishments, took the author to the Library of Congress, where she investigated the diaries and journals of presidents from George Washington to Jimmy Carter as well as their families and staffs. *Booklist* reviewer Denise M. Wilms claimed, "[This] historical hodgepodge is entertaining, to say the least," while a *Publishers Weekly* critic said, "Trivia fans have taken to Seuling's other books.... They may do the same for her new collection."

In *Elephants Can't Jump and Other Freaky Facts about Animals,* Seuling organizes her information in eleven categories such as eating habits, dwellings, and reproduction and enhances her facts with humorous line drawings. *Appraisal* reviewer Althea L. Phillips wrote, "The trivia enthusiasts with an interest in animals will devour this book," while Nancy Murphy, writing in the same publication, noted that Seuling provides "a fresh outlook on some familiar bits of knowledge." *School Library Journal* reviewer Mavis D. Arizzi commented, "These unusual bits of information just might inspire some students to do further research into the characteristics of various animals." With *You Can't Sneeze with Your Eyes Open and Other Freaky Facts about the Human Body,* Seuling covers, in the words of *Appraisal* reviewer Renee E. Blumenkrantz, "amusing and amazing facts" about the body in general, body systems and functions, the brain, birth, death, disease, medical practices, and unusual beliefs. *School Library Journal* reviewer Denise L. Moll said, "Like Seuling's other books ... this one would be especially useful for booktalking or for suggesting for recreational reading." Writing in *Appraisal*, John R. Pancella observed, "The author is very good at this writing style...." Looking back on the "Freaky Facts" books, Seuling wrote, "I was fast becoming known for these books, and it worried me that I would be considered the Queen of Trivia instead of a bona fide writer of children's books, so I tried to steer away from them for a while. Every time I thought I had done my last freaky fact book, however, something came along to persuade me to do another one.... From the feedback I've received over the years ... I'd say that these books, with their short readable bits of funny or fascinating information, have turned more than a few reluctant readers onto reading, and that pleases me enormously."

In addition to working as an author, illustrator, and editor, Seuling has been a teacher at the Bank Street College, the Manuscript Workshop, and the Institute for Children's Literature, among other places, and has become recognized as an authority on writing for children. She wrote in *SAAS*, "I still try to do it all—write, illustrate, edit, and teach—sometimes to the point of frustration, because it's what I love to do.... I am pleased to have devoted my life to books for children, because I believe books will help young people to grow and think and see the world in all its variety." She once said, "My purpose is different for each book I create—to share an emotional experience, show some aspect of the world a little better, or more clearly; make it easier to get through a tough or stressful situation—and yet all this must be kept carefully hidden so that it doesn't frighten children away. So, on the surface, I want to make children laugh, to entertain them, tell them a good story, excite their interest. I feel fortunate to work at what I love so much—writing and illustrating children's books. Although it has never been easy, the rewards still outweigh the difficulties. Young people want to know more and more about the life around them, about people and relationships and feelings, and if we're truthful, we can support them in this quest for knowledge. Inevitably, it turns around, and we learn something from the kids."

Seuling concluded, "My advice to new writers is: be persistent. The saddest part of writing is the defeatism that is felt so early by writers. One's first work rarely gets published, but that is when our hopes and ideals are so high that they are easily dashed by rejection. It is a rough process, and if one can weather the first years, and keep writing in spite of the obstacles, the chances of success keep growing. A writer is a growing thing; we grow with each page we write, and therefore the more we write the more we learn and the better we become."

■ Works Cited

Arizzi, Mavis D., review of *Elephants Can't Jump and Other Freaky Facts about Animals, School Library Journal,* March, 1985, p. 171.

Blumenkrantz, Renee E., review of *You Can't Sneeze with Your Eyes Open and Other Freaky Facts about the Human Body, Appraisal,* fall, 1987, p. 49.

Flanagan, Kate M., review of *The Triplets, Horn Book,* April, 1980, p. 400.

Goldberger, Judith, review of *Just Me, Booklist,* June 15, 1982, p. 1372.

Review of *The Great Big Elephant and the Very Small Elephant, Bulletin of the Center for Children's Books,* October, 1977, pp. 36-37.

Review of *The Great Big Elephant and the Very Small Elephant, Publishers Weekly,* June 13, 1977, p. 108.

Haviland, Virginia, review of *The Teeny Tiny Woman: An Old English Ghost Tale, Horn Book,* August, 1976, pp. 591-92.

Review of *Just Me, School Library Journal,* May, 1982, p. 80.

Kochinski, Linda, review of *You Can't Eat Peanuts in Church and Other Little-Known Laws, School Library Journal,* October, 1975, p. 101.

Review of *The Last Cow on the White House Lawn and Other Little-Known Facts about the Presidency, Publishers Weekly,* May 15, 1978, p. 104.

Moll, Denise L., review of *You Can't Sneeze with Your Eyes Open and Other Freaky Facts about the Human Body, School Library Journal,* February, 1987, p. 84.

Murphy, Nancy, review of *Elephants Can't Jump and Other Freaky Facts about Animals, Appraisal,* autumn, 1985, pp. 35-36.

Pancella, John R., review of *You Can't Sneeze with Your Eyes Open and Other Freaky Facts about the Human Body, Appraisal,* fall, 1987, pp. 49-50.

Phillips, Althea L., review of *Elephants Can't Jump and Other Freaky Facts about Animals, Appraisal,* autumn, 1985, p. 35.

Seuling, Barbara, *Just Me,* Harcourt, 1982.

Seuling, Barbara, essay in *Something about the Author Autobiography Series,* Volume 24, Gale, 1997, pp. 217-33.

Review of *The Teeny Tiny Woman: An Old English Ghost Tale, Publishers Weekly,* April 12, 1976, p. 66.

Review of *The Teeny Tiny Woman: An Old English Ghost Tale, School Library Journal,* May, 1976, p. 75.

Review of *The Triplets, Kirkus Reviews,* April 1, 1980, p. 437.

Wilms, Denise M., review of *The Last Cow on the White House Lawn and Other Little-Known Facts about the Presidency, Booklist,* September 1, 1978, p. 53.

■ **For More Information See**

PERIODICALS

Booklist, October 1, 1975, p. 241; May 1, 1982, p. 1163; February 15, 1985, p. 848; July, 1992, p. 1947.

Bulletin of the Center for Children's Books, July-August, 1975, p. 185; October, 1988, pp. 53-54.

Kirkus Reviews, July 15, 1978, pp. 752-53.

School Library Journal, May, 1975, p. 73; November, 1975, p. 83; September, 1977, p. 115; November, 1980, p. 67; August, 1982, p. 122.

Voice of Youth Advocates, October, 1997, p. 270.

—*Sketch by Gerard J. Senick*

*   *   *

SHYER, Christopher 1961-

■ **Personal**

Born May 9, 1961, in New Rochelle, NY; son of Robert M. (a business executive) and Marlene (a writer; maiden name, Fanta) Shyer. *Education:* University of Vermont, B.A., 1983; Columbia University, M.B.A., 1987. *Hobbies and other interests:* Skiing, travel.

■ **Addresses**

Home—Sleepy Hollow, NY. *E-mail*—Ichabodz@ ix.netcom.com. *Agent*—Alice Martell, Martell Agency, 555 Fifth Ave., New York, NY 10017.

■ **Career**

Zyloware Corporation (suppliers of eyeglasses and sunglasses), Long Island City, NY, vice-president, 1989—. *Member:* NetGALA, Columbia Club.

■ **Awards, Honors**

Washington Irving Book Selection, Westchester Library Association, 1997, for *Not Like Other Boys.*

■ **Writings**

(With Marlene Fanta Shyer) *Not Like Other Boys* (nonfiction), Houghton, 1996.

■ **Sidelights**

Christopher Shyer, together with his mother, Marlene Fanta Shyer, a children's book author, journalist, and novelist, have succeeded in telling their difficult story effectively in alternating chapters. *New York Times Book Review* contributor M. P. Dunleavy described *Not Like Other Boys* as "the heartfelt and sometimes harrowing" memoir of a mother and her gay son, a "dual coming out" that discusses not only homosexuality but "the sin of smallmindedness." The two authors relate progressively Shyer's mother's first suspicions when Chris was five, his unhappy childhood, miserable adolescence, comfortless visits to psychotherapists in search of "normalcy," and finally his adulthood, when he openly revealed his sexual orientation and found acceptance within his family.

Rebecca C. Burgee in *School Library Journal* praised the "well written" account with its honest expression of fears and conflicting emotions, recommending the title as "a strong choice for any collection" and concluding that "it is a hopeful book for today's society." Charles Harmon pointed out in *Booklist* that *Not Like Other Boys* "reveals what being gay is like for both the gay person and fellow family members." Shyer himself declares without compunction: "It is homophobia that should be in the closet."

■ **Works Cited**

Burgee, Rebecca C., review of *Not Like Other Boys, School Library Journal,* October, 1996, p. 166.

Dunleavy, M. P., review of *Not Like Other Boys, New York Times Book Review,* May 12, 1996, p. 18.

Harmon, Charles, review of *Not Like Other Boys, Booklist,* January 1 & 15, 1996, p. 764.

Shyer, Christopher, *Not Like Other Boys,* Houghton, 1996.

*   *   *

SRBA, Lynne

■ **Personal**

Born in Ohio; daughter of Joe (an aerospace engineer) and Theresa (a silicon water technician; maiden name, Ply) Srba; married Reid Maness (in public relations and marketing), September, 1985. *Education:* Attended Old Dominion University; Columbus College of Art and Design, B.F.A.; graduate study at University of Wisconsin—Milwaukee; North Carolina State University, Master's Degree, 1981.

■ Addresses

Home—6104 Glen Oak Ct., Raleigh, NC 27606. *Office*—201 East Davie St., Studio 205, Raleigh, NC 27601.

■ Career

Chapel Hill Newspaper, Chapel Hill, NC, illustrator, 1976-77; Duke University, Office of Publications, Durham, NC, illustrator and graphic designer, 1977-78; Research Triangle Institute, graphic designer and illustrator, 1978-85; Lynne Srba Graphics, Raleigh, NC, artist and owner, 1978—. North Carolina State University, teacher of illustration technique, 1979; Meredith College, adjunct faculty member, 1991-93; Children's Hospital of the King's Daughters, art therapy instructor.

■ Awards, Honors

Nearly thirty regional and national awards for illustration, design, and original art, including national award for annual report design, American Red Cross, 1994, and awards from Wake Visual Arts Association, Printing Industry of the Carolinas, International Association of Business Communicators, Triangle Advertising Federation, and U.S. Society for Technical Communication.

■ Illustrator

Susan Firer, *My Life with the Tsar,* New Rivers Press (St. Paul, MN), 1979.

Stephen A. Wainwright, *Axis and Circumference,* Harvard University Press (Cambridge, MA), 1988.

Hope Benton, *Whoa, Nellie!* (with parent and teacher guide by Beatrice H. Benton-Borghi, Barbara Beck, and Margaret Cloern), Open Minds, 1996.

Hope Benton, *Best Friends* (with parent and teacher guide by Beatrice H. Benton-Borghi, Barbara Beck, and Margaret Cloern), Open Minds, 1996.

Hope Benton, *A Thousand Lights* (with parent and teacher guide by Beatrice H. Benton-Borghi, Barbara Beck, and Margaret Cloern), Open Minds, 1996.

Hope Benton, *Down the Aisle* (with parent and teacher guide by Beatrice H. Benton-Borghi, Barbara Beck, and Margaret Cloern), Open Minds, 1996.

Johnny Ray Moore, *Howie Has a Stomach Ache,* Seedling Publications, 1996.

Rozland Grace, *Why is Johnny Special?,* BMF Press, 1998.

Betty Erickson, *Use Your Beak,* Seedling Publications, 1998.

Also designed book cover for *The Control of Boilers,* by Sam G. Dukelow.

LYNNE SRBA

■ Sidelights

Lynne Srba told *SATA:* "I am an artist living in Raleigh, North Carolina. I have traveled extensively in the United States and Europe studying, teaching, drawing, and painting. My background is in portraiture, illustration, and design. I am continually working with universities, colleges, museums, publishers, agencies, individuals, and corporations. I have art in galleries, museums, books, and private and corporate collections in the United States and other countries.

"I paint and draw angels, past and present, and the landscapes and seascapes they inhabit. These angels are, in fact, the friends, family, and animals we love. Pets are the angels of the universe: the comforters, healers, and peacemakers. Pets don't care if you are successful, beautiful, well-dressed, or rich. 'Just come home, feed me, take me out, stay with me as much as you can, or take me with you.' This is what my dog wants."

STEELHAMMER, Ilona 1952-

■ Personal

Given name is pronounced Ee-*lone*-a; born April 27, 1952, in Morton, WA; daughter of Marion (a logger) and Lydia (an antiques dealer; maiden name, Schuettler) Mullins; married Norman Steelhammer (a developer and certified public accountant), September 19, 1972; children: Cecelia, Emily, Brett. *Education:* Attended college.

■ Addresses

Home—3813 Ives Rd., Centralia, WA 98531. *Office*—Common Folk Co., 125 East High St., Centralia, WA 98531.

■ Career

Artist working in oils and acrylics, 1977—. Common Folk Co. (retail store for antiques, gifts, and art), Centralia, WA, founder and operator, 1990—. Artwork includes limited edition prints and greeting cards.

■ Awards, Honors

Award from Rotary International, 1988, for the poster "Polio Plus"; award from Providence Hospital, Centralia, WA, 1991, for the poster "Festival of Trees."

■ Illustrator

Stephen Cosgrove, *Chores,* Ideals Children's Books (Nashville, TN), 1988.
Stephen Cosgrove, *The Nosey Birds,* Ideals Children's Books, 1988.
Stephen Cosgrove, *Kind and Gentle Ladies,* Ideals Children's Books, 1988.
Stephen Cosgrove, *The Picnic,* Ideals Children's Books, 1988.
Stephen Cosgrove, *The Fine Family Farm,* reprinted, Forest House Publishing, 1996.
Stephen Cosgrove, *Lady Lonely,* reprinted, Forest House Publishing, 1996.

■ Work in Progress

Designing a poster for another festival of trees; illustrating a line of greeting cards for Common Folk Co.

■ Sidelights

Ilona Steelhammer told *SATA:* "I have been an artist forever, since my grade school days. For years, while I was doing art shows, people had been suggesting that I should illustrate children's books. I thought so, too. What a great challenge! Finally one day, author Stephen Cosgrove stepped into my art booth, and asked, 'Have you ever thought of illustrating children's books?' I was lucky—within one week he had taken four of my limited edition prints and written story lines for them. The

ILONA STEELHAMMER

characters I called Common Folk would now become 'simple folk' for the series.

"It was a challenging experience. I completed one book per month and met every deadline. It was my new job, and I worked every day, painting for eight hours per day. I became very focused and learned a great deal fast. I painted to scale, which I believe is the way to go. It was rewarding to see the story come alive in my paintings. The hardest part was painting the same people (in clothing) over and over so many times. The fun part was putting different things into the paintings that I personally love—things from my own family's home, such as my parents' street address on a village home or favorite quilt patterns and colors in bedding.

"The day the finished books arrived was one of my most memorable days. Seeing a whole complete book with the script was too good to be true. I will never forget it. Everyone should keep believing in his or her dreams. The universe has its way of helping people realize them. I am very grateful for all of the blessings that have come my way.

"The best art in the world (to me) is children's art work. The best age group is from three to six years old, before children start trying to make the work perfect and redoing it. Because we moved often while I was growing up, I only have one piece of art work from my own childhood: my 'family book' from the first grade. My mother saved it for me, and I love her more for it."

* * *

STINSON, Kathy 1952-

■ Personal

Born April 22, 1952, in Toronto, Canada; daughter of Douglas and Joyce (Gallinger) Powell; married Peter Carver; children: Matthew, Kelly.

■ Addresses

Home—R.R. #4, Rockwood, Ontario N0B 2K0, Canada. *E-mail*—kathy.stinson@sympatico.ca.

■ Career

Elementary school teacher, 1971-76; preschool program instructor, 1980-83; freelance writer, 1982—. Travelled to England as member of Canadian Children's Book Centre international writers' exchange, 1987. *Member:* Writers' Union of Canada, Canadian Children's Book Centre, Canadian Society of Children's Authors, Illustrators, and Performers (former treasurer), PEN Canada, Amnesty International.

■ Awards, Honors

I.O.D.E. (Toronto Chapter) award, 1982, for *Red Is Best;* Bicentennial Civic Award of Merit, City of Scarborough, 1996.

■ Writings

FICTION

Seven Clues in Pebble Creek, Lorimer, 1987.
The Great Pebble Creek Bike Race, Lorimer (Toronto), 1994.
Fish House Secrets (young adult novel), Thistledown Press (Saskatoon, Saskatchewan), 1992.
One Year Commencing . . . (young adult novel), Thistledown Press, 1997.

PICTURE BOOKS

Red Is Best, illustrated by Robin Baird Lewis, Annick Press (Toronto), 1982, revised edition, Oxford University Press, 1997.
Big or Little?, illustrated by Robin Baird Lewis, Annick Press, 1983.
Mom and Dad Don't Live Together Any More, illustrated by Nancy Lou Reynolds, Annick Press, 1984.
Those Green Things, illustrated by Mary McLoughlin, Annick Press, 1985, illustrated by Deirdre Betteridge, Annick Press, 1995.
The Bare Naked Book, illustrated by Heather Collins, Annick Press, 1986.
Teddy Rabbit, illustrated by Stephane Poulin, Annick Press, 1988.
The Dressed Up Book, illustrated by Heather Collins, Annick Press, 1990.

Who Is Sleeping in Aunty's Bed?, illustrated by Robin Baird Lewis, Oxford University Press, 1991.
Steven's Baseball Mitt: A Book about Being Adopted, illustrated by R. Lewis, Annick Press, 1992.

Author's works have been translated into several languages, including French, Polish, Japanese, Spanish, Finnish, and Danish, and have been published in braille.

JUVENILE NONFICTION

Writing Picture Books: What Works and What Doesn't, Pembroke (Markham, Ontario), 1991.
The Fabulous Ball Book, illustrated by Heather Collins, Oxford University Press, 1993.
Writing Your Best Picture Book Ever, illustrated by Alan and Lea Daniel, Pembroke, 1994.

■ Adaptations

Red Is Best and *Big or Little?* have been adapted for filmstrip, Society for Visual Education (Chicago), 1987.

■ Work in Progress

Over the Edge, a work of adult fiction; *Wanting to Know the Taste of Cream Soda,* a young adult novel; *Mr. Elliot's Story, Kristy and Maisie, Mrs. Muddle Goes to the Beach,* and *Nana Felicity's Chair,* juvenile fiction and picture books.

■ Sidelights

Although best known as an author of picture books, Kathy Stinson has also achieved critical success for her juvenile and young adult fiction and nonfiction. Active in promoting high-quality children's literature in her native Canada, Stinson has seen several of her own works, including *Red Is Best* and *Big or Little?,* published in both Great Britain and the United States and translated into numerous languages. "Deft handling of thorny contemporary issues is one of Kathy Stinson's hallmarks," noted Marie Campbell, reviewing the author's young adult novel *Fish House Secrets* for *Canadian Children's Literature.*

Born in Toronto in 1952, Stinson worked as a teacher of young people for several years before beginning a family of her own. It was while she was raising her two children, Matthew and Kelly, that she began to seriously pursue the "someday I would like to write a book" dream that had nagged her for several years. Her children would be the inspiration for her first two books: *Red Is Best* and *Big or Little?,* which showed, according to John Ferns of *Canadian Children's Literature,* that Stinson "knows children well and has listened to them with both amusement and love."

A little girl's enthusiastic praise for the color red serves as the focus of *Red Is Best.* Red socks help her to jump higher; red boots let her take giant steps; red pajamas scare bad-dream monsters away; and red barrettes make her hair feel "happy" all day. In fact, she wants

What do you hold in ...
Round hands?
Rubber hands?
What-time-is-it hands?
You'll-meet-a-tall-dark-handsome-
stranger hands?
And what do you hold in ...
Those hands?

Kathy Stinson introduces the various parts of the body in her picture book about youngsters dressing up in costumes. (From *The Dressed Up Book,* illustrated by Heather Collins.)

everything to be red, even over her mother's lighthearted objection. Called a "cheerful, good humoured book" by a *Junior Bookshelf* reviewer, *Red Is Best* contains repetitive words and phrases that critics believe make it useful for beginning readers as well as a book to be read at story time. *Big or Little?,* Stinson's second picture book, would follow in the same vein, as the events of a young boy's day show him to be "big"—capable of doing some things himself—and yet also "little." Commenting that both books accurately reflect the mind-set of most three- and four-year-olds, *Quill & Quire* reviewer Susan Walker opined that *Red Is Best* and *Big or Little?* "hold true to the small child's often perverse way of thinking ... and the text for both is simple and straightforward."

Among Stinson's other picture books are *Those Green Things,* wherein a young girl repeatedly jokes with her mother, asking "What are those green things?," in reference to all sorts of harmless household objects that in the child's imagination become slithery, slimy creatures. In *Teddy Rabbit* a young boy is devastated after he loses his favorite toy on the Toronto subway. "Few [readers] could fail to be moved by the child's plight," according to a *Canadian Children's Literature* reviewer, who praised the work for its "satisfying conclusion." And in *Who Is Sleeping in Aunty's Bed?,* a family visit to a favorite aunt turns into a game of musical beds when not enough sleeping spots for moms, dads, kids, and dogs can be found; and besides, Aunty snores. "Anyone who has experienced the fun and frustration that can occur in pursuit of a good night's sleep will enjoy *Who Is Sleeping in Aunty's Bed?,*" according to *Canadian Materials* contributor Patricia Fry.

In addition to her lighthearted fiction, Stinson has authored several books that deal with social issues that young people are often exposed to at an early age.

Steven's Baseball Mitt: A Book about Being Adopted reflects a young boy's efforts to find his own identity in an adopted family, while in *Mom and Dad Don't Live Together Any More,* a little girl's fears for her future and her way of life are answered by Stinson with expressions of individual caring on the part of each parent. "The tone of the book conveys sympathy for the child's distress," noted Gwyneth Evans in *Canadian Children's Literature,* "but also a calm, reflective acceptance of things as they are." And dealing with *children* as they are, Stinson created *The Bare Naked Book* and its companion volume, *The Dressed Up Book. The Bare Naked Book* provides young people with a relatively detailed introduction to the parts of their bodies, from "runny noses" and "itchy noses" to "pushing arms," "belly buttons," and other parts below. "This approach is a good one for older toddlers and preschoolers who are becoming aware of each others' bodies as well as their own," according to Lucy Young Clem in *School Library Journal.* Commenting on the fact that completely nude bodies—of babies and toddlers—occur infrequently in the book, and that most illustrations consist of semi-clad bodies going about their daily affairs, *Appraisal* critic Georgia L. Bartlett noted that "the authors have skillfully presented nudity within a natural context," such as while getting ready for bath-time. *The Dressed Up Book* looks at a child's anatomy from the other extreme, in the context of dressing up in costumes. "Stinson's text encourages parent and child to talk about the body as the story advances," Anne Gilmore of *Quill & Quire* noted, discussing the book's child characters rummaging through a closet and transforming themselves into all sorts of personas, disguising their heads, eyes, shoulders, and the like in the process.

In addition to picture books for youngsters, Stinson has also directed her writing talents to juvenile and young adult novels. Her work, *Seven Clues in Pebble Creek,* and its follow-up volume, *The Great Pebble Creek Bike Race,* focus on a group of boys spending the summer in rural Canada. In *Seven Clues,* eight-year-old Matt Randall and his friend, David, expect to spend a boring vacation until Matt receives a postcard that tells him to search for a "different sort of treasure" that will reap him rewards. While noting that the story lacks strong character development, *Canadian Materials* critic Pauline Henaut praised the work as appealing to reluctant male readers. In the sequel, *The Great Pebble Creek Bike Race,* Matt and friends David and Amanda are pitted against each other in a local contest, the prize being a brand-new racing bike. The real story, however, revolves around Matt's changing relationships and his efforts to remain friends with two boys who dislike each other, allowing "young readers [to] gain insight into human relationships at different levels," according to *Canadian Materials* contributor Gillian Martin Noonan.

Fish House Secrets concerns troubled teens Chad and Jill. Fifteen-year-old Chad is still recovering from the shock of his mother's death in a car accident when he meets Jill, a teen who is temporarily hiding out on Chad's family's property in Nova Scotia. Together, the two help each other sort out the emotional issues in their own lives. In addition, Stinson's protagonists help the reader of *Fish House Secrets* gain "acceptance—of people who are ultimately flawed; of accidents that bring both disaster and unexpected joy," according to *Canadian Children's Literature* reviewer Campbell. While noting that neither Stinson's plot nor "technique" are innovative, Margaret Mackey praised the author's first young adult novel in *Canadian Materials,* writing that Stinson "has made a satisfying whole out of her

Stinson investigates various facts about balls and games played with balls in her informational book illustrated by Heather Collins.

entwined narratives" and that *Fish House Secrets* should be popular among teen readers.

In addition to continuing to write for both toddlers and teens full time, Stinson visits young people in schools and libraries throughout Canada. She also runs workshops for adults who want to write for children. The recipient of Scarborough, Ontario's Bicentennial Civic Award of Merit, Stinson has devoted some of her time to several writer-in-residence programs, both at local libraries and Canada-wide through electronic media.

■ Works Cited

Bartlett, Georgia L., review of *The Bare Naked Book, Appraisal,* summer, 1987, pp. 87-88.

Campbell, Marie, review of *Fish House Secrets, Canadian Children's Literature,* Number 75, 1994, pp. 75-76.

Clem, Lucy Young, review of *The Bare Naked Book, School Library Journal,* April, 1987, p. 90.

Evans, Gwyneth, review of *Mom and Dad Don't Live Together Any More, Canadian Children's Literature,* Numbers 39-40, 1985, p. 129.

Ferns, John, review of *Red Is Best, Canadian Children's Literature,* Number 30, 1983.

Fry, Patricia, review of *Who Is Sleeping in Aunty's Bed?, Canadian Materials,* November, 1991, p. 355.

Gilmore, Anne, review of *The Dressed Up Book, Quill & Quire,* July, 1990, p. 24.

A family laughingly adapts to crowded sleeping arrangements during a visit to a favorite aunt's house. (From *Who Is Sleeping in Aunty's Bed,* written by Kathy Stinson and illustrated by Robin Baird Lewis.)

Henaut, Pauline, review of *Seven Clues in Pebble Creek,*
Canadian Materials, July, 1988, p. 132.

Mackey, Margaret, review of *Fish House Secrets, Cana-*
dian Materials, October, 1992, p. 272.

Noonan, Gillian Martin, review of *The Great Pebble*
Creek Bike Race, Canadian Materials, November/
December, 1994, p. 223.

Review of *Red Is Best, Junior Bookshelf,* June, 1984, p.
121.

Review of *Teddy Rabbit, Canadian Children's Litera-*
ture, Number 51, 1988, p. 100.

Walker, Susan, review of *Big or Little?, Quill & Quire,*
August, 1983, p. 34.

■ For More Information See

PERIODICALS

Canadian Children's Literature, Number 44, 1986, p.
91; Number 45, 1987, pp. 95-96; Number 51, 1988,
p. 76; Number 62, 1991, p. 96; Number 67, 1992,
pp. 84-85.

Canadian Materials, July, 1990, p. 182; March, 1992, p.
98; October, 1992, p. 266.

Junior Bookshelf, August, 1992, p. 144; December,
1993, p. 222.

Quill & Quire, June, 1992, p. 37; July, 1994, p. 61.

School Librarian, August, 1992, p. 99.

School Library Journal, August, 1983, p. 58; April,
1985, p. 83; February, 1986, p. 101; April, 1986, p.
80.

*   *   *

STOCKDALE, Susan 1954-

■ Personal

Born October 3, 1954, in Miami, FL; daughter of Grant
Stockdale (a former ambassador to Ireland) and Alice
Boyd Magruder Proudfoot (an author and poet); married Todd S. Mann (president of a health care company); children: Chelsea, Justin. *Education:* Studied with
illustrator Luis de Horna, Instituto de Cultura, Spain,
1974-75; studied with printmaker Ansai Uchima, Sarah
Lawrence College, 1975; Occidental College, B.A. (art;
cum laude), 1976.

■ Addresses

Home—Atlanta, GA; and c/o Simon & Schuster Children's Books Division, 15 Columbus Circle, New York,
NY 10023.

■ Career

Artist. Textile designs have been purchased by apparel
industry companies. Worked previously in public relations. *Exhibitions:* Has exhibited her work in Atlanta,
GA; Alexandria, VA; and Washington, D.C. *Member:*
Society of Children's Book Writers and Illustrators.

■ Writings

(And illustrator) *Some Sleep Standing Up* (picture
book), Simon & Schuster, 1996.

■ Work in Progress

Nature's Paintbrush: The Patterns and Colors Around
You, for Simon & Schuster.

■ Sidelights

Seeing a napping flamingo during a trip to the zoo with
her children inspired Susan Stockdale to write and
illustrate her first book, *Some Sleep Standing Up.* "We
saw a flamingo that was sound asleep while standing on
one leg," the author told *SATA.* "We all thought that
was just amazing, and started talking about the different
ways animals sleep." When a trip to the library produced no whimsical books on the subject, Stockdale
decided to write her own. "My art work has always
included images of animals in fanciful settings, so the
subject matter was perfect for me."

■ For More Information See

PERIODICALS

Booklist, September 1, 1996, p. 140.

Kirkus Reviews, April 15, 1996, p. 610.

SUSAN STOCKDALE

School Library Journal, April, 1996, p. 131.

* * *

STODDARD, Sandol 1927-
(Sandol Stoddard Warburg)

■ Personal

Born December 16, 1927, in Birmingham, AL; daughter of Carlos French and Caroline (Harris) Stoddard; married Felix M. Warburg, April 2, 1949 (divorced, June 14, 1963); married William A. Atchley (a doctor), June 1, 1974; children: (first marriage) Anthony, Peter, Gerald, Jason. *Education:* Bryn Mawr College, A.B. (magna cum laude), 1959; San Francisco State College, graduate study.

■ Career

Writer.

■ Awards, Honors

One of ten best picture books of 1960, *New York Herald Tribune,* for *The Thinking Book;* Children's Book Showcase honor, 1977, for *Free; Saint George and the Dragon* was named a distinguished book of 1983 by the American Library Association.

■ Writings

FOR CHILDREN; AS SANDOL STODDARD WARBURG

The Thinking Book, illustrated by Ivan Chermayeff, Atlantic-Little, Brown, 1960.
Keep It Like a Secret, illustrated by Chermayeff, Atlantic-Little, Brown, 1961.
(Adaptor) *Saint George and the Dragon: Being the Legend of the Red Cross Knight from the "Faerie Queene" by Edmund Spenser,* illustrated by Pauline Baynes, Houghton, 1963.
My Very Own Special Particular Private and Personal Cat, illustrated by Remy Charlip, Houghton, 1963.
Curl Up Small, illustrated by Trina Schart Hyman, Houghton, 1964.
I Like You, illustrated by Jacqueline Chwast, Houghton, 1965.
From Ambledee to Zumbledee: An A-B-C of Rather Special Bugs, illustrated by Walter Lorraine, Houghton, 1968.
Growing Time, illustrated by Leonard Weisgard, Houghton, 1969.
Hooray for Us, illustrated by Jacqueline Chwast, Houghton, 1970.
On the Way Home, illustrated by Dan Stolpe, Houghton, 1973.

FOR CHILDREN; AS SANDOL STODDARD

Free, illustrated by Jenni Oliver, Houghton, 1976.
Five Who Found the Kingdom: New Testament Stories, illustrated by Robert Sabin, Doubleday, 1981.
Bedtime Mouse, illustrated by Lynn Munsinger, Houghton, 1981.

The Doubleday Illustrated Children's Bible, illustrated by Tony Chen, Doubleday, 1983, portions published as *A Child's First Bible,* Dial, 1990.
Bedtime for Bear, illustrated by Lynn Munsinger, Houghton, 1985.
The Rules and Mysteries of Brother Solomon: A Picture Book, illustrated by Jana Winthers Newman, Paulist Press, 1987.
(Compiler) *Prayers, Praises, and Thanksgivings,* illustrated by Rachel Isadora, Dial, 1992.
Turtle Time, illustrated by Lynn Munsinger, Houghton, 1995.
What Are Roses For?, illustrated by Jacqueline Chwast, Houghton, 1996.

OTHER

The Hospice Movement: A Better Way of Caring for the Dying (adult nonfiction), Stein & Day, 1978, revised, Vintage, 1992.

■ Adaptations

The Thinking Book was adapted as a Reading Incentive Film starring Sidney Poitier, Bank Street College, 1969; *Growing Time* was translated into Japanese and made into a Japanese film, 1975; *Curl Up Small* was adapted as a film by John Korty.

■ Sidelights

Sandol Stoddard was raised in two worlds: both within the austere, solemn, self-contained social landscape of New England and amid the warm, gracious, outgoing atmosphere of the South. With published books under both her own name and her name from a former marriage, Sandol Stoddard Warburg, Stoddard's gentle stories for young children include *The Thinking Book, Curl Up Small, Bedtime Mouse,* and the more recent *Turtle Time* and *What Are Roses For?,* as well as several books based on Christian teachings.

Born in Alabama in 1927, Stoddard was raised in New Haven, Connecticut, and attended private schools in New England before enrolling in college. While attending Bryn Mawr, Stoddard began to rebel against the social strictures confining her—and many other women of her generation—to a role as wife and dedicated mother, despite her education and her creative drive. Continuing her rebellion after college graduation, she married unconventionally and moved to the more relaxed culture of the West Coast, where she raised four children while attempting to find the time to indulge her passion for writing. Her earliest books, which include *The Thinking Book* and *Keep It Like a Secret,* were according to Stoddard a reflection of her effort to understand life at its most basic, to "get down to the very simplest, barest bones of things." Since then, she has studied and perfected her craft, and has attempted to understand the source of her creativity and personal faith: as she wrote in *On the Way Home,* "We who seek make a journey of mystery together, though there are times when we may not touch hands; for those of us who dare, alone and in the dark, to move forward on the path toward truth have begun already, in our various and separate ways, the long journey home."

Among Stoddard's earliest works for children are *Curl Up Small, Free,* and the humorous alphabet book *From Ambledee to Zumbledee: An A-B-C of Rather Special Bugs. Curl Up Small* depicts baby animals eager to go out and explore the world around them, despite their need for a mother's care. In *Free,* a fierce tiger demands the only rose flowering in an isolated garden where children play; after he finally steals it, the rose kills him. From the tiger's grave, another equally beautiful bloom grows, which is enjoyed by Free, the only child remaining, who bravely returns to her garden home. A *Publishers Weekly* reviewer stated that *Free* "ought to appeal to those with developed insights."

A series of twenty-six silly bug species decorate the text and drawings of Stoddard's *From Ambledee to Zumbledee,* while in *Growing Time* the author contemplates a far more serious topic: the death of a family pet. When Jamie's dog, King, who had practically been raised alongside him, finally dies of old age, the young boy must come to terms with mortality and learn to accept and love King's replacement—a new, frisky puppy. *Horn Book* reviewer Diane Farrell praised Stoddard's treatment of death in what the critic termed "a beautifully written, sensitive treatment" of the subject "in terms that are meaningful to children." And a *Publishers Weekly* critic agreed, maintaining that the author "has made death not beautiful, but understandable."

More recent picture books written by Stoddard include several tales that involve that most dreaded part of childhood: bedtime. In *Bedtime Mouse,* illustrated by Lynn Munsinger, an imaginative young girl envisions her toys dancing around her room while she gets ready for bed. Young readers will enjoy "the sparkling rhymes," according to a *Publishers Weekly* critic, and will anticipate their own bedtimes, where they can "meet all the exuberant creatures that dance in the heroine's dreams." A young bear named Small feels differently, however, and in *Bedtime for Bear* he fusses about everything, from his pajamas to the arrangement of his blankets, in order to stay up later. Finally, with the help of his grandmother, Small settles in and falls asleep, ending a story that *School Library Journal* contributor Connie M. Hornyak considered "worth sharing . . . with nighttime procrastinators." Stoddard and Munsinger teamed up once again for *Turtle Time,* the story of a baby turtle that is quite comfortable retreating into its shell for "a lot of turtle naps." A *Publishers Weekly* commentator called *Turtle Time* "another winning sleepy-time tale" from Stoddard and Munsinger, and the critic commended Stoddard's "graceful intertwining of nonsense and truth."

In addition to her stories for children, Stoddard has written several books that introduce young readers to Christian history and teachings. In collaboration with illustrator Tony Chen, she created *The Doubleday Illustrated Children's Bible,* in which she arranged over one hundred biblical stories as separate tales, adding

A young girl devises a getting-ready-for-bed poem about a baby turtle who hides in his shell at naptime. (From *Turtle Time,* written by Sandol Stoddard and illustrated by Lynn Munsinger.)

historical footnotes but eliminating peripheral material that might confuse or distract young readers from the central message. While praising Stoddard's method, Ann A. Flowers had mixed opinions about the text, noting in her *Horn Book* critique: "In general, the retellings are smooth and straightforward but lacking in the beauty and grandeur of language that prevails in the great translations." However, Flowers summed up the work as "an attractive, commendable introduction to the Bible, excellent for reading aloud." Stoddard and Chen abridged their *Illustrated Children's Bible* into a work for younger children that was published as *A Child's First Bible.*

Other books by Stoddard that are grounded in the Christian faith include *Five Who Found the Kingdom,* a collection of New Testament tales which focus on young people who met and were influenced by Jesus. "The stories follow Biblical theory, portraying Jesus of Nazareth as a healer of the sick whose life was destined from birth and who changed the lives of those he encountered," noted *School Library Journal* contributor Jane E. Gardner in a positive assessment of the book. In *Prayers, Praises, and Thanksgivings,* Stoddard collects devotional sayings from a variety of religions and cultures. Praised by *Booklist* reviewer Carolyn Phelan as "a refreshing source of brief, unsentimental prayers and devotional poems for children," *Prayers, Praises, and Thanksgiving* contains the works of Gandhi, Edna St. Vincent Millay, Sir Thomas More, Archbishop Desmond Tutu, and Muhammad, among its many other sources. "The blending of all these voices . . . ," noted Nancy Vasilakis in *Horn Book,* "reinforces our awareness that we all belong to one human family."

Stoddard once explained to Lee Bennett Hopkins in *Books Are by People,* "In writing, one tries to be more and more honest all the time—more and more comprehensive . . . . In the major efforts, one gives all of oneself each time, developing a feeling of affection, even passion; a work is like the feeling a passionate woman has for her newborn baby or a passionate gardener has for his newest rose, which always seems the most perfect ever."

■ Works Cited

Review of *Bedtime Mouse, Publishers Weekly,* December 18, 1981, pp. 70-71.

Farrell, Diane, review of *Growing Time, Horn Book,* August, 1969, p. 404.

Flowers, Ann A., review of *The Doubleday Illustrated Children's Bible, Horn Book,* February, 1984, p. 78.

Review of *Free, Publishers Weekly,* May 31, 1976, p. 198.

Gardner, Jane E., review of *Five Who Found the Kingdom: New Testament Stories, School Library Journal,* February, 1982, p. 81.

Review of *Growing Time, Publishers Weekly,* March 17, 1969, p. 57.

Hornyak, Connie M., review of *Bedtime for Bear, School Library Journal,* January, 1986, pp. 61-62.

Klein, Harriet, review of *Free, School Library Journal,* October, 1976, p. 112.

Phelan, Carolyn, review of *Prayers, Praises, and Thanksgivings, Booklist,* November 12, 1992, p. 426.

Stoddard, Sandol, interview with Lee Bennett Hopkins, *Books Are by People,* Citation Press, 1969.

Stoddard, Sandol, *On the Way Home,* Houghton, 1973.

Stoddard, Sandol, *Turtle Time,* Houghton, 1995.

Review of *Turtle Time, Publishers Weekly,* January 30, 1995, p. 99.

Vasilakis, Nancy, review of *Prayers, Praises, and Thanksgivings, Horn Book,* March-April, 1993, p. 223.

■ For More Information See

PERIODICALS

Booklist, June 1, 1969, p. 1129; February 1, 1984, p. 812.

Bulletin of the Center for Children's Books, November, 1965, p. 52; December, 1965, p. 71; October, 1969, pp. 33-34; December, 1992, p. 124.

Horn Book, October, 1968, p. 555; August, 1981, pp. 426-27.

Kirkus Reviews, December 1, 1981, p. 1464; February 1, 1991, p. 177; January 15, 1996, p. 142.

Publishers Weekly, October 21, 1968, p. 51; February 26, 1988, p. 199.

School Library Journal, October, 1981, p. 136; May, 1991, p. 90; April, 1995, p. 118; December, 1996, p. 107.

SUSI, Geraldine Lee 1942-

■ Personal

Surname is pronounced *Sue-*see; born July 19, 1942, in New York, NY; daughter of Harold C. and Wilhelmina Mary (Howell) Reinhardt; married Ronald A. Susi (a career military pilot and elementary school teacher), June 17, 1962; children: Mark, Lori, Scot, Sheri Susi Nygaard. *Education:* Attended Elmira College, 1960-62, and Eastern New Mexico University, 1962; Texas Tech University, B.S., 1965; Troy State University, M.A., 1974; additional study at George Mason University, 1987—. *Hobbies and other interests:* Art, sewing, stained glass, gardening, skiing and biking, travel, cooking.

■ Addresses

Home—7939 Kettle Creek Dr., Catlett, VA 20119. *Electronic mail*—rsusi@mnsinc.com.

■ Career

Reading and mathematics specialist and teacher in Gwinn, MI, 1975-78; elementary reading specialist at elementary and junior high schools in Fairfax County, VA, 1978-97.

■ Writings

Looking for Pa: A Civil War Journey from Catlett to Manassas, 1861 (historical novel; with teacher's guide), illustrated by Douglas P. French, EPM Publications (McLean, VA), 1995.

Contributor to periodicals, including *Language Arts Journal* and *Reading Teacher Journal.*

■ Work in Progress

A sequel to *Looking for Pa: A Civil War Journey from Catlett to Manassas,* following the Harding family and describing "how the Civil War affects them as the fighting continues to escalate throughout Virginia"; researching the effects of the Civil War on the average citizen, with additional sequels in mind.

■ Sidelights

Geraldine Lee Susi told *SATA:* "I find it impossible to live in Virginia and not be transformed by the history that surrounds me. From the forming of the Jamestown colony to the American Revolution and the Civil War, Virginia has been an influential part of the making of America. I live in the heart of all this. Every day, as I drive to and from my job as a reading specialist, my route takes me through the battlefields of First and Second Manassas (also known as the Battles of Bull Run).

"Traveling through this historically preserved area gives me the sense of going back in time. In my imagination characters come to life, as I weave them into the rich

GERALDINE LEE SUSI

historical fabric of the Civil War. My story begins right where I live, and I have walked every road and trail that my characters have walked.

"As a reading teacher, I wanted to write a story that would 'hook' the reader, while presenting accurate history as the background. Much to my delight, adults as well as youngsters have enjoyed *Looking for Pa*. It is an exciting read-aloud book for parents and teachers alike. Calling upon my years of teaching experience, I prepared a teacher's guide to accompany this novel, making it an excellent addition to any school's American history study.

"Now that I am retired, I make presentations to elementary schools showing students the process involved in writing and publishing a book. I enjoy meeting young people and promoting writing as a lifelong skill and possible career choice."

■ For More Information See

PERIODICALS

Voice of Youth Advocates, October, 1995, p. 225.

*   *   *

SUZANNE, Jamie
See ZACH, Cheryl (Byrd)

SWAMP, Jake 1941-

■ Personal

Native American name, Tekaronianeken; born October 18, 1941, on Akwesasne Mohawk Nation Reservation, near Rooseveltown, NY; son of Leon (Native American name, Ioratekah; a rigger and farmer) and Charlotte (Native American name, Tekonowakweni; a homemaker; maiden name, Papineau) Swamp; married Judy Point (Native American name, Kanerataronkwas; a homemaker), September 2, 1961; children: Andrew Aroniawente, Angela Kahentethah, Glen Iawentanawen, Philip Karoniase, Leona Kaneratiosta, Kahontineh, Skahendowaneh. *Education:* Attended high school. *Politics:* "Great law of peace." *Religion:* Traditional religion, Longhouse.

■ Addresses

Home and office—Mohawk Nation, P.O. Box 366, Rooseveltown, NY 13683. *Agent*—Michael Collyer, 1 Dag Hammarskjold Plaza, New York, NY 10017-2299.

■ Career

Ironworker in Utica, NY, for nearly thirty years; Mohawk Nation Council, Wolf Clan chief, 1969—; CKON-FM Radio, manager; American Friends Service Committee, director of Environmental Justice Project, 1988-90; Akwesasne Freedom School, director. *Member:* Tree of Peace Society (president; chairperson), Metropolitan Peace Museum, Fenimore Cooper Farmers Museum.

■ Awards, Honors

Peacebuilder Award, New York State Dispute Resolution Association, 1996; Media Award, National Arbor Day Foundation, 1998.

■ Writings

Giving Thanks: A Native American Good Morning Message, illustrated by Erwin Printup, Jr., Lee & Low (New York City), 1995.

■ Work in Progress

A children's book about Mohawk ironworkers; a children's book about the importance of names.

■ Sidelights

Jake Swamp told *SATA:* "The book *Giving Thanks* was written in response to the need of children to be secure in the natural environment. If children in the world were all exposed to the teachings of the book, they would have a common sharing of knowledge as a base for understanding. For many years I have traveled worldwide, planting trees for peace, based on the history of the peacemaker who emerged a thousand years ago to bring peace to the Iroquois Nations. As a result of coming in contact with many different cultures, I

JAKE SWAMP

suddenly realized that the world needs to have a common base of sharing. I believe it will be through everyone's children that our world will become peaceful."

■ For More Information See

PERIODICALS

Horn Book, January, 1996, p. 94.
Kirkus Reviews, September 1, 1995, p. 1289.
Publishers Weekly, August 28, 1995, p. 112.

*   *   *

SZEKESSY, Tanja

■ Personal

Born in Berlin, Germany; daughter of Tamas (a radiologist) and Maria Charlotte (maiden name, Kietzmann; present surname, Marlott) Szekessy. *Education:* Hochschule der Kuenste Berlin, degree in design, 1996, M.A., 1997.

■ Addresses

Home—Kantstrasse 49, 10625 Berlin, Germany.

■ Career

Freelance designer and illustrator.

■ Awards, Honors

First prize, Berlin Cartoon Contest, 1993; Book of the Month Award, German Academy of Children and Youth Literature, 1996, for German edition of *A Princess in Boxland.*

■ Writings

A Princess in Boxland (self-illustrated), translated by J. Alison James, North-South Books (New York City), 1996.

■ Work in Progress

A book about a snowman who makes a bet with a snow rabbit; a story about "how children live in big cities without losing their sense of humor."

■ Sidelights

Tanja Szekessy told *SATA:* "Writing and illustrating children's books allows me to create a world in which I can ask any question there may be. The questions may be important or unimportant. The children who get into this world by reading and seeing the book then tell me the answers. That means they tell me stories I never put into it. This magic is what I like, and any subject can be used for it.

TANJA SZEKESSY

"I also value books that give answers to children who may have questions of their own, but I leave those to other clever persons. Meanwhile, I try to make some doubtful riddles, hoping that some day I will be a real magician who can make sorrow disappear from children's hearts and make cheerfulness appear there instead. That's the purpose of children's books."

■ For More Information See

PERIODICALS

Horn Book Guide, fall, 1996, p. 279.
Publishers Weekly, June 17, 1996, p. 64.
School Library Journal, July, 1996, p. 74.*

U–V

URY, Allen B. 1954-

■ Personal

Born January 17, 1954, in Chicago, IL; son of Bernard E. (an owner of a public relations agency) and Helen B. (a homemaker) Ury; married Rene Dangler (a literacy tutor), December 18, 1977; children: Robert Nathan. *Education:* University of Wisconsin—Madison, B.A., 1975. *Politics:* "Moderate Democrat." *Religion:* Jewish.

■ Addresses

Home and office—625 Rhine Lane, Costa Mesa, CA 92626. *Agent*—Anne McDermott, Coast-to-Coast Talent Group, 4942 Vineland, North Hollywood, CA. *Electronic mail*—ABU625@aol.com.

■ Career

Public relations account executive, 1977-88; screenwriter, Costa Mesa, CA, 1985—. Screenplay analyst and lecturer, 1993—. *Member:* Phi Beta Kappa.

■ Writings

CHILDREN'S BOOKS

The Hunt and More Fright with a Bite, Troll, 1996.
A Fate Worse Than Death: More Fright with a Bite, Troll, 1996.
Scary Stories for Sleepovers: Lost in Horror Valley, Lowell House (Los Angeles, CA), 1996.
Scary Stories for Sleepovers: The Living Ghost, Lowell House, 1996.
Scary Stories for When You're Home Alone, illustrated by Bernard Custodio, Lowell House, 1996.
More Scary Stories for When You're Home Alone, Lowell House, 1996.
Scary Mysteries for Sleep-Overs, illustrated by Mia Tavonatti, Price, Stern, Sloan (Los Angeles, CA), 1996.
More Scary Mysteries for Sleep-Overs, illustrated by Mia Tavonatti, Price, Stern, Sloan, 1996.

ALLEN B. URY

Duh! Heir Head and Other Stories Even Dumber Than "Dumb and Dumber," Lowell House, 1996.
Duh! Brain, Brain Go Away, and Other Stories Even Dumber Than "Dumb and Dumber," Lowell House, 1997.
Crawlers: Home Ick-o-Nomics and Other Tasty Tales, TorKids (New York City), 1997.
Still More Scary Stories for When You're Home Alone, illustrated by Eric Reese, Lowell House, 1997.
Still More Scary Mysteries for Sleep-Overs, illustrated by Mia Tavonatti, Price, Stern, Sloan, 1997.

Even More Scary Mysteries for Sleep-Overs, illustrated by Mia Tavonatti, Price, Stern, Sloan, 1997.
Crawlers: The Roaches' Revenge, TorKids, 1997.
Scary Stories for Sleep-Overs: Tomb of Eternity, NTC Contemporary Publishing, 1997.

OTHER

The Jigsaw Murders (screenplay), Concorde Pictures, 1988.
Freddy's Nightmares: Killer Instinct (for television), New World Television, 1988.

■ Work in Progress

Danger Man, an original comedy screenplay.

■ Sidelights

Allen B. Ury told *SATA:* "I've wanted to be a writer for as long as I can remember. In junior high and high school, I wrote and performed in numerous original plays, musicals, and sketch reviews. By college, I had set my sights on Hollywood, and—being rather impatient—graduated in only three-and-a-half years from the University of Wisconsin—Madison with a degree in radio, television, and film.

"Although my original creative forays were in movies and television—a field in which I continue to be active—I stumbled into juvenile horror on the urging of my literary agent. As it turned out, I was reading one of the *Scary Stories for Sleepovers* books to my then eight-year-old son, so I had a pretty good handle on the format. One book assignment has led to dozens of others, including humor and nonfiction.

"Getting paid to scare little kids is fun. Besides, there is still a lot of the 'little kid' left in me, even after all these years. Making up stories is a great way to make a living."

■ For More Information See

PERIODICALS

School Library Journal, July, 1996, p. 87.

*   *   *

van der MEER, Ron 1945-

■ Personal

Born March 24, 1945, in Amsterdam, Netherlands; son of Albert (a blacksmith) and Lucy (Dinkgreve) van der Meer; married Atie van der Linde (an author), August 26, 1966; children: Mara, Simone. *Education:* Attended Royal College of Fine Art, the Hague, Netherlands, 1965-69, and Royal College of Art, London, 1969-72.

■ Career

Author and illustrator; self-employed artist, designer, and paper engineer. Van der Meer Paper Design Ltd.,

Langley, Berkshire, director, 1985—. Research Fellow at Goldsmith's College, University of London, and Design Research Department, Royal College of Art, 1972-73; visiting teacher in drawing techniques with a drawing aid, Chorley Wood School for Girls with Little or No Sight, 1972-75; visiting lecturer, Goldsmith's College, University of London, 1972-76; lecturer, Graphic Design department, St. Martin's School of Art, 1973-85; visiting teacher in typography and calligraphy, Eton College, 1974-77; lecturer in Graphics Information department, Royal College of Art, 1976—; visiting lecturer, Middlesex Polytechnic, 1977-78. Designer and creator of games for Royal Society ROSPA and Globe Education; designer of toys and jigsaw puzzles Toy Trumpet Co. Designer of pop-up television commercial for Dettol, 1983; design consultant for Design Council, London. *Exhibitions:* "Playthings for the Handicapped Child," Royal College of Art, 1971; "50 Odd Posters," RCA Galleries, 1972; "Woven Structures," Camden Art Centre, 1973; G.P.O. Galleries, the Hague, 1973; "Letter, Sign, Symbol," Nederlandse Kunst-stichting (Netherlands Institution of Art), 1975; "50 Drawings for the Blind," Whitechapel Art Gallery, 1975. *Member:* Friends of the Royal Academy, Authors Society.

■ Awards, Honors

Honorable mention and prize, C.B.S. American Competition, 1971, for animated short film "Christmas"; honorable mention and prize, Chicago Film Festival's Students Competition, 1972, for animated short film "Freedom"; with Atie van der Meer, runner-up for Mother Goose Award "for most exciting newcomers to British illustration," 1979, for *My Brother Sammy* and *Sammy and Mara;* Utah Children's Informational Award, 1979, for *Your Amazing Senses;* Redbook Award, 1984, and American Award for best pop-up book, 1985, for *Sailing Ships.*

■ Writings

SELF-ILLUSTRATED, EXCEPT AS NOTED

(Catalogue with text) *Fifty Drawings by the Blind Made with Ron van der Meer's Drawing Aid,* Whitechapel Art Gallery (London), 1975.
(With Frank Muir) *Frank Muir's Big Dipper,* Heineman (London), 1981.
The World's First Ever Pop-Up Games Book, Heineman, 1982.
The Pop-Up Book of Magic Tricks, Heineman, 1983, Viking, 1983.
The Case of the Kidnapped Dog, Macmillan (London), 1983.
(With Alan P. McGowan) *Sailing Ships Pop-Up Book,* illustrated by Borje Svensson, Viking Penguin, 1984.
Majesty in Flight: Nature's Birds of Prey in Three Dimensions, Abbeville Press (New York), 1984.
(With Sharon Gallagher) *Inside the Personal Computer: An Illustrated Introduction in Three Dimensions,* Abbeville Press, 1984.

(With John Hedgecoe) *The Working Camera: The World's First Three-Dimensional Guide to Photography Made Easy*, Harmony Books (New York), 1986.

(With Raymond Briggs) *The Snowman: A Pop-Up Book with Music*, Hamish Hamilton, 1986.

(With Maxim Jakubowski) *The Great Movies—Live! A Pop-Up Book*, Simon & Schuster, 1987, published as *The Great Movie Lives*, Ebury (London), 1987.

(With Richard Smith) *The Good Health Kit*, Ebury, 1987.

(With Lesley Anne Ivory) *Kittens*, Aurum, 1988, published as *Kittens: An Abbeville Pop-Up Book*, Abbeville Press, 1990.

(With Babette Cole) *Babette Cole's Beastly Birthday Book*, Heineman, 1990, Doubleday, 1991.

Panda Comes to Stay, illustrated by Graham Ralph, BBC Books, 1991.

Spider in the Bath, illustrated by Graham Ralph, BBC Books, 1991.

(With Lesley Anne Ivory) *Little Angels*, Knopf, 1992.

The Birthday Cake: A Lift-the-Flap Pop-Up Book, Random House, 1992.

(With Christopher and Helen Frayling) *The Art Pack: A Unique, Three-Dimensional Tour through the Creation of Art through the Centuries—What Artists Do, How They Do It, and the Masterpieces They Have Given Us*, Knopf, 1992, Ebury, 1992.

(With Babette Cole) *The Bible Beasties*, Harper, 1993, Marshall Pickering, 1993.

The Fantastic Fairy Tale Pop-Up Book, illustrated by Fran Thatcher and Tracey Williamson, Random House, 1993.

(With Michael Berkeley) *The Music Pack: A Unique Three-Dimensional Tour through the Creation of Music over the Centuries: What Musicians Do, How They Do It, and the Masterpieces They Have Given Us*, Knopf, 1994, Ebury, 1994.

(With Bob Gardner) *Math Kit: A Three-Dimensional Tour through Mathematics*, Simon & Schuster, 1994, published as *The Maths Pack Is Like No Other Book You Have Ever Seen*, Cape (London), 1994.

Family Bear Pop-Up Book, illustrated by Thomas Rohner, Simon & Schuster, 1994.

Bugz: An Extraterrestrial Pop-Up Book, Running Press (Philadelphia, PA), 1994.

Beauty and the Beast Pop-Up, Random House, 1995.

(With Ron Fisher) *The Earth Pack: Tornadoes, Earthquakes, Volcanoes: Nature's Forces in Three Dimensions*, National Geographic Society, 1995.

(With Frank Whitford) *The Kid's Art Pack*, Knopf, 1995.

My First Nursery Books, Random House, 1995.

Brain Pack: An Interactive, Three-Dimensional Exploration of the Mysteries of the Mind, Running Press, 1996.

Market Day, Random House, 1996.

The Pick and Shop Marketplace, illustrated by Fran Thatcher, Random House, 1996.

(With Deyan Sudjic) *The Architecture Pack*, Knopf, 1997.

WITH ATIE VAN DER MEER, EXCEPT AS NOTED

Basil and Boris in London, Evans Brothers (London), 1978.

Basil and Boris in North America, Evans Brothers, 1978.

Sammy and Mara, Hamish Hamilton (London), 1978.

My Brother Sammy, Hamish Hamilton, 1978.

Naughty Sammy, Hamish Hamilton, 1979.

Sammy and the Cat Party, Hamish Hamilton, 1979.

Oh Lord!, Macmillan, 1979.

Penny and the Piglets, Heineman, 1980.

Joey, Heineman, 1980.

I'm Fed Up, Hamish Hamilton, 1981.

Monster Island, Holt, 1981, published as *Monster Island Pop-Up Book*, Holt, 1981.

Funny Fingers, Heineman, 1982.

Fungus the Bogeyman Pop-Up Book, Hamish Hamilton, 1982.

Who's Afraid?, Hamish Hamilton, 1983.

The Ghost Book, Macmillan (London), 1983.

Where's the Mouse?, Blackie (Glasgow), 1983.

Where Is the Baby?, Blackie, 1983.

What Is Missing?, Blackie, 1983.

Who Eats What?, Blackie, 1983.

My Train, Blackie, 1983.

My Plane, Blackie, 1983.

My Motorbike, Blackie, 1983.

My Car, Blackie, 1983.

What Colour?, Blackie, 1984.

What Shape?, Blackie, 1984.

Who's Real?, Blackie, 1984.

Where's the Apple?, Blackie, 1984.

Roaring Lion Tales Pop-Up Book, Blackie, 1984.

First Arabian Pop-Up Book, Blackie, 1984.

Animals, Purnell (London), 1985.

My Boat, Blackie, 1985.

My Lorry, Blackie, 1985.

My Rocket, Blackie, 1985.

My Circus, Blackie, 1985.

My Truck, Blackie, 1985.

Circus, Purnell, 1986.

I'm Hungry: Spin Me and See What I Like!, Methuen (London), 1986.

Magic, Purnell, 1986.

Monsters, Purnell, 1986.

What Will the Caterpillar Be?, Methuen, 1986.

Who Eats the Bone?, Methuen, 1986.

Who Is in the Water?, Methuen, 1986, Price Stern Sloan, 1986.

Who Lives Here?, Methuen, 1986.

Who Changes into What?, Price Stern Sloan, 1986.

Who Eats What?, Price Stern Sloan, 1986.

Your Amazing Senses: 36 Games, Puzzles, and Tricks That Show How Your Senses Work, Simon & Schuster, 1987, Child's Play, 1987.

(With Gerald Hawksley) *Little Chunky Bus*, Blackie, 1987.

(With Gerald Hawksley) *Little Chunky Lorry*, Blackie, 1987.

(With Gerald Hawksley) *Little Chunky Train*, Blackie, 1987.

Playthings: A Turning Picture Book, Hamish Hamilton, 1987.

Surprise: A Turning Picture Book, Hamish Hamilton, 1987.

Things That Work: A Turning Picture Book, Hamish Hamilton, 1987.

Who's Hiding? A Turning Picture Book, Hamish Hamilton, 1987.

Pigs at Home: A Picture Word Book, Aladdin Books, 1988.

Jumping Animals, Child's Play International, 1989.

Jumping Children, Child's Play International, 1989.

Jumping Monsters, Child's Play International, 1989.

Amazing Animal Senses, Joy Street Books (Boston), 1990, Child's Play International, 1990.

Fun with Animals: A Spinning Wheel Book, Putnam, 1990.

Fun with Numbers: A Spinning Wheel Book, Putnam, 1990.

Fun with Shapes: A Spinning Wheel Book, Putnam, 1990.

What Is the Time?, Carnival, 1990.

Funny Hats: A Lift-the-Flap Counting Book with a Surprise Gift, Random House, 1992, World International, 1992.

Whose Footprints Are These?, Price Stern Sloan, 1992.

Funny Shoes, Aladdin Books, 1994.

ILLUSTRATOR

(With Atie van der Meer) Alain Presencer, *Goldilocks and the Three Bears,* Methuen, 1986.

(With Atie van der Meer) Alain Presencer, *Hansel and Gretel,* Methuen, 1986.

(With Shirley Hughes) Penelope Leach, *The Baby Pack,* Cape, 1990; published as *The Baby Kit,* Summit, 1990.

Vera van der Meer, *Family Bear,* World International, 1992.

Designer of an educational alphabet, published in a book on alphabets by Fletcher/Spencer, 1973. Redesigner of *Eton Chronicle,* 1974. Creator and illustrator, with Jill Kent, of "Fred, Mags and Creep" series for Macmillan Education, 1976. Contributor of drawings and text, "Rainbow Programme," Thames Television, 1980. Designer and creator of greeting cards, including *Nursery Rhyme Cards,* Heineman, 1982; *Pop-Up Christmas Greeting Cards from the Victoria & Albert Collections,* 1983; *Animal Greeting Cards, Cage Cards,* and *Fungus the Bogeyman Pop-Up Cards,* Hunkydory, 1984; and *Flower Cards* and *Butterfly Cards,* Hunkydory, 1985. Designer of novelty jumping boxes *Little Red Riding Hood, The Ugly Duckling, Hansel and Gretel,* and *Cinderella,* all published by Blackie, 1984. Designer of *Pop-Up Calendar Flowers,* Abbeville, 1984. Designer of *Five Fairy Tale Toy Theatres: Sleeping Beauty, Cinderella, The Three Little Pigs, Goldilocks and the Three Bears,* and *Little Red Riding Hood,* all published by Blackie, 1985.

■ Sidelights

Called "one of the most innovative of paper engineers" by *Publishers Weekly,* van der Meer is the creator of pop-up books, flap books, and other interactive titles for young children that are praised for their ingenuity, usefulness, and audience appeal. In addition, he is the author and illustrator of several well-received picture books that are celebrated for their humor, attention to detail, and subtle lessons as well as for the color and vibrancy of their illustrations. A popular and prolific author/illustrator who often collaborates with his wife Atie, van der Meer characteristically creates concept books, although several of his works are realistic or pure fantasy. Van der Meer blends facts and fun to address topics of special interest to children, such as colors, numbers, shapes, transportation, animals and the natural world, the arts, cameras, computers, and the human body; he also bases his works on some of his audience's favorite subjects, such as ghosts, monsters, and extraterrestrials; mysteries and surprises; and folk and fairy tales. Van der Meer consistently designs his works so that young readers will find a variety of activities on every double-page spread. His books include such devices as moveable parts, optical allusions, three-dimensional glasses, scratch-and-sniff pictures, and rubber band constructions. In addition, van der Meer enhances his creations by including glossaries, pamphlets, cassettes, CDs, and, in a pop-up book about music, even tiny drumsticks to increase the knowledge and foster the enjoyment of his audience. Van der Meer often collaborates with specialists and other professionals to create his informational books. Although some observers note that van der Meer's texts, although accurate, are too simple, and regard his interactive books as ephemeral non-literature, most reviewers consider him an exceptional book designer whose artistic sensibility and technical skill have helped to raise the standards of the toy book.

From *Jumping Animals,* a picture book with pop-up paper engineering written and illustrated by Ron and Atie van der Meer.

Born in Amsterdam, van der Meer attended the Royal College of Fine Arts, the Hague, before moving to England to study at the Royal College of Art in London; he and Atie van der Meer and their children Simone and Mara—the latter appears as a character in the popular "Sammy" series of picture books—currently reside in Berkshire, England. Since 1985, van der Meer has been the director of van der Meer Paper Design Ltd.; he has also worked in design research and has taught drawing at a school for the blind, typography and calligraphy at the preparatory school Eton College, and design at the university level. In addition to his many books for children, van der Meer has designed toys, games, puzzles, calendars, and greeting cards; he is also the creator of television commercials and two award-winning animated short films, has served as a design consultant, and has held several exhibitions of his art.

Among the most acclaimed of the van der Meers' early works is the "Sammy" series of picture books about an extended family with two small children; the series includes *My Brother Sammy, Sammy and Mara, Naughty Sammy,* and *Sammy and the Cat Party.* In the first two books preschooler Mara describes her mother's pregnancy and watches her new little brother grow and develop; a reviewer in *Junior Bookshelf* notes of the first volume, "Mothers about to produce a second child might find this helpful to show to their first child," while *Growing Point* critic Margery Fisher observes of both books, "A smart, youngish grandmother plays a convincing part in stories which are honest without gimmickry, properly individualised, and complemented by brightly coloured portraits." Writing in *School Library Journal,* Gemma DeVinney says of all four volumes, "Many kids (and their parents) will readily relate to the featured family's near-chaotic near-disasters. The colorful illustrations are well executed and have real pizazz."

One of the most acclaimed of van der Meer's early works is *Oh Lord!,* a picture book lauded for depicting the creation of the world in an especially charming manner. Designed in cartoon format, *Oh Lord!* features God with a detachable halo who is, in the words of *Junior Bookshelf* reviewer Marcus Crouch, "credible, fallible, kind, and firm." God is assisted in his six-day endeavor by two red-haired, anatomically correct cherubs, who are used as the models for Adam and Eve. Although he takes a few false steps and is hindered a bit by the mischievous cherubs, God is finally able to finish his task and retire—with the cherubs in tow—to a chaise lounge on a beach for a well-earned rest. Crouch concludes, "The van der Meers here do for God what Raymond Briggs did for Father Christmas, they give him a human personality and show him subject to some of the weaknesses that plague mankind." *Booklist* reviewer Barbara Elleman notes that while various groups of adults may object to some of the story's elements, "youngsters will relate to the childlike approach that is infused throughout this sly, gentle spoof." In another *Booklist* review, Elleman adds, "Some of the results [of God's attempts to create] are hilarious, and all are joyfully pictured." Writing in *School Library Journal,*

From *Funny Shoes,* written and illustrated by Ron and Atie van der Meer.

Mary I. Purucker says, "The crisp pen-and-ink illustrations filled in with clear, bright colors illuminate this folk-like interpretation of Genesis with innocence and humor."

One of van der Meer's earliest solo successes is *Monster Island,* a pop-up book about two vacationing children who arrive on an island by balloon and blissfully miss the outrageous creatures and volcanoes that appear around them. Older children will appreciate "the irony," writes a reviewer in *School Library Journal,* while younger children will appreciate "the colors, motion and monsters." Although *School Librarian* contributor Margaret Meek says that *Monster Island* is "another book for adults to buy as a toy," a reviewer in *Junior Bookshelf* notes, "What rivets attention are the garish colours and the ingenious pop-up devices."

Sailing Ships Pop-Up Book is a concept book that van der Meer co-authored with Dr. Alan P. McGowan, head of the department of ships at the National Maritime Museum in Greenwich, England. Tracing the development of vessels over the last five thousand years, this work includes thread for young readers to rig the sails of the ships depicted. The companion volume, which van der Meer wrote without a collaborator, is *Majesty in Flight: Nature's Birds of Prey in Three Dimensions.* Writing of both works in the *New York Times Book Review,* Carol Brightman says, "The soaring falcon in Ron van der Meer's *Majesty in Flight* [and] the galleon in his and Alan McGowan's *Sailing Ships ...* are triumphs of graphic engineering."

With *Your Amazing Senses: 36 Games, Puzzles, and Tricks That Show How Your Senses Work,* Ron and Atie van der Meer provide young readers with, in the words of a critic in *Kirkus Reviews,* an "entertaining introduction to the five senses, with intriguing hands-on activities." The authors highlight four to eight activities on each page which explain such subjects as sight-singing and learning the Braille alphabet. *School Library Journal* contributor Alice R. Arnett adds, "The text is basically accurate, and the illustrations are colorful and well coordinated with the text." Another of the van der Meers' pop-up books to be published in the late 1980s is *Kittens*, which depicts the young animals at play; a reviewer in *Junior Bookshelf* queries, "Is it a book? Is it a toy? Whatever you decide you cannot fail to be enchanted by the ingenious paper engineering of its four prettily designed spreads." With *Pigs at Home*, the van der Meers invite youngsters to match labels to items in what *Growing Point* reviewer Margery Fisher calls a "jauntily idiosyncratic human/porcine home," while a critic in *Publishers Weekly* adds, "Bold shapes, plenty of details and the easygoing porkers ... make this visit worth a repeat."

The van der Meers began the 1990s with *Amazing Animal Senses*, a concept book that uses moveable parts to explore a variety of animal survival techniques. Writing in *School Library Journal*, Eva Elisabeth Von Ancken predicted, "As an introduction to nature study or as a supplement to more serious works, it will find a place in the library and classroom." Soon after the publication of this volume, van der Meer produced one of the most acclaimed of his works with *The Art Pack: A Unique, Three-Dimensional Tour through the Creation of Art through the Centuries—What Artists Do, How They Do It, and the Masterpieces They Have Given Us.* Working with Christopher Frayling, an instructor at the Royal College of Art, and Frayling's wife Helen, a painter, van der Meer invites his readers to literally reach into great works of art and to use a variety of devices—including a taped audio tour of twenty famous paintings and a removable pocket dictionary of art terms—to learn about their history, their composition, and their creators. *New York Times Book Review* contributor D. J. R. Bruckner claims that van der Meer "has outdone himself" and that *The Art Pack* "does what few books on art have done: it makes art tremendously exciting, challenging, fascinating, and familiar.... This book is a spoiler; it makes film or television shows on art look flat, and it will make readers want to reach out in galleries and museums." Bruckner concludes, "Is 'The Art Pack' a toy? Surely, and a most intelligent one. Mr. van der Meer and the authors wisely assume the child survives in us.... Their story makes curiosity explode and the test of their book is that it tempts the reader into all kinds of experiments not even hinted at in its pages; it makes the constructed world look different."

The Art Pack sold approximately 150,000 copies over a two-year period; its success prompted several other "Pack" books, such as *The Music Pack: A Unique Three-Dimensional Tour through the Creation of Music Over the Centuries: What Musicians Do, How They Do It, and the Masterpieces They Have Given Us* and *The Earth Pack: Tornadoes, Earthquakes, Volcanoes: Nature's Forces in Three Dimensions*. In *The Music Pack*, a collaboration with composer/broadcaster Christopher Berkeley, van der Meer creates pop-up musical instru-

ments and orchestra layouts as well as scales and time signatures; the book also includes information on the composers plus a compact disc containing twenty compositions by Bach, Debussy, Handel, Mozart, Verdi, Wagner, and other artists. A reviewer in *Publishers Weekly* acknowledges that "a great deal of ingenuity has gone into creating [the pop-ups]" and that *The Music Pack* has "plenty of novelty value." In *The Earth Pack*, a collaboration with Ron Fisher, van der Meer uses interactive devices to demonstrate earthquakes, hurricanes, blizzards, and other natural events; a booklet of terms and an audiotape are included. Published by the National Geographic Society, *The Earth Pack* is described by *Booklist* reviewer Ilene Cooper as "more expensive than many interactive books but longer and more substantial as well."

Van der Meer has also received special notice for *Math Kit: A Three-Dimensional Tour through Mathematics*, a concept/pop-up book on which he collaborated with English mathematics instructor Bob Gardner. A critic in *Kirkus Reviews* calls *Math Kit*, which explains mathematical processes ranging from subtraction to calculus as well as mathematical accomplishments like the Great Pyramids of Egypt, "a magnificently produced volume—more like a game book than an instructional manual—that might amuse even the most die-hard math hater."

■ Works Cited

Arnett, Alice R., review of *Your Amazing Senses, School Library Journal*, February, 1988, pp. 70-71.

Brightman, Carol, "Toy Books in the Age of Packaging," *New York Times Book Review*, November 11, 1984, pp. 50-51.

Bruckner, D. J. R., "A Hands-On History of Art," *New York Times Book Review*, September 6, 1992, p. 27.

Cooper, Ilene, review of *The Earth Pack, Booklist*, February 1, 1996, p. 942.

Crouch, Marcus, review of *Oh Lord!, Junior Bookshelf*, February, 1980, p. 19.

DeVinney, Gemma, review of *My Brother Sammy* and others, *School Library Journal*, August, 1980, p. 58.

Elleman, Barbara, review of *Oh Lord!, Booklist*, February 1, 1980, p. 772.

Elleman, Barbara, review of *Oh Lord!, Booklist*, February 15, 1985, p. 853.

Review of *The Fantastic Fairy Tale Pop-Up Book, Publishers Weekly*, July 19, 1993, p. 253.

Fisher, Margery, review of *My Brother Sammy* and *Sammy and Mara, Growing Point*, May, 1979, p. 3529.

Fisher, Margery, review of *Pigs at Home, Growing Point*, January, 1989, p. 5102.

Review of *Kittens, Junior Bookshelf*, December, 1988, p. 296.

Review of *The Math Kit, Kirkus Reviews*, November 1, 1994, p. 1473.

Meek, Margaret, review of *Monster Island, School Librarian*, December, 1981, pp. 319-20.

Review of *Monster Island, Junior Bookshelf*, June, 1982, p. 95.

Review of *Monster Island, School Library Journal,* October, 1983, p. 125.

Review of *The Music Pack, Publishers Weekly,* September 19, 1994, p. 58.

Review of *My Brother Sammy, Junior Bookshelf,* June, 1979, p. 155.

Review of *Pigs at Home, Publishers Weekly,* October 14, 1988, p. 71.

Purucker, Mary I., review of *Oh Lord!, School Library Journal,* March, 1980, p. 125.

Review of *Your Amazing Senses, Kirkus Reviews,* November 15, 1987, p. 1634.

Review of *Your Amazing Senses, Publishers Weekly,* December 11, 1986, p. 67.

Von Ancken, Eva Elisabeth, review of *Amazing Animal Senses, School Library Journal,* March, 1991, p. 209.

■ For More Information See

PERIODICALS

Children's Book Watch, March, 1995, p. 1.

Growing Point, January, 1984, p. 4198; September, 1986, p. 4684; November, 1986, p. 4710.

New York Times Book Review, March 23, 1980, p. 34; November 11, 1984, p. 50.

Publishers Weekly, December 11, 1987, p. 67; August 31, 1990, p. 63; August 24, 1992, p. 78; May 2, 1994, p. 308.

Times Educational Supplement, November 11, 1994, p. 19.

Washington Post Book World, December 13, 1987, p. 9.*

—Sketch by Gerard J. Senick

W

WALLNER, Alexandra 1946-

■ Personal

Born February 28, 1946, in Germany; came to the United States in 1952, naturalized citizen, 1964; daughter of Severin (a physician) and Hildegard (an artist; maiden name, Waltch) Czesnykowski; married John C. Wallner (an illustrator), July 16, 1971. *Education:* Pratt Institute, B.F.A., 1968, M.F.A., 1970. *Hobbies and other interests:* Gardening, making pressed flower collages.

ALEXANDRA WALLNER

■ Addresses

Home—2227 Mt. Vernon St., Philadelphia, PA 19130. *Agent*—Kirchoff/Wohlberg, Inc., 866 United Nations Plaza, New York, NY 10017. *Office*—Greywood Studio.

■ Career

American Home, New York City, assistant art director, 1972-73; *New Ingenue,* New York City, associate art director, 1973-75; freelance illustrator and writer, 1975—. Illustrator for Kevin Corbett Designs, 1984, Portal Publications, 1985, and Argus Communications, 1986; co-owner of Greywood Studio. Educator and lecturer at writing conferences.

■ Writings

The Adventures of Strawberry Shortcake and Her Friends, illustrated by Mercedes Llimona, Random House, 1980.
Strawberry Shortcake and the Winter that Would Not End, illustrated by Mercedes Llimona, Random House, 1982.

SELF-ILLUSTRATED

Munch: Poems and Pictures, Crown, 1976.
Ghoulish Giggles and Monster Riddles, Whitman, 1982.
Twelve Days of Christmas, Warner, 1989.
Jingle Bells, Warner, 1989.
Silent Night, Warner, 1989.
Deck the Halls, Warner, 1989.
Since 1920, Doubleday, 1992.
Betsy Ross, Holiday House, 1994.
Beatrix Potter, Holiday House, 1995.
The First Air Voyage in the United States: The Story of Jean-Pierre Blanchard, Holiday House, 1996.
An Alcott Family Christmas, Holiday House, 1996.
Laura Ingalls Wilder, Holiday House, 1997.
The Farmer in the Dell, Holiday House, 1998.

ILLUSTRATED WITH HUSBAND, JOHN WALLNER

Kerby on Safari, Avon, 1984.

Bonnie Larkin Nims, *Where Is the Bear?,* Whitman, 1988.

David A. Adler, *A Picture Book of Abraham Lincoln,* Holiday House, 1989.

David A. Adler, *A Picture Book of George Washington,* Holiday House, 1989.

David A. Adler, *A Picture Book of Benjamin Franklin,* Holiday House, 1990.

David A. Adler, *A Picture Book of Thomas Jefferson,* Holiday House, 1990.

David A. Adler, *A Picture Book of Helen Keller,* Holiday House, 1990.

David A. Adler, *A Picture Book of Christopher Columbus,* Holiday House, 1991.

David A. Adler, *A Picture Book of Florence Nightingale,* Holiday House, 1992.

David A. Adler, *A Picture Book of Robert E. Lee,* Holiday House, 1994.

David A. Adler, *A Picture Book of Davy Crockett,* Holiday House, 1995.

David A. Adler, *A Picture Book of Patrick Henry,* Holiday House, 1995.

David A. Adler, *A Picture Book of Paul Revere,* Holiday House, 1995.

David A. Adler, *A Picture Book of Thomas Alva Edison,* Holiday House, 1996.

David A. Adler, *A Picture Book of Patrick Henry,* Holiday House, 1996.

David A. Adler, *A Picture Book of Louis Braille,* Holiday House, 1997.

ILLUSTRATOR

Martha Gamerman, *Trudy's Straw Hat,* Crown, 1977.

Malcolm Hall, *The Friends of Charlie Ant Bear,* Coward, McCann & Geoghegan, 1980.

Joanne E. Bernstein and Paul Cohen, *Un-Frog-Gettable Riddles,* Whitman, 1981.

Jean Bethell and Susan Axtell, *A Colonial Williamsburg Activities Book: Fun Things to Do for Children 4 & Up,* Colonial Williamsburg Foundation, 1984.

Marcia Leonard, *King Lionheart's Castle,* Silver Press, 1992.

Teddy Slater, *Alice Meets the Aliens,* Silver Press, 1992.

Gary Hines, *The Christmas Tree in the White House,* Henry Holt, 1998.

Also illustrator of children's textbooks; author and illustrator of stories for children's magazines.

■ Work in Progress

A book on Abigail Adams.

■ Sidelights

Alexandra Wallner told *SATA:* "I have always enjoyed writing and drawing. I had a lonely childhood, with no brothers or sisters, and always living where there were no children my age. To entertain myself I made up stories and fantasies and wrote short books and comic strips."

At the age of six, Wallner emigrated from her native Germany to the U.S. with her parents. "I spoke no English until the first grade and learned [my new language] by reading comic books: *Donald Duck, Uncle Scrooge, Little Lulu, Katy Keene, Archie*—not a bad way for a person to learn a language; pictures and words right there together. I loved the bright colors and clever stories.

"My mother was an artist, greatly influenced by the 'Trash Can School' of art. She painted town scenes, bar scenes, and portraits and also wrote humorous stories. I was greatly influenced by her, and, I suppose, subconsciously I was imitating her.

"After high school I studied art at Pratt Institute and received my BFA and MFA degrees. I started my career at *American Home* because I wanted to start somewhere in commercial art. It was in my position with *New Ingenue* that I really learned typography, layout, illustration, and graphic design. When my husband, who is also an illustrator, started his studio, he was having so much fun with illustration, that I decided I would do it too. I'm glad I made this decision.

"Since 1990, I've been writing and illustrating my own stories. I'm very interested in history. I like to write biographies of interesting famous people, particularly women, who did not have easy lives but overcame difficulties gracefully, women like Betsy Ross, Beatrix Potter, Laura Ingalls Wilder, and Louisa May Alcott. In the midst of a difficult life the last three women turned to writing to express themselves. I feel a close kinship with them.

"Since 1995, I've been teaching writing and illustrating for children's picture books at the International Women's Writing Guild summer conference. Its important to me to share my knowledge with other women. I encourage them to write brief stories. At the end of one week, they have made a small book. Their sense of accomplishment is tremendous. I am also involved in the IWWG's Mentor Program which helps high school girls complete a writing project by the end of a school term. I encourage people to express their creativity with art and writing, because that is what I do. It helps me understand the world."

In Wallner's self-illustrated work *Betsy Ross,* she reveals to the reader that Ross may not have been the seamstress who made the first American flag. She also describes Ross's Quaker life, multiple marriages, and upholstery business. According to Deborah Stevenson in *Bulletin of the Center for Children's Books,* the author moves Ross "from a cameo role to a starring part ... using her to explain early American urban life." Wallner takes "pride in detail," noted *Five Owls* reviewer Mary Bahr Fritts. Describing Wallner's illustrations, Carolyn Phelan, a critic in *Booklist,* stated that "bright color and many details ... tell the story and recreate" that time period in American history.

Regarding *Beatrix Potter,* a reviewer for the *New Jersey Education Association* noted that Wallner makes the life story of the British author "accessible to readers" with "simple text and appealing illustrations." Potter grew up in a very restrictive household and spent most of her time in solitude, writing and drawing. Potter filled notebooks with sketches of plants and animals. She became not only a well-known children's author but later a prominent British conservationist. Wallner's illustrations "express her [Potter's] many periods of loneliness," stated a reviewer in *School Library Journal.* A critic in the *New Advocate* remarked that Wallner's "exquisite illustrations provide detailed glimpses into late nineteenth-century English life."

Noted author Laura Ingalls Wilder, who wrote about growing up in pioneer country in such works as *Little House on the Prairie,* was the subject of another of Wallner's biographies for children. Wilder's father dreamed of making a living off the land, and so the family traveled west until they came to the prairie, where they made their home. Some of the events and places along the way became material for Wilder's later writings. Pamela K. Bomboy, a reviewer in *School Library Journal,* stated that *Laura Ingalls Wilder* is an "accurate, concise beginning biography" with "folk-art" illustrations that range from a rendering of "patterned fabrics of pioneer clothing to a panoramic view of a sea of prairie grass." Marilyn Bousquin, a critic in *Horn Book,* described the book as a "seamless interdependence" of word and picture that "captures both the hard realities of pioneer life and the hearthlike warmth of Laura's family life."

■ Works Cited

Review of *Beatrix Potter, New Advocate,* Spring, 1996, p. 163.
Review of *Beatrix Potter, New Jersey Education Association Review,* March, 1996.
Review of *Beatrix Potter, School Library Journal,* December, 1996, p. 45.
Bomboy, Pamela K., review of *Laura Ingalls Wilder, School Library Journal,* November, 1997.
Bousquin, Marilyn, review of *Laura Ingalls Wilder, Horn Book,* November/December, 1997, p. 647.
Fritts, Mary Bahr, review of *Betsy Ross, Five Owls,* March, 1994, p. 87.
Phelan, Carolyn, review of *Betsy Ross, Booklist,* February 15, 1994, p. 1086.
Stevenson, Deborah, review of *Betsy Ross, Bulletin of the Center for Children's Books,* March, 1994, p. 237.

■ For More Information See

PERIODICALS

Booklist, February 15, 1994, p. 1086; September 1, 1996, p. 138.
Bulletin of the Center for Children's Books, January, 1998, p. 181.
Kirkus Reviews, September 1, 1992, p. 1136.
Publishers Weekly, September 30, 1996, p. 91.

School Library Journal, May, 1991, p. 87.

* * *

WANGERIN, Walter, Jr. 1944-

■ Personal

Born February 13, 1944, in Portland, OR; son of Walter M. (an educator) and Virginia (Stork) Wangerin; married Ruthanne Bohlmann, August 24, 1968; children: Joseph Andrew, Matthew Aaron, Mary Elisabeth, Talitha Michal. *Education:* Concordia Senior College (now Concordia Theological Seminary), B.A., 1966; Miami University, Oxford, Ohio, M.A., 1968; Christ Seminary, Seminex, M.Div., 1976. *Religion:* Lutheran.

■ Addresses

Home—Box 1218, Valparaiso, IN. *Office*—Huegli Hall, Valparaiso University, Valparaiso, IN 46383.

■ Career

Worked variously as a migrant pea-picker, lifeguard, and inner city youth worker; KFUO-Radio, St. Louis, MO, producer and announcer, 1969-70; University of Evansville, Evansville, IN, instructor in English literature, 1970-74; pastor of churches in Evansville, 1974-85; ordained Lutheran minister, 1976; Valparaiso University, Valparaiso, IN, Jochum Professor in English and Theology, 1991—.

■ Awards, Honors

Best Children's Book of the Year designation, *New York Times,* 1978, National Religious Book Award for children/youth, 1980, and American Book Award for science-fiction paperback, 1981, all for *The Book of the*

WALTER WANGERIN, JR.

Dun Cow; *Thistle* was chosen as a *School Library Journal* Best Book of 1983; Gold Medallion Book Award, 1985, for *Ragman and Other Cries of Faith;* Gold Medallion Book Award, Evangelical Christian Publishers Association, 1986, for *Potter, Come Fly to the First of the Earth;* Best Fiction designation, Association of Logos Bookstores, 1986, for *The Book of Sorrows;* Book of the Year, *Virtue,* 1987, for *As For Me and My House: Crafting Your Marriage to Last;* Gold Medallion Book Award, 1988; Gold Medallion Book Award, 1993, *Reliving the Passion: Meditations on the Suffering, Death, and Resurrection of Jesus as Recorded in Mark;* Gold Medallion Book Award, 1996, for *The Book of Genesis: A Selection from the Best-Selling Book of God.*

■ Writings

FOR CHILDREN

The Glory Story, Concordia (St. Louis, MO), 1974.

God, I've Gotta Talk to You, Concordia, 1974.

(With A. Jennings) *A Penny Is Everything,* Concordia, 1974.

The Baby God Promised, Concordia, 1976.

The Bible: Its Story for Children, Rand McNally (Chicago), 1981, as *The Bible: The Book of God for Children,* Zondervan (Grand Rapids, MI), 1997.

O Happy Day!, Concordia, 1981.

Thistle, illustrated by Marcia Sewall, Harper (New York City), 1983, illustrated by Bryna Waldman, Augsburg (Minneapolis), 1995.

My First Book about Jesus, illustrated by Jim Cummins, Rand McNally, 1983.

Potter, Come Fly to the First of the Earth, illustrated by Daniel San Souci, Chariot Books (Elgin, IL), 1985.

Elisabeth and the Water-Troll, Harper, 1986.

In the Beginning There Was No Sky: A Story of Creation, illustrated by Lee Steadman, T. Nelson (Nashville), 1986.

Branta and the Golden Stone, illustrated by Deborah Healey, Simon & Schuster (New York City), 1993.

The Crying for a Vision, Simon & Schuster, 1994.

Probity Jones and the Fear Not Angel, illustrated by Tim Ladwig, Augsburg Fortress, 1997.

The Bedtime Rhyme, Augsburg Fortress, 1998.

FOR ADULTS

The Book of the Dun Cow, Harper, 1978.

Ragman and Other Cries of Faith (essays), Harper, 1984.

The Book of Sorrows (sequel to *The Book of the Dun Cow*), Harper, 1985.

The Orphean Passages: The Drama of Faith, Harper, 1986.

A Miniature Cathedral: Poetical Exercises Presented in Three Cycles (verse), Harper, 1986.

As for Me and My House: Crafting Your Marriage to Last, T. Nelson, 1987.

Miz Lil and the Chronicles of Grace, Harper (San Francisco), 1988.

The Manger Is Empty: Stories in Time, Harper, 1989.

Mourning into Dancing, Zondervan, 1992.

Reliving the Passion: Meditations on the Suffering, Death, and Resurrection of Jesus as Recorded in Mark, Zondervan, 1992.

Measuring the Days: Daily Reflections with Walter Wangerin, HarperSanFrancisco, 1993.

Little Lamb, Who Made Thee? A Book about Children and Parents, Zondervan, 1993.

The Book of God: The Bible as a Novel, Zondervan, 1996.

Whole Prayer: Speaking and Listening to God, Zondervan, 1997.

God's Story Is My Story: Essays on Hearing and Telling the Word, Augsburg Fortress, 1997.

The Book of Genesis: A Selection from the Best-Selling Book of God, Zondervan, 1997.

Contributor of essays to periodicals, including *Christianity Today* and *Leadership.*

■ Sidelights

Acclaimed storyteller and theologian Walter Wangerin, Jr. completed his first novel when he was in middle school. He has since written poetry, short stories, science fiction, essays, and children's literature. His most notable work is the 1978 novel *The Book of the Dun Cow.* Called a "master storyteller" by *Twentieth-Century Young Adult Writers* contributor Tracy J. Sukraw, Wangerin excels at what Sukraw described as "books in which he resurrects the fable and fairy tale ... and fills them with rich, multi-level stories that are unique for their modern resonance and elusive use of symbols and religious parallels."

Born in Portland, Oregon, in 1944, Wangerin obtained his B.A. from Concordia Senior College. In college, Wangerin did not follow the traditional course of proceeding straight from Concordia to the seminary. Instead, he went on to earn a master's degree from Miami University in Oxford, Ohio, studying literature "with the idea ... that this was where I could learn writing better." During those studies he became interested in Medieval English literature and studied a variety of languages, including Greek, Latin, Anglo-Saxon, and German. After graduation, still unsure of his career path, Wangerin worked at a variety of jobs—as a migrant pea-picker, a lifeguard, a youth worker in the inner city, and even as a radio announcer and producer—before deciding to pursue a religious vocation.

Despite the fact that writing has never been his predominate career, Wangerin once told *SATA* that ambitions to be a writer influenced much of his childhood and early adulthood. "[People have] tendencies to do certain things, and either those tendencies wear themselves out, or they never have any approval or any success, or they naturally pass away. I always had a tendency to read, and it was very, very natural also to write. I always had the tendency to tell stories.... I can point to different times along the way where someone's encouragement shaped [that] tendency.... I remember a teacher in high school, in a creative writing course. We had written short stories and mine was one that he particularly singled out, and the phrase that he used was, 'Wangerin can write the eyes out of a turkey at fifty paces.' For him, that was just a tossed-off comment, but it was also a sensitive one that established in my mind that there was goodness in my work. I wasn't seeking praise, and I don't think I made a big thing out of it at the time. It was just one of those tiny little tacks that I think turned tendency into an art, an activity."

There would be times, even when Wangerin was engaged in a fulfilling occupation, that he "rather pined not be able to give full attention to writing," as he explained to *SATA*. However, when he accepted a position as full-time pastor of a Lutheran congregation in Illinois, a parish in the inner city, he "made a commitment both before these people and before my wife, and definitely before the Lord, that I would stay here for a good long time." Because his duties as pastor of a church allowed him some flexibility, Wangerin used his mornings to work on the manuscript for his first full-length novel, *The Book of the Dun Cow.*

The Book of the Dun Cow became quite popular—indeed, almost a cult favorite—with both children and adults alike, and was named a best children's book by the *New York Times*. The story, a fantasy involving animal characters, deals with the ageless struggle between good and evil, a characteristic theme throughout much of Wangerin's fiction. In the book, varying species of animals isolate and represent specific human characteristics: the proud rooster Chauntecleer, the faithful dog Mundo Cani, and the hideous snake Wyrm, who lies in the dark, damp earth. All animals possess the power of speech. They exist in an ancient world, a world where "the earth was still fixed in the absolute center of the universe.... And the sun still traveled around the moored earth, so that days and nights belonged to the earth and to the creatures thereon, not to a ball of silent fire." Through one of Wyrm's henchmen, a rooster-toad hybrid named Cockatrice, evil rises to the surface of the earth and threatens the peaceful farmyard. Only through the loss of many animal's lives in battle, the maternal Dun Cow's gift of her horn as a potent weapon against evil, and the ultimate self-sacrifice of Mundo Cani can good retain sway, causing Chauntecleer to question the cost of its victory: "it is entirely possible even to kill the enemy, and still to be defeated by the battle," the rooster realizes.

The Book of the Dun Cow proved popular with reviewers: some described the work as a classic romance, and others praised it as a work of fantasy on par with J. R. R. Tolkien's *Lord of the Rings*. "Wangerin provides some riveting images," noted Laura Geringer in her *School Library Journal* summation of the work: "rhythmic—at times, hypnotic, at times amusing—dialogue among the creatures of field and barnyard; and, most compelling of all, a poignant love story." A *Junior Bookshelf* critic took a slightly different approach, calling *The Book of the Dun Cow* "a long book, a difficult book at times, in places even a dull book ... but beyond any question a very good book and perhaps a great one." And a contributor for the *Bulletin of the Center for Children's*

Books summed up Wangerin's work by saying, "In its length, its complexity, its creation of a whole and vivid animal world, this is superb.... [Its] style: witty, sophisticated, and polished, with dialogue that is as dramatic as it is entertaining."

Despite its categorization as such by critics, Wangerin did not intend *The Book of the Dun Cow* as an allegory. "What I understand allegory to be is not what this book is," Wangerin once explained. "I'm not sure how clearly people use that term always, or how reviewers use that term. Maybe they're right in their definitions. But I understand an allegory to be a kind of code language, or even a codal use of character and event so that a character in a story equals some concept, some idea, or some character outside the story, and every quality neatly fits into the qualities of this thing outside. So you need an interpretive key to understand what's going on, and especially to understand it on a deeper level.... I think sometimes people mean by [calling a piece of writing an] allegory that meaning can be found in it. I'll accept that.... But even so, I would not say as an author that I first conceived meaning, then conceived a way to present it, then turned the meaning into a story and hoped that people would get the meaning. In fact, it's much simpler than that—I just wrote the story."

The overwhelmingly positive critical reception Wangerin received after publishing *The Book of the Dun Cow*

Probity, a present-day African American girl, attends the events of the first Christmas through the intervention of an angel. (From *Probity Jones and the Fear Not Angel*, written by Wangerin and illustrated by Tim Ladwig.)

would affect his attitude toward his next book. "When I suddenly [saw] how other people [had] expectations and how they read *The Book of the Dun Cow,* unconsciously the freedom I [had] to move left or right [became] restricted. Some good things come from [critical] response, and it always gives me pleasure when people are pleased, but I do have to be careful to keep [each new book] on its own track and not be swayed by other people's expectations or their ... interpretations, which may not have been what I had in mind."

The sequel to *The Book of the Dun Cow,* titled *The Book of Sorrows,* continues the story of Chauntecleer the Rooster as he attempts to regain his emotional balance after proving victorious in the devastating war against the forces of Wyrm. Saddened by the death of his friend Mundo Cani and believing that the dog's sacrifice should have been his to make, Chauntecleer goes in search of the evil Wyrm to destroy him, only to discover that the redemption he sought by such efforts has been thwarted by Wyrm's prior death. While Catherine Chauvette would note in *School Library Journal* that, compared to its successor, *The Book of Sorrows* is "its sequel," but "not its equal," *Booklist* contributor Stephanie Zvirin contended that Wangerin's second novel "has much to recommend it: the vivid confrontations between good and evil take on an almost visual dimension."

Since the success of *The Book of the Dun Cow* and its sequel, Wangerin has written several more books, including theological books for adults, several collections of essays, and a number of children's books. In *Potter, Come Fly to the First of the Earth,* a boy named Potter, saddened and sickened by the death of his best friend, takes out his rage on a bird pecking near his window. Realizing he has injured the bird, he attempts to help it; the bird, a magical creature, gives Potter the ability to leave his body in the form of a dove and fly over the Earth. A witness to the death and rebirth of the mythic phoenix, Potter returns to his human form with a greater appreciation for life, death, and love. *Elisabeth and the Water-Troll* finds a young girl also suffering from the death of a loved one—this time her mother. A water troll who lives in a nearby well hears her tears fall, takes pity on Elisabeth, and brings her to his dwelling in an attempt to console her. Her neighbors, fearing and misunderstanding the monstrous-looking troll and believing the girl to have been kidnapped, attack it. The troll dies willingly, knowing that he has shown the young girl the ultimate power of love.

In *The Crying for a Vision,* Wangerin roots his tale in Lakota myth. Orphaned Waskn Mani is different than the other boys in his tribe, having no interest for the hunt. Instead, his search for his mother leads him to confrontations with a fierce warrior named Fire Thunder, who caused his mother's disappearance after she accepted the advances of Waskn's father—a star creature—over those of Fire Thunder. Realizing that his mother had joined those magical beings able to change form, Waskn recognizes that his is also a special destiny; he ultimately sacrifices himself in an effort to restore the

peace among his people that Fire Thunder's hostility threatens. Calling *The Crying for a Vision* "possibly the best book written for young adults in years," a *Kirkus Reviews* critic described the cadence in Wangerin's work as "simultaneously familiar and foreign, like another language we have only just discovered we understand." Lisa Dennis noted in her *School Library Journal* review that while the work contains "challenging structure," an advanced vocabulary, and a deeply spiritual focus, "Those able to appreciate this masterfully told tale will be richly rewarded."

Wangerin offered the following for "those who (wisely) labor to possess writing skills: First the skill, then the significance. You can have dazzling skill without significance; but what a waste! Beauty that moves us without purpose is ultimately dangerous to us; we will give it our own purpose, and we will not be so careful as the artist might have been; we will allow evil designs to creep in, greed, racism, the division of the peoples (for example, Hitler's vile use of Wagner); we may go so far as to kill others in body and spirit by your beauty, dear artist. For God's sake, don't present us with works both sweet and hollow at the soul of them. On the other hand, significance presented without skill (the sweaty labor of a right and proper craft!) will either expand into bombasts or diminish into petty squabble. Without skill, there will seem to be no significance at all; and that, too, is a dreary waste."

■ Works Cited

Review of *The Book of the Dun Cow, Bulletin of the Center for Children's Books,* January, 1979, p. 92.

Review of *The Book of the Dun Cow, Junior Bookshelf,* October, 1980, p. 260.

Chauvette, Catherine, review of *The Book of Sorrows, School Library Journal,* August, 1985, p. 88.

Review of *The Crying for a Vision, Kirkus Reviews,* November 15, 1994, p. 1546.

Dennis, Lisa, review of *The Crying for a Vision, School Library Journal,* January, 1995, p. 138.

Geringer, Laura, review of *The Book of the Dun Cow, School Library Journal,* October, 1978, p. 160.

Sukraw, Tracy J., essay in *Twentieth-Century Young Adult Writers,* St. James Press, 1994.

Wangerin, Walter, *The Book of the Dun Cow,* Harper, 1978.

Zvirin, Stephanie, review of *The Book of Sorrows, Booklist,* June 15, 1985, p. 1418.

■ For More Information See

PERIODICALS

Booklist, February 15, 1986, p. 874; November 1, 1993, p. 524; December 15, 1994, p. 747.

Bulletin of the Center for Children's Books, December, 1983, p. 80; January, 1995, p. 179.

Detroit News, January 20, 1980.

Kirkus Reviews, May 1, 1985, p. 397; March 1, 1991, p. 325.

New York Times Book Review, December 10, 1978.

Publishers Weekly, June 17, 1983, p. 73; March 21, 1986, p. 64; September 12, 1986, p. 36; February 15, 1991, p. 90; September 6, 1993, p. 96; September 30, 1996, p. 92; November 4, 1996, p. 47.
School Library Journal, November, 1983, p. 84; April, 1986, p. 93; May, 1987, p. 94; May, 1991, p. 96; October, 1993, p. 134.
Washington Post Book World, December 4, 1978.

*   *   *

WARBURG, Sandol Stoddard
See STODDARD, Sandol

*   *   *

WARREN, Andrea 1946-

■ Personal

Born October 30, 1946, in Norfolk, NE; daughter of James V. (a public school administrator) and Ruth (an executive director of a charitable organization; maiden name, Wilson) Warren; married Jay Wiedenkeller, November 22, 1981; children: Alison, Brendon (deceased), Kymberly, Derek. *Education:* University of Nebraska, B.S., 1968, M.A. (English), 1971; University of Kansas, M.S. (journalism), 1983. *Hobbies and other interests:* Reading, Tai Chi, quilting, travel, theater.

■ Addresses

Home and office—4908 West 71st St., Shawnee Mission, KS 66208-2309. *Agent*—Regina Ryan, 251 Central Park West, New York, NY 10024. *Electronic mail*—AWKansas@aol.com.

■ Career

High school English teacher in Hastings, NE, 1969-79; University of Kansas, Lawrence, writer and editor, 1979-81; Golf Course Superintendents Association of America, Lawrence, editor of national magazine, 1981; freelance writer, 1982—. *Member:* American Society of Journalists and Authors, Writers Place of Kansas City, Orphan Train Heritage Society of America.

■ Awards, Honors

Boston Globe-Horn Book Award, nonfiction category, 1996, American Library Association Notable Book citation, Notable Children's Trade Book in the Field of Social Studies, National Council for Social Studies/ Children's Book Council, Book of Distinction, *Hungry Mind Review,* best book in social studies for grades kindergarten through six, Society of School Librarians International, Best Children's Nonfiction, Society of Midland Authors, 1997, Literature Choice, 1997, all for *Orphan Train Rider: One Boy's True Story.*

ANDREA WARREN

■ Writings

JUVENILE

Coming on Strong, Scholastic, Inc. (New York City), 1986.
Searching for Love, Bantam (New York City), 1987.
Orphan Train Rider: One Boy's True Story, Houghton (Boston, MA), 1996.
Pioneer Girl: Growing Up on the Prairie, Morrow (New York City), 1998.

FOR ADULTS

Recovering from Breast Cancer, HarperCollins (New York City), 1991.
(With husband Jay Wiedenkeller) *Everybody's Doing It: How to Survive Your Teenagers' Sex Life (and Help Them Survive It, Too),* Penguin (New York City), 1993.

Contributor of more than a hundred articles to magazines and newspapers, including *Ladies' Home Journal, American Health, Reader's Digest, American Education, Good Housekeeping,* and *The World & I.*

■ Work in Progress

Research on the airlift of orphans from Saigon in April 1975.

■ Sidelights

Andrea Warren told *SATA:* "I have had a varied career, though all of it has in some way connected me to words and the joy of writing, or teaching writing. Under different circumstances, I would have first become a working journalist. Instead, it was a foregone conclusion that I would become a teacher, and no surprise that I selected English as my field, since reading and writing were always my great passions.

"My other teaching assignments included world history, debate, and creative writing. I moved to Lawrence, Kansas, in the summer of 1979, and for the next two years worked as an editor on a women's equity grant studying women in school administration. Shortly before I completed my master's degree in magazine journalism, I was hired to edit a golf magazine. I then worked briefly as a newspaper reporter while starting my freelance writing career, which took off in 1983. I also taught writing and communication workshops and a magazine writing seminar.

"My first two books were young adult novels. The next two were adult trade books. I then moved to history for young readers when I wrote *Orphan Train Rider* and *Pioneer Girl*. At least for the foreseeable future, I will continue to write for young readers, loosely defined as grades five through ten. Those were the years in my life when I was an insatiable reader.

"I grew up in a tiny Nebraska town, and our public library was my refuge. I still remember books I read and re-read there. At the time it never occurred to me that someday I could write books. In fact, it took me several decades to confront my desire to write full time. I kept waiting for someone to tell me to do it—to give me permission. I finally had to give myself permission, and it was the hardest and the easiest thing I've ever done.

"*Orphan Train Rider* came readily as a subject. Ever since I first learned of them when I was a child, I had been interested in the orphan trains and the one hundred fifty thousand American children who rode the rails to new homes. *Pioneer Girl* grew out of my interest in sharing with my readers what it was really like to grow up on the prairie. The book tells the true story of a Nebraska pioneer who lived in a sod house and spent her childhood working hard to help her parents.

"My next book will be about the airlifting of three thousand orphans from Saigon in the final days of the Vietnam war. My adopted daughter, Alison, was one of those children. Like the last two, this book will be for younger readers. I hope it will also find a crossover audience with adults.

"My interests typically lie in the stories of ordinary people and how they work through the challenges of their own lives. I have a special interest in children caught up in tragic circumstances beyond their control, but I have also written many magazine stories about adults who find themselves in extraordinary difficulties, which they meet with grace, perseverance, and courage. When I come across this type of story, I find it irresistible.

"While I love fiction, I am happy at present writing nonfiction history. I might have majored in history and devoted my teaching career to it except for one major problem: I so often found it boring. Wars and treaties and successions of kings and presidents didn't interest me nearly so much as the people behind the facts. I loved historic literature, like *War and Peace,* which taught me the facts, but did so almost surreptitiously because I was so engrossed in the lives of the characters. I have tried to pattern my writing for children in the same way.

"I write every weekday. I keep regular office hours and, when I'm not on the phone or handling billings or some such thing, I am writing. I meet weekly with two other writers here in Kansas City who also make their living by freelancing magazine articles and books, and we critique each others' work and offer support for the vagaries and difficulties of the writer's life. Although my children are grown and away from home, I love working at home, and I have a sunny office that I always enjoy. I share my life with my husband, Jay, and feel fortunate to do so."

■ **For More Information See**

PERIODICALS

Booklist, July, 1996, p. 1826.
Horn Book, January-February, 1997, pp. 35-39.
Ladies' Home Journal, December, 1997, p. 80.
Library Journal, April 1, 1993, p. 118.
School Library Journal, August, 1996, p. 162.
Writer's Digest, July, 1988, p. 72.

*   *   *

WASHINGTON, Donna L. 1967-

■ **Personal**

Born October 6, 1967, in Colorado Springs, CO; daughter of Don Lowell (a career military officer) and

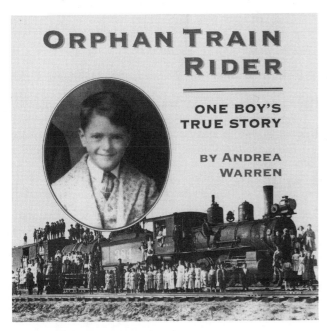

Warren writes alternate chapters about the history of the orphan trains, which carried homeless youngsters west to be adopted, and the true story of Lee Nailling, who rode the train to Texas in 1926.

Gwendolyn Yvonne (a professional cake decorator) Washington; married David William Klibanow (a social worker), December 31, 1995; children: Devin McKenzie. *Education:* Northwestern University, B.S. (speech), 1990. *Politics:* Democrat. *Religion:* Unitarian Universalist.

■ Addresses

Home and office—114 Windsor Dr., Wake Forest, NC 27587. *Electronic mail*—QBOT5@aol.com.

■ Career

Storyteller and actress. Sunday school teacher, 1995—. Member of board of directors for social service agency for people with developmental disabilities, 1994-96. *Member:* National Storyteller's Association (NSA), Illinois Humanities Scholar.

■ Writings

The Story of Kwanzaa (picture book), illustrated by Stephen Taylor, HarperCollins, 1996.
A Pride of African Tales, illustrated by James Ransome, HarperCollins, 1997.

■ Work in Progress

Are You Gonna Be Here When John Gets Here? for Hyperion Press; a young adult fantasy novel.

■ Sidelights

Donna L. Washington's first children's book introduces readers to Kwanzaa. *The Story of Kwanzaa* describes the seven-day festival of African and African-American pride and heritage, including a discussion of the holiday's origins and an explanation of various activities and the events or principles they symbolize. A *School Library Journal* reviewer maintained that Washington's work is "a useful addition in a still small group of books." A *Kirkus Reviews* critic called *The Story of Kwanzaa* "a fine primer on a holiday that is fast gaining recognition."

■ Works Cited

Review of *The Story of Kwanzaa, Kirkus Reviews,* September 15, 1996, p. 1409.
Review of *The Story of Kwanzaa, School Library Journal,* October, 1996, p. 42.

■ For More Information See

PERIODICALS

Booklist, September 1, 1996, p. 138.
Publishers Weekly, September 30, 1996, p. 88.*

WILLIAMS-ANDRIANI, Renee 1963-
(Renee Andriani)

■ Personal

Born September 6, 1963, in Avon, CT; daughter of Henry A. II and Josette (an editor; maiden name, Hubert) Williams; married Vince Andriani (an illustrator), October 17, 1992; children: Maggie. *Education:* Rhode Island School of Design, B.F.A.

■ Addresses

Home—2815 West 82nd St., Leawood, KS 66206. *Office*—Hallmark Cards, Inc., No. 200, Kansas City, MO 64141. *Agent*—Judy Sue Goodwyn-Sturges, 154 West Newton St., Boston, MA 02118.

■ Career

Hallmark Cards, Inc., Kansas City, MO, designer for Shoebox Greetings, 1985—. Freelance illustrator of children's books.

■ Illustrator

P. J. Petersen, *The Amazing Magic Show,* Simon & Schuster (New York City), 1994.
Stephen Krensky, *A Good Knight's Sleep,* Candlewick Press (Cambridge, MA), 1996.
Andris Zoltners, Prabhakant Sinha, and Stuart Murphy, *The Fat Firm: The Transformation of a Firm from Fat to Fit,* McGraw (New York City), 1997.
Rick Walton, *Really Really Bad School Jokes,* Candlewick Press, 1998.

UNDER NAME RENEE ANDRIANI

Still Married after All These Years, Hallmark Card, 1990.
Hennie M. Shore, *Angry Monster Workbook,* Center for Applied Psychology, 1995.
Hennie M. Shore and Lawrence Shapiro, *Anybody Can Bake a Cake,* Center for Applied Psychology, 1995.

■ Sidelights

Renee Williams-Andriani told *SATA:* "I was fortunate to be born to parents who, though not formally involved in the arts themselves, did all they could to foster my creative interests. Growing up, I doodled on reams and reams of scrap paper that my dad brought home from the office. Later he and my mom were kind enough to go into hock to get me through art school.

"I love illustrating for children and the endless variety of challenges it offers. I also love working for Hallmark, because I get to be funny all day long! My pearls of wisdom are: honor your deadlines, keep an eye on trends, and try not to burn bridges!"

■ For More Information See

PERIODICALS

Booklist, December 1, 1994, p. 666.
School Library Journal, March, 1995, p. 185.*

*   *   *

WILLIAMS-GARCIA, Rita

■ Personal

Born April 13 in Jamaica, Queens, NY; father was in the U.S. Army; mother was a domestic servant; married Peter Garcia; children: Michelle, Stephanie. *Education:* Graduated from Hofstra University; pursuing a master's degree in creative writing at Queens College; also studied dance under Alvin Ailey and Phil Black. *Hobbies and other interests:* Chess, playing Tetris, jogging, sewing.

■ Addresses

Home—Jamaica, NY.

■ Career

Writer; Interactive Market Systems, New York City, manager of software distribution and production. Has also worked as a dancer and reading teacher. *Member:* Authors Guild, Society of Children's Book Writers and Illustrators.

■ Awards, Honors

Notable Books for Children and Young Adults citation, American Library Association (ALA), 1991, for *Fast Talk on a Slow Track; Booklist* Editors' Choice selection, 1995, Best Books for Young Adults citation, ALA, and Coretta Scott King Honor Book selection, ALA, both 1996, all for *Like Sisters on the Homefront;* PEN/ Norma Klein Award for Children's Fiction, 1997.

■ Writings

Blue Tights, Lodestar, 1988.
Fast Talk on a Slow Track, Lodestar, 1991.
Like Sisters on the Homefront, Lodestar, 1995.

■ Sidelights

"Focusing her attention on contemporary African American youth," writes Susan P. Bloom in *Twentieth-Century Young Adult Writers,* "Rita Williams-Garcia informs her fictional teenagers with her own experiences as student, as teacher, as dancer." Her three young adult novels to date show young black men and women living and coping with difficulties in an honest, uncontrived manner. "Williams-Garcia's portrayal of these urban black adolescents and their worlds feels genuine, neither sensationalized nor romanticized," declares *Horn Book* contributor Rudine Sims Bishop. "Her work is marked by an authentic rendering of the styles and cadences of

RITA WILLIAMS-GARCIA

urban black language, some touches of humor, and strong, dynamic characterization." Together with such African American writers as Jacqueline Woodson, Dolores Johnson, and Angela Johnson, says Bishop, Williams-Garcia "show[s] great promise, and with continuing support and nurturing ... may well turn out to be among the most prominent African-American literary artists of the next generation."

"I was born in Queens, New York, at the tail end of the fifties," Williams-Garcia told Susan Pais, Phyllis Brown, Ann Gartner, and Kay E. Vandergrift in a specially-conducted interview posted on their web page. "My father was in the army so we traveled by car across the country. Our first stop was to Arizona when I was three—a sweeping contrast to our Far Rockaway projects." Williams-Garcia's family then settled in the California town of Seaside, where Rita and her siblings spent their childhood. "We played a lot outdoors; we were very athletic children," she explained to *Booklist* interviewer Hazel Rochman. "We were always doing things. My sister was an artist. My brother was into math. I loved words; I just thought that was normal. To characterize me as a kid, you could say that I was definitely a geek."

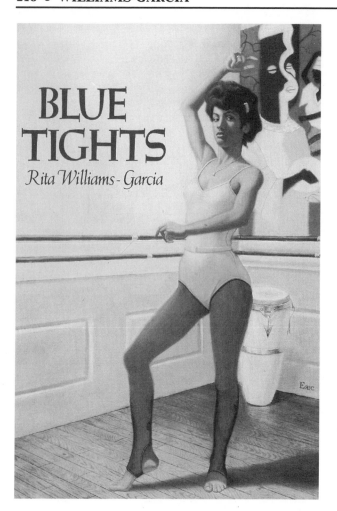

Williams-Garcia's story centers on Joyce Collins, a young African American student who discovers herself through dance.

Perhaps the most important influence on Williams-Garcia's life, she says, was her mother, whom she calls "Miss Essie." "My sister, brother and I grew up thinking our mother, 'Miss Essie,' discovered Pop Art," the author stated in a publisher's biography released by Penguin Books. "When she wasn't cleaning, working or in school, Miss Essie painted every little thing that needed color."

Williams-Garcia developed her reading skills early in life. She recalls in her webpage interview that she taught herself to read at age two by learning to associate letters with their sounds, partly through looking at billboards and partly through the efforts of her older sister, who would often share her books with her. By the time she entered school, Williams-Garcia was already an accomplished reader and a writer of poetry and stories, "mostly adventures that involved the heroic exploits of my sister Rosalind, brother Russell and I."

Williams-Garcia was exposed to racial issues while growing up during the 1960s. She remembers discussing race relations and racism in the classroom in the aftermath of the 1968 riots and the assassination of Dr. Martin Luther King, Jr. At the age of twelve, Williams-

Garcia left California for Georgia for six months, then settled in Jamaica, New York. In the sixth grade, she reported in her webpage interview, she went looking for literature for young adults that featured black protagonists. She discovered biographies of historical figures, such as Harriet Tubman and Sojourner Truth, and a single novel (*Mary Ellen, Student Nurse*), but little else. "When I brought this up to the school librarian ... she gave me three books about a West African girl who would rather hunt with her father, the chief, than do traditional girl things," the author recalled. "I'll pay a king's ransom to know the title and author of the aforementioned books!" Her teachers encouraged her to write for herself, and at the age of fourteen she published her first story in *Highlights* magazine.

"None of my characters are truly me," Williams-Garcia stated in her interview, "although there is always some aspect of me in each and every one. Joyce in *Blue Tights* is a voluptuous teen with dance inside of her. Denzel in *Fast Talk* is a bright young man who must face himself.

Afraid of failure, Denzel Watson begins selling candy door-to-door instead of returning to Princeton University after he experiences the pressing workload at the prestigious school.

Gayle in *Like Sisters on the Homefront* has lived through a lot of pain but refuses to acknowledge it. That's where similarities between myself and my characters pretty much end. Outside of watching football and baseball with my sister, my adolescence was uneventful."

When Williams-Garcia enrolled in Hofstra University, she temporarily dropped writing for other activities. "In college, real life seemed to displace my need to 'make' stories," she explained in the Penguin publishers biography, "so I didn't write for nearly three years. (Real life was running my dance company and being political)." She declared a major in economics, auditioned for dancing roles in musicals, and performed community outreach work through her sorority, Alpha Kappa Alpha. In her senior year in college, Williams-Garcia enrolled in a creative writing class. She combined her outreach work—teaching high school girls remedial reading—with her writing workshop training and penned an early version of the story that became *Blue Tights.*

Blue Tights is partly based on Williams-Garcia's own experiences, but it is mostly a conglomeration of the stories of many young women. The book tells the tale of Joyce Collins, an ambitious African American girl who loves to dance and exhibits great talent. However, Joyce finds that she is shut out of her school's European-oriented dance program because the dance instructor believes her body shape is not suited to ballet. Besides dealing with this great disappointment, Joyce has to come to terms with her home life—she has been raised by an often absent mother and a religiously fanatic aunt—and her identity. "A volatile combination of worldliness and innocence," Bishop states, "Joyce seeks love and popularity in all the wrong places and with all the wrong people." "Williams-Garcia does not shy away from the harsh circumstances that define Joyce and her family," explains Bloom. "Aunt Em's severe treatment of Joyce stems from a horrific self-induced coat hanger abortion she suffered in her adolescence. Williams-Garcia provides less sensational, daily evidence of the grinding poverty that eats at this family." "Through her work with an African-American dance troupe," Bishop concludes, Joyce "discovers her own special talents as a dancer and achieves a new appreciation of her own self-worth."

It took Williams-Garcia several years to get *Blue Tights* published. While she worked on the book, revising and collating the stories she had assembled from her own life and the lives of her reading students, she went to work for a marketing company in Manhattan, churning out manuscripts on an old typewriter in the company mailroom. The manuscript of *Blue Tights* (originally titled *Blue Tights, Big Butt*), however, kept returning to the author with depressing regularity. Editors complained that the protagonist had a poor self-image and was too focused on her appearance. "The letters I got back from editors and agents were more or less on the same lines," the author explained to Rochman. "Can you make the girl older, about 17, if there's going to be

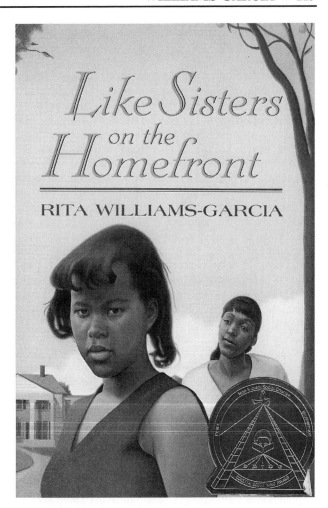

A streetwise teen mother finds adjusting to the ways of her rural relatives difficult until she forms a special bond with her great-grandmother.

any kind of sexual content in the book? Or, this is not a good role model; she's not positive; she doesn't have anything uplifting to offer to young African American women growing up; can you do something about her attitude? Can you do something about all these references to black culture? Readers aren't going to understand them. Can you make it more universal?"

Williams-Garcia continued to write and submit stories during the 1980s until her job was cut in a company restructuring. In the meantime she had married and given birth to two daughters. She brought the *Blue Tights* manuscript to Lodestar Books, a publishing house known for its history of publishing challenging books. The novel was released in 1988 and won recognition from many reviewers. "By writing about urban black teenagers and a young girl who aspires to be a dancer," Nancy Vasilakis states in *Horn Book*, "Rita Williams-Garcia incorporates a setting and a subject that she obviously knows well." "The novel vividly evokes [Joyce's] neighborhood and the rigor and joy of her dancing," writes a *Booklist* critic, adding, "Joyce's sexual conflicts are treated with candor." "Joyce's understanding is believably paced and powerfully realized," declares a *Publishers Weekly* reviewer, "and her story is uplifting."

While Joyce Collins's story becomes uplifting through her realization of her own potential and self-respect, Denzel Watson's story, in *Fast Talk on a Slow Track*, becomes uplifting in the way he deals with failure while moving from high school to college. Denzel, the smooth-talking valedictorian of his high school, attends a summer program for minority students at Princeton University. Denzel had relied on his winning personality throughout high school, but he quickly discovers that he cannot use the same tricks in college. "While he is involved with the summer program, he struggles with the feeling of inadequacy and decides not to return to Princeton in the fall," writes Jo Holtz in *Voice of Youth Advocates*. "For the first time in his life, he feels like a failure." Denzel turns to a part-time job as a door-to-door salesman to regain his self-esteem, and experiments briefly with the world of black street culture. Finally, however, he bows to family pressure and resolves to enter Princeton in the fall, "to find that, with a little humility and some serious study, he *can* hack it," explains a *Kirkus Reviews* contributor. "The author puts it to her college-bound readers: When the time comes, will *they* have what it takes to step up to a new, very challenging world?"

Fast Talk on a Slow Track won as much favorable attention from reviewers as *Blue Tights* had. It was also cited on the American Library Association's list of Notable Books for Children and Young Adults. "Williams-Garcia writes just as authoritatively about teenage boys as she did about girls in her first novel," states Nancy Vasilakis in *Horn Book*. "She understands the forces and fears driving a young man in search of his true self." "Teens everywhere," writes Hazel Rochman in *School Library Journal*, "will be able to identify and commiserate with Denzel as he goes through his options, gains confidence, and matures."

The heroine of *Like Sisters on the Homefront*, fourteen-year-old Gayle, also has her own set of problems and needs to gain maturity in order to cope with them. After she becomes pregnant for a second time (her first pregnancy resulted in a son, Jose, now seven months old), her mother takes her to an abortion clinic and then ships her off to the family home in Georgia. At first Gayle feels uncomfortable in the rural environment; she is away from her boyfriend and homegirls and has to cope with her uncle's disapproval, her aunt's insistence on proper child care for her young son, and her cousin Cookie's religious standards. She begins to change when her aunt gives her the responsibility of caring for her great-grandmother, Great, who is sick and near death. The relationship between Great and Gayle deepens as the old woman's condition worsens. Great "exhibits a strength of spirit and a stubbornness that Gayle recognizes in herself," writes reviewer Nancy Vasilakis in *Horn Book*. "Great understands Gayle, too. 'When you lay down your deviling,' she tells her great-granddaughter, 'you'll be stronger than those who lived by the rule all their lives.'"

Great finally chooses Gayle to receive the Telling, the source of family history that keeps the family together. "Strong-willed, self-absorbed, and impulsive," states Vasilakis, Gayle "is not unlike the heroine of Williams-Garcia's earlier novel, *Blue Tights*, imbued with a lively mix of naivete and worldliness, particularly in sexual matters, that gives her characterization depth and vibrancy." "Painting Gayle as a hard-edged, high-spirited young woman clearly headed for either trouble or triumph," states Deborah Stevenson in *Bulletin of the Center for Children's Books*, "Williams-Garcia breathes life into what could have been a stereotypical portrait of a trash-talking, streetwise city teen, and while its scales are tipped in favor of a responsible life, the book is honest enough to acknowledge the pleasures of the other kind."

Williams-Garcia plans to continue her pattern of writing strong, hard-hitting books about African-American teens living in the modern world—not in times of great crisis, but in the small crises of everyday life. "I really don't think we deal with the complex issues of our young people's lives," she told Rochman. "We tell them about racism and those kinds of things ... but then there's that real person who has to deal with the fact that he is not a symbol, he is not a model, he is a real, flesh-and-blood person who makes mistakes and has to keep moving and learning and accepting all these things as part of life.... It's what you come to know about yourself that is more important than any big thing that might happen to you."

■ Works Cited

Bishop, Rudine Sims, "Books from Parallel Cultures: New African-American Voices," *Horn Book*, September-October, 1992, pp. 616-20.

Bloom, Susan P., "Rita Williams-Garcia," *Twentieth-Century Young Adult Writers*, St. James Press, 1994, pp. 709-10.

Review of *Blue Tights*, *Booklist*, December 15, 1987, pp. 696-97.

Review of *Blue Tights*, *Publishers Weekly*, November 13, 1987, p. 73.

Review of *Fast Talk on a Slow Track*, *Kirkus Reviews*, February 1, 1991, pp. 179-80.

Holtz, Jo, review of *Fast Talk on a Slow Track*, *Voice of Youth Advocates*, June, 1991, pp. 104-05.

Pais, Susan, Phyllis Brown, Ann Gartner, and Kay E. Vandergrift, compilers and interviewers, "Learning about Rita Williams-Garcia," http://www.scils.rut gers.edu/special/kay/williamsgarcia.html.

"Rita Williams-Garcia" (publishers' release), http://www.penguin.com/usa/childrens/bios/garcia.html.

Rochman, Hazel, review of *Fast Talk on a Slow Track*, *School Library Journal*, April, 1991, p. 143.

Rochman, Hazel, "The Booklist Interview: Rita Williams-Garcia," *Booklist*, February 15, 1996, pp. 1002-03.

Stevenson, Deborah, review of *Like Sisters on the Homefront*, *Bulletin of the Center for Children's Books*, September, 1995, p. 34.

Vasilakis, Nancy, review of *Blue Tights, Horn Book,* March-April, 1988, pp. 215-16.

Vasilakis, Nancy, review of *Fast Talk on a Slow Track, Horn Book,* July-August, 1991, p. 466.

Vasilakis, Nancy, review of *Like Sisters on the Home-front, Horn Book,* November-December, 1995, pp. 748-49.

■ For More Information See

BOOKS

Children's Literature Review, Volume 36, Gale, 1995.

PERIODICALS

ALAN Review, winter, 1996.

Booklist, April 1, 1991, p. 1561.

Bulletin of the Center for Children's Books, January, 1988, p. 106; June, 1991, pp. 253-54; September, 1995, p. 34.

Dance, November, 1993, p. 81.

Kirkus Reviews, December 1, 1987, p. 1680.

Publishers Weekly, February 8, 1991, pp. 58-59.

School Library Journal, June-July, 1988, p. 120.

Voice of Youth Advocates, August, 1988, p. 136.*

—*Sketch by Kenneth R. Shepherd*

*   *   *

WINN, Bob
See SEULING, Barbara

*   *   *

WINTON, Tim 1960-

■ Personal

Born in 1960, in Western Australia; children: three. *Education:* Attended Curtin University, Perth.

■ Career

Writer.

■ Awards, Honors

Vogel Award, Allen & Unwin Australia, 1981, for *An Open Swimmer;* Miles Franklin Award, Arts Management Party Limited (Australia), 1984, for *Shallows,* and 1992, for *Cloudstreet;* Deo Gloria Prize for religious writing, 1991, for *Cloudstreet;* Best Books for Young Adults, American Library Association, 1992, for *Lockie Leonard, Human Torpedo; The Riders* was shortlisted for the Booker Prize, 1995; Commonwealth Writers Prize best novel award, South East Asia and South Pacific section, 1995, for *The Riders.*

■ Writings

FOR YOUNG PEOPLE

Jesse, illustrated by Maureen Prichard, McPhee Gribble (Melbourne, Victoria, Australia), 1988.

Lockie Leonard, Human Torpedo, McPhee Gribble (South Yarra, Victoria, Australia), 1990, Little, Brown (Boston), 1991.

The Bugalugs Bum Thief, illustrated by Carol Pelham-Thorman, Puffin (Ringwood, Victoria, Australia), 1991.

Lockie Leonard, Scumbuster, Piper (Chippendale, New South Wales), 1993, Macmillan, 1993.

Lockie Leonard, Legend, Pan (Chippendale, New South Wales), 1997.

Blueback: A Fable for All Ages, Macmillan (South Melbourne), 1997.

NOVELS

An Open Swimmer, Allen & Unwin (Sydney, Australia), 1982.

Shallows, Graywolf Press (St. Paul, MN), 1984.

That Eye, the Sky, McPhee Gribble (Fitzroy, Victoria, Australia), 1986, Atheneum (New York City), 1987.

In the Winter Dark, McPhee Gribble (Melbourne, Australia), 1988.

Cloudstreet, McPhee Gribble (Melbourne, Victoria), 1991, Graywolf Press, 1992.

The Riders, Macmillan (Chippendale, New South Wales), 1994, Scribner (New York City), 1995.

The Collected Shorter Novels of Tim Winton (includes *Open Swimmer, That Eye, the Sky,* and *In the Winter Dark*), Picador (London), 1995.

SHORT STORIES COLLECTIONS

Scission and Other Stories, McPhee Gribble (Fitzroy, Australia), 1985.

Minimum of Two, McPhee Gribble, 1987, Atheneum, 1988.

Blood and Water: Stories (contains "Minimum of Two" and "Scission"), Picador (London), 1993.

OTHER

(With Trish Ainslie and Roger Garwood) *Land's Edge,* Pan Macmillan with Plantagenet Press (Chippendale, New South Wales), 1993.

(With Bill Bachman) *Local Color: Travels in the Other Australia,* The Guidebook Company (Hong Kong), 1994.

Contributor to books, including "My Father's Axe," *The Oxford Book of Australian Short Stories.* Also the author of film scripts.

■ Adaptations

Lockie Leonard, Human Torpedo was adapted by Paige Gibbs for the stage, and performed by Perth Theatre Company; *That Eye, the Sky* was adapted for stage by Justin Monjo and Richard Roxburgh, 1994, and released as a movie in 1995, starring Peter Coyote. *The Riders* was optioned for filming by Jan Chapman in 1995.

■ Sidelights

Australian writer Tim Winton has won critical acclaim for novels featuring richly evoked settings and roundly drawn characters who embark on journeys of self-discovery. An avowed Christian, Winton also incorporates religious themes and imagery into his adult novels and short stories, and some critics have remarked that universal questions of good and evil, humanity and brutality lie beneath his characters' dilemmas. *Los Angeles Times Book Review* writer Carolyn See described Winton as "a novelist, a great one, because against all evidence and odds, he reminds us of what it is to be human, and reminds us to be proud of our humanity."

Winton has written several novels, film scripts, short stories, and books for young people. *Shallows* was the first of his novels to find its way into American bookstores, appearing in 1984—the same year it won Australia's esteemed Miles Franklin Award for literature. Set in a small Australian seaside town, the novel focuses on a community still clinging to its more prosperous past as an important whaling center. "Have a Whale of a Time in Angelus," the civic billboards proclaim, while the town suffers economic decline engendered by the growing obsolescence of the whaling industry; whales stranded in shallow coastal waters provide a metaphor for the characters' moral strandedness. Queenie Coupar, a descendant of the town's first family, and her urban-transplant husband Cleve are central to the story, as is her wealthy grandfather and the story of the whaling industry itself with its salty, sometimes violent personnel and the blood and gore that accompany the hunt and slaughter. Winton's novel describes the disintegration of the town's status quo when Greenpeace activists arrive to protest the remnants of the whaling industry.

Shallows was praised by reviewers for its evocation of the whale and the activities aboard a whaling ship, with *Los Angeles Times* reviewer Carolyn See comparing the novel to Herman Melville's classic *Moby Dick*. The critic contended that Winton's use of the whale leitmotif, "so definitively used by Melville, is here new and startling." Other reviewers were equally laudatory, although Elizabeth Ward, writing in the *Washington Post Book World,* faulted Winton for "some excesses. He typically writes in a dense, economical, heavily physical style ... but he also likes to feature snot, nose-pickings, vomit and so forth to an extent which can be distasteful." Yet Ward also noted that "*Shallows* is that rare thing, not historical fiction, but fiction which brings the history of a place to life." Stuart Evans of the London *Times* praised Winton's creation of the cast of characters and the novel's portrayal of "pride, loneliness, longing for love, and the struggle between nostalgic heroics and the heroism of compassion."

That Eye, the Sky is the first of Winton's works to overtly explore religion. Mary Ellen Quinn of *Booklist* lauded the "original style that reflects the exuberance of the ten-year-old narrator" and labeled the book "enormously appealing." The story is set in rural Western Australia and is narrated by a young boy named Morton Flack, whom everyone refers to as Ort. *Washington Post* reviewer Ward called the designation of Ort as the

Tim Winton's award-winning novel describes the disruption of the status quo in a small Australian seaside town when Greenpeace activists arrive to protest the whaling industry in the community. (Cover photo by Robert Garvey.)

novel's storyteller and spiritual center "a cunning stroke, since the naivete of the child's mind allows for, or renders artistically possible, the visionary and miraculous elements that in the end redeem the family's suffering." The suffering in question has been brought on by a number of incidents: Ort's parents are former free-spirits of the 1960s, pining for their past, and his father has recently suffered a disabling car accident that has left him incapacitated. Ort's grandmother lives with the family and is also bedridden and possibly afflicted with senile dementia. His teenage sister Tegwyn longs to leave the family home, which is surrounded by dying trees and a mysterious glowing cloud that hovers above at night.

As *That Eye, the Sky* begins, another ex-hippie enters the Flack household in the person of evangelical preacher Henry Warburton. He soon becomes an integral, if not destructive, part of their lives: baptizing Ort and his mother, helping take care of Ort's invalid father, and having his way with Tegwyn. Ort confides in Warburton of his strange visions of the sky, which seems to be keeping watch on him in the form of a giant eye, and of the other apparitions that plague the boy. However,

Warburton is not a typical cleric, and eventually his hypocrisy sets a series of events in motion that conclude the novel.

Writing again about Winton for the *Washington Post*, Ward found some technical flaws with *That Eye, the Sky*, namely in young Ort's ability to recall very long passages of adult conversation. Yet the critic granted that Winton's "use of natural imagery—of moon and cloud, sky and water and dying trees—to suggest Ort's experience of the ineffable is as graceful as a poet's." Garrett Epps, writing in the *New York Times*, described the book as "a thoroughly engaging story of childhood, tragedy and faith," that should not be dismissed because of unfamiliar Australian slang terms, while a *Publishers Weekly* reviewer concluded that "unforeseen effects end the wrenching story that proves love like Ort's can prevail against hell itself."

Cloudstreet, set just after World War II in Australia, is about an unlucky gambler, Sam Pickles, who has inherited a large house in Perth. Since he and his wife prefer not to work, they rent half of the house to the Lamb family. The Lambs are radically different from the Pickles, and the clashes and bond between the two over the years in their coexistence form the basis of the novel. *Voice Literary Supplement* contributor Joy Press called Winton's style in *Cloudstreet* "mellifluous yet veined with pathos ... it grabs you with its stream of words, and then gradually slows down to the pace of life." Noting that the author's verbiage is "sometimes overripe," Press maintained: "that only adds to its charm, and Winton balances the ballast with his wonderful silences, those mesmeric moments listening to the house breathe or the terrible pauses before bad luck strikes."

In *The Riders,* Winton chronicles the destruction of a young Australian family who have moved to Ireland. Scully is building a home for his wife, Jennifer, and their seven-year-old daughter when Jennifer leaves the pair. Distraught, the father and daughter search for her throughout western Europe, and in some ways the novel becomes a chase mystery, rife with clues and frantic travels, but the dilemma is never resolved. The "riders" of the title are a quartet of phantom horsemen who appear to Scully in his darkest moments. He becomes more obsessed with finding his wife, but the trauma suffered by his daughter because of the breakup is only exacerbated by his behavior and eventually brings him back from the edge.

Along with his other works, Winton has also written several popular books for young adults, including *Lockie Leonard, Human Torpedo,* and *Lockie Leonard, Scumbuster*. In his first *Lockie Leonard* story, Lockie and his family have just moved to a small town in time for him to begin high school. Lockie finds it a bit difficult fitting in: he lives on the wrong side of the tracks, his father is a cop, and he's obviously a city boy. His talent for surfing, however, win him leadership in the surfing club and the attention of the most popular girl in school. Maeve Visser Knoth, writing in *Horn*

Book, observed that although the situation is not new to young-adult fiction, "the dialogue and characters ... are fresh and original." She concluded that Winton has introduced a "lovable, vulnerable adolescent" who deals with his coming-of-age "with humor if not grace." A *Publishers Weekly* critic predicted that the author's "dry, typically Down Under wit" and his use of unfamiliar, somewhat daunting Australian slang "should charm young readers on this side of the equator."

In *Lockie Leonard, Scumbuster,* Lockie becomes involved with trying to do something about the industrial pollution problem, while going through his usual falling in and out of love, and having his share of ups and downs in school. *School Librarian* contributor Patricia Peacock noted that Winton's ending "is typically off-beat and funny." She also maintained that young readers will enjoy the stories "without noticing the underlying wisdom of Tim Winton's observations."

In a *Publishers Weekly* interview, Michelle Field commented that landscape in Winton's books often comes across as the really strong, reassuring element in the characters' lives. "I guess it is a non-European notion of mine," Winton responded. "A European grows up surrounded by both landscape and human doings; but my experience is that 'human doings' seem pretty paltry in the Australian landscape. Ayers Rock, for instance, would blow anything man might build right out of the water. This engenders a perspective which, I think, you resist at your peril."

■ Works Cited

Epps, Garrett, review of *That Eye, the Sky, New York Times,* May 17, 1987, p. 50.

Evans, Stuart, review of *Shallows, Times* (London), August 7, 1986.

Knoth, Maeve Visser, review of *Lockie Leonard, Human Torpedo, Horn Book,* March-April, 1992, pp. 212-3.

Review of *Lockie Leonard, Human Torpedo, Publishers Weekly,* November 22, 1991, p. 57.

Peacock, Patricia, review of *Lockie Leonard, Scumbuster, School Librarian,* May, 1996, p. 77.

Press, Joy, review of *Cloudstreet, Voice Literary Supplement,* April, 1992, p. 5.

Quinn, Mary Ellen, review of *That Eye, the Sky, Booklist,* March 15, 1987, p. 1095.

See, Caroyln, review of *Minimum of Two, Los Angeles Times Book Review,* May 23, 1988.

See, Carolyn, review of *Shallows, Los Angeles Times Book Review,* July 7, 1986.

Review of *That Eye, the Sky, Publishers Weekly,* January 23, 1987, p. 63.

Ward, Elizabeth, review of *Shallows, Washington Post Book World,* August 10, 1986, p. 5.

Ward, Elizabeth, review of *That Eye, the Sky, Washington Post,* April 3, 1987.

Winton, Tim, interview with Michelle Field, *Publishers Weekly,* May 29, 1995, pp. 62-63.

■ For More Information See

PERIODICALS

Booklist, December 15, 1991, p. 761.
Books for Keeps, March, 1996, p. 12.
Kirkus Reviews, January 1, 1987, p. 20.
Magpies, July, 1991, p. 29; November, 1993, p. 23.
Publishers Weekly, March 6, 1995, p. 23.
Times Literary Supplement, June 13, 1986, p. 645;
    October 10, 1986, p. 1130; September 3, 1993, p.
    23; February 17, 1995, p. 20.*

*   *   *

WONG, Janet S. 1962-

■ Personal

Born September 30, 1962, in Los Angeles, CA; daughter of Roger and Joyce Wong; married Glenn Schroeder (an attorney); children: Andrew. *Education:* University of California at Los Angeles, B.A., 1983; Yale University, J.D., 1987.

■ Addresses

Home and office—Medina, WA. *Electronic mail*—janet-swong@hotmail.com.

JANET S. WONG

■ Career

Attorney in Los Angeles, CA, 1987-91; writer in Los Angeles and Medina, WA, 1991—. Writer in residence, University of Southern California Writing Project, 1995; visiting author, Singapore Society for Reading and Literacy, 1997. Public speaker and performer in Los Angeles and Medina, 1994—. Arbitrator/mediator, Arts Arbitration and Mediation Services, 1989-95.

■ Awards, Honors

Books for the Teen Age Citation, New York Public Library, and Notable Trade Book in the Field of Social Studies Citation, National Council for the Social Studies/Children's Book Council, 1996, William White Award Master List, 1998-99, all for *A Suitcase of Seaweed and Other Poems;* IRA Celebrate Literacy Award, Foothill Reading Council, 1998.

■ Writings

Good Luck Gold and Other Poems, Margaret K. McElderry Books/Simon & Schuster, 1994.
(Self-illustrated) *A Suitcase of Seaweed and Other Poems,* Margaret K. McElderry Books/Simon & Schuster, 1996.

Contributor to *Marvelous Math: A Book of Poems,* selected by Lee Bennett Hopkins, Simon & Schuster, 1997, and *I Am Writing A Poem About,* edited by Myra Cohn Livingston, McElderry Books, 1997.

■ Work in Progress

The Rainbow Hand: Poems about Mothers, for McElderry/Simon & Schuster; *The Trip Back Home,* for Harcourt; *Apple Pie Fourth of July,* for Harcourt; *Behind the Wheel: Poems about Driving,* for McElderry; *This Next New Year,* for Frances Foster/Farrar Straus; *Night Garden: Poems from the World of Dreams,* for McElderry; *BUZZ,* for Harcourt.

■ Sidelights

Janet S. Wong is an Asian American children's poet whose works employ a variety of voices and poetic styles to explore her own heritage. Born in the United States, Wong is the daughter of a Korean-born mother and a Chinese-born father, and all three cultures have found a place in her books. In a review of the 1994 work *Good Luck Gold and Other Poems* in *Voice of Youth Advocates,* Anthony Manna referred to Wong as "a fresh new talent" who has "distinctive gifts as a consciously cultural poet."

Good Luck Gold is a collection of forty-two poems told from the point of view of Asian American children, offering insight into their lives. Written in rhyme, free verse, haiku, and other styles, the pieces explore everyday subjects such as food and shopping, as well as deeper topics, including racism, illness, and divorce. Several reviewers expressed the overall impression that

A suitcase of seaweed

and other poems

by Janet S. Wong

Wong's collection of original poems, addressing experiences drawn from her own life, employ three viewpoints—American, Korean, and Chinese—and various forms, from free verse to haiku. (Cover illustration by Janet S. Wong.)

Good Luck Gold is a powerful, positive contribution to Asian American poetry for young people. Manna commented that the best pieces in this work are "characterized by technical competence and genuine emotional force." Writing in *Bulletin of the Center for Children's Books*, Deborah Stevenson noted that the book will be enjoyable to children from a variety of ethnic backgrounds.

Wong continued to explore her own mixed background in *A Suitcase of Seaweed and Other Poems*, published in 1996. The book is divided into three sections of poems—Korean, Chinese, and American—representing the poet's identity. As *Horn Book* contributor Nancy Vasilakis pronounced, "The quiet, lyric poems acknowledge proudly, subtly, and with occasional touches of irony and humor the distinct strands within the weave of cultures of which she is a part."

Each section is introduced with a short personal memoir; Hazel Rochman commented in *Booklist* that these are "as interesting as the poems." As in *Good Luck Gold*, the pieces are often written from a child's point of

view, and explore topics such as family relations—particularly those between parent and child—and the poet's deeper Asian roots. Reviewers commented that many of her subjects are universal and will be appreciated by children from all backgrounds. Manna noted in *Voice of Youth Advocates* that Wong's best poems are "small, precise, and perfectly pitched observations that imply ... a wide range of subtle thoughts and feelings."

Wong told *SATA:* "Since the time I was supposed to have learned all about fractions and decimals, I have known I would not be a mathematician. I knew, too, I never would be a neurosurgeon, which my father once wanted me to be. But I never thought I would be a poet, either. As far as I can remember—and at least since fourth grade—I remember hating poetry. I can't say, honestly, that I read much of it, but I did not like what I read—especially when I had to read it aloud! So why do I write poetry now?

"One Saturday in September 1991 I attended a workshop on writing for children. Myra Cohn Livingston, one of the speakers ... recited the title poem from her book *There Was A Place and Other Poems....* The next thing I knew, I was blinking back tears. What a powerful piece of writing!

"I like poems that are not afraid to talk about painful things. I like poems that make you laugh, or cry; poems that grab you and make you read them again; poems that make you think.

"Poetry is, in a way, like shouting. Since you can't yell at the top of your lungs for a very long time, you have to decide what you really need to say, and say it quickly. In a way, too, I suppose, poetry is like math. An idea for a poem is a problem that needs to be solved—and for me, the fun is in finding an answer."

■ Works Cited

Manna, Anthony, "Should We Read (More) Poetry (More Often)?: Seven New Collections Tell Why," *Voice of Youth Advocates,* October, 1995, pp. 201-3.

Manna, Tony, review of *A Suitcase of Seaweed and Other Poems, Voice of Youth Advocates,* October, 1996, pp. 241-42.

Rochman, Hazel, review of *A Suitcase of Seaweed and Other Poems, Voice of Youth Advocates, Booklist,* April 1, 1996, p. 1362.

Stevenson, Deborah, review of *Good Luck Gold and Other Poems, Bulletin of the Center for Children's Books,* January, 1995, p. 181.

Vasilakis, Nancy, review of *A Suitcase of Seaweed and Other Poems, Horn Book,* July-August, 1996, p. 475.

■ For More Information See

PERIODICALS

Booklist, November 15, 1994, p. 600.

Bulletin of the Center for Children's Books, April, 1996, p. 282.

School Library Journal, January, 1995, p. 133.

Teaching and Learning Literature, March-April, 1997, pp. 62-70.

*   *   *

WURTS, Janny 1953-

■ Personal

Born December 10, 1953, in Bryn Mawr, PA. *Education:* Hampshire College, B.A. (creative writing and illustration), 1975; attended Moore College of Art.

■ Addresses

Office—Frazer, PA. *Agent*—c/o HarperCollins, Inc., 1000 Keystone Industrial Park, Scranton, PA 18512.

■ Career

Fantasy and science-fiction writer and illustrator. Worked as a laboratory assistant in the Astronomy College of Hampshire College.

■ Writings

NOVELS

Sorcerer's Legacy, Ace, 1982.
The Master of White Storm, Penguin/ROC, 1992.
Fugitive Prince (first volume of "Alliance of Light"), HarperPrism, 1997.

"CYCLE OF FIRE" SERIES

Stormwarden, Ace, 1984.
Keeper of the Keys, Ace, 1988.
Shadowfane, Ace, 1988.

"EMPIRE" SERIES

(With Raymond E. Feist) *Daughter of the Empire,* Doubleday, 1987.
(With Feist) *Servant of the Empire,* Doubleday, 1990.
(With Feist) *Mistress of the Empire,* Doubleday, 1992.

"THE WARS OF LIGHT AND SHADOW" SERIES

The Curse of the Mistwraith, HarperCollins (London), 1993.
Ships of Merior, HarperCollins, 1995.
Warhosts of Vastmark, HarperCollins, 1996.

SHORT STORIES

That Way Lies Camelot, HarperPrism, 1996.

■ Sidelights

Janny Wurts is an author and illustrator of science fiction whose dual career originated in her lifelong interest in space and the fantastic. As an illustrator she has created book covers for James Blish's *A Case of Conscience,* for *Best SF of the Year 13,* and for her own books, the first of which—*Sorcerer's Legacy*—was published in 1982. A tale of wizardry, court intrigue, and escapades in another world, the book was recommended for older readers of young-adult fantasy as "an emotion-

ally intense and gripping story" by Peggy Murray in *Voice of Youth Advocates.*

Stormwarden, the well-regarded first volume in Wurts's "Cycle of Fire" series, combines elements of fantasy and science fiction. The story takes place in a distant world dominated by demons, where the survivors of humanity, guarded by their spaceship's computer, try to thwart the demons' plans for hegemony. The plot follows three young humans who take different, though intertwined, paths to maturity. Reviewer Peter Kobel, writing in *Booklist,* found the work an "engrossing fantasy.... [which is] fast paced and intelligently written." Two reviewers for *Fantasy Review*—Fred Runk and Diana Waggoner—found the novel's ambitions to outrun its achievements; but Hal Hoover, a *Voice of Youth Advocates* contributor, was of the opinion that the novel's various story threads were "masterfully woven to a final conclusion."

"The Cycle of Fire" series continues with *Keeper of the Keys* and *Shadowfane.* Discussing *Shadowfane, Booklist*'s Roland Green praised Wurts as "excellent at world building and characterization." *Voice of Youth Advocates* contributor Deborah L. Dubois called the book a "well-written fantasy," but suggested that its violence detracts from its appeal as a young adult library purchase.

Wurts has also published another collection of fantasy novels, the "Empire" series, in collaboration with Raymond E. Feist, while continuing with solo projects as well. One such tale, *The Master of White Storm,* is set in the mythical Eleven Kingdoms and centers on two galley slaves who lead a rebellion against wizard masters. *Booklist*'s Roland Green found the novel's opening section, the slave revolt, "gripping, [and] superlatively well realized." Although finding the continuity between scenes less effective than the individual scenes themselves, Green maintained that the book supports Wurts's reputation for "fantasy more unconventional and intelligent than not."

Wurts instituted a new series, "The Wars of Light and Shadow," with the novel *The Curse of the Mistwraith.* The plot follows the adventures of two half-brothers, one the master of light and the other the master of shadows, as they attempt to overcome their suspicions of each other in order to unite against the Mistwraith, a force that has kept the world of Athera in its thrall. A commentator in *Publishers Weekly* found the book "entertaining and readable" but suggested that the plot was made to bear the weight of too much foreshadowing of sequel volumes. More than one critic admired the novel's characterizations and setting: *Library Journal* contributor Jackie Cassada called attention to "elaborate and vivid world-building and complex protagonists," while Candace Smith of *Booklist* noted "strongly sympathetic characters and a well-conceived setting." The novel, Smith predicted, would "hook readers of epic fantasy." The success of *The Curse of the Mistwraith* prompted HarperCollins to publish a sequel, *Ships of Merior.* Weighing in at 928 pages compared to

The Curse of the Mistwraith's 688, *Ships of Merior* finds the half-brothers deadly enemies after their defeat of the Mistwraith. "Wurts," wrote a reviewer for *Publishers Weekly*, "creates a complex, beautiful world."

Wurts has been praised for both her fantasy and science fiction tales. When her collection of short stories, *That Way Lies Camelot*, was assessed by a *Kirkus Reviews* commentator, the critic praised the works that were pure fantasy and judged the hard science fiction stories in the group "reminiscent of the original *Star Trek* and Robert Heinlein's juveniles—and better than either." Similarly, *Voice of Youth Advocates* contributor Christy Tyson asserted that *That Way Lies Camelot* "will delight and satisfy readers of both fantasy and science fiction."

■ Works Cited

Cassada, Jackie, review of *The Curse of the Mistwraith, Library Journal*, February 15, 1994, p. 188.

Review of *The Curse of the Mistwraith, Publishers Weekly*, December 6, 1993, p. 60.

Dubois, Deborah L., review of *Shadowfane, Voice of Youth Advocates*, April, 1989, p. 48.

Green, Roland, review of *The Master of White Storm, Booklist*, March 15, 1992, p. 1344.

Green, Roland, review of *Shadowfane, Booklist*, November 1, 1988, p. 452.

Hoover, Hal, review of *Stormwarden, Voice of Youth Advocates*, June, 1985, p. 141.

Kobel, Peter, review of *Stormwarden, Booklist*, December 1, 1984, p. 484.

Murray, Peggy, review of *Sorcerer's Legacy, Voice of Youth Advocates*, June, 1983, p. 101.

Runk, Fred, review of *Stormwarden, Fantasy Review*, February, 1985, p. 28.

Review of *Ships of Merior, Publishers Weekly*, January 30, 1995, p. 89.

Smith, Candace, review of *The Curse of the Mistwraith, Booklist*, February 1, 1994, p. 997.

Review of *That Way Lies Camelot, Kirkus Reviews*, December 15, 1995, p. 1738.

Tyson, Christy, review of *That Way Lies Camelot, Voice of Youth Advocates*, October, 1996, p. 222.

Waggoner, Diana, review of *Stormwarden, Fantasy Review*, February, 1985, p. 28.

■ For More Information See

BOOKS

Weinberg, Robert, *Biographical Dictionary of Science Fiction and Fantasy Artists*, Greenwood Press (Westport, CT), 1988, pp. 299-300.

PERIODICALS

Voice of Youth Advocates, April, 1998, p. 62.*

Y–Z

YOUNG, John
See MACINTOSH, Brownie

*   *   *

ZACH, Cheryl (Byrd) 1947-
(Jennifer Cole; Jamie Suzanne)

■ Personal

Born June 9, 1947, in Clarksville, TN; daughter of
Smith Henry (a military non-commissioned officer) and
Nancy (a sales manager; maiden name, LeGate) Byrd;
married Q. J. Wasden, June 2, 1967 (divorced, September, 1979); married Charles O. Zach, Jr. (president of a
die casting company), June 20, 1982 (died, 1990);
children: (first marriage) Quinton John, Michelle Ni-
cole. *Education:* Austin Peay State University, B.A.,
1968, M.A., 1977. *Politics:* Democrat. *Religion:* Episcopalian.

■ Addresses

Home—Clarksville, TN.

■ Career

Writer, 1982—. Harrison County High School, MS,
English teacher, 1970-71; Dyersburg High School,
Dyersburg, TN, English teacher, 1978-82. Freelance
journalist, 1976-77. *Member:* Romance Writers of
America, Society of Children's Book Writers and Illus-
trators (regional advisor), PEN, Phi Kappa Phi.

■ Awards, Honors

Golden Medallion Award for best young adult novel,
Romance Writers of America, 1985, for *The Frog
Princess,* and 1986, for *Waiting for Amanda;* Rita
Award finalist, Romance Writers of America, for *Look-
ing Out for Lacey* and *Paradise;* Rita Award, Romance
Writers of America, for *Runaway;* inducted into Ro-
mance Writers of America Hall of Fame, 1996 (first
young adult author to be so honored).

CHERYL ZACH

■ Writings

FOR CHILDREN

Benny and the Crazy Contest, Bradbury, 1991.
Benny and the No-Good Teacher, illustrated by Janet
    Wilson, Bradbury, 1992.
Here Comes the Martian Mushroom, Willowisp, 1994.

YOUNG ADULT ROMANCE NOVELS

The Frog Princess ("First Love" series), Silhouette,
    1984.
Waiting for Amanda, Silhouette, 1985.
Fortune's Child, Silhouette, 1985.
Looking Out for Lacey, Fawcett, 1989.

Paradise, HarperCollins, 1994.
Dear Diary: Runaway, Berkley, 1995.
Dear Diary: Family Secrets, Berkley, 1996.
Kissing Caroline ("Loves Stories" series), Bantam, 1996.
Carrie's Gold, Avon, 1997.

YOUNG ADULT ROMANCE NOVELS; UNDER PSEUDONYM JENNIFER COLE

Three's a Crowd, Fawcett, 1986.
Star Quality, Fawcett, 1987.
Too Many Cooks, Fawcett, 1987.
Mollie in Love, Fawcett, 1987.

"SWEET VALLEY TWINS" SERIES; UNDER PSEUDONYM JAMIE SUZANNE

Second Best, Bantam, 1988.
The Class Trip, Bantam, 1988.
Left Behind, Bantam, 1988.
Jessica, the Rock Star, Bantam, 1989.
The Christmas Ghost, Bantam, 1989.

"SMYTH VS. SMITH" SERIES

Oh, Brother, Lynx Books, 1988.
Stealing the Scene, Lynx Books, 1988.
Tug of War, Lynx Books, 1988.
More Than Friends, Lynx Books, 1989.
Surprise, Surprise, Lynx Books, 1989.
Growing Pains, Lynx Books, 1989.

"SOUTHERN ANGELS" SERIES

Hearts Divided, Bantam, 1995.
Winds of Betrayal, Bantam, 1995.
A Dream of Freedom, Bantam, 1995.
Love's Rebellion, Bantam, 1995.

"MIND OVER MATTER" SERIES

The Mummy's Footsteps, Avon, 1997.
Phantom of the Roxy, Avon, 1997.
Curse of the Idol's Eye, Avon, 1997.
The Gypsy's Warning, Avon, 1997.
The Haunted Beach, Avon, 1997.
The Disappearing Raven, Avon, 1997.

OTHER

Twice a Fool (adult romance novel), Harlequin, 1984.
Los Angeles (juvenile nonfiction), Simon & Schuster, 1989.

Contributor of articles, poems, and stories to magazines and newspapers, including *Writer, Romance Writers Report,* and *Fiction Writers Monthly.* Zach's books have been published in French, German, Dutch, and Swiss.

■ Sidelights

In 1985, award-winning young adult author Cheryl Zach was walking on a street in Honolulu, Hawaii, when she "had an epiphany—a moment when time seems to stop and you receive a sudden insight or revelation," as she explained in her essay in *Something about the Author Autobiography Series (SAAS).* She realized, "I was living my dream. And I felt a surge of joy." Zach, who began her career writing young adult romance novels because

In Zach's historical novel, Hannah helps fellow slaves find their freedom via the Underground Railroad and even attempts a daring escape herself.

of an agent's marketing decision and spent some time writing under a pseudonym for the "Sweet Valley High" series, may well be pleased about her success as a writer. Some of the series for which she has written have been very well received by young readers, and her work for the series "Southern Angels" has received positive critical attention. The first young adult author to be inducted into the Romance Writer's of America Hall of Fame, Zach has won praise for her ability to empathize with her characters, to write suspenseful works, and to integrate historical detail into the settings and plots of her novels.

Zach's parents were both from Tennessee, where she was born after World War II. Due to her father's career in the U.S. Army, the family moved around a great deal and Zach spent her childhood in different parts of the United States, and in Europe. As Zach recalled in *SAAS,* she began to develop her skills as a writer when she was a young child by making up stories. Zach's love of history began in elementary school, when she read "an American history textbook ... like a novel." In addition, Zach began to experience some of the situations which would emerge as themes in her novels for young adults. Notable among these was her temporary separation from her parents, when her father was stationed in Germany and her mother was in the hospital with tuberculosis. "I know that somewhere inside me lingers the feelings of a little kid whose parents have gone away." Finally, in part because her family moved around so frequently, she "felt different from the crowd" in high school, and "never, ever felt typical."

Zach went to Austin Peay State University, where she majored in English and minored in history. She became active in drama, the college literary magazine, the drill team, band, and a sorority. It was at this point that she first began to submit articles and stories for publication to magazines and journals. She won the college English Award when she graduated in 1968. Despite winning this award and her limited success publishing articles, she was not able to begin her professional career as a writer immediately. Zach had eloped in college, and in 1969, she and her husband had a son. "There are people who are able to write with small children, but I wasn't one of them," she remarked in *SAAS*. "With no help with childcare, I accomplished very little writing."

Still, Zach was able to begin work as a high school English teacher in Mississippi. There, in addition to the usual challenges of teaching young adults, Zach dealt with the problems of racial integration. She worked as hard as she could to become an effective teacher despite the tension in the school. She also, as she wrote in her sketch in *SAAS*, "discovered that I genuinely like my teenaged students, despite—or perhaps because of—the fact that my own adolescence was not a comfortable time. This empathy would later be an important factor when I once again began writing seriously."

Zach spent some time in graduate school before leaving with her husband and young son for Scotland. After a few years there, she returned to Tennessee and graduate school, and later, she worked once again as a high school teacher. She also had another child, a girl. "I taught sophomores and seniors, the last an age level I loved because in the twelfth grade we studied English literature and composition ... my students were a joy." Despite her enthusiasm for teaching and her appreciation for her students, Zach was not completely satisfied with her career. "I still had a strong desire to write. I sometimes felt that something inside me would die if I gave up writing, and I would lose a piece of myself, perhaps never to be found again." She began to write obsessively, in between teaching, grading papers, and caring for her son and daughter. Zach also began serious attempts to publish her work. She attended writers' conferences and began to consult more experienced writers. One of the most important things she learned at these conferences was that "writing is a business."

In 1979, Zach and her husband divorced. She then remarried in 1982 and moved to Los Angeles. Although her children were teased about their accents and took some time to adjust (inspiring the book *Here Comes the*

Martian Mushroom based on her daughter's experience moving from a small town in Tennessee to Los Angeles), Zach soon found the move to be a beneficial one when she was finally able to devote herself full-time to writing. "After years of snatching thirty minutes here and an hour there, having the whole day to write made me so happy I almost floated off the chair. I wrote and wrote." Zach also took advantage of the many resources available to writers in the Los Angeles area, attending conferences and meeting with literary agents. Finally, one agent suggested that she write an adult romance novel.

As Zach worked on the proposal for the adult romance novel, she kept thinking of another story that "had been suggested by something that happened while" she was "teaching high school. Taking a real event and then changing almost everything—which is how fiction writers work—I wrote a story about a high school girl who is the new girl at school (I know how that felt!) and who is elected class president as the result of a practical joke that backfires. She has to prove herself to the other kids,

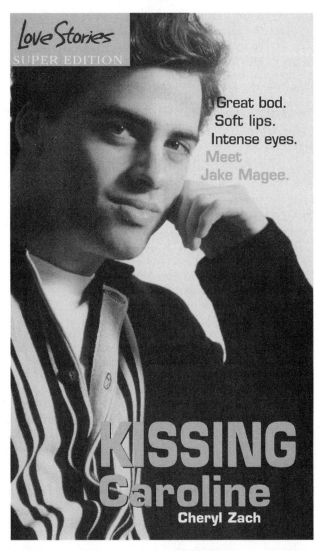

Part of the "Love Story" series, *Kissing Caroline* tells of Jake Magee, who plays matchmaker for his friend Caroline until he realizes that he is in love with her.

and even more to herself. I wrote this book mainly for myself." After Zach won a contract for the adult romance novel, her agent suggested they market the story about the new girl as a young adult romance.

As Zach completed the adult romance novel, yet another character captured her attention: "this girl—her name was Amanda—kept looking over my shoulder and I could barely write the book I was supposed to be writing. Finally, I had to stop and write the first chapter of her story, then finish the adult novel, then go back and write Amanda's book, which sold right away." Zach's first two romance novels for young adults—the ones she wrote as she worked on her first adult novel—met with immediate success and won Romance Writers of America awards.

One of these first romance novels, *Waiting for Amanda,* follows the story of a young woman, Mandy, determined to make a life for herself and her younger sister after the death of their mother. The girls move to Kentucky to live with an elderly great-aunt, where Mandy gradually learns to cope with her anger and develops a romance with a local boy. According to Lorelei Neal of *Voice of Youth Advocates,* the story is "thought-provoking."

The Frog Princess begins with a prank. Despite—or because of—her unpopularity, Kelly is elected ninth-grade class president. Gradually, the uncomfortable, self-conscious girl rises to the challenges of her leadership position and even loses weight. As Judie Porter of *School Library Journal* noted, however, the story does not end as many young adult romance novels do. Instead of getting the popular guy, Kelly develops a relationship with one that's "not-so-popular." Betsy Hearne of *Booklist* appreciated the "nice glimpse" of Kelly's relationship with her single mother.

Zach's novel *Fortune's Child* takes up the story of a girl much different from Kelly. Melissa is rich, beautiful, and intelligent, and to top it off she dates a football hero. Nevertheless, Melissa finds herself distressed when her father has an affair with his secretary. Her grades fall and her relationship with the jock deteriorates. She begins some difficult soul-searching with an intelligent and attractive Vietnamese boy. In the process, explained Jo Ellen Broome of *Voice of Youth Advocates,* Melissa "learns the meaning of ... true friendship."

After writing *Fortune's Child,* Zach worked on a novel for a new series "about three teenaged sisters in California." The book, *Three's a Crowd,* was, according to Zach, "a best-seller on the teen list of one of the bookstore chains." So she accepted an offer to work on the "Sweet Valley Twins" series, eventually completing five books.

With the intention of using her real name again, Zach wrote some of the books in the "Smyth vs. Smith" series. The stories in these books draw on Zach's "experiences as a step-parent. With so many step or blended families in America today, I thought this was a

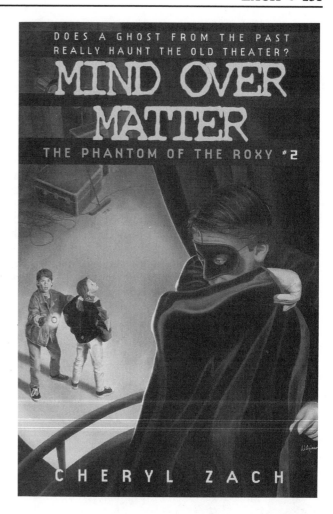

In the second book of Zach's "Mind Over Matter" series, twelve-year-old Quinn and his cousin Jamie investigate a series of accidents at the Roxy Theater.

situation to which many teens could relate, and about whose hilarious and poignant moments they would enjoy reading." *Oh, Brother!,* the first book in the series, begins when the Smyth family (a woman and her teenaged daughter and son) moves to Florida to join the Smith family (a man and his teenaged son and daughter). Even before the wedding, the children of the Smyth-Smith union are at each other's throats. They gradually learn to get along, however. Meticulous Maxine and her new step-sister, Stephanie, grow closer, and Bill and Hal overcome their problems with one another. A reviewer in *Publishers Weekly* remarked, the novel "has a pleasant, readable style and premise many readers will relate to."

Zach is also the author of a nonfiction book for young people about Los Angeles, titled, aptly enough, *Los Angeles.* She explained that she "used some of" her "own photographs in this book." She and her husband would "drive 'till I found a likely spot, then I'd select a camera and snap a roll of film, while Chuck offered helpful advice. This would be my first hardcover book, and I dedicated it to my husband Chuck, just as I had also done in my very first novel."

Around the time *Los Angeles* was published, Zach learned her husband, who ran a tool and die company, was diagnosed with lymphoma (a type of cancer). As he needed a great deal of care, and as the couple wanted to spend more time together, Zach devoted less of her time to writing. Though Chuck Zach fought the cancer through chemotherapy, his health eventually deteriorated, and he died in 1990. After her husband's death, Zach decided to return to live in her hometown in Tennessee. It was not until she was settled in Clarksville that Zach began to write again. She began work on a series "about four girls who live through the drama and danger of the Civil War. These books involved a lot of research, which I always find fascinating. I read old diaries and journals and stacks of history books. I traveled to Charleston where the war began ... and visited battlefields and museums and old homes ... across the South." Zach's books in the "Southern Angels" series have won praise from various critics.

Sixteen-year-old Elizabeth of *Hearts Divided* falls for a young Union soldier she meets at her boarding school. When war breaks out, Elizabeth's loyalties are torn: she's a Southern girl in love with a Northern soldier.

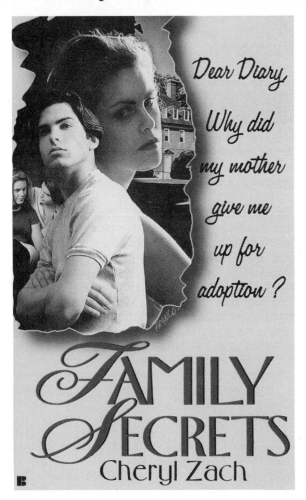

A high school senior stricken with leukemia, Sarah must fight strict adoption agency rules to locate her biological parents in hopes of finding a matching bone marrow donor.

Before too long, Elizabeth is forced to make a difficult choice. According to Sandra L. Doggett of *School Library Journal,* the novel's readers will "watch Elizabeth grow from a flirty teenager to an independent-thinking woman capable of making valuable contributions."

The heroine in *Winds of Betrayal* also finds her love life overturned by the Civil War. Victorine, a young Creole woman, is very pleased with her arranged engagement to Andre, but she does not understand his lack of enthusiasm for the Confederate cause. As the war rages around her and she becomes a doctor's assistant, she realizes that her fiance's character is flawed. She also begins to fall in love with the doctor, despite the fact that he is not a Creole. "Historical detail is carefully woven into a tightly crafted plot that keeps the pages turning," observed Ann Bouricius of *Voice of Youth Advocates.*

A Dream of Freedom follows the story of Hannah, a black slave. When the war comes, Hannah's employment as a seamstress in Charleston, South Carolina, ends, and she must return to her owner's plantation. Hannah, however, has learned a great deal from her life in the city, and she has met some interesting people, including a free man she begins to love. Hannah risks her life to free other slaves. As the war progresses and as she pursues her dream of freedom, Hannah becomes increasingly bold. *A Dream of Freedom* features more than just an adventurous heroine and a historical setting—according to Patsy H. Adams in *Voice of Youth Advocates,* readers "find drama, danger, intrigue, and love" in this novel.

Mystery and adventure in the Amazon distinguish the plot of *Paradise.* Ana, an American girl who has grown up in both New York and Rio de Janeiro, arrives in Brazil to meet her father and spend her vacation. When she learns that her father has gone to the Amazon, she follows him and finds a suspicious scene instead of her father. Ana gets lost in the jungle, but she is saved by a young college student who is working with his botanist mother in the Amazon. At first, Brad distrusts Ana, but he eventually grows to love her and believe in her as the two struggle to find Ana's father. "Ana is a brave heroine.... She becomes a champion of the rain forest...." explained Sarah A. Hudson of *Voice of Youth Advocates.* As Barbara Jo McKee of *Kliatt* noted, Zach writes with detail about jungle wildlife, and "conservation facts abound...." *Paradise* was a finalist for the Rita Award from the Romance Writers of America.

Zach wrote another young adult romance, *Dear Diary: Runaway,* after reading "a riveting newspaper story." This novel explores the troubles of a girl through her diary entries. Readers enter Cassie's story when she is still just friends with Seth, and follow along as Cassie and Seth develop a romantic relationship. Cassie becomes pregnant, and her strict father sends her to a girls' home. Feeling responsible for the pregnancy and his future child's welfare, Seth attempts to free Cassie. Although they have good intentions, the fleeing teenagers soon find themselves in a situation beyond their control. Anne O'Malley of *Booklist* described this "suspenseful teen romance" as "a page-turner." After her third nomination, Zach finally won a Rita award from the Romance Writers of America for *Runaway*.

Although Zach continues to write fiction for young people in her comfortable study at home in Clarksville, Tennessee, she draws on and adds to a supportive community of writers and editors through electronic mail. She also speaks to other writers at conferences and workshops. In addition to receiving letters from her readers, Zach visits with children in schools, because, as she claimed in *SAAS,* "it's great fun to meet some of my readers in a classroom setting,"

■ Works Cited

Adams, Patsy H., review of *A Dream of Freedom, Voice of Youth Advocates,* April, 1996, pp. 33-4.

Bouricius, Ann, review of *Winds of Betrayal, Voice of Youth Advocates,* April, 1996, p. 34.

Broome, Jo Ellen, review of *Fortune's Child, Voice of Youth Advocates,* February, 1986, p. 389.

Doggett, Sandra L., review of *Hearts Divided, School Library Journal,* October, 1995, p. 161.

Hearne, Betsy, review of *The Frog Princess, Booklist,* December 1, 1984, pp. 528-29.

Hudson, Sarah A., review of *Paradise, Voice of Youth Advocates,* April, 1995, p. 30.

McKee, Barbara Jo, review of *Paradise, Kliatt,* November, 1994, p. 17.

Neal, Lorelei, review of *Waiting for Amanda, Voice of Youth Advocates,* June, 1985, p. 124.

Review of *Oh, Brother!, Publishers Weekly,* September 9, 1988, p. 138.

O'Malley, Anne, review of *Dear Diary: Runaway, Booklist,* January 1 & 15, 1996, p. 822.

Porter, Judie, review of *The Frog Princess, School Library Journal,* January, 1985, p. 89.

Zach, Cheryl, comments in *Something about the Author,* Volume 58, Gale, 1990, pp. 195-97.

Zach, Cheryl, essay in *Something about the Author Autobiography Series,* Volume 24, Gale, 1997.*

—*Sketch by R. Garcia-Johnson*

*   *   *

ZURBO, Matt(hew) 1967-

■ Personal

Born July 17, 1967, in Australia; son of John and Sandra Zurbo; married, wife's name Gwendolynne. *Hobbies and other interests:* B-rated movies, comics, cars from the 1970s, the bush, Australian Rules Football.

■ Addresses

Home—Cobweb Gully, 40 Apollo Bay Post Office 3233, Australia.

MATT ZURBO

■ Career

Writer; factory worker and mountain worker.

■ Writings

Blow Kid, Blow!, illustrated by Jeff Raglus, Puffin (Ringwood, Australia), 1996.
Idiot Pride (young adult), Puffin, 1997.
I Got a Rocket, illustrated by Dean Gorissen, Puffin, 1997.
Stealing the World, illustrated by Dean Gorissen, Puffin, 1998.

Also author of *Hot Nights, Cool Dragons* (young adult), and *Eight Ball* (short stories).

■ Work in Progress

The Big "So What!", a self-illustrated juvenile work; *Book of Tattoos,* an adult fantasy; *Hard Cream,* a work of adult fiction.

■ Sidelights

Matt Zurbo told *SATA:* "I grew up in the inner city, then moved to the cold, wet forests of the Otway Ranges in search of work. These days I move to and from city and bush, chase work as an unskilled laborer, and make time to write at night.

"I am a self-taught writer who never went past high school. I have no idea when or why I started writing. Mostly, I guess I took it on because I both wanted to tell colorful, odd stories, and I had (or thought I had) something to say. For me, writing is a fabulous physical sensation: the working of words, ideas, and convictions into stories, images, and rhythms. I also like the work ethic of writing something complex so that it reads simple and fun.

"My roots are important to me. With *Blow Kid, Blow!* I wanted to inspire working class kids with a story in which they could take pride. I wanted a positive, cool message to run underneath (not over) a jazzy story line.

"I want to inspire kids, people, to do things—to have grit, passion, a sense of worth. I want my stories to be cool, and maybe a little tough, and to carry underlying strengths and messages."

■ For More Information See

PERIODICALS

Age, July 5, 1997.
Magpies, May, 1997, p. 39.
Reading Time, August, 1997, p. 35.
Sydney Morning Herald, May 1, 1997.
Weekend Australian, June 14, 1997.